Professional ADO 2.5

David Sussman
James M. Conard
Brian Matsik

Ian Blackburn
Tim McCarthy
John Papa
Simon Robinson

Wrox Press Ltd. ®

Professional ADO 2.5

© 2000 Wrox Press

Reprinted: April 2000

Published by Wrox Press Ltd, Arden House, 1102 Warwick Road, Acocks Green, Birmingham, B27 6BH, UK
Printed in the United States
ISBN 1-861002-75-0

Trademark Acknowledgements

Wrox has endeavored to provide trademark information about all the companies and products mentioned in this book by the appropriate use of capitals. However, Wrox cannot guarantee the accuracy of this information.

Credits

Authors
David Sussman
James M. Conard
Brian Matsik
Ian Blackburn
Tim McCarthy
John Papa
Simon Robinson

Technical Editors
Julian Skinner
Andrew Tracey

Technical Reviewers
Richard Anderson
Tore Bostrup
Joseph Bustos
Michael Corning
David Elmqvist
Todd Lewis
Robert MacDonald
Craig McQueen
Sophie McQueen
John Mendler
J. Boyd Nolan
Carl Prothman
Simon Robinson
Eric Wilson
Neil White

Development Editor
Greg Pearson

Project Manager
Tony Berry

Design/Layout
Tony Berry
Mark Burdett
Jonathan Jones
John McNulty

Figures
William Fallon
Jonathan Jones

Cover
Chris Morris

Index
Alessandro Ansa
Michael Brinkman
Martin Brooks
Andrew Criddle

Managing Editor
Joanna Mason

About the Authors

David Sussman

David has spent most of his professional life as a programmer, encompassing Assembler, Unix, C, and a variety of MS technologies. He is now a full time writer living in a quiet, rural village in Oxfordshire. He dreams of one day being able to perform a five ball Mills Mess. And no, he still hasn't got fit.

Acknowledgements

A few thanks are in order. Firstly to James, for agreeing to write this book with me, and to the other authors who filled in gaps in our knowledge, and rescued us when deadlines got tight. Thanks guys. For John Franklin at Wrox, who like a true film hero leapt in front of me and took the bullets when deadlines got very tight. And of course to the editors - Julian and Andrew have worked incredibly hard pulling my vague ramblings into something resembling English.

James M. Conard

James M. Conard (MCT, MCSD, MCSE) is a developer, trainer and author residing in the Southeastern United States. He specializes in MTS/COM(+), ADO, XML, SQL Server and related Windows DNA technologies from a Visual Basic perspective. James frequently teaches and mentors other developers on Windows DNA technologies and consults small to medium sized companies on how to leverage DNA technologies to solve real-world business problems. You can email James at `JConard@dnamentor.com`.

Acknowledgements

First off, I would like to thank my esteemed co-author David Sussman. From the first specification to the last hour, Dave has played an invaluable role in the success of this book, not only for his material, but also for his ideas and input. I would also like to thank Brian Matsik, Johnny Papa and Simon Robinson for filling the gaps with your expertise.

I would also like to thank everyone at Wrox for making this book come together so smoothly. A special thanks to John Franklin, Dominic Shakeshaft, Tony Berry, and Greg Pearson for allowing me to participate in this project. I hope I exceeded your expectations and I apologize for all of my delays. Thanks to Julian Skinner and Andrew Tracey – you guys did a great job of polishing the rough spots and working out the details of chapter integration between seven separate authors. I look forward to participating with all of you on future projects.

I would like to personally thank my parents who taught me the value of hard work and persistence. I also want to thank my loving wife Amanda for her patience over the seven months. Thanks to my best friend Jeremy Cox for his wisdom and thanks to my brothers for antagonizing me about Linux. Finally, most importantly, I would like to thank the Lord Jesus Christ for his grace to accomplish goals that I could have never have accomplished on my own. I'm frequently reminded of Luke 1:37, which reads: "For with God nothing shall be impossible."

If anyone has any questions or comments about this acknowledgement, topics covered in the book, or consulting, please email me at the address above. Although I cannot respond individually to everyone's questions, I am happy to assist where I can.

Brian Matsik

Brian is an MCSD and MCT as well as the President of OOCS in Charlotte, NC. He specializes in training, web development, and database technologies. Currently he is figuring out how to add more hours into the day or work twice as fast. You can reach Brian at brianmat@oocs.com. Brian has also worked on *Professional InterDev 6 Programming* and *VBScript Programmer's Reference*, both from Wrox Press.

Acknowledgements

For the first time I would like to thank Tracy as my wife and not my fiancée. Her understanding and support keeps me going. I would like to thank everyone that has helped me along the way and especially to Tweety Stewart and David Poston for showing me that I am fully capable of writing and expressing my ideas. Their influence has helped me tremendously in my career and I cannot thank them enough.

Ian Blackburn

Ian is a technical trainer and consultant specializing in Microsoft products and the Internet within a wide range of industries. He runs his own company, Blackburn IT Services Ltd (http://www.bbits.co.uk), as well as being a shareholder of, and technical consultant to, Computer Literacy Ltd, a Microsoft Solution Provider based in London. He is an MCSE and an MCP+I.

Dedication

This book is dedicated to my wife, Stephanie; my daughter, Rebecca; and my son, Thomas. Thanks for putting up with all the work! Now it's time to play for a while….

Acknowledgements

Thanks to everyone at Wrox for the hard work they have put in to getting this book together.

Tim McCarthy

Tim is a Microsoft Certified Solution Developer (MCSD) and Microsoft Certified Trainer (MCT) living in San Diego. He is a Principal Engineer for InterKnowlogy, and specializes in building distributed applications utilizing Visual Basic and the Microsoft Backoffice products. Tim is currently spending his free time getting ready for the upcoming Suzuki Rock 'n' Roll Marathon in San Diego.

John Papa

John Papa has been developing business solutions for e-Commerce, Internet, Intranet and LAN based solutions since 1994. John is certified in the critical technological areas of Microsoft solutions and has merited the MCP, MCSD and MCT. He has published several technical books on how to implement leading edge technologies in a business solution such as Professional ADO RDS with ASP and SQL Server 7.0 Programming Unleashed. He also shares his experiences in the field by being regularly published in such trade journals as Microsoft Internet Developer (MIND) magazine and Visual Basic Programmers Journal (VBPJ).

His knack for developing databases that model a business's every data work flow have earned him and Blue Sand Software recurring business from their customers. John commitment to the customer's needs and quality are evident in his work, writings and speaking engagements, and are reinforced by a high customer satisfaction rate. John can be reached at johnp@bluesand.com.

Acknowledgements

Foremost, I would like to thank my family. To my wife, Colleen, thank you for supporting me through long nights and endless weekends of preparing this book. You are my rock, which without, I would certainly fall. To my baby girl Haley, my little miracle, for spending late nights with me while I write this book and for teaching me that it is possible to type and rock a baby at the same time. To my mother, Peggy, thanks for everything you've inspired me to become and especially for the support and the enduring love you've freely given. Although it may seem otherwise at times, I'll always love you. To my father, John, I can only hope to become half of the man you are. You are my best friend and I am very proud to be your son. To my sisters Julie, Sandy, Laurie and Debbie, thank you for staying so close. Our family is the source from which I have always drawn my strength. And to my Kadi girl, for keeping me company on long nights of writing. Without you all, I could never have come so far.
--Johnny Papa

"Two roads diverged in a wood, and I --
I took the one less traveled by,
And that has made all of the difference."
--Robert Frost

Simon Robinson

Simon Robinson lives in Lancaster, in the UK, where he shares a house with some students. He first encountered serious programming when he was doing his PhD in physics, modelling all sorts of weird things to do with superconductors and quantum mechanics. The experience of programming was nearly enough to put him off computers for life (though oddly, he seems to have survived all the quantum mechanics), and he tried for a while being a sports massage therapist instead. But then he realised how much money was in computers and wasn't in sports massage and rapidly got a job as a C++ programmer/researcher instead. (Simon is clearly the charitable, deep, spiritual, type, who understands the true meaning of life).

His programming work eventually lead him into writing, and he now makes a living mostly writing great books for programmers. He is also an honorary research associate at Lancaster University, where he does research in computational fluid dynamics with the environmental science department. You can visit Simon's web site at `http://www.SimonRobinson.com`.

Table of Contents

Chapter 2: The ADO Environment   29

Chapter 6: Data Shaping

Chapter 7: ADO and XML

Chapter 8: Internet Publishing 281

Chapter 11: Performance Tuning ADO   391

Chapter 12: Directory Services   427

Chapter 13: Exchange Server   469

Chapter 14: RDS: Remoting Your Data   487

Chapter 15: Developing OLE DB Providers 511

Chapter 16: Creating an OLE DB Provider for the Windows NT/2000 Registry — 539

Appendix F: RDS Object Summary 847

Appendix G: RDS Constants 855

Appendix H: ADOX Object Summary 859

Introduction

What Is This Book About?

ActiveX Data Objects, or ADO, is the latest high-level data access technology advanced by Microsoft. The release of ADO revolutionized data access by providing a universal means of accessing data from both relational and non-relational sources. ADO has been growing steadily in functionality since its inception: ADO 2.1 added extensions for data definition and security, and support for multi-dimensional data. ADO 2.5, to be released with Windows 2000, adds even more functionality, including two completely new objects for manipulating streams of text or binary data, and for managing objects within the file system. It also includes a new data provider for accessing web resources.

Who Is This Book For?

This book is aimed at developers who are already using ADO for their basic data access needs, but who want to develop their knowledge of this exciting technology. This book will provide a wealth of both background information on ADO and practical examples which will enable you to harness the full power of ADO in your applications. Most of the examples are in Visual Basic, so a good knowledge of this language is assumed. The book also contains examples in JavaScript, VBScript, ASP and Visual C++.

Like all of the Wrox *Professional* series of books, this is designed to give in-depth information that will be useful for the developer. This book is **not** a primer of ADO. We won't be showing you how to open a recordset or build a connection string, since we are assuming that you will already have performed these basic operations many times. If you are unfamiliar with ADO, you should look out for our forthcoming book *Beginning ADO*. Until then, you might like to check out *Beginning ASP Databases* if you want to use ADO chiefly from ASP.

What Does This Book Cover?

This book covers almost every aspect of programming with ADO. Each chapter deals with an advanced topic which will help you achieve a thorough understanding of ADO and demonstrate how you can take of advantage of ADO's more powerful features in your data-centric applications.

Chapter 1: An Introduction to Data Access

This chapter discusses a number of data access technologies introduced prior to ADO, examining the needs that ADO was designed to meet.

Chapter 2: The ADO Environment

This chapter looks at a number of technologies that are used in conjunction with ADO, including the data access technologies supplied with MDAC and the technologies used within the Windows DNA strategy.

Chapter 3: The Cursor Service

In this chapter, we look at the features provided by the OLE DB Cursor Service, such as sorting, filtering and searching through recordsets, and batch updates. We also look at the Synchronization Service, which is managed by the Cursor Service, and which is responsible for synchronizing cached recordsets with the data store.

Chapter 4: Recordset Persistence

This chapter discusses the role of the OLE DB Persistence Provider, which is used to save ADO recordsets to a file. We look at some situations in which this is useful, and examine what happens when a recordset is transferred across process or machine boundaries.

Chapter 5: Asynchronous Processing and Event Notification

In this chapter, we look at ADO events. We also discuss asynchronous processing, with particular emphasis on the COM+ environment.

Chapter 6: Data Shaping

Data shaping involves creating hierarchical recordsets – recordsets nested within other recordsets. This chapter deals with creating and manipulating these hierarchical or shaped recordsets.

Chapter 7: ADO and XML

After a quick introduction to XML, we examine the XML-Data schemas which ADO uses to persist data in XML format. We then look at how to use XML in ADO-based data-centric applications.

Chapter 8: Internet Publishing

In this chapter, we discuss the Internet Publishing Provider, and see how to use this together with the new `Record` and `Stream` objects. We use these to develop a complete web-site management application using ADO and client-side JavaScript.

Chapter 9: Multi-Dimensional Data

ADO Multi-Dimensional (ADOMD) was introduced with ADO 2.1, and allows us to work with multi-dimensional OLAP data. In this chapter, we examine the ADOMD object model and learn how to use this to create working OLAP solutions.

Chapter 10: ADOX: Data Source Definitions and Security

ADOX, the ADO Extensions for DDL and Security, was also introduced in ADO 2.1. This provides a unified object model for modifying database schemas and for managing security. In this chapter, we look at the objects, methods and properties of ADOX, plus we also take a quick look at SQL-DMO, an alternative to ADOX for SQL Server databases.

Chapter 11: Performance Tuning ADO

This chapter looks at some of the performance issues related to ADO. We take a quick look at some of the tools available for performance testing ADO and discuss some of the ways in which you can get the maximum performance from your ADO-based application.

Chapter 12: Directory Services

After an introduction to Directory Services, we look at the ADSI interfaces and the ADSI LDAP provider, and learn how to use these in conjunction with ADO. In a final section, we look at using ADSI from C++.

Chapter 13: Exchange Server

In this chapter, we take a quick preview of the new Exchange Provider and using ADO with Exchange 2000 Beta.

Chapter 14: RDS: Remoting Your Data

This chapter looks at Remote Data Services, and the facility this technology provides for transferring ADO recordsets across the Internet or an intranet. We see how RDS allows us to manipulate data on the client and then update the database on the server.

Chapter 15: Developing OLE DB Providers

One of the most powerful features of OLE DB (the underlying technology behind ADO) is the ability to create custom providers for any type of data source. In this chapter, we look at how you can build your own OLE DB data provider.

Chapter 16: Creating an OLE DB Provider for the Windows NT/2000 Registry

Having seen the theory in the previous chapter, we now go on to develop a complete simple provider for the Windows Registry.

Chapter 17: ADO in Action

The last chapter demonstrates some of the most powerful features of ADO in action by developing an application which can access many different types of data store.

Data Transfer: A Business-to-Business Case Study

After we've seen what ADO 2.5 has to offer, it's time to put these techniques into action by building a complete e-commerce application. This case study develops a business-to-business application using ADO, data shaping and XML for the automated transferral of data to and from product suppliers.

Finally, we also provide a large reference section which contains detailed information on the ADO, ADOX and ADOMD object models, constants and dynamic properties. In addition, we provide references for the RDS object model and RDS constants, and for ADO data types and errors.

What You'll Need to Use This Book

To get the most from this book, you will need to have ADO 2.5, which is shipped with Windows 2000 and MDAC 2.5. However, many of the examples will also work with ADO 2.1. Ideally, you will be running Windows 2000 or Windows NT 4.0, but most of the samples will also work with Windows 98 or 95.

Most of the examples use Visual Basic, so you will need VB installed. A few of the examples use ASP, for which you will need either IIS (automatically installed with Windows NT/2000) or PWS (supplied on the Windows 95/98 CD). Some of these examples require ASP 3.0, shipped with IIS 5.0 and Windows 2000.

Throughout most of the book, Microsoft SQL Server 7.0 is used as the data source, although Chapter 10 chiefly uses Access 2000, which currently has better support for ADOX. Chapter 9 requires an OLAP server (such as Microsoft OLAP Server, supplied with SQL Server 7.0, but not installed by default; note that this cannot be installed on Windows 95/98).

Conventions

We use a number of different styles of text and layout in the book to help differentiate between the different kinds of information. Here are examples of the styles we use and an explanation of what they mean.

Bullets appear indented, with each new bullet marked as follows:

❑ **Important Words** are in a bold type font.

❑ Words that appear on the screen, such as menu options, are in a similar font to the one used on screen, for example the File | New... menu. The levels of a cascading menu are separated by a pipe character (|).

❑ Keys that you press on the keyboard, like *Ctrl* and *Enter*, are in italics.

Code has several styles. If it's a word that we're talking about in the text, such as a For...Next loop or a file name like Default.asp, we'll use this font. If it's a block of code that is new, important or relevant to the current discussion, it will be presented like this:

```
Dim objCmd As ADODB.Command
Set objCmd = New ADODB.Command
```

Sometimes, you'll see code in a mixture of styles, like this:

```
Dim objCmd As ADODB.Command
Set objCmd = New ADODB.Command
objCmd.CommandText = "authors"
objCmd.CommandType = adCmdTable
```

The code with a white background is code we've already looked at, or that has little to do with the matter at hand.

Advice, hints, background information, references and extra details appear in an italicized, indented font like this.

> **These boxes hold important, not-to-be forgotten, mission-critical details that are directly relevant to the surrounding text.**

These formats are designed to make sure that you know what it is you're looking at. We hope they make life easier.

Tell Us What You Think

We've worked hard on this book to make it useful. We've tried to understand what you're willing to exchange your hard-earned money for, and we've tried to make the book live up to your expectations.

Please let us know what you think about this book. Tell us what we did wrong, and what we did right. This isn't just marketing flannel: we really do huddle around the email to find out what you think. If you don't believe it, then send us a note. We'll answer, and we'll take whatever you say on board for future editions. The easiest way is to use email:

feedback@wrox.com

You can also find more details about Wrox Press on our web site. There, you'll find the code from our latest books, sneak previews of forthcoming titles, and information about the authors and editors. You can order Wrox titles directly from the site, or find out where your nearest local bookstore with Wrox titles is located.

Customer Support

If you find a mistake, please have a look at the errata page for this book on our web site first. If you can't find an answer there, tell us about the problem and we'll do everything we can to answer promptly! Just send us an email:

support@wrox.com

or fill in the form on our web site:

http://www.wrox.com/Contacts.asp

An Introduction to Data Access

Welcome to Professional ADO 2.5 Programming! In this first chapter, we're going to discuss briefly the history and evolution of data access technologies, so that we can effectively understand the role and purpose of ActiveX Data Objects (ADO) today. In particular we're going to:

❑ Discuss the importance of data in the Information Age.

❑ Define the benefits and problems with previous data access technologies such as Native APIs, Open DataBase Connectivity (ODBC), Data Access Objects (DAO), and Remote Data Objects (RDO).

❑ Examine the role of the Component Object Model in the evolution of data access technologies.

❑ Understand how the Universal Data Access (UDA) strategy solves the problems with these previous data access technologies.

❑ Briefly discuss each of the Microsoft Data Access Components (MDAC) that implements the UDA strategy.

By the end of this chapter, you should understand how data access technologies have evolved in the last decade, the direction they are going and why. You should also be able to answer the important question, "Why Universal Data Access?"

Data-Centric Applications in an Information Age

The Twentieth Century is undoubtedly best regarded as the Information Age. Whether you like it or not, every day information plays a more crucial role in our lives than the day before. We utilize a number of modern devices such as fax machines, cell phones and computers in an attempt to keep us connected with society and communicating a wide variety of information. Our society is simply information driven.

Over the last 60 years, the rate and method in which we receive information has rapidly changed. One of the most significant changes since the invention of the telephone – or even since that of the printing press – is the use of the Internet as a universal information delivery mechanism. In the 1860s it took eight days for the Pony Express to deliver a letter 2,000 miles across the western half of the United States. Today, the Internet enables large volumes of data to be transferred around the world faster, cheaper and more reliably than ever before. But the Internet is much more than just a communications tool.

The Internet is becoming a central part of our lives and it's making a difference to how we work, learn and play. Last year approximately 148 million people used the Internet not only to communicate, but also to perform tasks such as paying bills, shopping and planning vacations. According to the United States Internet Council (`http://www.usic.org`), by the end of the year 2000, the Internet will play an essential role in the lives of an estimated 320 million people worldwide.

Information in Businesses

When we consider the essential role that information plays in our day-to-day lives, it's not surprising that an estimated 90% of today's business applications are **data-centric**. Data-centric applications are designed solely for accessing, displaying and manipulating data.

As companies everywhere realize that the effective use of information can provide them with strategic advantages over their competitors, access to this information is being required in new scenarios and the complexity of the information continues to grow. For example, today more and more users need the ability to work with data in mobile environments. Important data is no longer *just* stored in mainframes and Database Management Systems (DBMSs) such as Microsoft SQL Server and Oracle. Many organizations now *also* need the ability to use information seemlessly from email systems, file systems and all types of documents. Many of these changes are a direct result of the impact the Internet has on today's businesses. For example, a typical company might manage its customers as contact records in a Microsoft Exchange public folder, store purchase orders as emails, save invoices as Microsoft Excel spreadsheets and maintain product information as Adobe Acrobat Documents (PDFs).

However, even though these aspects of data have changed, the fundamental requirement of data-centric applications remains the same: to access, display and manipulate data. Instead, the data access technologies have rapidly evolved to provide access to this complex data in these new scenarios. But, before we discuss the current direction of data access technologies, let's briefly review the history of data access over the last few years and see how data access technologies have evolved to meet the needs of developers. By understanding the evolution of data access technologies over the last decade, we can have a better understanding of how ADO not only satisfies traditional requirements, but also the data access requirements of the present.

History of Data Access

In May 1989, Microsoft jointly released their first database product called Ashton-Tate/Microsoft SQL Server 1.0, along with Ashton-Tate, the makers of dBase. However, with very few front-end applications or development tools, Ashton-Tate/Microsoft SQL Server 1.0 had a very limited user base by mid-1990.

This was the classic chicken-or-egg scenario. Microsoft decided to concentrate on the database system first and then quickly provide the tools and data access technologies needed by developers.

> **In this book, we'll use the terminology** *database* **and** *data source* **very strictly. A data source is any piece of software that stores and manages data. A database is a data source that stores its data in a tabular, row-column format.**

In the summer of 1990, Microsoft released SQL Server 1.1. This was much more than an upgrade to the bugs in the 1.0 version; in fact, Microsoft SQL Server 1.1 was a milestone release. Not only did version 1.1 mark the end of the Ashton-Tate and Microsoft agreement, but it also provided support for an important new client platform, Windows 3.0. Windows 3.0, released shortly before SQL Server 1.1, shipped with an API called DB-Library that enabled applications developed in C to access Microsoft SQL Server databases. As a result, Microsoft SQL Server 1.1 was one of the first database products which fully supported the popular Windows 3.0 operating system.

But this was just the beginning. Over the last decade, Microsoft has been aggressively releasing data access technologies that meet the rapidly evolving demands of their customers. As the requirements of applications became more sophisticated, so did the data access technologies. This can be thought of as a cause-and-effect relationship. These technologies include ODBC, Jet/DAO, RDO and finally ADO and OLE DB.

The timeline overleaf illustrates the rapid evolution of data access technologies over the last decade, beginning with Microsoft initiating the ODBC Specification in 1988 and ending in Feburary 2000 with the release of the Microsoft Data Access Components (MDAC) version 2.5, which includes ADO 2.5.

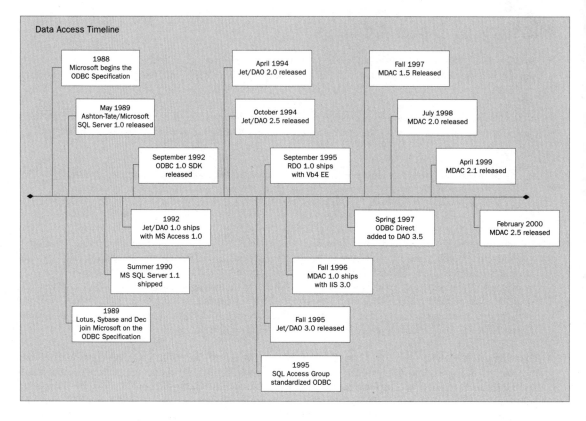

Data Access Timeline

1988 Microsoft begins the ODBC Specification	**April 1994** Jet/DAO 2.0 released	**Fall 1997** MDAC 1.5 Released
May 1989 Ashton-Tate/Microsoft SQL Server 1.0 released	**October 1994** Jet/DAO 2.5 released	**July 1998** MDAC 2.0 released
September 1992 ODBC 1.0 SDK released	**September 1995** RDO 1.0 ships with Vb4 EE	**April 1999** MDAC 2.1 released
1992 Jet/DAO 1.0 ships with MS Access 1.0	**Spring 1997** ODBC Direct added to DAO 3.5	**February 2000** MDAC 2.5 released
Summer 1990 MS SQL Server 1.1 shipped	**Fall 1996** MDAC 1.0 ships with IIS 3.0	
1989 Lotus, Sybase and Dec join Microsoft on the ODBC Specification	**Fall 1995** Jet/DAO 3.0 released	
	1995 SQL Access Group standardized ODBC	

Native APIs

Native APIs are programming interfaces designed for use against a specific DBMS. For example, to execute and retrieve results from SQL statements for data stored in a SQL Server database, you might previously have used the DB-Library. If your data were stored in an Oracle database, you would use Oracle's native API, OCI (Oracle Call Interface).

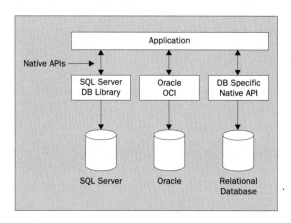

> Even today, most database systems still support their own native API for backwards compatibility with existing applications. However, native APIs are no longer commonly used, and are not recommended for use with new applications.

Problems with Native APIs

While native APIs typically deliver very high-performance data access, they all share three common, but significant problems:

❑ Native APIs are specific to a given language and operating system.

❑ New versions of database products typically broke compatibility with existing applications.

❑ Native APIs can only be used for a specific database system.

Native APIs are Specific to Languages and Operating Systems

Native APIs are usually implemented as DLLs with associated header (.h) and library (.lib) files provided for the use of developers. As a result, native APIs aren't easily used from languages other than C or C++.

Some database vendors created extensions to their native APIs that would support languages other than C or C++. One example of such an extension is VBSQL. VBSQL is a high-performance, API-based interface that enables applications developed in Visual Basic to access Microsoft SQL Server databases. VBSQL is implemented as a thin layer on top of the existing DB-Library native API. Almost every method of VBSQL can map back to a corresponding method in the DB-Library. Another example of a language-dependent version of a native API is the DB-Library for Borland (BLDBLIB.LIB).

Since native APIs were typically implemented as API-based DLLs, they were also specific to a given operating system. For example, if you were developing a 16-bit Windows application that accessed a SQL Server database, you would use the 16-bit version of DB-Library. For an MS-DOS application, you would need to use the MS-DOS version of DB-Library.

This approach of providing separate versions of a native API for each language or operating system was not a long-term solution to fixing the language- and operating system-dependent problems of native APIs. If extensions were to be developed for each language or operating system, this would mean that developers would have to learn a handful of complex APIs for each database system. Additionally, database vendors would have the nightmare of trying to maintain and support separate versions of a native API.

New Versions of Database Products Broke Compatibility with Existing Applications

API-based DLLs are usually closely tied to the implementation details. As a result, when a new version of a database system was released, a new version of the native API typically had to be released along with it to expose the new functionality and features provided by the database system. In other words, a native API couldn't simply be upgraded to provide support for a new version of a database and still provide backwards compatibility. Vendors would usually release the new version of the native API with a different filename. Customers that wanted to upgrade to the newest version of a database system were also required to rebuild and redeploy their applications. As you can imagine, this made upgrading database systems a costly venture. An example of such a problem occurred with SQL Server's native API, DB-Library. Today there are two versions of DB-Library provided for 16-bit Windows, `MSDBLIB3.LIB` and `W3DBLIB.LIB`. `MSDBLIB3.LIB` is the recommended DB-Library for use in 16-bit Windows, but `W3DBLIB.LIB`, the older version, also still ships with the newest version of SQL Server in order to provide backwards compatibility with existing applications.

Native APIs Can Only Be Used for a Specific Database System

The most frustrating problem with native APIs was that code written using one database's native API wasn't portable to another database system's native API, because there was no conformance or standardization with the programming interface itself. For example, if you'd developed an application against Oracle's native API (OCI), and you wanted to convert your database to Microsoft SQL Server, you would have needed to rewrite all of your OCI-specific data access code to support SQL Server's native API, DB-Library. Companies were effectively tied to a database vendor because it was too costly to rewrite data access code in entire applications. Incidentally, most database vendors did not mind this problem and were in no rush for standardization.

The database-specific aspect of native APIs was also costly for independent software vendors (ISVs) developing resellable software solutions. Vendors had to develop, support and maintain separate versions of an application or write database-specific code for each database system they wanted their application to support.

During this time the client/server revolution was occurring. Companies were learning that with a client/server architecture they could make use of the centralized management features mainframes provided on less expensive server machines and they could distribute processing load to very cheap desktop computers. New database systems were being released to take advantage of this client/server architecture. Users needed the ability to retrieve, analyze and manipulate data stored in these relational databases spread across the network from client workstations to servers to mainframes. Developers, users and administrators all needed a 'universal' data access technology that would support all relational databases. Additionally, this data access technology needed to be extensible and have an open architecture, so that future database systems could be supported without requiring major rewrites of client applications

The Need for Standardization

These three common problems were unlikely all to be addressed with a single solution. Today, we can look back and say that it's obvious that native APIs really needed the language-independent, multi-platform and versioning features of Microsoft's Component Object Model (COM). However, the OLE 2.0 specification, the foundation for the Component Object Model, was still several years away from being finalized and many people at that time did not realize the potential benefits of binary, reusable components.

Standardization of data access APIs was definitely the problem with the highest priority. Applications needed the ability to access multiple relational database systems using the same, standardized data access API. Applications needed Open DataBase Connectivity (ODBC).

ODBC and the ODBC API

In September 1992, after four years of working on a specification jointly with several other companies, Microsoft officially released the first version of the Open DataBase Connectivity (ODBC) Software Development Kit (SDK). ODBC is a platform-independent, industry-standard software architecture designed to solve the problems of native APIs by allowing applications to access any relational database using the same standardized API, known as the ODBC API. These relational databases can range from local databases such as Access to enterprise-level databases such as SQL Server and Oracle.

The idea behind using the same standardized API was that applications could be developed in a consistent way regardless of the database system they accessed. With ODBC, companies could easily upgrade database systems and change database vendors without the costly software development changes.

ODBC Architecture

The key to Open DataBase Connectivity providing access to any relational database can be found in ODBC's architecture. The ODBC architecture is composed of two main components: the ODBC Driver Manager and the ODBC driver.

ODBC Driver Manager

The ODBC Driver Manager is a Windows DLL (`ODBC.dll` or `ODBC32.dll`) that provides a static API on which applications can call methods. The Driver Manager is a generic software layer that has no knowledge of specific databases. The ODBC Driver Manager acts as an abstraction layer, hiding applications from a database-specific software component known as the **ODBC driver**. This abstraction allows an application to be developed the same way regardless of the underlying database.

ODBC Drivers

An ODBC driver is a database-specific software component that is responsible for establishing connections with the database system, submitting SQL statements to the database, modifying the syntax of the SQL statement if necessary and returning resultsets or error messages to the calling application. Each database system has its own specific ODBC driver. To access a different database system, an application can simply change its selection of ODBC drivers without modifying source code, assuming a compatible SQL grammar was used. Some ODBC drivers are simply layers on top of the existing native API. However, most ODBC drivers are independent of the database's native API, and the ODBC driver delivers comparable performance to the native API.

When an application wants to perform an operation against a database, it calls the appropriate method on the ODBC API, specifying the SQL command to be executed and the **ODBC Data Source Name** the application wants to execute the SQL statement against. An ODBC Data Source Name contains the connection information required to establish an ODBC connection to a particular database system. This connection information usually includes the database server, the database name, the ODBC driver and possibly the user name and password to use when connecting to the database. When the Driver Manager processes these method calls, it first dynamically loads and initializes the ODBC driver for the requested Data Source Name, if it hasn't done so already. The Driver Manager then calls a corresponding method on the ODBC API which is implemented by the loaded ODBC driver. To minimize the confusion caused by the fact that there are two implementations of the ODBC API, the implementation of the ODBC API provided by an ODBC driver is also referred to as the Service Provider Interface (SPI). The ODBC driver is responsible for communicating with the database, executing SQL statements and returning resultsets and errors to the application:

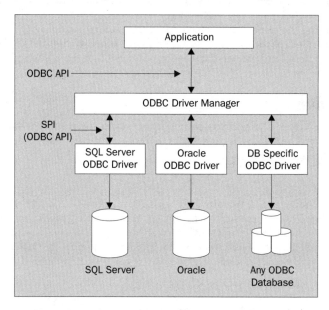

It's important to understand that even though the APIs implemented by the ODBC Driver Manager and the ODBC driver are almost the same, the Driver Manager still serves a very important purpose. The Driver Manager is designed to hide the details of loading the appropriate ODBC driver from the application. Since the ODBC drivers are dynamically loaded by the Driver Manager according to the configuration of the requested ODBC Data Source Name, the ODBC Data Source Name can easily be changed to use a different ODBC driver or a different database, without modifying any source code or recompiling the application.

Surprisingly, even with the abstraction layer provided by the Driver Manager, ODBC typically provides high performance. However, in some situations, data access through ODBC can be slower than data access using the equivalent native API because ODBC drivers may not be able to take advantage of certain database-specific features through the ODBC architecture. Additionally, ODBC can also be slower than the corresponding native API because some ODBC drivers are simply layers over the native API.

Standardization

Over the years, ODBC has become a widely accepted industry standard for accessing relational databases. Although Microsoft initially started the specification for ODBC in 1988, by the fall of 1989 three other companies, Lotus, Sybase and Dec became involved in defining the specification. It was clear that for ODBC to become an *industry* standard and not just a database vendor consortium, an independent standards body should be responsible for defining and maintaining the specification. In June 1990, Microsoft turned over the specification for ODBC to the SQL Access Group. The Structured Query Language had already become an ANSI standard in 1986 and an ISO standard in 1987. The ODBC specification was to be defined by the same standards body that defined SQL. This support for SQL and the influence of SQL as an industry standard would later contribute to the success of ODBC.

While Microsoft officially released the ODBC 1.0 SDK in September 1992 and used ODBC in most of their products by 1994, the ODBC specification wasn't finalized by the SQL Access Group until 1995. This final draft of the ODBC specification detailed three conformance levels for ODBC drivers, and the ODBC API functions and SQL grammar that must be supported at each level. Today, just as the Structured Query Language is the international standard for retrieving and manipulating data in a relational database, Open DataBase Connectivity is an international standard for communicating with a database system.

A large variety of ODBC drivers are currently available from both Microsoft and other third party vendors. Since ODBC is a platform-independent architecture, a number of ODBC drivers are available not only for Windows platforms, but also for the Macintosh and various flavors of Unix. Additionally, if an ODBC driver is not available for your database or OS platform, you can develop your own custom ODBC driver.

Problems with the ODBC API

With its high-performance, open architecture, broad industry support and international standardization, Open DataBase Connectivity was a major step forward for data access technologies, but it was not perfect and it still suffered from one major problem. The ODBC API was designed for use by C programmers and its frequent use of pointers, structures and other C-specific programming elements made it difficult or impossible to use from other programming languages and tools. During this time, Delphi and Visual Basic were starting to gain recognition and acceptance for their rapid application development (RAD) capabilities. However, the complexity of the ODBC API was the limiting factor when using these development tools.

Since the ODBC API was designed to support any relational database, it might take several lines of complex code performed in exactly the correct order just to accomplish a simple task. It was becoming evident that an object-based data access interface would eliminate many of the unnecessary complexities of the procedural/handle-based ODBC API. Ideally, this object-based interface would be language- and tool-independent, allowing one version of the data access interface to be used from multiple environments.

The Solution was Found in COM

In 1993 OLE version 2.0 was released and it introduced the revolutionary concept of component-based programming. With component-based programming, applications could be assembled by simply utilizing off the shelf or custom components. The Component Object Model (COM), a subset of the original OLE 2.0 collection of technologies, defined the standard for these (COM) components. Besides the reusability, COM components also provided a number of other important benefits, including language-independence and location-independence, to mention just two. This means reusable binary components could be used from any programming language or tool that supported COM, and regardless of the component's physical location. Microsoft quickly applied the benefits of COM components to solve the problems of the ODBC API by developing two COM component-based layers on top of the ODBC API called **Data Access Objects (DAO)** and **Remote Data Objects (RDO)**.

Data Access Objects (DAO)

A few months after Microsoft officially released the ODBC 1.0 SDK, Microsoft also released their first desktop database system for Windows, named Microsoft Access 1.0. Microsoft Access 1.0 was a powerful, but easy-to-use desktop database product that quickly gained popularity. Behind the scenes, Access used the Microsoft Jet Database Engine, known simply as Jet. Jet implements functionality that allows users to manipulate and query data stored in three types of databases:

❑ **Microsoft Access Databases (MDB)** – Microsoft Access Databases are the native database file format for the Jet database engine and as a result they usually provide the best performance over the other types of databases supported by Jet.

❑ **Indexed Sequential Access Method (ISAM) Databases** – The ISAM databases supported by the Jet database engine include Paradox, dBase, Btrieve, Excel and FoxPro. The Jet database engine can work with these ISAM databases directly without changing their structure or converting database formats.

❑ **ODBC Data Sources** – The Jet database engine can access any database that supports ODBC and has an ODBC driver. This includes databases such as Microsoft SQL Server, Oracle, and Sybase SQL Server.

The Jet engine provides a high level of flexibility by allowing all three types of databases to be accessed concurrently. However, the Jet engine is not limited to retrieving and manipulating data in these databases; it also provides support for data definition language (DLL) statements, security management and database maintenance.

The main problem with the first version of the Jet database engine was that it did not have a programming interface. Without a simplified programming interface, the success of the Jet database engine would be severely limited.

Jet Database Engine 1.1

In May 1993, Microsoft shipped Jet 1.1 with Microsoft Access 1.1 and Microsoft Visual Basic 3.0. The new Jet 1.1 data engine had a number of improvements and bug fixes over the first release, but most importantly Jet 1.1 shipped with an interface for using the database engine programmatically. This interface was **Data Access Objects (DAO) 1.1**. DAO was a COM (also known as OLE Automation) component that gave custom applications most of the power and flexibility of the Jet 1.1 database engine in a simple object model. Since DAO was an OLE Automation (COM) component, DAO was also language-independent, enabling any programming language or toolset that supported OLE Automation to take advantage of DAO and the Jet 1.1 database engine. Developers using these programming languages/toolsets could now retrieve and manipulate data using a more flexible and organized object hierarchy rather than complex and sequential ODBC API functions.

Visual Basic 3.0 also shipped with the Jet data control, which allowed applications to be 'bound' quickly to databases through the Jet database engine. When used carefully and combined with the flexibility of DAO, data binding was a very useful feature. One thing was certain: creating data-centric applications had never been easier.

Today the Jet database engine supports many more features and DAO exposes all of Jet's functionality. DAO has become one of the most widely used and accepted data access technologies by all types of developers. This is partly due to the fact that DAO builds on the success of ODBC.

Problems with DAO

Even with its great success and popularity, the earlier versions of DAO also had a significant problem. While DAO provided access to ODBC data sources, the Jet data engine had much more overhead than the ODBC API. Some performance overhead when accessing ODBC data sources is to be expected when you consider that DAO and Jet were layers on top of the ODBC API; however, the performance penalties caused by Jet were simply unacceptable in many situations, forcing most developers to resort back to the complex ODBC API when they needed to access ODBC data sources. Additionally, DAO doesn't provide support for some of the more complex features of larger Relational Database Management Systems (RDBMSs) such as support for server-side cursors, multiple resultsets and stored procedures. For Microsoft Access and ISAM databases DAO/Jet was a proven winner, but most developers still needed a COM-based, high-performance data access technology for ODBC data sources.

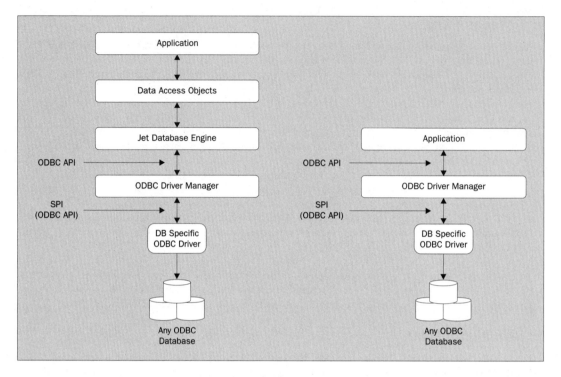

As you can see from the above diagram, DAO (left) provides much worse performance when accessing ODBC Data Sources, compared to using the ODBC API (right) directly. This is because together DAO and the Jet database engine add two additional layers on top of the ODBC API implemented by the ODBC Driver Manager. However, with Microsoft Access or ISAM databases, the Jet database engine bypasses ODBC.

Remote Data Objects (RDO)

In September 1995, in an attempt to answer both the performance problems of DAO/Jet with ODBC databases and the complexity problems of the ODBC API, Microsoft shipped Remote Data Objects (RDO) 1.0 with the 32-bit Enterprise Edition of Visual Basic 4.0. RDO is a thin, COM-based wrapper on top of the ODBC API designed to provide high-performance data access to ODBC Data Sources while providing the simplicity of DAO. The RDO object model was designed to take advantage of the more complex features of RDBMSs, such as client and server-side cursors, multiple resultsets, parameterized queries and stored procedures.

RDO is a much smaller data access interface than DAO. RDO does not provide support for data structure modification or security because RDO was designed purely for data access to ODBC data sources. But the most important difference between DAO and RDO is that RDO does not use the Jet database engine. Instead, as you can see from the diagram opposite, RDO is a thin layer on top of the ODBC API that simplifies data access to ODBC Data Sources without sacrificing performance. In fact, in most situations, RDO's performance is nearly the same as using the ODBC API directly.

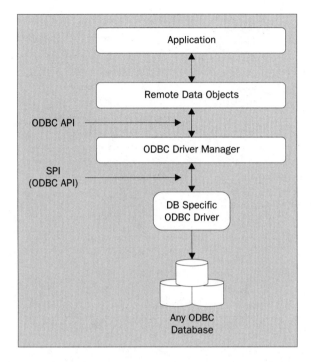

RDO also provides the flexibility for developers to use the ODBC API and RDO together by exposing attributes about the underlying ODBC connections through the RDO object model. This provides an easy upgrade path for applications that currently use the ODBC API, but want to move to a COM-based data access technology.

With the introduction of RDO, developers had two data access technologies to choose from. RDO was usually the technology of choice for ODBC data sources, while DAO still played an important role in working with Microsoft Access and ISAM databases when performance was a higher priority than compatiblity with multiple database systems. As a result, developers were often faced with the difficult, but important, design decision of choosing the appropriate data access technology for a given situation.

ODBCDirect

While RDO is COM-based and is therefore language-independent, licensing restrictions limit the use of RDO to developers who own the Enterprise Edition of a Visual Studio development tool. Many applications still used DAO and needed costly redevelopment to take advantage of the performance benefits provided by RDO. In the spring of 1997, Microsoft released DAO 3.5, first with Office 97 and later with Visual Basic 5.0. DAO 3.5 included support for a new operational mode of DAO called ODBCDirect. ODBCDirect mode allows applications to use DAO when accessing ODBC Data Sources without suffering from the unacceptable performance penalties of the Jet database engine. As you can see from the following diagram, ODBCDirect mode effectively makes DAO a layer on top of RDO. In ODBCDirect mode, when methods and properties are invoked on DAO objects, DAO forwards the calls to the corresponding methods and properties on RDO objects.

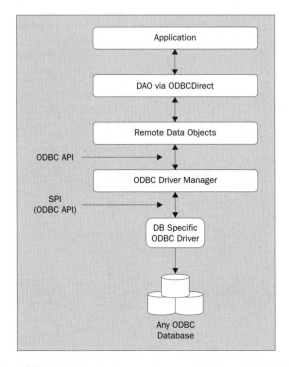

While you might think that adding DAO as a layer on top of RDO would result in the same performance problems that DAO had on top of Jet, it's important to remember that the performance problems of DAO when accessing ODBC data sources were caused by the Jet database engine and not by the DAO programming interface. ODBCDirect enables any programming language or toolset that supports COM to take advantage of the performance benefits of RDO without rewriting existing DAO code or worrying about licensing issues.

The Data Access Needs of the Present

During 1995-1996, the use of the Internet was becoming more widespread. Businesses were starting to recognize the value of the Internet as an application platform, rather than just a new advertising tool. Companies like Amazon and Dell were breaking new ground in the areas of business-to-consumer (B2C) and business-to-business (B2B) e-commerce. Both internet and non-internet data-centric applications were being developed to help companies compete in this global market. But these new data-centric applications were faced with a number of new requirements, including:

❑ **Access to non-relational data** –Many businesses began to realize that important data was being stored in new formats such as calendars, emails, newsgroup postings, streaming video, and image files. From file systems to Exchange folders, data-centric applications needed the ability to retrieve and manipulate data in these various non-relational data sources either by using a single data access technology or by first converting the data into a relational format so it could be accessible via ODBC. However, organizations also still needed the ability to make use of existing data stored in legacy data sources such as mainframes, minicomputers and relational client/server databases.

❑ **Access to distributed data** – Not only was there a need to access both relational and non-relational data sources, but also these data sources were scattered in a variety of locations. Many organizations were globalizing and the simple approach of having a single database system was not practical. Instead, these 'enterprise' organizations were replicating or distributing data sources to multiple locations in order to provide faster data retrieval and manipulation, improved fault tolerance and increased scalability. Data-centric applications needed the ability to access data seamlessly, regardless of its physical location.

❑ **Access to data in disconnected environments** – More than 40 percent of the personal computers sold to corporations today are laptops, intended to be used in a mobile, disconnected environment. Disconnected environments add a number of other complexities to a data-centric application. Usually these complexities are related to the transfer and management of data in a multi-user, connectionless environment. In this type of environment, users usually need to bring sets of data down locally for disconnected viewing, modification, addition or deletion of data and then merge their changes to the shared network data source(s) system once they connect to the network again. Unfortunately, this level of functionality required a fair amount of custom code and a well thought-out design. Data-centric applications needed a standard approach to temporarily caching data on local workstations.

❑ **Scalable data access** – Contrary to what some developers think, scalability is not just another Microsoft buzzword. Scalability actually is the real-world situation of an application meeting the growing needs of a business. As a business grows more and more users might need to use your data-centric application. Applications typically need the ability to 'scale', to meet this demand from additional users with little or no modification. In no other area is the need for scalability more evident than with internet applications. The number of users in an internet system can grow by leaps and bounds in a very short space of time. It's important to understand that scalability is a distinct concept from that of high performance. Performance is the rate at which *a user* is able to perform operations. Scalability is the support for a large number of users while also providing high performance for each concurrent user.

A well-designed, distributed architecture is actually the key to scalability and as a result, the requirement for scalable data access usually goes hand-in-hand with distributed data and disconnected environments. Usually the best technique to achieve scalability involves spreading application processing across multiple machines. Ironically, when you look at today's typical client workstation, most of them are often under-worked and they have more processing power than they know what to do with, making them perfect targets for data-centric applications.

In addition to a distributed architecture, data-centric applications can also achieve scalability by performing operations quickly, pooling connections to data sources and reducing the number of locks held during transactions.

Existing Data Access Technologies Couldn't Satisfy these Requirements

There was a growing need for a solution: not only to the data access problems faced in the past, such as performance, complexity, and language-dependence, but *also* these new requirements developers were facing. ODBC couldn't satisfy these new requirements in its current form. While ODBC could access both desktop and client/server database systems, it was designed for relational databases, and a very specific set of data types. Since RDO is a layer on top of the ODBC API, it suffered from the same problems. DAO, on the other hand, did provide access to diverse databases, but it was notorious for its slow performance when accessing ODBC data sources. ODBC, with its broad industry support and international standardization, was clearly here to stay, but it wasn't a solution for accessing non-relational data sources.

Different APIs

Currently developers creating data-centric applications were becoming buried under the vast number of APIs. Each data source, both relational and non-relational, had its own COM components and/or APIs.

When developing data-centric applications, you would have to choose the data access technology based on the type of data you were accessing. Often, the choice would also depend on a combination of several additional factors such as the applications performance requirements, the programming language or toolset you were using and the timeframe you had available to develop the application. For example:

❑ To retrieve data from a Microsoft SQL Server database you would use DB-Lib, RDO, ODBC API, or DAO.

❑ To manipulate data stored in an ISAM database such as Btrieve, FoxPro or dBase, you would use DAO/Jet.

❑ To access the registry, performance monitor data, Windows NT/2000 user and group accounts or the Windows NT/2000 Event Log, you would use the Win32 API.

❑ To access files and directories you might use the Win32 API, the Scripting Runtime or Active Directory Service Interfaces (ADSI).

❑ To define SQL Server security and database objects such as tables, rules and stored procedures programmatically you would use the SQLDMO Object Library

❑ To manipulate MTS/COM+ component information that is stored in the MTS/COM+ catalogs you would use the MTS Admin Type Library or the COM+ Admin Type Library.

❑ To access the Microsoft Repository, you would use the complex Repository interfaces.

❑ To access Exchange folders or Personal Folder Files, you could use MAPI, the Collaboration Data Objects (CDO) library or the Outlook object library.

❑ To retrieve data over the Internet, you could use the HTTP protocol and the Microsoft Internet Controls, or any one of hundreds of third-party components.

Possible Solutions

Some companies, such as IBM and Oracle, believe the solution to the requirements made of today's data-centric applications is to store all types of data into a single database structure. While this 'universal' database approach provides centralized management of all data, it requires the costly conversion and movement of data. Additionally, non-relational, non-structured data would have to be stored in a relational, structured format. The universal database approach also does not make use of current investments in existing hardware and software.

Microsoft has approached these new data-centric application requirements from the data access perspective, which seems much more logical. Microsoft believes that developers need a universal way to access all types of data sources regardless of the data types, the data format or the data's location without being required to build problematic data conversion and movement routines. Microsoft's answer to these new requirements is to leave data exactly where it is and provide developers with **Universal Data Access (UDA)**.

Universal Data Access

The Universal Data Access (UDA) strategy, introduced during the fall of 1996, is Microsoft's solution to the challenges developers are facing when creating today's data-centric applications. But UDA is not simply a new data access technology. Instead, UDA is a strategy or methodology, implemented as a framework of technologies that provide high-performance access to any type of data source, both relational and non-relational, and possibly scattered across multiple locations and operating systems. Microsoft's Universal Data Access strategy provides a number of advantages to data-centric applications including:

❑ **Simplified development** – With UDA, you will no longer be required to use a data access API specific to the data source you are accessing. Instead, you can use the same UDA technologies to access any type of data source regardless of the data format, data type or internal storage mechanism. Furthermore, the UDA technologies are designed to provide consistent high-performance data access in any development architecture. Developers can use the same data access technologies for single-user desktop applications to mission-critical, n-tier internet systems. This eliminates much of the guess-work previously required when designing today's data-centric applications.

❑ **Interoperability** – UDA is designed to provide interoperability with both existing legacy data sources and today's new data sources, so that data-centric applications can both make use of current technology investments and be easily extended to support new data sources and types of data. UDA is a vendor-neutral, open-architecture solution that does not require data to be moved to a 'universal' database or storage format nor does it require data sources to implement any changes or additional functionality. This level of true interoperability has allowed UDA technologies to quickly gain broad industry support and work with all popular database products.

❑ **Reliability** – Today's data-centric applications must be more reliable than ever before. Since the Internet is a global network, most internet applications are responsible for running 24 hours a day, 7 days a week and 365 days a year. The UDA technologies achieve the required reliability for these mission-critical, data-centric applications by building upon the success and avoiding the failures of previous data access interfaces such as ODBC, RDO, and DAO.

❑ **High performance and scalability** – High performance and scalability were very important design goals for the UDA technologies. Of course, performance and scalability are relative issues that can only be measured against other data access technologies. However, the UDA technologies have delivered performance that is very comparable to that of native APIs and the ODBC API. The key to the high performance and scalability benefits of the Universal Data Access technologies are found in the pluggable architecture of COM components. When additional functionality beyond basic data retrieval and manipulation is needed, separate components can be dynamically loaded to implement this functionality and then later released when they are no longer needed.

The UDA technologies also provide integrated support for client-side data caching and manipulation while possibly being **disconnected** from the centralized server. After changes are made, the data can then be efficiently marshaled across the network and the changes can be merged into the data source. This batch processing approach in data-centric applications can result in excellent scalability, because clients require fewer network roundtrips and less processing by the server, whereas in typical client/server or internet application scenarios, *each* operation invoked by the client results in a complete round trip. We'll discuss data caching and transfer again briefly in Chapter 2 and in more detail in Chapter 3.

Based on COM

If you're familiar with the Component Object Model (COM), you will probably realize that these benefits are not exclusive to UDA technologies. COM components have provided these benefits for years. However, the COM support found in the UDA technologies is not limited simply to the COM-based APIs exposed by a handful of components. The UDA technologies support and utilize COM components and COM interfaces internally to provide Universal Data Access. This level of support for COM is strategic because the UDA technologies build on the success of a 6+ year old technology, which is very widely implemented. With the release of COM+ in Windows 2000, COM has been extended to provide transaction processing, simplified administration, concurrency management, resource pooling, asynchronous (queued) components, dynamic load balancing, object pooling and publish and subscribe events. We'll examine how the UDA technologies use COM and discuss more about COM+ in the next chapter.

UDA is Implemented as a Collection of Technologies

It is important to remember that UDA is only a strategy or concept, and not a physical implementation. Developers can take advantage of UDA using any of the following four integrated technologies:

❑ **ODBC** – As we have already seen, Open DataBase Connectivity (ODBC) is a software architecture designed to allow applications to access any relational database using the same standardized ODBC API. As an international standard and widely accepted data access technology, ODBC can be used to access almost every database in use today. The Universal Data Access strategy effectively builds upon the success of ODBC by supporting access to *any* ODBC database through OLE DB. This support for ODBC databases is one example of how the UDA technologies provide interopability with existing data sources.

❑ **OLE DB** – OLE DB is a low-level or system-level programming interface that effectively serves as the foundation of the Universal Data Access strategy. Where ODBC was designed to access *only* relational databases, OLE DB allows data-centric applications to access *any* type of data source including not only relational databases, but also hierarchical and semi-structured data sources such as legacy mainframe data, e-mail systems and directory services. However, as a system-level programming interface, OLE DB can only be accessed directly from applications developed in C++.

❑ **ADO** – Where OLE DB is the *system-level* programming interface that implements the Universal Data Access strategy, ActiveX Data Objects (ADO) is the *application-level* programming interface. ADO is designed for high-performance data access in *all* development scenarios, regardless of the data source, the programming language, or the application's physical architecture. ADO combines the ease of use found in DAO and RDO with the extensibility of OLE DB. The relationship between ADO and OLE DB can be compared to that of RDO and ODBC. Just as RDO was a thin wrapper over the ODBC API, ADO is a thin COM-based object model over OLE DB.

❑ **RDS** - Remote Data Services (RDS) are a high-level set of COM components built on top of several fundamental ADO and OLE DB components. In addition to providing a simplified programming interface on top of ADO and OLE DB, RDS also provides several unique features that facilitate the development of distributed, data-centric applications.

As you can see from the following diagram, OLE DB is the center of the integrated UDA technologies. Through OLE DB, applications can access any data source including ODBC databases. Instead of accessing OLE DB directly, applications can also code to the simpler ADO or RDS object models:

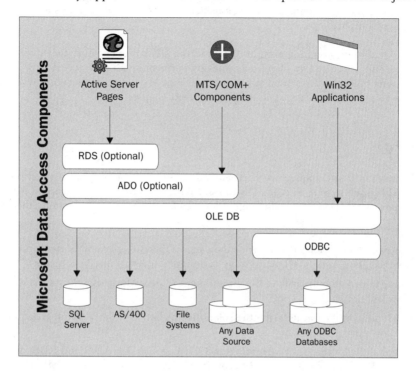

MDAC

Collectively these technologies are also known as the Microsoft Data Access Components (MDAC). However, it's important not to confuse UDA with MDAC. UDA is nothing more than a strategy or scheme for accessing any type of data stored in any data source, whereas MDAC is the redistributable set of technologies (ODBC, OLE DB, ADO and RDS) that *implement* the Universal Data Access strategy.

The ODBC, OLE DB, ADO and RDS run-time components are packaged and distributed under the MDAC umbrella because they are all integrated and inter-dependent on one another. For example, ADO and RDS depend on OLE DB for almost their entire functionality, while OLE DB requires the ODBC Driver Manager and the appropriate ODBC drivers to be installed to access ODBC databases.

Distribution of these four technologies as a single unit can also reduce versioning, setup and maintenance problems that are commonly associated with previous data access APIs. MDAC also maintains its own version numbers and always installs components to the same location. When a new version of ADO, for example, is released, it is always packaged in a new version of MDAC and distributed as part of the complete unit, rather than being distributed as an individual component. In most situations, this packaging and distribution approach eliminates many of the 'DLL Hell' problems that can occur when a system is running incompatible versions of components. However, this benefit of MDAC can easily be lost when applications attempt to install only subsets of MDAC, such as only the ADO or only RDS, with their application.

As of version 2.5, all MDAC releases will be packaged in operating systems and operating system service packs. This is an attempt to reduce further the administration effort required to keep machines running the most current versions of the MDAC components. Packaging the Microsoft Data Access Components in operating systems and service packs will also allow developers to avoid redistributing them with custom applications.

N-tier and 3-tier systems designed around the Windows DNA model can reduce even further the administration effort required on client machines by performing all data access in MTS or COM+ objects executing on centrally located application servers. We'll discuss the Windows DNA model and its role in the Universal Data Access strategy in the next chapter.

Summary

In this brief but important chapter, we've discussed the evolution of data access technologies beginning with native APIs, such as SQL Server's DB-Library API, up to the recent release of Microsoft Data Access Components (MDAC) 2.5, which includes ADO version 2.5. After reading this chapter you should:

❑ Understand the problems with prior data access technologies and understand how the Universal Data Access (UDA) strategy is designed to solve these problems

❑ Be able to describe the role of the Component Object Model (COM) in the evolution of data access technologies

❑ Be able to identify and describe the relationships between the technologies that implement the UDA strategy

❑ Understand why the UDA technologies (ODBC, OLE DB, ADO and RDS) are collectively packaged and distributed as the Microsoft Data Access Components (MDAC).

Now that we have a "bird's eye view" of Microsoft's UDA strategy and MDAC, in the next chapter we shall discuss each of the Microsoft Data Access Components in more detail, and examine how they help us towards the lofty goal of Universal Data Access.

2

The ADO Environment

In the last chapter, we discussed the evolution of data access technologies over the last decade and we briefly introduced the Microsoft Data Access Components (MDAC). In this chapter, we're going to look at the environment in which ADO is used. This chapter therefore consists primarily of a review of some of the technologies which are frequently used with ADO. We'll start by "digging deeper" into each of the present day technologies that compose MDAC, focusing primarily on ADO and OLE DB. Then, after a quick look at XML (another approach to standardizing data manipulation, and an increasingly important element in many data-centric applications), we will look at the architecture of the n-tier Windows DNA applications in which ADO is most frequently used. In particular, we're going to:

❑ Analyze OLE DB as the foundation of MDAC and the Universal Data Access (UDA) strategy.

❑ Understand the key role of the OLE DB interfaces.

❑ Define the three types of components that compose the OLE DB architecture: OLE DB data providers, service providers and consumers.

❑ Look at examples of each of these types of OLE DB components.

❑ Discuss the benefits of ADO as the primer data access technology

❑ Analyze the difference between the ADODB and ADOR object libraries

❑ Define the role of XML in relationship to the Microsoft Data Access Components

❑ Understand the role of RDS in relationship to ADO and OLE DB

❑ Discuss the Windows DNA architecture and n-tier development

❑ Examine several of the key technologies available for each tier

❑ Analyze the role of ADO and the features it provides for developing n-tier, data-centric applications

By the end of this chapter, you should have a comprehensive understanding of how ADO works and the features and benefits it provides.

ODBC

Open DataBase Connectivity, as we saw in the previous chapter, is a software architecture designed to allow applications to access any relational database using the same standardized ODBC API. Almost every relational database in use today can be accessed through ODBC. ODBC is an international standard and widely accepted data access technology. There are many ODBC drivers, available both from Microsoft and from third party vendors.

If you remember from our discussion on the history of data access, the main problem with ODBC is that it is designed solely for relational databases which are capable of processing SQL statements. Why then is ODBC considered a component of the Universal Data Access strategy? The only reason ODBC is considered a UDA component is for interoperability with existing relational databases. As an international standard with broad industry support, developers were not going to switch from using ODBC or RDO in their data-centric applications to OLE DB or ADO. Microsoft recognized this fact. So, instead of making developers choose between ODBC and OLE DB (or ADO), OLE DB and ADO have provided support for ODBC databases since their initial version 1.0 release. OLE DB effectively builds upon the success of ODBC by making any ODBC database appear as an OLE DB data source. This compatibility with existing ODBC databases provides an important migration path from ODBC to OLE DB or ADO. Applications can use OLE DB or ADO for both non-relational *data sources* that have support for OLE DB and relational *databases* that don't yet have support for OLE DB, but currently support ODBC. Organizations can also make use of their current investments in ODBC. Eventually, OLE DB will probably replace ODBC as the chief data access technology on the Windows platform. But for now, ODBC will continue to be supported with proprietary data access technologies such as the ODBC API, RDO and DAO and with current data access technologies such as OLE DB, ADO and RDS.

Don't worry if the relationship between ODBC and OLE DB sounds confusing. We'll discuss how OLE DB provides support for ODBC later in this chapter, but for now the important thing to understand is that the OLE DB architecture provides interoperability with existing ODBC databases.

OLE DB

OLE DB is a low-level or system-level programming interface that effectively serves as the foundation of the Universal Data Access strategy. Where ODBC was designed to access *only* relational databases, OLE DB allows data-centric applications to access *any* type of data source including relational databases, but also hierarchical and semi-structured data sources such as legacy mainframe data, e-mail systems and directory services. You could say that ODBC provided Universal *Database* Access where OLE DB provides Universal *Data* Access.

OLE DB can also provide access to non-persistent data sources or temporary data such as memory and processes. Virtually anything that can be considered data could be exposed and accessed through OLE DB. Additionally, OLE DB does not require applications to use a specific query language or command syntax, nor does it impose any restriction on data types. In fact, OLE DB can actually manage complex data types such as references to COM objects. How is OLE DB able to provide this level of flexibility?

> The key to the OLE DB, the system-level implementation of Microsoft's Universal Data Access strategy, lies in OLE DB's use of COM components and interfaces.

OLE DB is designed entirely as a COM-based data access technology. Unlike other data access interfaces that limit their COM support to their object model, OLE DB uses COM interfaces and COM components internally to provide access to diverse data sources and to implement reusable services on top of data sources. This intrinsic support for COM also explains the name OLE DB, which probably should have been named COM DB.

Providing UDA Through Interfaces

Implementing a solution that provides Universal Data Access is similar to answering the classic question, "Is the glass half-full or half-empty?" Of course, the answer to this question depends on your perspective. OLE DB takes the "half-full" perspective and looks at the similarities between data sources, instead of the differences. OLE DB defines an extensible set of COM interfaces that expose data in a standard format. In other words, to a data-centric application or a **consumer**, data is data, regardless of the data's native format or type of data source. As a result, these COM interfaces effectively form an abstraction layer between the data-centric application and the data source. The following diagram illustrates this concept. Notice that the data-centric application communicates only with OLE DB through the standard OLE DB interfaces. As a result, the data-centric application is totally unaware of the implementation details of OLE DB and the underlying data source:

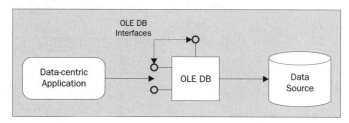

I know what some of you are probably thinking. Didn't ODBC drivers act as an "abstraction layer" between data-centric applications and a database? Yes, ODBC drivers also provide an abstraction layer. However, because ODBC drivers were not implemented using COM interfaces, this abstraction layer was too closely tied to the data access implementation and was not extensible.

We'll discuss the components that implement these COM interfaces to form this abstraction layer in more detail later, but first let's examine how OLE DB can also provide extensibility through the use of these COM interfaces.

> **Unfortunately, these OLE DB interfaces can only be used directly from C++ because of their complexity. However, ADO exposes almost all of OLE DB's functionality through a simplified object model and a handful of dual-interface COM components that can be used from any programming language or toolset that supports COM.**

Factored Interfaces

In the Microsoft Component Object Model, a single instance of a COM component – a COM object – can implement one or more interfaces. Each interface defines and exposes a set of functionality that is implemented by the COM component. For example, let's consider an `Orders` component for an e-commerce application that implements three interfaces: `IOrderInformation`, `IPlaceOrder` and `IProcessOrder`. As you can see in the following diagram, these three interfaces separate and group the functionality provided by our `Orders` component. The `IOrderInformation` defines methods for managing general order information such as the `OrderID`, the `OrderDate` and the items on the order; the `IPlaceOrder` interface defines methods for managing data associated with placing an order such as credit card information and billing information; and the `IProcessOrder` interface defines methods for shipping orders, tracking orders and accepting returns:

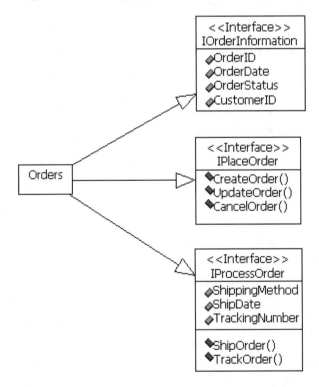

This process of dividing a COM component's functionality into well-organized sets of COM interfaces is sometimes called **interface factoring**. Why is understanding interface factoring with COM objects important to understanding OLE DB and ADO? Because interface factoring is a key to how OLE DB (and ADO) can provide access to diverse data sources without imposing any restrictions on these data sources or the data being accessed. In other words, interfaces are the key to OLE DB's extensibility and flexibility. OLE DB provides only eight COM objects but over five times as many interfaces. These OLE DB interfaces group related sets of functionality provided by the eight OLE DB objects, just as the `IOrder`, `IPlaceOrder`, and the `IProcessOrder` interfaces group related functionality of the `Orders` component in the previous diagram. OLE DB provides two important benefits through this interface factoring:

❑ **Simplified data-centric applications** – Interface factoring reduces the complexity of data-centric applications by allowing applications to use only the interfaces needed for the task at hand. If an application needs to access relational data, it doesn't need to worry about interfaces provided for hierarchical or *semi-structured* data. Of course, ADO hides all the details of using OLE DB interfaces; however, as we will see later in this chapter, the ADO object model and development using ADO is inherently simple because of OLE DB's support for interface factoring.

❑ **Extensible data sources** – Interface factoring allows data sources to provide support only for the interfaces required to expose the data source's functionality. For example, if a data source manages relational data, it only needs to support the OLE DB interfaces required to expose relational data. A data source is not required to support functionality for features it doesn't provide. However, if an existing data source wants to provide extended functionality or support for an additional data format, the data source simply supports the appropriate set of additional OLE DB interfaces. Existing data-centric applications will not require any changes and new applications can be developed to take advantage of the new features.

> Data sources themselves aren't actually responsible for implementing the OLE DB interfaces. Instead, a data source-specific COM component called an OLE DB data provider is actually responsible for this task. However, for the context of this discussion, it's easier simply to think of the data source as implementing the functionality behind the OLE DB interfaces.

The first version of OLE DB only provided a core set of interfaces that enabled data to be exposed in a relational (row-column) format. With OLE DB 2.5, there are now four groups of OLE DB interfaces that are designed to expose different types of data or provide extended functionality to existing types of data. These four sets of OLE DB interfaces include:

❑ OLE DB interfaces for tabular or relational data

❑ OLE DB interfaces for multi-dimensional data (OLAP)

❑ OLE DB interfaces for DDL and Security

❑ OLE DB interfaces for Semi-Structured Data

Since the main subject matter of this book is ADO, we won't discuss these sets of OLE DB interfaces in any detail. Besides, by now you're probably wondering how these OLE DB interfaces fit into the big picture and what they have to do with ADO? To address these issues, we need to take a look at the OLE DB architecture.

OLE DB Architecture

OLE DB is an open-architecture model that is divided into three general types of COM components:

❑ **OLE DB Data Providers** – OLE DB data providers are COM components that implement the OLE DB interfaces. When methods are called on these implemented interfaces, by OLE DB service providers or OLE DB consumers, the data provider is responsible for performing the requested operation against the data source. Unlike other components in the OLE DB architecture, a data provider is not dependent on any other OLE DB components in order to perform its operations. From a high-level perspective, OLE DB data providers are similar to ODBC drivers; they are both data source-specific software layers that are responsible for accessing and exposing data. The single, but significant, difference is that OLE DB data providers are accessed using COM'.

❑ **OLE DB Consumers** – OLE DB consumers are simply data-centric applications, components or tools that utilize or *consume* data through the OLE DB interfaces. You can think of OLE DB consumers as clients and the OLE DB data provider as the server. As the 'client', an OLE DB consumer makes requests for data retrieval and/or manipulation by calling methods on the appropriate OLE DB interfaces. The data-source specific OLE DB data provider acting as the 'server' processes these requests and returns results to the OLE DB consumer. The OLE DB consumer can then manipulate the data in a standard way using the OLE DB interfaces.

❑ **OLE DB Service Providers** – OLE DB service providers are probably the most interesting components of the OLE DB architecture. They implement standard services that extend the functionality of data providers. Examples of these services could include cursor engines, query processors and data conversion engines. Service providers are reusable COM components that effectively act both as an OLE DB data provider and as an OLE DB consumer because they both consume and produce data through the OLE DB interfaces. You can think of OLE DB service providers as the 'middle tier' between the OLE DB consumer ('client') and the OLE DB data provider ('server'). Where data providers and consumers are required component layers when accessing data using OLE DB, the use of service providers is entirely optional. However, we often use not just one, but several, OLE DB service providers together. Of course, you should bear in mind that the more layers you have for retrieving and manipulating data, the more the performance of the data-centric application degrades.

The following diagram illustrates the role of these three types of OLE DB components within the OLE DB architecture. Notice that the optional OLE DB service provider(s) both consume and expose data through the OLE DB interfaces. Communication between these OLE DB components typically occurs within the same process, although it can also occur across process and machine boundaries using industry-standard network protocols such as Microsoft's Distributed COM (DCOM) or HTTP.

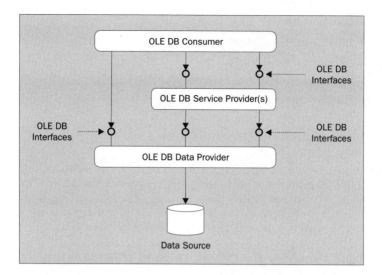

Where does ADO fit into the OLE DB architecture? ADO is actually a high-level OLE DB consumer that abstracts developers from the details of the OLE DB objects, interfaces and even the OLE DB architecture. Nevertheless, the more you understand about the underlying OLE DB architecture, the better you'll be able to make use of ADO as an OLE DB consumer. When you call functions or properties on ADO objects, ADO simply forwards the method calls to the appropriate OLE DB service(s) or data provider(s).

Since ADO is the application-level implementation of UDA and based entirely on OLE DB, it is helpful to spend a little time understanding the OLE DB architecture. Let's look at each type of component in the OLE DB architecture in more detail.

OLE DB Data Providers

As we have seen, an OLE DB data provider is simply a COM component that exposes data through the OLE DB interfaces. The details of the underlying data source are completely encapsulated by the OLE DB data provider. As a result, the data source can range in features and complexity from a full DBMS, such as SQL Server or Oracle, to a simple ASCII text file. From the OLE DB consumer's perspective, it is irrelevant what data source the data originates from, regardless of the data provider involved or the complexity of the data source from which the data originated, because the consumer accesses and manipulates data through the OLE DB interfaces.

Microsoft currently provides a number of OLE DB data providers for both relational and non-relational data sources. These OLE DB data providers include:

- ❑ Relational OLE DB data providers
    - ❑ OLE DB provider for ODBC
    - ❑ OLE DB provider for SQL Server
    - ❑ OLE DB provider for Jet
    - ❑ OLE DB provider for Oracle

❑ Non-relational providers

    ❑ OLE DB provider for AS/400

    ❑ OLE DB provider for Index Server

    ❑ OLE DB provider for Internet Publishing

    ❑ OLE DB provider for Active Directory

    ❑ OLE DB provider for Microsoft Exchange

    ❑ OLE DB provider for OLAP

In addition to this comprehensive list of OLE DB data providers available from Microsoft, there are also a number of data providers available from third-party vendors such as Merant (http://www.merant.com) and ISG Navigator (http://www.isgnavigator.com). Furthermore, custom OLE DB data providers can also be developed for virtually any data source. Let's discuss each of these OLE DB data providers that are currently provided by Microsoft.

Microsoft OLE DB Provider for ODBC Drivers (MSDASQL)

When Microsoft released MDAC 1.0 back in the fall of 1996, the first and only OLE DB Provider available was the Microsoft OLE DB Provider for ODBC drivers (MSDASQL). This was a strategic move because in OLE DB's first version, consumers such as ADO could access *any* relational database that had an ODBC driver. Additionally, organizations could make use of their current investments and experience in ODBC.

MSDASQL effectively acts as a conversion layer, mapping OLE DB interfaces to ODBC APIs. MSDASQL receives calls by ADO and other OLE DB consumers through its standard OLE DB interfaces. It interprets these calls and invokes the corresponding ODBC APIs, which in turn send the requests to an ODBC driver. After the data source has processed a request to modify or retrieve data, any results are returned back to the ODBC driver and then to MSDASQL. Finally, MSDASQL exposes a standard OLE DB rowset that is accessible by OLE DB consumers or service providers through the tabular OLE DB interfaces:

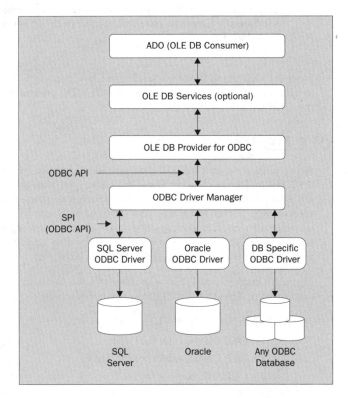

OLE DB Service Providers with MSDASQL

Since MSDASQL exposes data from an ODBC data source through OLE DB, OLE DB service providers can provide additional functionality on top of the data. For example, by using MSDASQL to access ODBC databases, an OLE DB service provider called the Client Cursor Engine (CCE) can be used to provide searching, filtering and sorting capabilities for data within an OLE DB rowset. This additional functionality is otherwise available when accessing the same data with the ODBC API, DAO or RDO.

Native Data Providers

Since the release of MDAC 2.0, Microsoft has released a number of 'native' OLE DB data providers for various databases that are completely independent of ODBC. These native data providers communicate directly to the data source using the data source's native communication mechanism. With native data providers there is no need for an intermediate translation from one API to another. As a result, native data providers are data-source specific; unlike MSDASQL, which can be used to access several different database products.

> The term 'native data provider' is usually used when discussing relational databases. With non-relational data sources currently there is no distinction between 'native' and 'non-native' data providers. This is because all data providers for non-relational data sources use the native communication mechanism of the data source they are accessing.

Since the release of MDAC 2.0, Microsoft has provided three native providers for the following popular relational database systems:

- ❑ Microsoft SQL Server 7.0
- ❑ Microsoft Jet Database Engine
- ❑ Oracle 8.0

Native providers are much faster than using the OLE DB Provider for ODBC, because they eliminate the need both for the OLE DB to ODBC conversion process and for the ODBC driver and Driver Manager layers. For this reason, you should always use the native OLE DB data provider for the data source you are accessing, so long as one is available.

MSDASQL has provided an effective path for applications to migrate from ODBC-based data access technologies to OLE DB-based data access technologies. While MSDASQL is the default provider in ADO, applications can be changed to use a native data provider by specifying the native provider's programmatic ID (ProgID) when connecting to a data source.

Microsoft OLE DB Provider for SQL Server (SQLOLEDB)

One important native OLE DB data provider is the Microsoft OLE DB Provider for SQL Server (SQLOLEDB). SQLOLEDB is an OLE DB version 2.0-compliant provider that exposes data stored in Microsoft SQL Server 6.5 and 7.0 databases through the OLE DB interfaces.

Where MSDASQL maps OLE DB interfaces to the ODBC API, SQLOLEDB is implemented directly on top of the client network libraries used by Microsoft SQL Server 7.0. When SQLOLEDB processes method calls by a consumer or service provider, it simply packages and forwards SQL statements to the SQL Server data engine. Any resultsets returned from the SQL Server data engine are exposed by SQLOLEDB using the OLE DB tabular interfaces. Of course, between SQLOLEDB and the SQL Server data engine are standard network components responsible for packing and unpacking network packets.

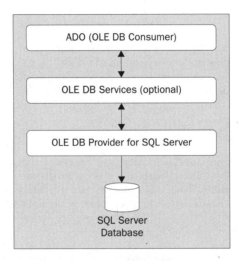

> The OLE DB provider for SQL Server can be used with both SQL Server version 6.5 and version 7.0. However, to use the OLE DB provider for SQL Server with SQL Server 6.5, a group of stored procedures known as the catalog stored procedures must first be upgraded by executing the `Instcat.sql` script against the 6.5 installation. `Instcat.sql` is included with the SQL Server 6.5 service pack 5a. For more information about using SQLOLEDB with SQL Server 6.5 and the `Instcat.sql` file, see the Microsoft Knowledge Base Articles #Q216519 and #Q197176.

MSDE

A discussion about SQL Server wouldn't be complete without a few words about the Microsoft Data Engine (MSDE). MSDE is a fully compatible version of the SQL Server 7.0 data engine that is designed to execute on client workstations. MSDE is optimized to host small databases (less than 2 Gb) that are accessed by only a handful of users. Actually, MSDE will intentially slow down when more than five concurrent users are connected to a database.

By developing against this freely distributable, but fully compatible, version of SQL Server, applications are provided with a migration path to the standard, small business or enterprise editions of SQL Server as an organization's needs change without requiring code changes. Since MSDE *is* the SQL Server data engine, MSDE fully supports the OLE DB provider for SQL Server (SQLOLEDB) and there is no difference between connecting to an MSDE database and a database hosted by any of these other editions of SQL Server 7.0. With the addition of MSDE, the SQL Server product line has become a scalable database system capable of satisfying the relational storage needs of any application.

OLE DB Provider for Microsoft Jet (JOLT)

MDAC 2.0 shipped with the first release of the OLE DB Provider for Microsoft Jet, sometimes referred to as JOLT. As you can probably guess by the name, the OLE DB Provider for Microsoft Jet uses the Microsoft Jet database engine to expose data stored in Microsoft Access databases (.mdb) and numerous ISAM databases including Paradox, dBase, Btrieve, Excel and FoxPro.

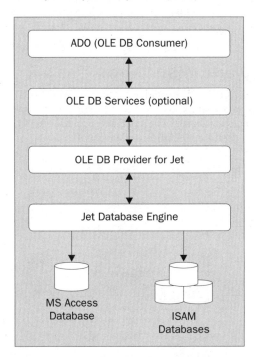

Considering the popularity of Access databases, a native provider for Microsoft Jet databases was a major step forward for the Universal Data Access strategy. Most developers working with Jet databases were typically using DAO because of its ease of use and high performance. The first release of the OLE DB Provider for Jet, version 3.51, delivered very competitive performance figures to DAO while providing an even easier COM-based object model in ADO. However, JOLT lacked functionality that was currently provided by DAO, especially in the areas of data definition and security. These limitations forced many developers to continue to use DAO when accessing Access and ISAM databases even though there was a native OLE DB data provider available for Microsoft Jet.

Nine months after the release of MDAC 2.0, which included version 3.51 of the OLE DB provider for Microsoft Jet, Microsoft released an MDAC upgrade called MDAC 2.1 SP1A. MDAC 2.1 SP1A, also known as MDAC 2.1 GA (Generally Available), included the Microsoft Jet 4.0 database engine (msjet40.dll) and version 4.0 of the OLE DB Provider for Microsoft Jet (msjetoledb40.dll). The OLE DB Provider for Microsoft Jet version 4.0 provided the following enhancements over the 3.51 version:

❑ **Support for all ISAM databases that are supported by Jet** – Version 3.51 of the OLE DB provider for Microsoft Jet only supported Microsoft Access databases. Version 4.0 supports all of the ISAM databases supported by the 4.0 version of the Jet database engine, including Paradox, dBase, Btrieve, Excel and FoxPro.

❑ **Compact and Repair support for Access Databases** – The Jet 3.51 OLE DB Provider did not include support for compacting or repairing Microsoft Access databases, a commonly used feature of DAO. Since the requirement of compacting and repairing databases is specific to Access databases, OLE DB did not define any standard interfaces to expose this functionality. Version 4.0 of the OLE DB provider for Microsoft Jet implements this functionality and exposes a provider-specific interface called `IJetCompact`. The `IJetCompact` interface is an example of an OLE DB provider extending its functionality by supporting additional interfaces. However, a consumer must be careful to degrade gracefully if a custom interface is not supported.

OLE DB Provider for Oracle (MSDAORA)

MDAC 2.0 also included the OLE DB Provider for Oracle (MSDAORA). MSDAORA is an OLE DB version 2.0-compliant provider that exposes OLE DB interfaces for retrieving and manipulating data stored in Oracle 7.3.3 or later databases. The OLE DB provider for Oracle is implemented as a layer on top of Oracle's Native API, the Oracle Call Interface (OCI).

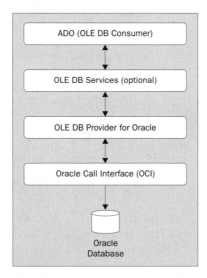

OLE DB Provider for AS/400 and VSAM (SNAOLEDB)

Data in an AS/400 or VSAM (Virtual Sequential Access Method) database can be accessed using SNAOLEDB, the OLE DB Provider for AS/400 and VSAM. SNAOLEDB is provided with Microsoft SNA Server, a comprehensive gateway and application integration platform for AS/400 and mainframe-based systems. This provider allows access to some of the most common non-relational storage systems in use today and supports all file types for AS/400 and most of the data types available in VSAM. This makes it a powerful tool in gaining access to indexed and sequential files at both a file and record locking level. The provider is designed to support the following AS/400 file types and VSAM data set file types:

❑ Keyed and non-keyed physical files

❑ Logical files with external descriptions

❑ Basic Sequential Access Method (BSAM) data sets

- ❏ Queued Sequential Access Method (QSAM) data sets

- ❏ Entry-Sequenced Data Sets (ESDS)

- ❏ Key-Sequenced Data Sets (KSDS)

- ❏ Fixed-length Relative Record Data Sets (RRDS)

- ❏ Variable-length Record Data Sets

- ❏ Partitioned Data Set (PDS) and Partitioned Data Set Extended (PDSE)

SNAOLEDB is designed to run under SNA Server 4.0 either as a server-based deployment or a client-based deployment.

For more information on using ADO to access an AS/400 system, see Craig McQueen's ASPToday article at `http://www.asptoday.com/articles/19990608.htm`*.*

OLE DB Provider for Microsoft Index Server (MSIDXS)

If you're not familiar with Microsoft Index Server, let me quickly brief you. Microsoft Index Server, also known as Microsoft Indexing Service, is a Windows NT/2000 service that provides indexing of files and directories to enable faster and more profitable searches. Basically, during periods of little or no system activity, Index Server transparently searches through files and directories and builds a **catalog** of information about each file. A catalog can be thought of as a database that consists of virtual tables or directories that contain the data indexed by the Index Server. Searches can then be quickly performed against the contents of these catalogs, rather than having to search through the physical files and directories.

Microsoft Index Server is fully integrated into Internet Information Server and as a result it is most commonly used to index web sites, email and news groups. Microsoft Index Server is also integrated in SQL Server 7 where it indexes databases to provide full-text searching functionality.

Index Server 2.0 shipped with the first version of the OLE DB Provider for Index Server (MSIDXS). MSIDXS allows developers to execute specially formatted SQL queries against the contents of Index Server catalogs, just as if they were another relational database system. Although it exposes these read-only query results in a tabular format, the OLE DB Provider for Index Server was a milestone release for OLE DB because it was one of the first OLE DB data providers that exposes data stored in a non-relational data source.

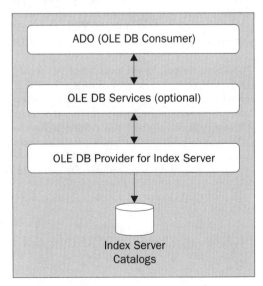

OLE DB Provider for Active Directory Services (ADsDSOObject)

A directory service is both a source of information about important objects and resources on a network, known as a **directory**, and a set of tools or **services** that enable users to use this information. A directory could include information about objects and resources such as printers, fax servers, applications, documents and user and group accounts. End users can quickly locate these important resources on the network by utilizing services or tools to query directories. Administrators can utilize services to manage and organize directories and their resources centrally. A directory service could be compared to the index in the back of this book. The index is an information source and, when queried for a particular keyword or keywords, it provides the page numbers where the keywords are discussed.

Currently there are a number of directory services available, including Windows NT4 directory services, Novel Netware directory services, Exchange directory services, and with the release of Windows 2000, Microsoft introduced the Active Directory Services. Active Directory Services extend the features and capabilities of the Windows NT4 directory services and are designed to scale from small workgroups to large enterprises. The Active Directory Services have become the standard directory service on the Windows platform. It has already been integrated within Windows Backoffice applications such as Exchange, Site Server and IIS, and is expected to be integrated into the next version of SQL Server, SQLServer 2000. This integration with the extensible Active Directory Services eliminated the need for applications to maintain their own application-specific directory service. However, with many organizations using a combination of these directory services on both Microsoft and non-Microsoft platforms, there was a need for a standardized API for multiple directory services. This is fulfilled by the Active Directory Service Interfaces (ADSI).

ADSI is similar to OLE DB, in that ADSI is also an architecture based on interfaces and providers. ADSI defines a single set of COM interfaces that provide standard access to multiple directory services. These interfaces are implemented by directory service-specific providers. Applications developed against the ADSI interfaces can query and manage resources in any directory service that supplies an ADSI provider. ADSI 2.5 includes providers for Active Directory Services, Windows NT 4.0 directory services, Novell NetWare Directory Services (NDS), and any other directory service that supports the Lightweight Directory Access Protocol (LDAP). Additionally, since most of the ADSI interfaces are COM-automation interfaces, they can be used from any COM-compliant development language or toolset, including Visual Basic, Visual Interdev, Visual J++, Visual C++, Microsoft Office and scripting languages such as Visual Basic Script and JScript.

Instead of making developers learn yet another API, Microsoft has fulfilled their commitment to Universal Data Access by providing the OLE DB Provider for Active Directory Services. The OLE DB provider for Active Directory Services (called ADsDSOObject) allows applications and components to query for read-only information about resources in almost any directory service through the Active Directory Service Interfaces. Additionally, the OLE DB provider for Active Directory Services also allows us to perform operations, such as searching, that cannot be performed directly through ADSI in some languages because some of ADSI's interfaces can only be used from C++. We'll discuss more about directory services and use the OLE DB Provider for Active Directory Services in Chapter 12.

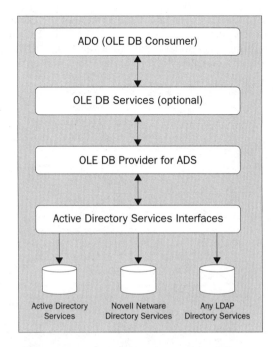

OLE DB Provider for Internet Publishing (MSDAIPP)

The OLE DB Provider for Internet Publishing (MSDAIPP) allows applications to access and manipulate folders and files across the HTTP protocol. These files and folders can be located on any Web server that supports either the FrontPage Web Extender (WEC) or the Web Distributed Authoring and Versioning (WebDAV) protocol extensions. The WEC protocol extensions are part of the FrontPage 2000 Server Extensions which can be installed on a variety of Windows NT4 and Unix web server products, including:

- ❏ Internet Information Server 3.0 – 5.0
- ❏ Apache Web Server 1.2
- ❏ Netscape Enterprise Server 3.0
- ❏ Netscape Fasttrack server 2.0
- ❏ Stronghold Apache-SSL Web Server
- ❏ O'Reilly WebSite 1.2

The WebDAV protocol is a powerful extension to the HTTP 1.1 standard that enables users to copy, move, edit, search and delete files and folders on a web server. WebDAV also effectively transforms a web server from a mere file server to a collaborative work environment by allowing users in diverse computing environments to view and edit files simultaneously. Since WebDAV is being built into the existing HTTP standard, web servers won't need to run an application on top of HTTP like WEC to provide this functionality. Additionally, WebDAV is an open standard based on HTTP and XML that will be available on *all* platforms. At the time of writing, WebDAV has not yet been standardized. However, Internet Information Server 5.0 provides support for the current specification today.

The OLE DB Provider for Internet Publishing can make use of the capabilities of WebDAV and integrate with legacy web servers through the use of the WEC (FrontPage) extensions. The OLE DB provider for Internet Publishing encapsulates the low-level WEC and WebDAV protocol operations and allows developers to access and manage files and folders on a web server just like any other data source.

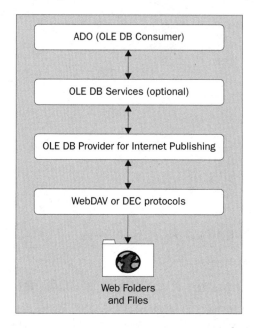

Version 1.0 of the OLE DB Provider for Internet Publishing was available with MDAC 2.1 packaged in Internet Explorer 5.0 and Office 2000. However, it was severely limited in functionality. MDAC 2.5, included with Windows 2000, ships with version 1.1 of the OLE DB Provider for Internet Publishing, which provides improved compliance with the WebDAV specification. But even more significant, MSDAIPP 1.1 supports the OLE DB interfaces for semi-structured data. The semi-structured OLE DB interfaces, IRow and IStream, are used to represent the hierarchical relationships of files and directories. We'll discuss more about WebDAV and WEC protocol extensions and utilize the OLE DB provider for Internet Publishing in Chapter 8.

OLE DB Provider for OLAP Services (MSOLAP)

The OLE DB Provider for OLAP Services (MSOLAP) allows access through OLE DB to multi-dimensional data from OLAP servers. The OLAP server we'll be looking at is the Microsoft OLAP Server, and is supplied with SQL Server 7.0 (although it is not installed by default), and the OLE DB Provider for OLAP Services is supplied with MDAC. OLAP, or Online Analytical Processing, is a technique for allowing data to be analyzed according to multiple "dimensions" – that is, looking at the same data but from a different conceptual viewpoint. For example, we could use OLAP to examine sales data according to product type, geographical location and time dimensions, such as sales of soft drinks in Florida in the second quarter of the year 2000. Granted, we could achieve this with a standard SQL query, but OLAP allows us to "drill down" into each of the dimensions without requerying the data source. For example, if we needed more detailed information about the geographical spread of our sales, we could drill down into the "location" dimension to examine the sales in a specific county or city within the state.

Version 2.1 of MDAC came with an entirely new set of ADO-related objects named ADO Multi-Dimensional, or ADOMD, which are designed specifically for dealing with multi-dimensional data of this kind. ADOMD is a layer on top of OLE DB for OLAP, which is a set of interfaces and methods allowing providers to expose multi-dimensional data and consumers to access that data. Because of this extended functionality, querying an OLAP server also requires a special set of extensions to the SQL language, known as MDX (Multi-Dimensional Expressions).

The MSOLAP Provider is designed for working with these OLE DB for OLAP objects. These are accessible through ADOMD, which acts as the OLE DB consumer. MSOLAP also supports the MDX extensions which allow us to build OLAP queries. ADOMD, OLAP and MDX are discussed in much greater detail in Chapter 9.

OLE DB Provider for Microsoft Exchange (ExOLEDB)

It has long been an aspiration of ADO programmers to be able to access Exchange mail server via ADO, but until the release of Exchange 2000 (currently in beta), there has been no OLE DB provider for Exchange data. Exchange 2000 introduces a feature named the Web Store, which maps onto the Exchange Information Store and provides many of the features of a web server and a file system.

The OLE DB Provider for Exchange, ExOLEDB, is supplied with Exchange 2000 and allows us to connect to an item in the Web Store in a very similar way to accessing web files and directories with the OLE DB Provider for Internet Publishing. As with MSDAIPP, ExOLEDB uses the semi-structured ADO `Record` object to expose the hierarchical structure of the Web Store. And also like MSDAIPP, this provider leverages the powerful WebDAV protocol. We will discuss accessing the Exchange 2000 Web Store from ADO in Chapter 13.

Custom OLE DB Providers

At this point, I'm sure you're probably wondering: what happens if you need access to a data source that does not provide an OLE DB data provider and does not support ODBC? Do you have to resort to using data-source specific APIs? Fortunately, OLE DB allows developers to create custom OLE DB data providers that can expose *any* data source. For example, custom OLE DB data providers could be developed for data sources such as:

❑ Microsoft Repository

❑ Personal Address Book

❑ Windows Registry

❑ Scheduled Tasks

❑ Windows Media content

❑ Shared Memory

These are just a few examples from the virtually endless list of possible data sources that could be exposed by custom OLE DB data providers. By exposing a data source using a custom OLE DB data provider, applications and components can access and manipulate data using standard data access APIs such as OLE DB, ADO and RDS. Additionally, you can take advantage of existing OLE DB Service providers to add functionality on top of the data source and the data provider.

While the most common reason to implement a custom OLE DB data provider is to provide access to a custom or non-typical data source that doesn't already have a data provider, custom OLE DB data providers can also be developed to provide additional or custom functionality on top of an existing OLE DB data provider. For example, a custom OLE DB data provider for SQL Server could implement data integrity rules and internally utilize the SQLOLEDB provider for the actual data access to SQL Server databases. This type of custom OLE DB data provider would effectively be acting as an OLE DB service provider because it is both consuming and producing OLE DB data.

As you will realize, the ability to develop custom OLE DB data providers is the key to Universal Data Access because it enables standardized access to data sources beyond Microsoft's own products and the popular relational database systems. In Chapter 15 we'll discuss more about this vital functionality, and in the following chapter we'll go on to create a custom OLE DB data provider for the Windows NT/2000 Registry.

OLE DB Consumers

OLE DB consumers are probably the simplest section of the OLE DB architecture. As I mentioned earlier, OLE DB consumers are simply data-centric applications, components or tools that utilize or **consume** OLE DB data through the OLE DB interfaces exposed by OLE DB data providers and/or service providers. An OLE DB consumer creates an instance of a provider's **Data Source Object** and uses a hierarchy of OLE DB objects to perform operations against a data source through the data provider. And that's it. Consuming data from OLE DB data providers and/or service providers is the *only* responsibility of an OLE DB consumer.

Unfortunately, if you want to develop an OLE DB consumer you must resort to C++ because of the complexity of the OLE DB interfaces. However, you can utilize ADO from any language that supports COM. As we discussed earlier, ADO is actually a high-level OLE DB consumer that abstracts developers from the details of the OLE DB objects, interfaces and even the OLE DB architecture. Besides ADO, Microsoft also provides serveral products that, among other things, make use of the OLE DB for data access and effectively act as OLE DB consumers. These products include:

❑ **SQL Server Distributed Query Processor (DPQ)** – SQL Server 7's Distributed Query Processor (DPQ) provides the ability to execute T-SQL statements that retrieve data from any data source that has an OLE DB data provider. In fact, you can make use of this functionality to perform heterogeneous joins using a combination of data from a SQL Server database and any other data source that has an OLE DB data provider. For example, you could use the OLE DB provider for Oracle to join a `products` table in an Oracle database with a `customers` table in a SQL Server database. The possible combinations of data sources are virtually limitless because OLE DB is an extensible architecture. SQL Server implements distributed queries statically through the use of Linked Servers and the OPENQUERY function and dynamically through the use of the new T-SQL OPENROWSET function. Consult the SQL Server documentation for more details about this powerful feature.

❑ **Data Transformation Services** – SQL Server 7 also provides an even more impressive new feature called Data Transformation Services (DTS). DTS is a set of tools and COM components that provide the ability to transfer data between any OLE DB data sources. Although Data Transformation Services is installed with SQL Server 7, don't let that fool you. DTS is the ultimate OLE DB consumer and a great example of UDA because DTS can consume data through the OLE DB interfaces from virtually *any* standard or custom OLE DB data providers.

In addition to providing the ability to transfer data structure and data between any OLE DB data sources, DTS also allows custom operations, called transformations, to be applied to the data as it is transferred. A transformation could be as simple as changing the format of data, or it could be as complex as performing data validation and business rules through scripts written in either VBScript or JScript.

An operation such as importing and exporting data, applying a transformation, or executing a program is known in DTS as a **task**. Groups of tasks are defined, sequenced, and persisted in **packages**. Packages can be stored in the SQL Server MSDB database, the Repository or in a DTS file. A DTS package can be executed manually from SQL Enterprise Manager or automatically based on a defined schedule.

There are three different ways to create, manage and execute packages:

- ❏ **DTS Programming Interfaces** – DTS provides a set of COM-automation components that can allow developers to create custom applications that extend the capabilities of the DTS Import and Export Wizards and the DTS Designer. Using the DTS components, an application can programmatically define and execute packages that include complex data conversions and transformation tasks between various OLE DB data providers. Since the DTS components are COM-automation components, they can be used in any development tool or language that supports COM-automation, such as Visual Basic, Visual C++, Visual J++, and Office and scripting languages such as Visual Basic Script and JScript.

- ❏ **DTS Import and Export Wizards** – While the DTS components are extremely powerful and flexible, most DTS operations are performed using the simple step-by-step Import and Export Wizards. The Import and Export Wizards provide a number of customizable options including the ability to configure column mappings and transformations; package saving, scheduling and replication capabilities; and the option of transferring entire tables or only the results of complex queries.

- ❏ **DTS Designer** – The DTS designer is a graphical user interface (GUI) built into SQL Enterprise Manager that can be used to design, execute and visualize the workflow of complex, multi-data source packages. The DTS designer provides more flexibility and control than the DTS Import and Export Wizards while providing abstraction from the more complex DTS components.

OLE DB Service Providers

As I mentioned, OLE DB service providers are probably the most interesting components of the OLE DB architecture. Why? Because OLE DB service providers play a dual role as both OLE DB consumers and OLE DB providers. OLE DB service providers implement standard services for data exposed through OLE DB that extend the functionality of data providers. To understand the significant role of OLE DB service providers and their benefits, let's first reflect back on ODBC for a moment.

Up until this point, with the exception of the support for COM interfaces, the OLE DB architecture is similar to the ODBC architecture. We have OLE DB data providers that are similar to ODBC drivers and OLE DB consumers that are simply the client applications that are consuming or using the data. With ODBC, additional functionality beyond simple data access and data manipulation, such as client cursor services or distributed transactions, must be implemented by the ODBC driver. If another ODBC driver wanted to provide the same services, it was required to develop the same functionality. As a result, several implementations of common services developed, with each service varying in functionality.

OLE DB service providers, the effective 'middle-tier' of the OLE DB architecture, are designed to separate common data access services into sets of reusable COM components. This componentization of common data access services provides the following benefits:

❑ **Standard Services that can be used with most OLE DB data providers** – OLE DB service providers provide generic implementations of common services that are not tied to any specific OLE DB data provider. As a result, there is only one implementation of a given service and OLE DB consumers can utilize the same services that always provide the same functionality, regardless of the data source or the data provider being used. OLE DB service providers can even add functionality on top of ODBC databases when using the OLE DB provider for ODBC, and custom data sources when full or OSP custom data providers are developed. However, it's important to note that in some situations, data providers might require certain OLE DB service providers to be disabled. This might be the case with older data providers or data providers that don't meet the few requirements for supporting service providers. Specific OLE DB service providers can be enabled or disabled through the OLEDB_SERVICES registry entry for the provider, or this can be performed by the OLE DB consumer.

❑ **Minimizing the requirements of OLE DB data providers** – OLE DB service providers make it easier to expose a custom data source because they minimize the requirements of developing custom OLE DB data providers. OLE DB data providers all support a base level of functionality, by implementing a standard set of OLE DB interfaces. Any additional functionality needed above that base level can be accessed from existing OLE DB service providers. For example, if we want to develop a custom OLE DB data provider for the Windows Registry, we only need to worry about exposing data stored in the Registry and implementing any data source-specific functionality. Through the use of OLE DB service providers, our OLE DB data provider for the Windows Registry can automatically support OLE DB services such as the Client Cursor Service, transaction enlistment and session pooling.

❑ **Extensibility with existing OLE DB data providers** – This benefit of OLE DB service providers goes hand-in-hand with the first two, just from a different perspective. Most OLE DB service providers act as a middleman between the OLE DB consumer and the data provider. As data moves from the data provider to the consumer and vice-versa, it passes through the OLE DB service providers that implement the requested functionality on top of the data. The service providers consume data using the standard OLE DB interfaces and then expose data using the same or a different set of OLE DB interfaces, depending on the type of functionality the service provider provides. This design allows for transparent plug-and-play usage of OLE DB service providers. As new OLE DB service providers become available, they can easily be plugged into this architecture to extend the functionality of new and existing data-centric applications.

❑ **High performance** – OLE DB service providers are designed to *supplement* intelligently the functionality of data providers. OLE DB service providers are only used when the consumer requests functionality, in the form of an OLE DB interface, that is *not* natively supported by the OLE DB data provider. Whether the data provider or a service provider implements the requested functionality is completely transparent to the consumer. Either way, the OLE DB consumer's requests are serviced in the most direct and efficient way possible. To maximize performance and minimize overhead further, most of the OLE DB service providers are implemented as a number of seperate components. This way only those services needed at any one time are loaded into memory.

There are a total of six OLE DB service providers currently provided in MDAC that play a crucial role in data-centric applications both individually and when combined in use together. These six OLE DB service providers include:

❏ Transaction enlistment – Transaction enlistment is a core OLE DB service that allows Microsoft Transaction Server (MTS) or COM+ automatically to register or enlist an instance of a MTS/COM+ component within a distributed transaction. Consequently, any work performed by the MTS/COM+ object will automatically be performed within the protection of a distributed transaction. We'll discuss MTS and COM+ in more detail later in ths chapter.

❏ Session Pooling – OLE DB session pooling is a core OLE DB service that automatically pools OLE DB Sessions, which are essentially connections to an OLE DB data provider. When an OLE DB consumer requests an OLE DB session, it will automatically be provided with an existing session if one already exists for the specified data provider and data source. We'll examine OLE DB session pooling in detail in Chapter 11.

❏ Persistence Provider – The OLE DB Persistence Provider gives us the ability to save an entire set of data to a stream, so that it can be stored in a file or object, or transferred across the network. We'll discuss using the Persistence Provider from ADO in Chapter 4.

❏ Cursor Service – The OLE DB Cursor Service is a core service provider that allows an OLE DB consumer to search, sort, filter and manipulate data in local memory without being connected to a data provider. The Cursor Service, also known as the Client Cursor Engine (CCE), is frequently used in combination with several other OLE DB Service Providers. We'll discuss using the Cursor Service from ADO in Chapter 3.

❏ DataShape Provider – The OLE DB DataShape Provider effectively allows applications to create hierarchial models of data based on the relationships between the data. These hierarchial sets of data can be nested to any level and are easily accessible to the OLE DB consumer. We've dedicated the entire Chapter 6 to discussing the details of the Data Shape Provider.

❏ (Data) Remoting Provider – The OLE DB Remoting Provider provides the ability to utilize an OLE DB Data Provider that resides on a remote machine. The Remoting Provider utilizes the OLE DB Cursor Service and the Persistence Provider to transfer data across DCOM or the HTTP or HTTPS protocols. The OLE DB Remoting Provider is essentially a subset of the functionality available through the Remote Data Services (RDS). We'll briefly discuss RDS later in this chapter and we'll utilize it extensively in Chapter 14.

> The Client Cursor Engine, Session Pooling and Transaction Enlistment are sometimes referred to as OLE DB service components instead of OLE DB service providers because they are invoked manually by the OLE DB consumer or data provider, whereas the term 'service provider' is reserved for components that transparently reside between the consumer and data provider. In this book, we will not differentiate between service components and service providers, but instead use the term 'service provider' consistently.

Although each of the service providers can be used independently, they are often used together. In fact, some OLE DB service providers actually depend on the functionality of others. For example, the Persistence Provider is used in conjunction with the Remoting Provider when transferring data from remote data sources across DCOM or the HTTP protocol. We'll discuss and use each of these OLE DB service providers throughout the course of this book.

ActiveX Data Objects (ADO)

Where OLE DB is the system-level programming interface that implements Universal Data Access, ActiveX Data Objects is the application-level programming interface. ADO is designed for high-performance data access in *all* development scenarios, regardless of the data source, the programming language, or the application's physical architecture. ADO has become the data access technology of choice for developing data-centric applications that range from single-user database front-ends to n-tier distributed applications and everything in between, including scalable internet and intranet applications. ADO combines the ease of use found in DAO and RDO with the extensibility of OLE DB.

It's important to understand that OLE DB and ADO are not separate technologies. ADO is implemented as a COM-based OLE DB consumer – an integrated component of the OLE DB architecture. As an OLE DB consumer, ADO accesses OLE DB interfaces implemented by OLE DB service providers or data providers and exposes these complex OLE DB interfaces as COM-automation objects that can be used from any programming language. In other words, ADO utilizes OLE DB data and service providers to retrieve and manipulate data and then exposes this data and functionality through a simple, COM-based object model. This is illustrated in the following diagram.

> **The relationship between ADO and OLE DB can be compared to that of RDO and ODBC. Just as RDO was a thin wrapper over the ODBC API, ADO is a thin COM automation-based object model over the complex OLE DB Interfaces.**

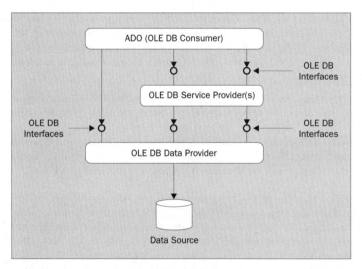

When methods are invoked on ADO objects, behind the scenes ADO forwards the method call to the appropriate OLE DB service provider or data provider that implements the requested functionality. ADO simply provides abstraction from the complexity of OLE DB. In fact, you could develop data-centric applications using ADO without having any knowledge of OLE DB. However, since OLE DB is the foundation for ADO and the entire Universal Data Access strategy, the more you understand about the underlying OLE DB architecture, the better you'll be able to take advantage of ADO's capabilities.

In addition to the capabilities inherited from OLE DB, ADO provides a number of benefits of its own. We will look at these next.

Programming Language/Toolset Independence

Today's data-centric applications are rarely developed using one programming language or toolset. Instead, applications are assembled using a combination of integrated development environments such as Visual Basic, Visual Interdev, Visual C++ and Visual FoxPro. Data-centric applications can also be constructed using Microsoft Office and other third-party products that use the VBA engine. On the internet development side, it sometimes seems as though Internet Explorer and Internet Information Server (IIS) provide more scripting languages and technologies than available acroynms. Thankfully, ADO can be used with any programming language or tool that supports COM. But how is this possible; after all, OLE DB is based entirely around COM, but the OLE DB interfaces and objects can only be used in C++? What's different about ADO?

ADO supports COM automation by implementing all ADO components as **dual-interface** COM components. Without going into detail about COM interfaces and binding, the term 'dual interfaces' basically means that applications can either bind directly to ADO's type library and discover functionality at design time, or they can bind to the ADO type library and call methods on IDispatch interfaces at run-time. Applications developed using Visual C++, Visual J++ and Visual Basic can use either or both types of binding, while scripting languages such as VBScript, JScript and PerlScript must use the Automation (IDispatch) interfaces.

This language/toolset independence provided by ADO and COM automation allows you, as a developer, to choose the tool that is appropriate for the data-centric application you are developing or the tool you are the most comfortable with, instead of the tool that is appropriate for the data access technology. For example, if you need to create mission-critical MTS/COM+ components you might use Visual C++ and ATL. For example, for web-based, dynamic user interfaces, you might use DHTML with Visual Basic Script or JScript.

> **Don't worry if you don't understand all of this COM terminology. A detailed knowledge of COM is not required to use ADO from Visual Basic and scripting languages. However, the more you understand about the Component Object Model, the better you'll be able to utilize ADO.**

Circular Object Model

The ADO object model is organized in a circular structure and composed of only five main objects: Connection, Command, Recordset, and the two new objects introduced in ADO 2.5, Record and Stream. This circular object model allows any of the main objects to be created independently and then programmatically 'attached' to other objects, or ADO will implicitly create the associated objects for you as they are needed. For example, if you want to open a Recordset against a data source, you can simply create a Recordset object just as you would any other COM object and call its Open method. You are not required to first create a Connection or Command object.

This programming model is much more flexible than the traditional hierarchical models used by OLE DB, DAO and RDO, which require us to work down the entire object model to perform even a simple operation. With ADO, we can create only the objects that deliver the functionality we need without the memory and processing overhead of creating numerous parent objects.

ADO's circular object model is depicted in the following diagram:

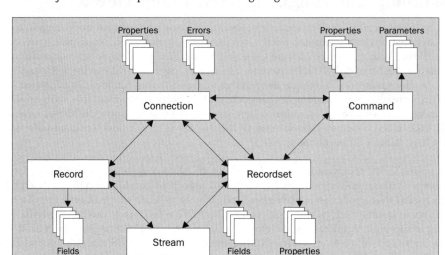

One of the main benefits of ADO's object model is that it decreases the amount and complexity of code required. In the following VB code example, when the Open method is called on the rsAuthors Recordset object, ADO implicitly creates an Connection object using the connection information specified in the ActiveConnection parameter, and retrieves all of the records from the authors table in the pubs database.

```
Dim rsAuthors As ADODB.Recordset

'create the rsAuthors ADODB.Recordset
Set rsAuthors = New ADODB.Recordset

'open a connection to the pubs Database and
'...retrieve all of the records from the authors table
rsAuthors.Open Source:='SELECT * FROM authors', _
               ActiveConnection:='Provider=SQLOLEDB;Password=;' & _
                                 'User ID=sa;Initial Catalog=pubs;' & _
                                 'Data Source=JConard'

'close the connection to the Data Source
rsAuthors.ActiveConnection.Close

'release our rsAuthors ADODB.Recordset
Set rsAuthors = Nothing
```

Once the Recordset has been opened, we can use it to perform our desired operation (for example, displaying the data to the user), and then close and release it from memory. Implicit object creation is great for performance when you only need to perform single operations because there is very little object creation overhead.

In addition to simplified development, the ADO object model also promotes object reuse. Let's add some code to our previous example so that it also returns a `Recordset` with all of the records in the `titles` table. If we specify the connection string in the `Open` method's `ActiveConnection` parameter for our `rsTitles Recordset` as well as for our `rsAuthors` recordset, we would cause ADO implicitly to create two `Connection` objects and two physical data source connections. Instead, to avoid this overhead, let's only specify the connection string when opening the `rsAuthors` recordset and let's reuse the implicitly created `Connection` object in the `ActiveConnection` parameter of the second `Recordset`'s `Open` method. Alternatively, we could have explicitly created a `Connection` object and specified it in the `ActiveConnection` parameter of our `Recordset`'s `Open` method or the set the `ActiveConnection` property of our `Recordset` objects:

```
Dim rsAuthors As ADODB.Recordset
Dim rsTitles As ADODB.Recordset

'create the rsAuthors ADODB.Recordset
Set rsAuthors = New ADODB.Recordset

'create the rsTitles ADODB.Recordset
Set rsTitles = New ADODB.Recordset

'open a connection to the pubs Database and
'...retrieve all of the records from the authors table
rsAuthors.Open Source:='SELECT * FROM authors', _
                ActiveConnection:='Provider=SQLOLEDB;Password=;' & _
                                  'User ID=sa;Initial Catalog=pubs;' & _
                                  'Data Source=JConard'

'retrieve all of the records from the Titles table
'...using the ADODB.Connection that was implicitly created for '...the last
Recordset
rsAuthors.Open Source:='SELECT * FROM authors', _
                ActiveConnection:=rsAuthors.ActiveConnection

'close the connection to the Data Source
'...we only need to do this on one reference to the Connection
rsAuthors.ActiveConnection.Close

'release our rsAuthors ADODB.Recordset
Set rsAuthors = Nothing

'release our rsTitles ADODB.Recordset
Set rsTitles = Nothing
```

As you can imagine, the Data Access Group probably invested a lot of time in the design of ADO's object model, but it was definitely well worth it. The ADO object model is faster, more scalable and easier to use than previous data access technologies such as RDO and DAO, simply because of a better object model design.

ADO is an Extensible and Open Architecture Data Access Technology

You might have noticed on the last diagram that the ADO 2.5 object model provides a `Properties` collection for almost every object. This `Properties` collection allows ADO to expose dynamically provider-specific properties for the OLE DB data and service providers being used.

For example, when establishing a connection to our pubs SQL Server 7.0 database using the OLE DB Provider for SQL Server, several provider-specific properties and their default values are added to the `Connection` object's `Properties` collection when the SQLOLEDB provider is specified. One of these properties, `"Integrated Security"` allows us to specify that Windows NT/2000 Integrated Security should be used for authentication. This allows us to connect to the pubs SQL Server 7 database using the security credentials of the currently logged-in user.

```
Dim conDataSource As ADODB.Connection

'create an instance of an ADODB.Connection
Set conDataSource = New ADODB.Connection

'use the OLE DB Provider for SQL Server
conDataSource.Provider = 'SQLOLEDB'
'connect using Windows NT/2000 authentication
conDataSource.Properties('Integrated Security').Value = 'SSPI'

'connect to the pubs database on the Jconard machine
conDataSource.Open 'Initial Catalog=pubs;Data Source=JConard;'

'close our connection to the Pubs database
conDataSource.Close

'release our instance of the ADODB.Connection
Set conDataSource = Nothing
```

Many properties are read-only, or can only be modified before performing certain key operations. In this example, we can only set the `"Integrated Security"` property after specifying the provider of SQLOLEDB but before calling the Open method on our ADO Connection object. Once our `conDataSource` ADO `Connection` object is opened, the `"Integrated Security"` property becomes read-only.

This collection of dynamic properties makes ADO an exensible data access technology that is capable of utilizing any OLE DB data or service provider. `"Integrated Security"` is one example of a provider-specific property that applies only to `Connection` objects. Since the `"Integrated Security"` property is specific to the SQLOLEDB provider, it wouldn't make sense for it to be implemented as a static property of an ADO `Connection` object. Instead, the `Properties` collection offers a technique for extending the functionality of the standard ADO objects while still keeping the ADO object model very simple and easy-to-use.

A list of the dynamic properties exposed by some of the main OLE DB data providers and service providers can be found in Appendix C.

Developing with ADO or OLE DB

When you consider the benefits ADO provides on top of those already provided by the OLE DB architecture, why would you ever develop your own OLE DB consumer? The only possible reason is performance. By writing many lines of low-level C++ code against the complex OLE DB interfaces you avoid the minimal overhead of the ADO object model and gain a slight performance advantage that may be required for mission-critical data-centric applications. I believe the benefits of ADO far outweigh the minimal performance advantages of developing custom OLE DB consumers (although this task is greatly simplified from Visual C++ by the ATL Consumer Templates). However, if you need to develop fully-functional custom OLE DB service or data providers, unfortunately you must resort to developing directly against the complex OLE DB interfaces.

ADODB and ADOR

ActiveX Data Objects are available in two different 'flavors': ADODB and ADOR.

ADODB

The ADODB library is the full version of ADO that can be used to perform any ADO operation. ADODB is packaged as an in-process COM server named `msado15.dll`. Yes, that's correct: even version 2.5 of ADODB is packaged in the file `msado15.dll`. By using the ADODB library, you have access to all the ADO components and thus all the capabilities of ADO. As you can see in the following diagram, the ADODB library contains the ADO object model we met earlier:

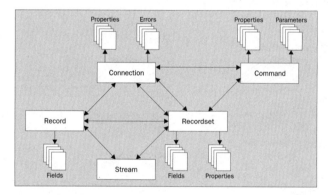

ADOR

The ADOR (ActiveX Data Objects Recordset) library was designed to be a lightweight, subset of the ADODB library. The ADOR library includes only the `Recordset`, `Field` and `Property` objects and the `Fields` and `Properties` collections:

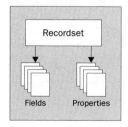

Since the ADOR library doesn't include most of the main ADO objects, such as the `Connection`, `Command`, `Record` and `Stream` objects, ADOR does not provide the full functionality of ActiveX Data Objects. Instead, ADOR – also implemented as an in-process COM server named `msador15.dll` – was originally designed to allow client applications to manipulate, sort and filter data with the convenience of a `Recordset` object without the overhead of the entire ADO object model. Internet applications developed for Internet Explorer 4.x could depend on the availability of ADOR because it was included with IE 4.x's default installation.

ADODB vs. ADOR

The relationship between the ADODB and ADOR libraries was once very clear, but has become very confusing. With ADO 1.5, the `ADODB.Recordset` and the `ADOR.Recordset` were implemented as separate components that provided exactly the same functionality. The ADOR library could be used without any dependency on the ADODB library.

Since ADO 2.0, the `ADOR.Recordset` component is no longer implemented as a separate, independent component. Instead, the ADOR library actually relies on ADODB for its functionality. A quick look at the `ADODB.Recordset` and the `ADOR.Recordset` keys in the Registry using the `RegEdit` utility shows that both objects share the same GUID (Global Unique Identifier). In fact, if you unregister and re-register `msado15.dll` you will find that it registers both the `ADODB.Recordset` and the `ADOR.Recordset` ProgIDs. ADOR is effectively acting as a type library with interface and component definitions, but without any implementation or registration code.

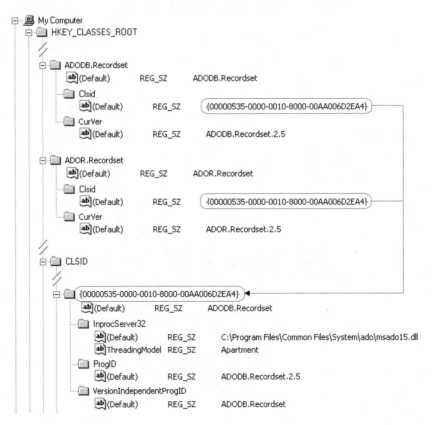

All this means that you can continue to create `Recordset` objects using the `ADOR.Recordset`'s `ProgID`; however, in doing so you are unnecessarily creating a dependency for two files. The `msador15.dll` file (ADOR) is providing the type library and the `msado15.dll` file (ADODB) is providing the implementation. On the other hand, if you create `Recordset` objects using the `ADODB.Recordset ProgID`, you will use the type library located in the same file as the implementation, `msado15.dll`, the same file that contains the implementation for the `Recordset` component.

> **As of ADO 2.0 the `ADODB.Recordset` and the `ADOR.Recordset` are implemented as the same component. However, both `ProgIDs` are still supported for backwards compatibility.**

You can also continue to use `Recordset` objects created with either `ProgID` interchangeably, as you could when they were separate components, because the definitions for both the `ADODB.Recordset` and the `ADOR.Recordset` implement the same inbound interfaces. For example, let's revise our previous example that retrieves all of the records from the `authors` table in the `pubs` SQL Server 7.0 database so that the records are returned into an object of the type `ADOR.Recordset` instead of one defined as an `ADODB.Recordset`.

```
Dim rsAuthors As ADOR.Recordset
Dim conDataSource As ADODB.Connection

'create an instance of an ADODB.Connection
Set conDataSource = New ADODB.Connection

'open a Connection to the Pubs SQL Server 7 database
conDataSource.Open 'Provider=SQLOLEDB;Password=;' & _
                   'User ID=sa;Initial Catalog=pubs;Data Source=iswin2k'

'retrieve all of the records from the authors table
Set rsAuthors = conDataSource.Execute('SELECT * FROM authors')

'close our recordset
rsAuthors.Close

'close and destroy the connection to the Pubs database
conDataSource.Close
Set conDataSource = Nothing
```

In this code example, the return value from our `ADODB.Connection` object's `Execute` method is placed in a variable of the type `ADOR.Recordset`, even though the `Execute` method is defined as returning an `ADODB.Recordset`. Again, this is possible because the both the `ADODB.Recordset` and the `ADOR.Recordset` implement the same inbound interfaces.

While you would think that since an `ADOR.Recordset` is actually implemented as an `ADODB.Recordset`, a `Recordset` object would have the same functionality no matter which `ProgID` was used to create it. However, this is not the case. ADO 2.0 added support for events to the `Connection` and `Recordset` components. To expose these events the `ADODB.Recordset` definition was modified to implement an additional interface. However, the `ADOR.Recordset` definition does not implement this outgoing (event) interface. Consequently, `Recordset` objects defined as an `ADOR.Recordset` cannot take advantage of events but `Recordset` objects defined as `ADODB.Recordsets` can. By using the OLE/COM object viewer utility that comes with Visual Studio 6.0, we can view the Interface Definition Language (IDL) statements for each library and see the differences in the type library definitions for the `ADODB.Recordset` and the `ADOR.Recordset`. For sake of space, I've trimmed out the other ADO component and interface definitions from this example:

```
// Generated .IDL file (by the OLE/COM Object Viewer)
//
// typelib filename: msado15.dll
[
 uuid(00000205-0000-0010-8000-00AA006D2EA4),
 version(2.5),
 helpstring('Microsoft ActiveX Data Objects 2.5 Library'),
 helpfile('ado210.chm'),
 helpcontext(00000000)
]
library ADODB
{
 [
 uuid(00000535-0000-0010-8000-00AA006D2EA4),
 helpcontext(0x0012c903),
 licensed
 ]
coclass Recordset {
 [default] interface  Recordset;
 [default, source] dispinterface RecordsetEvents;
 };
 };

// Generated .IDL file (by the OLE/COM Object Viewer)
//
// typelib filename: msador15.dll

 [
 uuid(00000300-0000-0010-8000-00AA006D2EA4),
 version(2.5),
 helpstring('Microsoft ActiveX Data Objects Recordset 2.5 Library'),
 helpfile('ado210.chm'),
 helpcontext(00000000)
]
library ADOR
{
 [
 uuid(00000535-0000-0010-8000-00AA006D2EA4),
 helpcontext(0x0012c903),
 licensed
 ]
coclass Recordset {
 [default] interface _Recordset;
 };
 };
```

ADODB and ADOR Summary

Today there are no advantages to using ADOR because it relies upon ADODB for its functionality and consequently ADOR (`msador15.dll`) can no longer be distributed without the full version of ADO (`msado15.dll`). Besides, Internet Explorer 5.x installs a subset of MDAC 2.1 which includes ADO (both the ADODB and the ADOR libraries), OLE DB and ODBC but does not include any ODBC drivers or OLE DB data providers. The `ADOR.Recordset` also lacks support for `Recordset` events. However, despite these aspects, ADOR will continue to be supported for backwards compatibility – and that is the only reason for still using ADOR.

> **In this book unless otherwise specified, when we discuss the** `Recordset` **component we are referring to the** `ADODB.Recordset` **and not the** `ADOR.Recordset`, **although they can be used interchangeably and provide the same functionality, with the exception of** `Recordset` **events.**

Language Specifics

As I have already mentioned, today's data-centric applications are usually developed using a combination of development tools and languages. While ADO is a language-independent implementation of the Universal Data Access strategy due its support for COM automation, different development environments provide various features that enhance the usability of ADO. These features fall into two categories:

- ❑ **ADO Object Model enhancements** – Some development languages hide the implementation details of COM more than others do. In particular, Visual Basic and scripting languages such as VBScript and JScript almost completely abstract developers from COM components and interfaces where development tools such as Visual C++ and Visual J++ require extensive knowledge of COM. However, these development languages usually offer more low-level control than is available with Visual Basic or scripting languages. Since ADO is based entirely on COM, as a COM server and an OLE DB consumer, a development tool's support for COM directly affects its support for ADO.

- ❑ **Integrated Development Environment (IDE) tools** – Several development environments provide integrated tools designed to reduce the complexity of ADO or abstract developers from writing ADO code. The goal of these tools is to reduce the time required to develop applications that use ADO by simplifying development as much as possible without making major sacrifices in flexibility or performance.

> **Most of the examples in this book will use Visual Basic or scripting languages because of the extensive knowledge of COM that is required to use ADO in Visual C++ and Visual J++.**

Let's discuss two of the most popular development environments (Visual C++ and Visual Basic) and look at some of the features of developing ADO-based applications in these environments. A Data Environment very similar to that of Visual Basic is also provided by Visual Interdev.

Visual C++ 6.0

ADO is really designed for use by Visual Basic and scripting clients, which means that the documentation for C++ developers is a bit skimpy. In fact, it is only VB and scripting clients who *must* use ADO for data access purposes. If you are programming in C++, you have a choice of whether to use ADO or to use the underlying OLE DB interfaces directly – and the implicit assumption tends to be that you will prefer to use OLE DB directly for performance reasons. Since ADO acts as a wrapper and simply calls up the underlying OLE DB interfaces, there is always a slight performance hit by going through ADO as opposed to using OLE DB directly – though unless performance really is an absolute key priority you are unlikely to really notice the difference.

The other factor to consider is that if you are using Microsoft's Active Template Library (ATL), you will have available the ATL Consumer template classes, which themselves provider high-performance implementations of boilerplate code that calls up OLE DB. Although OLE DB is by any standards a lot harder and more complex than ADO to learn, these classes do a lot of the work for you, so your code ends up no more complex than if you'd used ADO. These classes are also rather better documented in MSDN than using of ADO from C++. On the other hand, you have a steep learning curve before you can use them, since you will need to be familiar with not only ATL, but also the OLE DB interfaces *and* the way that the ATL Consumer classes work.

We therefore have three options for coding data access clients in C++, and these are summarized in the following table.

Option	Description
Raw OLE DB	This means you access the OLE DB interfaces with your own code. This is very hard to code, but it does lead to efficient code. You need to learn OLE DB first, though!
ATL OLE DB Consumer templates	Access OLE DB interfaces mostly through the ATL template classes. Roughly as efficient as using raw OLE DB, and much easier to code up. But you need to be familiar with OLE DB, ATL and the template classes themselves.
ADO	This leads to code of similar size to code using the ATL Consumer templates. The only knowledge required is ADO. However, documentation on how to do this is sparse.

Since this is an ADO book we're going to concentrate on the third option – that of using ADO! And if you've got this far reading this book, it's a fairly safe bet that you already know in principle how to use the ADO objects. We're also assuming that you are already familiar with ATL and COM, so all that is really needed is to know what header files etc. to call up and what the names of the classes you need to use are. So the purpose of this section isn't to give you a complete set of examples on how to use ADO with C++ from scratch. Over the next couple of pages we are simply going to point you in the right direction to where the relevant header files are and what the main points to look for in creating ADO objects in C++ are.

If you want more detailed information on coding ADO clients in C++, you might want to check up Wendy Sarrett's book, 'Visual C++ Database Programming Tutorial', also published by Wrox.

Header Files etc.

COM classes for use in VB are always defined in a type library – and the type library in question is currently `msado20.tlb`, which you can import in the normal way. In the case of the ADO objects, Microsoft has supplied an IDL file and two C++ headers. The IDL file is `MSADO15.IDL` (the name of this file has been kept the same, even though ADO has now progressed well beyond version 1.5). This IDL file contains all the interface definitions and constant definitions you'll need in human-readable form. The C++ header files are:

File	Description
Adoid.h	Contains the GUIDs for interfaces and coclasses
Adoint.h	Contains C++ class definitions for the interfaces

In C++ the usual choice is between `#importing` the type library and `#including` the C++ header files – and in the case of ADO, either approach will work. Here we demonstrate using the header files. In order to use `Adoid.h`, you will also need to link to the library `Adoid.lib`. With these settings, the following code fragment will create a new `Connection` object:

```
#include <windows.h>
#include <adoid.h>
#include <adoint.h>

int main (int argc, char *argv[])
{
   // other processing
   hr = CoInitialize(NULL);

   ADOConnection *pConnection;

   HRESULT hr;
   hr = CoCreateInstance(CLSID_CADOConnection, NULL, CLSCTX_INPROC_SERVER,
                         IID_IADOConnection, (void**)&pConnection);

   // other processing
   return 0;
}
```

This code illustrates that the objects are created using `CoCreateInstance()`, in the normal way corresponding to VB's New command. The ADO objects are all in-process servers, hence the `CLSCTX_INPROC_SERVER` flag. The names of the classes in C++ are simply `ADOConnection`, `ADOCommand` etc., while the relevant `CLSIDs` and `IIDs` are formed by prefixing `CLSID_C` and `IID_I` to the name of the class (for example, `CLSID_CADOCommand` and `IID_IADOCommand`). The same is true for all the main ADO objects.

Once the objects have been created in this way, you can simply call up their methods as usual. Since there is virtually no documentation in this area, if you do encounter problems you're usually best off examining the ADO header files themselves to find out the names of the classes etc.

We're not going to give a full example here, since we are assuming that you are able to code COM clients in general using C++. However, we will remark on the use of variants in ADO – since ADO makes heavy use of this datatype, which is not generally encountered outside VB and COM interfaces specifically designed for VB and scripting use.

Variants

Variants are the standard way in which VB stores any object for which the type is not explicitly defined. For example the statements:

```
Dim var
```

And:

```
Dim objConnection As Object
```

Will both cause a variable of type `Variant` to be created.

In C++ terms, a `VARIANT` is a structure (note that it is capitalised for its definition in the C++ header file) consisting of a discriminated union. That is to say, it is a union of members of all the different data types that might conceivably be stored in the `Variant`, along with a member variable, `vt`, which indicates which of these members actually contains valid data. The full structure is complex, but the gist of it can be gained from the first few lines of its definition:

```
struct    tagVARIANT
        {
// stuff removed for clarity
        VARTYPE vt;
// variables reserved for future use removed for clarity
        union
            {
            LONG lVal;
            BYTE bVal;
            SHORT iVal;
            FLOAT fltVal;
            DOUBLE dblVal;
            VARIANT_BOOL boolVal;
            _VARIANT_BOOL bool;
            SCODE scode;
            CY cyVal;
            DATE date;
            BSTR bstrVal;
            IUnknown __RPC_FAR *punkVal;
            IDispatch __RPC_FAR *pdispVal;
```

The `vt` member is of type `VARTYPE`, which is simply an unsigned short. The main possible values are as follows:

```
enum VARENUM
    {VT_EMPTY     = 0,
     VT_NULL      = 1,
     VT_I2        = 2,
     VT_I4        = 3,
     VT_R4        = 4,
     VT_R8        = 5,
     VT_CY        = 6,
     VT_DATE      = 7,
     VT_BSTR      = 8,
     VT_DISPATCH  = 9,
```

```
VT_ERROR      = 10,
VT_BOOL       = 11,
VT_VARIANT    = 12,
VT_UNKNOWN    = 13,
VT_DECIMAL    = 14,
VT_I1         = 16,
VT_UI1        = 17,
VT_UI2        = 18,
VT_UI4        = 19,
VT_I8         = 20,
VT_UI8        = 21,
```

The values are fairly self-explanatory; for example, VT_BSTR for a string, VT_I4 for a standard integer, and VT_I2 for a shorter one! vt should be set to one of the above values, and may also be bitwise OR'd with several values that indicate other information about the value. The most important such value is VT_ARRAY, which indicates that the Variant actually contains an array of the datatype in question rather than a single value.

What this all means is that, for example, the VB statement:

```
Dim var
var = 3
```

would translate into C++ as:

```
VARIANT var;
var.vt = VT_I4;
var.lVal = 3;
```

Helper Classes: CComVariant and _variant_t

Dealing with raw structures in C++ isn't always the easiest way to code, and as a result two classes have been made available to assist in dealing with Variants. These classes to some extent automate the process of storing and retrieving particular types of information in Variants. To be honest, of these two classes, CComVariant is by far the more useful since it has many more overloaded operations defined – so we've only mentioned _variant_t for the sake of completeness. _variant_t is defined in the file comdef.h, which you will need to #include if you wish to use it.

CComVariant encapsulates all the functionality of _variant_t and a lot more. It is supplied with the Active Template Library (ATL), which comes with your Visual Studio 6 installation. To use it you need to #include the file atlbase.h.

We don't have space here to cover CComVariant in detail – the easiest way to find out all it does is to examine its definition in atlbase.h. But essentially it allows Variants to be treated as normal variables. For example, to assign an integer (VT_I4) to a variant you can simply write

```
CComVariant var;
var = 3;
```

CComVariant is actually derived from the VARIANT structure rather than encapsulating it – this means it's fine to use pointers to CComVariants directly in COM method calls that nominally require pointers to VARIANTs.

Arrays

Arrays in VB are more complex. And, unfortunately, there are no helper classes in C++ to make the work easier. Essentially, an `Array` in VB is a data structure known as a `SAFEARRAY` in C++. This data structure contains the data in the array, as well as a series of member variables that give information about the size and dimensionality of the array. Usually a `SAFEARRAY` will be contained in a `VARIANT`, and indicated by the `VT_ARRAY` flag in the `VARIANT`'s `vt` member variable, while a member variable called `parray` holds a pointer to the actual `SAFEARRAY` structure. This is the standard way that a `Variant` in VB can contain an array of data.

The `SAFEARRAY` can be accessed by means of a set of Windows API functions, which are documented with examples in MSDN. The main functions you will need to look up are `SafeArrayCreate()`, which actually creates a new `SAFEARRAY` with the given dimensions, and `SafeArrayAccessData()` to get to the data in the `SAFEARRAY`.

Visual Basic 6.0

Visual Basic 6.0 provides a graphical user interface (GUI) tool called the **Data Environment (DE)** that allows developers to create and manage ADO `Connection` and `Command` objects visually at design time. As you can see in the following diagram, the Data Environment simplifies the development of data-centric applications by abstracting Visual Basic developers from the ADO object model. Instead of typing redundant code, the DE allows developers to keep their hands on their mouse by using a set of graphical property pages to configure properties for reusable ADO `Connection` and `Command` objects at design time:

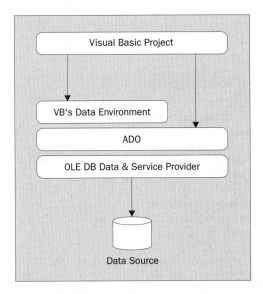

The Data Environment supports multiple connections to various data sources through the data source's OLE DB data provider. Each connection can have any number of `Command` objects that are based on stored procedures, SQL statements, tables, views or synonyms. Additionally, the Data Environment allows us to create groups of command objects that expose hierarchical recordsets. In this case, we simply use the DE's graphical user interface to define a hierarchy of ADO command objects and the Data Environment will automatically generate the complex Shape syntax that's required to create hierarchical recordsets using the OLE DB Shaping service provider (MSDataShape).

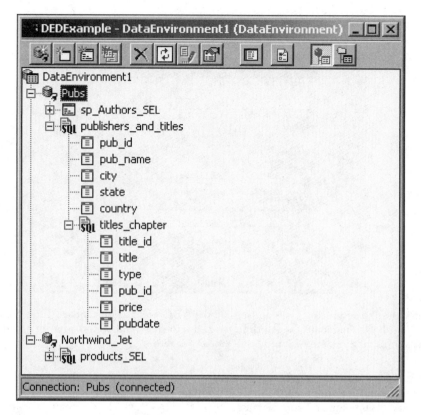

After ADO Connection and Command objects have been defined in the Data Environment, they can be used two different ways: as a data source when performing data binding and programatically through Visual Basic code.

ADO Commands and Connections as a Data Source

If you want to utilize data binding in your Visual Basic application, during design time you can simply drag Command objects or individual fields in the Data Environment and drop them on a Visual Basic form or Data Report. The DE will automatically create controls on the form or Data Report and set the DataSource, DataMember and DataField properties for these new control(s).

By default, the controls created by the DE are based on the data type of each field. However, using the Data Environment you can assign a specific type of control to each field or change the default control assigned to each data type. Instead of displaying each field independently, a data bound grid control can be used to display all of the results from a Command object and a hierarchical flex grid control can be used to display the results from a hierarchical group of Command objects. The screenshot overleaf shows an example of binding a Command object from the Data Environment to both a DataGrid control and to standard controls on a Visual Basic form:

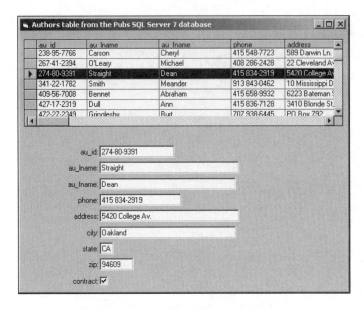

At run-time, the DE automatically establishes all the ADO connections and executes the Command objects. Visual Basic then loads the appropriate data into each data bound control, based on the values in the DataSource, DataMember and DataField properties.

Programmatically

As mentioned above, at run-time the Data Environment creates ADO Command and Connection objects for each command and connection configured in the Data Environment designer. These ADO Connection and Command objects and the resulting Recordset objects can be accessed through the Data Environment's object model which is exposed at run-time. This object model is a subset of the full ADO object model that dynamically changes based on the design-time configuration.

The Data Environment's object model exposes a single Recordset object for each Command that is configured to return a Recordset. This same Recordset is used for databinding and exposed by the Data Environment's object model in two different ways: through the Rs... properties and through the Recordsets collection.

The Data Environment's object model exposes each Recordset object as a property with the same name as the Command object that returned it, but preceded by rs to indicate that the property returns a Recordset object. For example, if we have a Command defined in the Data Environment with the name cmd_Authors_SEL, the Data Environment exposes the Recordset returned from this Command as a property with the name of rscmd_Authors_SEL:

```
'MoveFirst in our Recordset created by the Data
'...Environment using the Property procedure
DataEnvironment1.rscmd_Authors_SEL.MoveFirst
```

The Data Environment's object model also provides a Recordsets collection that contains references to the same ADO Recordset objects that are exposed by the property procedures. The Recordsets collection allows developers to loop through all the Recordset objects created by the Data Environment without knowing the name assigned to the Recordset.

```
'MoveFirst in our Recordset created by the Data Environment
'...using the Recordsets collection
DataEnvironment1.Recordsets(1).MoveFirst
```

When an application is loaded, each `Recordset` object is initially closed until a method is executed on the Data Environment or a control is bound to a `Command` in the Data Environment.

In addition to the `Recordset` objects that are automatically created by the Data Environment, you can also return a new, separate `Recordset` by executing the ADO `Command` objects exposed by the Data Environment object model. The `Commands` collection contains a reference to each ADO `Command` object that was defined during design-time and created by the Data Environment at run-time. As you can see in this example, the `Command` objects returned from the `Commands` collection are actually `ADODB.Command` objects, so they provide exactly the same functionality:

```
Dim rsTitles As ADODB.Recordset

'use a With statement to reduce the amount of code

With DataEnvironment1.Commands('cmd_Titles_SEL_byPubID')
    'set the pub_id parameter
    .Parameters('pub_id').Value = '0736'

    'execute this command object and return a Recordset
    Set rsTitles = .Execute()
End With
```

Each configured ADO `Command` is also exposed as a method of the Data Environment object. However, when a `Command` object is executed as a method it cannot return a `Recordset` object. In this example we execute our ADO `Command`, `cmd_Authors_INS`, by calling a method with the same name on the `DataEnvironment1` object variable.

```
DataEnvironment1.cmd_Authors_INS '111-11-1111', 'Conard', 'James', '555-555-5555'
```

As you can imagine, the Data Environment can greatly simplify the development of data-centric applications in Visual Basic by building upon the ADO object model. In addition to the Data Environment, Visual Basic 6.0 also provides the ability to develop class modules called Data-Aware Class Modules that can act as sources for ADO data or consumers or ADO data. For more information about using these VB-specific features, please refer to "Professional Visual Basic 6 Databases", also published by Wrox Press.

RDS

Remote Data Services (RDS), the final component of the Microsoft Data Access Components, is very simple technology after you have the prerequisite knowledge of ODBC, OLE DB and ADO. RDS is a high-level set of COM components built on top of the following ADO and OLE DB components:

❑ ADO `Recordset` object

❑ Client Cursor Engine OLE DB service provider

❑ Remoting OLE DB service provider

❑ Persistence OLE DB service provider

RDS makes use of these ADO and OLE DB components to provide a high-level set of simple client and server COM components that facilitate an intelligent process of managing data called **batch processing**. Batch processing is the process of retrieving data from a remote data source, disconnecting from the data source, manipulating the data on the client machine and finally reconnecting and merging any changes to the data back into the data source. This process results in increased scalability and performance for the overall data-centric application because it minimizes the number of network round trips required.

Data is transferred or **marshaled** across machine boundaries in the form of **disconnected** ADO Recordset objects using DCOM, HTTP or HTTPS. A disconnected recordset is simply an ADO recordset that is not associated with an ADODB.Connection object and is therefore not connected to a data source. Disconnected recordsets are managed in memory by the OLE DB Cursor Service which also provides scrolling, searching and filtering capabilities without re-executing queries or involving the data source in any way. Existing records within a disconnected recordset can be modified or deleted and new records can be added. A disconnected recordset object can also be persisted to a file in either a binary format called Advanced Data TableGram (ADTG) or in Extensible Markup Language (XML) format and later reloaded, using the OLE DB Persistence Provider. When working with SQL-based data, the disconnected recordset can simply be reconnected to the data source and the recordset's copy of the data can be intelligently re-synchronized with the data source's.

Although today disconnected recordsets and features such as persistence and synchronization can be utilized through the ADO object model, this was not always the case. With MDAC 1.0, these features were only available through a set of components called Advanced Data Connector (ADC). With MDAC 1.5, disconnected recordsets and batch processing were made available through the ADO object model and ADC was renamed to Remote Data Services (RDS) to reflect this change. We'll discuss more about batch processing and disconnected recordsets in Chapter 3.

If these batch processing features found in RDS are also available through the ADO object model, what is the role of RDS today? Where ADO is designed to be the data access technology that can be used in any environment, RDS is designed specifically for use in internet and intranet scenarios. As a web-based Universal Data Access technology, RDS provides two powerful features that are not available through the ADO object model. These features are:

❑ **DHTML Data Binding** – One of the RDS client components, appropriately named the DataControl, is an ActiveX control that provides the ability to bind disconnected ADO Recordset objects to standard HTML elements on a web page such as input boxes, hyperlinks and tables. The DataControl exposes a simplified set of properties and methods that can be invoked through script to retrieve and manage disconnected ADO Recordset objects. The DataControl works with a generic RDS server component called the DataFactory that uses the appropriate OLE DB provider to perform the actual data retrieval and manipulation with the remote data source. We'll discuss DHTML data binding in more detail later in this chapter.

❑ **Remote Component Instantiation** – Probably the most powerful features of RDS is the ability to create and invoke methods on a remote COM(+) or MTS object across DCOM or the HTTP or HTTPS protocols. Where the DataFactory component only provides generic data access functionality requiring business logic and custom data access functionality to reside on the client machine, remote COM(+) or MTS components allow our business logic and data access code to be embedded in binary, resuable components that execute on the server. When methods are invoked on these COM(+) or MTS components, they can return disconnected

ADO `Recordset` objects which can then be used with the `RDS.DataControl` and DHTML data binding. The ability to instantiate remote components is implemented through the use of another simple RDS client component called `DataSpace`. The `DataSpace` component is also automatically used by the `DataControl` component to instantiate and work with the generic `DataFactory` component.

As you can see, even though batch processing and disconnected recordset capabilites are available through the ADO object model, RDS simplifies the process of batch processing and provides powerful features for developing web-based data-centric applications. Of course batch processing, DHTML data binding and the RDS components can become confusing topics because they involve several different components on both the client and the server. Don't worry! We'll look at these RDS components in detail and utilize them to implement DHTML data binding in Chapter 14.

XML

You've probably heard a lot of hype in the last year or so about Extensible Markup Language (XML). But everyone seems to have a different opinion as to what exactly XML is and what benefits it brings. Many people think that XML is a programming language or a replacement for HTML. Some skeptics think that XML is just a lot of hype. XML is none of these things.

> In a nutshell, Extensible Markup Language (XML) is an industry standard specification for describing data.

However, this one-sentence definition doesn't really suffice. To understand what XML really is and understand its benefits, we need to look at an example. The following example is an XML-formatted list of books and their authors:

```
<booklist>
   <book>
      <title>Professional ADO 2.5</title>
      <authorlist>
         <author>James Conard</author>
         <author>David Sussman</author>
      </authorlist>
   </book>
   <book>
      <title>ADO 2.1 Prog Ref</title>
      <authorlist>
         <author>David Sussman</author>
      </authorlist>
   </book>
</booklist>
```

As you can see, XML is a tag-based markup language similar to HTML. In fact, both XML and HTML are derived (albeit in different ways) from Standard Generalized Markup Language (SGML), a complex, industry-standard format for storing documents. However, unlike HTML which describes the document's layout, XML describes the data itself. For example, in the previous XML-formatted data, there are two book records defined with the `<book>` and `</book>` tags. Each book has a title, between the `<title>` and `</title>` tags, and a list of authors between the `<authorlist>` and `</authorlist>` tags.

Why is there so much hype surrounding this simple data format? Because as a text-based data format XML has two main benefits:

- ❑ **XML is extensible.** – XML, by definition, is extensible to describe any type or structure of data. Unlike HTML, where each tag is interpreted by the browser, with XML tags have no intrinsic meaning. As a result, XML allows for an unlimited set of tags. It's up to the XML author to define tag names that best describe the data. The tag names that are choosen must be understood only by the application(s) that will be processing the data. In additon to support for an unlimited set of tags, as we saw in the previous example, XML can also be used to represent **semi-structured data**. Semi-structed data is data that tends to be organized in a hierarchy with each level possibly having a different stucture.

- ❑ **XML is evolving as an industry standard.** – In Febuary 1998, after extensive work by several leading companies, XML 1.0 became a Recommendation, the final stage of the World Wide Web Consortium's (W3C) standardization process. As a soon-to-be industry standard, XML provides interopability between applications, platform-independence and a universal format for data exchange. But how can XML be an industry standard with everyone defining their own tags? Good question! The XML 1.0 specification defines the rules for the formatting of XML data and not the tags themselves. For example, the XML specification states that each opening tag must have a corresponding closting tag, defines reserved characters, and defines the syntax for inserting comments.

The XML 1.0 Specification is available at the Web site of the World Wide Web Consortium, at `http://www.w3c.org`.

The XML Document Object Model (DOM)

To utilize XML-formatted data, it must first be parsed and interpreted. While you could develop a parser yourself, there are a number of XML parsers available for almost every platform in use today. For Windows platforms, Microsoft includes the **Microsoft XML Parser (MSXML)** with Internet Explorer 5.0. MSXML provides the ability to open an XML-formatted file or string and manipulate and edit the data through a set of COM components that comprise the **Document Object Model (DOM)**. The DOM is another W3C standard that defines the API for which XML-formatted data should be exposed by an XML parser. MSXML fully supports W3C's Level 1 specification and provides additional features that make it easier for developers to work with XML-formatted data.

Uses of XML

Again, almost every developer has a different idea of how XML applies to them. But as I see it, there are three *general* uses for XML: separating data from presentation; data exchange; and data persistence. Let's briefly discuss each of these three uses.

Seperating Data from User Interface

The typical web page has meaningful data intermingled within various HTML tags that define how the data should be displayed. As a result, it's very difficult for applications to utilize data found in web pages. XML was designed primarily to separate this meaningful data from HTML tags. This seperation of the data from the user interface provides several benefits including:

❑   Multiple views of the data – When data is separated from the user interface, the user interface can dynamically support rearranging, sorting, filtering or grouping the data without requiring the data to be downloaded from the server again. For example, our list of books could be sorted by the book's title, grouped by the author, or filtered for a specific subject. Performing these operations on the client machine within the web browser can greatly increase the performance and scalability of the entire application.

❑   Local manipulation of data – XML-formatted data can easily be manipulated using the simple XML DOM through client-side script. For example, in the case of our book list, authors and books could be added, out-of-print books could be removed from the list and author names could be updated to adjust for any mis-spellings. Again, this local processing of data increases scalability and performance because a round tip to the server is not required for each data manipulation operation.

❑   Batch processing – After data has been manipulated on the client machine only the changes need to be submitted to the server. Additionally, the web page can request an updated copy of the XML-formatted data in the background without requiring the user to referesh the page. This batch processing model streamlines an application's user interface and increases scalability.

Data Exchange

While XML provides several benefits when developing HTML-based user interfaces, it is also a highly effective format for exchanging data between applications or between components within an application. These applications or components can be scattered across various platforms and communicate using virtually any protocol. Additionally, because XML-formatted data is self-describing, the applications participating in the data exchange don't require any prior information about the data's format or structure. For example, XML could be used to transfer data between different database systems such as Oracle and SQL Server. In this case, these database manufacturers would not have to agree on a proprietary format, but instead they could both independently provide support for importing and exporting XML-formatted data and instantly provide interopability with any other data source that also supports XML.

Data Persistence

Finally, XML is also an ideal format for peristing data. Again, because XML is standardized, this persisted data could be interchanged with diverse applications across multiple platforms. But even more significant, XML is an ideal format for data persistence because it doesn't require any manual parsing or file manipulation code. Instead, you can use one of the many XML parsers currently available, including the easy-to-use MSXML which supports the standard Document Object Model.

> Please note that I'm not suggesting that you should throw out all of your database systems and replace them with XML-formatted data files. XML, like any technology, has its uses in the appropriate scenarios. The challenge is to identify those scenarios and use XML appropriately depending on the needs of your application.

XML vs. UDA

As I mentioned, XML is not the solution to every problem and it is not a replacement for your current Data Sources. Rather, it's simply a new way of accessing data. Wait a minute! Doesn't that mean XML conflicts with ADO? After all, the UDA strategy is about accessing all types of data. XML and ADO both have their own role.

Unfortunately, ADO and OLE DB, for the most part, are platform-specific technologies that are limited to the Windows operating systems. XML introduces the ability to expose data in a standard format so it can be utilized from any environment. But don't throw ADO out of the door just yet! The interoperability provided by XML doesn't come without a price. Currently, there are no data sources available that provide native access to data in XML format. As a result, data must be obtained through other data access technologies and converted to XML. As you can imagine, this process can be terribly inefficient when compared to simply accessing data in its existing format through ADO and OLE DB. Even if there were data sources that natively supported XML, the XML DOM – which is essentially the data access technology for accessing XML-formatted data – lacks the functionality and features that are available through ADO. However, that said, converting data to XML format presents tremendous opportunities for interoperability with multiple applications running in various environments. For example, the following diagram illustrates how data can be stored in its existing data source. This data can be accessed through the ADO and OLE DB technologies and then used directly by applications running on a Windows platform, or the data can be exposed in XML format so it can be leveraged from any application running in any environment:

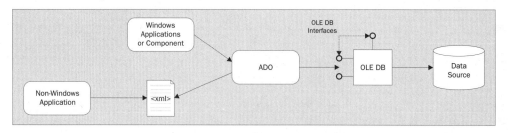

To aid in this conversion process, ADO and OLE DB have provided intrinsic support for XML since ADO 2.1. Currently, this support is limited to saving or **persisting** an ADO Recordset in XML format to a file or object implementing the IStream interface. However, the next version of ADO is expected to provide full support for XML-formatted data. We'll discuss more about XML, the XML DOM, and ADO's integrated support for XML-formatted data in Chapter 7.

Windows DNA

While 90% of applications are data-centric (meaning that their primary requirement is to access and manipulate data), it is important to remember that data access is just one aspect of developing applications. There are a number of other factors involved in developing today's data-centric applications including:

- ❏ User interface design
- ❏ Implementing security
- ❏ Leveraging reusability and extensibility
- ❏ Integrating with existing systems
- ❏ Providing fault tolerance and error handling
- ❏ Delivering high performance and scalability
- ❏ Simplifying deployment, support and maintenance
- ❏ Implementing business rules and logic

What exactly is Windows DNA and what does it have to do with solving these requirements? Windows DNA, like XML, means different things to different people. Everyone seems to have a different opinion of what Windows DNA means to them and the benefits of Windows DNA vary based on who you ask.

From my perspective, Windows DNA is a programming model or blueprint for designing and developing distributed component-based applications by utilizing a comprehensive set of products and services. Like UDA, Windows DNA is an umbrella terminology that groups together several products and services. However, Windows DNA has a much broader scope because it groups together products and services that satisfy *all* aspects of developing applications, including the requirement for Universal Data Access. Windows DNA maps these abstract requirements of developing data-centric applications to an infrastructure of physical products and services that are available today.

I like to think of Windows DNA as a puzzle. Technologies such as ADO, COM+, DHTML, etc. appear as scattered, unrelated pieces of the puzzle. Windows DNA is about connecting these separate pieces of development technologies into an integrated infrastructure of services all based around the industry standard COM and XML specifications. It's important to understand that Windows DNA didn't define the puzzle pieces – Windows DNA doesn't provide physical products and services. Windows DNA is just a conceptual way of placing the puzzle pieces or grouping various technologies together to make the development of high performance, reliable and scalable applications simpler.

DNA actually makes developing applications easier because it is all about utilizing existing products and services to minimize the amount of infrastructure code required to create an application. Just think about all the times that you wrote hundreds of lines of code to provide transaction processing, message queuing, security, or custom database access in your applications. Now imagine all of these development requirements being lifted off your shoulders, and instead Microsoft will take care of these details for you, by providing you with a set of efficient and programmable services, leaving you to concentrate on the business requirements of the application. Yes, this is the general concept behind component-based programming, but Windows DNA takes the idea of a reusable infrastructure beyond simple email components and grid controls to sophisticated run-time services.

Windows DNA is not just about utilizing the newest technologies or the hottest acronyms. Windows DNA is about picking up the ugly, ragged-edged puzzle piece off the floor and finding a place for it in your puzzle. In other words, Windows DNA is also about interoperability, or using what's already there, with existing legacy systems, so that you can make use of and extend current technology investments. DNA's support for open, industry and internet standards such as HTML and XML enables this interoperability with legacy systems on a variety of platforms without sacrificing anything when used with the newest technologies on sophisticated operating systems such as Windows 2000.

I'm sure you won't be surprised to hear that the Windows Distributed interNet Architecture is about leveraging the Internet. The Internet has become a great platform for developing data-centric applications for two main reasons:

❑ It allows developers to create applications that are platform-independent without making developers learn a new proprietary language.

❑ It provides a flexible mechanism for deploying applications and therefore exchanging and sharing information.

The Windows DNA technologies can be used to develop both web-based and standard Win32 data-centric applications.

3-tier and n-tier Architecture

Windows DNA applications are divided up into three or more *logical* tiers or layers. Components in each of these tiers perform a specific type of processing. While the names of these tiers vary depending on the source, in this book we will define the three basic tiers as follows:

User Services

The **User Services tier**, sometimes referred to as the **Presentation Services**, is an application's user interface. The user interface in a three-tier or n-tier application is responsible for allowing the user to view and manipulate data, and performing simple data formatting and validation. However, business logic and data access functionality is completely separated from the User Services tier, although from the user's perspective, the User Services tier *is* the entire application, because the user is totally unaware of any other tiers or application layers. Typically, user services are developed using the Win32 API or technologies built on top of the Win32 API such as Visual Basic forms or Microsoft Foundation Classes. However, many user services are also being developed using internet technologies, such as DHTML, because of the multi-platform capabilities and the reduced deployment and maintenance efforts required.

Business Services

The **Business Services tier**, also referred to as the middle tier, is responsible for encapsulating business rules and other application-specific functionality. The Business Services tier is centrally located between the User Services and the Data Services tiers. Since business rules have the highest likelihood of changing, separating them from both the user interface and the data sources results in more manageable applications. As business rules change, you only have to implement the changes in the centrally-located Business Services tier instead of making changes to *every* user interface or *every* data source.

In addition to reduced management, centrally locating business rules also promotes reusability. Business rules can be implemented once and utilized by different types of user interfaces and various data sources. For example, the Business Services tier could be implemented as a handful of COM+ components that bridge both Win32 and internet-based user interfaces with various data sources such as SQL Server databases, Active Directory Services and Microsoft Exchange folders.

Data Services

The **Data Services tier** is responsible for retrieving, manipulating and storing data. Although the Data Services implement logic related to the storage and integrity of data such as rules, constraints and data relationships, all business-related logic is completely separated and implemented in the Business Services tier. The Data Services tier encapsulates all aspects of data access, manipulation and storage. If anything about the data source changes, only the data services need to be modified to reflect the changes.

The Data Services tier is typically composed of COM components that utilize ADO, OLE DB or ODBC to access a variety of data sources such as SQL Server and Oracle databases, Microsoft Exchange folders, and Active Directory Services. However, the Data Services tier can also be composed of data source-specific interfaces such as stored procedures, triggers or views.

This 3-tier model is illustrated in the following diagram:

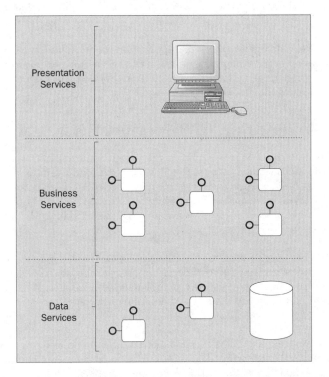

Some applications further sub-divide the standard User Services tier, Business Services tier, or Data Services tier. For example, you might decide to divide the Business Services into data-centric and user-centric tiers, thus having a total of four tiers. This type of application is often referred to as an n-tier application because it is divided into more than three tiers.

> It's important to understand that the 3-tier and n-tier application models are logical
> and not physical. The terminology 'tier' does not necessarily mean a separate physical
> machine. It simply refers to a separate, logical section of an application. Of course,
> placing all the tiers on a single machine defeats the purpose of distributed
> applications. However, using only two separate machines (one machine for the
> Presentation Services and another for the Business and Data Services) is not
> uncommon. Nor is it uncommon to have multiple machines for a single tier.

Dividing applications into these separate tiers or sections, can reduce the complexity of the overall
application and therefore reduce development time and cost. For example, developers can specialize in
the design and development of a specific tier or tiers. Common services can also be easily identified and
shared across multiple applications.

Additionally, because the 3-tier and n-tier application models are logical, they provide an incredible
level of flexibility. Logical tiers can be arranged physically based on the security, reusability, scalability,
performance and management requirements in any given situation. For example, if simplified
management is the primary goal of an application, the Business Services and Data Services tiers could
be physically located on shared servers instead of client machines. If scalability is the primary goal, both
the User Services and the Business Services tiers could be physically located on underworked client
workstations.

While Windows DNA didn't define the 3-tier application model, Windows DNA simplifies 3-tier and n-
tier application development by mapping products and services to specific tiers. We'll discuss these
specific products in more detail in the following section, but first let's understand the essential role of
the Component Object Model (COM) in Windows DNA.

COM is the Foundation of Windows DNA

Just as the Component Object Model (COM) is the foundation for OLE DB and ADO, both COM and
its networked version, Distributed CCOM (DCOM), are the foundation of Windows DNA. Going back
to our puzzle analogy, you can think of COM and DCOM as the outer border of puzzle pieces. The
border of a puzzle serves as a structure for holding together the puzzle as one cohesive unit, just as
COM and DCOM serve as the structure for holding together Windows DNA and allowing various
products and services to interoperate.

In a nutshell, COM is a specification for developing language-independent, reusable software
components called COM components. COM components encapsulate code and functionality and
expose this functionality through one or more implemented interfaces. Each interface defines a set of
methods that can be called by any other COM components or applications to untap a component's
encapsulated functionality.

In Windows DNA applications, COM components can be used on any tier of the n-tier application
model. For example, in the following diagram, the clsCustomer_Bus component encapsulates
business-related logic and acts as the mediator between the User Services and the Data Services tiers.
The clsCustomerTx_ds and the clsCustomerN_ds components encapsulate data access and
manipulation code. The functionality implemented by these three components is exposed by each
component's default interface and handful of methods the interface defines:

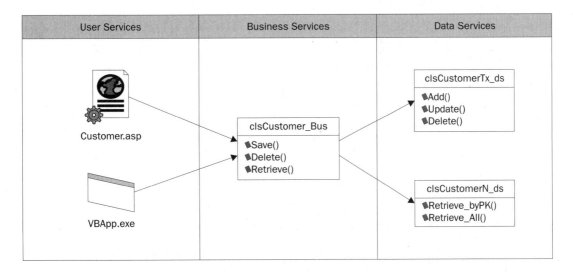

DCOM as the Transport

Since its inception, COM has provided the ability for components and applications to communicate across threads and processes. Distributed COM, or DCOM (often called 'COM with a longer wire'), extended COM to provide communication across physical machine boundaries. Today, when discussing communication between components, the terms COM and DCOM are often used interchangably.

> **In Windows DNA, DCOM acts as the glue that transparently connects COM components, DNA services, and applications across both logical tiers and physical process and machine boundaries.**

DCOM is supported on several popular operating systems including all variations of Windows, various flavors of Unix and even Sun Solaris. Communication with components can occur across different protocols such as TCP/IP, IPX/SPX, and HTTP (with Windows NT 4, Service Pack 4)!

But most importantly, DCOM provides **location transparency** by completely abstracting COM components and clients from these communication details. Location transparency allows applications or COM components to communicate with other COM components in exactly the same way regardless of the physical location of the component, the operating system hosting the component or network protocol, if any, that is used. Additionally, DCOM's location transparency is what makes it possible for an application designed around the *logical* 3-tier and n-tier application models to be *physically* arranged based on its security, reusability, scalability, performance and management requirements.

COM and DCOM are actually infrastructures in themselves. COM is not just the foundation for ADO, OLE DB and the Window Distributed interNet Architecture, but rather, COM is the foundation for almost every product on the Microsoft platform. This brief, one-page overview of COM and DCOM does not even begin to do such an important technology justice. I recommend referring to the Wrox family of COM/DCOM-related books for an in-depth look at this important infrastructure technology.

DNA Technologies – The Pieces of the DNA Puzzle

Windows DNA simplifies the development of 3-tier and n-tier applications by providing an infrastructure of products and services that complement the 3-tier and n-tier application models. While most Windows DNA technologies are targeted at providing a set of functionality for a specific tier, it's important to remember that Windows DNA is an open and flexible architecture. Windows DNA technologies can be used on any tier(s) in a logical 3-tier or n-tier model. Furthermore, you don't have to use or learn about every technology to design and develop Windows DNA applications. Instead, you can employ the technologies you need arranged logically and physically as you see fit.

Let's discuss briefly some of the most common technologies that comprise Windows DNA, so we better understand the role ADO plays in Windows DNA applications.

> **The products and technologies that comprise Windows DNA are fairly complex. Most warrant entire books in themselves. The simple, 'nutshell definitions' as I like to call them, that follow only begin to explain these important DNA technologies. The goal here is not to gain a vast amount of knowledge about every Windows DNA product, but instead introduce the various technologies and terminology we will be utilizing throughout this book.**

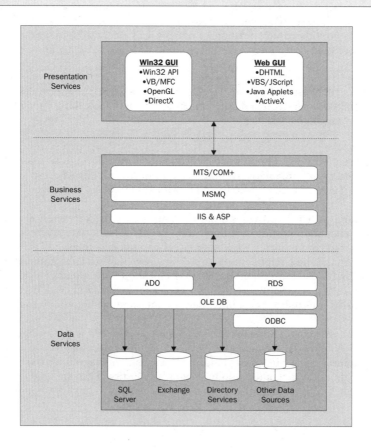

User Services

As we have seen, the User Services tier consists of the graphical interface displayed to the user and is the only part of the application the user interacts with. The physical implementation of the User Services tier is probably the most variable of the three tiers. Client machines hosting the User Services tier can range from handheld HP/C or PalmPCs to high-performance desktop workstations. Traditionally, user interfaces were implemented as applications, but with the explosion of the Internet, the introduction of intranets, and the improvements made with development tools and technologies in recent years, more and more User Services are being developed using Web-based technologies. Web-based User Services provide reduced maintenance, simplified deployment and operating system independence, however this often comes at the price of reduced functionality and features. Eventually, as web-based technologies and development tools improve, the distinction between Web-based interfaces and traditional application interfaces will be eliminated – at least from the user's perspective. However, until then, Windows DNA defines a broad range of products and technologies for developing the User Services tier, including:

❑ Dynamic HTML (DHTML)

❑ Win32 API

Let's discuss each of these products and technologies in more detail.

DHTML

HTML pages by themselves can be eye-pleasing, but they are static and limited in functionality. Changing a web page's contents or layout after it has loaded requires a request to the server and a reload of the page, ultimately resulting in lower performance, limited scalability and frustrated users. Dynamic HTML (DHTML) is a group of technologies implemented in the browser that allow developers to create more interactive and functional web pages. DHTML provides a language-independent and easy-to-use object model for HTML pages. The DHTML object model, based on the World Wide Web Consortium's (W3C) standard Document Object Model (DOM), exposes all elements of an HTML page as programmable objects with properties, methods and events. This object model allows scripts written in JavaScript or VBScript to modify the style, content, and structure of a Web page without reloading it. HTML elements such as text boxes, command buttons, images and text can dynamically added, removed or modified. These elements can be dynamically positioned anywhere on the page and even layered on top of other elements without reloading the page.

While the ability to modify the style, content and structure of a Web page dynamically is important for developing interactive web sites, web-based user interfaces serve no purpose in data-centric applications unless they provide the ability for users to view and manipulate data. DHTML also introduces the powerful ability to bind standard HTML elements on a Web page such as input boxes, <DIV> tags and tables to a **Data Source Object** (**DSO**). A DSO is a COM component that synchronously or asynchronously retrieves data from a data source and exposes this data through the standard OLE DB Simple Provider (OSP) interfaces. The OSP interfaces are COM-automation compatible interfaces layered on top of the complex OLE DB interfaces required for Level 0 and Level 1 OLE DB conformance. As the acronym suggests, the OSP interfaces are designed to expose only simplistic, tabular data. In Chapters 15 and 16, we'll use these OSP interfaces to develop custom OLE DB data providers.

Internet Explorer ships with a number of Data Source Objects ranging in functionality and capabilities, including:

❑ **Tabular Data Control** – The Tabular Data Control (TDC) is a simple DSO that provides access to data stored in text files. The TDC can asynchronously download these text files from a URL and temporarily store them on the client machine where they can serve as a data source in disconnected scenarios. Most Database Management Systems (DBMSs), such as SQL Server, provide the ability to export data to text files.

❑ **JDBC DSO** – The JDBC Data Source Object is a Java applet that provides read-only access data sources that support Java DataBase Connectivity (JDBC).

❑ **XML DSO** – In Internet Explorer 5, XML data islands can be embedded in an HTML page using the XML tag. Internet Explorer automatically parses the XML data and exposes it through the OSP interfaces. The XML DSO also provides support for binding hierarchical data. Since Internet Explorer itself implements the XML DSO, it does not require the use of a Java applet or an ActiveX control which might not be enabled due to the client's security settings. As the popularity and mainstream usage of XML data increases, the XML DSO is becoming the most popular way to perform DHTML data binding. We'll discuss DHTML data binding to XML data in more detail in Chapter 7.

❑ **HTML DSO** – While not as widely used as the XML DSO, Internet Explorer's MSHTML component can parse an HTML document looking for tags with an ID attribute and expose data between these tags through the OSP interfaces. Data binding to an HTML DSO is much more complicated than using the XML DSO because the HTML DSO tries to use HTML for something it was never designed for. HTML was designed as a markup language for defining page layout, unlike XML, which was designed for describing data.

❑ **Remote Data Services (RDS)** – RDS is a more sophisticated DSO that can obtain data from any OLE DB data source. Unlike other DSOs, RDS provides the ability to update, insert and delete data because it can access data directly in it's native format. As we discussed earlier, RDS also provides the ability to create a MTS or COM+ object on the local or remote machine, call methods on the component to obtain a disconnected ADO Recordset and then use the Recordset as the source of the data. Don't worry if you didn't catch all of that. We'll discuss more about this involved process while we implement DHTML data binding using RDS in Chapter 14.

Data exposed by a Data Source Object can be bound to standard HTML elements using any of a handful of HTML attributes. Of course, these attributes can also be modified dynamically using the DHTML object model. Additionally, each DSO provides a Recordset property that returns an ADO Recordset representing the data the DSO managed by the DSO. Scripts can use this Recordset object to implement any required functionality that's not possible using the simple data binding attributes alone.

With the combination of an easy-to-use object model and a flexible, but simple, data binding architecture based on ADO and OLE DB, DHTML enables developers to create scalable, high-performance and sophisticated User Services.

Win32 API

It's important to remember that Windows DNA is not just about developing Internet applications. DNA provides interoperability in several areas including at the User Services tier. Many user interfaces have already been developed using the Win32 API or a language-specific library that simply abstracts developers from the Win32 API such as the Visual Basic run-time or Microsoft Foundation classes.

Win32 applications still offer the most functionality and flexibility, but with user interface technologies such as DHTML the benefits of developing Win32 applications are diminishing. For one thing, Win32 applications are of course tied to the Windows platform. Additionally, Win32 applications usually result in more maintenance and support costs than equivalent internet or intranet applications. However, Win32 applications will remain popular for developing the User Services tier because of their rapid development and almost unlimited capabilities. It's important to note that the development of the User Services tier is not exclusive to one technology. Many data-centric applications developed around Windows DNA provide a variety of user interfaces, implemented using a variety of technologies.

Business Services

Arguably, the Business Services tier is the most sophisticated tier because it is responsible for bridging multiple user interfaces (User Services) with multiple data sources (Data Services). The Business Services tier is usually implemented as groups of COM components. These COM components encapsulate business logic and application-specific operations. Thankfully, Microsoft provides the following integrated products and technologies that simplify the development of complex, middle-tier business components:

- ❑ MTS
- ❑ MSMQ
- ❑ COM+
- ❑ IIS & ASP

Let's discuss each of these products and technologies in more detail.

MTS

Microsoft Transaction Server (MTS) is a programming model for developing, deploying and managing secure, high-performance, scalable and robust COM components. If you didn't absorb all of that, don't worry. As an extension of COM and DCOM, MTS is a fairly comprehensive and complex product. This simple one-sentence definition is not sufficient to emphasize what MTS provides to distributed, component-based systems. But although it is difficult to define in a single sentence what exactly MTS is, understanding Microsoft Transaction Server's objective is very simple: MTS is designed to make the development of reliable, scalable, and high-performance COM components easier.

How does MTS make developing components easier? It allows developers to create multi-user, *feature-rich* components in basically the same way that we currently create single-user COM components packaged as in-process DLL servers. MTS abstracts developers from the complex details of distributed component development by using a programmable infrastructure. This abstraction allows the developer to focus primarily on the business logic for the application instead of worrying about complicated multi-user issues such as concurrency, connection pooling or security.

MTS's programmable infrastructure is composed of several services that contribute to increased scalability, increased reliability and simplified administration of distributed, component-based systems. These infrastructure services include:

❑ Declarative transactions

❑ Multi-user concurrency

❑ Thread pooling and management   ⸍

❑ Resource pooling

❑ Role-based security

❑ Fault tolerance

❑ MTS Explorer

❑ Scriptable Administration Objects

❑ Deployment packages

❑ Static load balancing

We will now look briefly at each of these services in turn.

Declarative Transactions

MTS provides a transaction model that eliminates the complex transaction-processing code required for distributed transactions coordinated by the Microsoft Distributed Transaction Coordinator (MS DTC). MTS's transaction model also *transparently* merges distributed transactions with COM components.

MTS transactions are implemented through the use of **declarative attributes** that are specified externally to a component's implementation. MTS automatically handles the complex and redundant details of beginning and committing or aborting transactions by interacting with MS DTC on the behalf of your component. Any operations your components perform against data sources are automatically being performed within a distributed transaction.

A single component can perform operations against several different types of resources within a single MTS transaction. For example, an MTS object could perform an operation against a SQL Server database and send a Microsoft Message Queue Server (MSMQ) message within the same MTS Transaction.

MTS also allows transactions seamlessly to span multiple objects. Simply by changing a component's transaction support level, an MTS object can execute in its own transaction, or it can be comprised of or combined with other MTS objects as part of a larger transaction. Multi-object transactions allow MTS components a much greater degree of flexibility and it enhances MTS component reuse without requiring code changes.

Multi-User Concurrency

When a distributed application provides services to multiple users, it can receive simultaneous calls from clients. As a result, most distributed applications must be concerned about issues such as concurrency and thread management. However, MTS shields you from these issues and allows you to create components that execute in a multi-user, distributed environment just as you would create a component that services a single user. MTS accomplishes this amazing task using *activities*. An activity is nothing more than a group of objects executing on the behalf of a *single* client. By grouping a single client's objects together into a logical activity, they are isolated from all other activities and objects. One client's work cannot interfere with another's. This simple concept is very important in On-Line Transaction Processing (OLTP) systems, such as MTS, to ensure the integrity of data and prevent deadlock situations.

Thread Pooling and Management

The multi-user concurrency and thread pooling/management features of Microsoft Transaction Server go hand-in-hand. MTS automatically manages a pool of up to 100 threads. One thread is used by each activity, until there are more activities than available threads, in which case activities begin to share threads. By using a physical thread per activity instead of a physical thread per object, MTS can be scaled to support many objects without consuming too many resources.

Resource Pooling

Resource pooling provides an efficient way of dispensing non-durable or temporary resources, such as threads, data source connections, or memory blocks, by providing an MTS object with a recycled resource instead of creating a new one. After a resource has been used, it is made available for reuse by the same or another MTS object. This reuse or recycling of resources is completely transparent to the MTS object consuming the resource. Resource pooling can significantly improve performance and scalability because resources can be reused from a pool faster than they can be created. Additionally, memory usage is reduced because multiple objects can share the same resource.

Non-durable resources are managed by and reside in the memory of an in-process server called a Resource Dispenser. One of the most common types of such non-durable resources are connections to data sources that control persistent storage, such as a database, a file system, or Exchange folders. For example, the ODBC Driver Manager acts as a Resource Dispenser for managing and pooling ODBC database connections. This type of resource pooling is known as connection pooling. With OLE DB sessions or ADO connections, the OLE DB Service Component provides a type of resource pooling known as *session pooling*.

Role-based Security

MTS security builds on top of the security infrastructure already provided by Windows NT and COM, by introducing the concept of roles. Roles provide an abstraction layer for components from physical Windows NT user and group accounts, which are prone to change and offer no flexibility.

During development, developers can define roles and determine what security permission the roles are granted. At deployment time, an administrator can simply map specific Windows NT user and group accounts to these same roles. This eliminates the decision-making required by the system administrator and makes the development and deployment of secure, component-based systems much easier.

Roles also offer a much more natural way of administering security. Instead of thinking about which components a particular user or group should have permission to, you can think about security in terms of the role(s) than an individual plays within the organization.

Approaching security in this manner is also much more appealing to system administrators because an understanding of COM and components is not required. An administrator simply adds or removes the Windows NT user and group accounts that belong to MTS role(s) using MTS Explorer.

For defining permissions, MTS offers developers two types of application security: declarative security and programmatic security. Both types only assign permissions through roles, and not through individual Windows NT user or group accounts. Although both declarative and programmatic security can be used independently, they provide the most powerful and flexible security model when used together.

Declarative security allows you to define authorization permissions for roles without writing a line of code. MTS automatically verifies that the caller belongs to a required role when a method call is made. MTS currently supports declarative security at three different levels: package (process), component, and interface.

Programmatic security allows us to supplement and extend declarative security by implementing code in our MTS components. MTS programmatic security is based on two functions of the MTS programming model. These two functions allow a component to have more control over security by manually checking whether or not the direct caller is in a particular role. When used in combination with declarative security, programmatic security can extend simple authorization checking to providing different behavior based on the direct caller's role.

While role-based declarative security is the recommended approach to implementing secure MTS components, the MTS security model is very flexible. The MTS security model also allows you to revert to the legacy technique of programmatically checking Windows NT user account names.

Fault Tolerance

Microsoft Transaction Server maintains internal consistency and integrity checking to ensure that all the components it manages are working properly. MTS objects cannot generate exceptions outside the object. So, when an MTS object fails, any unhandled errors will be written to the Windows NT Event Log and will result in the termination of the current process hosting the object, without raising an error to the calling client. This immediate termination of the process due to a failing MTS component is known as **Fail-fast**. Fail-fast is a very important safety feature because terminating the process reduces the chance that an error may go undetected. Undetected errors can lead to corrupt data and even system failures.

MTS also adds an additional layer of fault tolerance by allowing MTS components to execute in a separate process. *All* the components within a process are isolated from components in another process. This type of fault tolerance, known as **fault isolation**, makes MTS a much more stable run-time environment for COM components because if one component fails, it only causes the process and all the components in the process to fail, rather than all the processes on the system.

MTS Explorer

Microsoft Transaction Server stores configuration information about each component, each **package** (group of components), and security settings in the Windows System Registry. This collection of information is known as the MTS catalog. Instead of having developers and administrators access the registry directly to manipulate the MTS catalog, MTS provides a graphical user interface (GUI) administration tool named **MTS Explorer** (or Transaction Server Explorer). MTS Explorer allows an administrator to modify the MTS catalog in a controlled manner with a simple point and click of the mouse.

From MTS Explorer you can perform any MTS administration task, including:

❑   Adding, removing and configuring MTS components

❑   Adding, removing and configuring MTS packages (groups of components)

❑   Assigning permissions and controlling security

❑   Deploying packages for installation on other MTS servers

❑   Exporting and importing components to and from other MTS machines

The MTS Explorer is implemented as a **Microsoft Management Console (MMC)** snap-in. MMC is a feature that provides a common management environment for custom administration components called **snap-ins**. By implementing management applications as MMC snap-in components, they can be accessed from the same single user interface.

Scriptable Administration Objects

The easiest and most straightforward way to perform MTS administration tasks is through MTS Explorer. However, MTS also provides a programmable interface to the MTS catalog called the Scriptable Administration Objects. The Scriptable Administration Objects allow us to perform administrative operations through code rather than through MTS Explorer. Because the Scriptable Administration Objects are dual-interface COM components, we can use them from any tool or language that supports COM, including VBScript and JScript, that executes within a web page or the Windows Scripting Host. The Scriptable Administration Objects allow us easily to write scripts or applications to automate a routine task or create an enhanced version of the MTS Explorer.

Deployment Packages

The deployment of a distributed, component-based application is notorious for being one of the most frustrating and difficult stages in the development process. Fortunately, MTS provides help in the area of deployment by allowing us to export a package from the MTS catalog using either MTS Explorer or the Scriptable Administration Objects. Exporting a package creates a deployable package file that can be used to install a package on another MTS machine or used as a backup. Additionally, MTS also creates a client-side setup program when a package is exported. When the client-side setup program is executed on a client machine, it performs all of the necessary installation and configuration for the client computer to instantiate the MTS components.

Static Load Balancing

Microsoft Transaction Server allows an administrator to distribute components across multiple servers running MTS simply by dragging and dropping components across machines using MTS Explorer. Client machines must then be reconfigured to instantiate components on the appropriate machine.

As you can see, MTS provides a whole range of services to components besides just transaction processing, as the name Microsoft Transaction Server implies. Most of these services are automatic and require little or no additional code to be implemented by the MTS components using these services. Remember, the simple objective of MTS is to make developing COM components easier. Microsoft Transaction Server 2.0 has done a good job of fulfilling this objective on the Windows NT platform.

MSMQ

Microsoft Message Queue (MSMQ), also known as Windows 2000 Messaging Services, provides reliable, asynchronous communication between components and applications. With message queuing, components or applications can send text or binary data in the form of messages to a queue where they are temporarily stored until the receiving application or component removes them from the queue at its convenience. After the sender places a message in a queue, they can perform other tasks without waiting on a response from the recipient. On the other end, the recipient is guaranteed eventually to receive the message, even if the recipient is disconnected from the network or the recipient application is not even running.

In addition to improved fault tolerance and reliability, message queuing can also be used to improve performance and scalability. If a server is temporarily busy or unavailable, a client can send the request, in the form of a message, to the server's queue and the server can process and optionally reply to the request at its convenience. Additionally, multiple servers can share the same queue or queues effectively, providing dynamic load balancing of client request(s).

Message queuing could be compared to the real-world scenario of calling a company for technical support. When you call technical support, you can usually either wait on the phone to talk to a customer service representative or leave a voice mail and be called back at a later time. By leaving a voice mail, you ensure that someone will receive your message. You can then proceed with other tasks without waiting on the phone, just as message queuing frees the sender of the message to perform other tasks while it waits for a response from the receiving application. Additionally, just as you are unaware of which technical support representative will return your call, clients sending messages to a queue are unaware of which machine will process the request.

MSMQ is implemented as a set of COM components that enable developers to create applications that make use of these general benefits of message queuing and a number of additional MSMQ-specific benefits including:

❏ Prioritized messages

❏ Encryption and signature services

❏ Automatic notification through events

❏ Support for MS DTC transactions

❏ Interoperability with other message queuing systems

COM+

COM+, the latest revision to the Component Object Model delivered in Windows 2000, represents a unification of the COM, DCOM, MTS and MSMQ programming models. This unified architecture, also known as **Windows Component Services**, makes it significantly easier to develop components because the distinction between MTS and COM is eliminated:

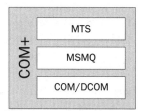

However, COM+ encompasses more than just the merging of the COM, DCOM, MTS and MSMQ programming models and administration. COM+ also picks up where MTS left off, by continuing to provide an infrastructure of robust and flexible services, leaving developers to focus on business problems and their solutions. In addition to enhancing and extending support for existing services originally provided by MTS, such as declarative transactions, role-based security and component management, COM+ adds the following services:

❏ **Dynamic Load Balancing** – According to Microsoft, intrinsic support for dynamic load balancing has been one of the most requested additions to DCOM and MTS. COM+ provides a dynamic load balancing service that intelligently creates COM+ objects on the available server performing the least amount of processing. COM+'s implementation of dynamic load balancing is completely transparent to the COM+ components and the clients, and it requires no additional code or changes to existing code. Dynamic load balancing will only be available with the AppCenter Server edition of Windows 2000.

❑ **Object Pooling** – Object pooling, also sometimes called called object recycling, is the process of reusing existing component instances instead of instantiating new ones. Object pooling reduces the amount of time it takes for the COM+ run time to provide the client with an object. It can ultimately result in higher performance and increased scalability in some situations.

❑ **Compensating Resource Managers** – All of the COM+ services we've discussed up to now are designed to enhance the scalability and performance of component-based applications. However, COM+ also provides a new feature called the **Compensating Resource Manager (CRM)** that provides an infrastructure that enhances COM+'s support for transaction processing. Compensating Resource Managers are pairs of COM+ components that allow a non-transactional resource to participate in transactions managed by the Microsoft Distributed Transaction Coordinator (MS DTC). For example, CRMs could be developed to provide transactional access for resources such as file systems, memory or the Windows 2000 registry. Transactional COM+ components can then access these resources through the CRM's interface(s) and all operations performed by both the transactional COM+ components and the CRM would be protected by an MS DTC Transaction. Should the transaction be aborted, the CRM is responsible for performing the *compensating* or opposite action to undo any previous operations.

❑ **Queued Components** – The integration of MSMQ into the COM+ programming model is found in COM+'s support for queued components. Queued components allow clients to invoke methods asynchronously on COM+ components via a transparent MSMQ message. To the client, there is no difference between instantiating and calling methods on a queued component compared to any other COM+ component. However, behind the scenes queued components rely on a complex architecture that uses MSMQ messages to marshal method calls, parameters and return values from the client to the server. Queued components eliminate the need for developers to implement their own architecture to support asynchronous communications between components using MSMQ.

❑ **Loosely Coupled Events (LCE)** (Publish/Subscribe events) – COM+ also introduces a new asynchronous event system known as **Loosely Coupled Events** (**LCE**). Unlike the existing connection point event system used in COM, LCE is designed more for broadcasting information in a distributed system and allows the component that raises an event and the components that receive the event not to be in direct communication.

The COM+ event system is composed of a **publisher** and a **subscriber,** which are new terms for server and client respectively. The publisher is the COM+ component that will initiate the event, where subscribers are the clients that will process the event. Between the publisher and the subscriber is a COM+ component called the **EventClass** that acts as a mediator between the publisher and the subscriber. The EventClass is the key to the COM+ event system because it removes the need for a direct communication between the subscriber and the publisher. This simplifies the development of COM+ components that raise events (publishers) because they raise events on the EventClass the same way, regardless of the number or location of the subscribers. The EventClass is responsible for broadcasting events to all the subscribers.

As in MTS, COM+ components can easily take advantage of most of these services simply by changing declarative attributes that are external to the implementation of the component. COM+ services can also be combined together to provide the desired functionality for a component. For example, when used together, dynamic load balancing and object pooling can greatly improve the scalability and performance of COM+ components.

Windows Component Services is a strategic step in the evolution of COM that further simplifies the development of reliable, high-performance, and scalable component-based systems by providing an infrastructure of integrated products and services.

IIS and ASP

Internet Information Server (IIS) is Microsoft's extremely successful web server product available on the Windows NT and Windows 2000 platforms. In Windows DNA, IIS acts as the link between the User Services and Business Services tiers by serving web pages and all types of data across the Internet and Intranets using a variety of web-based protocols including HTTP, HTTPS and FTP.

The key technology that has made IIS so successful as a web server is Active Server Pages (ASP). ASP is a language-neutral, server-side scripting environment used to develop dynamic internet and intranet applications. When a file with an .asp extension is requested across the HTTP or HTTPS protocols, IIS executes the embedded server-side script in the ASP file and returns the results of the script to the client. ASP files are typically used to deliver dynamic content in the form of HTML pages. However, ASP can also be used to expose dynamically any sort of 'data' that's used in the User Services tier, including DHTML, XML and client-side scripts.

The server-side scripts in Active Server Pages can be written using any language that provides an Active Scripting engine. IIS includes the VBScript and the JScript scripting engines. While these scripting languages are very popular and easy to use, they are also interpreted and limited in functionality. As a result, they provide limited performance and scalability. Hopefully, the next version of ASP (codenamed ASP+) will resolve this issue by providing the ability to create Active Server Pages using native or compiled Visual Basic or Visual C++ code. However, only time will tell.

Instead of embedding business logic in Active Server Pages and dealing with the limitations of the scripting languages, it is recommended to encapsulate business logic and data access code in MTS or COM+ components. Script in the Active Server Pages can simply create and call methods on MTS or COM+ objects to perform most of the work.

> *For more information on using components with ASP, see 'Beginning Components for ASP' from Wrox Press, ISBN 1-861002-88-2.*

In addition to the ability to use MTS and COM+ components, ASP and IIS are completely integrated with Microsoft Transaction Server. This integration of IIS and MTS/COM+ allows ASPs to utilize MTS or COM+ services such as declarative transactions, connection/session pooling and object pooling. Additionally, Active Server Pages can be configured to participate in transactions along with MTS/COM+ and MSMQ. Such a page is called a **Transactional Active Server Page**.

Data Services

The Data Services tier is responsible for retrieving and manipulating data while abstracting the Business Services tier from the details of data storage and integrity. Like the Business Services tier, the Data Services tier is also typically implemented as a set of MTS or COM+ components. However, where the MTS/COM+ components in the Business Services tier are responsible for encapsulating business logic, the Data Service components utilize the technologies such as ADO, OLE DB, ODBC, CDO and the XML DOM to access and expose a variety of underlying data sources. Besides these external data access interfaces, the data services tier can also be composed of data source specific interfaces such as stored procedures, triggers or views. Additionally, these data access technologies are often layered on top of one another. For example, a COM+ data service component might use ADO (and thus OLE DB) to call stored procedures implemented in a SQL Server database.

Data access and manipulation is just one aspect of the Data Services tier. The Data Services tier also encompasses the data sources themselves. Some of these data sources that could be considered part of the Windows DNA Data Services tier include:

- ❑ SQL Server databases
- ❑ Jet databases
- ❑ Exchange folders
- ❑ Active Directory Services
- ❑ Oracle databases
- ❑ Index Server
- ❑ AS/400s

Since we've discussed these data sources already during our discussion of the OLE DB data providers, we won't discuss them in any more detail here. However, it's important to note that this is not an exclusive list. Any application that manages or stores data can be considered a data source, and we've already seen how the Universal Data Access technologies can provide access to any data sources.

ADO and n-tier Applications

Although the primary role of ADO in an n-tiered application is to provide data access interact with the data source(s) on the Data Services tier, it's important to understand that in a data-centric application, data is just that – central to the entire application, not just one specific tier or layer. In other words, even though the data source is only accessed from the Data Services tier, data manipulation and processing is performed on **every** tier. For example, let's consider the n-tier application that we discussed earlier. Our User Services tier, which consists of an Active Server Page and a Visual Basic application, is responsible for presenting and gathering data from the user. The User Services tier instantiates and calls methods on the clsCustomer_Bus component, which composes the Business Services tier. This component applies any business rules and forwards the data retrieval or data manipulation request to an instance of either the clsCustomerTx_ds or the clsCustomersN_ds components in the Data Services tier. These Data Service components carry out the data retrieval or data manipulation request by interacting with the actual data source(s). Any results from the Data Services components, including data returned from a query, are returned through the Business Services tier and then finally reach the User Services. The architecture of this n-tier application is depicted in the following diagram:

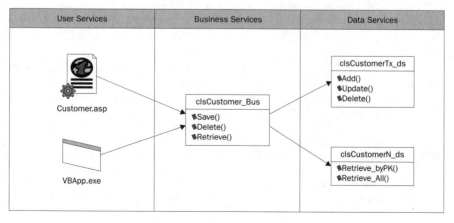

Previous data access technologies, such as DAO and RDO, have provided very little help in the way of managing and working with data after it has been retrieved from the data source. Unlike these data access technologies, ADO *exposes* several features that facilitate the development of n-tier, data-centric applications. Notice that I used the term "exposes". It's important to understand that ADO does not try to add any functionality of its own. Instead, ADO relies on the pluggable component architecture of OLE DB, with OLE DB's Service Components, to add features and enhancements on top of the features supplied by the OLE DB data provider. Some of these features include:

❑ **Disconnected Recordsets** – Undoubtedly, one of the most powerful features exposed by ADO is the ability to disconnect an open ADO `Recordset` object completely from the OLE DB data provider and data source. After a recordset has been disconnected, its data can be searched, sorted, filtered and manipulated without requerying or involving the OLE DB data provider or data source in any way. Disconnected recordsets can greatly improve the overall scalability and performance of a data-centric application because expensive data source connections can be pooled or released when a recordset is disconnected. Additionally, since any operations performed against a disconnected recordset don't involve the data provider, disconnected recordsets can also reduce the number of network round trips. Because of these benefits combined with the features and flexibility of a `Recordset` object, a disconnected recordset is ideal for transferring data across tiers in a Windows DNA, n-tier application. Disconnected recordsets are implemented by the underlying OLE DB Cursor Service.

❑ **Batch Processing** – Batch processing is the intelligent process of manipulating (updating, inserting, and deleting) data within a disconnected recordset and then reconnecting the recordset to the data provider and applying any pending changes to the data source in **batches** or groups. Batch processing is ideal for Windows DNA, n-tier applications because it minimizes the number of network round trips and enables disconnected or off-line scenarios. Since disconnected recordsets and batch processing are so closely tied, you should not be surprised to hear that batch processing is also implemented by the OLE DB Cursor Service.

❑ **Fabricated Recordsets** – Fabricated recordsets (or createable recordsets, as they're sometimes called) are simply ADO `Recordset` objects that are created and populated with data programmatically, rather than by an OLE DB data provider. Just like disconnected recordsets, fabricated recordsets also support searching, sorting, filtering and manipulating data without involving an OLE DB data provider. However, unlike disconnected recordsets, fabricated recordsets cannot be be used with batch processing. Fabricated recordsets represent the awesome ability to quickly and easily retrieve and package data in the form of an ADO `Recordset` object from various data sources in which there is no OLE DB data provider currently available. Additionally, a fabricated `Recordset` object can serve as a sophisticated data type that can be created and passed across tiers within a Windows DNA, n-tier application. You guessed it! This feature is also implemented by the underlying OLE DB Cursor Service.

❑ **Shaped Recordsets** – If you have been writing data access code for any length of time, then you are probably very familiar with combining data from two or more tables into one recordset through a SQL join. However, joins are typically not the best way to expose data that contains a parent-child (one-to-many) relationship, because joins effectively flatten the relationship into a tabular format (row-column). As a result, a recordset populated as the result of a join operation typically has a lot of repeated data. Shaped recordsets, also appropriately known as **hierarchical recordsets**, are an effective replacement for joins. Shaped recordsets are simply ADO recordsets that contain another recordset, sometimes called a chapter, in one or more fields. In other words, a field in the parent recordset would contain an entire recordset of its own. Recordsets can be nested to expose any depth of parent/child relationships.

Depending on the situation, shaped recordsets can usually result in higher performance and scalability in n-tier applications when compared to join operations because data is not repeated, and so there is less data to transfer across the network. However, in some situations when dealing with very few records, a shaped recordset could actually represent more overhead than its join counterpart because of the structural overhead of the Recordset object. The functionality behind shaped recordsets is implemented by the OLE DB Shape Provider.

❑ **Recordset Persistence** – Another powerful feature that's accessible from an ADO Recordset object is **recordset persistence**. Recordset persistence is the ability to save or persist an entire ADO Recordset object including its data, structure and properties either to a file or to another object that implements the IStream interface. Some of the objects that currently implement the IStream interface include ADO's new Stream object, ASP's Response object and MSXML's DOMDocument object, to name but a few. The recordset can be persisted in either a proprietary binary format called Advanced Data TableGram (ADTG) or in XML format. After a recordset has been persisted, the same or another Recordset object can be populated from the file or object to which the Recordset was previously persisted. As you can imagine, recordset persistence can be used in a number of ways, including situations where the User Services tier needs the ability to work with data in off-line and disconnected scenarios. Recordset persistence is also used behind the scenes when remoting a recordset across process or machine boundaries. Recordset persistence is implemented by the OLE DB Persistence Provider, although the OLE DB Cursor Service is also utilized when opening a previously persisted recordset.

❑ **Remoting Recordsets** – As I briefly mentioned earlier, an ADO Recordset object can be remoted across process and machine boundaries using either DCOM or either HTTP or HTTPS protocol. This is possible because an ADO Recordset, unlike most objects, is automatically persisted or **marshaled** to a data stream when it is passed across processes (or machines) and recreated when it reaches the destination. Since the entire Recordset is marshaled and then reconstructed, the original Recordset object can be destroyed, thus freeing resources for other uses and increasing scalability of the overall data-centric application. Furthermore, this behavior is ideal for Windows DNA, n-tier applications because the logical tiers usually represent physical machine boundaries. Recordsets can actually be remoted in a number of ways, but no matter how remoting is intiated, the OLE DB Persistence Provider and the OLE DB Cursor Service are always involved. The OLE DB Remoting Provider can also be explicitly invoked to access a remote data source using an OLE DB data provider on a remote server, just as if the data provider were installed on the local machine.

❑ **Connection Pooling** – To circumvent the performance problems typically associated with creating a connection to an OLE DB data provider and data source, OLE DB provides a feature known as **resource pooling**. However, don't let the name fool you. OLE DB resource pooling, also known as **session pooling**, is the process of reusing an existing OLE DB Session, the underlying OLE DB equivalent of an ADO Connection, if one is already available. If a session matching the user authentication and connection properties is not available in the pool, one will automatically be created. When an application releases an ADO Connection, the underlying OLE DB Session is not destroyed, but placed back within the pool for future reuse. The OLE DB core components are responsible for managing the size and inventory of the pool. OLE DB resource pooling plays a curcial role in scalability and performance especially on the Data Services tier of an n-tier, data-centric application. By default, OLE DB session polling is enabled for ADO.

Although these features are well-suited for n-tier, data-centric application development, it's important not to forget that ADO provides the same high-performance data access regardless of the architecture of the application. ADO is the single data access technology that you need to know for everything from desktop to client/server to n-tier development. Every one of these features can also be utilized in a single-machine, single-user scenario.

Summary

In this rather lengthy chapter we've discussed a number of topics, including:

- ❏ The role of ODBC and the OLE DB Provider for ODBC (MSDASQL) in MDAC and the UDA strategy
- ❏ The features and functionality available when using ADO in various development environments such as: Visual Basic, Visual Interdev and Visual C++
- ❏ The ADO Recordset library and its relationship to the full ADODB library
- ❏ The role of Remote Data Services (RDS) in comparison to ADO
- ❏ The technologies available for each tier in a n-tier application

We concluded this chapter with a discussion about the features ADO provides that facilitate the development of Windows DNA, n-tier applications. In the next chapter, we're going to discuss and implement some of these features such as disconnected recordsets, fabricated recordsets and batch processing.

3

The Cursor Service

In Chapter 2, we learned that ADO is an OLE DB consumer that simply exposes the functionality provided by OLE DB service providers and data providers through a circular, COM-automation object model. The fact is that ADO never performs any operations on its own. Instead ADO always relies upon the flexible component architecture of OLE DB, where OLE DB service providers add features and enhancements on top of the functionality supplied by the data provider. When methods are invoked on ADO objects, behind the scenes ADO forwards the request down to the appropriate OLE DB provider that implements the appropriate OLE DB interface(s) and thus the requested functionality.

Exposing all types of data sources in a standard way was only one of the design goals of OLE DB. OLE DB was also designed to provide:

❑   Access to distributed data

❑   Access to data in disconnected environments

❑   Scalable data access

In this chapter we're going to see how the OLE DB Cursor Service fulfills these three design goals. Additionally, we'll learn how to leverage the functionality of the Cursor Service from the ADO object model. You'll see that when combined with the Cursor Service, ADO becomes an extremely powerful data access technology that can be utilized to solve many of the challenges you will encounter when developing Windows DNA *n*-tier applications.

OLE DB Cursor Service

Many of ADO's powerful features, such as **disconnected recordsets**, **fabricated recordsets** and **batch processing**, are provided by the OLE DB Cursor Service. The OLE DB Cursor Service, also known as the Client Cursor Engine (CCE), is a central OLE DB service provider that was originally integrated within RDS 1.0 and 1.5, then known as Advanced Data Connector (ADC). Today the Cursor Service exists as a separate OLE DB Service Provider (MSDACE.DLL) and is included with MDAC 2.0 and later.

The OLE DB Cursor Service uses technology which was originally developed for Visual FoxPro to provide a data caching mechanism that temporarily stores data and metadata in the form of an **OLE DB Rowset** in local memory. A Rowset is the OLE DB equivalent of an ADO Recordset. Each ADO Recordset object is simply a wrapper on top of exactly one underlying OLE DB Rowset. The Rowset managed by the Cursor Service can either originate from an OLE DB data provider or other service provider as the result of a data request made by the consumer, or the Rowset can be created by the consumer. The Cursor Service provides the ability to scroll, sort, filter and search for data within the Rowset without re-executing queries or involving the data provider and data source in any way. In the typical scenario where the data source resides on a remote server, performing these operations locally within a consumer's cached copy of data can greatly improve the performance and scalability of the overall data-centric application.

In addition to read-only, data-fetching capabilities, the OLE DB Cursor Service also supports data manipulation (updates, inserts, deletes) within the Rowset. When working with SQL-based data, any changes can intelligently be re-synchronized with the data source. This data remoting process can also result in increased scalability and performance in transactional applications because data manipulation operations are applied to the data source in batches, thus minimizing the number of expensive network round trips required.

Don't worry, we'll be discussing each of these features supplied by the OLE DB Cursor Service in more detail, but first let's understand how the Cursor Service works within the OLE DB Architecture and learn how to invoke the Cursor Service from ADO.

Cursor Service in the OLE DB Architecture

Although rowsets managed by the Cursor Service can be created by the OLE DB consumer, typically they originate from an OLE DB data provider or from another service provider. Normally, when an ADO Recordset is opened, the specified data provider or service provider(s) processes the data request and exposes any resulting data to ADO (the OLE DB consumer) in the form of an OLE DB Rowset. ADO consumes the OLE DB Rowset through the OLE DB interfaces and exposes it as an ADO Recordset. This Rowset represents a subset of data within the actual data source. As a result, all subsequent operations within the Rowset involve the data provider and the data source. The following diagram illustrates this process where an ADO Connection is established to a data provider (left) and an ADO Recordset is opened against the connection (right). Thankfully, this data-retrieval process is only slightly different when the OLE DB Cursor Service is involved:

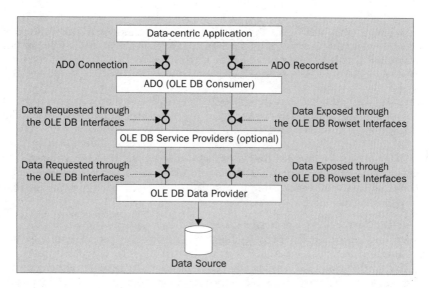

The Cursor Service conveniently positions itself between the OLE DB provider exposing the Rowset and the OLE DB consumer (ADO) consuming the Rowset. As a result, the Cursor Service is able to temporarily store or **cache** rowsets produced by an OLE DB data provider or service provider and expose the cached Rowset to the OLE DB consumer. However, the integration of the Cursor Service within the OLE DB architecture is completely transparent because of the abstraction provided through the use of the OLE DB interfaces. The Cursor Service simply consumes data through the OLE DB Rowset's interfaces, performs the caching process, and exposes the cached data through the same OLE DB Rowset interfaces. Additionally, the Cursor Service implements several custom interfaces that provide extended functionality on top of the cached data:

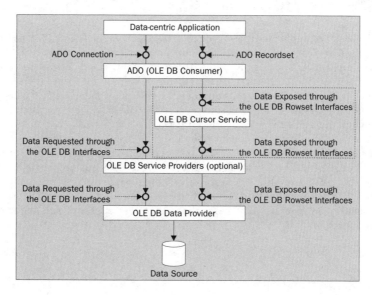

> **The caching process performed by the OLE DB Cursor Service involves duplicating the *source rowset* that is exposed by the data or service provider into a separate *cached rowset* that is exposed and managed by the Cursor Service.**

Despite what you might think, this caching process is not quite as simple as a memory copy. Keeping with our high-level view of OLE DB, the caching process performed by the OLE DB Cursor Service can be broken down into a three-step process:

❑ **The Cursor Service first determines basic metadata about the source rowset.** This 'basic metadata' includes fundamental column information such as the number of columns, and the name and datatype of each column. The Cursor Service begins constructing the cached rowset using this metadata.

❑ **Next, the Cursor Service performs the actual data copy.** The Cursor Service populates its newly created cached rowset by fetching and copying *every* record from the source rowset. If the source rowset contains 10,000 records then 10,000 records will be copied to the cached rowset. The cached rowset's data will reside primarily in memory, although when working with large rowsets it may be necessary for the Cursor Service temporarily to store some data on disk. This entire copying process can be performed synchronously or asynchronously.

❑ **Finally, the Cursor Service retrieves extended metadata and closes the source rowset.** If the data source is SQL-based and the source rowset was opened in **batch optimistic** mode, the OLE DB Cursor service will determine extended metadata such as the column, table, and catalog information about the data source from which the source rowset's data originated. This extended metadata information is stored as properties with the cached rowset and it can later be used by the **Synchronization Service** to keep the cached rowset in synchronization with the data source. We'll look at this extended metadata and the Synchronization Service in more detail later in this chapter.

After the Cursor Service duplicates the source rowset, ADO (as the OLE DB consumer) consumes and exposes the cached rowset to the data-centric application as a fully functional ADO `Recordset`. From the data-centric application's perspective, a recordset based on a cached rowset, a 'cached recordset' if you will, is no different to any other recordset. However, behind the scenes there are some differences that affect the behavior of the recordset. Subsequent requests for data within the cached recordset do not involve the data provider or the data source. Instead data is fetched, scrolled, searched and manipulated within the cached rowset by the OLE DB Cursor Service. Assuming that the recordset was not opened in read-only mode, data can also be modified, inserted or deleted within the cached rowset. However, because the cached rowset is a local *copy* of data from the data source, any changes are not visible to other consumers. The Cursor Service is responsible for tracking changes and providing the consumer with not only the modified column values, but also the original value and the last read (underlying) value. The cached rowset can later be intelligently re-synchronized with the data source to apply any outstanding changes. Finally, when the cached recordset is closed, the corresponding cached rowset will be destroyed.

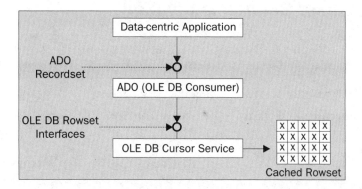

The OLE DB Cursor Service manages each cached rowset independently and does not share common data or metadata. In the scenario where two ADO recordsets are opened against the same data source and the Cursor Service caches the results, the Cursor Service will *always* create and manage two independent cached rowsets instead of one shared rowset, even though the data and metadata (column names, base tables, etc.) might be exactly the same. Consequently, data-fetching operations (sorting, filtering, Move, etc.) or data manipulation operations (update, insert, delete) performed against one cached rowset/recordset will not affect any other rowsets/recordsets managed by the Cursor Service.

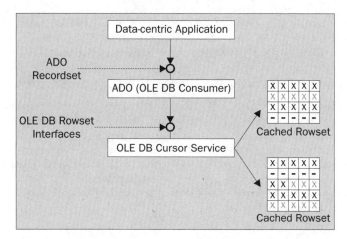

While the Cursor Service and its entire caching process are completely hidden from ADO, it's important to understand what is going on behind the scenes so that we can make intelligent decisions when designing the architecture of an application. For example, knowing that the Cursor Service creates a duplicate of the rowset exposed by an OLE DB data or service provider, we probably wouldn't want the Cursor Service to be involved with a recordset containing ten thousand records. Instead we should always limit the size of the recordsets to maximize the performance and scalability of the Cursor Service.

> It's important to remember that software component layers, such as the OLE DB Cursor Service, don't exempt us from *understanding* about a particular layer. Instead they simply exempt us from *developing* that particular layer.

When the Cursor Service is Invoked

Now that we understand how the OLE DB Cursor Service operates within the OLE DB architecture, let's discuss the scenarios in which it is used. When an ADO recordset is opened against an OLE DB data or service provider, the Cursor Service can become involved in one of two ways:

❑   An OLE DB service provider requires the Cursor Service

❑   The data consumer explicitly requests the Cursor Service

Let's look at these two scenarios in more detail.

An OLE DB Service Provider Requires the Cursor Service

Remember, OLE DB services are designed to be modular, single-purpose components that can be plugged into and removed from the OLE DB architecture as needed. As a result, they are frequently used in combination with each other. The Cursor Service is a dependency of almost every OLE DB service provider, including the OLE DB Persistence Provider, the OLE DB Remoting Provider and the OLE DB Shape Provider.

Typically the OLE DB Cursor Service caches rowsets exposed by an OLE DB service provider, as we depicted in the earlier diagrams. However, this is not always the case. Some OLE DB service providers require the Cursor Service to produce a cached rowset, so they can easily scroll through the rowset's records multiple times while performing the service operation. We'll discuss how the Cursor Service is used in conjunction with the OLE DB Persistence Provider in Chapter 4.

The Data Consumer Explicitly Requests the Cursor Service

ADO developers can invoke the OLE DB Cursor Service by setting the `CursorLocation` property of an ADO `Recordset` object to `adUseClient` before opening it. Really, requesting the Cursor Service is that simple! In the following example we instantiate and open an ADO recordset to retrieve all of the records from the `authors` table in the `pubs` SQL Server database. But before we open the recordset, we specify `adUseClient` for the `Recordset`'s `CursorLocation` property. As a result, subsequent operations within the opened recordset will be performed using the OLE DB Cursor Service and the local copy of data, or the cached rowset, without involving the OLE DB data provider (SQLOLEDB) or the data source (pubs database):

```
Dim rsAuthors As ADODB.Recordset

'create a new instance of an ADODB.Recordset
Set rsAuthors = New ADODB.Recordset

With rsAuthors
    'use the Microsoft OLE DB Cursor Service
    .CursorLocation = adUseClient

    'retrieve all of the records from the Authors table in the Pubs SQL Server db
    .Open Source:="SELECT * FROM authors", _
          ActiveConnection:="Provider=SQLOLEDB;Initial Catalog=pubs; " & _
                            "Data Source=jconard;User ID=sa;Password=;", _
          CursorType:=adOpenStatic, LockType:=adLockReadOnly
```

```
    Do While .EOF = False
        'print each author's last name and first name to the debug window
        '...Note: these operations are performed using the cached data
        Debug.Print .Fields("au_lname").Value & ", " & .Fields("au_fname").Value

        'move to the next record
        .MoveNext
    Loop
End With


'close our open Recordset
'...Note: this will cause the cached rowset to be destroyed
rsAuthors.Close

'destroy our instance of the ADODB.Recordset
Set rsAuthors = Nothing
```

In the example above, note that the `CursorType` parameter in the `Recordset` object's `Open` method is set to `adOpenStatic`. Static cursors are the only type of cursors supported by the OLE DB Cursor Service. ADO will automatically default to `adOpenStatic` for the `CursorType` when the `CursorLocation` is set to `adUseClient`. We also specified the default `LockType` of `adLockReadOnly`. As a result we will not be able to update, insert or delete records in our `rsAuthors` recordset. We'll discuss the other possible `LockTypes` that can be used with the OLE DB Cursor Service later in this chapter.

You might have noticed that the ADO `Connection` object also provides a `CursorLocation` property. When the `CursorLocation` property on an ADO `Connection` object is set to `adUseClient`, any recordsets opened against that connection will use the OLE DB Cursor Service. This includes `Recordset` objects returned from a call to an ADO `Connection` object's `Execute` method or `Recordset` objects that are explicitly opened by calling their `Open` method. In the following example, both the `rsAuthors` and `rsTitles` ADO `Recordset` objects will automatically inherit the `CursorLocation` property value of `adUseClient` from the `conPubs` ADO `Connection`, even though these `Recordset` objects are opened in different ways:

```
Dim conPubs As ADODB.Connection
Dim rsAuthors As ADODB.Recordset
Dim rsTitles As ADODB.Recordset

'create a new instance of an ADODB.Connection
Set conPubs = New ADODB.Connection

'create a new instance of an ADODB.Recordset
Set rsAuthors = New ADODB.Recordset

'establish a connection to the Pubs SQL Server database
conPubs.Open ConnectionString:="Provider=SQLOLEDB;Initial Catalog=Pubs;" & _
                              "Data Source=jconard;User ID=sa;Password=;"

'use the Microsoft OLE DB Cursor Service
conPubs.CursorLocation = adUseClient
```

```
'retrieve all of the records from the Authors table
rsAuthors.Open Source:="SELECT * FROM Authors", _
              ActiveConnection:=conPubs, CursorType:=adOpenStatic, _
              LockType:=adLockReadOnly

'retrieve all of the records from the Titles table
Set rsTitles = conPubs.Execute("SELECT * FROM Titles")

'Show message boxes if the CursorLocation is adUseClient for these Recordsets
If rsAuthors.CursorLocation = adUseClient Then
    MsgBox "The 'rsAuthors' ADO Recordset is using the OLE DB Cursor Service!"
End If

If rsTitles.CursorLocation = adUseClient Then
    MsgBox "The 'rsTitles' ADO Recordset is using the OLE DB Cursor Service!"
End If

'close our open Recordsets
'...Note: this will cause the cached rowsets to be destroyed
rsAuthors.Close
rsTitles.Close

'close our connection to the Pubs SQL Server Database
conPubs.Close

'destroy our ADODB.Recordset and Connection instances
Set rsAuthors = Nothing
Set rsTitles = Nothing
Set conPubs = Nothing
```

The previous example also demonstrates how the CursorLocation property can be used after an ADO Recordset has been opened to determine whether or not the OLE DB Cursor Service is being used. The dynamic Server Cursor property can also be used for the same purpose, except that this property appropriately returns False when the OLE DB Cursor Service is managing the recordset's data:

```
If rsAuthors.Properties("Server Cursor").Value = False Then
    MsgBox "The 'rsAuthors' ADO Recordset is using the OLE DB Cursor Service!"
End If
```

You ADO veterans who have been around since the version 1.0 days might remember a CursorLocation constant value of adUseClientBatch. With ADO 1.5 the adUseClientBatch constant was renamed to adUseClient. However, both the adUseClient and the adUseClientBatch constants are still supported for backwards compatibility and both constants have a value of 3 so either one could actually be used. The adUseClientBatch constant is now marked as hidden in the ADODB type library. Consequently, new applications should use the adUseClient constant instead.

Cursor Service Capabilities and Features

The OLE DB Cursor Service facilitates two powerful features that have revolutionized the development of data-centric applications especially within distributed, n-tier environments. These two features are:

❑ **Disconnected recordsets**

❑ **Fabricated recordsets**

The Cursor Service also provides sorting, filtering and searching for data within a disconnected or fabricated recordset. These features allow operations to be off-loaded to the OLE DB consumer without requiring the data provider and data source to be requeried. Ultimately, fewer requests to the data source results in higher performance and scalability in a data-centric application because it allows for efficient utilization of all available resources. Let's learn how to leverage these powerful features.

Disconnected Recordsets

Recordsets that utilize the OLE DB Cursor Service by setting the `CursorLocation` property to `adUseClient` are almost totally self-sufficient. After one of these recordsets has been opened, data can be searched, sorted, fetched and manipulated within the recordset without involving (sometimes expensive) round-trips to the data provider and data source. Instead, these operations are performed by the OLE DB Cursor Service using the cached OLE DB rowset which resides in local memory. Since the data provider and data source are no longer needed after a recordset that utilizes the Cursor Service has been opened, why not simply disconnect from the data provider and data source completely? Welcome to the powerful feature of disconnected recordsets.

A **disconnected recordset** is simply an ADO `Recordset` that has been disconnected from the data provider and instead utilizes the OLE DB Cursor Service for its `Rowset` implementation. In straightforward terms, a disconnected recordset is an ADO `Recordset` that has been *both*:

❑ Opened with a `CursorLocation` of `adUseClient`

❑ Disconnected by setting its `ActiveConnection` property to `Nothing`

Really, it's that simple! These are the *only* qualifications for creating disconnected recordsets and what's more, there are no exceptions to these rules. Let's take a look at disconnected recordsets in action. In the following example we'll implement a method named `GetAuthorsRS` that, when invoked, returns a disconnected ADO recordset containing all of the records from the `authors` table in the `pubs` SQL Server database:

```
Public Function GetAuthorsRS() As ADODB.Recordset
    Dim rsAuthors As ADODB.Recordset

    'create a new instance of an ADODB.Recordset
    Set rsAuthors = New ADODB.Recordset

    'use the Microsoft OLE DB Cursor Service
    rsAuthors.CursorLocation = adUseClient
```

```
        'retrieve all of the records from the Authors table
        '...from the Pubs SQL Server database
        rsAuthors.Open Source:="SELECT * FROM Authors", _
                    ActiveConnection:="Provider=SQLOLEDB;Initial Catalog=Pubs; " & _
                                    "Data Source=jconard;User ID=sa;Password=;", _
                    CursorType:=adOpenStatic, LockType:=adLockBatchOptimistic

        'disconnect from the Data Provider and data source
        Set rsAuthors.ActiveConnection = Nothing

        'return the disconnected Recordset
        Set GetAuthorsRS = rsAuthors

        'release our local reference to the rsAuthors ADODB.Recordset
        Set rsAuthors = Nothing
    End Function
```

If disconnected recordsets are this simple to implement, why then is there so much confusion in the development community on this subject? The main reason is because the qualifications for creating a disconnected recordset are exclusive. Remember, both the CursorLocation must be set to adUseClient *and* the ActiveConnection must be set to Nothing . Many developers run into difficulty with disconnected recordsets because they release the reference to the Connection, but forget to open the Recordset with a CursorLocation of adUseClient. The CursorLocation property will default to using server-side cursors (adUseServer). If you attempt to disconnect an ADO Recordset that is using server-side cursors instead of the OLE DB Cursor Service you will receive the following run-time error:

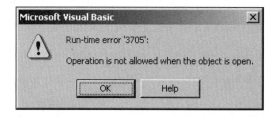

It's important to note that a recordset's ActiveConnection should not be closed before the recordset has been disconnected. If the connection that was used to open a disconnected recordset is closed before the recordset is disconnected, ADO will also automatically close any open Recordset objects associated with that connection. This behavior is true no matter how the connection was established. For example, the following function will open a recordset using an explicit connection (Connection object) and end up returning a closed Recordset object because the connection is closed before the recordset is disconnected:

```
Public Function GetAuthorsRS() As ADODB.Recordset
    Dim conDataSource As ADODB.Connection
    Dim rsAuthors As ADODB.Recordset

    'create a new instance of an ADODB.Connection
    Set conDataSource = New ADODB.Connection
```

```
'create a new instance of an ADODB.Recordset
Set rsAuthors = New ADODB.Recordset

'establish a connection to the data source
conDataSource.Open "Provider=SQLOLEDB;Initial Catalog=Pubs; " & _
                   "Data Source=jconard;User ID=sa;Password=;"

'use the Microsoft OLE DB Cursor Service
rsAuthors.CursorLocation = adUseClient

'retrieve all of the records from the Authors table
rsAuthors.Open Source:="SELECT * FROM Authors", _
               ActiveConnection:=conDataSource, _
               CursorType:=adOpenStatic, LockType:=adLockBatchOptimistic

    'close the connection
    conDataSource.Close

    'disconnect from the data provider and data source
    Set rsAuthors.ActiveConnection = Nothing

    'return the disconnected Recordset
    Set GetAuthorsRS = rsAuthors

    'release our local reference to the rsAuthors ADODB.Recordset
    Set rsAuthors = Nothing
End Function
```

The solution to this problem is to simply close the connection after disconnecting the recordset. For example, we could just switch the two lines of highlighted code in the last example:

```
    'disconnect from the Data Provider and data source
    Set rsAuthors.ActiveConnection = Nothing

    'close the connection
    conDataSource.Close
```

Another common cause for problems with disconnected recordsets is actually not specifically related to the OLE DB Cursor Service or the disconnected recordset feature. Instead, this problem stems from improper usage of `Recordset` object references. However, it frequently shows itself when dealing with disconnected recordsets because disconnected recordsets are typically returned from method calls. In our previous example, we returned a reference to our disconnected recordset `rsAuthors`, which effectively creates two references within the `GetAuthorsRS` method. Let's take a look at the last few lines of that method again:

```
    'disconnect from the Data Provider and data source
    Set rsAuthors.ActiveConnection = Nothing

    'return the disconnected Recordset
    '...NOTE: After this line there are two Recordset object references
    Set GetAuthorsRS = rsAuthors
```

```
'release our local reference to the rsAuthors ADODB.Recordset
Set rsAuthors = Nothing
```

The statement `Set GetAuthorsRS = rsAuthors` actually causes another reference to be made to the `rsAuthors` recordset. When another reference is made to an existing recordset, it is just that – another *reference* to an *existing* ADO `Recordset`. It is *not* a duplicate recordset. Remember, an ADO `Recordset` object represents *exactly one* underlying OLE DB `Rowset`. Any operations (method or property calls) performed on one reference effect the state of the same `Recordset` Object and the same OLE DB `Rowset`. For example, in the following diagram, three object references point to the same `Recordset` object. The single `Recordset` object has exactly one OLE DB `Rowset` which manages the actual data. Each reference will have the same current record, the same values for each field, etc., because each reference represents the same `Recordset` object which exposes the same OLE DB `Rowset`:

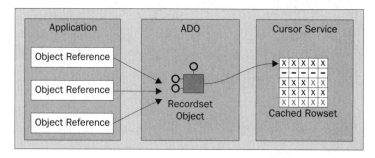

Many developers mistakenly call the `Close` method on one `Recordset` object reference not realizing that the method call effects all other references to the same `Recordset` object. The following diagram illustrates this problem, again with three `Recordset` object references. The first object reference (`rs1`) is created when the `Recordset` component is instantiated. The second (`rs2`) and third (`rs3`) `Recordset` object references simply point to the same `Recordset` object. However, the problem occurs when the third reference (`rs3`) calls the `Close` method, causing the underlying OLE DB `Rowset` to be destroyed and the shared `Recordset` object to become empty. Any subsequent operations performed against the recordset's data using either of the other two references will return an error because the `Recordset` has been closed and the underlying OLE DB `Rowset` no longer exists:

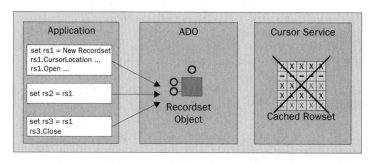

This behavior explains why we don't call the `Close` method on our `rsAuthors` Recordset object reference in the final lines of our `GetAuthorsRS` method. Instead, we simply release our temporary reference to the `Recordset` object after a reference has been placed in the return value in the line above:

```
'disconnect from the Data Provider and data source
   Set rsAuthors.ActiveConnection = Nothing

   'return the disconnected Recordset
   '...NOTE: After this line there are two Recordset object references
   Set GetAuthorsRS = rsAuthors

   'release our local reference to the rsAuthors ADODB.Recordset
   Set rsAuthors = Nothing
```

As I mentioned, this behavior is not specific to disconnected recordsets or the OLE DB Cursor Service; however, it often shows itself in methods that return disconnected recordsets. The only real solution to this issue is to keep track of your object references carefully.

Reconnecting a Disconnected Recordset

A disconnected recordset can be reconnected to the same or to a different data provider and data source simply by setting the `Recordset`'s `ActiveConnection` property to an open ADO `Connection` object or to a valid `ConnectionString`. The following example creates a method named `ResyncRecordset` that reconnects to the data provider and data source and refreshes a disconnected recordset passed as a parameter named `rs` with the current values from the `pubs` SQL Server database. Finally the `ResyncRecordset` method disconnects the recordset which was specified as the `rs` parameter and returns it to the caller:

```
Public Function ResyncRecordset(ByVal rs As ADODB.Recordset) _
                                            As ADODB.Recordset

    If rs.LockType <> adLockBatchOptimistic Then
       'Resync is not supported with any other than adLockBatchOptimistic
       Err.Raise vbObjectError + 2000, _
                Description:="Resync is only supported with a " _
                        & "LockType of adLockBatchOptimistic!"
       'exit this procedure
       Exit Function
    End If

    'reconnect the passed recordset to the pubs SQL Server database
    rs.ActiveConnection = "Provider=SQLOLEDB;Initial Catalog=Pubs; " & _
                        "Data Source=jconard;User ID=sa;Password=;"

    'resync all records the passed Recordset with the data source
    rs.Resync adAffectAll, adResyncAllValues

    'disconnect from the Data Provider and data source
    Set rs.ActiveConnection = Nothing

    'return the disconnected Recordset
    Set ResyncRecordset = rs
End Function
```

With just a few lines of code we can acquire a disconnected recordset containing all of the author records and then later refresh the disconnected recordset with the values from the data source by calling our `ResyncRecordset` method:

```
Dim rsAuthors As ADODB.Recordset

'get a disconnected recordset containing all of the authors
Set rsAuthors = GetAuthorsRs()

'Refresh our recordset with the values from the data source
Set rsAuthors = ResyncRecordset(rsAuthors)

'close and release our disconnected recordset
rsAuthors.Close
Set rsAuthors = Nothing
```

Typically, disconnected recordsets are reconnected to the data provider and data source so that any pending changes performed in the cached rowset can be applied to the data source. We'll discuss more about reconnecting a disconnected recordset to the data source and performing resynchronization when we discuss the Synchronization Service later in this chapter.

Fabricated Recordsets

Although recordsets that utilize the OLE DB Cursor Service are typically composed of results returned from a query, they can also be created and opened without connecting to a data provider and data source. Such a recordset is appropriately called a **fabricated recordset**, a **programmatic recordset** or a **creatable recordset**.

A fabricated recordset is simply an ADO `Recordset` that has been created completely from scratch. Fields must be appended and data must be inserted manually, instead of being automatically generated as the result of a query. Behind the scenes the OLE DB Cursor Service is responsible for managing these fields and data in a new OLE DB `Rowset`. Fabricated recordsets can be utilized as sophisticated data types for packaging parameter values, exposing data sources that don't have an OLE DB data provider, or for simply storing temporary data within an application.

To create a fabricated recordset, you must first create and add all of the fields to an instance of an ADO `Recordset` by calling the `Append` method of the `Recordset` object's `Fields` collection. Then the `Recordset` object must be opened without specifying an ADO `Connection` object or a `ConnectionString`. ADO will automatically utilize the OLE DB Cursor Service and create a new underlying OLE DB `Rowset` when a recordset is opened without a connection. Finally, data can be inserted into the fabricated recordset using the `AddNew` method just like normal.

In the following example, we create a method named `GetStatesRS` that returns an ADO `Recordset` containing the `Abbreviation` and `Name` for every state in the U.S. Instead of retrieving this static data from a data source and returning it in the form of a disconnected recordset, in this example we'll create and return a fabricated recordset that is manually loaded with every state's `Abbreviation` and `Name`. Not only do fabricated recordsets provide a much more scalable and robust solution for managing this type of *static* data, but also this approach is easier to deploy, administrate and reuse for future applications. In situations where the data at hand is more prone to change, I recommend storing it in the data source and using disconnected recordsets rather than fabricated recordsets. To conserve space, this code example only adds a few of the states to the recordset:

```
Public Function GetStatesRS() As ADODB.Recordset

    Dim rsStates As ADODB.Recordset
    Dim vFieldNames As Variant

    'create a new instance of an ADODB.Recordset
    Set rsStates = New ADODB.Recordset

    'use the Microsoft OLE DB Cursor Service
    rsStates.CursorLocation = adUseClient

    With rsStates.Fields
        'append our Abbreviation and StateName fields
        .Append "Abbreviation", adVarChar, DefinedSize:=2
        .Append "StateName", adVarChar, DefinedSize:=25
    End With

    With rsStates
        'open the fabricated recordset
        .Open

        'get the FieldNames in an array for the AddNew method
        vFieldNames = Array("Abbreviation", "StateName")

        'add the Abbreviation and name for each State to the fabricated recordset
        .AddNew FieldList:=vFieldNames, Values:=Array("AL", "Alabama (AL)")
        .AddNew FieldList:=vFieldNames, Values:=Array("AK", "Alaska (AK)")
        .AddNew FieldList:=vFieldNames, Values:=Array("AZ", "Arizona (AZ)")
        .AddNew FieldList:=vFieldNames, Values:=Array("AR", "Arkansas (AR)")
        .AddNew FieldList:=vFieldNames, Values:=Array("CA", "California (CA)")
        .AddNew FieldList:=vFieldNames, Values:=Array("CO", "Colorado (CO)")
        .AddNew FieldList:=vFieldNames, Values:=Array("CT", "Connecticut (CT)")
        .AddNew FieldList:=vFieldNames, Values:=Array("DE", "Delaware (DE)")
        .AddNew FieldList:=vFieldNames, Values:=Array("FL", "Florida (FL)")
        '...
    End With

    'return the fabricated recordset
    Set GetStatesRS = rsStates

    'release our local reference to the rsStates ADODB.Recordset
    Set rsStates = Nothing
End Function
```

After a fabricated recordset has been manually populated with data by calling the AddNew method, virtually any operations can be performed against the data. For example, the OLE DB Cursor Service allows a fabricated recordset's data to be manipulated, searched, sorted and filtered without ever requiring a connection to an OLE DB data provider and data source. With this level of functionality, a fabricated recordset can be used as a sophisticated datatype in many different situations. We'll discuss several of these situations in a moment, but first let's take a look at the Append method a little more closely.

Append Method

Notice in the previous example that we call the Append method of the Fields collection twice to append both our Abbreviation and StateName fields:

```
With rsStates.Fields
    'append our Abbreviation and StateName fields
    .Append "Abbreviation", adVarChar, DefinedSize:=2
    .Append "StateName", adVarChar, DefinedSize:=25
End With
```

The Append method has the following syntax and parameters:

```
Recordset.Fields.Append (Name As String, [Type As DataTypeEnum], _
                         [DefinedSize As Long], _
                         [Attrib As FieldAttributeEnum = adFldUnspecified]
                         [FieldValue As Variant])
```

Parameter	Type	Description	Default
Name	String	The name of the field object. Each field name must be unique. Also, the name should not be 'ASC' or 'DESC' because those names will conflict with sorting keywords.	
Type	DataTypeEnum	The data type of the new field.	adEmpty
DefinedSize	Long	The defined size in characters or bytes of the new field. The default value depends on the Type of the field.	
Attrib	FieldAttributeEnum	The attributes for the new field.	adFldUnspecified
FieldValue	Variant	The value of the new field. This parameter is only valid when appending fields to a Record object, not a Recordset.	

The most common cause for problems when creating fabricated recordsets occurs when appending fields. Unfortunately, fields can only be appended to a closed recordset that does not have an active connection. Calling the Append method while the Recordset object is open or after the recordset has an active connection will cause a run-time error. Fields cannot be appended to a disconnected recordset because a disconnected recordset is not closed.

Deleting Fields

If for some reason you wish to remove a field from a fabricated recordset, you can do so by calling the `Delete` method of the `Recordset` object's `Fields` collection. Simply specify the name or index of the `Field` you want to delete as a parameter. You should note that the `Delete` method, just like the `Append` method, will raise a run-time error when called on an open recordset. In the following example, we append three fields to our fabricated recordset and then delete one of them before opening the recordset:

```
Dim rsFabricated As ADODB.Recordset

'create a new instance of an ADODB.Recordset
Set rsFabricated = New ADODB.Recordset

'use the Microsoft OLE DB Cursor Service
rsFabricated.CursorLocation = adUseClient

With rsFabricated.Fields
    'append our LastName, FirstName and Phone fields
    .Append "LastName", adBSTR
    .Append "FirstName", adBSTR
    .Append "Phone", adBSTR

    'remove the Phone field from the fabricated recordset
    .Delete "Phone"
End With

'open the fabricated recordset
rsFabricated.Open
```

I know this example doesn't make much sense, but that's really because the `Delete` method doesn't make much sense. Remember, a field can only be deleted from a recordset that is not open. However, when a fabricated recordset is closed all of the fields are automatically destroyed anyway. The only time you can really use the `Delete` method is after a field has been appended, but before the recordset is opened – as in the previous example. However, even in this scenario the `Delete` method doesn't serve any really useful purpose when used with fabricated recordsets. The `Delete` method does play an important role when used with `Record` objects, as we'll discuss in Chapter 8

Sorting

The OLE DB Cursor Service provides the ability to sort a cached rowset based on the values of one or more fields. This functionality is exposed through an ADO `Recordset`'s `Sort` property. The `Sort` property can be set to a comma-separated list of field names that indicate the fields the recordset should be sorted on and optionally the direction of the sort. By default each field specified in the `Sort` property will be sorted in ascending order. However, you can use the optional keywords `ASC` or `DESC` for each field to specify that the field's data should be sorted in ascending or descending order. The syntax for the `Sort` property is actually the same as the `ORDER BY` clause of an SQL `Select` statement.

For example, in the following code we'll call our `GetAuthorsRS` method that we created earlier in this chapter to acquire a disconnected recordset containing all of the author data from the pubs SQL Server database. After we have obtained the disconnected recordset we'll sort on the author's last name (au_lname) and first name (au_fname) and print the sorted recordset to the debug window:

```
Dim rsAuthors As ADODB.Recordset

'get a disconnected recordset containing all of the Authors
Set rsAuthors = GetAuthorsRs()

With rsAuthors
    'sort the recordset by the Author's lastname and firstname in Ascending order
    .Sort = "au_lname ASC, au_fname ASC"

    'Print the Sorted Recordset
    Debug.Print vbCrLf & "AUTHORS **********************************" & vbCrLf

    Do While .EOF = False      'print each author's last name and first name to the
debug window
        '...Note: these operations are performed using the cached data
        Debug.Print vbTab & .Fields("au_lname").Value & ", " & _
                            .Fields("au_fname").Value

        'move to the next record
        .MoveNext
    Loop
End With

'close and release our disconnected recordset
rsAuthors.Close
Set rsAuthors = Nothing
```

From the application's perspective, setting a `Recordset` object's `Sort` property to a valid sort string causes ADO to resort the recordset's data and reposition to the first record. However, behind the scenes the OLE DB Cursor Service performs a little magic to execute sorting operations as efficiently as possible. Instead of physically repositioning the data in the underlying OLE DB `Rowset`, the Cursor Service creates a temporary index for each field specified in the `Sort` property if an index for the field does not already exist. This temporary index simply maps the new row positions to the physical rows in the actual rowset. In this sense, you can think of a sort operation as providing a *view* of the existing OLE DB `Rowset`, instead of reorganizing the rowset or creating an entirely new rowset.

Local indexes can also be created and removed through the use of an ADO `Field` object's dynamic `Optimize` property. If a local index already exists on a field specified in the `Sort` property, then the OLE DB Cursor Service will not create a temporary index on that field, but will instead use the existing index. We'll discuss more about creating and removing local indexes using the `Optimize` property later in this chapter.

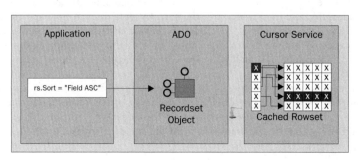

Since the Cursor Service does not physically rearrange the data, a sorting operation is very fast. When you need to perform multiple sort operations on the same data, the Cursor Service provides a scalable alternative for sorting as opposed to re-querying the data source to retrieve data in a sorted order.

To reset the rows to their original order, the `Sort` property must be set to an empty string. This will also cause the OLE DB Cursor Service to delete any temporary indexes. Local indexes created through the use of a `Field` object's dynamic `Optimize` property will not be deleted:

```
'reset the recordset to its original sort order
rsAuthors.Sort = ""
```

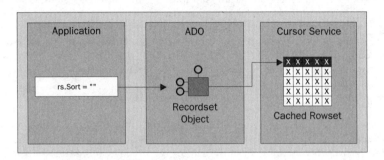

Unlike the `Find` method and the `Filter` property, which can be used with several OLE DB data providers, the `Sort` property requires the use of the OLE DB Cursor Service. It doesn't matter whether the recordset is fabricated, disconnected or still connected to a data source, as long it was opened with a `CursorLocation` of `adUseClient`.

> It's important to note that the OLE DB Cursor Service will raise a run-time error if you attempt to sort on a field with a data type of `adBSTR`, `adVariant` or `adIDispatch` because fields of these datatypes are pointers to data instead of a literal value.

Searching

The OLE DB Cursor Service also supports searching through a cached rowset for the first record matching a specified set of criteria. This functionality is exposed by ADO through a `Recordset` object's `Find` method. The `Find` method is defined as follows:

```
Find (Criteria As String, [SkipRows as Long], _
      [SearchDirection as SearchDirectionEnum], [Start as Variant])
```

The required `Criteria` parameter is used to specify a *single* search condition in the form of `FieldName-Operator-Value`. The `FieldName` can be the name of any field in the recordset. The `Operator` can be any one of the following: `'>'` (greater than), `'<'` (less than), `'='` (equal), `'>='` (greater than or equal), `'<='` (less than or equal), `'<>'` (not equal), or `'LIKE'` (pattern matching). Finally, the `Value` expression identifies the number, string or date value to search for in the specified field. String values must be enclosed in either single quotes or pound/hash signs (#) and date values must be enclosed in pound signs. Double quotes will not work. When using the `LIKE` operator, an asterisk (*) or a percent sign (%) can be used at the end or the beginning of the value, as wildcards for one *or more* occurrences of any character or substring. With a few exceptions, this basic syntax for the criteria string is actually the same as the syntax for a `WHERE` clause in an SQL statement. But enough with all of the syntax details, let's look at an example of using the `Find` method.

> The `Find` **method only supports one search condition. If you try to specify multiple search conditions using the** `AND` **or** `OR` **keywords the OLE DB Cursor Service will raise a run-time error. If you need to specify multiple search conditions you should use the** `Filter` **property.**

In the following code, we'll define a method named `FindAuthorRecord` that provides searching for an author record matching a specified last name. Within our `FindAuthorRecord` method we'll first obtain a disconnected recordset containing all of the author records by calling the `GetAuthorRS` method that we created earlier. Then we'll search for a record with the `au_lname` field equal to the passed `sAuthorLastName` parameter:

```
Private Sub FindAuthorRecord(ByVal sAuthorLastName As String)
    Dim rsAuthors As ADODB.Recordset

    'get a disconnected recordset containing all of the Authors
    Set rsAuthors = GetAuthorsRs()

    'find the record with a value in the au_lname field equal to the parameter
    rsAuthors.Find "au_lname = #" & sAuthorLastName & "#"

    'close and release our disconnected recordset
    rsAuthors.Close
    Set rsAuthors = Nothing
End Sub
```

To execute our new `FindAuthorRecord` method simply invoke it, passing a valid last name for the `sAuthorLastName` parameter:

```
FindAuthorRecord "O'Leary"
```

Notice in our `FindAuthorRecord` method that we placed pound/hash signs around the variable's value in the `Find` method's `Criteria` parameter. We could have used single quotation marks around the value instead. However you will receive a run-time error with using single quotation marks when a value contains an apostrophe, as in the name `'O'Leary'`. This problem also occurs when using pound/hash signs around a value that contains a pound/hash sign. The only real solution is to use the appropriate separating character based on the data being searched.

While we've just utilized the `Find` method to perform a simple search within a disconnected recordset, our new `FindAuthorRecord` method is pretty useless because we don't check to see whether or not any records were found. When the `Find` method is executed against our disconnected recordset, the OLE DB Cursor Service performs the search within the underlying OLE DB `Rowset` and always changes the current record position. If a record was found that meet the specified criteria, then the recordset's position is set to the first matching record. If no match is found, the recordset's position is set to either the end-of-file (`EOF`), when searching forward, or the beginning-of-file (`BOF`), when searching backward.

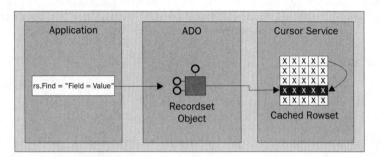

Knowing this, let's revise our `FindAuthorRecord` method to print a message to the debug window indicating whether or not a record was found:

```
Private Sub FindAuthorRecord(ByVal sAuthorLastName As String)
    Dim rsAuthors As ADODB.Recordset

    'get a disconnected recordset containing all of the Authors
    Set rsAuthors = GetAuthorsRs()

    'find the record with a value in the au_lname field equal to the parameter
    rsAuthors.Find "au_lname = #" & sAuthorLastName & "#"

    If ((rsAuthors.EOF = False) And (rsAuthors.BOF = False)) Then
        'we found the specified Author Record
        Debug.Print "The author with the last name of '" & _
                sAuthorLastName & "' was found at position #" & _
                rsAuthors.AbsolutePosition
    Else
        'we didn't find the specified Author Record
        Debug.Print "The author with the last name of '" & sAuthorLastName & _
                "' was not found!"
    End If

    'close and release our disconnected recordset
    rsAuthors.Close
    Set rsAuthors = Nothing
End Sub
```

When a `Recordset` object's `Find` method is invoked, by default the OLE DB Cursor Service will perform the search beginning at the *current record* and search to the end of the rowset. However, in most situations this default behavior is not adequate because the entire rowset is not being searched. To ensure that you are searching all of the records, you should use the `Find` method's `SearchDirection` and `Start` optional parameters.

The `SearchDirection` parameter can be set to either the constant `adSearchForward` (default), to search forward in the recordset, or `adSearchBackward` to search backward in the recordset. The `Start` parameter allows you to specify a bookmark for the location to begin the search from. The `Start` parameter can also be set to the constant value `adBookmarkFirst`, to begin the search at the first record in the recordset, or `adBookmarkLast` to begin from the last record in the recordset.

In the following example, we'll revise our `FindAuthorRecord` method to ensure that we are searching through each record in our disconnected recordset by specifying a value of `adSearchForward` for the `SearchDirection` parameter and a value of `adBookmarkFirst` for the `Start` parameter. Alternatively, we could accomplish the same goal by specifying a value of `adSearchBackward` for the `SearchDirection` parameter and a value of `adBookmarkLast` for the `Start` parameter.

```
Private Sub FindAuthorRecord(ByVal sAuthorLastName As String)
    Dim rsAuthors As ADODB.Recordset

    'get a disconnected recordset containing all of the Authors
    Set rsAuthors = GetAuthorsRs()

    'find the record with a value in the au_lname field equal to the parameter
    '...and search forward, starting at the beginning of the recordset
    rsAuthors.Find "au_lname = #" & sAuthorLastName & "#", _
                SearchDirection:=adSearchForward, Start:=adBookmarkFirst

    If (rsAuthors.EOF = False) Then       'we found the specified Author Record
        Debug.Print "The author with the last name of '" & _
                sAuthorLastName & "' was found at position #" & _
                rsAuthors.AbsolutePosition
    Else
        'we didn't find the specified Author Record
        Debug.Print "The author with the last name of '" & sAuthorLastName & _
                "' was not found!"
    End If

    'close and release our disconnected recordset
    rsAuthors.Close
    Set rsAuthors = Nothing
End Sub
```

Notice in this example, that it is only necessary to check for the end-of-file (EOF) because we are searching forward. If searching backwards we should check for the beginning-of-file (BOF) to know whether or not a record was found.

The `SkipRecords` parameter is an integer value that indicates the offset for the starting position of the search. If a value is specified for the `Start` parameter, then the `SkipRecords` parameter will be the offset from that value. If the `Start` parameter is not specified, then the `SkipRecords` parameter will be an offset from the current record. For example, a value of 1 in this parameter would cause the search to begin at the next row from the start position in the search direction, a value of 2 would cause the search to begin at two rows ahead of the start position in the search direction, and so on. The `SkipRecords` parameter can also bet set to a negative number to begin the search before the start position.

Before you dismiss the `SkipRecords` parameter as having no practical use, let me show you one. As I mentioned, when a search is performed if a match is found the recordset's position is moved to the matching record. However, if you call the `MoveNext` method, the next record will not necessarily meet the criteria you specified when you executed the `Find` procedure. To find more than one record that matches our criteria, we can execute the `Find` method within a loop, specifying a `SkipRecords` parameter of 1 to begin the search at the next record from the current record. The following example defines a method named `FindEachAuthorRecordLike` that uses this technique to find each author record with a similar last name to the value specified in the `sAuthorLastName` parameter:

```
Private Sub FindEachAuthorRecordLike(ByVal sAuthorLastName As String)
    Dim rsAuthors As ADODB.Recordset

    'get a disconnected recordset containing all of the Authors
    Set rsAuthors = GetAuthorsRs()

    With rsAuthors
        'find the first record with a au_lname value similar to the parameter
        '...and search forward, starting at the beginning of the recordset
        .Find "au_lname LIKE #" & sAuthorLastName & "#", _
            SearchDirection:=adSearchForward, Start:=adBookmarkFirst

        Do While Not .EOF
            'we found a match from our last search
            '...since we're searching forward, EOF would
            '...be true if Find couldn't locate a record

            'print a message to the debug window containing the Author's Last and
            '...First name and the Absolution position of the found record
            Debug.Print "The found author's name is '" _
                    & .Fields("au_lname").Value _
                    & ", " & .Fields("au_fname").Value & "'" & vbCrLf _
                    & "The record's position = " & .AbsolutePosition

            'execute the same find again starting at the next record
            '...(from the current record moving forward) by specifying
            '...a value of 1 in the SkipRecords parameter
            .Find "au_lname Like #" & sAuthorLastName & "#", _
                    SearchDirection:=adSearchForward, SkipRecords:=1
        Loop
    End With

    'close and release our disconnected recordset
    rsAuthors.Close
    Set rsAuthors = Nothing
End Sub
```

To test our `FindEachAuthorRecordLike` method, simply invoke it, passing a value of `'S*'` for the `sAuthorLastName` parameter to display a message box for each author with a last name beginning with `'S'`:

```
FindEachAuthorRecordLike "S*"
```

As you can see, the code to find each record matching the specified criteria is actually pretty simple. However, a `Recordset` object's `Filter` property, which we'll discuss in just a moment, is much easier and faster to use than repeatedly invoking the `Find` method as in the previous example.

Unlike the `Sort` property, the `Find` method can also sometimes be called when using server cursors because it is supported by some OLE DB Data Providers in addition to the OLE DB Cursor Service. However, the OLE DB Cursor Service provides a scalable alternative to relying on the data provider to provide searching. Since the Cursor Service performs searches against an OLE DB rowset cached in *local* memory, it doesn't require any involvement by the data provider or data source. As a result, there is less network traffic, quicker searches and less processing overhead on the data source.

Filtering

While sorting and searching are powerful features, in my opinion, the most useful data-fetching feature provided by the OLE DB Cursor Service is filtering. Filtering allows you to view only a subset of the records within an ADO `Recordset`, by temporarily hiding records that don't meet the specified criterion. Filtering is exposed by ADO through a `Recordset` object's `Filter` property. The `Filter` property sets and returns a variant value that can contain either a criterion string in the same syntax as the `Find` method's `Criteria` parameter, an array of bookmarks that point to records in the `Recordset`, or a constant value defined by the `FilterGroupEnum` enumeration.

In the following example, we'll create a generic method named `FilterAuthorRecordLike` that lists each author with a similar last name to the passed `sAuhorLastName` parameter. This scenario is exactly the same as our `FindEachAuthorRecordLike` method that we created in the last section. However, instead of calling the `Find` method repeatedly, we'll simply call the `Filter` property once to exclude any records that don't meet the criterion:

```
Private Sub FilterAuthorRecordLike(ByVal sAuthorLastName As String)
    Dim rsAuthors As ADODB.Recordset

    'get a disconnected recordset containing all of the Authors
    Set rsAuthors = GetAuthorsRs()

    With rsAuthors
        'filter the recordset so it only contains the records
        '...where the au_lname field's value is similar (like)
        '...to the sAuthorLastName parameter
        .Filter = "au_lname Like #" & sAuthorLastName & "#"
    End With

    'close and release our disconnected recordset
    rsAuthors.Close
    Set rsAuthors = Nothing
End Sub
```

As I mentioned, the `Filter` property effectively hides records that don't meet the specified criterion. From the data-centric application's perspective the hidden records don't even exist in this `Recordset`, although they actually still reside in the underlying OLE DB `Rowset` and still take up memory. To reflect the filter operation, ADO also adjusts the values of certain properties such as the `AbsolutePosition`, the `AbsolutePage`, the `RecordCount` and the `PageCount`. The following diagram illustrates this behavior when the `Filter` property is called. The shaded records in the diagram represent the hidden records that didn't meet the `Filter` property's criteria and the highlighted record represents the `Recordset`'s position on the current record after the `Filter` property call:

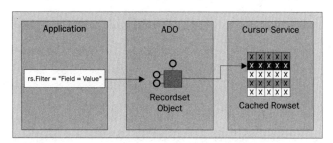

Let's revise our `FilterAuthorRecordLike` method so each name and `AbsolutePosition` for each author record remaining in the recordset is displayed in the debug window:

```
Private Sub FilterAuthorRecordLike(ByVal sAuthorLastName As String)
    Dim rsAuthors As ADODB.Recordset

    'get a disconnected recordset containing all of the Authors
    Set rsAuthors = GetAuthorsRs()

    With rsAuthors
        'filter the recordset so it only contains the records
        '...where the au_lname field's value is similar (like)
        '...to the sAuthorLastName parameter
        .Filter = "au_lname Like #" & sAuthorLastName & "#"

        Do While Not .EOF
            'now loop through each record in our filtered recordset

            'print a message to the debug window containing each Author's
            '...Last and First name and the Absolution position of the record
            Debug.Print "The found author's name is '" _
                & .Fields("au_lname").Value _
                & ", " & .Fields("au_fname").Value & "'" & vbCrLf _
                & "The record's position = " & .AbsolutePosition

            'move to the next record in the filtered recordset
            .MoveNext
        Loop
    End With

    'close and release our disconnected recordset
    rsAuthors.Close
    Set rsAuthors = Nothing
End Sub
```

We can invoke our `FilterAuthorRecordLike` method by simply calling it and specifying a last name to filter for in the `sAuthorLastName` parameter:

```
FilterAuthorRecordLike "S*"
```

As I mentioned, the criterion string used by the `Filter` property is the same format as the criterion string used in the `Find` method's `Criteria` parameter. Even the same rules apply for the formatting of values, comparison operators, and wildcards. However, unlike the `Find` method, the `Filter` property allows multiple criteria to be specified by using the logical operators `AND` and `OR`.

In the following example, we'll modify our `FilterAuthorRecordLike` method to filter author records that have both a similar last name and first name:

```
Private Sub FilterAuthorRecordLike(ByVal sAuthorLastName As String, _
                              ByVal sAuthorFirstName As String)

    Dim rsAuthors As ADODB.Recordset

    'get a disconnected recordset containing all of the Authors
    Set rsAuthors = GetAuthorsRs()

    With rsAuthors
        'print the RecordCount before the filter is been applied
        Debug.Print "UnFiltered Recordset's Recordcount: " & .RecordCount

        'filter the recordset so it only contains the records
        '...where the au_lname field's value is similar (like)
        '...to the sAuthorLastName parameter
        .Filter = "(au_lname Like #" & sAuthorLastName & "#)" & _
                    " AND " & "(au_fname Like #" & sAuthorFirstName & "#)"

        'print the RecordCount after the filter has been applied
        Debug.Print "Filtered Recordset's Recordcount: " & .RecordCount

        Do While .EOF = False
            'now loop through each record in our filtered recordset

            'print a message to the debug window containing each Author's
            '...Last and First name and the Absolution position of the record
            Debug.Print "The found author's name is '" _
                    & .Fields("au_lname").Value _
                    & ", " & .Fields("au_fname").Value & "'" & vbCrLf _
                    & "The record's position = " & .AbsolutePosition

            'move to the next record in the filtered recordset
            .MoveNext
        Loop
    End With


    'close and release our disconnected recordset
    rsAuthors.Close
    Set rsAuthors = Nothing
End Sub
```

There is no precedence between the AND and OR logical operators and the criterion clauses can be joined together with parentheses, as in the previous example. However, you cannot group criteria clauses that are joined by an OR operator and join the group to another clause with the AND operator. For example, the following filter is invalid because the two criterion groups are joined by an AND operator and one criterion group uses an OR operator:

```
rsAuthors.Filter = "(au_lname LIKE #P*# OR au_lname LIKE #H*#)" & _
                   " AND (au_fname LIKE #S*#)"
```

Once you've finished with the filtered recordset, you can destroy the filter by setting the Filter property either to the constant adFilterNone or to an empty string. The OLE DB Cursor Service will then expose all of the records in the cached rowset and ADO will reposition to the first record:

```
'Show all the Author records in the Recordset now by clearing our filter
rsAuthors.Filter = adFilterNone
```

Filtering has several uses, especially for presenting data in a data-centric application's User Interface. One popular use is to retrieve a disconnected recordset containing all of the possible records the user is interested in and then providing multiple views of the recordset's data simply by changing the Filter property. In this situation, the OLE DB Cursor Service manages the underlying OLE DB Rowset and performs the Filter operation in local memory, so you don't have to worry about the overhead of transferring each filtered rowset across the network. Of course, you must also consider the overhead of caching many records in local memory. If you wish, the Filter property can also be used with some OLE DB data providers when using server cursors. Consult your data provider's documentation for more details.

Indexes

The OLE DB Cursor Service doesn't support the use of indexes through a Recordset's Index property, as you might expect. Instead, the creation and destruction of local indexes on specific fields in a cached rowset can be controlled through the use of a Field object's dynamic Optimize property. By setting this property to True, the Cursor Service will create a local index for the respective field. A value of False will cause the index to be destroyed.

In the following example, we'll revise our FindAuthorRecord method that we created earlier so that it creates a local index on the last name (au_lname) field of our disconnected recordset before performing the search:

```
Private Sub FindAuthorRecord(ByVal sAuthorLastName As String)
    Dim rsAuthors As ADODB.Recordset

    'get a disconnected recordset containing all of the Authors
    Set rsAuthors = m_objPubsNonTx.GetAuthorsRs()

    'create an index on the au_lname field
    rsAuthors.Fields("au_lname").Properties("Optimize").Value = True
```

```
'find the record with a value in the au_lname field equal to the parameter
'...and search forward, starting at the beginning of the recordset
rsAuthors.Find "au_lname = #" & sAuthorLastName & "#", _
                SearchDirection:=adSearchForward, Start:=adBookmarkFirst

If ((rsAuthors.EOF = False) And (rsAuthors.BOF = False)) Then
    'we found the specified Author Record
    MsgBox "The author with the last name of '" & sAuthorLastName & _
            "' was found at position #" & rsAuthors.AbsolutePosition
Else
    'we didn't find the specified Author Record
    MsgBox "The author with the last name of '" & sAuthorLastName & _
            "' was not found!"
End If

'close and release our disconnected recordset
rsAuthors.Close
Set rsAuthors = Nothing
End Sub
```

The OLE DB Cursor Service will automatically take advantage of existing indexes to provide higher performance when performing sorting, finding and filtering operations. Remember, if an index is not created on a field specified in the Sort property, the OLE DB Cursor Service will automatically create one and then destroy it when the Sort property is cleared. To avoid the overhead of index creation and destruction for each sort operation, you should create a local index using the Optimize property before performing multiple sort operations on the same column.

The Synchronization Service

The Synchronization Service is responsible for synchronizing a cached OLE DB Rowset managed by the Cursor Service with the data source from which the Rowset's data originated. A cached rowset can become out of sync with the data source for two reasons:

❑ **Records have been manipulated within the data source.** In On-line Transaction Processing (OLTP) systems it is likely that many users will be manipulating data concurrently in a shared data source. Since a cached rowset is a static snapshot of data, it must be manually refreshed with the current values from the data source to see changes made by other users. We'll refer to this process as **refreshing**.

❑ **Records have been manipulated within the cached rowset.** In this situation, insertions, updates and deletions performed against the cached rowset residing in local memory must be applied to the data source. This process is known as **batch updating**.

In a nutshell, the Synchronization Service resynchronizes the cached rowset with the originating data source by executing SQL statements against the data source. For this reason, the Synchronization Service can only be used with data sources that support the standard SQL Statements: SELECT, UPDATE, INSERT and DELETE. Thankfully, all of the details of construction and execution of these SQL statements are completely encapsulated by the Synchronization Service. Our only responsibilities as ADO developers are to:

- ❑   Enable the Synchronization Service when opening a recordset
- ❑   Invoke resynchronization by calling methods on the `Recordset` object

> **The name Synchronization Service is a bit misleading. Actually the Synchronization 'Service' isn't a separate OLE DB Service Component, but instead it represents functionality that is integrated within the OLE DB Cursor Service.**

Enabling the Synchronization Service

By default the Synchronization Service is disabled and cannot be utilized to perform resynchronization. To enable the Synchronization Service, an ADO `Recordset` must be opened with both a `CursorLocation` of `adUseClient` and a `LockType` of `adLockBatchOptimistic`. We already know that a `CursorLocation` of `adUseClient` tells ADO to utilize the OLE DB Cursor Service for its underlying `Rowset` implementation, but what are the effects of changing the `LockType` to `adLockBatchOptimistic`?

When a recordset is opened with a `LockType` of `adLockBatchOptimistic` the OLE DB Cursor Service performs two additional tasks when creating a cached rowset later that allow resynchronization to be performed by the Synchronization Service. The Cursor Service:

- ❑   Enables changes to the OLE DB Rowset
- ❑   Retrieves extended metadata information

These two operations are the reasons for the significant performance hit when opening a recordset with the `LockType` of `adLockBatchOptimistic` versus a `LockType` of `adLockReadOnly`. Let's discuss these two stages in more detail and understand why this performance hit occurs.

> **It's worthwhile to note that the Synchronization Service is also enabled when a `Recordset` is opened with a `CursorLocation` of `adUseClient` and `LockType` of `adLockOptimistic`. However, the `Recordset` object behaves slightly different than one explicitly opened with a `LockType` of `adLockBatchOptimistic`. In particular, data manipulation operations (updates, inserts or deletes) are performed both within the cached OLE DB `Rowset` and directly against the data provider and data source. If the `Recordset` is disconnected, then the changes will only be performed within the cached `Rowset`, but as long as the `LockType` is set to `adLockOptimistic`, it is not possible to apply any pending changes to the data source. One last peculiarity, when a disconnected `Recordset` with a `LockType` of `adLockOptimistic` is passed to another process, the `LockType` is automatically adjusted to `adLockBatchOptimistic` and the `Recordset` begins behaving accordingly. For the context of this chapter, we will focus our discussion to recordsets with a `LockType` of `adLockBatchOptimistic`.**

Enables Changes to the OLE DB Rowset

By default, a `Recordset` object's `LockType` property will be set to `adLockReadOnly`, which results in a read-only cached rowset. When a recordset is opened with a `LockType` of `adLockBatchOptimistic`, the OLE DB Cursor Service will create a cached rowset that supports data manipulation. Data can be inserted, updated and deleted within the cached rowset using the standard `Recordset` methods: `AddNew`, `Update` and `Delete`. However, since the cached rowset resides in local memory, these changes are not managed by the data source, nor are they visible to any other users. As a result, no rows are actually locked in the data source until the changes in the cached rowset are actually applied to the data source.

❑   To track changes to data in a cached rowset and resolve conflicts when performing resynchronization, the OLE DB Cursor Service manages not one, but *three* independent values for each field. These values are exposed by ADO through corresponding properties on a `Field` object. These three properties are:

❑   **Value.** A `Field` object's `Value` property sets or returns the *current* value for a field within the cached rowset. However, the `Value` property may not reflect the actual value stored in the data source because of changes made in the cached rowset or because of changes made in the data source by other users. The `CancelBatch` and `CancelUpdate` methods can be used to reset a field's value to its original value, effectively undoing any changes.

❑   **OriginalValue.** The read-only `OriginalValue` property returns the value stored in the field *before* any changes were made in the cached rowset. If the `OriginalValue` is different to the `Value` property then the field's value has been changed in the cached rowset. On the other hand, if the `OriginalValue` is different to the `UnderlyingValue` then the field's value has been changed in the data source.

❑   **UnderlyingValue.** The read-only `UnderlyingValue` property returns the value of the field as stored in the data source. Although the `UnderlyingValue` is initially the same as the `OriginalValue`, the `UnderlyingValue` will be different if the field's value has been changed in the data source. The `UnderlyingValue` must be manually refreshed by calling a `Recordset` object's `Resync` method.

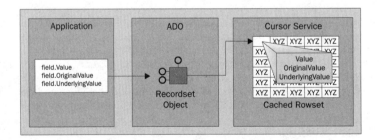

Retrieves Extended Metadata

In addition to creating a cached rowset that supports data manipulation, when a recordset is opened with a `LockType` of `adLockBatchOptimistic`, the OLE DB Cursor Service also retrieves extended metadata about the data source. This extended metadata is later used by the Synchronization Service to construct SQL queries that are executed against the data source when performing resynchronization The following five metadata attributes are managed for each field defined in the rowset:

❑ **BaseColumnName.** The `BaseColumnName` attribute stores the name of the column/field in the data source from which the Rowset's data originated. The value for this attribute will typically be the same as the field's name unless an alias was used. If the column's name cannot be determined or the column was derived from a calculation, the value for this attribute will be `Null`.

❑ **BaseTableName.** The `BaseTableName` attribute stores the name of the table in the data source from which the rowset's data originated. The value for this attribute will be `Null` if the table's name cannot be determined.

❑ **BaseSchemaName.** The `BaseSchemaName` attribute stores the name of the schema in the data source from which the rowset's data originated. The value for this attribute will be `Null` if the schema's name cannot be determined.

❑ **BaseCatalogName.** The `BaseCatalogName` attribute stores the name of the catalog or database from which the rowset's data originated. The value for this attribute will be `Null` if the catalog name cannot be determined.

❑ **KeyColumn.** Finally, the `KeyColumn` attribute stores a Boolean value that indicates whether (`True`) or not (`False`) the column/field is a key column used to uniquely identify a row. In the case of SQL Server, this attribute will be set to `True` for columns with either a Primary Key, a Unique Key or a Unique Constraint. Any fields with this attribute set to `True` are referred to as `KeyColumns` and are used in the `WHERE` clause of a `SELECT`, `UPDATE` or `DELETE` statement issued by the Synchronization Service to ensure that these operations only affect a single row.

These five metadata attributes effectively describe the data source from which the cached rowset's data originated. Without this metadata the Synchronization Service would have no way to construct SQL statements used to perform resynchronization. As you can see in the following diagram, the Cursor Service manages these attributes at the field level and they are exposed through the ADO object model as read-only dynamic properties of an ADO `Field` object:

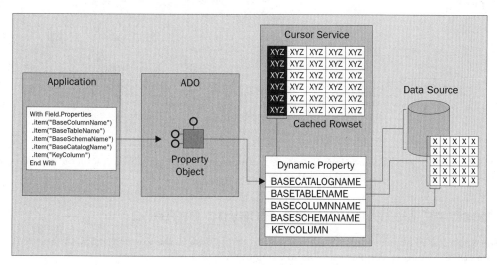

Even though fabricated recordsets can be opened with a `LockType` of
`adLockBatchOptimistic`, resynchronization cannot be performed with fabricated
recordsets because they lack each of these required metadata attributes.
Unfortunately, the values for these metadata attributes cannot be set manually
because they do not even exist for fields of a fabricated recordset. Hopefully a future
version of ADO will overcome this limitation, but until then resynchronization is
limited to recordsets whose data originated from a data provider.

Invoking the Synchronization Service

As I mentioned, a cached rowset can become out of sync with the data source because either the cached
rowset's data has been changed or the data source's data has been changed. ADO provides two methods
to perform resynchronization, one for each situation. These methods are: `Resync` and `UpdateBatch`.

Basically, the `Resync` method refreshes a cached rowset with the current data from the data source. The
`UpdateBatch` method is a little more interesting. The `UpdateBatch` method applies any changes
within the cached rowset to the data source. The `UpdateBatch` method is much more complex than
the `Resync` method because it involves inserting, updating and deleting data and resolving multi-user
conflicts. In the following diagram, Client A manipulates data within its cached rowset and applies the
changes to the data source by calling the `UpdateBatch` method and Client B is calling the `Resync`
method to refresh its cached `rowset` with the Data Source:

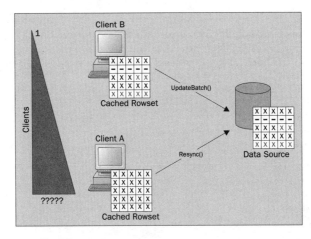

Let's discuss the `Resync` and `UpdateBatch` methods in more detail and implement the code required
to use these methods with disconnected recordsets.

Refreshing Data using the Resync method

The `Recordset` object's `Resync` method refreshes the data in the `Recordset` with the current values
from the data source. The `Resync` method is defined as follows:

```
Resync([AffectRecords As AffectEnum = adAffectAll], _
       [ResyncValues As ResyncEnum = adResyncAllValues])
```

To understand how the Resync method works, let's take a look at an example. In the following code we'll first acquire a disconnected recordset containing all of the records from the authors table in the pubs SQL Server database. To shorten the amount code in this example, we'll simply call our GetAuthorsRS method that we created earlier in this chapter to obtain this disconnected recordset. Next, we'll modify an individual record in the authors table by executing an SQL UPDATE statement. Finally, we'll reconnect our disconnected recordset and call the Resync method to refresh the recordset with the change:

```
Private Sub ModifyDataAndResyncRecordset()
    Dim sAuthorID As String
    Dim rsAuthors As ADODB.Recordset
    Dim conDataSource As ADODB.Connection

    'create a new instance of an ADODB.Connection
    Set conDataSource = New ADODB.Connection

    'establish a connection to the data source
    conDataSource.Open "Provider=SQLOLEDB;Initial Catalog=Pubs; " & _
                    "Data Source=jconard;User ID=sa;Password=;"

    'get a disconnected recordset containing all of the Authors
    Set rsAuthors = GetAuthorsRs()

    'get the first Author's ID (au_id) into a variable
    sAuthorID = rsAuthors.Fields("au_id").Value

    'update a record in the data source using the Author's ID
    '...as a parameter. The change will be immediate.
    conDataSource.Execute "UPDATE Authors SET au_lname ='Conard' " & _
                    " WHERE au_id = '" & sAuthorID & "'"

    With rsAuthors
        'our disconnected recordset is now out of sync with the data source
        '...first reconnect it and then refresh it's data
        Set .ActiveConnection = conDataSource
        .Resync

        'find the record we updated in our disconnected Recordset
        .Find "au_id = '" & sAuthorID & "'", SearchDirection:=adSearchForward, _
                                Start:=adBookmarkFirst

        If .EOF = False Then
            'display the Record in a messagebox
            MsgBox "au_id: " & .Fields("au_id").Value & vbCrLf & _
                    "au_lname: " & .Fields("au_lname").Value
        End If
```

```
    End With

    'close and release our disconnected recordset
    rsAuthors.Close
    Set rsAuthors = Nothing  _
End Sub
```

As you can see, from our perspective refreshing a recordset is quite simple. That's because the Synchronization Service abstracts us from all of the complexities of resynchronization. When the Resync method is called, behind the scenes the Synchronization Service performs the following three operations:

❑ Constructs a SQL SELECT statement

❑ Executes the SELECT statement

❑ Replaces the record's values with the data returned from the SELECT statement

Constructs a SQL SELECT Statement

First, the Synchronization Service constructs a SQL SELECT statement using the metadata attributes obtained by the Cursor Service when the recordset was opened. This SELECT statement consists of two parts: the column list and the row identifier. The column list is composed using each field's BaseColumnName attribute. The row identifier section is simply the WHERE clause that compares each KeyColumn against its original value from the recordset in an attempt to ensure that exactly one record is returned when the statement is executed. The idea here is that a record's KeyColumn(s) uniquely identify a record and the values in these columns hardly ever change. But instead of using literal values in this comparison, the SELECT statement is parameterized to include a question mark in the place of a literal value. This allows for faster execution of the SELECT statement because values don't have to undergo conversion. For example, the following SELECT statement is constructed by the Synchronization Service when the Resync method is called in the previous code example:

```
SELECT "au_id","au_lname","au_fname","phone","address","city","state","zip",
       "contract"
  FROM "Pubs".."Authors"
  WHERE "au_id"=?
```

Notice in this example that each object name (column, table, catalog and schema name if we had one) is enclosed in double quotation marks. The Synchronization Service formats SQL statement in this way to provide support for extended character sets and object names that include spaces.

When a recordset contains data derived from a join operation, instead of creating a single SELECT statement that contains a join, the Synchronization Service will construct a SELECT statement for each unique BaseTableName. To understand how this works, let's look at a simple scenario.

The following diagram illustrates the simple one-to-many relationship between the publishers and titles tables in the Pubs SQL Server database and some simple data in both tables. Some of the columns from these tables have been omitted for this example.

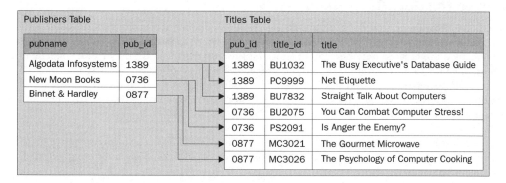

As you can see, each record in the `publishers` table has one or more records in the `titles` table. To retrieve the matching data from these two tables we might execute the following SELECT statement when opening a recordset:

```
SELECT publishers.pub_id, publishers.pub_name, titles.title_id, titles.title
    FROM publishers
    INNER JOIN titles
    ON publishers.pub_id = titles.pub_id
```

Based on our previous example, the recordset would have the following structure and data:

pub_id	pubname	title_id	title
1389	Algodata Infosystems	BU1032	The Busy Executive's Database Guide
1389	Algodata Infosystems	PC9999	Net Etiquette
1389	Algodata Infosystems	BU7832	Straight Talk About Computers
0736	New Moon Books	BU2075	You Can Combat Computer Stress!
0736	New Moon Books	PS2091	Is Anger the Enemy?
0877	Binnet & Hardley	MC3021	The Gourmet Microwave
0877	Binnet & Hardley	MC3026	The Psychology of Computer Cooking

When the `Resync` method is called on this `Recordset`, the Synchronization Service will construct not one, but two SELECT statements because there are two base tables involved. The column names will be assigned to the appropriate SELECT statement based on which base table the column belongs to. These two SELECT statements will look similar to the following:

```
SELECT "title_id","title" FROM "Pubs".."titles" WHERE "title_id"=?
SELECT "pub_id","pub_name" FROM "Pubs".."publishers" WHERE "pub_id"=?
```

These independent SELECT statements are both constructed to return only a single row by comparing each table's `KeyColumn` against its original value from the recordset. Why does the Synchronization Service issue two independent queries instead of performing a join? For performance reasons joins are a very costly operation for a database system to perform when compared to single table queries. By constructing (and executing) a separate query for each base table, the Synchronization Service eliminates a huge amount of overhead that would otherwise be incurred by the database system.

Executes the SELECT Statement

Next, the Synchronization Service submits the SELECT statement(s) to the data provider for execution, using the original values from the recordset's KeyColumn(s) as parameter(s). While the SELECT statement(s) are created only once as a result of a Resync method call, they can be executed multiple times, once for each record that should be refreshed. This is another reason why the SELECT statement(s) are parameterized instead of simply having a literal value in the WHERE clause. The Resync method's AffectRecords parameter allows you to control which records are refreshed, and effectively, the number of times the SELECT statement is executed.

In the case of our previous code example, the Synchronization Service simply executes the single SELECT statement repeatedly for each record being refreshed, specifying a different author ID (au_id) for each execution:

```
? = '111-11-1111'

SELECT "au_id","au_lname","au_fname","phone","address","city","state","zip",
    "contract"
  FROM "Pubs".."Authors"
  WHERE "au_id"=?
```

Refreshes the Recordset with the Returned Data

Finally, the Synchronization Service replaces the value(s) for each field in the cached rowset with the value for each field in the single record returned from the execution of the SELECT statement. The Resync method's *ResyncValues* parameter allows you to control which values are refreshed. We'll discuss more about this parameter in a moment. This step will be performed for each SELECT statement that is executed.

The following diagram illustrates the three steps performed by the Synchronization Service when the Resync method is invoked on a Recordset object. For sake of space the data provider has been omitted from the diagram, but in actuality the Synchronization Service relies on the data provider for all interaction with the data source:

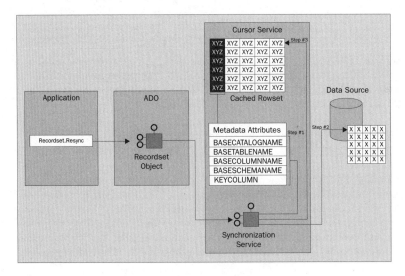

Monitoring the Synchronization Service

Since we're accessing the `pubs` SQL Server database and using the Microsoft OLE DB Provider for SQL Server (SQLOLEDB) we can take advantage of the Visual Studio Analyzer (VSA) events raised by SQLOLEDB. After loading VSA and creating an Analyzer Project, simply set up a filter for the **SQL Server OLEDB** component and the `QuerySend` event under the category **All Regular Events->Database**. Now execute the code in the previous example. When the `Resync` method is called, it will flood the VSA Event Viewer with a VSA event for each execution of the `SELECT` statement.

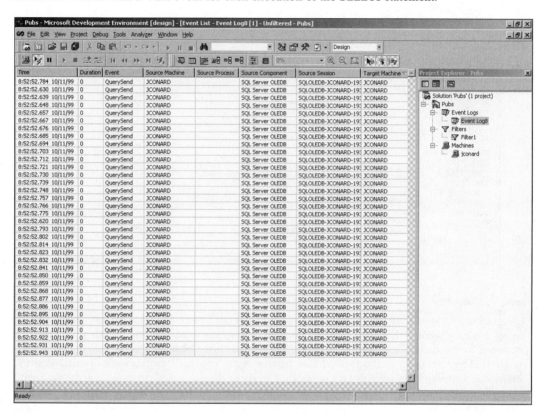

If you take a closer look at one of these `QuerySend` events, you'll notice the parameterized `SELECT` statement in the `Arguments` field for the event. Unfortunately there's no way to view the value(s) that were specified for the parameters for each execution from Visual Studio Analyzer, but nevertheless the information exposed by VSA is essential to understanding how the Synchronization Service works and the performance impact of using it. Visual Studio Analyzer is an invaluable tool for gathering performance statistics, performing debugging and troubleshooting ADO and the SQLOLEDB Provider. We'll discuss more about VSA and utilize it extensively in Chapter 11.

> **When the data source is a Microsoft SQL Server Database, you can also use the SQL Server Profiler tool for monitoring the behavior of the Synchronization Service. Unlike VSA, the SQL Server Profiler does show the value(s) used for the parameters in the `SELECT` statements. However, the SQL Server Profiler is not as powerful as Visual Studio Analyzer because it only allows you to monitor SQL Server events.**

Field ▽	Value
Arguments	SELECT "au_id","au_lname","au_fname","phone","address","city","state","zip","contract" FROM "Pubs".."Authors" WHERE "au_id"=?
Category	Database
Causality ID	{D88C9F54-988C-4FF1-BF00-B9887187C6A7}
Correlation ID	SQLOLEDB077124B692CB43F698872C07AA2EB2CC
Duration	42667
Duration (ms)	4
Dynamic Event Data	0
Event	QuerySend
Exception	
Full Category	All Regular Events::Database
Return Value	
Security Identity	Administrator
Source	SQL Server OLEDB
Source Component	SQL Server OLEDB
Source Handle	
Source Machine	JCONARD
Source Process	
Source Process ID	1992
Source Session	SQLOLEDB-JCONARD-1992-93923528
Source Thread	6b4
Target Component	SQL Server OLEDB
Target Handle	
Target Machine	JCONARD
Target Process	VB6
Target Process ID	1992
Target Session	SQLOLEDB-JCONARD-1992-93923528
Target Thread	6b4
Time	19:05:30.209 10/8/99
Type	Outbound

Event - Event Log2 [5] - Unfiltered - Pubs

Resync vs. Requery

Since a SELECT statement is executed on a record-by-record basis, the Resync method will not be able to see any new records that were inserted into the data source even if these records would have been returned by the original query. Additionally, any records inserted or deleted within the recordset will be unaffected by a Resync method call. These behaviors are why the Recordset object's Requery method is different from the Resync method. Where the Resync method issues a separate query for each record to be refreshed, the Requery method repopulates the recordset by re-executing the original statement that created the recordset. Any new records in the underlying data source will be included in the recordset after the Requery method has been called.

Conflicts with the Resync Method

The Synchronization Service will be unable to refresh an individual record's value(s) in either of the following two situations:

❑ The corresponding record in the data source has been deleted.

❑ The value for one of the *Key Columns* (field with the KeyColumn dynamic property set to True) has been changed for the corresponding record in the data source.

In either of these situations, the Synchronization Service will raise the following run-time error and remove the conflicting record(s) from the recordset:

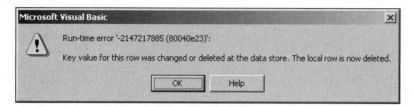

To demonstrate the behavior of the Synchronization Service in these situations, let's create a method that updates the `KeyColumn` for a record in the data source before calling the `Resync` method. When the `Resync` method is called, we'll trap the run-time error and filter the recordset so we can see the number of records that were conflicting:

```
Private Sub UpdateKeyColumnAndResyncRecordset()
    Dim rsAuthors As ADODB.Recordset
    Dim sAuthorID As String
    Dim conDataSource As ADODB.Connection

    'create a new instance of an ADODB.Connection
    Set conDataSource = New ADODB.Connection

    'establish a connection to the data source
    conDataSource.Open "Provider=SQLOLEDB;Initial Catalog=Pubs; " & _
                    "Data Source=jconard;User ID=sa;Password=;"

    'get a disconnected recordset containing all of the Authors
    Set rsAuthors = GetAuthorsRs()

    'get the first Author's ID (au_id) into a variable
    sAuthorID = rsAuthors.Fields("au_id").Value

    'Update the Key Column (au_id) for a record in the data source
    conDataSource.Execute "UPDATE Authors " & _
                    " SET au_id = '123-45-6777'" & _
                    " WHERE au_id = '" & sAuthorID & "'"

    With rsAuthors
        'our disconnected recordset is now out of sync with the data source
        '...first reconnect it and try to refresh its data
        Set .ActiveConnection = conDataSource

        'show the Recordcount before peforming calling Resync
        MsgBox "Total Number of records in the Recordset: " & .RecordCount

        'will trap any errors in-line for this example
        On Error Resume Next

        'Attempting a Resync after a record has been deleted in the
        '...data source will through a run-time error -2147217885
        .Resync
```

```
        If Err.Number = -2147217885 Then
            'filter for conflicting records

            'This is not required, it just allows us to
            '...see the number of conflicts
            .Filter = adFilterConflictingRecords

            'we can't access the data for any conflicting records,
            '...but we can see the number of records with conflicts
            MsgBox "Conflicting Records: " & .RecordCount
        End If
    End With

    'turn off the Resume Next
    On Error GoTo 0

    'close and release our disconnected recordset
    rsAuthors.Close
    Set rsAuthors = Nothing
End Sub
```

Filtering for conflicting records can only be performed *immediately* after the Resync method has been called. Conflicting records will always have a status of adRecDBDeleted, regardless of the actual reason for the conflict. Unfortunately we cannot access the values for any field of a conflicting record or perform any operations on that record because it has been marked for removal from the recordset by the Synchronization Service. In fact, the first method or property call on the Recordset object without a filter will cause the conflicting records to be permanently removed from the recordset. This is why the filtering for conflicting records can only be performed *immediately* after a Resync method call. For example, in the following code sample we'll remove our filter for conflicting records and display the RecordCount for the entire Recordset. Notice that this RecordCount will be one less than the total number of records before the Resync method was called because there was one conflicting record:

```
'<code snipped>

With rsAuthors
    'our disconnected recordset is now out of sync with the data source
    '...first reconnect it and try to refresh it's data
    Set .ActiveConnection = conDataSource

    'show the Recordcount before peforming calling Resync
    MsgBox "Total Number of records in the Recordset: " & .RecordCount

    'will trap any error's in-line for this example
    On Error Resume Next

    'Attempting a Resync after a record has been deleted in the
    '...data source will through a run-time error -2147217885
    .Resync

    If Err.Number = -2147217885 Then
        'filter for conflicting records
```

```
         'This is not required, it just allows us to
         '...see the number of conflicts
         .Filter = adFilterConflictingRecords

         'we can't access the data for any conflicting records,
         '...but we can see the number of records with conflicts
         MsgBox "Conflicting Records: " & .RecordCount
      End If

         'turn off our filter
         .Filter = adFilterNone

         'show the Recordcount now
         MsgBox "Total Number of records in the Recordset: " & .RecordCount

      End With

      '<code snipped>
```

Probably the most common cause for problems with the `Resync` method arises from the Synchronization Service not being able to uniquely identify a record. This problem presents itself as an ugly run-time error with the description Insufficient key column information for updating or refreshing:

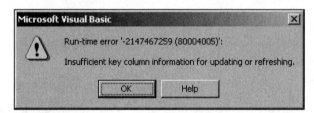

In this situation the Synchronization Service will not be able to refresh any records because either there are no keycolumns in the `Recordset`.

The reason for this error will vary depending on the data provider. In the case of the SQL Server OLE DB Provider, this error will occur *only* because the base table does not have a Primary Key, a Unique Constraint or a Unique Index. With the Jet OLE DB Provider, this error will also occur because the base table does not have a Primary Key or because the Jet Provider cannot determine the `KeyColumn`(s).

> **SQL Server will automatically determine the `KeyColumns` for the base table(s) when a recordset is opened; however, with Access databases the Primary Key columns must be included in the `SELECT` statement that populated the recordset for the Synchronization Service to be able to perform resynchronization.**

AffectRecords Parameter

By default, the `Resync` method's *AffectRecords* optional parameter will be set to the constant `adAffectAll`, which will cause all of the records in the recordset to be refreshed. Other valid settings for this parameter are `adAffectGroup`, which causes all records in the current filter to be refreshed, and `adAffectCurrent`, which causes only the current record to be refreshed. You should try to minimize the number of records affected by the `Resync` method through the use of the `AffectRecords` parameter because the Synchronization Service executes a separate `SELECT` statement for each that will be refreshed. Lastly, the `AffectRecords` parameter also supports a constant value of `adAffectAllChapters` that is supposed to cause the Synchronization Service to refresh all of the chapters within a shaped `Recordset`. However, currently this constant has no affect. To refresh chapters of a shaped `Recordset`, you must call the `Resync` method on each chapter.

ResyncValues Parameter

The `ResyncValues` optional parameter specifies which values are refreshed with data from the data source. This parameter will default to a value of `adResyncAllValues` which, appropriately, causes all the values for each field to be refreshed. If a field's value has been changed in the recordset and the change has not been applied to the data source, the change will be overwritten with the current value from the data source. To preserve any local updates, you should use the `adResyncUnderlyingValues` constant for the `ResyncValues` parameter. This setting will cause the Synchronization Service to *only* replace the underlying value and not affect either of the other two values. As a result, pending changes are not affected. Additionally, this option is very useful when resolving conflicts that occur as a result of an `UpdateBatch` method call. After invoking the `Resync` method with a value of `adResyncUnderlyingValue` for the `ResyncValues` parameter, you can simply compare a field's underlying value against its original value to know whether or not a record has been updated in the data source. We'll discuss more about resolving conflicts with batch updating later in this chapter.

> Although the `Resync` method would be useful for read-only recordsets, it can only be called on recordsets that were opened with a `LockType` of `adLockBatchOptimistic` (or `adLockOptimistic`). The reason is that the Cursor Service does not obtain the metadata attributes required to construct SQL queries when a recordset is opened in read-only mode.

Performing Batch Updates

Where the `Resync` method refreshes a recordset with the current values from the data source, the recordset object's `UpdateBatch` method is used to apply any pending changes in the recordset to the data source. These pending changes, also referred to as **local changes**, include any records inserted, updated or deleted within the recordset that have not yet been applied to the data source. The `UpdateBatch` method is defined as follows:

```
UpdateBatch([AffectRecords As AffectEnum = adAffectAll])
```

The syntax looks simple enough, doesn't it? Before we dive into all the details of the UpdateBatch method, let's take a quick look at the method in action. In the following example, we'll first acquire a disconnected recordset containing all of the records from the authors table in the pubs SQL Server database by calling our GetAuthorsRs method. Next, we'll insert, update and delete records in this disconnected recordset by simply calling the Recordset object's AddNew, Update and Delete methods as normal. Finally, we'll reconnect our disconnected recordset and call UpdateBatch method to apply these pending changes in the recordset to the data source:

```
Private Sub ManipulateDataAndApplyChanges()
   Dim rsAuthors As ADODB.Recordset

   'get a disconnected recordset containing all of the Author records
   Set rsAuthors = GetAuthorsRs()

   With rsAuthors

      'find and update the record for the Author with
      '...as Last Name (au_lname) of 'Greene'
      .Find "au_lname = #Greene#", SearchDirection:=adSearchForward, _
                           Start:=adBookmarkFirst

      If .EOF = False Then
         'the record was found, update it
         .Update Fields:="contract", Values:=True
      End If

      'find and delete the record for the Author with
      '...as Last Name (au_lname) of 'Smith'
      .Find "au_lname = #Smith#", SearchDirection:=adSearchForward, _
                           Start:=adBookmarkFirst

      If .EOF = False Then
         'the record was found, update it
         .Delete AffectRecords:=adAffectCurrent
      End If

      'add a new record into our disconnected Recordset
      .AddNew FieldList:=Array("au_id", "au_lname", "au_fname", "address", _
                        "city", "state", "zip", "contract"), _
            Values:=Array("987-65-4321", "Conard", "James", _
                     "123 Somwhere Dr.", "Tampa", "FL", "33610", True)

      'After these local changes, our disconnected recordset
      '...is now out of sync with the data source

      'First reconnect the disconnected recordset...
      .ActiveConnection = "Provider=SQLOLEDB;Initial Catalog=Pubs;" & _
                     "Data Source=jconard;User ID=sa;Password=;"

      'Now apply the changes to the data source
      '...if a conflict occurs and error will be raised here.
      .UpdateBatch
   End With
```

```
      'close and release our disconnected recordset
    rsAuthors.Close
    Set rsAuthors = Nothing
  End Sub
```

Not only is the syntax for the `UpdateBatch` method simple, but as you can see in this example, utilizing it to apply pending changes in a recordset to the data source is also easy. Just like with the `Resync` method, the Synchronization Service encapsulates all of the complex details of resynchronization when the `UpdateBatch` method is called. However, the role of the Synchronization Service is inherently more complex when the `UpdateBatch` method is invoked. This is partially due to the fact that the `UpdateBatch` method can result in one of three different types of SQL statements (`UPDATE`, `INSERT` and `DELETE`) being created for each record affected, instead of simply a single `SELECT` statement being created for all records, as is the case with the `Resync` method. Additionally, the Synchronization Service must deal with complex multi-user concurrency scenarios when updating existing data.

When the `UpdateBatch` method is called, behind the scenes the Synchronization Service performs the following three operations:

❑ Builds the necessary SQL statements

❑ Executes the SQL statements

❑ Refreshes the affected record(s) in the recordset

Builds the Necessary SQL Statements

First the Synchronization Services determines which rows have been inserted, updated or deleted in the recordset but not yet applied to the data source and builds the appropriate SQL statement for *each* of the these records. The Cursor Service maintains a status value for each record. This status value, which is exposed through the `Recordset` object's read-only `Status` property, is used by the Synchronization Service to determine pending changes. Initially, before any data is manipulated each record's status is appropriately set to `adRecUnmodified`. Deleted records will have a status of `adRecDeleted`, updated records will have a status of `adRecModified` and inserted records will have a status of `adRecNew`.

For updated records, the Synchronization Service constructs an SQL `UPDATE` statement that consists of three parts: the new values, the row identity and the concurrency checks. The new values section is simply a list of each column that has been modified and the new value for that column. The row identity is used to ensure that the `UPDATE` statement only affects a single row. The concurrency checks consist of conditions used to ensure that the single record being updated has not been modified since it was last read. We'll discuss more about concurrency checking and conflicts later in this section.

`INSERT` and `DELETE` statements constructed by the Synchronization Service are much simpler. Since `INSERT` statements don't have to worry about row identity or concurrency, they only consist of a list of columns and new values. `DELETE` statements, on the other hand, only consist of a row identity to ensure that exactly one record is deleted.

In the case of our previous example, the Synchronization Service will construct the following three SQL statements:

```
DELETE FROM "Pubs".."Authors"
   WHERE "au_id"=?

UPDATE "Pubs".."Authors"
   SET "contract"=?
   WHERE "au_id"=? AND "contract"=?

INSERT INTO "Pubs".."Authors" ("au_id","au_lname","au_fname",
   "phone","address","city","state","zip","contract")
VALUES (?,?,?,?,?,?,?,?,?)
```

Executes the SQL Statements

Next, the Synchronization Service groups the SQL Statements together into batch(es) and submits each batch to the data provider for execution. A batch can contain any combination of semi-colon separated UPDATE, INSERT and DELETE statements that affect the same base table. If multiple base tables are being manipulated then there will be at least one batch for each base table. With our previous UpdateBatch code example, the Synchronization Service combines all three of the SQL statements into a single batch because the statements are all affecting the Authors table:

```
DELETE FROM "Pubs".."Authors" WHERE "au_id"=?;
UPDATE "Pubs".."Authors" SET "contract"=? WHERE "au_id"=? AND "contract"=?;
INSERT INTO "Pubs".."Authors" ("au_id","au_lname","au_fname","phone","address",
   "city","state","zip","contract")
VALUES (?,?,?,?,?,?,?,?,?)
```

By default 15 SQL statements will be concatenated together and executed as a single batch. However, this number is adjustable through the Recordset object's dynamic Batch Size property. Some data sources do not support multiple statements or require a special syntax for separating statements. In these situations you should change the Batch Size property to 1 prior to calling the UpdateBatch method to ensure that there is only one statement per batch. We'll utilize this property later in this chapter.

The Synchronization Service executes UPDATE, INSERT and DELETE statements in batches instead of individually in an attempt to minimize the number of network roundtrips. This simple technique can provide a significant performance advantage especially over large networks such as an intranet or the Internet. However, the performance advantages of batches depend on the type of network and the data provider being used, another reason for having an adjustable batch size.

Refreshes the Affected Record(s) in the Recordset

Finally, if the execution of a batch was successful, by default the Synchronization Service will automatically refresh the values for the affected records with the values from the data source. Why is refreshing the rowset with values from the data source necessary? Many data sources provide default values, auto-incrementing values or rules/constraints that affect data being inserted or updated. Additionally, most database systems provide a timestamp value for each record that is used by the Synchronization Service for managing concurrency. By refreshing affected records in the recordset after apply changes, the Synchronization Service ensures that the rowset managed by the Cursor Service is in synchronization with the data source at the point in time when the UpdateBatch method is called. By default the Synchronization Service will only refresh autoincrement columns for inserted records. However, this behavior can be controlled and disabled through the Recordset object's dynamic Update Resync property. We'll discuss more about the dynamic Update Resync property later in this section.

The Synchronization Service will also reset the status for the all records affected by the `UpdateBatch` method. Inserted and updated records will be reset to `adRecUnmodifed`. Deleted records will be changed to `adRecDBDeleted` and removed from the recordset. However, if any error(s) should occur while executing the batch, the Synchronization Service will preserve the pending record(s) status so that the error(s) can be resolved and the `UpdateBatch` method can be called again to reapply the remaining, pending changes to the data source. Failure can occur for a variety of reasons including: network connectivity errors, metadata changes, concurrency conflicts, and constraint violations. The challenge with utilizing the `UpdateBatch` method is not calling the method itself, but to handle these errors gracefully.

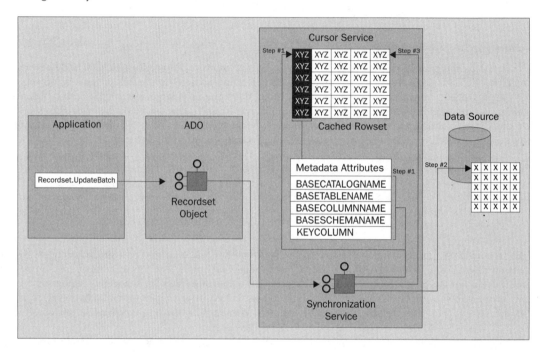

Optimistic Batch Updating

When a recordset is opened with a `LockType` of `adLockBatchOptimistic`, the Cursor Service does not hold any locks on the underlying data except during the initial read and subsequent `UpdateBatch` or `Resync` method calls. This results in higher scalability and performance and allows recordsets to be disconnected from the data provider and data source. However, since no locks are held, users can concurrently change the same data. To deal with these multi-user concurrency issues, the Synchronization Service includes concurrency checks within the `WHERE` clause of an `UPDATE` statement to ensure that a record has not been changed since it was last read. These concurrency checks compare a field's `UnderlyingValue` in the `Recordset` against its current values in the data source. If the record has changed since the Cursor Service last read it, then the `UPDATE` statement will not affect any records and the record will be marked as conflicting. In the `UPDATE` statement constructed by the Synchronization Service when our previous example is executed, the concurrency checks consist of the `'Contract'=?` section in the `WHERE` clause:

```
UPDATE "Pubs".."Authors" SET "contract"=? WHERE "au_id"=? AND "contract"=?;
```

As you can see in this example, in addition to the KeyColumn(s) which are used to uniquely identify a row, the Synchronization Service will compare each column that is being updated against its last read value.

Since this default concurrency checking behavior is not adequate for all situations, it can be customized through the Recordset object's dynamic Update Criteria property. Using this property you can tell the Synchronization Service to perform concurrency checking by comparing only key columns, only row timestamps, or the entire row instead of comparing the changed columns.

When an UPDATE statement issued by the Synchronization Service does not affect any records, a conflict has occurred. Conflicts, also referred to as **collisions**, can occur for one of two reasons:

❑ The record being updated has been deleted from the data source

❑ The record being updated has been modified in the data source

For example, in the following code we'll define two methods named UpdateTitleRecord and CreateConflict. The UpdateTitleRecord method will acquire a disconnected recordset containing all of the records from the titles table, update a record in the disconnected recordset and finally reconnect to the data source and apply the pending change by calling the UpdateBatch method. The CreateConflict method will be called by the UpdateTitleRecord method to create a conflict in the titles table. This method is only provided to demonstrate how conflicts occur and how to resolve them. Let's define the UpdateTitleRecord method first:

```
Private Sub UpdateTitleRecord()
    On Error GoTo ErrorHandler

    Dim rsTitles As ADODB.Recordset

    'create a new instance of an ADODB.Recordset
    Set rsTitles = New ADODB.Recordset

    With rsTitles
        'use the Microsoft OLE DB Cursor Service
        .CursorLocation = adUseClient

        'retrieve all of the records from the Titles table
        '...from the Pubs SQL Server database
        .Open Source:="SELECT * FROM Titles", _
              ActiveConnection:="Provider=SQLOLEDB;Initial Catalog=Pubs; " & _
                                "Data Source=jconard;User ID=sa;Password=;", _
              CursorType:=adOpenStatic, LockType:=adLockBatchOptimistic

        'disconnect from the Data Provider and data source
        Set .ActiveConnection = Nothing

        'find and update the record for the Title with
        '...title_id of 'PC9999'
        .Find "title_id = #PC9999#", _
              SearchDirection:=adSearchForward, _
              Start:=adBookmarkFirst
```

```
        If .EOF = False Then
            'the record was found, update it
            .Update Fields:=Array("title", "pubdate"), _
                    Values:=Array("Net Etiquette for 2000", "2/1/00")
        End If

        If .EOF = False Then
            'the record was found, update it
            .Update Fields:=Array("title", "pubdate"), _
                    Values:=Array("Professional ADO 2.51", "2/1/00")
        End If

        'After these local changes, our disconnected recordset
        '...is now out of sync with the data source

        'First reconnect the disconnected recordset...
        .ActiveConnection = "Provider=SQLOLEDB;Initial Catalog=Pubs;" & _
                    "Data Source=jconard;User ID=sa;Password=;"


        'before we apply the changes, create a conflict in the data source
        '...NOTE: this is only done for demonstration.
        CreateTitleConflict

        'Now apply the changes to the data source...
        .UpdateBatch
    End With

    'close and release our disconnected recordset
    rsTitles.Close
    Set rsTitles = Nothing

ExitProcedure:
    'exit this procedure
    Exit Sub

ErrorHandler:
    MsgBox "The following error occured: " & vbCrLf & _
            "Description: " & Err.Description & vbCrLf & _
            "Number: " & Err.Number
End Sub
```

Now let's define the `CreateTitleConflict` method that simply creates a conflict by updating the same title record in the data source:

```
Private Sub CreateTitleConflict()
    Dim conDataSource As ADODB.Connection

    'create a new instance of an ADODB.Connection
    Set conDataSource = New ADODB.Connection
```

```
        'establish a connection to the data source
        conDataSource.Open "Provider=SQLOLEDB;Initial Catalog=Pubs; " & _
                          "Data Source=jconard;User ID=sa;Password=;"

        'create a conflict by Updating the pubdate for the title record
        '...with the title_id of 'PC9999'
        conDataSource.Execute _
                "UPDATE Titles SET pubdate = '2/15/99' WHERE title_id = 'PC9999'"

        'close and release our ADO Connection
        conDataSource.Close
        Set conDataSource = Nothing
End Sub
```

> Since the values are hard-coded in the `CreateTitleRecord` method, a conflict will only be raised the first time this method is executed. If you want to test this conflict resolution example multiple times, you must either adjust the title records back to their original values after each execution or change the `CreateTitleRecord` method appropriately to generate a conflict.

When the `UpdateBatch` method is called and a conflict occurs, the Synchronization Service will raise the run-time error 'Row cannot be located for updating. Some values may have been changed since it was last read'. This generic error message can be misleading because it is also raised when a conflict occurs because a record has been deleted in the data source.

Unfortunately, conflicts cannot be resolved automatically by the Synchronization Service. Instead, we must implement code to resolve conflicts when they do occur. While it is possible to perform conflict resolution without any user intervention, most of the time the user must decide whether they want to overwrite the other user's changes or cancel their own changes. Implementing conflict resolution can be broken down into a three-step process:

1. Determine which records conflicted. Conflicting records are assigned a status of `adRecConcurrencyViolation`. While we could scroll through the entire recordset looking for records with this status, there is an even easier way. We can simply filter the `Recordset` to include only conflicting records by setting the `Recordset` object's `Filter` property to `adFilterConflictingRecords`.

2. **Refresh the conflicting record's underlying value.** Next, we must refresh the conflicting record's underlying values with the current values from the data source. This can be accomplished with the `Recordset` object's `Resync` method by specifying a value of `adResyncUnderlyingValues` for the `ResyncValues` parameter. If this value is not specified, the `Resync` method will refresh all of the values for the record(s), thus erasing any pending changes. In the situation where the conflict occurred because the record has been deleted from the data source, the Synchronization Service will raise an error and remove the record from the recordset. As we discussed earlier, this is the normal behavior of the Synchronization Service when the `Resync` method is called.

3. **Overwrite the existing data or cancel the pending changes.** Finally, we have to decide whether to overwrite the existing data in the data source with our own changes or cancel our own pending changes in the recordset. Usually a default cannot be assumed so this decision requires user intervention. Overwriting the existing data can be accomplished simply by calling the `UpdateBatch` method again. The Synchronization Service always behaves the same way when the `UpdateBatch` method is called, but this time (hopefully) the record's underlying values are in synchronization with the data source because they were just refreshed by calling the `Resync` method. Remember, the record's underlying values are used by the Synchronization Service in the `WHERE` clause of the `UPDATE` statement to ensure that the record has not been changed since it was last read. If we decide to cancel our own pending changes we can do so by either calling the `Recordset` object's `CancelBatch` method which will replace each field's value with its underlying value, or by calling the `Resync` method again specifying a value of `adResyncAllValues` for the `ResyncValues` parameter

Let's implement conflict resolution in our `UpdateTitleRecord` method that we just created. First modify the error handler to trap the conflict error and call a method named `ConflictResoution` passing it the recordset containing the conflict records:

```
ErrorHandler:
    'an error occured, check the Error number and handle it appropriately
    If Err.Number = -2147217864 Then
        'a conflict occured, let's call our general conflict resolution procedure
        '...passing it our Recordset
        ConflictResolution rsTitles

    Else
        'some other error occured
        MsgBox "The following error occured: " & vbCrLf & "Description: " & _
              Err.Description & vbCrLf & "Number: " & Err.Number
    End If
```

The `ConflictResolution` method is a generic implementation of the conflict resolution steps we just discussed. After filtering and refreshing the underlying values for the conflicting records (steps 1 and 2), this method displays a simple message box that tells the user about the problem and asks whether or not to overwrite the other user's changes. If the user answers **Yes**, then the `UpdateBatch` method is called again to apply the pending changes. If the user answers **No**, then the `Resync` method is called to refresh all of the values for the pending records with the current values from the data source.

```
Private Sub ConflictResolution(ByRef rs As ADODB.Recordset)
    On Error GoTo ErrorHandler
```

```
      Dim lMsgBox As Long

      With rs
          'Step #1 - Determine which Records conflicted
          .Filter = adFilterConflictingRecords

          'Step #2 - Refresh the conflicting records underlying value
          .Resync AffectRecords:=adAffectGroup, ResyncValues:=adResyncUnderlyingValues

          'Step #3 - Overwrite the existing data or cancel the pending changes
          lMsgBox = MsgBox("The update you performed has conflicted with an " & _
                        "update performed by another user." & vbCrLf & _
                        "Do you wish to overwrite their changes?", _
                        vbQuestion Or vbYesNo Or vbDefaultButton2)

          If lMsgBox = vbYes Then
              'the user wishes to overwrite the existing data,
              '...call the UpdateBatch method again
              .UpdateBatch AffectRecords:=adAffectGroup

          ElseIf lMsgBox = vbNo Then
              'the user wishes to preserve the existing data,
              '...and cancel their own changes
              '.CancelBatch AffectRecords:=adAffectGroup
              .Resync AffectRecords:=adAffectGroup, ResyncValues:=adResyncAllValues
          End If
      End With


  ExitProcedure:
      'exit this procedure
      Exit Sub

  ErrorHandler:
      'an error occured, check the Error number and handle it appropriately
      If Err.Number = -2147217885 Then
          'a record has been removed from the recordset that was
          '...deleted in the data source.
          MsgBox "The record(s) you updated have been deleted from the data source."
      Else
          'some other error occured
          MsgBox "The following error occured: " & vbCrLf & "Description: " & _
                Err.Description & vbCrLf & "Number: " & Err.Number
      End If
  End Sub
```

This is a very simple example of resolving conflicts. In most situations, you should present the user with their changes and the current data from the data source, so they can intelligently decide what to do in this situation. SQL Server Enterprise Manager, for example, presents users with a more friendly dialog window:

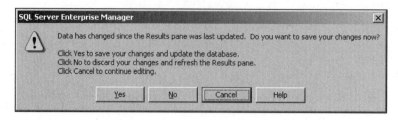

We are also assuming in our `ConflictResolution` example that the record's values have not been modified from the time we called the `Resync` method in step 2 to the time we call the `UpdateBatch` method in step 3. If the record's values had changed in this short amount of time, then the `UpdateBatch` method would again fail because the record's underlying values in the recordset would again be out of sync with values from the data source.

Customizing Updating Using the Dynamic Properties

The default behavior of the Synchronization Service is adequate for most situations. However, what happens when you need the Synchronization Service to behave differently when applying pending changes in a recordset to the data source? Do you have to abandon the `UpdateBatch` method and resort to manually applying local changes to the data source? Thankfully, the answer is no. The Synchronization Service's behavior can be customized through the `Recordset` object's dynamic properties. Three of the dynamic properties that warrant a discussion here are:

❑   `Batch Size`

❑   `Update Resync`

❑   `Update Criteria`

Batch Size Dynamic Property

The `Batch Size` dynamic property can be used to change the number of SQL statements that are included in a single batch. The default batch size is 15. For example, the following line of code can be added to our `ManipulateDataAndApplyChanges` method that we created earlier to force the Synchronization Service to execute each SQL statement in a separate batch:

```
'tell the Synchronization service to submit one statement at a time
rsAuthors.Properties("Batch Size").Value = 1
```

While this is a valid scenario for using the `Batch Size` property, especially with data providers or data sources that do not support batches, typically you'll want to go in the other direction with the `Batch Size` property and submit several statements at one time. However, you should not change the `Batch Size` property to a large value (above 50) without adequate memory and proper testing with your network topology.

Update Resync

The Update Resync dynamic property can be used to control what values, if any, in the recordset are refreshed for records affected by an UpdateBatch method call. This property can be set to any of the following values defined by the ADCPROP_UPDATERESYNC_ENUM enumeration:

❏ adResyncNone. The adResyncNone constant specifies that no values should be refreshed when the UpdateBatch method is called. This setting is generally not recommended when records are being updated or inserted in the data source because the recordset will not have the current values after the update or insert and therefore a subsequent call to the UpdateBatch method for the same records will result in conflicts.

❏ adResyncAutoIncrement. The adResyncAutoIncrement constant specifies that auto-incrementing columns such as autonumber and identity columns for inserted records should be refreshed when the UpdateBatch method is called. This setting is the default for the Update Resync property.

❏ adResyncConflicts. The adResyncConflicts constant specifies that the underlying values for conflicting records should be refreshed when the UpdateBatch method is called. This setting effectively eliminates the need to refresh conflicting records' underlying values (via the Resync method) when performing conflict resolution because the Synchronization Service will do so automatically only when a conflict occurs.

❏ adResynchUpdates. The adResyncUpdates constant specifies that all of the values should be refreshed for updated records when the UpdateBatch method is called. When performing updates, the Update Resync property should always include this setting to ensure that subsequent updates can be performed on the same data.

❏ adResyncInserts. The adResyncInserts constant specifies that all of the values for newly inserted records should be refreshed when the UpdateBatch method is called. You should use this setting when you want the recordset to include default values added by the data source when a record is inserted.

❏ adResyncAll. The adResyncAll constant specifies that *all* of the values should be refreshed for all inserted and updated records when the UpdateBatch method is called. This setting will also cause the Synchronization Service to refresh the underlying values for conflicting records.

It's important to understand that these settings are not mutually exclusive. The adRsyncAutoIncrement, adResyncUpdates, adResyncInserts, and adResyncConflicts values can be used in various combinations simultaneously. The adResyncAll would produce the same affect as setting the Update Resync property to all four of these settings.

Let's take a look at an example of using the Update Resync property. In the following code, we'll revise the ManipulateDataAndApplyChanges method that we created earlier in this section so that all of the values for inserted or updated records are refreshed. So it's easier to watch the SQL statements in Visual Studio Analyzer as they're submitted to the SQLOLEDB Provider, we'll also specify a Batch Size of 1. For the sake of space, I've omitted the error handling and conflict resolution code:

```
Private Sub ManipulateDataAndApplyChanges()
    Dim rsAuthors As ADODB.Recordset
```

```
'get a disconnected recordset containing all of the Author records
Set rsAuthors = GetAuthorsRs()

With rsAuthors
    'find and update the record for the Author with
    '...as Last Name (au_lname) of 'Greene'
    .Find "au_lname = #Greene#", SearchDirection:=adSearchForward, _
                            Start:=adBookmarkFirst

    If .EOF = False Then
        'the record was found, update it
        .Update Fields:="contract", Values:=True
    End If

    'find and delete the record for the Author with
    '...as Last Name (au_lname) of 'Smith'
    .Find "au_lname = #Smith#", SearchDirection:=adSearchForward, _
                            Start:=adBookmarkFirst

    If .EOF = False Then
        'the record was found, update it
        .Delete AffectRecords:=adAffectCurrent
    End If

    'add a new record into our disconnected Recordset
    .AddNew Fieldlist:=Array("au_id", "au_lname", "au_fname", _
                        "address", "city", "state", "zip", "contract"), _
                    Values:=Array("987-65-4321", "Conard", "James", _
                                "123 Somwhere Dr.", "Tampa", "FL", _
                                "33610", True)

    'After these local changes, our disconnected recordset
    '...is now out of sync with the data source

    'First reconnect the disconnected recordset...
    .ActiveConnection = "Provider=SQLOLEDB;Initial Catalog=Pubs;" & _
                        "Data Source=jconard;User ID=sa;Password=;"

    'tell the Synchronization service to submit one statement at a time
    '...so it's easier to watch the behavior of the Synchronization Service
    '...from Visual Studio Analyzer
    .Properties("Batch Size").Value = 1

    .Properties("Update Resync").Value = adResyncInserts Or adResyncUpdates

    'Now apply the changes to the data source...
    .UpdateBatch

End With

'close and release our disconnected recordset
rsAuthors.Close
Set rsAuthors = Nothing
End Sub
```

By using Visual Studio Analyzer, we can see that the Synchronization Service submits five batches when the `UpdateBatch` method is called in our previous example. Two of these batches consist of SELECT statements that refresh a record's values after an UPDATE or INSERT statement because the Update Resync dynamic property was set to `adResyncInserts` and `adResyncUpdates` before the `UpdateBatch` method was called:

```
DELETE FROM "Pubs".."Authors"
    WHERE "au_id"=?

UPDATE "Pubs".."Authors" SET "contract"=@P1 WHERE "au_id"=? AND "contract"=?

SELECT "au_id","au_lname","au_fname","phone","address","city",
       "state","zip","contract","id","stamp" FROM "Pubs".."Authors"
    WHERE "au_id"=?

INSERT INTO "Pubs".."Authors"
    ("au_id","au_lname","au_fname","address","city","state","zip",
     "contract")
VALUES (?,?,?,?,?,?,?,?)

SELECT "au_id","au_lname","au_fname","phone","address","city",
       "state","zip","contract","id","stamp" FROM "Pubs".."Authors"
    WHERE "au_id"=?
```

Update Criteria

The `Update Criteria` dynamic property can be used to control how much concurrency checking is included in the WHERE clause of an UPDATE statement issued by the Synchronization Service. This property can be set to one of the following four values defined by the `ADCPROP_UPDATECRITERIA_ENUM` enumeration:

❑ `adCriteriaKey`. The `adCriteriaKey` constant specifies that only the `KeyColumns` should be used to detect conflicts. This setting effectively tells the Synchronization Service not to include any concurrency checking in the WHERE clause because the `KeyColumns` compose the row identity which is required in every UPDATE and DELETE statement to ensure that exactly one record will be affected.

❑ `adCriteriaAllCols`. The `adCriteriaAllCols` constant specifies that conflicts should be detected by comparing the underlying values for the recordsets' fields against the current values for all columns in the data source.

❑ `adCriteriaUpdCols`. The `adCriteriaUpdCols` constant specifies that the recordset's underlying value should be compared against the data source's current value for only the columns being updated. This is the default setting for the `Update Criteria` property.

❑ `adCriteriaTimeStamp`. The `adCriteriaTimeStamp` constant specifies that the recordset's timestamp should be compared against the data source's timestamp to detect conflicts. If this setting is specified and the data source does not have a timestamp column then the Synchronization Service behaves as if the `adCriteriaCols` setting were specified.

Batch Updating with Multi-table Recordsets

When the `UpdateBatch` method is called on a `Recordset` which contains data derived from multiple base tables, the behavior of the Synchronization Service will vary depending on several factors including: the columns affected, the values of certain dynamic properties and the operation being carried out (`UPDATE`, `INSERT` or `DELETE`). Before we discuss each of these different factors and their effects on the Synchronization Service, let's look at our simple scenario of the `publishers` and `titles` tables again.

As we discussed earlier, there is a one-to-many relationship between the `publishers` and `titles` tables in the SQL Server database. Each record in the `publishers` table has a relationship to one or more records in the `titles` table. This relationship is illustrated in the following diagram. Note that some of the columns from these tables have been omitted for this example.

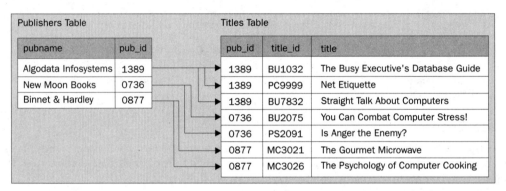

The following code retrieves a disconnected recordset containing the joined data from these two tables, which is referred to as a **multi-table recordset**, and then later reconnects the recordset and calls the `UpdateBatch` method to apply any pending changes. We'll modify this code example throughout this section as we examine the behavior of the Synchronization Service in various scenarios when manipulating data in a multi-table recordset.

```
Private Sub ManipulateMultiTableRSAndApplyChanges()
    Dim rsPublishersAndTitles As ADODB.Recordset
    Dim sSource As String

    'create a new instance of an ADODB.Recordset
    Set rsPublishersAndTitles = New ADODB.Recordset

    'build the SQL SELECT statement to retrieve
    '...a joined Recordset containing the Publishers
    '...and their corresponding titles
    sSource = "SELECT publishers.pub_id, publishers.pub_name, " & _
            "titles.title_id, titles.pubdate, titles.title " & _
            "FROM publishers INNER JOIN titles " & _
            "ON publishers.pub_id = titles.pub_id"

    With rsPublishersAndTitles
```

```
                      'use the Microsoft OLE DB Cursor Service
                      .CursorLocation = adUseClient

                      'execute our SELECT statement againist the Pubs SQL Server database
                      .Open Source:=sSource, _
                            ActiveConnection:="Provider=SQLOLEDB;Initial Catalog=Pubs; " & _
                                              "Data Source=jconard;User ID=sa;Password=;", _
                            CursorType:=adOpenStatic, LockType:=adLockBatchOptimistic

                      'disconnect from the Data Provider and data source
                      Set .ActiveConnection = Nothing

                      'reconnect the disconnected recordset...
                      .ActiveConnection = "Provider=SQLOLEDB;Initial Catalog=Pubs;" & _
                                          "Data Source=jconard;User ID=sa;Password=;"

                      'Now apply the changes to the data source...
                      .UpdateBatch
                  End With

                  'close and release our disconnected recordset
                  rsPublishersAndTitles.Close
                  Set rsPublishersAndTitles = Nothing
              End Sub
```

Inserting or Updating Records into a Multi-Table Recordset

When a record is inserted or updated in a recordset that was populated as a result of a join operation and only a single base table's columns are affected, the Synchronization Service will construct and execute a *single* SQL statement to carry out the operation. For example, the following AddNew method call only affects the columns from the titles table in our multi-table recordset:

```
.AddNew Fieldlist:=Array("title_id", "title", "pubdate"), _
        Values:=Array("PROADO", "Professional ADO 2.5", "1/1/2000")

'reconnect the disconnected recordset...
.ActiveConnection = "Provider=SQLOLEDB;Initial Catalog=Pubs;" & _
                    "Data Source=jconard;User ID=sa;Password=;"

'Now apply the changes to the data source...
.UpdateBatch
```

When the UpdateBatch method is called to apply this pending change, the Synchronization Service will only construct and execute a single INSERT statement because only the titles table was affected by the AddNew method call:

```
INSERT INTO "Pubs".."titles" ("title_id","pubdate","title") VALUES (?,?,?)
```

As you can see, in this situation the behavior of the Synchronization Service is straightforward. However, if more than one base table is affected by an AddNew or Update method call then the Synchronization Service will construct and execute an SQL Statement for each base table. For example, the following call to the AddNew method affects columns in both the titles and publishers tables:

```
'add a new record into our disconnected Recordset
.AddNew FieldList:=Array("title_id", "title", "pubdate", "pub_id", "pub_name"), _
        Values:=Array("PROMTS", "Professional VB6 MTS", "6/1/1999", "9912", _
                    "Wrox Press, Ltd.")

'reconnect the disconnected recordset...
.ActiveConnection = "Provider=SQLOLEDB;Initial Catalog=Pubs;" & _
                    "Data Source=jconard;User ID=sa;Password=;"

'.Properties("Unique Table").Value = "publishers"

'Now apply the changes to the data source...
.UpdateBatch
```

Because the columns that are affected by this AddNew method call originate from two different base tables, when the UpdateBatch method is called the Synchronization Service constructs two separate SQL INSERT statements. These INSERT statements will be executed in separate batches because the Synchronization Service groups statements together by the base table the statement will affect:

```
INSERT INTO "Pubs".."titles" ("title_id","pubdate","title") VALUES (?,?,?)

INSERT INTO "Pubs".."publishers" ("pub_id","pub_name") VALUES (?,?)
```

Based on this behavior of the Synchronization Service we can draw two conclusions about inserting or updating records in a recordset derived from a join operation:

❑ **If you want to insert or update a record in one base table, simply assign values to columns only from the table you want to manipulate.** For example, if we only want to add a new record to the titles table in our previous example, then add a new record to the joined recordset, but only assign values to the columns from the titles table.

❑ **If you want your insert or update operation to affect multiple tables, simply assign values to columns from the appropriate base tables.** It's worthwhile noting that when inserting records into a recordset derived from a join, you must ensure that all required fields are supplied with a value. Otherwise one of the SQL INSERT statements could succeed and another could fail. This requirement does not apply when updating records because an SQL UPDATE statement only affects the columns that were modified, unless of course you are explictly setting a required field to null.

Unless you take measures to control the behavior of the Synchronization Service, there are two significant problems that can occur when columns from multiple base tables are affected by an Update or AddNew method call. These two problems are:

❑ The relationship between the tables is not established because the joined column is only affected in one base table.

❑ The order of INSERT statements violates the relationship between the affected tables.

> Generally, you do not have to worry about these problems when updating a record in a multi-table recordset, unless you wish to update the joining column, in which case these problems might become relevant. However, with most normalized databases it is not very likely that you would want to change the joining column's value in this manner.

Relationships Not Established

In our previous example, when the AddNew method and values are supplied for both the titles and publishers tables, you might have noticed that the Synchronization Service only inserted a value for the pub_id column in the publishers table, even though this column was used in the JOIN operation that populated the recordset. Here was the code again that called the AddNew method:

```
'add a new record into our disconnected Recordset
.AddNew FieldList:=Array("title_id", "title", "pubdate", "pub_id", "pub_name"), _
        Values:=Array("PROMTS", "Professional VB6 MTS", "6/1/1999", "9912", _
                "Wrox Press, Ltd.")
```

When the UpdateBatch method is called, take a second look at the SQL statements created and executed by the Synchronization Service. Notice that the pub_id column is only listed in the INSERT statement for the publishers table and not in the INSERT statement for the titles table:

```
INSERT INTO "Pubs".."titles" ("title_id","pubdate","title") VALUES (?,?,?)

INSERT INTO "Pubs".."publishers" ("pub_id","pub_name") VALUES (?,?)
```

As you can see, the Synchronization Service does not automatically establish relationships between joined tables when inserting records. Instead you must perform the following two tasks to *manually* establish the relationships between the inserted records:

❑   Return the joining columns in the SELECT list. If the joining columns have the same name, you should use an alias for the columns. Otherwise you will be unable to address the columns in the recordset's Fields collection by name.

❑   Provide the same value for the joining columns. If the joining columns are not assigned the same value then the inserted records will not have a relationship between each other. In the typical situation where the relationship between base tables is implemented through the use of Primary Key and Foreign Key constraints, the insert will fail if the joining columns are not assigned a value.

The following code revises the ManipulateMultiTableRSAndApplyChanges method that we created earlier to satisfy these two requirements. Notice that the pub_id column from the publishers table is returned with the alias Publishers_PubID and the pub_id column from the titles table is returned with the alias Titles_PubID:

```vb
Private Sub ManipulateMultiTableRSAndApplyChanges()
    Dim rsPublishersAndTitles As ADODB.Recordset
    Dim sSource As String

    'create a new instance of an ADODB.Recordset
    Set rsPublishersAndTitles = New ADODB.Recordset

    'build the SQL SELECT statement to retrieve
    '...a joined Recordset containing the Publishers
    '...and their corresponding titles
    sSource = "SELECT publishers.pub_id AS Publishers_PubID, " & _
            "publishers.pub_name, titles.title_id, titles.pubdate, " & _
            "titles.title, titles.pub_id AS Titles_PubID " & _
            "FROM publishers INNER JOIN titles " & _
            "ON publishers.pub_id = titles.pub_id"

    With rsPublishersAndTitles

        'use the Microsoft OLE DB Cursor Service
        .CursorLocation = adUseClient

        'execute our SELECT statement against the Pubs SQL Server database
        .Open Source:=sSource, _
            ActiveConnection:="Provider=SQLOLEDB;Initial Catalog=Pubs; " & _
                            "Data Source=jconard;User ID=sa;Password=;", _
            CursorType:=adOpenStatic, LockType:=adLockBatchOptimistic

        'disconnect from the Data Provider and data source
        Set .ActiveConnection = Nothing

        'add a new record into our disconnected Recordset
        .AddNew Fieldlist:=Array("title_id", "title", "pubdate", _
                            "Titles_PubID", "Publishers_PubID", "pub_name"), _
                Values:=Array("PROADO", "Professional ADO 2.5", "1/1/2000", _
                            "9911", "9911", "Wrox Press, Ltd.")

        'reconnect the disconnected recordset...
        .ActiveConnection = "Provider=SQLOLEDB;Initial Catalog=Pubs;" & _
                            "Data Source=jconard;User ID=sa;Password=;"

        'Now apply the changes to the data source...
        .UpdateBatch
    End With

    'close and release our disconnected recordset
    rsPublishersAndTitles.Close
    Set rsPublishersAndTitles = Nothing
End Sub
```

When the UpdateBatch method is called in this example, the Synchronization Service constructs and executes the following two SQL INSERT statements which both include the pub_id column:

```
INSERT INTO "Pubs".."titles" ("title_id","pubdate","title","pub_id")
    VALUES (?,?,?,?)

INSERT INTO "Pubs".."publishers" ("pub_id","pub_name") VALUES (?,?)
```

However, in this last example the Synchronization Service also raises the following error message when the UpdateBatch method is called:

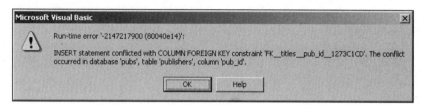

While we've satisfied the requirements to establish the relationship between the publishers and titles tables, this error occurs because of the order the INSERT statements are executed – which brings us to the next problem.

The Order the SQL Statements are Executed Violates the Relationship

The order in which the Synchronization Service executes INSERT and UPDATE statements depends on the order of columns in the initial SELECT statement that populated the recordset. By default, INSERT and UPDATE statements are executed in the reverse order in which the tables' columns appear in the SELECT statement. For example, in our previous code sample the batch that affected the titles table were executed first because the pub_id column from the titles table was last in the SELECT statement:

```
sSource = "SELECT publishers.pub_id AS Publishers_PubID, " & _
          "publishers.pub_name, titles.title_id, titles.pubdate, " & _
          "titles.title, titles.pub_id AS Titles_PubID " & _
          "FROM publishers INNER JOIN titles " & _
          "ON publishers.pub_id = titles.pub_id"
```

As we also saw in the last code sample, the order of SQL statements represents a significant problem when inserting records where a Primary Key and Foreign Key is used to enforce the relationship between base tables. Thankfully, instead of rewriting SQL SELECT statements, we can control the order of execution through a Recordset object's dynamic Unique Table property. In our previous code sample, we can ensure that the INSERT statement against the publishers table executes first by simply assigning the Unique Table dynamic property a value of 'publishers' before calling the UpdateBatch method:

```
'Force Updates and Inserts agaiinst the publishers table to execute first
.Properties("Unique Table").Value = "publishers"

'Now apply the changes to the data source...
.UpdateBatch
```

Deleting Records in a Multi-Table Recordset

When a record is deleted in a recordset that was populated as a result of a join operation, the Synchronization Service behaves quite differently when applying the change to the data source than it does with `INSERT` or `UPDATE` operations. In this situation the Synchronization Service constructs and executes two SQL `DELETE` statements, one for each base table. For example, the following code will find and delete the record with a `title_id` of `'PROADO'` and then reconnect and apply the change to the data source:

```
'find and delete the record with a title_id = 'PROADO'
.Find "title_id = #PROADO#", SearchDirection:=adSearchForward, _
                            Start:=adBookmarkFirst

If .EOF = False Then
    'the record was found, update it
    .Delete AffectRecords:=adAffectCurrent
End If

'reconnect the disconnected recordset...
.ActiveConnection = "Provider=SQLOLEDB;Initial Catalog=Pubs;" & _
                    "Data Source=jconard;User ID=sa;Password=;"

'Now apply the changes to the data source...
.UpdateBatch
```

When the `UpdateBatch` method is called, the Synchronization Service constructs and executes the two following `DELETE` statements:

```
DELETE FROM "Pubs".."titles" WHERE "title_id"=?

DELETE FROM "Pubs".."publishers" WHERE "pub_id"=?
```

In this case we don't run into any constraint violations because the child record from the `titles` table is deleted before the parent record. While you would assume that the `Unique Table` dynamic property could be used to control the order of execution for `DELETE` statements the same way it does for `INSERT` and `UPDATE` statements, this is not the case at all. Instead, when executing `DELETE` statements the `Unique Table` dynamic property tells the Synchronization Service which base table should be affected by the record deletion performed within the recordset. For example, if we set the `Unique Table` property to a value of `'titles'` before calling the `UpdateBatch` method the Synchronization Service will only delete the corresponding record from the `titles` table:

```
'Force Updates and Inserts againist the publishers table to execute first
'.Properties("Unique Table").Value = "publishers"

'or when performing a delete operation, force the delete
'...to only affect the titles table
.Properties("Unique Table").Value = "titles"

'Now apply the changes to the data source...
.UpdateBatch
```

This time when the `UpdateBatch` method is called, the Synchronization Service only constructs and executes one `DELETE` statement for the `titles` table:

```
DELETE FROM "Pubs".."titles" WHERE "title_id"=?
```

While this varying behavior of the Synchronization Service with respect to the `Unique Table` property is a pain to remember, this behavior with respect to deletes is probably appropriate for most situations. In most situations you'll probably only want a single record to be deleted from your child table (`titles`) instead of also deleting the record from the parent table (`publishers`), which most likely has other child records. Nevertheless, it would have been nice if a different dynamic property were supplied for specifying which table's record should be affected by a `DELETE` operation. As it stands, `DELETE` operations and `INSERT` operations cannot be applied at the same time if the values you need to specify in the `Unique Table` property are conflicting, as is the case in the last two examples. Unfortunately, the best approach to take when performing `UPDATE`, `INSERT` and/or `DELETE` operations within a multi-table recordset is to:

1. Carefully specify the column order in the `SELECT` statement that populates the recordset so that the `UPDATE`, `INSERT` and `DELETE` operations are applied to the base tables in the appropriate order.

2. Leverage the `Unique Table` property only for specifying which base table `DELETE` operations should affect.

> **Because of all of these annoying factors involved with manipulating data within a multi-table recordset and applying the changes with the `UpdateBatch` method, I strongly advise avoiding multi-table recordsets when leveraging the OLE DB Cursor and Synchronization Service's batch updating features. Shaped recordsets provide a wonderful alternative to multi-table recordsets and they do not suffer from these problems. We'll discuss more about the benefits and drawbacks of shaped recordsets in Chapter 6.**

Summary

In this chapter we've discovered a number of features that are provided by the OLE DB Cursor Service and are easily accessible through the ADO object model. Specifically, we learned:

- ❑ How to leverage disconnected recordsets, fabricated recordsets and batch processing

- ❑ Common pitfalls to watch out for when utilizing these features

- ❑ What the Cursor Service and/or Synchronization Service do behind the scenes when these features are utilized

- ❑ How to customize the default behavior of these services through a handful of dynamic properties

In the next chapter we're going to build upon our newly acquired knowledge and learn how to save or *persist* an ADO `Recordset` object in various environments.

Recordset Persistence

In the last chapter, we looked at the powerful features provided by the OLE DB Cursor Service: disconnected recordsets, fabricated recordsets and batch processing. In this chapter, we're going to examine the Microsoft OLE DB Persistence Provider and see how it can be used to *persist* or save ADO recordsets to a file. In particular, we will:

❑   Discuss the role of the Persistence Service in respect to other OLE DB Service Providers

❑   Look at the two ways a recordset can be persisted: manually and implicitly

❑   Define the two persistence formats: ADTG and XML

❑   Analyze the usefulness of persisting an ADO recordset to a file.

❑   Use recordset persistence with Active Server Pages to expose data across the Internet or across an intranet

❑   Examine what happens behind the scenes when an ADO recordset is transferred across process or machine boundaries

❑   Analyze the data and metadata that is persisted and learn how to control the behavior of implicit persistence

Without further delay, let's get started!

The OLE DB Persistence Provider

The OLE DB Persistence Provider, also known simply as **MSPersist**, is an OLE DB service provider that also plays a significant role in caching and transferring data within a data-centric application. MSPersist provides the ability to save or **persist** an entire OLE DB rowset including its data, metadata and current state into a data stream. Rowsets can be persisted in either a proprietary binary format called Advanced Data TableGram (ADTG) or in the industry-standard text format known as Extensible Markup Language (XML). Regardless of the format, the possibilities for using this data stream are virtually endless. For example, the data stream can be saved to a file on the local file system, saved to another object, stored in an MSMQ Message, or passed across processes or the network using a variety of different protocols (DCOM, HTTP, etc.). MSPersist can later be used to open the data stream and reconstruct the rowset in its entirety without reconnecting to the data provider and data source from which the rowset's data originated.

As an OLE DB service provider, MSPersist is frequently used in conjunction with other OLE DB service providers such as the Cursor Service, the Data Shaping Provider and the Remoting Provider. For example, MSPersist depends on the Cursor Service to provide data fetching, manipulation and searching capabilities on a rowset constructed from a data stream. As we'll see later in this chapter, the OLE DB Remoting Provider leverages both the Persistence Provider and the Cursor Service to pass OLE DB rowsets across process and machine boundaries using the DCOM or HTTP protocols.

When you consider the integration between these components, the history of rowset persistence is not surprising. Rowset persistence has existed in one form or another since MDAC 1.0. Like the Cursor Service, the Persistence Provider was initially integrated within Advanced Data Connector (ADC) 1.0, which is now known as RDS. In ADC 1.0, rowset persistence was limited to persisting an OLE DB Rowset for transfer across the network and recreating it on the other side. With MDAC 1.5, ADC's Rowset persistence functionality was enhanced to save some Rowset properties in addition to the rowset's data and metadata and it was moved to the OLE DB Cursor Service (MSADC.DLL). As a result, only rowsets created by the Cursor Service could be persisted. Finally with MDAC 2.0, rowset persistence found its permanent home as a separate OLE DB service provider with the filename MSDAPRST.DLL. As a separate service provider, the Persistence Service can persist a rowset created by any OLE DB data provider or service provider to a data stream. The OLE DB Persistence Provider can also be utilized two different ways:

❏   Explicitly by calling a `Recordset` object's `Save` or `Open` methods

❏   Implicitly when a recordset is passed across process boundaries

Now that we have a basic understanding of the Persistence Provider, let's discuss how we can leverage it in our data-centric applications.

Explicitly Persisting a Recordset

The OLE DB Persistence Provider can be invoked directly through an ADO `Recordset` object's `Save` and `Open` methods. These methods are defined as follows:

```
Save([Destination], [PersistFormat As PersistFormatEnum = adPersistADTG])

Open([Source], [ActiveConnection], _
     [CursorType As CursorTypeEnum = adOpenUnspecified], _
     [LockType As LockTypeEnum = adLockUnspecified], _
     [Options As Long = -1])
```

The Save method provides the to ability to persist the recordset as a data stream to file on the local file system or to any object that implements the IStream interface. When the Save method is called on an open ADO Recordset, behind the scenes ADO instantiates the OLE DB Persistence Provider and invokes methods on the new instance through the OLE DB interfaces. The Persistence Provider then saves the recordset's underlying rowset to a data stream and stores the data stream in either the file or object specified in the Save method's Destination parameter. By default, the rowset will be persisted in ADTG format; however, the Save method's PersistFormat parameter can be used to explicitly specify the format of the persisted data stream as either ADTG or XML. The persisted data stream, whether it be stored as a file or in another object, can be accessed and manipulated even if the recordset is disconnected or the Recordset object itself is closed.

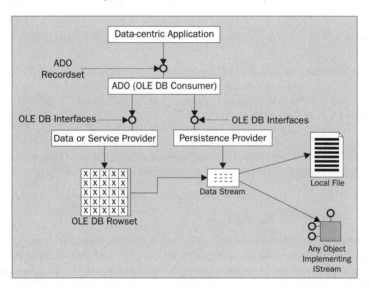

The Open method can be used to populate the Recordset object by reading the persisted data stream from a file or another object. In this situation, the Persistence Provider acts more like an OLE DB data provider than a service provider. An ADO connection can be established to MSPersist just like any other data provider. When a Recordset object's Open method is called against a connection to MSPersist, behind the scenes ADO forwards the request to the instance of the Persistence Provider represented by the connection. If no ActiveConnection is specified, ADO will automatically create an implicit connection to MSPersist. The Persistence Provider reads the data stream from the file or object specified in the Open method's Source parameter. The data and metadata from the data stream is interpreted by the Persistence Provider and used to create and populate a new OLE DB rowset. This forward-only, read-only rowset only provides basic data fetching capabilities. However, the OLE DB Cursor Service consumes the Persistence Provider's rowset and creates and exposes its own fully functional rowset that provides features such as forward and backward scrolling, data manipulation and searching. Finally, the Persistence Provider steps out of the picture and ADO interacts with the Cursor Service when operations are performed within the recordset.

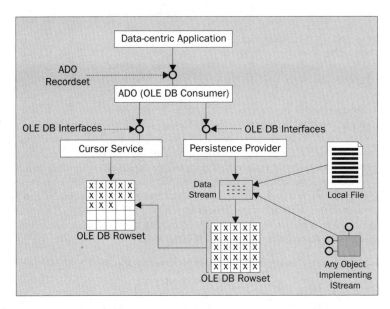

This process of loading a persisted data stream is a perfect example of the modular design of the OLE DB service provider architecture. Each service provider is designed to serve a single purpose. In the case of the Persistence Provider, it is only responsible for saving an OLE DB rowset to a data stream and creating an OLE DB rowset from an existing data stream. Instead of implementing data manipulation, searching and synchronization features, the Persistence Provider leverages the Cursor Service to provide this functionality. The benefit of this plug-'n'-play OLE DB service provider architecture for us as ADO developers is that an ADO recordset behaves consistently and provides the same functionality, regardless of whether it is disconnected, fabricated, shaped, remoted or populated from a persisted data stream.

Persisting a Recordset to a File

Once we understand how ADO interacts with the Persistence Provider when a `Recordset` object's `Save` and `Open` methods are called, utilizing these methods to persist a recordset to a file is extremely simple. For example, the following code defines a method named `SaveAuthorsToXMLFile` that retrieves all of the records from the `authors` table in the `pubs` SQL Server database and saves the entire recordset to a file on the local file system in XML format:

```
Private Sub SaveAuthorsToXMLFile()
    Const sFile As String = "c:\Authors.xml"
    Dim rsAuthors As ADODB.Recordset

    'create a new instance of an ADODB.Recordset
    Set rsAuthors = New ADODB.Recordset

    With rsAuthors
        'use the Microsoft OLE DB Cursor Service
        .CursorLocation = adUseClient
```

```
        'retrieve all of the records from the authors table
        '...in the Pubs SQL Server database
        .Open Source:="SELECT * FROM Authors", _
            ActiveConnection:="Provider=SQLOLEDB;Initial Catalog=Pubs; " & _
                             "Data Source=jconard;User ID=sa;Password=;", _
            CursorType:=adOpenStatic, LockType:=adLockBatchOptimistic

        'disconnect from the Data Provider and data source
        Set .ActiveConnection = Nothing

        If Dir$(sFile) <> "" Then
            'the destination file already exists, delete it
            Kill sFile
        End If

        'persist the Recordset to disk as an XML file
        .save Destination:=sFile, PersistFormat:=adPersistXML
    End With

    'close and release our rsAuthors Recordset
    rsAuthors.Close
    Set rsAuthors = Nothing
End Sub
```

Notice in this example that we delete the file if it already exists. If the file specified in the Save method's Destination parameter already exists, the Persistence Provider won't overwrite the file, but instead it will raise the following run-time error:

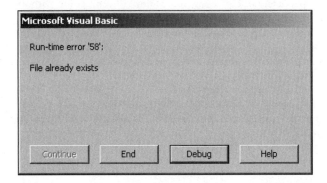

Since the recordset was persisted in XML format, after executing the SaveAuthorsToXMLFile method, we can open up the file in notepad or Internet Explorer 5.x to view its contents:

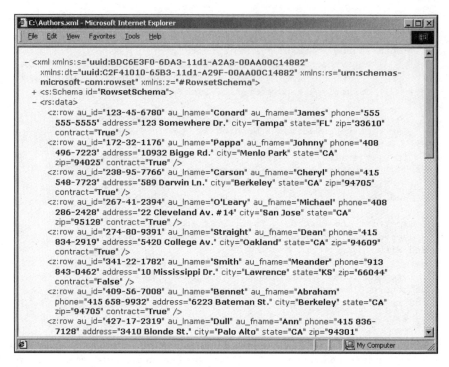

The fact that XML is a text-based, human-readable data format is one of the major benefits of using XML for recordset persistence. However, this benefit doesn't come without a cost. With all of its open and close tags, XML is a very verbose data format. Just to give you an idea of the size difference between the XML and ADTG formats, in the last example the persisted file took up 8.27 KB in XML format, even though only 25 records were persisted. By contrast, in the binary ADTG format the persisted file was only 3.2 KB – almost one-third of the size.

Opening a recordset from a file is almost as easy as saving a recordset to a file. In the following example, we'll define a method named `OpenAuthorsFromXMLFile` that populates a `Recordset` object using the data from the `Authors.xml` file that was created by calling the `SaveAuthorsToXMLFile` method. After the recordset has been opened, we'll simply print out the last name and first name for each author record to the debug window:

```
Private Sub OpenAuthorsFromXMLFile()
    Const sFile As String = "c:\Authors.xml"
    Dim rsAuthors As New ADODB.Recordset

    'create a new instance of an ADODB.Recordset
    Set rsAuthors = New ADODB.Recordset

    With rsAuthors
        'use the Microsoft OLE DB Cursor Service
        '.CursorLocation = adUseClient

        'retrieve all of the records from the Authors table
        '...in the Pubs SQL Server database
```

```
            .Open Source:=sFile, ActiveConnection:="Provider=MSPERSIST", _
                CursorType:=adOpenStatic, LockType:=adLockBatchOptimistic

        Do While .EOF = False
            'print each author's last name and first name to the debug window
            '...Note: these operations are performed using the cached data
            Debug.Print .Fields("au_lname").Value & ", " & .Fields("au_fname").Value

            'move to the next record
            .MoveNext
        Loop
    End With

    'close and release our rsAuthors Recordset
    rsAuthors.Close
    Set rsAuthors = Nothing
End Sub
```

In this example, we explicitly created a connection to the Persistence Provider by specifying
`"Provider=MSPERSIST"` for the `Open` method's `ActiveConnection` parameter. If the recordset does
not have an `ActiveConnection` when the `Open` method is called, ADO will automatically create an
implicit connection to the Persistence Provider and immediately release the connection after the
recordset has been populated. For example, the following code will also open a recordset from the file
specified in the `sFile` variable. In this example, the recordset will not have an `ActiveConnection`
after the `Open` method completes:

```
'retrieve all of the records from the Authors table
'...in the Pubs SQL Server database
.Open Source:=sFile, CursorType:=adOpenStatic, LockType:=adLockBatchOptimistic
```

After a recordset has been opened from a file, it can be used just like any other disconnected or
fabricated recordset. Data can be fetched, searched, sorted, filtered and manipulated within the
recordset. Additionally, the recordset can be connected to a data provider and resynchronized with the
data source.

For example, in the following code we'll revise our `SaveAuthorsToXMLFile` method that we created
earlier so that an author record is updated before persisting the recordset:

```
Private Sub SaveAuthorsToXMLFile()
    Const sFile As String = "c:\Authors.xml"
    Dim rsAuthors As ADODB.Recordset

    'create a new instance of an ADODB.Recordset
    Set rsAuthors = New ADODB.Recordset

    With rsAuthors
        'use the Microsoft OLE DB Cursor Service
        .CursorLocation = adUseClient

        'retrieve all of the records from the Authors table
        '...in the Pubs SQL Server database
        .open Source:="SELECT * FROM Authors", _
```

```
                ActiveConnection:="Provider=SQLOLEDB;Initial Catalog=Pubs; " & _
                        "Data Source=jconard;User ID=sa;Password=;", _
                CursorType:=adOpenStatic, LockType:=adLockBatchOptimistic

        'disconnect from the Data Provider and data source
        Set .ActiveConnection = Nothing

        'find and update the record with a au_lname = 'Conard'
        .Find "au_lname = #Conard#", SearchDirection:=adSearchForward, _
                        Start:=adBookmarkFirst

        If .EOF = False Then
            'the record was found, update it
            .Update Fields:="address", Values:="1010 Fairway Blvd."
        End If

        If Dir$(sFile) <> "" Then
            'the destination file already exists, delete it
            Kill sFile
        End If

        'persist the Recordset to disk as an XML file
        .save Destination:=sFile, PersistFormat:=adPersistXML

    End With

    'close and release our rsAuthors Recordset
    rsAuthors.Close
    Set rsAuthors = Nothing
End Sub
```

If you take a look at the persisted XML file, you'll see that the Persistence Provider saves the updated record's old value and new value as well as the status of each record (updated, inserted or deleted):

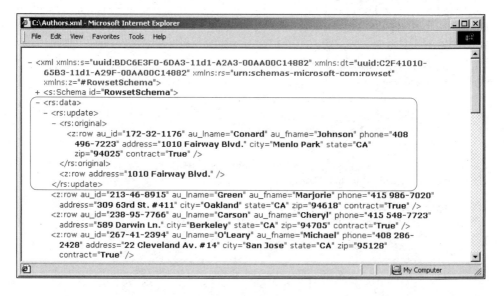

Now let's modify our `OpenAuthorsFromXMLFile` method so that after opening the XML file, it adds an author record to the recordset, reconnects to the data provider and data source and calls the `Recordset` object's `UpdateBatch` method to apply the pending changes in the recordset to the data source:

```
Private Sub OpenAuthorsFromXMLFile()
    Const sFile As String = "c:\Authors.xml"
    Dim rsAuthors As New ADODB.Recordset

    'create a new instance of an ADODB.Recordset
    Set rsAuthors = New ADODB.Recordset

    With rsAuthors
        'use the Microsoft OLE DB Cursor Service
        .CursorLocation = adUseClient

        'Open our persisted XML file which contains
        '...all of the Author records from the Pubs database
        .open Source:=sFile, ActiveConnection:="Provider=MSPERSIST", _
            CursorType:=adOpenStatic, LockType:=adLockBatchOptimistic

        'add a new record
        .AddNew FieldList:=Array("au_id", "au_lname", "au_fname", "contract"), _
            Values:=Array("543-21-1234", "Sussman", "David", True)

        'reconnect the disconnected recordset...
        .ActiveConnection = "Provider=SQLOLEDB;Initial Catalog=Pubs;" & _
                        "Data Source=jconard;User ID=sa;Password=;"

        'Now apply the changes to the data source...
        .UpdateBatch

    End With

    'close and release our rsAuthors Recordset
    rsAuthors.Close
    Set rsAuthors = Nothing
End Sub
```

> The `UpdateBatch` and `Resync` methods will fail with the common error Insufficient base table information for updating or refreshing if the metadata information about the data source was not persisted. This metadata information will only be saved if the persisted recordset was opened with a `CursorLocation` of `adUseClient` and a `LockType` of `adLockBatchOptimistic` or `adLockOptimistic`.

Persisting a Recordset to an Object

While the ability to persist a recordset to a file is extremely powerful, there are many situations when you might need the persisted recordset in the form of a string or array. The typical approach taken by many developers in the past has been to persist a recordset to a temporary file and then read this file back into a string or array. However, implementing this functionality requires several lines of ugly code. Moreover, the file system can easily become a performance and scalability bottleneck. Thankfully, ADO 2.5 and the Persistence Provider now allow recordsets to be persisted to any object that supports the `IStream` interface. A couple of the components that implement the `IStream` interface include:

- ❏ ADO's `Stream` object

- ❏ ASP's `Response` and `Request` objects

Let's discuss and look at some examples of using recordset persistence to each of these components.

Persisting Recordsets to an ADO Stream Object

The new ADO `Stream` object is designed to represent a stream of text or binary data. While it is typically used with OLE DB data providers that expose semi-structured data, such as the OLE DB Provider for Internet Publishing or the OLE DB Provider for Microsoft Exchange, the `Stream` object can also be used to persist a recordset in memory rather than on disk. A recordset can be persisted to an ADO `Stream` object simply by specifying a reference to a valid `Stream` object in the `Destination` parameter of a `Recordset` object's `Save` method. The Persistence Provider will write the recordset's metadata and data into the `Stream` object through the `IStream` interface instead of to the file system. Once a recordset has been persisted to a `Stream` object, the `Stream`'s contents can be read, manipulated, copied to another `Stream` object or saved to a file. The following code provides an example of utilizing this functionality by saving a recordset to a new `Stream` object in XML format and then printing the `Stream`'s contents to the Debug window:

```
Private Sub SaveAuthorsToStream()
    Dim rsAuthors As ADODB.Recordset
    Dim stmAuthors As ADODB.Stream

    'create a new instance of an ADODB.Recordset
    Set rsAuthors = New ADODB.Recordset

    'create a new instance of an ADODB.Stream
    Set stmAuthors = New ADODB.Stream

    With rsAuthors
        'use the Microsoft OLE DB Cursor Service
        .CursorLocation = adUseClient

        'retrieve all of the records from the Authors table
        '...in the Pubs SQL Server database
        .open Source:="SELECT * FROM Authors", _
            ActiveConnection:="Provider=SQLOLEDB;Initial Catalog=Pubs; " & _
                            "Data Source=jconard;User ID=sa;Password=;", _
            CursorType:=adOpenStatic, LockType:=adLockBatchOptimistic

        'disconnect from the Data Provider and data source
        Set .ActiveConnection = Nothing

        'persist the Recordset to the ADODB.Stream
        .save Destination:=stmAuthors, PersistFormat:=adPersistXML

        'simply print the Stream's contents to the debug window
        Debug.Print stmAuthors.ReadText(adReadAll)
    End With
```

```
    'close and release our Stream
    stmAuthors.Close
    Set stmAuthors = Nothing

    'close and release our Recordset
    rsAuthors.Close
    Set rsAuthors = Nothing
End Sub
```

A Recordset object can also be populated using the contents of a Stream object simply by calling a Recordset object's Open method and passing an open ADO Stream object for the Source parameter. For an example of this functionality, in the following code we'll create a method named DuplicateRecordset that, as the name implies, creates a duplicate of an ADO Recordset object. This is accomplished by persisting a recordset to a Stream object and then populating a new Recordset object using the contents of the Stream:

```
Public Function DuplicateRecordset(ByRef rsSourceRecordset As ADODB.Recordset) _
                                                    As ADODB.Recordset

    Dim stmData As ADODB.Stream
    Dim rsNewRecordset As ADODB.Recordset

    'create a new instance of a Stream and Recordset
    Set stmData = New ADODB.Stream
    Set rsNewRecordset = New ADODB.Recordset

    'persist the Source Recordset to our temporary stream
    rsSourceRecordset.save Destination:=stmData, PersistFormat:=adPersistADTG

    'now populate the New Recordset using the Stream's contents
    rsNewRecordset.open Source:=stmData

    'return a reference to our New Recordset object
    Set DuplicateRecordset = rsNewRecordset

    'close and release our temporary Stream object
    stmData.Close
    Set stmData = Nothing

    'release our procedure-level reference to the new Recordset object
    Set rsNewRecordset = Nothing
End Function
```

Notice that in this example we don't establish an explicit connection to MSPersist when the Recordset's Open method is called, as we have in past examples. For some reason, ADO doesn't like the combination of a connection string in the ActiveConnection parameter and an object reference in the Source parameter of the Recordset object's Open method. If you do attempt to establish an explicit connection to MSPersist when populating a recordset from a Stream object or any object implementing the IStream interface, ADO will raise the following run-time error:

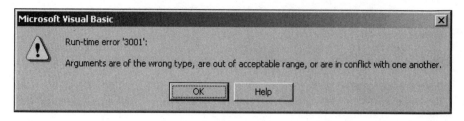

Unlike recordsets created by a `Recordset` object's `Clone` method, our `DuplicateRecordset` method will create a completely independent recordset that has its own underlying OLE DB rowset. As a result, data can be manipulated within one recordset without affecting the other. We can use the following code to illustrate this principle and test our new `DuplicateRecordset` method:

```
Private Sub TestDuplicateRecordsetMethod()
    Dim rsAuthors As ADODB.Recordset
    Dim rsAuthors2 As ADODB.Recordset

    'create a new instance of an ADODB.Recordset
    Set rsAuthors = New ADODB.Recordset

    With rsAuthors
        'use the Microsoft OLE DB Cursor Service
        .CursorLocation = adUseClient

        'retrieve all of the records from the Authors table
        '...in the Pubs SQL Server database
        .open Source:="SELECT * FROM Authors", _
            ActiveConnection:="Provider=SQLOLEDB;Initial Catalog=Pubs; " & _
                            "Data Source=jconard;User ID=sa;Password=;", _
            CursorType:=adOpenStatic, LockType:=adLockBatchOptimistic

        'disconnect from the Data Provider and data source
        Set .ActiveConnection = Nothing

        'duplicate the rsAuthors Recordset
        Set rsAuthors2 = DuplicateRecordset(rsAuthors)


        'delete all of the Records from the rsAuthors recordset
        Do While .EOF = False
            .Delete AffectRecords:=adAffectCurrent
            .MoveNext
        Loop
    End With

    'now display the Recordcounts for both Recordset's
    MsgBox "rsAuthors.RecordCount = " & rsAuthors.RecordCount
    MsgBox "rsAuthors2.RecordCount = " & rsAuthors2.RecordCount
```

```
      'close and release our Recordsets
      rsAuthors.Close
      Set rsAuthors = Nothing

      rsAuthors2.Close
      Set rsAuthors2 = Nothing
   End Sub
```

While these simple examples adequately demonstrate how recordset persistence works with the ADO `Stream` object, they don't do justice to emphasize the awesome capabilities the `Stream` object provides especially on the middle tier of an n-tier, data-centric application.

Persisting Recordsets to ASP's Response Object

As of ASP 3.0 (introduced in Internet Information Server 5.0), the `Request` and `Response` objects also support the `IStream` interface, and consequently these objects can be used as a source for populating a recordset and as a destination for persisting a recordset. Transfering data into and out of Active Server Pages across the HTTP or HTTPS protocols is a powerful technique that provides many benefits. In particular, it allows us easily to expose data on the Web, so it can be accessed by multiple client applications, possibly executing on various platforms. Moreover, the retrieved data can be manipulated locally and later transferred back to the web server where any pending changes can be applied to the data source. The following diagram illustrates an example of using this model for working with author records from the SQL Server pubs database:

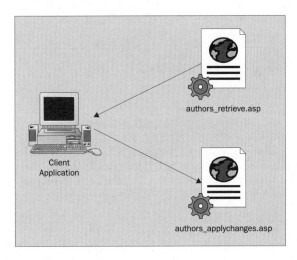

In this scenario, we might have an ASP page named `authors_retrieve.asp` which retrieves all of the author records from the SQL Server pubs database (using ADO of course), and persists the recordset to the ASP `Response` object. The recordset will be persisted in the format specified in the `PersistFormat` section of the `QueryString`. Consequently, the requesting application can specify the persistence format as a parameter in the URL. If no format is specified, by default the `authors_retrieve.asp` page will persist the recordset as XML. Let's take a look at the code for this page:

```asp
<%@ Language=VBScript %>
<% Option Explicit %>

<!-- METADATA TYPE="typelib"
            UUID="{00000205-0000-0010-8000-00AA006D2EA4}" -->

<%
    Dim rsAuthors

    'create a new instance of an ADODB.Recordset
    Set rsAuthors = Server.CreateObject("ADODB.Recordset")

    With rsAuthors
        'retrieve all of the records from the Authors table
        '...in the Pubs SQL Server database
        .Open "SELECT * FROM Authors", _
              "Provider=SQLOLEDB;Initial Catalog=Pubs;" & _
              "Data Source=jconard;User ID=sa;Password=;", _
              adOpenStatic, adLockBatchOptimistic

        'Persist the Recordset to the ASP Response object
        '...in the format specified
        if Request.QueryString.Item("PersistFormat") = "ADTG" then
            'persist the Recordset in ADTG format
            Response.ContentType = "multipart/mixed"
            .Save Response, adPersistADTG
        else
            'persist the Recordset in XML format
            Response.ContentType = "text/xml"
            .Save Response, adPersistXML
        end if

    End With
%>
```

We can test whether or not our `authors_retrieve.asp` page is working correctly simply by loading it in XML format using Internet Explorer 5.0. If you specify ADTG format when opening the page, Internet Explorer will attempt to download the file instead of displaying it:

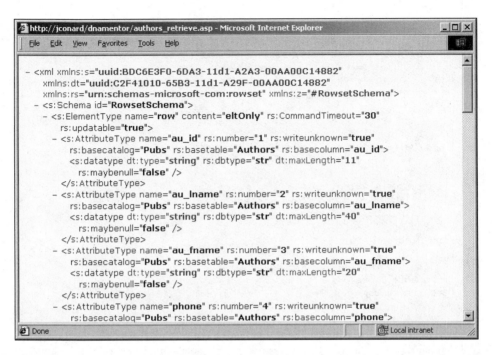

Once the author records are exposed by the `authors_retrieve.asp` page, we can develop a client application that uses this data. Since our ASP page supports XML, the client application could use an XML parser, such as the Microsoft XML Document Object Model (MSXML), to work with the author data. However, for the sake of this example, we'll assume that the client has ADO installed and is executing on a Windows platform. If you want to see an example of utilizing the XML DOM to manipulate XML data exposed by an ASP page, you can skip ahead to Chapter 7. Our simple client application will consist of one function named `OpenAuthorsFromASP` that, as the name suggests, opens an ADO `Recordset` by specifying the URL to the `authors_retieve.asp` page for the `Open` method's `Source` parameter. After the data has been streamed across HTTP and the recordset has been populated, our `OpenAuthorsFromASP` method will simply find and delete the author with the last name of `"Conard"`. Notice that we specify a persistence format of ADTG instead of XML. Since we are using ADO to manipulate the data in this example, we can sacrifice the interopability of the verbose XML format for the performance benefits of the streamlined, but proprietary, ADTG format:

```
Private Sub OpenAuthorsFromASP()
    Dim rsAuthors As New ADODB.Recordset

    'create a new instance of an ADODB.Recordset
    Set rsAuthors = New ADODB.Recordset

    With rsAuthors
        'use the Microsoft OLE DB Cursor Service
        .CursorLocation = adUseClient
```

```
            'Open the authors.asp page which streams a recordset
            '...containing all of the Authors records in ADTG format
            .open Source:="http://jconard/authors_retrieve.asp?PersistFormat=ADTG", _
                  ActiveConnection:="Provider=MSPERSIST", _
                  CursorType:=adOpenStatic, LockType:=adLockBatchOptimistic, _
                  Options:=adCmdFile

            'find and delete the record with a au_lname = 'Conard'
            .Find "au_lname = #Conard#", _
                  SearchDirection:=adSearchForward, _
                  Start:=adBookmarkFirst

        If .EOF = False Then
            'the record was found, delete it
            .Delete AffectRecords:=adAffectCurrent
        End If
    End With

        'close and release our Recordset
        rsAuthors.Close
        Set rsAuthors = Nothing
    End Sub
```

It's important to note that if the data returned from the `authors_retrieve.asp` page has just one extra character, ADO will fail when the `Recordset` object's `Open` method is called and raise the error message that you see below. To avoid this problem, you should always first test your data-exposing Active Server Pages using Internet Explorer 5.0 or later before attempting to open them from ADO.

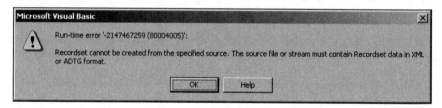

We haven't constructed much of a client application because we currently discard our changes when the `OpenAuthorsFromASP` method completes. Assumming that we can't simply establish an active connection to the to data source and call the `Recordset` object's `UpdateBatch` method directly from our client application, how can we apply our local changes to the data source? One technique is to submit the changed records back to the web server across HTTP. On the web server, our `authors_applychanges.asp` Active Server Page, can retrieve the data from the HTTP stream and apply any pending changes to the data source. We'll discuss the `authors_applychanges.asp` page in just a moment, but first let's implement the code in our client application's `OpenAuthorsFromASP` method to push the data back across the network.

In addition to providing an object model for accessing XML-formatted data, the MSXML library included with Internet Explorer 5.0 also introduces a powerful component named `XMLHTTP` that allows data easily to be sent to to and from web servers using the HTTP protocol. Although the `XMLHTTP` component was designed primarily for transferring XML-formatted data, it can actually be used to transfer data in any format, including ADTG.

In the following code, we'll revise our client application to utilize the XMLHTTP component to transfer the author records to the authors_applychanges.asp page. The first step to posting data across HTTP using an instance of the XMLHTTP component is to call its Open method. The Open method accepts three parameters: the HTTP method to use, the URL to connect to and a boolean value that indicates whether or not asynchronous communication should be used.

```
Private Sub OpenAuthorsFromASP()
    Dim rsAuthors As New ADODB.Recordset
    Dim objXMLHTTP As MSXML.XMLHTTPRequest
    Dim stmAuthors As ADODB.Stream

    'create a new instance of an ADODB.Recordset
    Set rsAuthors = New ADODB.Recordset

    'create a new instance of an MSXML.XMLHTTPRequest
    Set objXMLHTTP = New MSXML.XMLHTTPRequest

    'create a new instance of an ADODB.Stream
    Set stmAuthors = New ADODB.Stream

    With rsAuthors
        'use the Microsoft OLE DB Cursor Service
        .CursorLocation = adUseClient

        'Open the authors.asp page which streams a recordset
        '...containing all of the Authors records in ADTG format
        .open Source:="http://jconard/authors_retrieve.asp?PersistFormat=ADTG", _
            ActiveConnection:="Provider=MSPERSIST", _
            CursorType:=adOpenStatic, LockType:=adLockBatchOptimistic, _
            Options:=adCmdFile

        'find and delete the record with a au_lname = 'Conard'
        .Find "au_lname = #Conard#", _
            SearchDirection:=adSearchForward, _
            Start:=adBookmarkFirst

        If .EOF = False Then
            'the record was found, delete it
            .Delete AffectRecords:=adAffectCurrent
        End If

        'open a connection to the authors_applychanges.asp page
        objXMLHTTP.open "POST", _
                    "http://jconard/dnamentor/authors_applychanges.asp", _
                    varAsync:=False
```

Next, the Send method can be called on our instance of the XMLHTTP component to post data across HTTP to the destination we specified in the Open method. Unfortunately, the XMLHTTP component does not support the IStream interface, so instead of persisting the local recordset directly to our instance of the XMLHTTP component, we must first persist the recordset to an ADO Stream object, and then send the contents of the Stream object. Again, we'll use the ADTG format in preference to XML in this situation for higher performance:

```
'persist the Recordset's filtered records to a Stream in ADTG format
    .save Destination:=stmAuthors, PersistFormat:=adPersistADTG

    'send the contents of the stmAuthors Stream
    objXMLHTTP.send varbody:=stmAuthors.Read(adReadAll)
End With


    'close and release our Stream
    stmAuthors.Close
    Set stmAuthors = Nothing

    'close and release our Recordset
    rsAuthors.Close
    Set rsAuthors = Nothing
End Sub
```

> **Remember that to use the XMLHTTP component, you need to add a reference to Microsoft XML, version 2.0 to your project.**

That's all for our simple client application. Now we need to implement the `authors_applychanges.asp` Active Server Page that will receive the data from the client application and apply any pending changes to the data source. Thankfully, this code is also very straightforward. In the `authors_applychanges.asp` page will simply call the `Open` method of an ADO `Recordset` object, specifying the ASP `Request` object for the `Source` parameter. Once our recordset has been populated with the data posted to this ASP page, we can simply establish a connection to the SQL Server pubs database and apply any pending changes in the recordset to the data source by calling the `UpdateBatch` method as normal:

```
<%@ Language=VBScript %>
<% Option Explicit %>

<!-- METADATA TYPE="typelib"
            UUID="{00000205-0000-0010-8000-00AA006D2EA4}" -->

<%
    Dim rsAuthors

    'create a new instance of an ADODB.Recordset
    Set rsAuthors = Server.CreateObject("ADODB.Recordset")

    With rsAuthors
        'read in the data that was posted to this page
        .Open Request, , adOpenStatic, adLockBatchOptimistic, adCmdFile

        'reconnect to the Data source
        .ActiveConnection = "Provider=SQLOLEDB;Initial Catalog=Pubs; " & _
                            "Data Source=jconard;User ID=sa;Password=;"

        'apply the pending changes to the data source
        .UpdateBatch adAffectAll
    End With
%>
```

The simple example that we've covered in this section should help you understand the potential of persisting data to the ASP Response object and retrieving it from an ASP Request object. Granted, we could have leveraged ADO's new Stream object as a temporary data buffer instead of persisting and reading from the ASP Response and Request objects directly. However, that approach would result in much more overhead because an unnecessary ADO Stream object would have to be constructed, populated, read and finally destroyed. Consider the overhead of this process in an internet environment where virtually every millisecond counts.

In a production application, you would want to be sure to add conflict resolution and error handling code within the authors_applychange.asp page and within the client application. Thankfully, this task is not too difficult because XMLHTTP automatically retrieves and parses the response from a page when the Send method is called. Our authors_applychanges.asp page could simply persist any conflicting records back to the client application where the conflicts could be resolved by the user and resubmitted or discarded. In Chapter 7, we'll discuss a similar example that uses the XML DOM and DHTML data binding for the client side of the application.

Implicit Persistence

Up to this point, our discussion of recordset persistence has been limited to scenarios where the Persistence Provider is explicitly invoked through the Recordset object's Save and Open methods. However, the Persistence Provider can also be invoked implicitly as the result of a Recordset object being transferred across process or machine boundaries. Before we can understand exactly how this works, we need to discuss briefly some basics about object communication across process boundaries.

Normally, when an object is passed across processes, COM simply passes a reference to the object instead of the object itself. The actual object remains in the process in which it was created. Consequently, every method or property call on the reference travels across processes and possibly machine boundaries to wherever the actual objet resides. Cross-process method calls are significantly slower than in-process method calls because COM must package or **marshal** parameter values across process bounaries to the object's process where they are unpacked or **unmarshaled**. Marshaling and unmarshaling of parameters is managed by two layers called the proxy and the stub. The proxy resides in the client's process and acts, as its name suggests, as a proxy for the real remote object. The client communicates with the proxy as if it were the real object, and the proxy in turn communicates with another object, called the stub, which resides in the server process. The stub then passes the communication on to the object itself. The following diagram illustrates the interaction between the proxy and stub when methods are invoked on a remote object:

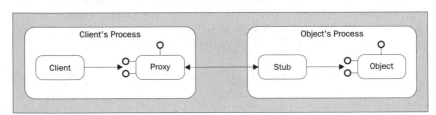

An ADO `Recordset` is a special type of component. When an ADO `Recordset` object is passed across processes, COM actually transfers the object itself including all of its data. As a result, subsequent method calls performed against the `Recordset` are performed within the client's process and do not require marshaling or the proxy/stub layers. This technique of marshaling the an entire object instead of simply a reference to the object is known as a Marshal By Value (MBV).

An ADO `Recordset` object's Marshal By Value support is provided by the OLE DB Peristence Provider. When an ADO `Recordset` object is passed across processes, the Persistence Provider automatically persists the entire `Recordset` to a data stream, so it can be transferred across process and possibly machine boundaries. When the data stream arrives in the client's process, it is used by MSPersist and ADO to construct a new ADO `Recordset`. Both the client's process and the original object's process now have their own copy of the `Recordset` object instead of sharing a reference to a single object. Since the entire `Recordset` object is effectively copied into the client's proces, the original object can be destroyed to free up resources for other objects to be created. The following diagram illustrates this process when a method is called on a object in another process and an ADO `Recordset` is passed as a parameter:

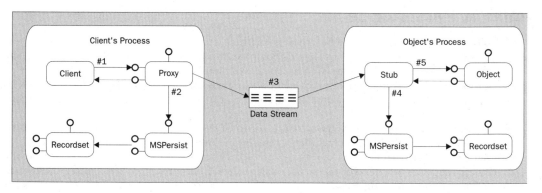

As you can see in the above diagram, we've broken this process down into five steps:

1. The client invokes a method on the object. Since the object resides in a separate process, the method is actually invoked on the proxy which, along with the stub, is responsible for managing cross-process communication.

2. The proxy marshals the parameters into a data stream so they can be sent across process and possibly machine boundaries. Since one of the parameters is a `Recordset` object which supports Marshal By Value, MSPersist is automatically invoked to persist the entire `Recordset` object including all of its data to the data stream.

3. The method call and parameters are sent to the stub which resides in the destination object's process.

4. The object's stub unmarshals the parameters from the data stream. MSPersist will automatically be invoked to reconstruct the `Recordset` object using the data and metadata persisted to the data stream.

5. Finally, the stub will invoke the method on the object, passing it all of the parameters, including a reference to the new `Recordset` object within the same process.

While this is the general role of Persistence Provider, its actual behavior can vary slightly depending on whether the Recordset object is passed by value or by reference.

> It's important to note that when an ADO Recordset object is passed to object within the same process (in-process), COM simply passes a reference to the Recordset object and the Persistence Provider is not involved in any way. This is true regardelss of whether the Recordset object is passed by reference or by value.

ByVal vs. ByRef

When an ADO Recordset object is passed across processes as a Byval parameter, the OLE DB Persistence provider persists and reconstructs the Recordset object as we just described. The Recordset is only passed across processes in one direction and will not be returned to the caller.

When an ADO Recordset object is passed across processes by reference to a method call, the Recordset is copied to the destination process, as is the case with a ByVal parameter, and then it is copied back to the caller after the method call has completed. This behavior is illustrated in the following diagram:

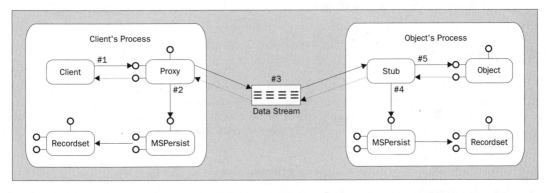

ByRef parameters are generally faster for in-process method calls, because data remains in its current location and only a reference to the data is passed. However, passing a recordset, or any data for that matter, across process boundaries as a ByRef parameter is a very expensive operation because data is marshaled in both directions. As a result, you should use ByVal parameters whenever possible. The only situation when method parameters should be declared as ByRef for an out-of-process component is when you want any changes to the parameter performed by the component to be reflected onto the client. For example, if we want to pass a Recordset object to a method in an out-of-process component which manipulates the Recordset's data, we might specify ByRef for the parameter's definition so that the client will see the changes within the Recordset.

MarshalOptions Property

By default, *all* of a recordset's data will automatically be persisted and marshaled across process boundaries. However, in many situations this behavior is undesirable. Consider the common scenario where a client application retrieves a disconnected recordset from a middle-tier object, manipulates the disconnected recordset's data locally, and passes the recordset back to a middle-tier object where the recordset is reconnected and any pending changes are applied to the data source. When the disconnected recordset is passed back to the middle-tier object, it is usually unnecessary for all of the recordset's data to be marshaled. After all, the middle-tier object is only interested in the pending changes. Thankfully, the ADO `Recordset` object provides a property named `MarshalOptions` that allows us to customize the behavior of the Persistence Provider when a `Recordset` object is marshaled across processes. The `MarshalOptions` property can be set to one of the following constant values:

❑   `adMarshalAll` – All records should be marshaled

❑   `adMarshalModifiedOnly` – Only pending changes – that is, records that have been inserted, updated or deleted – should be marshaled.

Simply changing the `MarshalOptions` property to `adMarshalModifiedOnly` before passing a disconnected `Recordset` object across processes can significantly increase the performance and scalability of your application. This is especially true when your disconnected recordset contains a large amount of data that has not been modified.

Summary

Recordset persistence is a powerful feature that has a virtually endless number of real-world applications. For example, recordset persistence can be used to store temporary data to a file, expose data across the Internet or accross an intranet, cache data in various environments, or convert data from proprietary formats to XML. In this chapter, we've discussed the details of recordset persistence in some of these scenarios. In particular, we:

❑   Explicitly persisted and opened an ADO `Recordset` to and from a local file

❑   Learned how to leverage ADO's new `Stream` object as a temporary data cache

❑   Exposed data in a `Recordset` object across HTTP using Active Server Pages

❑   Analyzed what occurs behind the scenes when an ADO `Recordset` is passed across process or machine boundaries

❑   Used the ADO `Recordset` object's `MarshalOptions` dynamic property to control the behavior of implicit persistence

In the next chapter, we'll continue with our overview of some of the issues raised by data access in a distributed application. Specifically, we will look at the topic of ADO events and asynchronous processing, and we'll see how ADO fits into the Windows DNA strategy.

5

Asynchronous Processing & Event Notification

What is Asynchronous Processing?

In most applications today, when a client makes a method call, it's blocked until the call returns. That is, the client cannot execute any code while it is waiting. This is known as **synchronous processing**. Asynchronous processing is when a method call starts a task and returns instantly, even if the task is not complete. The client goes about its business, while the component works on the task. When the task is complete, the component notifies the client that the result is ready. In this chapter we are going to explore the following:

- ❑ The different ways that the ADO object model enables us to implement asynchronous operations
- ❑ The factors to consider when using asynchronous processing with COM+ components
- ❑ Using MSMQ and ADO as a method of asynchronous communication
- ❑ Using COM+ Queued Components with ADO

All code examples will be in Visual Basic and SQL Server 7.0. We will be using the pubs database that ships with SQL Server. As an alternative to SQL Server, you can also use the Microsoft Data Engine (MSDE), which is freely distributable. All of the code will be available for download from www.wrox.com.

The Benefits

By using **asynchronous processing**, you can free the client to do other things while it's waiting. Asynchronous processing is also useful when clients need to be notified of interesting occurrences – for example, progress notification, changes in database values, or the arrival of messages. A client tells a component it wants to be notified when certain things happen, and the component sends notifications when those things occur. Both of these scenarios depend on **asynchronous notifications**, or **events**. The client application is doing other work, and then they receive a notification that an asynchronous request has completed, or that something else of interest has occurred.

A simple example of asynchronous processing in ADO might be in a desktop application when you have to fetch a very large number of records into a recordset. The users of the application would become very impatient if they were not able to continue their work while the recordset was loading. By using one of the ADO recordset events, you could execute the query and start the process of retrieving the recordset, immediately return control to the client, and then notify the user after the recordset had finished loading.

Asynchronous Operations in ADO 2.5

There are two common methods in the ADO object model that support asynchronous operations: `Open` and `Execute`. We will first take a look at the `Open` method. The `Connection`, `Record`, `Recordset`, and `Stream` objects all implement the `Open` method.

The Open Method

With the `Connection` object's `Open` method, the parameters are as follows: `Optional ConnectionString As String`, `Optional UserID As String`, `Optional Password As String`, and `Optional Options As Long` with a default value of -1. The parameter that allows us to asynchronously open a connection is the `Options` parameter. It takes a `ConnectOptionEnum` value as its input to determine if it will be asynchronous or not. The only `ConnectOptionEnum` value available is `adAsyncConnect`, or 16. The default `Option` value of -1 is for a synchronous connection. Here is an example of opening an asynchronous connection:

```
Dim cn As ADODB.Connection
Dim strConnection As String

strConnection = "PROVIDER=SQLOLEDB;Source=localhost;" _
& "Initial Catalog=pubs;User Id=sa;Password=;"

Set cn = New ADODB.Connection
cn.Open strConnection, , , adAsyncConnect
```

The Record object's Open method has the following arguments: Optional Source As Variant, Optional ActiveConnection As Variant, Optional CreateOptions As ConnectModeEnum, Optional Options As RecordOpenOptionsEnum, Optional UserName As String, and Optional Password As String. Like the Connection object, the parameter that we need to set in order to open a Record object asynchronously is the Options parameter. The value from RecordOpenOptionsEnum that we need to supply is adOpenAsync, or 4096. Since we can use the Record object to open a URL, it would really be nice to open the URL asynchronously due to the fact that sometimes internet connections can be quite slow. However, the OLE DB Provider for Internet Publishing does not currently support asynchronous connections. Here is what the code would look like if we could:

```
Dim recNode As ADODB.Record

Set recNode = New ADODB.Record
recNode.Open "", "URL=http://localhost/", , , adOpenAsync
```

Here is the error you will receive:

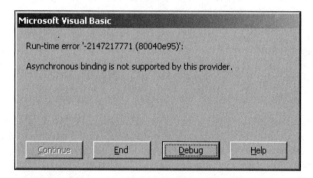

The Recordset object's Open method has the following arguments: Optional Source As Variant, Optional ActiveConnection As Variant, Optional CursorType As CursorTypeEnum with a default value of adOpenUnspecified, Optional LockType As LockTypeEnum with a default value of adLockUnspecified, and Optional Options As Long with a default value of -1. Like the Connection and Record objects, the parameter that we need to set in order to open a Record object asynchronously is the Options parameter. It takes an ExecuteOptionEnum value as its input to determine if it will be asynchronous or not. The only valid ExecuteOptionEnum values available for opening a recordset are adAsyncFetch (32), adAsyncFetchNonBlocking (64), adAsyncExecute (16), and adOptionUnspecified (-1).

To differentiate between the two options, `adAsyncFetchNonBlocking` opens a recordset asynchronously and the main thread will not block while retrieving rows. This means that you will only have access to the read-only properties of the `Recordset` and its objects until the `Open` operation has completed; control, however, will still be returned to the client. If the requested row has not been retrieved yet, the current row will automatically move to the end of the file. If you happen to open a `Recordset` object from a `Stream` object containing a persisted `Recordset`, such as an XML file, then `adAsyncFetchNonBlocking` will have no effect. The operation will be synchronous and blocking. The `adAsyncFetch` option only indicates that the remaining rows after the initial quantity specified in the `Recordset`'s `CacheSize` property should be retrieved asynchronously. The default `Option` value of −1 is for opening a recordset synchronously. Here is an example of opening a recordset asynchronously:

```
Dim strSQL As String
Dim strConnection As String
Dim rstAuthors As ADODB.Recordset

strSQL = "SELECT * FROM authors"
strConnection = "PROVIDER=SQLOLEDB;Source=localhost;" _
& "Initial Catalog=pubs;User Id=sa;Password=;"

Set rstAuthors = New ADODB.Recordset
With rstAuthors
        .CursorLocation = adUseClient
        .Open strSQL, strConnection, , , adAsyncFetch
End With
```

The `Stream` object's `Open` method has the following arguments: `Optional Source As Variant`, `Optional Mode As ConnectModeEnum` with a default value of `adModeUnknown`, `Optional Options As StreamOpenOptionsEnum` with a default value of `adOpenStreamUnspecified`, `Optional UserName As String`, and `Optional Password As String`. Like the other objects previously discussed, the parameter that we need to set in order to open a `Stream` object asynchronously is the `Options` parameter. The value from `StreamOpenOptionsEnum` that we need to supply is `adOpenStreamAsync`, or 1. If a `Stream` is opened asynchronously, then all operations (except for checking the `Stream`'s read-only properties) on the `Stream` are blocked until the `Open` operation has completed. Similar to the `Record` object, we can use the `Stream` object to open a file over HTTP. It would be really nice to open the file asynchronously, again due to the fact that sometimes internet connections get bogged down. However, Internet Publishing does not currently support asynchronous connections. Here is what the code would look like if we could:

```
Dim stm As ADODB.Stream

Set stm = New ADODB.Stream

stm.Open "URL=http://localhost/Test.txt", adModeRead, adOpenStreamAsync
stm.Charset = "ascii"
Debug.Print stm.ReadText
```

Although this code will compile flawlessly, we will get the exact same error as the one shown earlier; the data provider does not support asynchronous binding.

The Execute Method

The Connection and Command objects both implement the Execute method. With the Connection object's Execute method, the parameters are as follows: CommandText As String, Optional RecordsAffected As Variant, and Optional Options As Long with a default value of -1. The parameter that allows us to asynchronously execute a command from a Connection object is the Options parameter. It can take either CommandTypeEnum values, ExecuteOptionEnum values, or combinations of the two enumerations as its input. The only enumeration values that will determine if the action carried is asynchronous or not are adAsyncExecute (16), adAsyncFetch (32), and adAsyncFetchNonBlocking (64). The value of adAsyncExecute indicates that the command should execute asynchronously. The other two values have previously been discussed with the Recordset object, and are applicable when the Connection's Execute method will return a Recordset object. The default Option value of −1 is for a synchronous command execution that returns a Recordset. Here is an example of opening an asynchronous connection execute method:

```
Dim strSQL As String
Dim strConnection As String
Dim cn As ADODB.Connection

strConnection = "PROVIDER=SQLOLEDB;Source=localhost;" _
& "Initial Catalog=pubs;User Id=sa;Password=;"

strSQL = "UPDATE authors SET au_fname = 'Johnny' WHERE au_lname = 'Carson'"

Set cn = New ADODB.Connection
cn.Open strConnection
cn.Execute strSQL, , adAsyncExecute
```

With the Command object's Execute method, the parameters are as follows: Optional RecordsAffected As Variant, Optional Parameters as Variant (a variant array), and Optional Options As Long with a default value of -1. The parameter that allows us to asynchronously execute a command from a Command object is the Options parameter. It can take either CommandTypeEnum values, ExecuteOptionEnum values, or combinations of the two enumerations as its input. The only enumeration values that will determine if the action carried is asynchronous or not are adAsyncExecute (16), adAsyncFetch (32), and adAsyncFetchNonBlocking (64). The value of adAsyncExecute indicates that the command should execute asynchronously. The other two values have previously been discussed with the Recordset object, and are applicable when the Command's Execute method will return a Recordset object. The default Option value of −1 is for a synchronous command execution that returns a Recordset. Here is an example an asynchronous execute on a Command object:

```
Dim cmd As ADODB.Command
Dim strSQL As String
Dim strConnection As String

strConnection = "PROVIDER=SQLOLEDB;Source=localhost;" _
& "Initial Catalog=pubs;User Id=sa;Password=;"

strSQL = "UPDATE authors SET au_fname = 'Jerry' WHERE au_lname = 'Carson'"
```

```
Set cmd = New ADODB.Command
With cmd
    .ActiveConnection = strConnection
    .CommandType = adCmdText
    .CommandText = strSQL
    .Execute , , adAsyncExecute
End With
```

The Need for Events with Asynchronous Processing

When we execute a method asynchronously, we eventually need to be notified when the method has completed its action. For example, if we execute a long-running batch update query asynchronously, we would like to be notified when the query completes so we can see if the result was successful or not. In order to respond to events, we must set an event sink. A good analogy of this is tuning in to a specific channel to watch a sporting event. The sporting event is being broadcast, but we must tune to the right channel to watch the sporting event. In Visual Basic, we can set an event sink, or 'tune-in', to events by using the WithEvents keyword when dimensioning a variable for an object that issues events. Another way of receiving notification is to use callbacks. Callbacks are analogous to you giving an employee your phone number and saying, 'Call me back when you have finished the task I have assigned to you.' In the meantime, you continue to work on other tasks. In Visual Basic, you simply give the server object a reference to an instance of your client object, and the server will call a public method of your client object when it finishes its processing.

In this section, we will focus on using the events that the ADO 2.5 object model makes available.

Types of ADO Events

There are two main types of events in ADO:

❑   Will

❑   Complete

Will events are fired immediately after a method is called, but before the method is actually executed. They are a notification that a designated action will begin. Complete events are triggered immediately after a method has finished executing. They are a notification that a designated action has completed.

ADO events are also further grouped into two families:

❑   ConnectionEvents – pertain to the Connection object

❑   RecordsetEvents – pertain to the Recordset object

The following tables give a summary of the ADO events and their associated descriptions:

ConnectionEvent	Description
BeginTransComplete, CommitTransComplete, RollbackTransComplete	**Transaction Management** – Notification that the current transaction on the connection has started, committed, or rolled back.
WillConnect, ConnectComplete, Disconnect	**Connection Management** – Notification that the current connection will start, has started, or has ended.
WillExecute, ExecuteComplete	**Command Execution Management** – Notification that the execution of the current command on the connection will start or has ended.
InfoMessage	**Informational** – Notification that there is additional information about the current operation.

RecordsetEvent	Description
FetchProgress, FetchComplete	**Retrieval Status** – Notification of the progress of a data retrieval operation, or that the retrieval operation has completed.
WillChangeField, FieldChangeComplete	**Field Change Management** – Notification that the value of the current field will change, or has changed.
WillMove, MoveComplete, EndOfRecordset	**Navigation Management** – Notification that the current row position in a Recordset will change, has changed, or has reached the end of the Recordset.
WillChangeRecord, RecordChangeComplete	**Row Change Management** – Notification that something in the current row of the Recordset will change, or has changed.
WillChangeRecordset, RecordsetChangeComplete	**Recordset Change Management** – Notification that something in the current Recordset will change, or has changed.

Here is a code sample of how to use events in ADO. This example will demonstrate the EndOfRecordset event. Here is how we 'sink' the events for the Recordset in a Form or Class module:

```
Option Explicit
```

```
Private WithEvents rstAuthor As ADODB.Recordset
```

> **Note: You cannot use** `WithEvents` **in a Standard Module in Visual Basic. It must be in an object module, i.e. a Class Module or in a Form Module.**

Here is the code for looping through the authors table (Note that the variable `rstAuthors` is already declared above):

```
Private Sub GetAuthors()

    Dim strSQL As String
        Dim strConnection As String

    strConnection = "PROVIDER=SQLOLEDB;Data Source=localhost;" _
    & "Initial Catalog=pubs;User Id=sa;Password=;"

    strSQL = "SELECT * FROM authors"

    Set rstAuthor = New ADODB.Recordset
    With rstAuthor
        .Open strSQL, strConnection, , , adAsyncFetch
    End With
    rstAuthor.Close
    Set rstAuthor = Nothing

End Sub
```

This code asynchronously fetches rows from the authors table into the `rstAuthors Recordset` variable. Now, we will use an event to notify us when we have finished fetching all of the rows:

```
Private Sub rstAuthor_FetchComplete(ByVal pError As ADODB.Error, _
                                    adStatus As ADODB.EventStatusEnum, _
                                    ByVal pRecordset As ADODB.Recordset)

    If adStatus = adStatusOK Then
        Debug.Print "All rows have been retrieved!"
    End If

End Sub
```

Implications of Using ADO Events with COM+

Up until this point, we have discussed the benefits of asynchronous processing, the asynchronous operations available in ADO, and the events that ADO raises. We have not considered how asynchronous operations and events will perform in a COM+ component. If we wanted to put the above data access code into a COM+ application, this is what the code would look like for the Class Module:

```vb
Option Explicit

Implements ObjectControl

Private mobjContext As ObjectContext
Private WithEvents rstAuthor As ADODB.Recordset

Public Function GetAuthors() As ADODB.Recordset

On Error GoTo ErrorHandler

    Dim strSQL As String
        Dim strConnection As String

    strConnection = "PROVIDER=SQLOLEDB;Source=localhost;" _
    & "Initial Catalog=pubs;User Id=sa;Password=;"

    strSQL = "SELECT * FROM authors"


    rstAuthor.CursorLocation = adUseClient
    rstAuthor.Open strSQL, strConnection, , , adAsyncFetch
    Set rstAuthor.ActiveConnection = Nothing
    Set GetAuthors = rstAuthor
    mobjContext.SetComplete

ExitProc:
    Exit Function

ErrorHandler:
    mobjContext.SetAbort
    Resume ExitProc

End Function

Private Sub ObjectControl_Activate()

    Set mobjContext = GetObjectContext
    Set rstAuthor = New ADODB.Recordset

End Sub

Private Function ObjectControl_CanBePooled() As Boolean

    ObjectControl_CanBePooled = True

End Function

Private Sub ObjectControl_Deactivate()

    Set mobjContext = Nothing
    Set rstAuthor = Nothing

End Sub
```

Although this code will work, it is not recommended that you raise your own events in MTS or COM+. If you create an object that generates events, then that object must remain alive and active on the server, constantly monitoring for the conditions to trigger events. This means consuming lots of server resources, not to mention all of the network traffic that broadcasting events causes. These factors will greatly inhibit the scalability of the server. When developing components for MTS or COM+, they should be stateless. Again, if the components are not stateless, then they will be potentially eating up valuable server resources. If you do need events in COM+, you can use the COM+ Event Service, which uses a publisher-subscriber metaphor. However, the COM+ Event Service is beyond the scope of this book.

The rule with MTS and COM+ is to obtain resources late and release them early. The longer a client keeps a database connection open, the greater the possibility that another client may be blocked from using the database due to having too many connections open. With most databases, such as SQL Server, there are only a certain number of concurrent connections allowed according to the licensing that has been purchased. Therefore, if too many connections are open at the same time, another client may be blocked from connecting to the database.

MSMQ

After looking at ADO 2.5's asynchronous operations and events, you might have been a little bit discouraged to find that ADO events do not work too well with COM+ and the Internet Publishing Provider. The reason they do not is that events require an object to maintain its state, which is exactly the opposite of the statelessness paradigm of COM+ and HTTP. Before you start thinking that all distributed applications must operate synchronously using COM and DCOM, there is a solution to this dilemma. The answer is Microsoft Message Queuing Services (MSMQ). MSMQ Services makes asynchronous programming possible in a distributed environment. Not only does it handle asynchronous operations well, but it also offers built-in transactional support so message queues can participate in COM+ transactions. Just as with ADO events and ADO asynchronous operations, with MSMQ we can allow the client to make a request and still proceed with other work. The difference is, with MSMQ we do not even need the server to be available to process our request. We just put our request on the queue and as long as our request meets the criteria to go into the queue, then we go about our business. Our request is then forwarded to its proper destination and processed at a later time. This entire process can also be run under the context of a single transaction, since MSMQ integrates very well with COM+.

What is MSMQ?

A short definition for MSMQ is that it is a messaging middleware system that allows us to store and forward messages between applications. The messages that are stored and forwarded contain both metadata about the message itself, such as who the message is from, where it is going, and also the message data. What this buys us is scalability and reliability. A loosely coupled asynchronous system utilizing MSMQ may not necessarily be faster than a synchronous system communicating through COM or DCOM, but it can handle greater transaction throughput without failing. The loosely coupled system will result in greater scalability for the application.. This is because, with MSMQ, we can offload work that does not necessarily need to be done right away to another machine and not have to wait on that machine to finish processing the work. Since DCOM uses synchronous **Remote Procedure Calls** (**RPC**) to package up and marshal the bytes for executing methods, if one of the machines involved in the request becomes unavailable, the method request will fail. With MSMQ, you can make use of a message queue that resides on the client. The only synchronous call is just to place the message in the queue. Independent clients can send messages to other MSMQ server queues, and at the same time they can save the messages locally in case they cannot be delivered. This is how MSMQ can guarantee delivery, although it may not always be a timely delivery if the server queue happens to go down.

Who Needs MSMQ?

A modern example of a business that could benefit greatly from MSMQ is an e-commerce site. Typically, the goal of any online store is to consistently increase sales. This translates into a requirement of being able to accept a large number of orders in a short time period, such as during Christmas season. The key to being able to accomplish this goal is to have a system in place that can scale to meet the consumer demand. Let's take a closer look at how to architect this type of loosely coupled system.

When an order is placed online, several things must happen. The customer and order data must be validated, the credit card must be processed, the order must be confirmed, etc. The end result is that the order is processed and shipped to its destination. Now, if all of this processing is executed synchronously, i.e. while the user stares at an hourglass while the submit order button has been clicked, not too many users would want to come back to the site again. As a result of using this type of architecture, valuable server resources are being taken up on the web server processing someone's order that could be used to take someone else's order.

A logical way to partition the site would be to have a front-office and a back-office. The front-office would typically reside on or very near to a web server and would only do processing that is immediately required, such as validating an address or credit card number. It could then send the order to the client's message queue (Independent client MSMQ) to be asynchronously forwarded to the server's message queue, also known as the Primary Enterprise Controller (PEC) Server. In the event that the PEC was down, the MSMQ order message would be stored locally. The back-office would reside on another server or servers, depending on how complex the site is. The back-office's responsibility would be to pick up and process orders from the PEC queue, update inventory, adjust the status of orders, and any other activities that do not need to immediately occur when a customer places an order. By implementing this type of architecture, the front-office web site can maximize the number of orders it can handle and the back-office can systematically process each order and not interfere with any front-office processing.

Using MSMQ with ADO

The data that goes into the body of an MSMQ message can be just about any data type, such as strings, dates, integers, arrays, etc. It can also be any COM object that supports the IPersistStream interface. Therefore, since the ADO Recordset supports this interface, we can send one as the body of an MSMQ message.

Being able to send ADO Recordsets as the body of MSMQ messages is very useful for many reasons, such as:

❑ You do not need a special decoder ring in the receiving code to process the message. You simply re-instantiate the Recordset and begin working with it just as if you created it straight from a database.

❑ You can send a fairly large amount of data in a compact and efficient way.

❑ You can use the Recordset object to send method arguments to another component's methods.

As an example, we can send an MSMQ message having a body containing an ADO Recordset of just the au_id column of all of the authors that we would like to delete from the authors table. In the code that receives the MSMQ message, we simply reassign the contents of the body back to an ADO Recordset. Then we can use the metadata of the fields of the recordset object to build the parameters of an ADO Command object to delete the authors in the incoming ADO Recordset from the authors table.

We will demonstrate this by creating a simple Visual Basic Standard EXE project with a form and two command buttons, cmdSend and cmdReceive. In order to access the objects and properties of MSMQ, you need to set a reference to its object model. This is what your References dialog should look like:

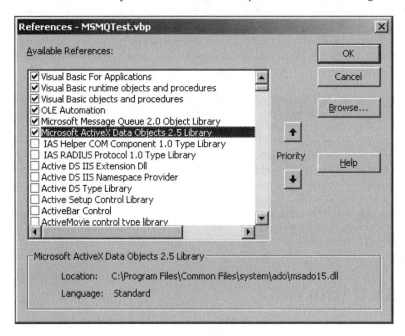

Here is the sending code for this example:

```
Private Sub cmdSend_Click()

On Error GoTo ErrorHandler

    'ADO object
    Dim rstSend As ADODB.Recordset

    Dim strConnection As String
    Dim strSQL As String

    'MSMQ objects
    Dim qInfo As MSMQQueueInfo
    Dim mSend As MSMQMessage
    Dim qSend As MSMQQueue
```

```vb
strConnection = "PROVIDER=SQLOLEDB;Source=localhost;" _
    & "Initial Catalog=pubs;User Id=sa;Password=;"

strSQL = "SELECT au_id FROM authors WHERE au_lname = 'Carson'"

'Set the root MSMQ object, the
'path of the queue, and the queue label
Set qInfo = New MSMQQueueInfo
qInfo.PathName = ".\PRIVATE$\RecordsetQ"
qInfo.Label = "My Recordset Queue"

'Create the queue
'Keep going if the queue already exists
On Error Resume Next
qInfo.Create
On Error GoTo 0

'Open the queue
Set qSend = qInfo.Open(MQ_SEND_ACCESS, MQ_DENY_NONE)

'Open a disconnected recordset
Set rstSend = New ADODB.Recordset
With rstSend
    .CursorLocation = adUseClient
    .Open strSQL, strConnection
    Set .ActiveConnection = Nothing
End With

'Instantiate the message object
Set mSend = New MSMQMessage

'Set the message label
mSend.Label = "Testing Recordset"

'Assign a recordset to the message body
mSend.Body = rstSend

'Send the message
mSend.Send qSend

'Close the queue
qSend.Close

'Clean up
ExitProc:
    Set rstSend = Nothing
    Set qInfo = Nothing
    Set mSend = Nothing
    Set qSend = Nothing
    Exit Sub
```

```
'Log any errors
ErrorHandler:
    App.LogEvent "Error:  " & Err.Description
    Resume ExitProc

End Sub
```

The first step that we take in this procedure is to initialize the connection string and the SQL string. Then we need to initialize the `MSMQQueueInfo` object, which acts as the root MSMQ object. Next we set the queue path and the name of the queue. In this example, we are creating a Private queue. This is because a private queue is the only type of queue you can use if the machine you are using is acting as a workgroup. If the machine is part of a network, then you can use a public queue. The next steps are to open the queue, build the recordset, and then assign the recordset object to the body of the message.

> **Please note that you need to use a disconnected recordset for this to work. This is because the recordset is being persisted as binary data into the message body.**

Finally, we send the message and close the queue. Here is what the new message will look like inside the MSMQ MMC snap-in:

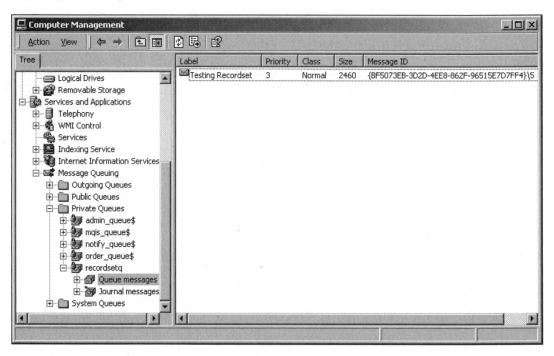

Here is the code for receiving the recordset message:

```vb
Private Sub cmdReceive_Click()

On Error GoTo ErrorHandler

    'ADO objects
    Dim rstReceive As ADODB.Recordset
    Dim cmd As ADODB.Command
    Dim fld As ADODB.Field

    Dim strConnection As String

    'MSMQ objects
    Dim qInfo As MSMQQueueInfo
    Dim qReceive As MSMQQueue
    Dim mReceive As MSMQMessage

    'Set the root MSMQ object
    'and path of the queue
    Set qInfo = New MSMQQueueInfo
    qInfo.PathName = ".\PRIVATE$\RecordsetQ"

    'Open the receiving queue
    Set qReceive = qInfo.Open(MQ_RECEIVE_ACCESS, MQ_DENY_NONE)

    'Get the receiving message
    Set mReceive = qReceive.Receive

    'Get the recordset from the message body
    Set rstReceive = mReceive.Body

    'Close the queue
    qReceive.Close

    'Connection string
    strConnection = "PROVIDER=SQLOLEDB;Source=localhost;" _
    & "Initial Catalog=pubs;User Id=sa;Password=;"

    'Set up the Command object
    'and define its parameters
    Set cmd = New ADODB.Command
    With cmd
        .ActiveConnection = strConnection
        .CommandType = adCmdStoredProc
        .CommandText = "usp_delete_author"
        .Parameters.Append .CreateParameter("RETURN_VALUE", adInteger, _
        adParamReturnValue, 4)
        For Each fld In rstReceive.Fields
            .Parameters.Append .CreateParameter("@" & fld.Name, fld.Type, _
            adParamInput, fld.DefinedSize)
        Next
    End With
```

```
        'Loop through the recordset and delete every
        'author in the recordset from the database
        With rstReceive
            Do Until .EOF
                For Each fld In rstReceive.Fields
                    cmd.Parameters("@" & fld.Name).Value = fld.Value
                Next
                cmd.Execute , , adExecuteNoRecords
                .MoveNext
            Loop
        End With

    'Clean up
    ExitProc:
        Set rstReceive = Nothing
        Set cmd = Nothing
        Set fld = Nothing
        Set qInfo = Nothing
        Set qReceive = Nothing
        Set mReceive = Nothing
        Exit Sub

    'Log any errors
    ErrorHandler:
        App.LogEvent "Error:  " & Err.Description
        Resume ExitProc

    End Sub
```

The first step that we take in this procedure is to again initialize the MSMQQueueInfo object. Also, we need to set the queue path and the name of the queue that we want to receive. Next, we open the queue, and retrieve the recordset from the body of the message. Since we have the information that we were after, we then close the queue. We then initialize and populate the parameters and properties of the Command object. This is a good example of using the metadata that the Field object contains to populate the data parameters of the Command object. Now that the Command object is ready, we loop through the recordset and execute the command to delete an author for every record in the recordset. Again we are using the metadata in the Field object for the parameter name and value. Since we could possibly be executing this stored procedure several times, we use the adExecuteNoRecords option of the Command object's Execute method. This improves performance by not returning an unnecessary Recordset object every time that the command is executed.

Here is the stored procedure used for the delete operation:

```
IF EXISTS (select * from sysobjects where id = object_id(N'[usp_delete_author]')
and OBJECTPROPERTY(id, N'IsProcedure') = 1)
DROP PROCEDURE [usp_delete_author]
GO
CREATE PROCEDURE usp_delete_author
    @au_id varchar(11)
AS
```

```
DELETE
FROM
      titleauthor
WHERE
      au_id = @au_id
DELETE

FROM
      authors
WHERE
      au_id = @au_id

RETURN(@@Error)
GO
```

COM+ Queued Components

Queued Components, a key feature of COM+ and based on MSMQ, provide an easy way to invoke and execute components asynchronously. Processing can occur without regard to the availability or accessibility of either the sender or receiver.

As mentioned previously when discussing MSMQ, DCOM uses synchronous RPC calls to marshal the data representing a COM call on another machine. The diagram below shows this:

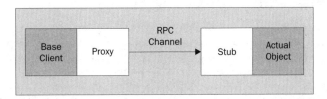

Queued Components, on the other hand, actually use MSMQ to handle the communication between the client-side proxy and the server-side stub, as shown below:

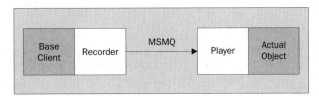

Queued Components consists of:

- ❏ Recorder (for the client side).
- ❏ Listener (for the server side).
- ❏ Player (for the server side).
- ❏ Message Mover tool to move messages from one queue to another.

Here is a more detailed diagram of the Queued Components architecture:

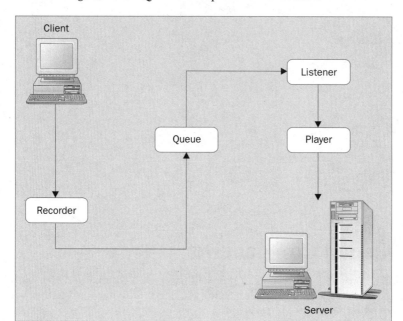

The Communication Process

When a client calls a method on a Queued Component, the client does not communicate with the actual COM object. Instead, the client is actually talking to a call recorder. This happens without the client knowing it; they still keep making COM calls as they normally would, but instead of getting marshaled to the server the calls are recorded on the client. As soon as the client releases the Queued Component, the Message Mover bundles up all of the COM calls and sends them asynchronously via an MSMQ message to the server on which the actual COM component is installed. The Listener on the server then uses MSMQ to read the message containing the bundled up COM calls sent by the client. Finally, the server then activates the Player to create the actual COM object and to play all of the recorded calls into it so they can then be executed.

Calling Queued Components

When using COM+, the way you instantiate your components dictates whether or not you will be making an asynchronous call through the Queued Components service or just a synchronous call through DCOM. If you use the `CreateObject` function to create your objects, then you will be using COM/DCOM. Here is a code sample of how to call a queued component:

```
Dim objAuthors As Pubs.Authors

Set objAuthors = GetObject("queue:/new:Pubs.Authors")
```

The Benefits

When designing new applications, you must consider the implication of coding components for synchronous processing versus asynchronous processing. Ultimately, the choice depends on the requirements of the specific application. Using queued processing offers advantages for certain applications, while writing an application using real-time, synchronous processing could be the best choice for another application. As a guideline, queued processing offers the following advantages over real-time processing:

- ❑ Component Availability
- ❑ Component Lifetimes
- ❑ Disconnected Applications
- ❑ Message Reliability
- ❑ Server Scheduling

Component Availability

A component may not be available because of server overload or networking problems. In a real-time processing application, if just one component of the transaction is not available, the entire process is blocked and cannot complete. An application using Queued Components separates the transaction into activities that must be completed now and those that can be completed at a later time. Messages are queued for later processing while the requesting component is free for other tasks.

Component Lifetimes

An application using Queued Components allows the server component to operate independently of the client. As a result, server components can complete more quickly. In a real-time system, the server component exists from the time it is created until the object is finally released. The server waits for the client to make method calls and for results to be returned, which negates the rapid cycling of server objects and limits server scalability.

Disconnected Applications

Sales of laptops, notebooks, and palm computers have created a need for applications that service mobile users. In a queued system, these users can work in a disconnected scenario when not connected to the server and later connect to the servers or databases to process their requests.

Message Reliability

Queued Components uses database techniques to protect data in a robust way. In the event of a server failure, all pending transactions are rolled back so that messages do not get lost.

Server Scheduling

An application using Queued Components is well suited to time-shifted component execution, which defers non-critical work to an off-peak period. This is the same concept that many of you have used in traditional batch mode processing. Similar requests can be executed one right after the other by the server, rather than requiring the server to react immediately to a myriad of different requests.

Writing Queued Components

Queued Components enhance the COM+ programming model to provide an environment in which components can be invoked either synchronously (real-time) or asynchronously (queued) – the component need not be aware of this environment. You simply write the COM component as you normally would, and then place the component into a COM+ Application. This is basically the same process as placing components in MTS in Windows NT 4.0. You then select from the Queuing dialog in the properties of your COM+ Application, whether or not you want the component to be queued, and whether or not the component will use the listener service to retrieve incoming calls via MSMQ. Here is what this dialog looks like:

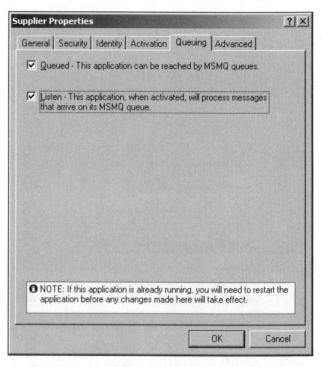

The next thing you need to do make sure your component's interfaces are marked as Queued. This lets COM+ know that it will receive incoming requests to this interface via MSMQ. This does not affect any outgoing calls made by this component to any other components. Here is what the Queuing Properties dialog box will look like:

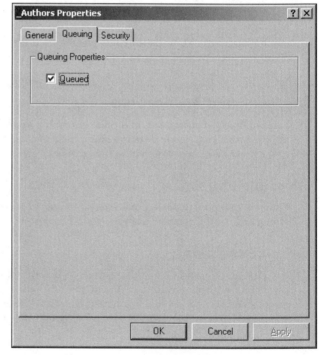

Do's and Don'ts of Writing Queued Components

❑ Do not return any values from your methods.

❑ Do not pass arguments by reference (ByRef); they must be passed by value (ByVal).

These rules seem pretty simple, but to implement them will probably change your style of programming a little bit. Most code that we write is usually written with the assumption that a client is always talking synchronously with the server. We usually use functions that return a Boolean or integer so we know whether or not our method succeeded or not. In order to use Queued Components, we must now write our code in a way that the server has everything it needs to carry our task. The server has no way of calling back to the client to get more information later.

Another subtle thing to watch out for is passing objects as arguments to methods. This includes those handy Dictionary and Collection objects we have gotten so accustomed to using to pass complex data in as a single parameter. Since all objects are passed by reference, these types of calls will fail with Queued Components. In my opinion, there are a few good ways to pass complex data to Queued Components. They are:

❑ A dimensioned array

❑ A persistable COM object (supports the IPersistStream interface)

❑ XML

ADO to the Rescue!

My favorite option is to use an ADO Recordset object to pass in several parameters to a method. As mentioned before, recordsets are persistable. **Therefore, they can be passed by value.** The ADO Recordset object is something that we should all be familiar with by now. It is both elegant and easy to work with. Here is an example of passing in an ADO Recordset as an argument to a public method:

```
Public Sub UpdateAuthor(ByVal rstAuthors As ADODB.Recordset)

      'Code here for updating each record
      'in the database

End Sub
```

Alternatively, we can also use ADO to persist a Recordset object as XML, and then pass XML as a string argument to a public method.

What about MSMQ?

Since Queued Components have so many benefits, do not require much extra effort at all to program, and also abstract MSMQ, you may be asking yourself, 'Why should I write code for MSMQ when I can just use Queued Components?' The main reason I can come up with is control. The more you abstract something, the less fine-grained control you will have. You cannot do everything with Queued Components that you can do with MSMQ directly. For example, with Queued Components you do not have control over the message format definition or the label of the message; but with MSMQ you do have control over these properties. It is the same reason why sometimes you may need to use the Win32 API, or Visual C++ instead of Visual Basic. It just depends on the degree of control you need and time and budget constraints.

Summary

In this chapter we have covered the following topics:

❑ Asynchronous processing

❑ Asynchronous events

❑ How ADO implements asynchronous processing and events

❑ Using asynchronous processing and events in COM+

❑ MSMQ as a method of asynchronous communication

❑ ADO's role with MSMQ

❑ COM+ Queued Components

❑ ADO's role with COM+ Queued Components

We have many choices available for doing work asynchronously. In today's world of distributed computing, the concepts that we have covered in this chapter are only going to become more and more useful. By choosing the right combinations and knowing when to use synchronous versus asynchronous calls, we will be able to make highly scalable, responsive, and fault-tolerant applications.

6

Data Shaping

This section covers the concepts and techniques behind ADO data shaping. We will explain what data shaping is, how to implement the SHAPE language and answer the all important question – 'Why would I ever use this?'

An Introduction to Data Shaping

One of the coolest, and arguably the most complex, technology implemented in ADO is data shaping. Data shaping allows you to develop hierarchical recordsets through an extension of regular SQL syntax. A hierarchical recordset is a standard recordset that contains a child recordset of related records. For instance, a customer's recordset could contain a recordset that holds all of the orders for that particular customer. Once you move to the next record in the customer recordset, the underlying recordset changes to contain the order information for that customer. These hierarchical recordsets can eliminate the need to dynamically re-query additional child recordsets in code since a shaped recordset returns as one object and can process whenever you navigate between rows in a recordset.

> A hierarchical recordset is a recordset (the parent recordset) that contains a field that is actually a pointer to another recordset (a child recordset) that is in some way related to the parent recordset.

Data shaping can be a bit overwhelming since the SHAPE syntax can be confusing. There is still limited documentation on shaping and there is very little you can compare the concepts to. I will try to remove some of the mystery and complexity behind shaped recordsets.

Another point to note about SHAPE queries is that the SHAPE language is not ANSI-SQL compliant. The MSDataShape provider acts as a translation layer between the SHAPE command and the SQL queries that are sent to the OLEDB provider or ODBC driver. The relationships between all of the objects is displayed in the following diagram.

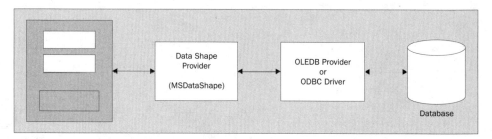

Prior to data shaping in ADO 2.0, developers needed to use queries that performed JOINs on database tables that were used to return related data. This was inefficient since there were a lot of duplicate records in the recordset. The following query would be used to return customers and orders:

```
SELECT Customers.CustomerID, Customers.CompanyName, Orders.OrderID,
Orders.OrderDate, Orders.EmployeeID, Orders.ShippedDate
FROM Customers INNER JOIN Orders ON Customers.CustomerID = Orders.CustomerID
```

The problem with this approach is that you must return the customer information for every order. You will note that in the output of the above query, the first two columns are repeated for every customer. You are being forced to transmit possibly hundreds of fields of repeating data which slows down your application and wastes bandwidth.

CustomerID	CompanyName	OrderID	OrderDate	EmployeeID	ShippedDate
CustomerID	CompanyName	OrderID	OrderDate	EmployeeID	ShippedDate
CustomerID	CompanyName	OrderID	OrderDate	EmployeeID	ShippedDate
CustomerID	CompanyName	OrderID	OrderDate	EmployeeID	ShippedDate
CustomerID	CompanyName	OrderID	OrderDate	EmployeeID	ShippedDate

The results of the query may better demonstrate this redundancy as you will see in the following table.

Customer ID	CompanyName	Order ID	OrderDate	Employee	Shipped Date
ALFKI	Alfreds Futterkiste	10692	03-Oct-1997	Peacock, Margaret	13-Oct-1997
ALFKI	Alfreds Futterkiste	10702	13-Oct-1997	Peacock, Margaret	21-Oct-1997
ALFKI	Alfreds Futterkiste	10835	15-Jan-1998	Davolio, Nancy	21-Jan-1998

Customer ID	CompanyName	Order ID	OrderDate	Employee	Shipped Date
ALFKI	Alfreds Futterkiste	10952	16-Mar-1998	Davolio, Nancy	24-Mar-1998
ALFKI	Alfreds Futterkiste	11011	09-Apr-1998	Leverling, Janet	13-Apr-1998
ALFKI	Alfreds Futterkiste	10643	25-Aug-1997	Suyama, Michael	02-Sep-1997
ANTON	Antonio Moreno Taquería	10365	27-Nov-1996	Leverling, Janet	02-Dec-1996
ANTON	Antonio Moreno Taquería	10856	28-Jan-1998	Leverling, Janet	10-Feb-1998
ANTON	Antonio Moreno Taquería	10682	25-Sep-1997	Leverling, Janet	01-Oct-1997
ANTON	Antonio Moreno Taquería	10677	22-Sep-1997	Davolio, Nancy	26-Sep-1997
ANTON	Antonio Moreno Taquería	10573	19-Jun-1997	King, Robert	20-Jun-1997
ANTON	Antonio Moreno Taquería	10507	15-Apr-1997	King, Robert	22-Apr-1997
ANTON	Antonio Moreno Taquería	10535	13-May-1997	Peacock, Margaret	21-May-1997

Data shaping was designed with these types of problems in mind and the need to be able to easily report on complex data. Enterprise Information Systems and data warehouses are more popular than ever, and the need to get to data is more important than ever.

There are three types of shaped recordsets: parent-child, parameterized hierarchies, and group-based hierarchies.

Firstly, we have a standard parent-child relationship. If we have an orders table and a customer table, then we can create a parent-child relationship through data shaping. If we relate the customer_id in the customers table to the customer_id in the orders table we will get a shaped recordset that looks like this:

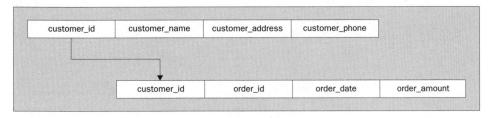

Using a SHAPE command we can generate this parent-child relationship:

```
SHAPE {SELECT * FROM customers}
APPEND ({SELECT * FROM orders} as rsOrders
RELATE customer_id to customer_id)
```

We will look at the syntax of the Shape command in more detail later in this section. But for now, it is important to note that we are able to return all of this information within one command and we can build complex hierarchical recordsets with relative ease.

Advances in Data Shaping

ADO 2.0 introduced the ability to shape data by adding the SHAPE syntax and hierarchical recordsets. The initial implementation of SHAPE was limited in how child recordsets could be processed.

ADO 2.1 added the ability to reshape a recordset, containing grandchild aggregates and parameterized commands, with COMPUTE statements.

ADO 2.5 does not extend data shaping. You can run all of the SHAPE examples in this chapter with ADO 2.1 as well as ADO 2.5.

What You Need to SHAPE

In order to implement data shaping with the majority of options, you will need at least ADO 2.0. If you plan on using some of the newer features such as reshaping, creating grandchild aggregates, or using parameterized commands then you will need ADO 2.1 or newer.

You will also need two providers: one will be for the data shaping and the other will be for the actual database server that you would like to use.

Finally you will need Visual Basic or a similar language to test the SHAPE commands. For our examples, we will be using the Northwind database. Specifically we will be using the SQL Server 7.0 version of Northwind, but the Access version should work for the majority of the examples.

Getting Help with SHAPE Commands

SHAPE commands can be difficult to verify and to build. In this section we will look at ways to view and build them with little effort.

Putting Together a SHAPE Testing Application

We really need to be able to test our queries and 'see' the results of the SHAPE commands to fully understand the SHAPE language and the relation of the recordsets. Here is a small test application that you can put together that will run a shape command and output the results to a hierarchical FlexGrid control.

Create a new Visual Basic application using the standard EXE template. On the default form add three controls: a textbox with the multiline property set to TRUE, a button, and a FlexGrid control. The FlexGrid is not in the toolbox by default, so we need to add it.

Right-click on the toolbar to get the popup menu. Select the **Components...** option from the menu:

You will then get the component window. Look for the **Microsoft Hierarchical FlexGrid Control** and check the box beside the entry. This will add the FlexGrid to your toolbox:

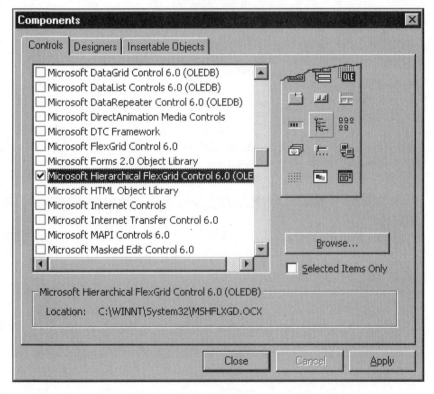

Add a FlexGrid on the form and give the controls the following names:

Textbox – `txtShapeCommand`

Button – `cmdExecute`

FlexGrid – `mshGrid`

In the `cmdExecute_OnClick` event add the following code:

```
Dim cn As ADODB.Connection, rs As ADODB.Recordset

Me.MousePointer = vbHourglass

Set cn = New ADODB.Connection
Set rs = New ADODB.Recordset
cn.Open "Provider=MSDataShape;Data Provider=SQLOLEDB.1;User ID=sa;" & _
        "Initial Catalog=Northwind;Data Source=SCREAMER;User Id=sa;"

On Error Resume Next
rs.Open txtShapeCommand.Text, cn, adOpenStatic, adLockReadOnly, adCmdText

If Err Then
  MsgBox "Error - " & Err.Number & ":" & Err.Description
End If

Set mshGrid.DataSource = rs

If Err Then
  MsgBox "Error - " & Err.Number & ":" & Err.Description
End If


rs.Close
cn.Close

Set rs = Nothing
Set cn = Nothing

Me.MousePointer = vbNormal
```

When you run the application your screen will look similar to the following screenshot. Enter the SHAPE command in the textbox and press the button. If the command is valid then the FlexGrid will populate with data and you can expand and collapse the data as needed. If there is an error then you will get a message box detailing the problem.

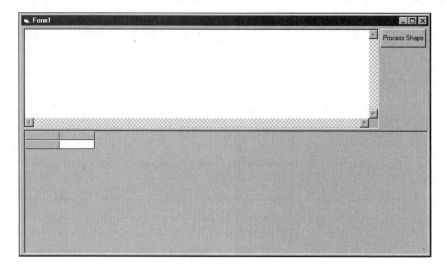

If your command is successful then you will see the data in the FlexGrid control:

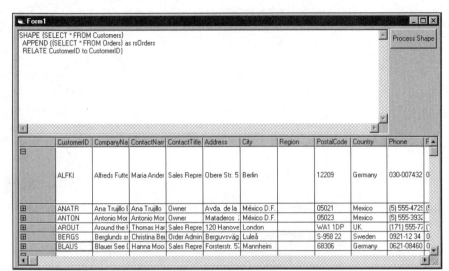

Using the Data Environment

It can be very difficult to create these complex SHAPE commands manually. If you are in need of assistance or would like to find an easy way to generate these commands, look no further than the data environment in Visual Basic. You can create these hierarchical queries easily and then copy and paste the SHAPE command in your application. Let's take a look at one of our queries and see how we can create this through the Data Environment.

Let's generate a simple SHAPE command that creates a COMPUTE BY statement.

First, we need to add the data environment to an existing Visual Basic project. We do this by selecting **Project -> Add Data Environment**, or under **Project->More ActiveX Designers->Add Data Environment**. This gives us a blank data environment window.

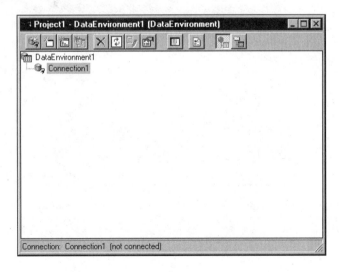

From this window we can right click on the **Connection1** entry and set a connection to our database. Select the **P**roperties menu item to configure the data connection:

We get our first connection dialog. We are asked to select a driver:

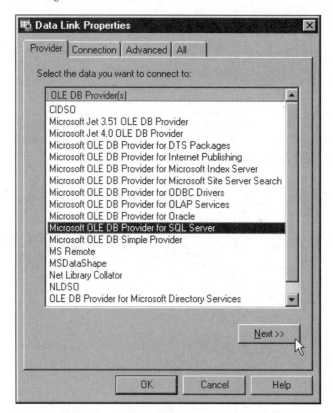

Your list may vary depending on the drivers you have installed. Since I am using the Northwind database from SQL Server I have selected the SQL Server OLE DB Provider. You could also select the OLE DB Provider for ODBC Drivers and use the old ODBC driver. However, this is used more for legacy drivers where native OLE DB providers are not yet available.

Once you've selected the provider press the **Next >>** button to configure it:

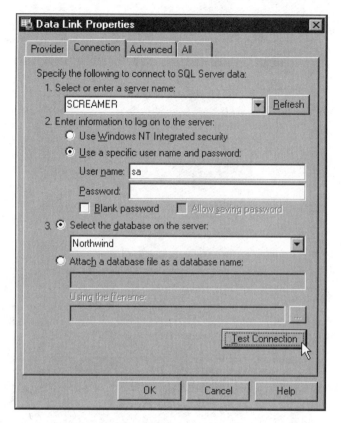

This screen will also vary depending on the OLE DB provider that you use. It is always a good idea to press the **Test Connection** button to verify your settings. If everything is configured properly you will get a success message.

Press the **OK** button on the connection settings dialog to return to the data environment window.

Once we have a valid connection we can once again right-click on the connection and select **Add Command** from the popup menu:

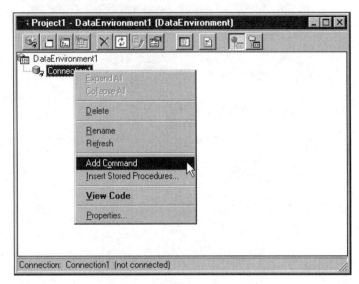

This gives us a new `Command` object. We select the properties of the new data `Command` object and we see the **Command1 properties** window. Here we set the type of object (table, stored procedure, view, or SQL statement) and any other required properties:

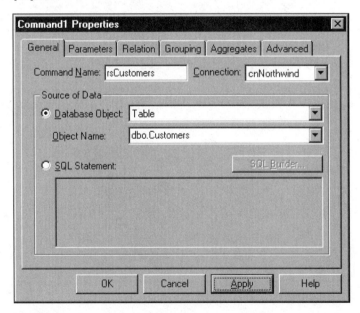

Once we have set up our information in the property pages we select the **OK** button and our command is now connected to the database and we can use it as-is. Unfortunately it is not very useful at the moment since this is nothing more than a straightforward `SELECT` statement.

If we right-click on the command we can select the Add Child Command entry in the pop-up menu. This will start to build our hierarchical recordset.

We go into the property pages for the new child command and set the recordsource information:

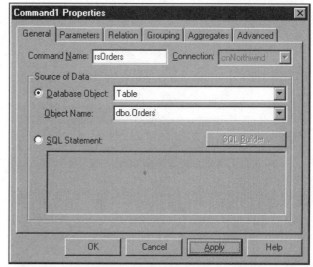

In order to link the child command to the parent command we must go to the Relation tab to set the relationship (the RELATE portion of the SHAPE command) to the parent Command object:

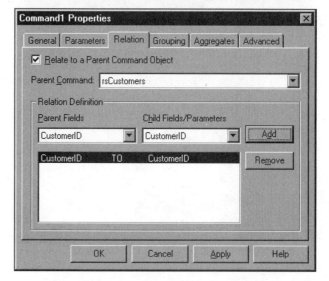

If we save the child command here we will have a hierarchical recordset built by the data environment. If we wanted to see the SHAPE command that this uses then we would select the parent command and right-click. From the popup-menu, selecting the Hierarchy Info entry would result in a dialog with all of the SHAPE information.

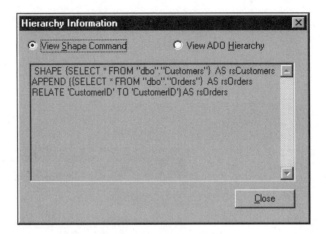

We can copy and paste this SHAPE command into our test application and run this command to verify the SHAPE statement. As you can see, this is a valid SHAPE statement that we can use in other applications.

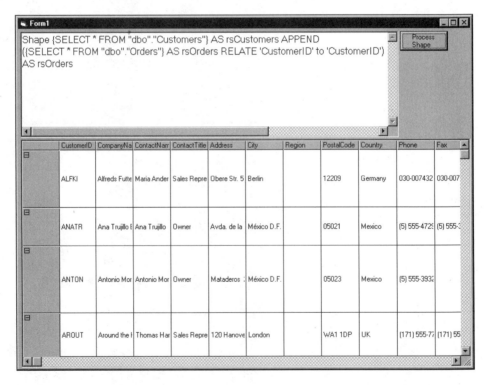

What we can then do is add another child command in the data environment. Up until now we have used the default names of command1 and command2. For clarity, let's rename command1 to Customers and command2 to Orders. Let's add a child command to Orders called OrderDetails that uses a SQL statement:

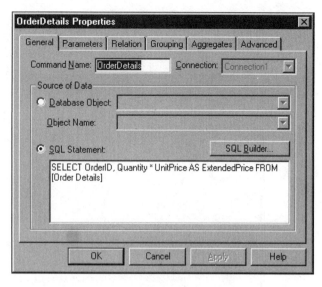

We now have a SHAPE command that is similar to one that we have already seen:

```
SHAPE {SELECT * FROM Orders}
APPEND ({SELECT [Order Details].OrderID,
 [Order Details].UnitPrice * [Order Details].Quantity as ExtendedPrice
 FROM [Order Details]}
RELATE OrderID TO OrderID) As rsOrderDetails,
SUM(rsOrderDetails.ExtendedPrice) AS OrderTotal
```

This is the same SHAPE command as the statement above with two exceptions:

❑ We have added a Customer parent recordset to the Orders recordset.

❑ We do not have an OrderTotal field.

We can generate the OrderTotal field by going to the properties of the Orders command and selecting the **Aggregates** tab. From here we can set up our SUM statement:

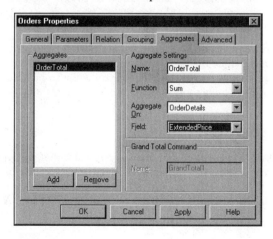

Our data environment now reflects this change by adding the additional field to the Orders command:

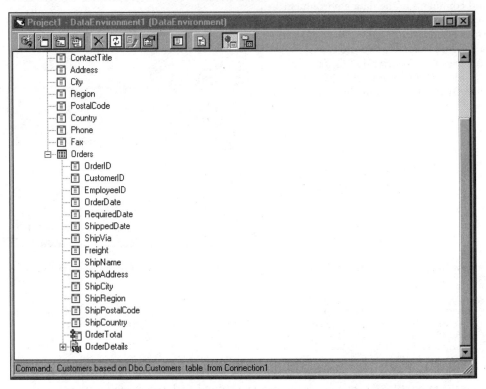

Our SHAPE command now looks like our SHAPE sample above. If we select the hierarchy information for the Customer recordset we get this SHAPE command (with some formatting applied):

```
SHAPE {SELECT * FROM "dbo"."Customers"} AS Customers
APPEND (( SHAPE {SELECT * FROM "dbo"."Orders"} AS Orders
APPEND ({SELECT OrderID, Quantity * UnitPrice AS ExtendedPrice
FROM [Order Details]} AS OrderDetails
RELATE 'OrderID' TO 'OrderID') AS OrderDetails,
SUM(OrderDetails.'ExtendedPrice') AS OrderTotal) AS Orders
RELATE 'CustomerID' TO 'CustomerID') AS Orders
```

You can use the data environment to generate complex SHAPE statements. This is much easier than trying to code these by hand since the data environment knows how to properly format the SHAPE statements without errors. By the end of this chapter you will also be able to build these complex queries, but it is always nice to have tools to make the job easier.

Shape Implementation

What does it take to SHAPE a recordset? Contrary to popular belief, you do not need astrologers and voodoo dolls to build correct SHAPE commands. All you need is a little background on how SHAPE commands work and how to properly structure a SHAPE query. The first order of business is to understand how to connect to a database in order to SHAPE a recordset. After we have created a proper connection we will begin shaping our data.

Shaping a Recordset

Data shaping requires that you specify two providers, unless you are manually creating recordsets that are not part of a relational database. The first provider is the service provider that will be the data shaping service for ADO. The second provider is the data provider that will be the actual database provider you use in creating normal connections. If you are programmatically creating recordsets then you will only use the service provider.

You must use the `MSDataShape` provider in order to execute a `SHAPE` command. For example, you can connect to the `pubs` database on SQL Server, for shaping, by executing the following commands:

```
Dim cn as New ADODB.Connection
cn.Provider = "MSDataShape"
cn.Open "Data Provider=SQLOLEDB.1;User ID=sa;Initial Catalog=Northwind;Data
Source=SCREAMER;User Id=sa;"
```

You can also combine the two commands above into one connection string using a `provider=` and a `data provider=` setting:

```
cn.Open "Provider=MSDataShape;Data Provider=SQLOLEDB.1;User ID=sa;" & _
        "Initial Catalog=Northwind;Data Source=SCREAMER;User Id=sa;"
```

You can also programmatically create a recordset that utilizes shaped recordsets. When creating recordsets programmatically, you need to specify that you are not using a data provider and you create the structure of the recordset (or recordsets) directly within the `SHAPE` command.

```
Dim rs As New ADODB.Recordset

rs.ActiveConnection = "provider=msdatashape;data provider=none;"

rs.Open "SHAPE APPEND new adInteger As CustomerID, New adVarChar(30) As Name," & _
    "((SHAPE APPEND new adInteger As CustomerID, New adCurrency As OrderTotal)" & _
    "RELATE CustomerID TO CustomerID) AS rsChild", , adOpenStatic, adLockOptimistic
```

This `SHAPE` command results in a recordset that has a parent and one child.

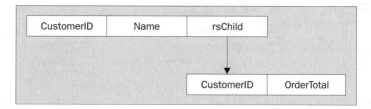

We have created a customer and order table directly within the `SHAPE` command and we can use this in the same manner as if the data had been returned from SQL Server or Access. The field types are `DataTypeEnum` constants from the ADO library. These constants are defined in Appendix B.

Shape Types

Data shaping provides several different types of recordsets that can be returned. They all operate the same way, but the function and execution are a bit different. We start with relational recordsets, move to parameterized recordsets, then we will get into computed and aggregate recordsets.

Relational recordsets represent the most basic form of SHAPE command, where you have a recordset that contains a related child recordset. Parameterized recordsets are similar to relational recordsets except that each child recordset is fetched when a parent moves the record pointer. Parameterized recordsets are also used when calling stored procedures that take parameters. Finally, aggregate recordsets compute values based on child records. You will see these in more detail in the following sections.

Relational Recordsets

Recordsets can be related, which is similar in fashion to a JOIN statement in SQL, except that you will see that related recordsets are more efficient and flexible than the old style of SQL JOIN. You can have a simple parent-child, parent-multiple child, parent-grandchild, parent-multiple grandchild, and even recordsets that have great grandchildren. We will look at the flexibility behind these recordsets in the following sections.

Parent-Child

A parent-child relationship between two tables is created by a simple SHAPE...APPEND syntax. A parent-child relationship would be similar to using a JOIN in SQL without the redundant row-by-row data that a JOIN returns. For instance, if you wanted a list of customers and orders, then you would need to return two recordsets and code for every time you move in either recordset or you could use a JOIN query to return the data as one table. The single table solution is the most common, but most inefficient because you are returning customer information on every row that you have order information. If a customer has placed 100 orders with you then you will duplicate the entire customer table 100 times. This makes for large recordsets and wasted network bandwidth. We can use the SHAPE command to produce the same results in a more efficient manner.

The basic syntax of the SHAPE command is:

```
SHAPE {select query}
APPEND ({next query} <recordset name>
RELATE child_field TO parent_field)  <recordset name>
```

To relate customers and orders you would use the following standard SHAPE syntax to generate the following command:

```
SHAPE {select * from customers}
APPEND ({select * from orders} as rsOrders
RELATE customer_id to customer_id)
```

Executing this SHAPE command will give the structure shown below. The entire Orders table is a child of the Customers table.

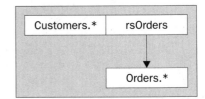

The key point to note here is that we are not duplicating customer data for each order row. Each parent record from the customers table has a field called `rsOrders` that contains a reference to the child recordset from the orders table and contains all of the fields from the orders table. As we move through the customer recordset we requery the child recordset to generate only the required information.

In Visual Basic you would access the child recordset with the following code:

```
Dim rsCustomers As ADODB.Recordset
Dim rsOrders As ADODB.Recordset
Dim SQL As String

Set cn = New ADODB.Connection
Set rsCustomers = New ADODB.Recordset

cn.Provider = "MSDataShape"
cn.Open "dsn=Northwind"

SQL = "SHAPE {SELECT * FROM Customers} "
SQL = SQL & "APPEND ({SELECT * FROM Orders} as rsOrders "
SQL = SQL & "RELATE CustomerID to CustomerID)"

rsCustomers.Open SQL, cn, adOpenStatic, adLockReadOnly, adCmdText

Do While Not rsCustomers.EOF
   Debug.Print "Company: " & rsCustomers.Fields("CompanyName").Value
   Set rsOrders = rsCustomers.Fields("rsOrders").Value
   Do While Not rsOrders.EOF
      Debug.Print Chr(9) & "Order Number: " & rsOrders.Fields("OrderID").Value
      rsOrders.MoveNext
   Loop
   rsOrders.Close
   rsCustomers.MoveNext
Loop

rsCustomers.Close
cn.Close

Set rsCustomers = Nothing
Set rsOrders = Nothing
Set cn = Nothing
```

Part of the output of this code would look as follows in the debug window in Visual Basic:

```
Company: The Big Cheese
 Order Number: 10310
 Order Number: 10708
 Order Number: 10805
 Order Number: 10992
Company: The Cracker Box
 Order Number: 10624
 Order Number: 10775
 Order Number: 11003
Company: Toms Spezialitäten
 Order Number: 10249
 Order Number: 10438
```

Each time we loop through a customer record we are returning the order records and looping through the child (orders) recordset.

Multiple Children

A parent record can have more than one child recordset. For instance, we would like to see all orders over 30 days old in one recordset and all new orders less than 30 days old in another recordset. We can use the SHAPE command to generate these two recordsets under the parent Customer table. If we modify our SQL statement above to look like the following then we will produce two child recordsets.

```
SQL = "SHAPE {SELECT * FROM Customers} "
SQL = SQL & "APPEND ({SELECT * FROM Orders "
SQL = SQL & "WHERE OrderDate < '" & Date - 30 & "' AND CustomerID = ?} "
SQL = SQL & "RELATE CustomerID to PARAMETER 0) as rsOver30Days, "
SQL = SQL & "({SELECT * FROM Orders "
SQL = SQL & "WHERE OrderDate >= '" & Date - 30 & "' AND CustomerID = ?} "
SQL = SQL & "RELATE CustomerID to PARAMETER 0) as rsUnder30Days"
```

In the above command we are using a parameterized query where PARAMETER 0 dynamically populates the CustomerID = ? parameter each time we move in the parent recordset. We can modify our loop to produce the report listed below.

```
Do While Not rsCustomers.EOF
    Debug.Print "Company: " & rsCustomers.Fields("CompanyName").Value
    Set rsOver30Days = rsCustomers.Fields("rsOver30Days").Value
    Debug.Print "OLD ORDERS"
    Do While Not rsOver30Days.EOF
        Debug.Print Chr(9) & "Order Number: " & _
            rsOver30Days.Fields("OrderID").Value & Chr(9) & "Order Date: " & _
            rsOver30Days.Fields("OrderDate").Value
        rsOver30Days.MoveNext
    Loop
    rsOver30Days.Close

    Debug.Print "NEW ORDERS"
    Set rsUnder30Days = rsCustomers.Fields("rsUnder30Days").Value
    Do While Not rsUnder30Days.EOF
        Debug.Print Chr(9) & "Order Number: " & _
            rsUnder30Days.Fields("OrderID").Value & _
            Chr(9) & "Order Date: " & rsUnder30Days.Fields("OrderDate").Value
        rsUnder30Days.MoveNext
    Loop
    rsUnder30Days.Close

    sCustomers.MoveNext
Loop
```

The figure below displays the Customers recordset with the two child recordsets for the orders over 30 days old as well as the recordset for the orders less than 30 days old.

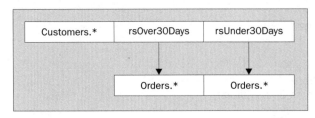

Here is the output for one of the companies in our database:

```
Company: Tortuga Restaurante
OLD ORDERS
 Order Number: 10276 Order Date: 8/8/96
 Order Number: 10293 Order Date: 8/29/96
 Order Number: 10304 Order Date: 9/12/96
 Order Number: 10319 Order Date: 10/2/96
 Order Number: 10518 Order Date: 4/25/97
 Order Number: 10576 Order Date: 6/23/97
 Order Number: 10676 Order Date: 9/22/97
 Order Number: 10842 Order Date: 1/20/98
 Order Number: 10915 Order Date: 2/27/98
NEW ORDERS
 Order Number: 11069 Order Date: 8/4/99
```

You can create as many child recordsets as necessary. You could follow this syntax to generate a shaped recordset of an invoice-aging summary for under 30 days, 30 days, 60 days, and 90 days. By using parameters within your SHAPE command you are creating an efficient means of data retrieval and you are retrieving data in ways that would require multiple temporary tables and calculations through traditional SQL syntax.

Parent-Child-Grandchild

We have seen child recordsets and multiple child recordsets (otherwise referred to as nested shapes) with ADO, but we can continue to add children to child recordsets. This is known as a parent-child-grandchild relationship. Taking our first example one step further, we can append the order details information to the recordset in order to see all of the line items of a given order for a specific customer. The syntax for this stays the same with the exception of an additional APPEND and SHAPE command.

This is the original source

```
SHAPE {SELECT * FROM Customers}
APPEND ({SELECT * FROM Orders} AS rsOrders
RELATE CustomerID to CustomerID)
```

Below is the recordset that is retuned from our SHAPE command.

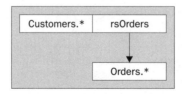

This is the source that has been updated to reflect the new grandchild OrderDetails table.

```
SHAPE {SELECT * FROM Customers}
 APPEND (( SHAPE {SELECT * FROM Orders} AS rsOrders
 APPEND ({SELECT * FROM [Order Details]} AS rsOrderDetails
 RELATE OrderID TO OrderID) AS OrderDetails)
 RELATE CustomerID TO CustomerID)
```

This yields a structure that is shown here:

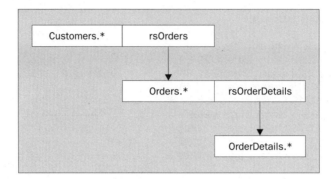

As you can see, we add a grandchild to a child by adding another APPEND clause to the current SHAPE command. We can go even further by appending to a grandchild through another APPEND clause. There is virtually no limit to the number of levels in an ADO shaped recordset.

So, if we take this query even further and determine that we want to be able to see the part details and then the vendor details for each part, we can really go overboard by adding two new APPEND clauses to form a new SHAPE:

```
SHAPE {SELECT * FROM Customers}
  APPEND (( SHAPE {SELECT * FROM Orders} as rsOrders
  APPEND (( SHAPE {SELECT * FROM [Order Details]} AS rsOrderDetails
  APPEND (( SHAPE {SELECT * FROM Products} AS rsProducts
  APPEND ({SELECT * FROM Suppliers} AS rsSuppliers
  RELATE SupplierID TO SupplierID) AS Suppliers)
  RELATE ProductID TO ProductID) AS Products)
  RELATE OrderID TO OrderID) AS OrderDetails)
  RELATE CustomerID TO CustomerID)
```

This SHAPE command yields this recordset structure (Ouch!):

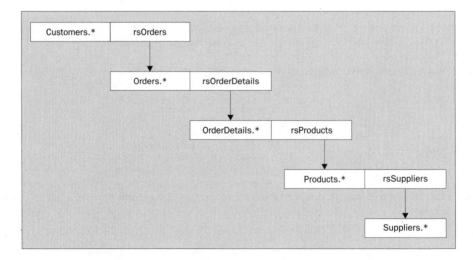

This example will take a little while to run (there is a lot going on here), but when it returns the FlexGrid will populate with the entire tree of data. Working from the inside out here is what our SHAPE does:

- ❑ Generate a SELECT * query on the Suppliers table

- ❑ Generate a SELECT * query on the Products table

- ❑ Relate suppliers and products by the SupplierID field

- ❑ Generate a SELECT * query on the OrderDetails table

- ❑ Relate OrderDetails and Products by the ProductID field

- ❑ Generate a SELECT * query on the Orders table

- ❑ Relate Orders to OrderDetails by the OrderID

- ❑ Generate a SELECT * query on customers

- ❑ Relate Customers to Orders by the CustomerID field

You can see that all of our examples use SELECT * queries. Obviously you would not want to do this in a production environment and would probably use a significant number of stored procedures in place of the SELECT * queries. We are doing this for demonstration purposes and to reduce the overall size of our SHAPE commands. In a production environment you should only return the rows that you need and should avoid SELECT * queries unless you are doing table scans on small tables.

We will look at some more complex SHAPEs that deal with aggregates and grouping in the next section. The basic idea will be the same; we work from the inside out to build our recordset.

Parameterized Recordsets

We looked at the simple SHAPE command in our first example and we can take the same code and generate a parameterized hierarchy. If we change the following code from:

```
SQL = "SHAPE {SELECT * FROM Customers} "
SQL = SQL & "APPEND ({SELECT * FROM Orders} as rsOrders "
SQL = SQL & "RELATE CustomerID to CustomerID)"
```

to:

```
SQL = "SHAPE {SELECT * FROM Customers} "
SQL = SQL & "APPEND ({SELECT * FROM Orders where CustomerID = ?} as rsOrders "
SQL = SQL & "RELATE CustomerID to PARAMETER 0)"
```

then we will see the same results in the debug window in Visual Basic. This method is more efficient than the first example because the data for orders is fetched on an as-needed basis, whereas a standard SHAPE command will pull all of the necessary data and generate the child records on the client. For this reason, you cannot disconnect a recordset shaped with parameters. You can only disconnect a recordset that uses the standard SHAPE...APPEND syntax. Keep that point in mind since you may need to decide between speed, bandwidth, and server resources.

You are able to use parameters on multiple levels of a SHAPE command. In our complex parent-child-grandchild relationship earlier in this chapter we used a standard RELATE option to set the primary key and foreign key relationships (RELATE SupplierID to SupplierID). As stated earlier, this is inefficient since all of the data for the recordset must be sent to the client at the time of creation. If we used a parameter then we would fetch the data as needed on a per record basis. Our parameter relationships would change the syntax of our SHAPE command.

```
SHAPE {SELECT * FROM Customers}
  APPEND (( SHAPE {SELECT * FROM Orders WHERE CustomerID = ?}
  APPEND (( SHAPE {SELECT * FROM [Order Details] WHERE OrderID = ?}
  APPEND (( SHAPE {SELECT * FROM Products WHERE ProductID = ?}
  APPEND ({SELECT * FROM Suppliers WHERE SupplierID = ?}
  RELATE SupplierID TO PARAMETER 0) AS Suppliers) AS Products
  RELATE ProductID TO PARAMETER 0) AS Products) AS OrderDetails
  RELATE OrderID TO PARAMETER 0) AS OrderDetails) AS Orders
  RELATE CustomerID TO PARAMETER 0) AS Orders
```

We still have the same structure that we had with our original SHAPE statement, but now we are not returning the child data until we navigate the recordset.

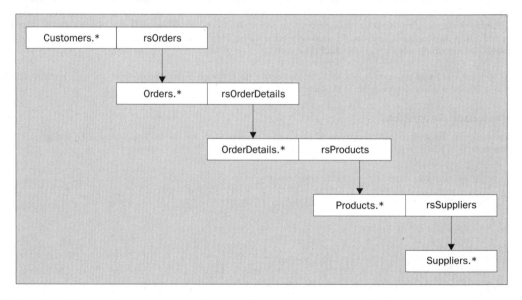

We lose the ability to disconnect from this recordset and we cannot marshal this recordset out of process, but it is more efficient than our original SHAPE command that returned all of the records. Our original command would allow us to persist the data, but all of the records would be sent over the wire to the application requesting the data. In an enterprise system you would quickly make enemies with the DBAs if you tried to pull this information on a database that has tens of thousands of customers with millions of orders (think of doing this with Amazon.com!). You need to balance the need for a persistent connection with available bandwidth and server resources.

As was noted above, you cannot marshal a parameterized shaped recordset out of process due to the fact that the recordset is built on an as-needed basis. If you send the recordset from a middle tier to a client, there is no way for the recordset to fetch the child records on subsequent calls.

Grouped/Aggregate Recordsets

The SHAPE language contains a COMPUTE command that you can use to generate a parent recordset on calculated values, or to group data. The COMPUTE command is different in the sense that, in contrast to most SHAPE commands, it generates a new parent rather than a new child.

The syntax for the COMPUTE command is as follows:

```
SHAPE {parent command} [AS] table-alias
COMPUTE table-alias [ ,field-list]
[BY field-list]
```

You can use the following commands in a COMPUTE statement:

❑ SUM()
❑ AVG()
❑ MIN()
❑ MAX()
❑ COUNT()
❑ STDEV()
❑ ANY()
❑ CALC()

The ANY operator will produce a non-calculated field on the parent recordset that the COMPUTE command creates. If you want to add the customer's name then you would specify the ANY(CustomerName) to the COMPUTE query.

Let's look at some examples of the COMPUTE command. This command gets a bit complex, so we will start with a normal SHAPE command and then add the COMPUTE command, so that you can see clearly how the COMPUTE command operates on a recordset.

Before we COMPUTE a recordset, let's see an example of using an aggregate function within a normal SHAPE command. We have looked at customers and orders, but we have not seen a report of the total order price for each customer and order. We will use the SUM() aggregate to report this information. Our SHAPE command would look as follows:

```
SHAPE {SELECT * FROM Orders}
APPEND ({SELECT [Order Details].OrderID,
  [Order Details].UnitPrice * [Order Details].Quantity as ExtendedPrice
  FROM [Order Details]}
RELATE OrderID TO OrderID) As rsOrderDetails,
SUM(rsOrderDetails.ExtendedPrice) AS OrderTotal
```

This SHAPE command returns a recordset that has shaped the OrderTotal information within the parent recordset:

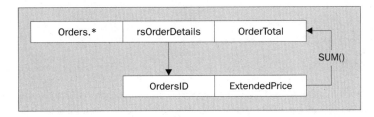

Using the SUM() function we were able to roll-up data to the parent recordset. The COMPUTE statement, on the other hand, would create a new parent recordset. Let's examine a statement with a COMPUTE in it.

The following SHAPE statement uses COMPUTE command to produce a recordset that groups Customers by CustomerID. This example does not show us much except for the creation of a new parent recordset.

```
SHAPE {SELECT * FROM Customers} as rsCustomers
COMPUTE rsCustomers BY CustomerID
```

What is produced is a new parent recordset:

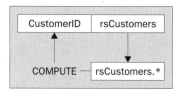

We can expand this SHAPE statement into something a little more meaningful by adding more detail information. If we take our query above, where we are calculating the line item total (ExtendedPrice), and roll the information up to a customer level to find the order totals, then we can produce a very detailed order report. We use the next SHAPE query to produce the desired output.

```
SHAPE
(SHAPE {SELECT Customers.CustomerID, Orders.OrderID
 FROM Customers INNER JOIN Orders
 ON Customers.CustomerID = Orders.CustomerID}
 APPEND ({SELECT [Order Details].Orderid,
 [Order Details].UnitPrice * [Order Details].Quantity as ExtendedPrice
 FROM [Order Details]} AS rsOrderDetails
 RELATE OrderID TO OrderID),
SUM(rsOrderDetails.ExtendedPrice) AS OrderTotal) AS rsOrders
COMPUTE rsOrders,
 SUM(rsOrders.OrderTotal) AS CustomerTotal
BY CustomerID
```

I know that this may look pretty complex now, but let's break the query down into manageable parts. First, we have the query that we used previously to find the line item totals. If we take the rsOrders and rsOrderDetails out of the SHAPE query then we are left with the changes that we made:

```
SHAPE
 <OLD SHAPE QUERY>
COMPUTE rsOrders,
 SUM(rsOrders.OrderTotal) AS CustomerTotal
BY CustomerID
```

All we have added is the COMPUTE and SUM() sections of the new SHAPE command. What we are creating is a new parent recordset that adds all of the order totals and groups by customer. What this produces is an outline with the parent totals:

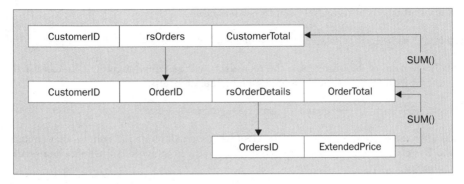

The `rsOrders` and `rsOrderDetails` are the original query and the `COMPUTE` command has added the new parent recordset that contains the `CustomerTotal` and `CustomerID` fields.

`COMPUTE` clauses can be the most confusing aspect of data shaping since the generation of a new parent recordset changes the entire hierarchy of the recordset structure. With a little practice you will be able to generate complex `COMPUTE` queries with little trouble. Remember to work from the inside out and test the queries incrementally since the ADO errors will only tell you where the error is, but it will not tell you the specific problem. This is the biggest area of frustration with ADO data shaping.

The SHAPE Language

Data shaping has a very complex grammar associated with the language. In this section the full `SHAPE` syntax along with the `APPEND` and `COMPUTE` commands are listed along with detailed information about the keywords and flags.

General SHAPE Syntax

We will start off with the simple `SHAPE` syntax. This is the foundation of data shaping and is the minimal implementation of the language:

```
SHAPE {parent-command} [[AS] table-alias]
APPEND ({child-command} [AS] child-table-alias]
RELATE parent-column TO child-column) [[AS] column-alias]
```

The most basic implementation of the `SHAPE` language is:

```
SHAPE {parent-command} [[AS] table-alias]
```

We can take the above command and use this on the SQL Server Northwind database to shape the customers table with the orders table:

```
SHAPE {select * from customers} AS customers
APPEND ({select * from orders} AS orders
  RELATE customer_id to customer_id) as orders
```

The first line generates the list of customers:

```
SHAPE {select * from customers} AS customers
```

And we append the child recordset from the orders table:

```
APPEND ({select * from orders} AS orders
```

And finally we need to determine how the recordsets will be joined together. We can use the `customer_id` field from each table to generate our relationship:

```
RELATE customer_id to customer_id) as orders
```

The alias after the RELATE command tells ADO what we will name the column that contains the child recordset. For clarity we could name the column `rsOrders` to avoid confusion when reading our SHAPE command.

When we are looping through our recordset we can assign the contents of the orders field to a recordset and then process the records within the child.

The full context of the SHAPE syntax is as follows:

Keyword	Notes
Parent-command, child-command	A query within braces {} and parenthesis () when using APPEND to append the child recordset to the parent.
	A previously shaped recordset.
	Another SHAPE command.
	The TABLE keyword followed by the table name.
Parent-column	A column in the recordset returned by the parent-command
Child-column	A column returned by the child-command
Table-alias	An alias that refers to the parent recordset
Child-table-alias	An alias that refers to the child recordset
Column-alias	The alias of the column that refers to the recordset appended to the parent

Column Type	Description
Data	Fields from a Recordset returned by a query command to a data provider, table, or previously shaped Recordset.
Chapter (child recordset)	A reference to another Recordset, called a chapter. Chapter columns make it possible to define a parent-child relationship where the parent is the Recordset containing the chapter column and the child is the Recordset represented by the chapter.
Aggregate	The value of the column is derived by executing an aggregate function on all the rows, or a column of all the rows of a child Recordset. Aggregate functions are described in more detail in the COMPUTE section of the SHAPE command syntax.

Column Type	Description
Calculated expression	The value of the column is derived by calculating a Visual Basic for Applications expression on columns in the same row of the Recordset. The expression is the argument to the CALC function. Calculated expressions are discussed in the COMPUTE section of the SHAPE syntax.
New	Empty, fabricated fields, which may be populated with data at a later time. The column is defined with the NEW keyword. (See NEW Keyword in the following table.)

NEW Keyword	Description
NEW (field type [(width | scale [, precision])])	Adds an empty column of the specified type to the Recordset.

SHAPE APPEND Commands

```
SHAPE {parent-command} [[AS] table-alias]
APPEND ({child-command} [AS] child-table-alias
RELATE parent-column TO child-column) [[AS] column-alias]
```

The {parent-command} and {child-command} can be one of the following:

- ❑ A query command within curly braces ('{}') that returns a Recordset object. The command is issued to the underlying data provider, and its syntax depends on the requirements of that provider. This will typically be Structured Query Language (SQL), although ADO doesn't require any particular query language. The parentheses ('()') are a required keyword; they append a chapter column to the parent which references the Recordset returned by the query command.

- ❑ The name of a previously shaped Recordset.

- ❑ Another SHAPE command.

- ❑ The TABLE keyword, followed by the name of a table.

table-alias and **child-table-alias** are references to the recordset returned by the command.

parent-column and **child-column** are fields in the parent-command and child-command respectively. These columns must be of the same datatype and length. You should follow the same rules as you would with a SQL JOIN command. The parent-column to child-column clause is a comma separated list of fields that should be related. This would be necessary if you are using composite keys in your database or there are multiple fields to join for the relationship between commands.

SHAPE COMPUTE Commands

```
SHAPE {child-command} [AS] table-alias
COMPUTE table-alias [, aggregate-command-field-list]
[BY grp-field-list]
```

{child-command} can be any of the following:

❑ A query command within curly braces ('{}') that returns a child Recordset object. The command is issued to the underlying data provider, and its syntax depends on the requirements of that provider. This will typically be Structured Query Language (SQL), although ADO doesn't require any particular query language.

❑ The name of a previously shaped `Recordset`.

❑ Another `SHAPE` command.

❑ The `TABLE` keyword, followed by the name of a table.

Aggregate-command-field-list is any of the aggregate commands of CALC expressions listed in the following tables.

Aggregate Functions	Description
SUM(recordset-name.column)	Calculates the sum of all values in the specified column.
AVG(recordset-name.column)	Calculates the average of all values in the specified column.
MAX(recordset-name.column)	Calculates the maximum value in the specified column.
MIN(recordset-name.column)	Calculates the minimum value in the specified column.
COUNT(recordset-name[.column])	Counts the number of rows in the specified alias or column.
STDEV(recordset-name.column)	Calculates the standard deviation in the specified column.
ANY(recordset-name.column)	The value of a column (where the value of the column is the same for all rows). Use this flag to specify a static field such as `CustomerID` or `OrderID` where you want the data to appear on each row.

Calculated Expression	Description
CALC(expression)	Calculates an arbitrary expression, but only on the row of the Recordset containing the CALC function. Any expression using these Visual Basic for Applications (VBA) functions is allowed: `Abs, Asc, Atn, CBool, CByte, CCur, CDate, CDbl, Chr, ChrB, ChrW, Chr$, ChrB$, CInt, CLng, Cos, CSng, CStr, Cvar, CVDate, CVErr, Date, Date$, DateAdd, DateDiff, DatePart, DateSerial, DateValue, Day, DDB, Error, Error$, Exp, Fix, Format, Format$, FV, Hex, Hex$, Hour, IIF, InStr, Int, IPmt, IRR, IsDate, IsEmpty, IsError, IsNull, IsNumeric, IsObject, LCase, LCase$, Left, LeftB, Left$, LeftB$, Len, Log, LTrim, LTrim$, Mid, Mid$, Minute, MIRR, Month, Now, NPer, NPV, Oct, Oct$, Pmt, PPmt, PV, QBColor, Rate, RGB, Right, RightB, Right$, RightB$, Rnd, RTrim, RTrim$, Second, Sgn, Sin, SLN, Space, Space$, Sqr, Str, Str$, StrComp, StrConv, String, String$, SYD, Tan, Time,Time$, Timer, TimeSerial, TimeValue, Trim, Trim$, TypeName, UCase, UCase$, Val, VarType , Weekday, Year`

Grp-field-list specifies the group order of the child recordset. This is equivalent to the GROUP BY clause in normal SQL syntax.

If the COMPUTE command does not contain a BY clause then there will be only one parent row where a BY clause will contain multiple parent rows for each unique value in the BY clause. Let's look at an example of using a BY clause and leaving the BY clause out.

First we will sum the totals for our orders using one of our past SHAPE commands that used a BY clause:

```
SHAPE
(SHAPE {SELECT Customers.CustomerID, Orders.OrderID
 FROM Customers INNER JOIN Orders
 ON Customers.CustomerID = Orders.CustomerID}
 APPEND ({SELECT [Order Details].Orderid,
 [Order Details].UnitPrice * [Order Details].Quantity as ExtendedPrice
 FROM [Order Details]} AS rsOrderDetails
 RELATE OrderID TO OrderID),
 SUM(rsOrderDetails.ExtendedPrice) AS OrderTotal) AS rsOrders
COMPUTE rsOrders,
 SUM(rsOrders.OrderTotal) AS CustomerTotal
BY CustomerID
```

The BY clause tells us to sum up the order totals by customer such that there is a parent row for each customer. Look at what is returned from our SHAPE sample application:

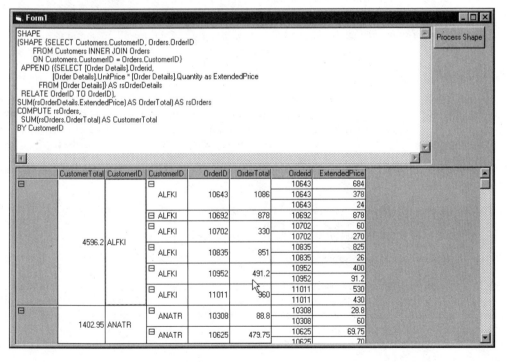

You can see that we have a **CustomerTotal** and **CustomerID** row for each customer since we used the BY clause on the CustomerID field. If we remove the BY clause then our data is dramatically different as you see in the next screenshot.

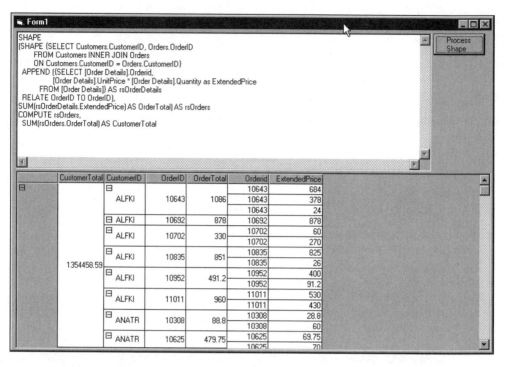

Instead of grouping by each customer we have created a grand total for all customers.

Reshaping

Recordsets that have been created with the data shape provider can be reshaped. Reshaping allows you to take recordsets built from the same connection and shape them as you would with a single SHAPE statement. You can take an existing recordset that has already been created and shape the recordset to display new data. You can use the AS operator to assign a name to a shaped recordset.

Data reshaping utilizes the names given to recordsets in SHAPE commands. Take one of our previous SHAPE commands:

```
SHAPE {SELECT * FROM Customers} as rsCustomers
  APPEND (( SHAPE {SELECT * FROM Orders} AS rsOrders
  APPEND ({SELECT * FROM [Order Details]} AS rsOrderDetails
  RELATE OrderID TO OrderID) AS OrderDetails)
  RELATE CustomerID TO CustomerID)
```

We have added the AS rsCustomers code to the first SHAPE command. What data shaping allows us to do is take the rsCustomers, rsOrders, or rsOrderDetails recordsets and use them in other SHAPE commands. We do not need to generate complex SHAPE statements; we can merely reuse some of the recordsets that we have already built. This allows us to break complex statements into much smaller statements and reuse existing recordsets without the need to transmit the same data to the client for each request.

For instance, we can take the SHAPE command:

```
SHAPE {SELECT * FROM Orders} AS rsOrders
```

and further shape the recordset later in our application by referring to the name rsOrders.

```
SHAPE {SELECT * FROM Customers}
  APPEND (rsOrders RELATE CustomerID TO CustomerID)
```

If we generated a recordset that had children (or grandchildren) such as:

```
SHAPE {select * from customers} as rsCustomers
APPEND ({select * from orders} as rsOrders
RELATE customer_id to customer_id)
```

Then we would be able to reshape both rsCustomers and rsOrders. For instance, we can reshape rsOrders by running a COMPUTE statement.

```
SHAPE {rsOrders}
COMPUTE rsOrders BY CustomerID
```

We can continue to shape the data from existing recordsets. Where is this really useful? Persisted recordsets. You can generate a complex SHAPE command and use the ADO Save() method to persist the recordset. At a later time you can generate reports or further analyze the data. This can be a very valuable tool if you have a traveling sales force and they would like the ability to analyze sales data while traveling away from the main system.

So, data reshaping is the ability to take existing shaped recordsets and modify the data that they represent. This has a great deal of potential, but it also has its limitations.

Limitations of Reshaping

There are some limitations when reshaping data. The main items that you need to keep in mind when reshaping are:

- ❏ The SHAPE command must refer to recordsets created by the same process on the same computer.
- ❏ The APPEND clause cannot be used to add new columns to an existing recordset.
- ❏ Reshaping of parameterized recordsets is not supported.
- ❏ You cannot reshape recordsets in an intervening COMPUTE clause or perform aggregate operations on any recordset other than the one being reshaped.

Summary

You can see that data shaping is not for the faint of heart, but the SHAPE command is not as complex as it first appears. If you create your SHAPE commands from the inside out and debug them in incremental steps then you will have much less trouble with SHAPE commands and you will be able to make one big problem become several small problems. Use the Visual Basic data environment to help build these queries and run the output thought the SHAPE test application that we built. Soon you will be generating enterprise reports at lightning speeds and reducing the amount of work that goes into generating a hierarchical recordset. SHAPE away!

7

ADO and XML

You might wonder what a chapter about XML is doing in a book about ADO. Well, unless you've been living in the outer reaches of Elbonia (along with the mud and pigs), you've probably noticed XML being talked about quite a lot. There's a simple reason for that – XML is an industry standard format for representing data. So, as far as we are concerned, it's just another form of data that we have to take into account.

This is actually an important point. The whole basis of UDA is the ability to access data from any source, so it's not only reasonable, but also imperative that we include XML.

So, in this chapter we're going to look at:

❑   What XML is and how it can be used to represent data

❑   An overview of the XML Document Object Model

❑   How XML fits into the ADO strategy

❑   How we can transfer XML data between the database and the client

❑   How we can transform XML data into a viewable format

All in all, there's a huge number of uses for XML. The interaction between ADO and XML isn't perfect, but it's only a matter of time before the integration is complete. Microsoft is actively working on this, not just from the ADO programmer's point of view, but because XML and ADO are used in many Microsoft products.

We're not going to go into great lengths describing everything about XML, as the subject area is too large. What we need to cover is how XML affects us as ADO programmers, and some of the surrounding areas where XML is useful. You might not like this (after all, databases work pretty well), but you're not going to be able to avoid XML for long. It's invading many aspects of data storage, so you'll have to know something about it.

Before we delve into ADO and it's use of XML, you need to understand a bit about XML, and how to use it to represent data.

What is XML?

If you're not familiar with XML, this section will give you an understanding of what it is, and why it is used to represent data. Even if you know what XML is and what it looks like, this section is still worthwhile, because we'll be concentrating on using XML for data representation.

One thing we're not really concerned with here is the discussion of using XML as a data transport mechanism, that is, for data in a transient state. If data is being transferred between two parts of a program (such as the client and the server) then XML is a good choice for this, but that's a design issue. We need to concentrate on the format of the data.

> To read more about XML, its history and current standing, then check out the Web site of the World Wide Web Consortium, at http://www.w3.org/TR/1998/REC-xml-19980210.

The Construction of XML

XML, or Extensible Markup Language, is just a way of using tags to mark up an area of a document. Hmm, what do we mean by *markup*? Well, let's use something we're familiar with – HTML is a markup language, and you can see what we mean by looking at the following HTML:

```
<HTML>
    <HEAD>
        <TITLE>Some groovy HTML page</TITLE>
    </HEAD>
    <BODY>
        Here is some text <B>with a bit in bold</B>
    </BODY>
</HTML>
```

This is pretty simple stuff. Each opening tag defines the start of something, and the closing tag defines the end. So, the <B> tag means "turn on bold", and </B> means "turn off bold". In HTML the markup identifies style and formatting, and these are applied by the browser when you view the page. The browser knows what these tags means and how to format the content within them.

XML bears some superficial resemblance to HTML, due to the fact that both languages derive, in different ways, from a common parent: Standard Generalized Markup Language, or SGML. This is not, in itself a language (despite its name), but a way of defining languages that are developed along its general principles. These languages are known as **SGML applications**, and HTML is one such application. XML, in contrast, is a simplified, lightweight version of SGML, and is itself used to define other languages, or **XML applications**.

What this means is that in XML the markup just identifies the data, and there is no implied meaning to the tags. In fact, the whole point about XML is that the tags are not predefined – we can name the tags whatever we like. So what use is this? Well, since the tags are marking up data, then they can relate to the data. For example, consider the `pubs` database from SQL Server, which has a `sales` table. In the database we get a table like this:

stor_id	ord_num	ord_date	qty	payterms	title_id
6380	6871	9/14/1994	5	Net 60	BU1032
6380	722a	9/13/1994	3	Net 60	PS2091
7066	A2976	5/24/1993	50	Net 30	PC8888
7066	QA7442.3	9/13/1994	75	ON invoice	PS2091
7067	D4482	9/14/1994	10	Net 60	PS2091
7067	P2121	6/15/1992	40	Net 30	TC3218
7067	P2121	6/15/1992	20	Net 30	TC4203
7067	P2121	6/15/1992	20	Net 30	TC7777
7131	N914008	9/14/1994	20	Net 30	PS2091
7131	N914014	9/14/1994	25	Net 30	MC3021
7131	P3087a	5/29/1993	20	Net 60	PS1372
7131	P3087a	5/29/1993	25	Net 60	PS2106
7131	P3087a	5/29/1993	15	Net 60	PS3333
7131	P3087a	5/29/1993	25	Net 60	PS7777
7896	QQ2299	10/28/1993	15	Net 60	BU7832
7896	TQ456	12/12/1993	10	Net 60	MC2222
7896	X999	2/21/1993	35	ON invoice	BU2075
8042	423LL922	9/14/1994	15	ON invoice	MC3021
8042	423LL930	9/14/1994	10	ON invoice	BU1032
8042	P723	3/11/1993	25	Net 30	BU1111
8042	QA879.1	5/22/1993	30	Net 30	PC1035

We could represent this in XML as follows:

```
<sales>
    <sale>
        <stor_id>6380</stor_id>
        <ord_num>6871</ord_num>
        <ord_date>1994-09-14 00:00:00.000</ord_date>
        <qty>5</qty>
        <payterms>Net 60</payterms>
        <title_id>BU1032</title_id>
    </sale>
    <sale>
        <stor_id>6380</stor_id>
        <ord_num>722a</ord_num>
        <ord_date>1994-09-13 00:00:00.000</ord_date>
        <qty>3</qty>
        <payterms>Net 60</payterms>
        <title_id>PS2091</title_id>
    </sale>
</sales>
```

This just shows the first two lines of the table in XML format. You can see that the tag names describe the data contents. For example, the Store ID is stored within the `<stor_id>` tags. All of the details for a sale are held within `<sale>` tags – the equivalent to a row in the database. All sales are held within the `<sales>` tags, the equivalent to the whole table.

None of this is very revolutionary, but it's important to remember that as far as XML is concerned, the tags don't mean a thing. We could equally well represent the sales data as:

```
<characters>
    <character>
        <pooh>6380</pooh>
        <tigger>6871</tigger>
        <piglet>1994-09-14 00:00:00.000</piglet>
        <kanga>5</kanga>
        <roo>Net 60</roo>
        <eeyore>BU1032</eeyore>
    </character>
    <character>
        <pooh>6380</pooh>
        <tigger>722a</tigger>
        <piglet>1994-09-13 00:00:00.000</piglet>
        <kanga>3</kanga>
        <roo>Net 60</roo>
        <eeyore>PS2091</eeyore>
    </character>
</characters>
```

Now I admit that for us humans the tags no longer bear any relation to the data they contain, but this doesn't really matter to XML. All it requires is a start tag, some data and an end tag. Obviously, it makes sense to use descriptive tags, but the important point to remember is that the tag names are not predefined.

Elements, Tags and Attributes

Before we start delving into XML it's important to get some definitions out of the way:

❑   A **tag** is the markup identifier, and is enclosed in angled brackets. For each opening tag, there must be a corresponding closing tag. For example, `<ord_num>` and `</ord_num>` are legal start and end tags.

❑   An **element** is a fully formed instance of a pair of opening and closing tags, including all the content between the tags. This content can consist of text, other XML elements, or a mixture of both.

❑   An **attribute** defines a property of a tag, and is enclosed within the opening tag.

Attributes are very similar to HTML attributes. For example, in the above XML document, we could use an attribute named `Format` to define the format in which an order date is stored:

```
<ord_date Format="yyyy-mm-dd">1994-09-14</ord_date>
```

Later in this chapter, we'll see how attributes can be used to hold XML data itself, rather than being used to define properties of the tags.

Well-Formed XML

Unlike HTML (at least, versions up to and including 4.0), XML must be **well-formed**. This means, among other things, that each opening tag must have a closing tag, and all attributes must be enclosed in quotation marks. For example, the following is not legal XML:

```
<ord_date Format=yyyy-mm-dd>1994-09-14</ord_date>
```

You may be used to this, since HTML allows attributes without quotes, but you can't get away with it in XML. Also, we cannot get away with omitting closing tags, as we frequently do in HTML. For example, in HTML we routinely misuse the `<P>` tag:

```
<P>
Here is a paragraph containing blah blah blah
<P>
Another paragraph of dull text
```

This is perfectly acceptable HTML. However, if we tried to convert this HTML into XML:

```
<Paragraph>
Here is a paragraph containing blah blah blah
<Paragraph>
Another paragraph of dull text
```

This would not be well-formed XML because there are no closing tags. Instead, we would need to write:

```
<Paragraph>
    Here is a paragraph containing blah blah blah
</Paragraph>
<Paragraph>
    Another paragraph of dull text
</Paragraph>
```

If we want an XML element without any content, there are two options. We can use a pair of opening and closing tags with no content between them:

```
<Paragraph></Paragraph>
```

Or we can use the shortened tag form:

```
<Paragraph />
```

Adding a trailing forward slash to the end of the tag name acts as a closing tag, and indicates that the tag is empty. Note that an empty tag can still have attributes.

Another feature of XML is that it is case-sensitive. Therefore, the following is not well-formed XML:

```
<Paragraph>some text</PARAGRAPH>
```

The opening and closing tags of an element must match exactly, including the case of the characters in the element name.

> As an aside, HTML 4.1 and XHTML are currently being worked on to make HTML well-formed. There are two advantages to this. The first is that well-formed HTML can be parsed by XML parsers. Secondly, a well-formed file is quicker to parse.

Root Elements

A well-formed XML document must also only have a single root element, which contains all the other XML elements. In our sales example, this was the tag `<Sales>`. So this is legal XML:

```
<Sales>
   . . . lots of XML here
</Sales>
```

But this isn't:

```
<Sales>
   . . . lots of XML here
</Sales>
<Sales>
   . . . lots more XML here
</Sales>
```

Here there are two root elements, so this is not a well-formed XML document.

Processing Instructions

Processing instructions are part of an XML document, but don't actually describe XML data. They are instructions to the XML parser describing certain features of the document.

A processing instruction is contained within a form of tag. The one you'll see most often is this:

```
<?xml version="1.0"?>
```

This identifies the version of XML used in the document. The current value and default is 1.0. This tag is also where you can indicate the character set used in the document:

```
<?xml version="1.0" encoding="iso-8859-1"?>
```

A list of the most common languages and their character sets is shown below:

Character Set	Language	Supported by IE Version
UTF-8	Unicode (8 bit)	4, 5
ISO-8859-1	Latin 1 (Western Europe, Latin America)	3, 4, 5
ISO-8859-2	Latin 2 (Central/Eastern Europe)	3, 4, 5
ISO-8859-3	Latin 3 (SE Europe)	4, 5
ISO-8859-4	Latin 4 (Scandinavia/Baltic)	4, 5
ISO-8859-5	Latin/Cyrillic	4, 5

Character Set	Language	Supported by IE Version
ISO-8859-6	Latin/Arabic	4 (if complex scripts are supported), 5
ISO-8859-7	Latin/Greek	3, 4, 5
ISO-8859-8	Latin/Hebrew	4 (if complex scripts are supported), 5
ISO-8859-9	Latin/Turkish	3, 4, 5
EUC-JP or Shift_JIS	Japanese	3, 4, 5

If you want to read more about the internationalization issue, then have a look at the W3C's page on this topic: `http://www.w3.org/International/`. *For more details about language support in Internet Explorer, check out MSDN, searching for* `'Character Set Recognition'`.

Special Characters

XML has a special set of characters that cannot be used in normal XML strings. These are:

Character	Must be Replaced With	Or With	Or With
&	&amp;	&#x26;	&#38;
<	&lt;	&#x3C;	&#60;
>	&gt;	&#x3E;	&#62;
"	&quot;	&#x22;	&#34;
'	&apos;	&#x27;	&#39;

For example, the following XML is illegal:

```
<Chapter>Asynchronous Processing & Events</Chapter>
```

Whereas the following is a well-formed XML element:

```
<Chapter>Asynchronous Processing &amp; Events</Chapter>
```

You don't need to worry about these characters when obtaining data from ADO, but if you are building your own XML data from other sources, then you need to code these characters accordingly. The last two columns show that you can use hexadecimal or decimal values as well as the special characters, although I find the special characters easier to read.

There are also other characters that can be described in this way, although they are not a requirement for XML itself. A few of these are shown below:

Character	Can be Replaced With	Or With	Or With
non-breaking space			
¢	&cent;	&#xA2;	&#162;
¥	&yen;	&#xA5;	&#165;
£	&pound;	&#xA3;	&#163;
©	&copy;	&#xA9;	&#169;
®	&reg;	&#xAE;	&#174;

This is not a complete list, so for other characters have a look at the MSDN section on character sets, under 'Web Workshop', 'DHTML, HTML & CSS'.

Validating XML

Since XML tags can be anything at all, how do you define which tag names are valid for a given document? After all, there's nothing to stop you using the character names from your favorite book. The solution is to use a **Document Type Definition** (**DTD**) or a **schema**.

Both DTDs and schemas perform a similar task – that of defining the structure of an XML document. We can associate a DTD or schema with an XML document. As we have seen, XML must conform to certain specific syntax rules, and an XML document which adheres to these is said to be **well-formed**. However, we can also check that the XML elements are not only correctly formatted, but that the data they contain has a specific structure. An XML document can be validated against an associated DTD or schema, and if it conforms to the specified definition, it is said to be **valid**.

The essence of this validation is to ensure that only the correct elements are supplied, and that their contents are correctly defined.

*If you want to validate an XML file against a schema or DTD, Microsoft provides a useful tool called the **XML Validator**. This is an HTML page which runs in IE5 and which validates XML documents and provides a limited amount of debug information. It displays error messages that are useful when you are trying to develop a schema or an XML document bound to a DTD, and can be downloaded from* http://www.microsoft.com/downloads/internet/samples/xml/xml_validator.

DTDs

DTDs were created by the W3C (as part of the original SGML specification) as a way of defining the structure and content of XML data. In order to associate a DTD with an XML document, we use a **document type declaration** (be careful to distinguish this from a document type *definition*, or DTD).

The easiest way to understand this is to see a DTD – let's use one for the sales data we saw earlier:

```
<!DOCTYPE sales [
   <!ELEMENT sales (sale)*>
   <!ELEMENT sale (stor_id|ord_num|ord_date|qty|payterms|
                   title_id)*>
   <!ELEMENT stor_id (#PCDATA)>
   <!ELEMENT ord_num (#PCDATA)>
   <!ELEMENT ord_date (#PCDATA)>
   <!ELEMENT qty (#PCDATA)>
   <!ELEMENT payterms (#PCDATA)>
   <!ELEMENT title_id (#PCDATA)>
]>
```

This might look pretty weird, but it's quite simple. Let's take it one line at a time. If the DTD is contained within the XML document (it can also be in another file), the document type declaration has the syntax:

```
<!DOCTYPE root_element_name [
   document_type_definition
]>
```

In our case, the DOCTYPE defines that the document consists of a root element called sales:

```
<!DOCTYPE sales [
```

Next we define this sales element, which can contain multiple sale elements. The * defines that zero or more instances of the sale element are allowed:

```
<!ELEMENT sales (sale)*>
```

Then we define the sale element, which consists of six other elements:

```
<!ELEMENT sale (stor_id|ord_num|ord_date|qty|payterms|
                title_id)*>
```

Finally, we define each individual element, stating the name of the element and the content which it can contain. PCDATA means that the element contains parsed character data – text which can be read by an XML parser. We do not define child elements or attributes, so these elements will be able to contain only text data:

```
    <!ELEMENT stor_id (#PCDATA)>
    <!ELEMENT ord_num (#PCDATA)>
    <!ELEMENT ord_date (#PCDATA)>
    <!ELEMENT qty (#PCDATA)>
    <!ELEMENT payterms (#PCDATA)>
    <!ELEMENT title_id (#PCDATA)>
]>
```

An example of XML that matches this DTD is the sales data we looked at earlier:

```
<sales>
    <sale>
        <stor_id>6380</stor_id>
        <ord_num>6871</ord_num>
        <ord_date>1994-09-14 00:00:00.000</ord_date>
        <qty>5</qty>
        <payterms>Net 60</payterms>
        <title_id>BU1032</title_id>
    </sale>
    <sale>
        . . .
    </sale>
</sales>
```

There is an outer element named `sales`, which consists of multiple `sale` elements. Each `sale` element consists of six others.

Schemas

Although this is quite easy, the DTD format does pose problems:

❑   There is no way to define the data type of elements. They are all just character data.

❑   It's not defined in XML syntax. It seems odd to have a format for defining XML, when that format isn't XML.

❑   It's not extensible because it uses a fixed format.

❑   We can have only one DTD per document, thus making inheritance impossible.

One of the ways around this is to use a **schema**. Schemas were originally introduced by Microsoft, AborText, Inso, and others, and have since been taken up by the W3C, although they aren't a standard yet.

The original proposal goes by the acronym XDR (meaning XML Data Reduced; this is described at `http://www.w3.org/TR/1998/NOTE-XML-data-0105/`). The XML Schema working draft (`http://www.w3.org/TR/xmlschema-1/`) is based largely on the earlier work. The example below uses the version of this implemented by IE5.

Schema Example

Using the above example, we have a schema that looks like this:

```
<?xml version="1.0"?>
<Schema xmlns="urn:schemas-microsoft-com:xml-data"
        xmlns:dt="urn:schemas-microsoft-com:datatypes">

   <ElementType name="stor_id" dt:type="string" />
   <ElementType name="ord_num" dt:type="string" />
   <ElementType name="ord_date" dt:type="date" />
   <ElementType name="qty" dt:type="i2" />
   <ElementType name="payterms" dt:type="string" />
   <ElementType name="title_id" dt:type="string" />


   <ElementType name="sale" content="eltOnly" model="closed">
      <element type="stor_id" />
      <element type="ord_num" />
      <element type="ord_date" />
      <element type="qty" />
      <element type="payterms" />
      <element type="title_id" />
   </ElementType>

   <ElementType name="sales" content="eltOnly" model="closed">
      <element type="sale" maxOccurs="*" />
   </ElementType>
</Schema>
```

This schema achieves much the same thing as the DTD above, but now the definition for the structure of the XML is itself in XML. Again, let's look at it in more detail. The first line defines the schema, and uses the xmlns attribute to define two namespaces. We'll be looking at namespaces a little later, but in essence they allow us to stop collisions between element names:

```
<Schema xmlns="urn:schemas-microsoft-com:xml-data"
        xmlns:dt="urn:schemas-microsoft-com:datatypes">
```

Next we have definitions for the fields. Each element in our XML document is defined by an <ElementType> element in the schema. Notice that schemas define elements in *reverse* order, the top-level elements being defined last. This is because we must define any elements before we can define them as children of another element. The <ElementType> elements for the fields have three attributes: the name attribute identifies the name of the element, and the type (prefixed by the dt namespace) identifies the data type of the element's content. Notice that unlike DTDs, we can specify the data type more accurately, rather than the vague character data of a DTD:

```
   <ElementType name="stor_id" dt:type="string" />
   <ElementType name="ord_num" dt:type="string" />
   <ElementType name="ord_date" dt:type="date" />
   <ElementType name="qty" dt:type="i2" />
   <ElementType name="payterms" dt:type="string" />
   <ElementType name="title_id" dt:type="string" />
```

Next we define the `sale` element, which contains details of each sale, again using an `<ElementType>` element. This has three attributes. The `name` attribute is of course set to `"sale"`. The `content` attribute defines what type of data can be contained within the element – in this case, `eltOnly` means that only other elements are allowed, and no text. The `model` attribute with a value of `"closed"` means that only the defined elements can be contained within the data. We'll look at the `content` and `model` attributes in more detail in a little while, when we look at XML-Data:

```
<ElementType name="sales" content="eltOnly" model="closed">
```

Now we can define the child elements for our `<sale>` element, specifying the types we've just created. Each of the child elements is defined in an `<element>` element within the parent's `<ElementType>` element. The `type` attribute specifies data type for the element's contents:

```
        <element type="stor_id" />
        <element type="ord_num" />
        <element type="ord_date" />
        <element type="qty" />
        <element type="payterms" />
        <element type="title_id" />
    </ElementType>
```

Finally, we define the outer `<sales>` element. Again, we set the content attribute to `"eltOnly"` and the model to `"closed"`. With this `<ElementType>` we need to add an `<element>` element for `<sale>`. By default, child elements can only occur once within the parent. To change this, we add a `maxOccurs` attribute with a value of `"*"`:

```
        <ElementType name="sales" content="eltOnly" model="closed">
            <element type="sale" maxOccurs="*" />
        </ElementType>
    </Schema>
```

Note that inline schemas are not recognized by the XML Validator – the schema must be placed in a separate file. This can be linked to the schema by adding the namespace definition xmlns="x-schema:*filename*" to the root element tag. The following is an example of an XML file which conforms to the above schema:

```
<?xml version="1.0"?>
<sales xmlns="x-schema:schema.xml">
    <sale>
        <stor_id>6380</stor_id>
        <ord_num>6871</ord_num>
        <ord_date>1994-09-14</ord_date>
        <qty>5</qty>
        <payterms>Net 60</payterms>
        <title_id>BU1032</title_id>
    </sale>
    <sale>
```

```
            <stor_id>6380</stor_id>
            <ord_num>722a</ord_num>
            <ord_date>1994-09-13</ord_date>
            <qty>3</qty>
            <payterms>Net 60</payterms>
            <title_id>PS2091</title_id>
        </sale>
    </sales>
```

This isn't really a great deal different from what the DTD does – it defines the elements that can appear in a valid XML data file. The great advantages of a schema are that it is defined in XML, which makes it highly customizable, and the addition of data types.

Microsoft XML-Data

As we saw in Chapter 4, an ADO recordset can be saved as XML by calling the Save method and specifying the save format as adPersistXML:

```
    rsSales.Save "sales.xml", adPersistXML
```

However, once you start using XML data with ADO you'll notice that the XML format Microsoft creates is unlike what we've seen up to now. For example, the sales details would look something like this:

```
<rs:data>
    <z:row stor_id="6380" ord_num="6871"
           ord_date="1994-09-14T00:00:00" qty="5"
           payterms="Net 60" title_id="BU1032" />
    <z:row stor_id="6380" ord_num="722a"
           ord_date="1994-09-13T00:00:00" qty="3"
           payterms="Net 60" title_id="PS2091" />
    <z:row stor_id="7066" ord_num="A2976"
           ord_date="1993-05-24T00:00:00" qty="50"
           payterms="Net 30" title_id="PC8888" />
    <z:row stor_id="7066" ord_num="QA7442.3"
           ord_date="1994-09-13T00:00:00" qty="75"
           payterms="ON invoice" title_id="PS2091" />
</rs:data>
```

Rather different isn't it? What's been done here is that instead of using elements for each individual item (field) of data, an element spans a whole row. Each field is represented by an attribute. (But note that using attributes isn't a requirement of XML-Data, and both elements and attributes are supported.)

One of the major reasons for choosing this attribute format for ADO data was the verbosity of XML elements. When dealing with data sets containing large amounts of repeated data, the XML files would get quite large because of the repeated opening and closing of tags. The attribute format is much terser, and therefore should be quicker to transfer. Microsoft is looking at providing an element format for ADO, but there are no definite plans for this as yet.

As a consequence of this format, the schema for sales details also looks rather different:

```
<xml xmlns:s="uuid:BDC6E3F0-6DA3-11d1-A2A3-00AA00C14882"
     xmlns:dt="uuid:C2F41010-65B3-11d1-A29F-00AA00C14882"
     xmlns:rs="urn:schemas-microsoft-com:rowset"
     xmlns:z="#RowsetSchema">
  <s:Schema id="RowsetSchema">
    <s:ElementType name="row" content="eltOnly"
                         rs:CommandTimeout="30">
      <s:AttributeType name="stor_id" rs:number="1"
                       rs:writeunknown="true">
        <s:datatype dt:type="string" rs:dbtype="str"
                    dt:maxLength="4" rs:fixedlength="true"
                    rs:maybenull="false" />
      </s:AttributeType>
      <s:AttributeType name="ord_num" rs:number="2"
                       rs:writeunknown="true">
        <s:datatype dt:type="string" rs:dbtype="str"
                    dt:maxLength="20"
                    rs:maybenull="false" />
      </s:AttributeType>
      <s:extends type="rs:rowbase" />
    </s:ElementType>
  </s:Schema>
</xml>
```

This structure is repeated for each field – we've cut it down here to show only a couple of fields. It's not so different from the first schema we looked at, and defines a single element, and then the fields are defined as attributes of the element. So, instead of using `<ElementType>` for each field, `<AttributeType>` is used instead. Within each attribute definition there is a detailed description of the data type, with attributes that identify properties such as the length of character fields, whether they can contain null values, and so on.

> *XML-Data currently has the status of a Note at the W3C. There are a number of other proposals covering the same topic, and these are being closely examined.*

Data Types

Since one of the good features of schemas is the ability to define data types, you need to know what those types are. When generating XML from ADO these will be filled in for you, but if you then need to manipulate the XML, or generate user interfaces for the XML data, then the data type could be useful. Listed below is the list of standard data types.

Type	Description
bin.base64	A binary object
bin.hex	Hexadecimal octets
boolean	0 or 1 (0 is false, and 1 is true)
char	A one character length string
date	A date, without the time. The format is yyyy-mm-dd
dateTime	A date, optionally with the time. The format is yyyy-mm-ddThh:mm:ss

Type	Description
dateTime.tz	A date, optionally with time and timezone. The format is yyyy-mm-ddThh:mm:ss-hh:mm. The timezone indicates the number of hours + or – GMT.
fixed.14.4	Fixed with floating point number, with up to 14 digits to the left of the decimal place and up to 4 to the right.
float	Floating point number
int	Integer number
number	floating point number
time	A time. The format is hh:mm:ss
time.tz	A time with an optional timezone. The format is hh:mm:ss-hh:mm
i1	An 8-bit integer (1 byte)
i2	A 16-bit integer (2 bytes)
i4	A 32-bit integer (4 bytes)
r4	A 4-byte real number
r8	An eight-byte real number
ui1	An 8-bit unsigned integer (1 byte)
ui2	A 16-bit unsigned integer (2 bytes)
ui4	A 32-bit unsigned integer (4 bytes)
uri	A Universal Resource Indicator
uuid	A set of hex digits representing a universally unique identifier. A GUID is an example of this.

The W3C also allows a set of types native to the XML language (usually called **primitive types**):

Type	Description
entity	Represents the XML ENTITY type
entities	Represents the XML ENTITIES type
enumeration	Represents an enumerated type
id	Represents the XML ID type
idref	Represents the XML IDREF type
idrefs	Represents the XML IDREFS type

Table Continued on Following Page

Type	Description
nmtoken	Represents the XML NMTOKEN type
nmtokens	Represents the XML NMTOKENS type
notation	Represents the XML NOTATION type
string	Represents a string type

We won't be looking at these primitive types in this book, but you will see uses of the standard data types later in the chapter.

ElementType

We saw the ElementType being used earlier, to define an XML element, and there are several attributes that this element can take:

Attribute	Description
content	Indicates the type of content for the element. This can be one of: empty, to indicate that the element cannot contain any content. textOnly, to indicate that only text is allowed in the element. eltOnly, to indicate that only elements can be contained within the element mixed, to indicate that the element can contain both text and elements.
dt:type	Identifies the data type of the element. This should be one of the data types described in the previous section.
model	Indicates whether the content can contain only what is defined in the schema, or if it can contain elements not defined in the schema. This can be one of: closed, to indicate that only defined elements are allowed. open, to indicate that any element is allowed.
name	Identifies the name of the element.
order	Identifies the ordering of defined elements. It can be one of: one, to indicate that only one of the defined elements is allowed. seq, to indicate that the elements must appear in the same order in which they are defined. many, to indicate that the elements can appear (or not appear) in any order.

The definition of what an open mode or a closed model means is confusing to many people. An open model allows elements that aren't defined in the schema, as long as those elements have their own namespace. If the elements don't have an explicit namespace they are taken to be part of the current schema namespace, and if they don't exist in the schema, then a validation error occurs.

AttributeType

Like the `ElementType`, the `AttributeType` also defines a set of attributes:

Attribute	Description
default	Identifies the default value of the attribute.
dt:type	Identifies the data type of the element. This should be one of the data types described in the previous section.
dt:values	If the data type is enumeration, then this identifies the enumerated values.
name	Identifies the name of the attribute.
required	Indicates whether or not the attribute is mandatory. This will be either yes or no.

One thing you might notice is that the ADO schema contains more attributes that those listed here. For example:

```
<s:AttributeType name="stor_id" rs:number="1"
                 rs:writeunknown="true">
```

The `rs:number` and `rs:writeunknown` attributes don't appear in the table listed above. That's one of the great beauties of XML – it's extensible, so you can add attributes if necessary. Both of these come from the recordset schema. The `rs:number` attribute defines a unique field number, and `rs:writeunknown` defines whether or not the attribute can be updated. Other attributes might be added, depending upon the cursor type. For example, the `store_id` changes to the following when a dynamic, editable cursor type is used:

```
<s:AttributeType name="stor_id" rs:number="1"
                 rs:writeunknown="true" rs:basecatalog="pubs"
                 rs:basetable="sales" rs:basecolumn="stor_id">
```

This has the addition of extra attributes to identify the catalog information, to allow updates to the data.

Namespaces

One thing you'll have noticed about the schema shown above is the use of prefixes and colons on the element and attribute definitions. This is the use of **namespaces**, which define the scope of the elements. For example, the first line of an ADO-produced XML file contains the following:

```
<xml xmlns:s="uuid:BDC6E3F0-6DA3-11d1-A2A3-00AA00C14882"
     xmlns:dt="uuid:C2F41010-65B3-11d1-A29F-00AA00C14882"
     xmlns:rs="urn:schemas-microsoft-com:rowset"
     xmlns:z="#RowsetSchema">
```

This defines an XML document, and then four namespaces:

- ❑ s is the Microsoft XML-Data schema
- ❑ dt is the Microsoft data types schema
- ❑ rs is the Microsoft recordset schema
- ❑ z is the individual row schema

Each of these namespaces is identified by a **Uniform Resource Indicator** (**URI**), which is a globally unique identifier. It just ensures that the namespace can be distinguished from other namespaces. You can use any name as the URI, although a Web site URL is often used. Remember though, that this is just an identifier – it doesn't link the schema to the URL in any way.

So what does a namespace really do? The main reason is the uniqueness issue – it allows you to define a schema for your data, and then apply that schema to elements. Any why is that useful? Because there's nothing to stop two schemas being used in the same XML document. Having a namespace means that you could have tags with the same name, but with different schemas. Even though the tags were named the same, they could be handled differently. For example, consider a tag called Contract. What format of data should this be? In the pubs database in SQL Server, the authors table has a field called contract, which is a Boolean field, indicating whether or not the author has a contract:

```
<contract>1</contract>
```

Another XML document, however, might use contract to indicate the path of a document containing the contract:

```
<contract>d:\authors\suss\contract.doc</contract>
```

If we have to process both XML documents, then we will need a namespace to indicate which form the data should take. For example, let's assume that we've modified the standard pubs data for the authors table, by adding in this second contract field, to determine the path of the Word document. To make the XML elements unique, we could use the following:

```
<xml xmlns:pubs="http://www.wrox.com/ms/PubsDB"
     xmlns:wrox="http://www.wrox.com/authors">
   <Author>
      <au_id>172-32-1111</au_id>
      <au_lname>Sussman</au_lname>
      <au_fname>Dave</au_fname>
      <pubs:contract>1</pubs:contract>
      <wrox:contract>
         d:\authors\suss\contract.doc
      </wrox:contract>
   </Author>
</xml>
```

If we were using the XML-Data format, then we can apply the namespaces to the attributes in a similar way:

```
<xml xmlns:pubs="http://www.wrox.com/ms/PubsDB"
     xmlns:wrox="http://www.wrox.com/authors">
   <Author au_id="172-32-1111" au_lname="Sussman"
           au_fname="Dave"
           pubs:contract="1"
           wrox:contract="d:\authors\suss\contract.doc">
   </Author>
</xml>
```

You'll see a lot of namespace prefixes when dealing with the Microsoft XML-Data format.

Schema Location

In contrast to the IE5-style schemas we saw earlier, when dealing with XML data from ADO, you'll find the schema included as part of the XML document:

```
<xml xmlns:s="uuid:BDC6E3F0-6DA3-11d1-A2A3-00AA00C14882"
    xmlns:dt="uuid:C2F41010-65B3-11d1-A29F-00AA00C14882"
    xmlns:rs="urn:schemas-microsoft-com:rowset"
    xmlns:z="#RowsetSchema">

    <s:Schema id="RowsetSchema">
      <s:ElementType name="row" content="eltOnly"
                              rs:CommandTimeout="30">
        . . .
      </s:ElementType>
    </s:Schema>

    <rs:data>
      <z:row stor_id="6380" ord_num="6871"
             ord_date="1994-09-14T00:00:00" qty="5"
             payterms="Net 60" title_id="BU1032" />
      . . .
    </rs:data>
</xml>
```

This means that you have to consider the fact that the schema is included as part of the XML document. So, the above XML has one root node (xml), and then under that it has two child nodes (s:Schema and rs:data). You'll see where this comes into play in a little while when we look at using the DOM.

Hierarchical XML Data

If you've used the Data Shaping service to create hierarchical recordsets, then you might have noticed that in previous versions of ADO you couldn't use the Save method of the Recordset object to persist the data in XML format. With ADO 2.5 you can now save these hierarchies in XML.

For example, consider the following shape command:

```
SHAPE {select * from titles}
APPEND ({select * from sales}
RELATE title_id TO title_id) AS rsSales
```

This constructs a parent recordset containing the book titles, and a child recordset containing the sales. The XML ADO produces for this caters for this hierarchy – a cut down version is shown below. The bold lines show the differences between a normal recordset in XML format and a shaped recordset in XML:

```
<xml xmlns:s='uuid:BDC6E3F0-6DA3-11d1-A2A3-00AA00C14882'
    xmlns:dt='uuid:C2F41010-65B3-11d1-A29F-00AA00C14882'
    xmlns:rs='urn:schemas-microsoft-com:rowset'
    xmlns:z='#RowsetSchema'>
    <s:Schema id='RowsetSchema'>
      <s:ElementType name='row'
                    content='eltOnly' rs:CommandTimeout='30'
                    rs:ReshapeName='DSRowset1'>
        <s:AttributeType name='title_id'. . .>
          <s:datatype dt:type='string' . . ./>
        </s:AttributeType>
        . . .
```

```
            <s:ElementType name='rsSales' content='eltOnly'
                           rs:CommandTimeout='30'
                           rs:ReshapeName='DSRowset2'
                           rs:relation='01000000006000000000000000'>
                <s:AttributeType name='stor_id' . . .'>
                    <s:datatype dt:type='string' . . ./>
                </s:AttributeType>
            </s:ElementType>
        </s:ElementType>
    </s:Schema>

    <rs:data>
        <z:row title_id='BU1032'
               title='The Busy Executive&#x27;s Database Guide'
               type='business      ' pub_id='1389'
               price='19.99' advance='5000' royalty='10'
               ytd_sales='4095'
               notes='An overview of . . .'
               pubdate='1991-06-12T00:00:00'>
            <rsSales stor_id='6380' ord_num='6871'
                     ord_date='1994-09-14T00:00:00' qty='5'
                     payterms='Net 60' title_id='BU1032'/>
            <rsSales stor_id='8042' ord_num='423LL930'
                     ord_date='1994-09-14T00:00:00' qty='10'
                     payterms='ON invoice' title_id='BU1032'/>
        </z:row>
    </rs:data>
</xml>
```

Here you can see that the row now contains the details for the book title. Each row also contains other elements (rsSales), containing the sales details. The schema has also changed to cater for this. The element type for the row not only contains attribute definitions for each field, but also another element type for the child recordset of the sales.

Schema Summary

We've only had a brief look at the XML-Data schema, although a more in-depth discussion would have been useful. The reason for this is that XML-Data is not a standard – it's one of a number of proposals that the W3C are considering for the definition of metadata. The W3C have not announced support for any particular schema, or indeed whether any will be used.

What Microsoft has proposed is a good solution, and I suspect they will continue to support the current format. However, if the W3C do adopt a schema as a standard then we have to consider that Microsoft will update their support. So that's one reason why I haven't gone into a great deal of detail – I don't want to document something until it is set in stone. It's best to keep your eye on both the W3C Web site (http://www.w3c.org) and the MSDN site (http://msdn.microsoft.com), as these will be updated as soon as a decision is made.

Another reason for not describing XML-Data in detail is that in many situations we don't really need to know anything about it. Much of the time we are only concerned with the data itself, and not the individual format in which it is laid out.

The XML Document Object Model

If you're used to programming COM objects then you'll understand the term "Object Model" – it is a representation of a set of objects and their relationships to one another. The **Document Object Model** (**DOM**) is a model for HTML and XML documents, and defines a standard way in which they can be accessed and manipulated.

If you're confused about how an object model can apply to XML data, then just think of a DOM document as an object that holds XML data. Just as a `Recordset` object holds data, so does a DOM object. XML data has a tree-like structure, so it's a good idea to think about nodes and lists of nodes.

The DOM and XML Data

You may well wonder what the DOM has to do with ADO – after all, ADO is really about data access isn't it? Yes it is, but the DOM is another way of representing XML data, so it's a good idea to understand a little about how it works, and how you can use it. We won't go into great depth, because we don't really need to, but there are some aspects of using the DOM that will be useful to you.

Before you can get data into a DOM object, you need to create it. The root object you need to create is a `DOMDocument`, in the `MSXML` library. For example:

```
Dim domXML As MSXML.DOMDocument
Set domXML = New MSXML.DOMDocument
```

The above shows a Visual Basic example – you should use the appropriate syntax for other languages. The important point is the object you are creating.

Now we have created the object, we have to consider how to get XML data into and out of the DOM document, and there are three ways of doing this.

Loading Data into the DOM

The first two ways of getting data into the DOM use methods of the `DOMDocument` object. If we have an existing XML file then we can use the `load` method:

```
domXML.load "c:\temp\sales.xml"
```

Alternatively, if the XML is contained in a string, we can use the `loadXML` method:

```
domXML.loadXML strXML
```

The third method is used to transfer the data directly from an ADO recordset into the DOM object, using the `Save` method of the `Recordset` object:

```
rsSales.Open "sales", "Provider=SQLOLEDB; . . ."

rsSales.Save domXML, adPersistXML
```

In previous versions of ADO you could only save to a file, but now you can also save to a stream. This is discussed in more detail under the persistence section of this chapter. For now we just want to show you that it can be done.

The DOM Structure

Once the data is in the DOM, you have to consider how it is stored. Let's recap on the XML data we'll be using here:

```
<xml xmlns:s="uuid:BDC6E3F0-6DA3-11d1-A2A3-00AA00C14882"
     xmlns:dt="uuid:C2F41010-65B3-11d1-A29F-00AA00C14882"
     xmlns:rs="urn:schemas-microsoft-com:rowset"
     xmlns:z="#RowsetSchema">

  <s:Schema id-"RowsetSchema">
    <s:ElementType name="row"  content="eltOnly"
                               rs:CommandTimeout="30">
        . . .
    </s:ElementType>
  </s:Schema>

  <rs:data>
    <z:row stor_id="6380" ord_num="6871"
           ord_date="1994-09-14T00:00:00" qty="5"
           payterms="Net 60" title_id="BU1032" />
        . . .
  </rs:data>
</xml>
```

This is an ADO-generated XML document for the sales table from the pubs database. When this is loaded into the DOM, it takes on the following structure:

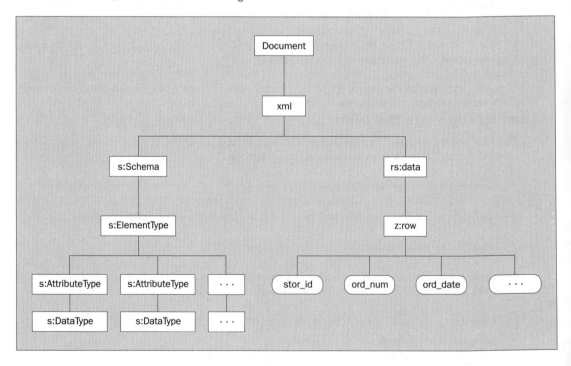

At the very top we have the document node. This is always the topmost node in the structure. Underneath that we have the XML data itself, contained in a node which represents the <xml> element. This XML data consists of two nodes – the schema and the recordset data, and each of these consists of its own XML elements. You can see how this structure maps onto the XML data.

What you'll also notice is that the data fields (stor_id, ord_num, etc.) appear as nodes of the z:row element, even though they are attributes in the XML data. This is because every structure in an XML document is managed as a node, albeit perhaps a node of a different type.

DOM Objects

Like the ADO object model, the DOM is made up from several basic objects:

❑   A Node object is a single node in the hierarchy.

❑   A NodeList object is a collection of Node objects.

❑   A NamedNodeMap object is a collection of Node objects that allows access by name as well as by index.

Since XML data caters for a variety of documents, there are different types of objects, for different types of nodes:

❑   A Document object is the root object for an XML document. The XML data always appears as a child node under this.

❑   A DocumentType object contains information about the document type declaration.

❑   An Element object represents an XML element.

❑   An Attribute (or Attr) object represents an XML attribute.

❑   A Text object represents the text of an attribute or element node. Note that text content of an element is stored in a child Text object, not directly in the Element object.

❑   A Comment object represents an XML comment (these are identical in format to HTML comments).

❑   A CDATASection contains unparsed character data, as stored in a CDATA section (used to store data which is ignored by the XML parser, and which therefore may contain otherwise illegal characters).

There are a few other objects, but we're not going to cover them here, since they are not really used in ADO. To get yourself into this node type mindset, it's a good idea to draw a picture. Let's take the sales information that we showed earlier, concentrating on just the recordset data:

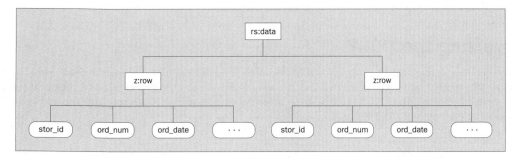

So, each row is a node, and each attribute (i.e. each field) is node too. So how do you go about getting access to this data? Simple, you use the built-in methods and properties of the DOM.

Node Properties

Assuming we have a DOM document full of XML data, we'll need some way to manipulate it. Keeping the above tree structure in mind, the following properties (supported by all Node objects) make this possible:

- ❑ childNodes, to return a NodeList of child nodes of the current node.

- ❑ firstChild, to return the first child of the current node.

- ❑ lastChild, to return the last child of the current node.

- ❑ parentNode, to return the parent of the current node.

- ❑ previousSibling, to return the previous node in the same level of the hierarchy.

- ❑ nextSibling, to return the next node in the same level of the hierarchy.

- ❑ nodeName, to return the name of the node.

- ❑ nodeValue, to return the value of the node.

- ❑ attributes, returns a collection of attributes for the node.

Another diagram will help make this easier to visualize:

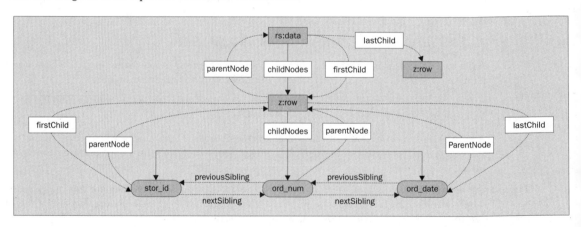

This shows clearly what each property refers to, and how the nodes are related.

Traversing the DOM

Having data in the DOM is not very useful if you can't get access to it. Let's assume we have the ADO sales data loaded into a DOM object, and see what some of the DOM methods and properties give us. The table below assumes we have a pointer to the root node of the DOM tree, and shows the method and what this method call returns.

Method	Returns
nodeName	#document
childNodes(0).nodeName	xml
attributes(0).nodeName	xmlns:s
attributes(2).nodeName	xmlns:rs
attributes(2).nodeValue	urn:schemas-microsoft-com:rowset
childNodes(0).childNodes(0).nodeName	s:Schema
childNodes(0).childNodes(1).nodeName	rs:data
childNodes(0).childNodes(1).childNodes(0).nodeName	z:row
childNodes(0).childNodes(1).childNodes(0).attributes(0).nodeName	stor_id

You can see that nodes contain other nodes, and you can just drill down through this structure. In fact, it's a recursive structure, so it's pretty easy to write recursive routines to traverse through it. Here's a simple Visual Basic example:

```
Private Sub TraversDOM()

    Dim domXML  As New MSXML.DOMDocument

    ' load the xml data into the DOM object
    domXML.Load "c:\temp\sales.xml"

    ' call the traversal routine, passing in
    ' the DOM object
    DumpNode domXML, 0

    Set domXML = Nothing

End Sub
```

This subroutine simply loads the XML file into a DOMDocument object and calls the recursive DumpNode sub. This sub takes as parameters the Node object to be displayed and an integer representing the level in the tree structure:

```
Private Sub DumpNode(nodNode As MSXML.IXMLDOMNode, intLevel As Integer)

    ' create two node objects for the
    ' atrributes and child nodes
    Dim nodAttr As MSXML.IXMLDOMNode
    Dim nodChild As MSXML.IXMLDOMNode

    ' print the node name and value
    Debug.Print Space(intLevel); nodNode.nodeName; vbTab; nodNode.nodeValue

    ' loop through the attributes
    If Not nodNode.Attributes Is Nothing Then
        For Each nodAttr In nodNode.Attributes
            Debug.Print Space(intLevel); "attr: "; _
                        nodAttr.nodeName; " ("; _
                        nodAttr.nodeValue; ")"
```

```
        Next
    End If

    ' loop through the children, and recurse, since they
    ' can contain other children.
    For Each nodChild In nodNode.childNodes
        DumpNode nodChild, intLevel + 1
    Next

End Sub
```

First we print the name and value of the node which was passed in (indented with the correct number of spaces for its level in the tree). We then loop through the node's attributes, displaying the name and value of each.

Finally, we loop through any children of the current node, and for each one in turn call the `DumpNode` sub. This time we pass in the current level plus one as the second parameter, increasing the level in the hierarchy by one place.

This gives the following result:

```
#document      Null
 xml     Null
 attr: xmlns:s (uuid:BDC6E3F0-6DA3-11d1-A2A3-00AA00C14882)
 attr: xmlns:dt (uuid:C2F41010-65B3-11d1-A29F-00AA00C14882)
 attr: xmlns:rs (urn:schemas-microsoft-com:rowset)
 attr: xmlns:z (#RowsetSchema)
  s:Schema      Null
  attr: id (RowsetSchema)
   s:ElementType      Null
   attr: name (row)
   attr: content (eltOnly)
   attr: rs:CommandTimeout (30)
   attr: rs:updatable (true)
    s:AttributeType      Null
    attr: name (stor_id)
    attr: rs:number (1)
    attr: rs:writeunknown (true)
    attr: rs:basecatalog (pubs)
    attr: rs:basetable (sales)
    attr: rs:basecolumn (stor_id)
     s:datatype      Null
     attr: dt:type (string)
     attr: rs:dbtype (str)
     attr: dt:maxLength (4)
     attr: rs:fixedlength (true)
     attr: rs:maybenull (false)
     . . .
  rs:data      Null
   z:row      Null
   attr: stor_id (6380)
   attr: ord_num (6871)
   attr: ord_date (1994-09-14T00:00:00)
   attr: qty (5)
```

```
attr: payterms (Net 60)
attr: title_id (BU1032)
z:row     Null
attr: stor_id (8042)
attr: ord_num (423LL930)
attr: ord_date (1994-09-14T00:00:00)
attr: qty (10)
attr: payterms (ON invoice)
attr: title_id (BU1032)
  . . .
```

One thing you notice here is that the elements themselves (`rs:data` and `z:row`, for example) have null values. You might think that's because they are empty nodes and the data is contained within attributes, but in fact the `nodeValue` for the element nodes would in any case be `Null`: the value of an element's content is contained in a child `Text` node.

DOM Summary

That's all were really going to cover of the DOM, otherwise we'll be turning this into an XML book. However, as I said at the beginning of the section, the DOM is just another way of representing data, so it's something we should be aware of, and it's useful to know how it works. We'll be seeing the DOM object in use in a few sections later in the chapter.

Microsoft is actively pursuing the closer integration of XML and ADO, so we really need to know more about it. Come to think of it, Microsoft is integrating XML with just about everything, so this knowledge is probably even more important than you think.

XML and ADO

OK, that's enough about the technical aspects of XML. You may think we've covered a lot of non-ADO stuff here, but there are a couple of good reasons for this. Firstly, XML is becoming increasingly important as a data transfer format, and secondly, XML management is being integrated into many development tools. So even though it's not strictly necessary to know all of this XML stuff, the more you understand about it, the better your chance of working with XML data.

So, let's look into ADO and see exactly what features it gives us. In the current version of ADO this really centers around the ability to get recordsets into and out of ADO as XML, but there are areas surrounding this that make for interesting programming. We'll look at various ways of transferring data into and out of ADO in XML format, and how it can be manipulated outside of ADO.

Persistence

The way ADO transfers data in XML format is via the Persistence Provider. In previous versions of ADO you could save (persist) a recordset in XML format to a file. The same mechanism is used in ADO 2.5, but has been enhanced by the addition of the **Stream** object (based upon the COM `IStream` interface).

The Stream is simply a way of accessing a chunk of memory, and provides two things:

❑ A way to access the contents of an object directly

❑ A way to transfer data between objects

The first of these will be covered in Chapter 8, when we look at Internet Publishing, and it's the second method we're interested in here. The way to think about this transfer between objects is just to think about a real stream, with water flowing between two places. You can put something into the stream at one end and it appears at the other end (come on, don't tell me you've never played Pooh Sticks!). In our object world, if two objects implement a Stream, then you can transfer data between them in a similar way.

The way that the Stream has been incorporated into ADO is in the Source argument of the Save and Open methods of the recordset.

Persisting to and from a Stream

To save a recordset to a Stream, we simply put the Stream object in place of the filename. For example:

```
rsSales.Save streamObject, adPersistXML
```

This has to be an existing, open Stream object (or an object that supports the IStream interface), and what you use depends on which environment you are in, and what you are trying to do. We'll be looking at specifics in a little while.

A similar method is used to open a recordset from a stream:

```
rsSales.Open streamObject, , , , adCmdFile
```

This is very simple, but because it uses a standard Stream interface, it's very powerful. To get a good idea of how flexible this is, consider the following:

❑ The Stream is supported by ASP 3.0, so you can save recordsets to the Response object, and open them from the Request object. This gives you a way to transfer recordsets as XML to and from a browser.

❑ CDO message bodies can be accessed via a Stream, therefore you could save recordsets to the body of a mail message. Likewise, you could open a recordset from a received mail message.

The Stream isn't only useful in persisting XML recordsets, as the Internet Publishing Provider and the Microsoft Exchange Provider both support the access of file contents via a Stream. We'll be looking at this in Chapter 8 and Chapter 13.

Data Updates

The XML data that ADO uses copes well with modification of the data set, handling inserts, deletions, and updates. These are handled by three elements that belong to the recordset namespace:

❑   rs:update for updated rows

❑   rs:insert for new rows

❑   rs:delete for deleted rows

Don't think that just because these are supported by XML that you have to code these yourself. In fact, the standard ADO methods are still used to update data, but the updated data, when converted to XML, has to contain this information. The reason is that if XML is being used as a data transport mechanism, then there needs to be some way to identify changed records.

Obviously, we're talking about a disconnected recordset here, so we'd be using client cursors, and batch optimistic locking. The updates would be shown if the data was transferred in XML format.

Updated Rows

These are rows that have been updated in the normal fashion, by just editing the values. For an update the original data is held within the rs:original element, whilst the changed fields are part of the rs:update element:

```
<rs:data>
  <rs:update>
    <rs:original>
      <z:row stor_id='6380' ord_num='6871'
             ord_date='1994-09-14T00:00:00' qty='5'
             payterms='Net 60' title_id='BU1032'/>
    </rs:original>
    <z:row payterms='Net 66'/>
  </rs:update>
```

Notice that the entire row is used as the original data. Because this is a disconnected recordset, the key information isn't persisted with it, so there's no way ADO knows which columns are used to uniquely identify a row.

Added Rows

For a new row, the rs:insert element contains the data added for new row. This row is added with the AddNew method of the recordset:

```
<rs:insert>
  <z:row stor_id='6380' ord_num='936g'
         ord_date='1999-08-17T00:00:00' qty='10'
         payterms='Net 90' title_id='BU1032'/>
</rs:insert>
```

Notice that there's no rs:original element this time, because there is no original row.

Deleted Rows

For a deleted row, removed with the `Delete` method, the `rs:delete` contains the deleted row.

```
    <rs:delete>
      <z:row stor_id='7066' ord_num='QA7442.3'
             ord_date='1994-09-13T00:00:00' qty='75'
             payterms='ON invoice' title_id='PS2091'/>
    </rs:delete>
  </rs:data>
```

These modifications are just part of the normal recordset, and when a batch update is performed on the server they will be applied to the source data.

ADO, XML and the Internet

It seems fairly obvious that the Internet has prompted the rise of XML, but it's also had a large impact on the development of ADO. In fact, the Internet is one of the reasons why ADO was developed, and was certainly why disconnected recordsets were created.

Chapters 3 and 4 talked about disconnected recordsets, and the whole idea of marshaling data, and it's a good idea to just think about transferring XML in a similar fashion. All we are doing is using XML as the format during the recordset marshaling.

Sending XML to the Browser

Since both ADO and ASP support the `Stream` we get the opportunity to pass XML data around easily between the web browser and the ASP server. The simplest way to perform this is as follows (we will use this ASP page to generate XML for subsequent pages, so save it with the name `XMLFromADO.asp`):

```
<%
    strConn = "Provider=SQLOLEDB; Data Source=" & _
              Request.ServerVariables("SERVER_NAME") & _
              "; Initial Catalog=pubs; User Id=sa; Password="

    Response.ContentType = "text/xml"
    Set rsSales = Server.CreateObject("ADODB.Recordset")
    rsSales.Open "sales", strConn

    rsSales.Save Response, 1     ' adPersistXML = 1
%>
```

This saves a copy of the recordset in XML format into the `Response` stream, which in ASP is what gets written to the browser. When it actually gets sent to the browser depends on whether buffering is on in the ASP page.

What you get (in IE) is the following:

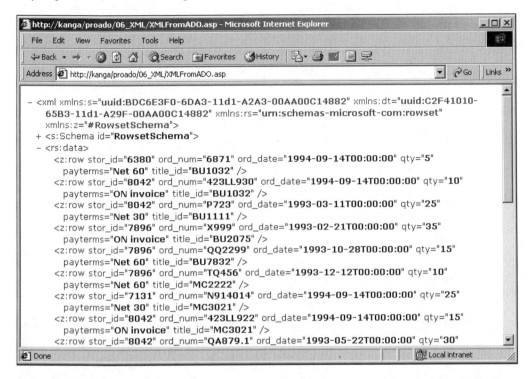

There's nothing particularly amazing about this, but it does show you how easy it is to transfer data in XML format to a browser.

Creating an XML Data Island

One of the areas where sending data directly to the browser is useful is in the creation of XML Data Islands. These are pockets of XML stored on the client, and used in the same way as RDS components, to manage the client data.

We can create a Data Island in IE with the XML tag:

```
<XML ID="dsoSales" SRC="XMLFromADO.asp"></XML>
```

The XMLFromADO.asp file would contain code similar to that shown above. We can now use this Data Island as a Data Source Object, perhaps using data binding to bind HTML elements (such as table cells) to the Data Island:

```
<TABLE DATASRC="#dsoSales">
    <TR><TD>
        <TABLE DATASRC="#dsoSales" DATAFLD="rs:data">
            <TR><TD>
                <TABLE DATASRC="#dsoSales" DATAFLD="z:row" BORDER="1">
                    <THEAD>
                        <TR>
```

```
                    <TD>Store ID</TD>
                    <TD>Order Number</TD>
                    <TD>Order Date</TD>
                    <TD>Quantity</TD>
                    <TD>Payment Terms</TD>
                    <TD>Title ID</TD>
                </TR>
            </THEAD>
            <TBODY>
                <TR>
                    <TD><SPAN DATAFLD="stor_id"></SPAN></TD>
                    <TD><SPAN DATAFLD="ord_num"></SPAN></TD>
                    <TD><SPAN DATAFLD="ord_date"></SPAN></TD>
                    <TD><SPAN DATAFLD="qty"></SPAN></TD>
                    <TD><SPAN DATAFLD="payterms"></SPAN></TD>
                    <TD><SPAN DATAFLD="title_id"></SPAN></TD>
                </TR>
            </TBODY>
        </TABLE>
    </TD></TR>
        </TABLE>
    </TD><TR>
</TABLE>
```

Notice that we have to have three bound tables – that's because of the way ADO creates its XML data, with the schema, the rowset data, and then the rows. The above data binding gives the following output:

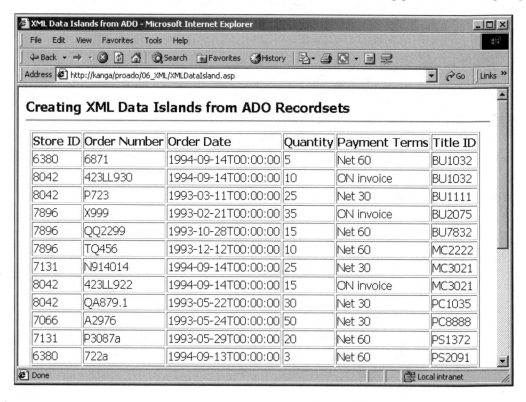

The important things to note are the way data binding works:

```
<TABLE DATASRC="#dsoSales">
    <TR><TD>
        <TABLE DATASRC="#dsoSales" DATAFLD="rs:data">
            <TR><TD>
                <TABLE DATASRC="#dsoSales" DATAFLD="z:row">
```

Because of the hierarchical nature of the XML data, we have to use a hierarchy of bound tables, each one binding to successive levels in the XML. If you find yourself getting confused by this layering then you can add the levels to the field name of the DATASRC attribute like so:

```
<TABLE DATASRC="#dsoSales">
    <TR><TD>
        <TABLE DATASRC="#dsoSales" DATAFLD="rs:data">
            <TR><TD>
                <TABLE DATASRC="#dsoSales" DATAFLD="rs:data.z:row">
```

This hierarchical data binding technique can be further used if your XML also has hierarchical data, such as books and then sales. For example, if we use the hierarchical XML we showed earlier in this chapter, we could do our data binding like so:

```
<TABLE DATASRC="#dsoSales">
    <TR><TD>
        <TABLE DATASRC="#dsoSales" DATAFLD="rs:data">
            <TR><TD>
                <TABLE DATASRC="#dsoSales" DATAFLD="rs:data.z:row">
                    <TR><TD>
                        <TABLE DATASRC="#dsoSales" DATAFLD="rs:data.z:row.rsSales">
```

Using XSL to Transform the Data Island

You don't have to use data binding to display the XML data, and you could easily use an XSL stylesheet. Since XSL is also an application of XML, you can load the XSL into a data island too, and then transform the XML on the client:

```
<XML ID="dsoSales" SRC="XMLFromADO.asp"></XML>
<XML ID="dsoXSL" SRC="SalesToTable.xsl"></XML>

<SPAN ID="spanData"></SPAN>

<SCRIPT LANGUAGE="JScript">

function dsoXSL.ondatasetcomplete()
{
    if (event.reason == 0)
        spanData.innerHTML = dsoSales.transformNode(dsoXSL.documentElement);
}

</SCRIPT>
```

In the above code, there are two data islands – one for the data and one for the stylesheet. When the stylesheet completes loading, the ondatasetcomplete event is fired, and we set the contents of a <SPAN> to contain the XML data transformed by the stylesheet. The stylesheet could look like this:

```
<xsl:stylesheet xmlns:xsl="http://www.w3.org/TR/WD-xsl">

    <xsl:template match="/">

        <TABLE BORDER="1">
            <TR>
                <TD>Store ID</TD>
                <TD>Order Number</TD>
                <TD>Order Date</TD>
            </TR>
            <xsl:for-each select="//rs:data/z:row">
                <TR>
                    <TD><xsl:value-of select="@stor_id"/></TD>
                    <TD><xsl:value-of select="@ord_num"/></TD>
                    <TD><xsl:value-of select="@ord_date"/></TD>
                </TR>
            </xsl:for-each>
        </TABLE>

    </xsl:template>

</xsl:stylesheet>
```

This just converts the XML into a table, using only three of the columns. The HTML tags are sent to the browser as they are, and thus rendered by IE5. We use an `<xsl:for-each>` element to iterate through every `<z:row>` element in the XML document, in a similar way to a Visual Basic `for...each` loop. We place `<TR>...</TR>` tags within this element, so that each iteration of the loop appears as a row in our HTML table. Within this row, we simply display each of our selected fields (the `@` symbol in front of the field names indicates that these are attributes of the `<z:row>` element) as table cells.

The advantage of this method is that you could load several different stylesheets from the server, and then cause user events (such as button clicks) to transform the data using the different styles.

For more information on using XSL in IE5, check out 'XML in IE5 Programmer's Reference', ISBN 1-861001-57-6.

Reading XML from the Browser

In the same way that we used the `Response` object to send XML data to the browser, we can use the `Request` object to open a recordset posted from the browser via the HTML `POST` method. For example, we could include this code in an ASP page on the server:

```
Dim rsData

Set rsData = Server.CreateObject("ADODB.Recordset")

rsData.Open Request, , , , adCmdFile
```

So not only do we have a way to send XML data to the client, but a way to retrieve it too. This adds yet another notch in favor of using ASP as a middle-tier component for Web applications.

However, there is an issue with this whole approach. The problem is how to get a modified XML data island back to an ASP page where we can call `UpdateBatch`. We can use the `XMLHTTP` object on the client and send the XML back like so:

```
var xmlhttp = new ActiveXObject("Microsoft.XMLHTTP");

xmlhttp.open("POST", "XMLReadFromRequest.asp", false);
xmlhttp.send(dsoSales.XMLDocument.xml);
```

This posts the XML stored in the data island (dsoSales) fine, which can be opened as a recordset from the Request, as shown above. This is where the problem lies, since the XML data island is really just a wrapper around two objects – the Recordset and the XML DOM document. Using the above code to send the data to an ASP page is fine, but what this sends is the contents of the XML DOM document, which doesn't keep track of changes. So, all the xml property represents is the latest view of the data in XML format.

It's the Recordset that is responsible for keeping track of the changes, so we need to get the XML from the Recordset, not from the DOM document. However, we need to get the data out of the Recordset in XML format. Easy, you might think, persist it to a Stream object, and then POST that back. Our code would then become:

```
var xmlhttp = new ActiveXObject("Microsoft.XMLHTTP");
var stmData = new ActiveXObject("ADODB.Stream");

// save in XML format (1 = adPersistXML)
dsoSales.Recordset.Save(stmData, 1);

xmlhttp.open("POST", "XMLReadFromRequest.asp", false);
xmlhttp.send(stmData.readText());
```

Since I've already said there's a problem, you won't be surprised to learn that this doesn't work. What's interesting though, is where it doesn't work – it's the Save method that fails, with this rather lovely message:

Hierarchical Recordset cannot be persisted because it was not generated by the Microsoft Data Shaping Service for OLE DB. To use it, specify 'Provider=MSDataShape' in the connection string.

Doh! At the time of writing this was still an outstanding bug, and I'm not sure whether it will be fixed for the final release. I do know that the XML/ADO integration is being worked on, so in future this will be solved.

Using the RDS Data Control

Luckily though, we don't need to panic, because the RDS data control actually works, proving this to be a problem with the XML data island. So, if we use the following code:

```
<OBJECT CLASSID="clsid:BD96C556-65A3-11D0-983A-00C04FC29E33"
        ID="dsoSales" HEIGHT="0" WIDTH="0">
   <PARAM NAME="URL" VALUE="XMLFromADO.asp">
</OBJECT>

<SPAN id="txtResult"></SPAN>

<BUTTON ID="cmdUpdateAll" TITLE="Save All Changes"
        ONCLICK="postXML()">Save</BUTTON>
```

```
<TABLE DATASRC="#dsoSales">
    <THEAD>
        <TR>
            <TD>Store ID</TD>
            <TD>Order Number</TD>
            <TD>Order Date</TD>
            <TD>Quantity</TD>
            <TD>Payment Terms</TD>
            <TD>Title ID</TD>
        </TR>
    </THEAD>
    <TBODY>
        <TR>
            <TD><INPUT TYPE="TEXT" DATAFLD="stor_id"></INPUT></TD>
            <TD><INPUT TYPE="TEXT" DATAFLD="ord_num"></INPUT></TD>
            <TD><INPUT TYPE="TEXT" DATAFLD="ord_date"></INPUT></TD>
            <TD><INPUT TYPE="TEXT" DATAFLD="qty"></INPUT></TD>
            <TD><INPUT TYPE="TEXT" DATAFLD="payterms"></INPUT></TD>
            <TD><INPUT TYPE="TEXT" DATAFLD="title_id"></INPUT></TD>
        </TR>
    </TBODY>
</TABLE>

<SCRIPT LANGUAGE="JScript">

function postXML()
{
    var xmlhttp = new ActiveXObject("Microsoft.XMLHTTP");
    var stmData = new ActiveXObject("ADODB.Stream");

    // save in XML format (1 = adPersistXML)
    dsoSales.recordset.Save(stmData, 1);

    xmlhttp.open("POST", "XMLReadFromRequest.asp", false);
    xmlhttp.send(stmData.readText());

    txtResult.innerHTML = xmlhttp.ResponseText;
}

</SCRIPT>
```

This is the same as the XML data island version, except that is uses the RDS data control. Another advantage is that the RDS data control doesn't require the nested tables to bind correctly to the hierarchical XML data.

Of course, we must now open the recordset in batch update mode, so we must change the line in XMLFromADO.asp where the recordset is opened:

```
rsSales.Open "sales", strConn
```

Since we want to perform batch updates, we will need to open the recordset with a lock type of adLockBatchOptimistic. We will also set the cursor type to adOpenStatic and the command type to adCmdTable:

```
rsSales.Open "sales", strConn, adOpenStatic, adLockBatchOptimistic, adCmdTable
```

We can now put the following code in the `XMLReadFromRequest.asp` file:

```
<!-- #INCLUDE FILE="Connection.asp" -->
<%
   Dim rsData

   Set rsData = Server.CreateObject ("ADODB.Recordset")

   rsData.CursorLocation = adUseClient
   rsData.Open Request, , adOpenKeyset, adLockBatchOptimistic, adCmdFile

   rsData.ActiveConnection = strConn
   rsData.UpdateBatch

   rsData.Close
   Set rsData = Nothing

   Response.Write "Data updated"
%>
```

This opens the `Recordset`, using the `Request` as the source of the recordset. Since the `Request` holds the XML data that has been `POST`ed back to us, we have an ADO recordset, in XML format, complete with changes. The `ActiveConnection` is then set to put to the server database, and `UpdateBatch` then updates the source data.

This page references the include file `Connection.asp`. This allows us to keep the connection details in one file, which simply contains the connection information and the reference to the ADO type library. The first line is the `METADATA` tag:

```
<!--METADATA TYPE="TypeLib"
            UUID="{00000205-0000-0010-8000-00AA006D2EA4}" -->
```

The `METADATA` tag identifies the ADO type library, which allows us to use the ADO constants without having to include them in the ASP file. You can also use the `FILE` attribute to reference the type library:

```
<!-- METADATA TYPE="TypeLib"
     FILE="C:\Program Files\Common Files\system\ado\msado15.dll" -->
```

This references the DLL directly, and works the same way as using the UID. The only difference is that the `FILE` method is less portable, since the default drive might not be `C:`.

The second part of the include file sets the connection string, using the current server name as the name of the SQL Server.

```
<%
   Dim strConn

   strConn = "Provider=SQLOLEDB; Data Source=" & _
             Request.ServerVariables("SERVER_NAME") & _
             "; Initial Catalog=pubs; User ID=sa; Password="
%>
```

If you are using a different database server, you should change the connection string accordingly.

So there you have an easy way of using XML as the format to transfer data to and from the client.

The SQL Server XML Preview

You can see how serious Microsoft is about XML by taking a look at the XML Preview for SQL Server. As its name suggests this is still a preview, and still actively under development, but it does show that Microsoft are working on different ways of transferring XML data to and from SQL Server.

The preview takes the form of an ISAPI DLL that passes SQL statements onto SQL Server, and takes the results and processes them into XML. Since it takes the form of an ISAPI DLL, the preview works by monitoring a virtual directory, and intercepting all calls to that site. The preview comes with a utility to specially register virtual directories.

So, how do you use it? It's pretty simple – all you do is add the SQL statement to the URL as a query string. For example:

```
Address  http://localhost/pubs?sql=select%20*%20from%20sales

  <?xml version="1.0" encoding="UTF-8" ?>
- <root>
    <row stor__id="6380" ord__num="6871" ord__date="1994-09-14 00:00:00.000" qty="5"
    <row stor__id="6380" ord__num="722a" ord__date="1994-09-13 00:00:00.000" qty="3"
    <row stor__id="7066" ord__num="A2976" ord__date="1993-05-24 00:00:00.000" qty="50
    <row stor__id="7066" ord__num="QA7442.3" ord__date="1994-09-13 00:00:00.000" qty=
        title__id="PS2091" />
    <row stor__id="7067" ord__num="D4482" ord__date="1994-09-14 00:00:00.000" qty="10
    <row stor__id="7067" ord__num="P2121" ord__date="1992-06-15 00:00:00.000" qty="40
    <row stor__id="7067" ord__num="P2121" ord__date="1992-06-15 00:00:00.000" qty="20
    <row stor__id="7067" ord__num="P2121" ord__date="1992-06-15 00:00:00.000" qty="20
    <row stor__id="7131" ord__num="N914008" ord__date="1994-09-14 00:00:00.000" qty='
        title__id="PS2091" />
```

The virtual directory has been set up as pubs, and any query to this URL goes through the new DLL. In the above screenshot, we've used the SQL argument to specify the SQL string for the data to be returned. Notice that by default there's no schema, but we can add one with extra commands on the end of the SQL statement. In fact, there are several valid commands, which give us quite a bit of control:

❑ We can specify the element form of XML instead of the attributes form (which ADO currently uses).

❑ We can return a DTD or a schema.

❑ We can specify a stored procedure instead of a SQL string, along with parameters.

❑ We can supply a template, which is a SQL query formatted in XML.

❑ We can supply an XSL stylesheet to format the data.

Not only does the preview allow retrieval of data in XML format, but it allows the updating of data via XML too. For example, the following XML inserts a new record into the `sales` table:

```
<root xmlns:sql="urn:schemas-microsoft-com:xml-sql">
    <sql:sync>
        <sql:after>
            <sales stor_id='7066' ord_num='QA7442.8'
                   ord_date='1998-09-13T00:00:00' qty='25'
                   payterms='ON invoice' title_id='PS2091'/>
        </sql:after>
    </sql:sync>
</root>
```

Here the `<sql:sync>` element tells the DLL that the data is to be synchronized with SQL Server, and the `<sql:after>` indicates the state of the new data. If this had been an update, then the old details would have been in a `<sql:before>` element. For deletions there would only be a `<sql:before>` – without a `<sql:after>` element, it means there is no data after the update – that is, the data should be deleted.

This demonstrates one of the really powerful features of this preview. One of the things that I've found really frustrating is there's no parity between this and the ADO XML format for updates. At the moment the preview is far more powerful than the ADO XML format, but I hope that over time we'll see them merge. If Microsoft is serious about the use of XML as a data transport mechanism, then we have to have consistency. Different formats from different companies is understandable, but from one company? Despite my reservations, you really should take a look at the preview, remembering that one point. It is a preview, and it's changing quite rapidly.

I'd recommend getting hold of a copy of this preview, since it's quite powerful, extremely fast, and offers a peek into what Microsoft might add into SQL Server itself in the future. The preview is available from `http://msdn.microsoft.com/workshop/xml/articles/xmlsql`, and since it's only 250K, it's not a great burden to download it.

Why Use XML?

One of the questions Microsoft people often get asked is why we should use XML when databases store the data, and ADO gives access to it? It's actually quite simple, and it's important to remember that XML is not out to replace ADO or databases. XML is, after all, just a text-based representation of data.

That doesn't in itself answer the question, so let's look at what XML and ADO can do:

❑   ADO is a method for accessing data from a variety of different data stores. The term 'accessing' encompasses many things – talking to data stores, manipulating records, and so on, but that's the primary focus of ADO. It provides no mechanism for representing the data visibly – that is, it's not a UI facility.

❑   XML is an open, text-based format, and thus allows data transfer between different systems.

❑   XML is a way of representing data, and in conjunction with XSL, allowing that data to be transformed.

This last point is probably the most important. XML and XSL allow data to be transformed into a visible format (such as HTML), and that includes ADO data. At the moment a lot of data is transformed from ADO through large ASP scripts on the server, or data binding on the client. I think the idea of writing a common set of XSL stylesheets to transform data into HTML, which could then be used at either the server or the client, could make programming easier. It separates the styling of the data from the data access, and in the long wrong, promotes better design.

Related Technologies

There are many technologies that use XML, and ADO is only one of them. It's a large and blossoming arena, and one that is going to invade many existing areas of the computer world. Some of these technologies I wanted to discuss in detail in this chapter, but then we'd end up with a 400 page chapter about XML! However, since these are important areas I believe they are worth investigation.

❑ Extensible Stylesheet Language, or XSL, is an XML based language that performs transformations of XML data into another format. This format can be another variety of XML, but XSL is most often used to transform XML into HTML for display in Web browsers. XSL was ratified on 16 November 1999, and encompasses two specifications – XSLT and XPath. For more details of these visit the W3C web site, at `http://www.w3c.org/`.

❑ HTML 4.1 and XHTML are what HTML should have been in the first place. As mentioned at the beginning of this chapter, HTML is pretty lax about things such as quotes around attribute values, and closing tags. HTML 4.1 and XHTML introduce the strictness of XML into HTML, which will mean that HTML files will be able to be processed by XML parsers.

❑ XLink and XPointer are extensions to XML to allow the linking between XML documents. This is pretty important if XML is to be used as a generic markup language.

❑ BizTalk is a Microsoft-hosted framework, to allow the easy transmission of XML data. Its premise is to define a set of standard XML tags for common business situations, such as publishing or EDI, using a central repository of XML tag specifications. The BizTalk body is not a standards organization, but is a community of standards users. You can read more about BizTalk at `http://www.biztalk.org`.

There are many other areas where XML is being used because it is a generic markup language. Check out the W3C Web site for more details.

Summary

This chapter has given you a brief look at XML and its use as a data format, especially in relation to ADO. It has only been a brief look, because there are many areas where the interaction between ADO and XML falls short of perfection. This may sound critical, but there is a reason for that. The problems (some of which I haven't detailed) really lie in the Internet Explorer area, and Microsoft's use of the XML DOM. Because these products are separate from ADO they've been not only developed by different teams, but also at a different pace, to different release schedules. I know for a fact that Microsoft is working on ways to rectify this, and future releases will provide more seamless integration.

So, what we've concentrated on has been:

❑ What XML is and how it is used to represent data.

❑ How a schema is used to define the metadata of the recordset, and enforce strictness upon the data.

❑ How you can use the implicit `Stream` support in both ADO and ASP to easily transfer XML recordsets from the server to the browser.

Because XML is such a big area we could have included more, but it's more important to explain the basics rather than just throw in every related topic. You'll see how XML is used more in Chapters 8 and 13, when we look at Internet Publishing and Microsoft Exchange Server.

8
Internet Publishing

Let's get one thing correct from the start. This chapter isn't about how to create web sites or the why and how of document publishing on the Internet. It does have some of those elements in it, but as you've been told several times already, this is an ADO book. So what we are really concerned with in this chapter is the OLE DB Provider for Internet Publishing.

This provider was released with ADO 2.1, but had very limited functionality, and it's only with this 2.5 release that its full potential has been realized. What it gives us is the ability to access data remotely from suitable web sites and from Exchange 2000 through ADO. So, in this chapter we're going to look at:

- ❏ The reasons why this management is necessary.
- ❏ How the Record and Recordsets are used together.
- ❏ How the provider manages URLs.
- ❏ How we can manipulate files remotely.
- ❏ How we can update files remotely.
- ❏ Where this will lead us in the future.

All in all it's a pretty exciting area, so let's dive in.

Resource Management

This whole chapter is really about the management of resources. I'm using the term **resource** as a generic description for a file or directory on a web server. This is an important point because although files provide the content for web sites, it's the directories that make up the structure, and managing the structure of your site is just as important as the content.

Having established the term resource, what do we mean by management? Isn't that done through some special tool, like the MMC for Microsoft IIS? Yes it is, but only to a certain degree. The IIS snap-in certainly allows the creation of site and virtual directories, how applications run within those sites, and certain permissions, but it really doesn't deal with the structure or content of the site once it's created. It can, but that's not its central role.

The Problem

So, once a site is created we are faced with several questions:

❑   How can I manage the resources within the site?

❑   How can I allow other users to manage the resources in a controlled way?

❑   How can I access the resources if I'm not in the office?

These are questions I'm sure many site administrators have asked themselves, and they are quite reasonable questions. Not only does the web have a huge amount of data available, but it's also growing at an alarming rate. We're constantly reading about information overload. I for one have enough trouble managing my own hard drive, let alone a web site exposed to the world.

Let's look at these questions in relation to a fictional web site, based around the Greek gods. Zeus has decided that the Pantheon of Gods is going online, with a main web site, which he will control, and sub-sites for several of his friends. He would like a structure similar to this:

Notice that Hera doesn't have a directory – she was always arguing with Zeus, and he isn't going to help her unless she asks nicely!

> **One important point is that this is a completely normal web site. It is not set up to use the FrontPage Server Extensions.**

How Can I Manage the Resources Within the Site?

'Managing the resources', said Zeus, 'what does that really mean?'

Well, there are several things to think about:

❑   You need to control the main site and the general structure, but you don't want your friends messing with the main pages.

❑   You want to be able to create new pages and edit the existing ones, move them around, delete them, and so on.

❑   You need to create the main pages to provide links to your friends' pages.

❑   You don't want to rely on a single tool, and you'd like to use a combination of tools to edit these pages – an image editor, HTML editor, and so on.

These aren't particularly complex issues, but it clarifies what the site management means.

How Can I Allow Other Users to Manage the Resources in a Controlled Way?

'I want my friends to create their own pages', said Zeus. 'I'll give them a helping hand and start them off, but I'd like them to manage their own set of pages in the same way that I do. I only want them to be able to edit their own pages, and not anyone else's.'

As with the main site, each of the sub-sites needs the same management control as the main site, but this time with a different user. So what you need is access control and namespace control. Each user can only edit their own section of the site.

How Can I Access the Resources If I'm Not in the Office?

'I don't want to be stuck in the office all of the time', Zeus chimed, 'so how can I manage the site remotely? Can I have the same management facilities as though I was in the office?'

You could use a dedicated tool that is integrated with the web server (such as FrontPage and the FrontPage Server Extensions), but this is a proprietary solution. What happens if you want to move your web site to another machine, or use a different editing tool? Or perhaps you're away and you've only got a browser. What you really need is the same functionality as though you were sitting in front of the server. You need to be able to create files, edit pages, and so on.

The Solution

The solution to all of these problems is to use Web Distributed Authoring and Versioning, or WebDAV for short. So what exactly is it? WebDAV is a W3C standard that extends HTTP 1.1 to include a set of new commands allowing the management of web resources. One of the reasons for the great success of the Web is the large-scale adoption of HTTP. If WebDAV is adopted to a similar degree, this will add a whole new set of functionality to the Web.

If you look at the way HTTP works at the moment, then it's pretty simple. From your browser you request a file (using GET), and that file is sent back to you. You can also send data back to the web browser using POST, or use DELETE to delete the file, but that's about it – HTTP doesn't allow you to do anything else with that file.

However, if we build support for WebDAV into your web server, then we automatically get a new set of commands, some of which are shown below:

❑ PROPFIND, to allow the retrieval of properties.

❑ PROPPATCH, to allow the updating of properties.

❑ MKCOL, to allow the creation of new collections (resources that contain other resources, such as folders).

❑ COPY and MOVE, to allow the copying and moving of resources within a namespace.

❑ LOCK, to lock a resource.

You can immediately see what sort of opportunities these give you. For example, PROPPATCH allows you to update values in a file on the server. COPY and MOVE allow you to manage files, and LOCK allows you to perform lock management. With just a few new HTTP commands we've suddenly answered many of those questions about resource management. Version management is still an issue, but we'll come to that later.

The real problem of course, is how you use these new commands. The first thing you need is a web server that supports them, and luckily IIS5 fully supports the standard (there's a list of other servers at the end of this chapter). The second thing you need is a client to make these command requests, and since not many people use HTTP commands directly, Microsoft has created the **OLE DB Provider for Internet Publishing**.

The Internet Publishing Provider

The whole idea behind this provider is that it's built on top of WebDAV, and uses the native HTTP commands. The great advantage of this is that you don't have to learn how to do all the nasty HTTP stuff, because ADO does it all for you.

To illustrate the use of this provider, we'll build a management tool using HTML and scripting. We could just as easily build this in Visual Basic (or any other COM-compliant language), but using HTML and scripting languages gives us a thin client approach. This tool only needs IE5 and ADO 2.5 installed on the client machine, whereas a Visual Basic application would require installation (with a setup program).

We're not going to detail every aspect of how the tool was built, because much of it is just the HTML side of things. What we'll concentrate on is the ADO usage. The full tool is well commented and available for download on the Wrox web site, along with a Visual Basic example.

Just so you can see what the final tool looks like, there's a screen shot below:

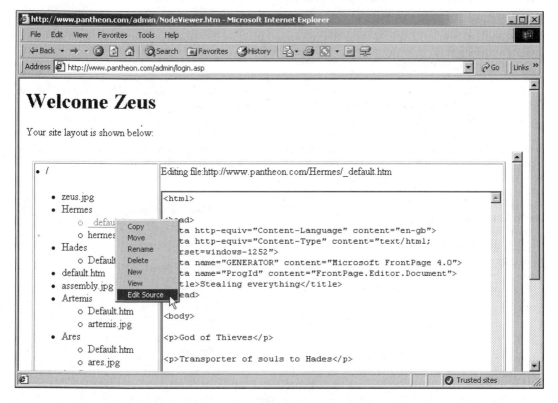

What we have is a list of files and directories on the left of the screen. A menu gives us options for managing those files, and the right-hand side of the screen displays the details for the selected option.

Because this is a web-based tool, the examples in this chapter will be in JavaScript, but they are extremely easy to translate into other languages. I'll gloss over some of the purely HTML and scriptlet-based parts of this tool, because they aren't really relevant to the ADO discussion.

If you'd like to emulate the site, then everything is downloadable from the Wrox site. I created a new web site on an existing machine for this, but you could just as easily use a virtual directory.

> As a word of warning, you might have trouble using some of the `Record` and `Stream` methods from ASP. At the time of writing I (and several other people) hit some security problems where URLs failed to open from ASP, but similar code worked fine in Visual Basic. As a workaround, I added the `IUSR_` account to the `Administrators` group, and this stopped the errors. Remember, though, that this is not a solution you should take on an exposed web server, since this could lead to a security breach. However, this solution should be fine for testing the code on a local server.

The Record and Recordset Objects

Before you can dive into coding you really need to see how the new `Record` object works, and how it is related to a recordset. The first thing to understand is that a **record isn't a row in a recordset** – it doesn't represent a single item in the recordset. What it does represent is a file or directory, in the context of a Document Source Provider.

The point to remember is that Document Source Providers manage resources. The Internet Publishing Provider is a Document Source Provider which is designed to manage resources on a web site. These resources are therefore files and directories, and a `Record` object represents an individual file or directory. The contents of a single directory (that is the files and directories directly under it) can be managed in a recordset. The easy way to think of this is that a single item is managed through a record and a collection of items is a managed through a recordset, where each row in the recordset represents a resource.

This is easiest explained by looking at the sample site. Let's first assume that the top-level URL we are dealing with is www.pantheon.com. This is a single item, so it's a `Record`. But, since it's a directory (or in this case a virtual site that points to a directory), it can contain files and sub-directories. So we can obtain a recordset of these:

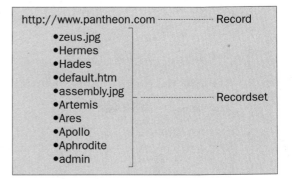

This recordset contains just the files directly under the top-level directory. Each of these files and directories can be opened as individual `Record` objects. So you can loop through the recordset using the details stored for each file or directory, and directly open that file or directory.

If the record is a directory, then it can contain files and directories of its own, so you can obtain a recordset of these:

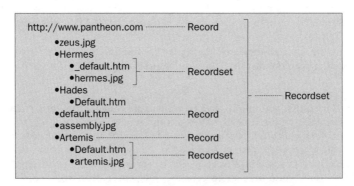

This gives us a way to process the files recursively from a web site. The important thing to remember is that individual files or directories can be opened as a `Record`, but together they are managed in a `Recordset`. This will be clearer when we show you how this works.

Semi-Structured Data

You may wonder why we have a Record object, since it seems as though the above structure could be modeled using hierarchical recordsets. At first glance it seems so, but when you look a little deeper this isn't necessarily so. If you think about a recordset, as shown in the above diagram, then it consists of files and directories. Each of these might have a different set of properties to the others. This isn't particularly easy to manage with the existing Recordset object, which is designed to handle rows of data where each row has the same set of properties as all of the other rows. XML is another good example of data without a set structure; we looked at this in the previous chapter.

A Recordset of files and directories does have a common set of properties, such as the name, full URL, size, modification date, and so on. But these aren't necessarily all of the properties for each file or directory. So the Record contains the properties for each individual file or directory. In other words, the same file can be represented either as a row in a Recordset, in which case it has a generic, limited set of properties, or as a Record object with a more specific set of properties. The row in the Recordset and the Record object are distinct representations of the same file.

When we look at the fields of the Record and Recordset you'll see how these properties are mapped into the Fields collection.

URL Management

Now that we've seen how the Record and Recordset objects are related, it's time to look at how to use them. The handling of URLs is managed through the Record object, so unsurprisingly we use the Open method, which has the following syntax:

```
Record.Open [Source], [ActiveConnection], [Mode],
            [CreateOptions], [UserName], [Password]
```

The arguments are as follows:

Argument	Type	Description
Source	Variant	The URL of the resource to be opened, or an open Recordset object
ActiveConnection	Variant	The connection string or Connection object that identifies the namespace for further operations
Mode	ConnectModeEnum	The access mode to use; the default is adModeUnknown
CreateOptions	RecordCreateOptionsEnum	Whether an existing resource should be opened, or a new resource created; the default is adFailIfNotExists.
Options	RecordOpenOptionsEnum	Specifies the open values; the default is adOpenRecordUnspecified.
UserName	String	The user ID to give authorization to the resource
Password	String	The user password to give authorization to the resource

Let's look at a few examples to examine this in more detail. The simplest way of using this is as follows:

```
var recURL = new ActiveXObject('ADODB.Record');
recURL.Open('URL=http://www.pantheon.com');
```

This simply opens the Record using the supplied URL as the source. Notice that for the connection details we specify URL= at the beginning of the URL. This is because the default OLE DB Provider is the one for ODBC drivers, which of course doesn't recognize URLs. So, you put URL= at the front of the connection details and ADO then switches to the OLE DB Provider for Internet Publishing.

In order to open records which represent directories, you will of course need to ensure that directory browsing is enabled on the Home Directory *tab of the web site's property pages.*

To open an individual file you do this:

```
recURL.Open ('URL=http://www.pantheon.com/admin/default.htm');
```

The above two examples just deal with a single file or directory, but if you plan to do more than just one file access, then you can use the ActiveConnection argument. This works in much the same way as when used to open a normal ADO Recordset, where it defines the connection to which all other actions apply. With the Record, the ActiveConnection does the same thing – it defines the namespace to which all other Record operations apply. In practice this identifies the root URL, meaning that no operations can go above that root (including relative URLs). For example:

```
recURL.Open ('default.htm',
             'URL= http://www.pantheon.com/Hermes');
```

Here we open the default.htm file, but our connection is defined as http://www.pantheon.com/Hermes. That means that the scope for all future operations is defined as http://www.pantheon.com/Hermes.

We can also use an existing Connection object:

```
conURL.Open ('URL=http://www.pantheon.com/Hermes');

recURL.Open ('default.htm', conURL);
```

Modes and Options

By default the access mode of a record when opened is adModeUnknown. To ensure that the correct mode is used when opening a Record you should pick one or more of the following ConnectModeEnum values:

Name	Value	Description
adModeRead	1	Indicates read-only permissions, meaning you cannot modify the Record.
adModeReadWrite	3	Indicates read/write permissions, indicating that you can modify the Record.
adModeRecursive	32	Used in conjunction with the ShareDeny values to propagate sharing restrictions to all sub-records of the current Record.
adModeShareDenyNone	16	Prevents others from opening connection with any permissions.
adModeShareDenyRead	4	Prevents others from opening connection with read permissions.
adModeShareDenyWrite	8	Prevents others from opening connection with write permissions.
adModeShareExclusive	12	Prevents others from opening connection to this Record.
adModeUnknown	0	Default. Indicates that the permissions have not yet been set or cannot be determined.
adModeWrite	2	Indicates write-only permissions.

What this means is that when opening a Record you have complete control over who else can access the resource at the same time. For example, to deny other users access to all files under a directory you could combine values:

```
adModeRead Or adModeShareDenyNone Or adModeRecursive
```

This opens the resource in read-only mode, but stops others from opening it in any mode.

There are some caveats to this at the moment though, since the versioning and access control portions of WebDAV are not ratified as a standard, and therefore are not implemented. There's a section at the end of the chapter explaining this in more detail.

As well as setting permissions, you can also define whether an existing resource should be opened or a new resource created. You do this with the CreateOptions argument, which can be one or more of the RecordCreateOptionsEnum values:

Name	Value	Description
adCreateCollection	8192	Create a new collection record (directory) at the specified URL.
adCreateNonCollection	0	Create a new record at the specified URL.

Table Continued on Following Page

Name	Value	Description
adCreateOverwrite	67108864	Overwrite any existing record at the specified URL.
adCreateStructDoc	-2147483648	Create a new structured document record at the specified URL.
adFailIfNotExists	-1	Fail if the URL does not exist.
adOpenIfExists	33554432	Open the record at the specified URL if it exists, rather than creating a new one.

By default the requested resource must exist when you try to open it, otherwise an error will be generated. To force the creation of a new resource you can use one of the adCreate options. For example:

```
recURL.Open ('NewFile.htm', conURL,
            adModeWrite, adCreateNonCollection);
```

This creates a new file. To create a directory, you create a collection:

```
recURL.Open ('NewDirectory', conURL,
            adModeWrite, adCreateCollection);
```

If you want to create a resource (file or directory), but don't want to overwrite it if it already exists you can add in another option:

```
recURL.Open ('NewDirectory', conURL, adModeWrite,
            adCreateCollection Or adOpenIfExists);
```

To force an existing file to be overwritten, you can use the overwrite flag:

```
recURL.Open ('NewFile.htm', conURL, adModeWrite,
            adCreateNonCollection Or adCreateOverwrite);
```

You should use this latter option with caution though, because you could easily overwrite an existing directory with a file. For example, the above Open statement creates a new file called NewFile.htm overwriting any existing copy. But, if the existing entry called NewFile.htm were a directory, the directory and all its children would be removed and replaced by the file.

When opening a resource you can also specify extra options, as used in the Options argument. The value can be one or more of the RecordOpenOptionsEnum values:

Name	Value	Description
adDelayFetchFields	32768	Delay fetching fields until they are requested
adDelayFetchStream	16384	Delay fetching the Stream until it is requested
adOpenAsync	4096	Open the Record asynchronously
adOpenSource	8388608	Open the source document at the URL, rather than the executed contents
adOpenURLBind	1024	Indicates that the connection string contains a URL

The first two options may improve performance when opening resources, since the fields of the Record and the default Stream object will not be generated until they are requested. The asynchronous flag behaves just like asynchronous use of connections and recordsets, and events are raised in the client through standard event handling code. We won't be showing this here because scripting languages don't support ADO events.

The adOpenSource value is more interesting, since (permissions willing) it allows us to open the actual source code of a page, rather than its output. This doesn't make much sense until you think of something like an ASP file, where opening the ASP file will open the results. Specifying adOpenSource will open the actual ASP source, rather than the executed contents of the page. You might think that this is a huge security risk, but don't worry – the source of a file can only be viewed if the permissions are set to allow this.

The option adOpenURLBind only needs to be used when a connection string doesn't specify URL= at the beginning. As mentioned earlier, the default OLE DB Provider is the one for ODBC, so we can either use URL= at the beginning of the connection string, or we can specify the adOpenURLBind to switch to the OLE DB Provider for Internet Publishing. We can also specify the MSDAIPP Provider explicitly in the Open method; for example:

```
Provider=MSDAIPP.DSO; Data Source=http://www.pantheon.com
```

This follows the more conventional form of Open, where we specify the Provider and the Data Source.

Security

The UserName and Password arguments of the Open method allow us to specify the security credentials to be used to connect to the requested resource. This works in conjunction with the security set up on the web server, and allows us to specify the user details.

For example, let's assume that Zeus has set up a user account for each of the gods who has a web site. He's used the standard security tools (IIS MMC and Windows Explorer) to set permissions for each directory, so that only the appropriate god has permissions to modify their own site, but they have permissions to view all sites. The Open command could now be this:

```
recURL.Open ('', 'URL=http://www.pantheon.com/Ares',
          adModeReadWrite, adFailIfNotExists,
          adOpenRecordUnspecified,
          'Ares', 'War');
```

If you are using a Windows 2000 network and IIS, you could easily use integrated security, but since other web servers support WebDAV this might not always be possible. However, the user name and password could easily be entered into a logon page and passed directly into the code that opens the required URL.

The Fields of a Record

Once you have a record open, you might well need to examine some of its properties. As mentioned earlier, these properties are mapped onto its Fields collection, a list of which is shown below. Descriptions of the data types can be found in Appendix B – they are the data type constants, found under DataTypeEnum:

Field	Type	Description
RESOURCE_PARSENAME	adVarWChar	The URL of the resource.
RESOURCE_PARENTNAME	adVarWChar	The URL of the parent resource.
RESOURCE_ABSOLUTEPARSENAME	adVarWChar	The absolute URL, including path.
RESOURCE_ISHIDDEN	adBoolean	Indicates whether or not the resource is hidden.
RESOURCE_ISREADONLY	adBoolean	Indicates whether or not the resource is read-only.
RESOURCE_CONTENTTYPE	adVarWChar	The likely use of the resource.
RESOURCE_CONTENTCLASS	adVarWChar	The MIME type of the resource.
RESOURCE_CONTENTLANGUAGE	adVarWChar	The resource language.
RESOURCE_CREATIONTIME	adFileTime	The time the resource was created.
RESOURCE_LASTACCESSTIME	adFileTime	The time the resource was last accessed.
RESOURCE_LASTWRITETIME	adFileTime	The time the resource was updated.
RESOURCE_STREAMSIZE	adUnsignedBigInt	Size of the default Stream.
RESOURCE_ISCOLLECTION	adBoolean	Indicates whether or not the resource is a collection – i.e. has children.
RESOURCE_ISSTRUCTUREDDOCUMENT	adBoolean	Indicates whether or not the resource is a structured document – e.g. a Word document.
DEFAULT_DOCUMENT	adVarWChar	The URL of the default document for a folder.
RESOURCE_DISPLAYNAME	adVarWChar	Display name of the resource.
RESOURCE_ISROOT	adBoolean	Indicates whether or not the resource is the root of a collection.
RESOURCE_ISMARKEDFOROFFLINE	adBoolean	Indicates whether or not the resource is marked for offline usage.

> **You should note that** RESOURCE_CONTENTTYPE **and** RESOURCE_CONTENTCLASS **might have their values reversed. At the time of writing they were as documented above, but this may have been corrected for the release.**

DAV Fields

There are also some fields that begin with DAV: – this stands for Distributed Authoring and Versioning, and these fields map onto the RESOURCE_ fields in the following way:

Field	DAV Field
RESOURCE_PARSENAME	DAV:lastpathsegment
RESOURCE_PARENTNAME	DAV:parentname
RESOURCE_ABSOLUTEPARSENAME	DAV:href
RESOURCE_ISHIDDEN	DAV:ishidden
RESOURCE_ISREADONLY	DAV:isreadonly
RESOURCE_CONTENTTYPE	DAV:getcontenttype
RESOURCE_CONTENTCLASS	DAV:getcontentclass
RESOURCE_CONTENTLANGUAGE	DAV:getcontentlanguage
RESOURCE_CREATIONTIME	DAV:creationtime
RESOURCE_LASTACCESSTIME	DAV:lastaccessed
RESOURCE_LASTWRITETIME	DAV:getlastmodified
RESOURCE_STREAMSIZE	DAV:getcontentlength
RESOURCE_ISCOLLECTION	DAV:iscollection
RESOURCE_ISSTRUCTUREDDOCUMENT	DAV:isstructureddocument
DEFAULT_DOCUMENT	DAV:defaultdocument
RESOURCE_DISPLAYNAME	DAV:displayname
RESOURCE_ISROOT	DAV:isroot
	DAV:getetag

The reason there are two sets of properties is that Internet Publishing is built on top of a protocol called WebDAV, and IIS 5.0 is a WebDAV server. It's therefore possible to use any WebDAV client to access IIS 5.0, so it must support the official set of DAV properties.

Traversing a Directory

To build any sort of URL and site management tool you'll need some way of displaying a list of files and directories under a URL. Because each directory can contain other directories, you can make this a recursive procedure. We start with a Record object get a recordset containing its children (i.e. its files and sub-directories). Then we loop through the records in the recordset, and if the individual row is a directory we can delve a level deeper. What we'll do is build up a string of HTML containing list items (in <UL> and <LI> elements), and set the innerHTML property of a SPAN to this HTML string. This causes the output to be rendered.

First, we start with some code to open the appropriate URL:

```
var recURL = new ActiveXObject("ADODB.Record");

recURL.Open('URL=http://www.pantheon.com');

spanNodes.innerHTML = TraverseTree(recURL);
```

Next comes the procedure for traversing through this tree structure:

```
function TraverseTree(recNode)
{
  var sNode = '';
  var rsChildren;
  var recChildNode = new ActiveXObject("ADODB.Record");

  // output the node name
  sNode = '<LI>' + recNode("RESOURCE_DISPLAYNAME") +
      '</LI>';

  // check to see if this node has children
  if (recNode.RecordType == adCollectionRecord)
  {
    // get any child nodes
    rsChildren = recNode.GetChildren();

    // loop through the children
    if (!rsChildren.EOF)
    {
      sNode = sNode + '<UL>';

      while (!rsChildren.EOF)
      {
        // does this child contain other children
        if (rsChildren("RESOURCE_ISCOLLECTION") == true)
        {
          // contains children, so we need to recurse
          recChildNode.Open(rsChildren);
          sNode = sNode + TraverseTree(recChildNode);
          recChildNode.Close();
        }
        else
        {
          // output the child name
          sNode = sNode + '<LI>' +
              recNode("RESOURCE_DISPLAYNAME") +
              '</LI>';
        }

        rsChildren.MoveNext();
      }
      sNode = sNode + '</UL>';
    }

    // close the child recordset
    rsChildren.Close();
  }

  rsChildren = null;
  recChildNode = null;

  return sNode;
}
```

What you end up with is the diagram you've already seen, with an indented list of nodes and files:

- zeus.jpg
- Hermes
  - _default.htm
  - hermes.jpg
- Hades
  - Default.htm
- default.htm
- assembly.jpg
- Artemis
  - Default.htm
  - artemis.jpg
- Ares
  - Default.htm
  - ares.jpg
- Apollo

Let's have a look at the code in more detail. The function accepts a Record object – this is the record for which we want to display the children:

```
function TraverseTree(recNode)
{
```

We have three local variables. The first, sNode, will be the string of HTML that we are building up. The second, rsChildren, will be a recordset of all the files and directories under the current Record. The third, recChildNode, will be used to create a new Record object when one of the rows in rsChildren is a directory:

```
var sNode = '';
var rsChildren;
var recChildNode = new ActiveXObject("ADODB.Record");
```

Once the variables have been declared, we can start to build up the HTML string, so we construct an <LI> element, the contents of which is the display name of the Record.

```
// output the node name
sNode = '<LI>' + recNode("RESOURCE_DISPLAYNAME") +
    '</LI>';
```

Now we need to see whether the Record is a collection record; that is, whether it is a directory. In our case this will always be so, but this routine is generic, so we add this in so that it can be used elsewhere.

```
// check to see if this node has children
if (recNode.RecordType == adCollectionRecord)
{
```

If the `Record` is a directory, then we need to get a recordset of its children, so we use the `GetChildren` method. This returns a standard ADO `Recordset`, each row of which will map to a file or directory, directly under the current `Record`:

```
// get any child nodes
rsChildren = recNode.GetChildren();
```

Now we can see if the `Record` actually has any children, and if so we add a `<UL>` element, to indent them:

```
// loop through the children
if (!rsChildren.EOF)
{
  sNode = sNode + '<ul>';
```

Now we can start to loop through the children:

```
while (!rsChildren.EOF)
{
```

To see if the row in the recordset refers to a file or a directory, we check the collection field. If `true`, then this is a directory, and if `false`, it's a standard file.

```
// does this child contain other children
if (rsChildren("RESOURCE_ISCOLLECTION") == true)
{
```

If the row refers to a directory, we need to recurse, because the directory can contain children of its own. So we open a new `Record` object, using the current row of the recordset as its source. This might seem confusing but it's easy to understand. If the initial `Record` points to www.pantheon.com, the recordset contains all of the files and directories under that directory. If we come to a row that is a directory, we want to open that directory as a `Record`, and pass that `Record` back into the current routine, where the process starts again.

```
// contains children, so we need to recurse
recChildNode.Open(rsChildren);
sNode = sNode + TraverseTree(recChildNode);
recChildNode.Close();
}
```

If the row doesn't refer to a directory, then it must be a file, so we can just add another `<LI>` element:

```
else
{
  // output the child name
  sNode = sNode + '<LI>' +
      rsChildren("RESOURCE_DISPLAYNAME") +
      '</LI>';
}
```

Then we can move onto the next row in the recordset.

```
            rsChildren.MoveNext();
    }
```

Once the rows in the recordset have been finished with, we have come to the end of the children for a particular `Record`, so we add the closing `</UL>` tag:

```
        sNode = sNode + '</ul>';
    }
    // close the child recordset
    rsChildren.Close();
}
```

Finally, we clear the memory used by the objects, and return the HTML string:

```
    rsChildren = null;
    recChildNode = null;

    return sNode;
}
```

At first sight, this routine might seem pretty confusing, but it's actually quite easy. Just draw your own directory structure, including the files and directories, and then follow through the routine by hand, and it becomes much clearer.

Adding URLs to the List Elements

As it stands, the routine is fine, but there's nothing you can do with the list of files and directories. You can't click on them because there is no intelligence built in. At the moment what we do is this:

```
// output the node name
sNode = '<LI>' + recNode ("RESOURCE_DISPLAYNAME") + '</LI>';
```

```
// output the child name
sNode = sNode + '<LI>' +
    rsChildren("RESOURCE_DISPLAYNAME") + '</LI>';
```

But what if we replace these two sections of code with the following:

```
// output the node name
sNode = FormatListItem(recNode);
```

```
// output the child name
sNode = sNode + FormatListItem(rsChildren);
```

We can now have a function that adds a little more detail to the `<LI>` elements:

```
function FormatListItem(rNode)
{
   return '<LI ONMOUSEDOWN="ProcessMouseDown(\'' +
       rNode("RESOURCE_ABSOLUTEPARSENAME") + '\'' +
       ', \'' + rNode("RESOURCE_CONTENTCLASS") + '\')"' +
       '>' + rNode("RESOURCE_DISPLAYNAME") + '</LI>';
}
```

This looks horrible at first sight, but it's really fairly simple. It uses three fields of the `Record` or `Recordset` which is passed into the function as `rNode`. What's being displayed is still the display name, but we've added a function to handle the `onMouseDown` event, so that when the user clicks on a list item, something happens. The returned HTML will look something like this:

```
<LI ONMOUSEDOWN="ProcessMouseDown
                ('http://www.pantheon.com/default.htm',
                'text/html')">default.htm</LI>
```

We pass the full URL of the resource and its MIME type into the `ProcessMouseDown()` function. This allows us to determine what type of resource it is (directory, specific type of file, etc.) so that we can process it accordingly.

I didn't use the `onClick` event because I wanted to display a context sensitive menu when the user clicks the right-mouse button. This just makes the scriptlet behave more like a normal application. We won't be looking directly at this `ProcessMouseDown()` function because all it does is set a couple of global variables (for the URL and MIME type) and display the menu. It's well documented though, so you can examine it in detail on your own. However, it is useful to see the menu:

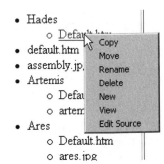

So what this is offering us is a choice. We can copy or move a file or directory, or even rename or delete it. We can also create new files, view the contents of files, or even edit the source of files. With this menu it's quite easy to see that we're building a remote administration and editing tool.

Visual Basic

The above examples have been in JScript, but the ADO operations would be similar in Visual Basic (although of course we wouldn't be building an HTML string). If we wanted a similar look to the above application, we would probably use a TreeView control, and add each file and directory as `Nodes` to the TreeView's `NodeList`.

Sample code is available for download from our web site which shows how easy this is.

Copying and Moving Files

If you've looked at the ADO documentation for the `Record` object then you'll have seen there are `CopyRecord` and `MoveRecord` methods. This makes it extremely simple for us to manipulate files on the web server, and both have the same syntax:

```
CopyRecord [Source], Destination, [UserName], [Password],
           [Options], [Async]

MoveRecord [Source], Destination, [UserName], [Password],
           [Options], [Async]
```

The `Source` identifies the URL of the file that is to be copied or moved. If this is left empty, then the current `Record` is taken as the source. The `Destination` is the URL of the file or directory. `UserName` and `Password` are the security credentials for the destination URL. `Async` is a Boolean value that identifies whether or not the action should be performed asynchronously.

The `Options` parameter specifies the behavior of the action and differs for copy and move. For a copy it can be one of the `CopyRecordOptionEnum` values, which are:

Name	Value	Description
adCopyAllowEmulation	4	If the `CopyRecord` method fails, simulate it using a file download and upload mechanism. This failure may happen if the destination doesn't support DAV.
adCopyNonRecursive	2	Copy the current directory, but not sub-directories.
adCopyOverWrite	1	Overwrite the existing file or directory.
adCopyUnspecified	-1	This is the default option, which specifies that recursive copying be performed, and the destination not be overwritten if it already exists.

For a move, `Options` can be one of the `MoveRecordOptionEnum` values:

Name	Value	Description
adMoveAllowEmulation	4	If the attempt to move the record fails, allow the move to be performed using a download, upload and delete set of HTTP operations. This could occur if the destination server doesn't support DAV.
adMoveDontUpdateLinks	2	Do not update hyperlinks of the source `Record`. By default, when moving a file, any hyperlinks in the file are updated to take into account the new destination, assuming the provider supports this behavior.
adMoveOverWrite	1	Overwrite the target if it already exists.
adMoveUnspecified	-1	This is the default option, which specifies that the destination should not be overwritten if it already exists, and the hypertext links should be automatically updated.

So, back to our utility: we can easily move and copy files. When a list item is selected, a global variable, `m_sItemURL`, is set to the full URL of the item, and then if either the **Move** or **Copy** option was selected, the right-hand side of the screen will display the following:

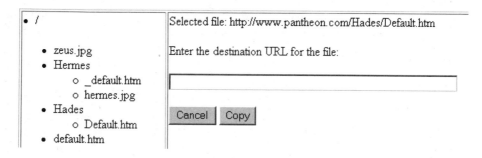

For a move, the text is slightly different and the button is labeled Move rather than Copy, but by and large it's the same. The text entry box has an ID of txtDestination.

So now when the button is pressed, we can call the following function, passing in either copy or move, depending upon the action:

```
function ProcessItem(sType)
{
    // close the record if open
    if (m_recNode.state == adStateOpen)
        m_recNode.Close();

    switch(sType)
    {
        case 'move':
            m_recNode.Open(m_sItemURL);
            m_recNode.MoveRecord ('', txtDestination.value);
            break;

        case 'copy':
            m_recNode.Open(m_sItemURL);
            m_recNode.CopyRecord('', txtDestination.value);
            break;
    }

    m_recNode.close();

    DisplayNode();
}
```

Both of these methods follow the same format. They open the URL as a Record, and then use the entered value as the destination for the copy or move operation.

The Scope of a Move

One important point to note about moving and copying files is that the scope of the connection limits where we can move the file to. For example, if our connection scope is http://www.pantheon.com/Artemis, then we cannot transfer files outside of that scope – that is, we cannot transfer to a directory higher than the scoped directory. This is a deliberate imposition to protect security.

If you do need to transfer files to and from different scopes then you'll need to open two different connections or Record objects with the different URLs as their scope. You can then use the Stream to read and write text between the Record objects.

Renaming Files

There isn't an explicit rename method for the Record, but renaming a file is just moving it to the same location, but with a different name. So, we can add another section to our ProcessItem function:

```
case 'rename':
    var iEnd = m_sItemURL.lastIndexOf('/') + 1;
    var sNewName = m_sItemURL.substr(0, iEnd) +
                   txtDestination.value;
    m_recNode.Open(m_sItemURL);
    m_recNode.MoveRecord('', sNewName);
    break;
```

Here we append the new name to the path of the URL and use the MoveRecord method.

Creating Files

If you flick back to the Open method, you'll remember that by default this fails if the URL doesn't exist. However, the CreateOptions argument allows us to specify one of the adCreate options. This allows us to create a new resource.

Before we can actually create the resource, we need to know whether it will be a file or a directory, so we offer the user a choice:

Now when the user presses the **Create** button, we can use either the adCreateNonCollection option to create a normal file, or the adCreateCollection option to create a directory.

```
case 'new':
    var sNewFile = m_sItemURL + '/' +
                    txtDestination.value;
    var iType;

    if (lstType.value == 'file')
        iType = adCreateNonCollection;
    else
        iType = adCreateCollection;

    m_recNode.Open(sNewFile, '', adModeReadWrite,
                    iType);
    break;
```

Notice that this will fail if the file already exists. If we wanted to ensure that the existing file was overwritten, we could add the adCreateOverwrite flag, like so:

```
m_recNode.Open(sNewFile, '', adModeReadWrite,
                iType + adCreateOverwrite);
```

However, this is a dangerous thing to implement by default, so you should really give the user some sort of warning. You can use error handling to check for an existing file:

```
try
{
    m_recNode.Open(sNewFile, '',
    adModeReadWrite, iType);
}
catch(e)
{
    if (e.number == -2147217768)
    {
        // file already exists
```

```
        var sMsg = 'This file already exists. ' +
                   'Are you sure you wish to overwrite it?\n\n' +
                   'Press OK to overwrite the file, ' +
                   'or Cancel to ignore the file creation.';

        if (confirm(sMsg))
            m_recNode.Open(sNewFile, '', adModeReadWrite,
                           iType + adCreateOverwrite);
        else
            return 0;
    }
    else
    {
        // some other error
        alert('Error: ' + e.description + ' (' + e.number + ')');
    }
}
```

Here we use the `try/catch` mechanism introduced in JScript 5.0. We try to create the new file, and if an error is raised we check the error number (these are documented in Appendix N). If the error indicates that the file already exists, we can use the `confirm()` function to get confirmation from the user. If the user really does want to overwrite the file, then we can add in the `adCreateOverwrite` flag, to force the the existing file to be overwritten.

In the downloadable code I've taken this confirmation even further, by checking what type the existing file is. If it's a directory, then I add another confirmation dialog just to be sure. This is a cross between paranoia and prudence, because overwriting a directory will destroy all the children of that directory, so it's possible to mess up badly!

Deleting Files

Deleting files is the simplest of our management actions, because we simply call the `DeleteRecord` method.

```
case 'delete':
    m_recNode.Open(m_sItemURL);
    m_recNode.DeleteRecord();
    break;
```

Streams

What we haven't covered so far is the ability to edit or view existing files. After all, wasn't this one of the great promises discussed at the beginning of the chapter? Yes it was, and the reason we haven't covered it yet is that everything we've done so far has been solely related to the `Record` and `Recordset` objects. To deal with the contents of a file we need to use the `Stream` object.

The `Stream` object is designed to allow access to the contents of a file. In effect the `Stream` is just a holder for a block of memory, and allows us to read and write data into it. Although the `Stream` object is new to ADO 2.5, streams have been around for many years as part of Windows and OLE programming, and are based on the `IStream` interface. In ADO we can open a `Stream` object either directly from a URL, or from an existing `Record` object.

So, let's have a look at how we'd use the `Stream` to view the contents of a file.

Reading the Contents of a File

In order to read a file's contents, we will open a Record, then open a stream from that Record, and finally display the contents of the stream in an HTML element:

```
recNode.Open(m_sItemURL, '', adModeRead, adOpenIfExists);

// open a stream from the record
stmNode.Charset = 'ascii';
stmNode.Open(recNode, adModeRead, adOpenStreamFromRecord);

spanContents.innerHTML = '<P>Viewing file:' + m_sItemURL +
                         '</P>' + stmNode.ReadText();

stmNode.close();
recNode.close();
```

There are three important points here. The first is this line:

```
stmNode.Charset = 'ascii';
```

By default, the contents of a file are Unicode-encoded, but we want to display the contents in an HTML element, so we set the character set to ascii, which forces ADO to convert the stream data.

The second step is get text data out of the file. For this, we use the ReadText method:

```
stmNode.ReadText()
```

This method simply returns the contents of the stream. We can also supply an argument to this method that identifies the number of characters to be read. This allows us to read chunks of data, rather than the whole file. However, by default all the characters are read from the file.

The third step is to display the contents of the stream:

```
spanContents.innerHTML = '<p>Viewing file:' + m_sItemURL +
                         '</p>' + stmNode.ReadText();
```

We display the contents of the file, plus some other text, as the innerHTML property of a SPAN. Because we set the innerHTML, IE will render the text for us if it contains HTML tags. The result is a page such as the following:

• /http://www.pantheon.com	Viewing file:http://www.pantheon.com/Hermes/_default.htm
• zeus.jpg • /Hermes	God of Thieves
○ _default.htm ○ hermes.jpg	Transporter of souls to Hades
• /Hades ○ Default.htm	postmaster@pantheon.com

Reading Images

To view an image we can't read the contents as a stream and display that, because HTML doesn't have a way of dealing with image data in the HTML code itself. The easiest way of doing this is to ignore the stream for the image, and just to set the innerHTML of the <SPAN>:

```
spanContents.innerHTML = '<P>Viewing file:' + m_sItemURL +
                         '</P>' + '<IMG SRC="' + m_sItemURL +
                         '"></IMG>' + '</DIV>';
```

Here we just use the URL of the selected item (as stored in the global variable m_sItemURL) as the SRC attribute for the IMG tag. Once again, as we set the innerHTML property, IE will render the HTML for us.

Editing the Contents

So we've got a simple way of viewing files, but what about editing them? This is pretty simple too, because we can use a similar technique. However, we don't want the contents to be rendered by IE, so we take a two-stage approach. First, we build up some HTML, consisting of a TEXTAREA (txtContents) and a BUTTON. The textarea will contain the file contents so that the user can edit them, and the button will allow the user to save any changes.

```
sHTML = '<P>Editing file:' + m_sItemURL + '</P>' +
        '<TEXTAREA ID="txtContents" ' +
        'STYLE="width:100%; height:85%"></TEXTAREA>' +
        '<BR><INPUT TYPE="BUTTON" ID="cmdSave"' +
        'ONCLICK="SaveStream()" VALUE="Save"></INPUT>';
```

Once the HTML string has been built, we set the innerHTML property of the SPAN to this value. Notice that we haven't yet read the contents of the stream – at this stage we've just built a container (txtContents) in which the contents can be edited:

```
spanContents.innerHTML = sHTML;
```

Now we have the textarea, we can set the innerText attribute to the contents of the stream:

```
txtContents.innerText = m_stmNode.ReadText();
```

Because it's the innerText attribute, IE doesn't render the contents as HTML, so we can see the actual content, including any HTML tags:

• /http://www.pantheon.com	Editing file:http://www.pantheon.com/Hermes/_default.htm

• zeus.jpg
• /Hermes
   o _default.htm
   o hermes.jpg
• /Hades
   o Default.htm
• default.htm
• assembly.jpg
• /Artemis
   o Default.htm
   o artemis.jpg
• /Ares
   o Default.htm
   o ares.jpg
• /Apollo
   o Default.htm
   o appollo.jpg
• /Aphrodite
	`<html>`
	
	`<head>`
	`<meta http-equiv="Content-Language" content="en-gb">`
	`<meta http-equiv="Content-Type" content="text/html; charset=windows-1252">`
	`<title>God of Thieves</title>`
	`</head>`
	
	`<body>`
	
	`<p>God of Thieves</p>`
	
	`<p>Transporter of souls to Hades</p>`
	
	`<p><a href="mailto:postmaster@pantheon.com">postmaster@pantheon.com</a></p>`
	
	`</body>`
	
	`</html>`

This can be edited like any text file. All that's required now is a way to save it.

Writing to a File

Saving the contents of the stream is fairly simple, although it's not just a case of calling a single method. What we have to remember is that the stream is really a memory manager. In a similar way to working with files, the `Stream` object keeps track of the current position in the stream, and has an end-of-stream similar to an end-of-file.

When we initially open a stream, we are automatically placed at position zero – that is, at the start of the stream. As we read in data from the stream, the current position moves with us. So, if we've read all of the contents, our current position will be at the end of the stream. If we write to the stream, this will cause data to be appended to the stream from the current position.

What we want to do, therefore, is to clear the current contents, and write the data from the textarea into the stream. To do this, we must first set the position back to the start of the stream:

```
function SaveStream()
{
    m_stmNode.Position = 0;
```

Then we set the end of the stream to be the current position. This has the effect of truncating the contents:

```
    m_stmNode.SetEOS();
```

Now we can use the `WriteText` method to write the contents of our textarea into the stream:

```
    m_stmNode.WriteText(txtContents.innerText);
```

And finally we can close the stream and tell the user that the contents have been saved:

```
    m_stmNode.Close();

    alert('New details saved');
}
```

There's no save command because the stream automatically flushes its contents to the actual file when the stream is closed.

Managing Local Files

One important thing to note about what we've shown so far is that all file handling has been managed by a URL. Specifically, this means a URL on a web server that supports DAV. If we wanted to copy the contents of a local file, there are two things we can do:

❏   If using Windows 2000 as a local machine, we could expose our local directories as a URL, and then we could use any of the above methods to copy files.

❏   Use something like the FileSystemObject, to give us a view of the local file system.

If using the latter method, we can use the LoadFromFile and SaveToFile methods of the Stream object. The former loads the contents of a local file into a stream, and the latter saves the stream contents to a local file. These methods have the advantage that they allow us to copy the contents directly into a stream. For example, the following Visual Basic code opens a file from a URL, opens the stream of the file's contents, and loads the stream with the contents of a local file:

```
Dim recNode As New ADODB.Record
Dim stmFile As New ADODB.Stream

recNode.Open "", _
             "URL=http://www.pantheon.com/Ares/default.htm", _
             adModeReadWrite
stmFile.Open recNode, adModeReadWrite, adOpenStreamFromRecord
stmFile.LoadFromFile "C:\data\TestFile.html"
```

Using the LoadFromFile method causes the existing contents of the stream to be overwritten. Since the Stream is bound to a Record object, the contents of the record are automatically reflected with the new contents of the stream.

Security

One very important point to note about this whole area is the security aspect. The first security consideration is the web site itself. We need to decide what sort of security credentials users will require to access our site.

We can set these from the Directory Security tab of the site's properties dialog. Selecting the Edit button from the Anonymous access and authentication control section allows to set the security mode:

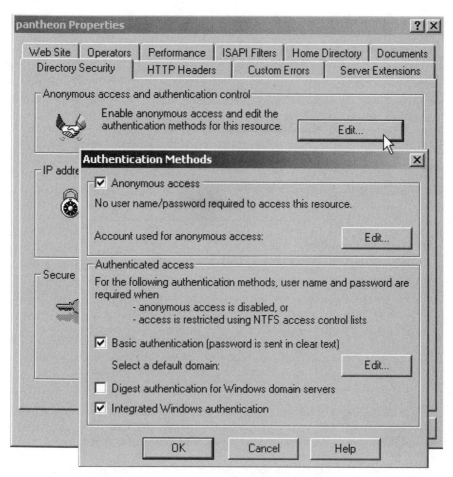

Anonymous access means that no security details are required to log in, unless file system permissions are in effect (more of this in a moment). If this option is cleared, then the settings in Authenticated Access come into play. Using Integrated Windows authentication is really only relevant if your users are logged into the Windows network, as their current logon details will be used to access the site. If you intend outside users to access the site, you can set basic authentication, and users will be presented with a login/password box before they can access the site. Note that under this option the username and password will be transferred as basic text (in base 64 UUEncoded format). This means that this information can easily be detected and decoded by network sniffing tools, so security is not absolute.

To restrict access to individual files and directories, we can use NTFS security. By default Everyone has Full Control:

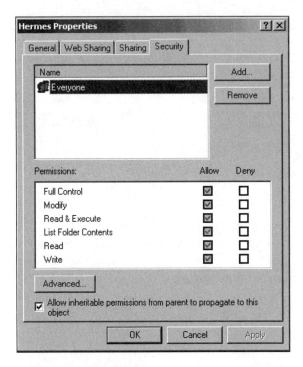

If you clear the inheritable permissions check box, you can remove the Everyone account and just add individual accounts, or copy the existing permissions and just give Everyone read permissions. You could then add the owner of the directory and give full permissions to that account.

Using NTFS permissions makes the file security extremely secure, and with IIS5 now supporting DAV, it's more important than ever that you secure your Web server.

> *If you'd like to read more detailed explanations of security, you should get hold of the Wrox Press book Professional Active Server Pages 3.0 (ISBN 1-861002-61-0), which covers IIS5 security in depth.*

Versioning and Locking

One aspect we haven't covered yet is that of locking and version control, and there's a simple reason for that. Currently, the Versioning part of the WebDAV protocol hasn't yet been finalized, so it's not actually implemented yet.

There is a working group discussing the specification at the moment, and although it's taking some time to put together, it's worth waiting for. The importance of a good versioning and locking protocol cannot be underestimated. As an ADO programmer, you're probably aware of locking, and the potential lost update problem, where another user overwrites your changes.

With WebDAV working over the Internet, and the greater delay between reads and updates, the whole process not only becomes more complicated, but also more important to manage correctly. The working group has to discuss features such as:

❑ **Basic Versioning** features are the type of features implemented by current source code control products. These allow the intent to change a resource (a check out), the submission of a changed resource (a check in), and the cancellation of a check out. These features are generally handled by locking the resource.

❑ **Advanced Versioning** handles the management (moving and copying) of locked resources.

❑ **Automated Versioning** allows new versions to be created automatically whenever a property of the resource is changed.

❑ **Version Branching** allows the standard linear version tree to be split into multiple branches. This would allow multiple editing of the resource at the same time. To go hand-in-hand with this, merge management is also required.

There are many more aspects to versioning, and you can clearly see the power they could give you. With a web server that supports a rich versioning system, you effectively have a source code control system that works over the Web. As a developer, doesn't that make the idea of working from home seem much easier?

Related Areas

Versioning isn't the only area that's being discussed in relation to WebDAV. There are a whole host of ideas being discussed, and some are being worked on to a great deal of detail by working groups. A few of these are listed below:

❑ **Advanced Collections** extend the basic WebDAV collections to cater for advanced features, such as references and ordering. References allow resources to be shared, since they act like symbolic links or shortcuts. A resource that is a reference has no body of its own, but points to another resource. Existing collections provide no capability for specifying the order of resources, so Advanced Collections will add this facility.

❑ **Access Control** will allow authentication permissions to be placed on resources, thus restricting who has access to resources, and what rights they have. At the moment under IIS5 this is handled by NTFS, but it's a good idea to allow WebDAV itself to have some sort of management capability in this area.

❑ **DAV Searching and Locating (DASL)** defines extensions to allow the searching of WebDAV servers. This will work in a similar way to indexing web servers, but has a wider remit.

❑ **Resource Description Framework (RDF)** is a framework for defining metadata, to allow greater interoperability by systems that exchange machine-understandable information. Like WebDAV, this is partly based upon XML.

There are many other areas where WebDAV could have an impact, and it's important to realize that it's not a static protocol. It's actively being worked on, and extensions will provide some very exciting possibilities.

Resources

If you'd like to read more about WebDAV, or any of the surrounding areas, then you should consider the following resources.

The home page of the WebDAV Working Group can be found at `http://www.ics.uci.edu/pub/ietf/webdav/`. If you'd like to learn more about the efforts of the working group then visit this site to see exactly what they are up to. If you'd like to participate in the working group then you only need to join the mailing lists – details of these can be found on this site.

You should also visit `http://www.webdav.org/` where there is a useful FAQ answering some of the common questions that crop up about DAV.

For more details on Resource Description Framework, visit the World Wide Web consortium site at `http://www.w3c.org`.

Summary

This chapter has been a departure from normal data access methods, where tables and queries are the norm. Given the way data is changing, it seems only natural that we have to take this into account when we need to access that data. We are used to dealing with recordsets and rows of data in relational databases, but now we have to consider documents too.

Web applications have already brought the use of remote data, especially RDS and other technologies like XML. With the ability to have applications run from everywhere, we also need the management capabilities to go with them, and WebDAV gives us that ability.

Reading between the lines of this chapter, the message has been WebDAV through and through, but we've shown how ADO, and in particular the OLE DB Provider for Internet Publishing, brings WebDAV easily to the developer. In particular we've looked at:

❑ What the `Record` object is, what it represents in relation to resources on a web server, and how it relates to a `Recordset`.

❑ How URLs are managed by the Internet Publishing Provider.

❑ How to manage resources on a web server.

❑ How to use the `Stream` object to access the contents of a file.

❑ How files can be edited remotely.

The samples we've shown are extremely simple to use, and the downloadable code is easily reusable. It's in the form of a scriptlet so you can just drop it into any web page and it should work fine as long as ADO 2.5 is installed on the client.

Because of this simplicity you should be able to extend this utility fairly easily, and turn it into a complete management tool.

9

Multi-Dimensional Data

ADOMD, or ADO for Multi-Dimensional Data to give it its full title, is probably the least used component of ADO. That's not to say that ADOMD isn't used much, but rather it's used much less than the main ADO components. This is mainly to do with what businesses use, and most of them use standard relational databases without any form of additional analytical processing engines. However, the analytical market is blooming and ADOMD is rapidly gaining ground.

ADOMD is specially designed to work with OLAP (On-Line Analytical Processing) data, which also explains its relative lack of use. In the past, OLAP systems have generally been expensive to purchase, and time consuming to set up and maintain. With the release of the Microsoft OLAP Services for SQL Server, we saw the introduction of a low-cost OLAP implementation, and ADOMD allows us to access these services very easily.

So, this chapter will look into ADOMD and see what sort of facilities it offers us, and examine some of the problems you might encounter. In particular we shall look at:

- ❏ The reasons why we have OLAP.
- ❏ The architecture of the Microsoft OLAP Services.
- ❏ The ADOMD object mode.
- ❏ How to use ADOMD to create working OLAP solutions.

What is OLAP?

The first thing to do is examine what On-Line Analytical Processing means. You won't be surprised to learn that it focuses around the manipulation of data. Since the rise of the PC, and especially the relational database, we've been storing increasing amounts of data. Much of this data has been, and for some while will continue to be, stored in relational databases, and therein lies one of the problems. They are great for storing data, and great for simple data extraction, but SQL isn't really designed for complex data analysis. It's great for standard set-based stuff, such as list of items and simple summaries, but it's not so good at deep analysis using several different tables and levels of complexity. This is where OLAP comes in, since its whole basis is the analysis of data from different viewpoints. For example, sales of products by time, location, consumer type, and so on. Whilst this is possible with standard SQL, it's much easier with OLAP.

To make a decision on the sort of analysis to be performed, you need to think about your data and what you want from it. In his latest book (Business @ the Speed of Thought, Warner Books), Bill Gates says 'How you gather, manage, and use information will determine whether you win or lose'. I believe that to be true – being able to analyze information quickly, and react on it, is critical as to which decisions are made.

OLAP makes this analysis as easy as possible, by:

❑ Pre-processing frequently used data. This speeds up the analysis because less calculation is required.

❑ Representing the data in a multi-dimensional way. Most relational systems only consider rows and columns, but OLAP allows more than two dimensions.

❑ Defining a special query language to make the data extraction easy.

These may not seem much, but combined they are quite powerful. The whole idea is to abstract the operational storage and provide an easier view for data analysis:

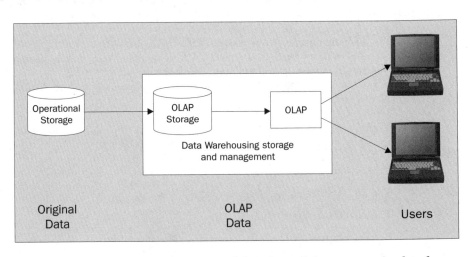

With OLAP systems, users don't access the actual operational data. Instead they request the data from the OLAP system, which stores the data in a format designed for analysis. This takes the form of one of the following:

- **Multidimensional OLAP** (**MOLAP**), where a multidimensional structure is used to store a copy of, and aggregations of, the original data. Since a complete copy of the data is held by the OLAP service, this provides the fastest response to queries, and is ideal for situations where the OLAP service is frequently queried.

- **Relational OLAP** (**ROLAP**), where only the aggregations are managed by the OLAP service. This type of storage provides slower response to queries than MOLAP, and is therefore more suited to data that isn't frequently queried.

- **Hybrid OLAP** (**HOLAP**) combines aspects of MOLAP and ROLAP, and is a compromise between the two storage types. The response time depends upon the query being issued. This type of storage is most suitable for summaries of large amounts of data, where queries require a rapid response.

Which of the three you use depends on what sort of queries you are going to be processing, the number of users, the amount of data, and how fast the queries need to be processed. In all three the OLAP service processes the query and returns the data appropriately, which removes some of the load from the source database. This is even more of an advantage if the OLAP service is running on a separate machine to the source database.

OLAP Data

To explain the use of OLAP, and ADOMD, we need some data so you can see what's happening. I'll be using the sample data supplied by the Microsoft SQL Server OLAP Services, for one simple reason – they are supplied with SQL Server, and you don't have to do anything other than install them. This means that you can get straight into OLAP without too much effort.

The sample data used is the `FoodMart` sample, based around an Access database. `FoodMart` is a supermarket chain and all of their sales details are stored in a database. You might initially think the analysis of this would be fairly easy, until you look at the entity-relationship model of the database:

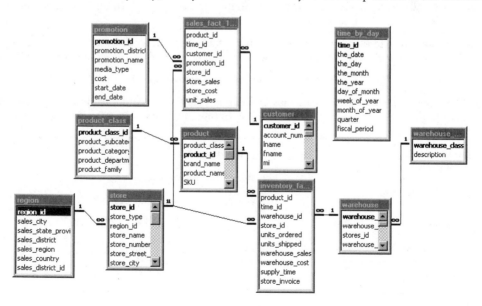

You can immediately see that this is isn't too complex, but decent analysis isn't that easy. Not only are there simple tables for the product, but details of the stores, the regions, types of products, the warehouse, and so on. Trying to produce figures linking all of these together would be rather complex. What OLAP does is to extract this information into a more manageable set of information. The following diagram concentrates on the warehouse side:

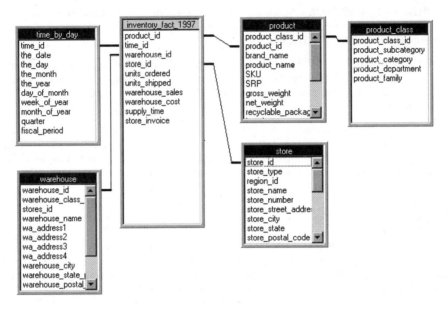

In OLAP terms the above diagram is defined as a **Cube**. A Cube is a subset of the data that is to be processed, and contains several elements:

- ❑ **A fact table**, to identify the actual information to be analyzed. In this case it is the `inventory_fact` table.

- ❑ **Dimensions**, to identify how the data in the fact table can be analyzed. These are the other tables in the diagram. A little later we'll look at how these can be broken down still further.

- ❑ **Levels** are `Dimensions` broken down into sub-categories.

The difference between `Dimensions` and `Levels` is a subtle one, and introduces the concept of a category of data and sub-categories. For example, in the sample data the `Dimensions` would be:

Dimension	Description
Store	The stores and locations.
Time	The years, months and quarters.
Product	The product names, groups, and brands.
Store Size in SqFt	The size of the stores in square feet.

Dimension	Description
Store Type	The types of the stores (Supermarket, Grocery, etc.)
Warehouse	The warehouse names and locations.

The `Product` dimension has several different levels:

Level Number	Name	Example
1	Product Family	Food
2	Product Department	Produce
3	Product Category	Fruit
4	Product subcategory	Fresh Fruit
5	Brand Name	High Top
6	Product Name	High Top Cantaloupe

This splitting of a category into levels gives the ability to drill down to a narrower focus. You'll see how this can be important when constructing queries a little later.

Two Dimensional Data

The greatest point about OLAP is that it allows you to view data from an analytical viewpoint, regardless of the underlying structure of the database. This is really important since databases are very often designed from an operational perspective.

One of the things we are aiming to do is produce figures like this:

	+ Product Family			
Store Type	All Products	+ Drink	+ Food	+ Non-Consumable
All	102,278.41	9,218.35	73,367.55	19,692.51
Deluxe Supermarket	32,251.87	3,554.97	22,143.27	6,553.63
Gourmet Supermarket	5,132.90	590.42	3,635.13	907.35
Mid-Size Grocery	5,274.34	437.32	3,661.14	1,175.88
Small Grocery	3,132.05	281.24	2,342.09	508.73
Supermarket	56,487.25	4,354.41	41,585.92	10,546.92

If you're used to relational databases, then this is similar to a crosstab query, and this is precisely why OLAP analysis is so good. Microsoft Access has special commands to perform crosstabs, but in standard SQL it's not so easy. You can do it using an intermediate table or by using some advanced SQL, but it's not very efficient. The OLAP services pre-process the data to make this kind of analysis easy.

To understand OLAP, and the data shown in the above diagram, we have to introduce some terms – **Axes** and **Axis**. Looking at the diagram these should be obvious – there are two Axes, one for the **Rows** and one for the **Columns**. When you are analyzing data using OLAP you'll always be dealing with at least these two Axes. What we've done with the above data is to map a Dimension (which is a representation of the structure of the data) onto an Axis (which is a representation of the way the data is analyzed in a single query).

Three Dimensional Data

The above diagram shows a simple set of data using two dimensions, where each Dimension was shown on an **Axis**. We have the product types along the **Columns** and the store types along the **Rows**. But OLAP has the facility to manage more Axes. In fact, the use of the term Cube is pretty good, because this automatically brings to mind three dimensions. For example, imagine that we wanted to add countries to this analysis. Using the third dimension could give us something like this:

Store Type	+ Product Family All Products	+ Drink	+ Food	+ Non-Consumable
All	102,278.41	9,218.35	73,367.55	19,692.51
Deluxe Supermarket	32,251.87	3,554.97	22,143.27	6,553.63
Gourmet Supermarket	5,132.90	590.42	3,635.13	907.35
Mid-Size Grocery	5,274.34	437.32	3,661.14	1,175.88
Small Grocery	3,132.05	281.24	2,342.09	508.73
Supermarket	56,487.25	4,354.41	41,585.92	10,546.92

Now we have the addition of a third axis – called **Pages**. Each page contains the data for a country, with a page for the summary information for all pages. With the OLAP facilities at hand this is pretty easy to do. You could equate this to the pages in a spreadsheet.

n-Dimensionsal Data

The SQL OLAP Services support a maximum of 63 Axes, so don't think you are restricted to only three. For example, if you wanted to extend the analysis shown in the above diagram by adding the Time Dimension onto a fourth Axis, you would end up with:

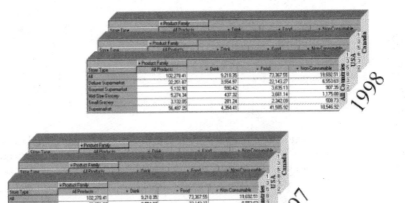

I've shown the fourth Axis as an extension backwards, but this was just to make it easier to draw the diagram. Conceptually it doesn't matter which way you extend the Axes.

There are only five named Axes (Columns, Rows, Pages, Sections and Chapters), but additional ones are named Axis(n), where n is the index.

Multiple Data per Axis

Something else that is also pretty easy in the OLAP world is the ability to show multiple sets of data on the same axis. If you wanted to show both the Store Type and the Country on the rows you can end up with this:

Store Type	+ Store Country	+ Product Family All Products	+ Drink	+ Food	+ Non-Consumable
All	All Stores	196,770.89	18,010.60	141,147.92	37,612.37
	+ Canada				
	+ Mexico				
	+ USA	196,770.89	18,010.60	141,147.92	37,612.37
Deluxe Supermarket	All Stores	61,860.15	6,923.76	42,380.16	12,556.22
	+ Canada				
	+ Mexico				
	+ USA	61,860.15	6,923.76	42,380.16	12,556.22
Gourmet Supermarket	All Stores	10,156.50	1,241.74	7,075.10	1,839.66
	+ Canada				
	+ Mexico				
	+ USA	10,156.50	1,241.74	7,075.10	1,839.66
Mid-Size Grocery	All Stores	10,212.20	882.69	7,226.60	2,102.92
	+ Canada				
	+ Mexico				
	+ USA	10,212.20	882.69	7,226.60	2,102.92
Small Grocery	All Stores	5,931.58	510.98	4,451.55	969.05
	+ Canada				
	+ Mexico				
	+ USA	5,931.58	510.98	4,451.55	969.05
Supermarket	All Stores	108,610.46	8,451.44	80,014.51	20,144.52
	+ Canada				
	+ Mexico				
	+ USA	108,610.46	8,451.44	80,014.51	20,144.52

Here we have the Store Type as the main category, and the Country as the sub-category.

Now you can see what sort of results can be achieved, it's time to examine how it can be done.

The OLAP Query Language

Since the OLAP data is pre-processed to some degree, we don't need to worry too much about things like totals. I don't mean that these can't be used, but that the OLAP service has already performed the aggregation for us. However, to get the data in this pre-processed form you can't use standard SQL because it is not designed to cope with multi-dimensional data, but you can use the OLAP extensions (MDX) for the SQL language.

In normal relational databases, you select the data you wish to see from tables or views. In the OLAP world it's similar, but there are extensions to the SQL language to cope with the multiple dimensions. We're not going to get into a deep discussion of this syntax here since it's pretty well documented (see the Microsoft SQL Server OLAP Services documentation), but a brief explanation will make things simpler later on in the chapter.

The basic query syntax is pretty much the same:

```
SELECT <axis_specification> [,<axis_specification>]
   FROM <cube_specification>
   WHERE <slicer_specification>
```

The first difference from standard SQL is the `axis_specification`, which allows us to select not only the source of the data, but also which axis it is to be placed on. For example, to see the Product details as the columns of the returned query you would use:

```
SELECT Product.Children ON COLUMNS
```

The data we are selecting is not only the Dimension, but also the depth of Levels to use. Using `Product.Children` gives us the following:

```
Food
Drink
Non-Consumable
```

That's because using `Children` says 'just give me the immediate children of this Dimension'. If we wanted to drill all of the way down to the lowest Level we would use:

```
SELECT Product.Members ON COLUMNS
```

This would give us:

```
Food
Baked Goods
Baking Goods
Produce
   Fruit
      Fresh Fruit
...
```

and so on.

To select the `Products` on the columns and the `Store Type` on the rows you would use:

```
SELECT Product.Children ON COLUMNS,
       [Store Type].Children ON ROWS
```

Notice how we enclose the Dimension with square brackets because its name contains a space.

To add a third dimension (such as the `Countries`, which in the sample data is held in the `Store` Dimension), you just add another axis:

```
SELECT Product.Children ON COLUMNS,
       [Store Type].Children ON ROWS,
       Store.Children ON PAGES
```

That's all there is to selecting data onto the axis. The next step is to identify where the data is coming from, and that's simply a matter of adding the Cube name:

```
SELECT Product.Children ON COLUMNS,
       [Store Type].Children ON ROWS
FROM Warehouse
```

Now this is just the simplest query; there is much more to the SELECT statement.

Multiple Data Sets on One Axis

One example of extra complexity in the SQL is where you wish to have multiple sets of data per axis, as in the earlier diagram, where we have Store Type and Store country along the rows. This is achieved by using the CROSSJOIN statement:

```
SELECT Product.Children ON COLUMNS,
    CROSSJOIN([Store Type].Children, Store.Children) ON ROWS
```

This works in the same way as a standard SQL CROSSJOIN, where each member of one set is matched with every member of the other sets. For example, if we have two sets:

Set	Children
One	b
	c
Two	d
	e

Then

```
CROSSJOIN (One.Children, Two.Children)
```

would give us:

```
b, d
b, e
c, d
c, e
```

This is pretty much like standard set manipulation in the math you learned way back in high school. If you look back to the diagram we showed earlier, you'll see how this can be effective:

Store Type	+ Store Country
All	All Stores
	+ Canada
	+ Mexico
	+ USA
Deluxe Supermarket	All Stores
	+ Canada
	+ Mexico
	+ USA

This was produced using the following:

```
CROSSJOIN ([Store Type].Children, Store)
```

Crossjoins are not limited to just two sets of data, and you could easily add a third:

```
CROSSJOIN([Store Type].Children, Store.Chilren, Time.Children)
    ON ROWS
```

Here we have the `Store Type` as the first Dimension, `Store` as the second and `Time` as the third. The OLAP service handles this just as easily as any other type of query.

When you use `CROSSJOIN`s you create **Members** within each Level. You'll see how these Members are used a little later. It's also worth noting the danger of using `CROSSJOIN`s, because they behave like standard set multiplication.

For two sets, the number of unique items returned by a `CROSSJOIN` is the number of items in the first set multiplied by the number of items in the second set. So for two sets of 10 items each, the resulting set would be 100 items. Add a third set to the `CROSSJOIN` and you again multiply by the number of items. This means that the results set from a `CROSSJOIN` can be quite large.

Slicing the Data

Slicing is an OLAP term that simply means the filtering of data, and there are two ways in which this can be done. The first is by adding the filter details to the `SELECT` statement. For example, to see only the `Food` column we could use:

```
SELECT {Food} ON COLUMNS,
```

We surround the item name with parentheses because we are dealing with a member of a set. To see both `Food` and `Drink` you would use:

```
SELECT {Food, Drink} ON COLUMNS,
```

Adding the `Children` or `Members` can be done here too:

```
SELECT {Food, Drink.Children} ON COLUMNS,
```

Alternatively you could see the `Drink` (which is the total for all `Drink` types) as well as the individual `Drink` types:

```
SELECT {Food, Drink, Drink.Children} ON COLUMNS,
```

The second method of filtering is to use a `WHERE` clause. For example, to limit a query to only show the figures for 1998 we could use:

```
SELECT Product.Children ON COLUMNS,
       [Store Type].Children ON ROWS
FROM Warehouse
WHERE ([1998])
```

The OLAP service recognizes 1998 as being a member of the `Time` dimension, but you can add the Dimension name to make things clearer:

```
WHERE (Time.[1998])
```

MDX Summary

The above section has only been a very quick look at the MDX language, but it should be enough to get you going. There are many more features available, all of which are documented in the help files for the OLAP services. For the purposes of what we'll be doing in this chapter, what's been covered so far is fine.

The important things to remember are that we'll be working with up to three axes – Rows, Columns, and Pages. We will also be using the `Children` and `Members` keywords to extract the details for each Dimension.

ADOMD Object Model

Now it's time to examine ADOMD, and see how it maps onto what you've learned about the OLAP services. Let's look at the object model first:

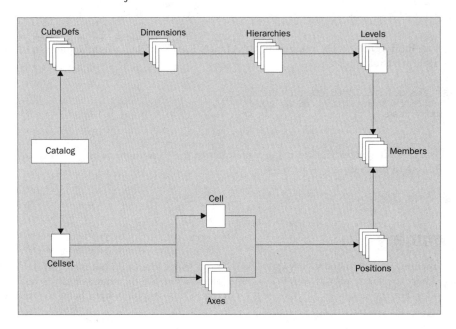

Most of these terms will be familiar, but let's explain the objects in more detail. The first set of objects (along the top in the above diagram) represent the structure of the data as held by the OLAP Services:

❑ Catalog, which is the container for all OLAP objects. This identifies the OLAP server, and the actual data server that supplies the original data.

❑ CubeDef, which is a container for a set of data. In our examples we'll be using the Warehouse as our CubeDef. A CubeDef doesn't represent how the data is shown – it just represents what the structures are and what they contain.

❑ Dimension, which is a distinct set of items. You've already seen that Time, Store and Store Type are dimensions – these are the top-level items upon which queries can be based.

❑ Hierarchy, which identifies the different ways in which the members of a Dimension can be aggregated.

❑ Level, which identifies the sub-elements in an individual Hierarchy. So, for the Time dimension we have three Hierarchies: Year, Quarter and Month.

❑ Member, which represents a unique item in a Level.

The second set of OLAP objects represent the data as it has been queried. So if you run a query against an OLAP server you get a set of data, which comprises:

❑ CellSet, which represents the whole set of data. The data is represented as an *n*-dimensional array, where there is a dimension for each Axis.

❑ Axis, which represents one of the physical axes of the CellSet. For example, the diagram above would require an Axis for the Rows and another Axis for the Columns. A third Axis for the Pages would be included if requested.

❑ Cell, which is a single cell, or item of data.

❑ Position, which is an individual row or column. A position represents a unique Row, Column or Page in a cellset. The intersection of Positions gives the unique position in the data array.

❑ Measure, which is a quantitative, numerical column, and is usually the name of the item that is shown in each cell. In our examples the measure has been the default measure, which is the Store Invoice – the amount invoiced by the store.

Some of these terms seem confusing, but they are pretty easy once you work through them. To show you how to do that we'll build a simple query interface as an HTML Scriptlet.

Using ADOMD

You've seen a few samples of OLAP data and what it might look like, and the lists above detail the ADOMD objects. However, you're probably still a little confused as to how these all fit together, so before we start the real coding and show you how to really use ADOMD, we'll have a preliminary exploration of the objects.

The samples we'll be using are based around the default FoodMart catalog, as supplied with the Microsoft OLAP Services for SQL Server, using the Warehouse cube. Other than installing the OLAP Services, you don't need to do anything else to get the FoodMart catalog set up.

> *For more information on installing the OLAP Services, see Chapter 18 of Professional Visual Basic 6 Databases, also by Wrox Press.*

Exploring the Objects

To open the Catalog, simply set the ActiveConnection property, either to a connection string or to an open Connection object. For a connection string, you specify two pieces of information – the OLE DB Provider name, and the name of the OLAP Server. For example, in Visual Basic you would do this:

```
Dim catData As New ADOMD.Catalog

catData.ActiveConnection = "Provider=MSOLAP; Data Source=Kanga"
```

This is similar to the connection string for SQL Server, except there's no need to specify the `Initial Catalog`, because there is only one catalog per OLAP Server. Setting the connection details automatically opens the `Catalog`, and then you can loop through the `CubeDefs`:

```
Dim catData  As New ADOMD.Catalog
Dim cubeData As ADOMD.CubeDef

catData.ActiveConnection = m_sConn

For Each cubeData In catData.CubeDefs
    Debug.Print cubeData.Name
Next
```

This gives the following output:

Sales
Warehouse
Warehouse and Sales

Delving one level deeper, to look at the Dimensions, we could use this code:

```
Dim catData  As New ADOMD.Catalog
Dim cubeData As ADOMD.CubeDef
Dim dimData  As ADOMD.Dimension

catData.ActiveConnection = m_sConn

For Each cubeData In catData.CubeDefs
    Debug.Print cubeData.Name
    For Each dimData In cubeData.Dimensions
        Debug.Print vbTab; dimData.Name
    Next
Next
```

This gives us the following output:

Sales
  Customers
  Education Level
  Gender
  Marital Status
  . . .
Warehouse
  Measures
  Product
  Store
  Store Size in SQFT
  Store Type
  Time

Warehouse
Warehouse and Sales
  Customers
  Education Level
  Gender
  . . .

I've cut out a few of the Dimensions from the `Sales` and `Warehouse and Sales` CubeDefs so it's easy to read. To save doing this again as we go deeper into the hierarchy, I'll concentrate on the `Warehouse` CubeDef, and the `Time` Dimension. I know that the data we'll be using only has one hierarchy, so we'll default to the first `Hierarchy` in the collection and look at the `Levels` and the `Members`, using this code:

```
Dim catData As New ADOMD.Catalog
Dim cubeData As ADOMD.CubeDef
Dim dimData As ADOMD.Dimension
Dim hierData As ADOMD.Hierarchy
Dim lvlData As ADOMD.Level
Dim memData As ADOMD.Member

catData.ActiveConnection = m_sConn

Set cubeData = catData.CubeDefs("Warehouse")
Set dimData = cubeData.Dimensions("Time")
For Each lvlData In dimData.Hierarchies(0).Levels
    Debug.Print lvlData.Caption
    For Each memData In lvlData.Members
        Debug.Print vbTab; memData.Caption; vbTab; _
                    memData.UniqueName
    Next
Next
```

This loops through the `Levels` and then for each `Level`, loops through the `Members`, printing out the `Caption` and the `UniqueName` properties. You'll see why they are required when you look at the output of this:

Year
  1997   [Time].[1997]
  1998   [Time].[1998]
Quarter
  Q1   [Time].[1997].[Q1]
  Q2   [Time].[1997].[Q2]
  Q3   [Time].[1997].[Q3]
  Q4   [Time].[1997].[Q4]
  Q1   [Time].[1998].[Q1]
  Q2   [Time].[1998].[Q2]
  Q3   [Time].[1998].[Q3]
  Q4   [Time].[1998].[Q4]

Month
```
1    [Time].[1997].[Q1].[1]
2    [Time].[1997].[Q1].[2]
3    [Time].[1997].[Q1].[3]
. . .
11   [Time].[1997].[Q4].[11]
12   [Time].[1997].[Q4].[12]
1    [Time].[1998].[Q1].[1]
2    [Time].[1998].[Q1].[2]
. . .
11   [Time].[1998].[Q4].[11]
12   [Time].[1998].[Q4].[12]
```

Once again I've cut a little text out here, but you can clearly see what we've got. The `Levels` comprise `Year`, `Quarter` and `Month`, but the `Members` probably contain more than you expected. You might have thought that the `Quarter`, for example, should only contain the quarters for a year, and the `Month` should only contain the months for a particular quarter. But, once you realize what's going on it's quite obvious. So, bear with the following explanations – I could have picked a simpler example, but then you'd probably have got confused when you looked at the Time dimension later. If I explain it now then at least you'll understand what's going on.

The thing to remember is that `Year`, `Quarter`, and `Month` are all at the same level in the object hierarchy – they are the `Levels`, and don't contain any data themselves. Whilst in real terms a year contains quarters, and a quarter contains months, in this example the years, quarters and months are just different ways we can look at the data.

If we pick one of those ways – `Year` for example – then underneath that are the items which make up the level. The `Year` contains two `Members` (`1997` and `1998`), because these are the only two years used within the data. If the sample data spanned a third year, then we'd see a third `Member`. Keep that in mind as you look at the `Quarter` – this contains all of the quarters for all of the data. So, since we have two years, and each year is broken down into four quarters, we have eight `Members` in the `Quarters` `Level`. The same applies for the `Months` – the `Members` contain all of the months for all of the data – two years equals 24 months.

If you flick back to the code you'll see that for each `Member` we printed the `Caption` and `UniqueName` properties. Since the `Members` can contain overlapping data (for example the month name repeated for two years), the `UniqueName` property contains, unsurprisingly, a unique name for the `Member`. This comprises the names of all items to uniquely identify the member. An analogy is in standard SQL where you use the table name and the column name to uniquely identify a column, for example, `authors.au_fname`.

Unless you're building a very complex query tool, or perhaps a customized management interface for the OLAP Services, then you probably won't use some of these ADOMD objects. What's more likely is that you'll be building something to allow users to query the data.

Creating Cellsets

Creating a cellset is extremely simple using the Open method, like this:

```
Dim cstData As New ADOMD.Cellset
Dim sConn As String
Dim sQuery As String

sConn = "Provider=MSOLAP; Data Source=Kanga"

sQuery = "SELECT Product.Children ON COLUMNS," & _
         " Time.Children ON ROWS," & _
         " [Store Type].Children ON PAGES" & _
         " FROM Warehouse"

cstData.Open sQuery, sConn
```

Now comes the interesting bit, because you have to get to grips with how the data is represented. We are now going through the set of objects shown at the bottom of the object model. So here we have the following:

- ❑ An Axes collection, which contains an Axis object for each axis selected. In the above query there will be three Axis objects in the collection – one each for the columns, rows, and pages.

- ❑ A Positions collection, which contains a Position object for each unique item in the Axis.

- ❑ A Members collection, which contains a Member object for each member in a Position.

- ❑ A Cell object, which represents an individual cell of data.

At this stage you might be a little confused, because there doesn't seem to be a way to get to the actual cells. There's no Cells collection, so where is the data? Well, the data is stored in an n-dimensional array (where n equals the number of axes), and you access the data through the Item property of the CellSet object. For example, the above query produces a three-dimensional array, which can be accessed as follows:

```
cstData.Item(0,0,0)
```

This returns the data in column 0, row 0, page 0. One of the things you have to watch for is that for a two dimensional query you only get a two-dimensional array:

```
cstData.Item(0,0)
```

The Item property is the default property, and can therefore be omitted, allowing us to access the data using this form:

```
cstData(0,0)
```

So, getting the data out from the cellset is pretty easy then – you can just loop through the dimensions. But what about the headings? Where are they stored? Well, that's where the collections come in. It may seem a roundabout way of managing the data, but it's actually quite efficient, because the headings are only stored once, and the data is in an easily accessible form.

When looking at the headings you once again need to put your thinking cap on, because what seems as though it should be stored in some form of hierarchy, isn't. Let's look at the three-dimensional query shown above, and use the following code:

```
Dim axsA As ADOMD.Axis
Dim posP As ADOMD.Position
Dim memM As ADOMD.Member
Dim lvlL As ADOMD.Level

For Each axsA In cstData.Axes
    Debug.Print axsA.Name
    For Each posP In axsA.Positions
        Debug.Print vbTab; posP.Ordinal
        For Each memM In posP.Members
            Debug.Print vbTab; vbTab; memM.Name
        Next
    Next
Next
```

Here we start with the Axes, printing out the name of each one. Then, for each Axis, we loop through the Positions, again printing the name. Finally, for each Position we print the Members. What this does becomes clear when you see the results.

Axis(0)
   0
     [Product].[All Products].[Drink]
   1
     [Product].[All Products].[Food]
   2
     [Product].[All Products].[Non-Consumable]
Axis(1)
   0
     [Time].[1997].[Q1]
   1
     [Time].[1997].[Q2]
   2
     [Time].[1997].[Q3]
   3
     [Time].[1997].[Q4]
Axis(2)
   0

   [Store Type].[All].[Deluxe Supermarket]
1
   [Store Type].[All].[Gourmet Supermarket]
2
   [Store Type].[All].[Mid-Size Grocery]
3
   [Store Type].[All].[Small Grocery]
4
   [Store Type].[All].[Supermarket]

The three Axes have obvious names. Within each Axis we have the numbered Positions – these represent the unique items within a cellset, and within each Position we have the Members. Each Position has a number that uniquely identifies its place within the Axis. This is the Ordinal, and can be used to index into the cellset. For example, to find out the data for the Food product, for Quarter 3, for Deluxe Supermarkets, we would use:

```
cstData(1, 2, 0)
```

You might be wondering why there are Positions as well as Members, since there seems to be only one Member per Position. Well, this becomes clearer when we do CROSSJOINs. For example, consider the following:

```
SELECT Product.Children ON COLUMNS,
    CROSSJOIN(Time.Children, Store.Children) ON ROWS
        [Store Type].Children ON PAGES
    FROM Warehouse
```

The data for Axis 0 and 2 (columns and pages) stays the same, but the rows are now made up from two different pieces of information. Our result for this axis would now be:

Axis(1)
  0
   [Time].[1997].[Q1]
   [Store].[All Stores].[Canada]
  1
   [Time].[1997].[Q1]
   [Store].[All Stores].[Mexico]
  2
   [Time].[1997].[Q1]
   [Store].[All Stores].[USA]
  3
   [Time].[1997].[Q2]
   [Store].[All Stores].[Canada]
  4
   [Time].[1997].[Q2]
   [Store].[All Stores].[Mexico]
  5
   [Time].[1997].[Q2]
   [Store].[All Stores].[USA]

Once again I've cut down the data, but you can clearly see what's happening. Each `Position` now has two members, and it's together that these make up the unique item on an `Axis`. Remember how a `CROSSJOIN` performs set multiplication, where every member of one `Dimension` is combined with every member of another `Dimension`. So, we have a single row that represents Q1 for Canada, a single for representing Q1 for Mexico, and so on. When using the `Children` this isn't so bad, since this only works at one level. However, `Members` contains the full hierarchy of elements for a `Dimension`, so performing `CROSSJOINS` with `Members` can be a lengthy process!

One important thing to remember is that it's still the `Position` that uniquely identifies an item. With a `CROSSJOIN`, the `Position` just happens to be made up from different members.

OK, that's enough about the overview of how to get data out of ADOMD. It's about time some practical examples were shown.

The OLAP Viewer Sample

There are some very simple ways to get query tools up and running, but building the query tool manually will teach you a lot more about ADOMD during the process, and you'll have a lot more control over what's being displayed.

What we are aiming for is an interface that looks like this:

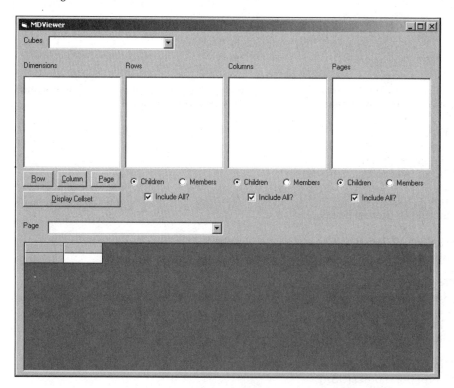

At the top we have a list box to allow selection of the CubeDef. Once selected, the Dimensions are displayed in a box underneath. There are three buttons to allow the selected Dimension to be added to a <u>R</u>ow, a <u>C</u>olumn or a <u>P</u>age, and radio buttons to determine whether the Children or the Members of each Axis are to be shown. If the Children are to be displayed then there's also the option of adding an Include All item, to summarize all items for that Dimension. Pressing the <u>D</u>isplay Cellset button will display an HTML table containing the selected data. The Rows, Columns, and Pages (and the radio buttons and check box) are implemented as a control array.

I won't go into all of the detail about building this sample, since some of it is purely VB. Instead I'll concentrate on the ADOMD code, and how it's used. The full code is available from the supporting web site, along with an HTML scriptlet that performs the same task.

Listing the Cubes

The first thing we need to do is display a list of the CubeDefs. If you remember from the sample earlier, we can just open the Catalog and then loop through the CubeDefs collection. This is performed in the Form_Open event. The Catalog object is held on a global variable, m_catData.

```
Private Sub Form_Load()

    Dim cubCube      As ADOMD.CubeDef        ' cube in catalog

    Set m_catData = New ADOMD.Catalog

    m_catData.ActiveConnection = m_sCatalog

    For Each cubCube In m_catData.CubeDefs
        cboCubeDefs.AddItem cubCube.Name
    Next

    Set cubCube = Nothing

End Sub
```

This simply loops through the CubeDefs collection, and adds the name of each Cube to the combo box.

Filling the Dimensions box

Now we need to fill the list box showing the Dimensions when the user picks a CubeDef. The principle is much the same as the previous example:

```
Private Sub cboCubeDefs_Click()

    Dim dimD        As ADOMD.Dimension
    Dim sCube       As String
```

```
lstDimensions.Clear
sCube = CStr(cboCubeDefs)
For Each dimD In m_catData.CubeDefs(sCube).Dimensions
    lstDimensions.AddItem dimD.Name
Next

Set dimD = Nothing

End Sub
```

This simply loops through the Dimensions for the selected CubeDef, adding the name of each dimension to the list box.

Building the Query

To build the query you have to assume that the user has selected some Dimensions and added them to the Row and Column list boxes. Using Pages isn't necessary, but we'll show you what's required for that too. What we're going to do here is construct an MDX SELECT statement, and this is done in two parts.

The outer part builds the overall structure of the query, and is run when the user clicks the Display Cellset button.

The first thing I do is ensure that at least one entry is in each of the Rows and Columns, so that we can build a valid query. Pages aren't mandatory, so I don't need to check that one.

```
Private Sub cmdDisplay_Click()

    Dim sQuery        As String

    If lstAxis(Rows).ListCount = 0 Or _
        lstAxis(Columns).ListCount = 0 Then
        MsgBox "You must select at least one " & _
                "row and one column"
        Exit Sub
    End If
```

Now I start with the SELECT statement, and add the details for the columns and rows. The QueryBuildIndex() function actually builds the *dimension* ON *axis* part of the query. We'll look at this function in a moment.

```
    sQuery = "select " & _
            QueryBuildIndex(Columns, "Columns") & ", " & _
            QueryBuildIndex(Rows, "Rows")
```

Having done the rows and columns we need to do the pages – but only if pages have been selected.

```
    If lstAxis(Pages).ListCount <> 0 Then
        sQuery = sQuery & ", " & _
                QueryBuildIndex(Pages, "Pages")
    End If
```

Finally we can add the source of the data – that is, the name of the `CubeDef`.

```
    sQuery = sQuery & " from " & cboCubeDefs
```

At this stage `sQuery` now contains a valid MDX query. Let's see how the inner bit of the query is built. This needs to build a string for the `Dimensions`, in one of several forms, since the user can select `Children`, `Members`, and an **Include All** item. It also needs to take account of multiple Dimensions, in which case a `CROSSJOIN` must be created.

The table below shows what we are aiming for, assuming that **Children** is selected.

Dimensions	All?	Query
Time	✓	`{[Time], [Time].Children}`
Time		`[Time].Children`
Time Store	✓	`CROSSJOIN({[Time], [Time].Children}, {[Store], [Store].Children})`
Time Store		`CROSSJOIN([Time].Children, [Store].Children)`

It's just a matter of checking a few options and building a string. Let's take a look at how it's done.

The `QueryBuildIndex()` function takes two arguments – the first is the axis index number, and the second is the name of the axis, and then we have a few variable declarations.

```
    Private Function QueryBuildIndex(iIndex As AxisEnum, _
                        sAxis As String) As String

        Dim sQuery       As String    ' query string
        Dim sType        As String    ' children or members
        Dim bChildren    As Boolean   ' true if Children selected
        Dim bAll         As Boolean   ' true if ball selected
        Dim sOn          As String    ' the On clause
        Dim iItem        As Integer   ' item in axis selection
        Dim sTemp        As String
```

The reason we have the axis index number is because the list boxes for the three axes are implemented as a control array, so we use this number to index into the array.

There are two Boolean variables, which identify whether or not the radio buttons or checkboxes are selected. The first identifies whether or not the **Children** radio button for this `Axis` is selected, and the second identifies whether or not the checkbox for the **Include All** item is selected:

```
bChildren = optChildren(iIndex).Value
bAll = chkAll(iIndex).Value
```

Next we identify the type of item to be displayed:

```
If bChildren Then
    sType = "Children"
Else
    sType = "Members"
End If
```

Now we can start constructing the string. If there are no items in the list box we just drop out. This shouldn't happen since we've checked this earlier, but it protects the function against failing if something odd does happen:

```
Select Case lstAxis(iIndex).ListCount
Case 0
    sOn = ""
```

Now we can construct the string for a single `Dimension`. If the **Children** option has been selected and the checkbox for **Include All** has been checked, then we need to use a different syntax. For **Include All** we include the name of the `Dimension` on its own, which will give us the summary row.

```
Case 1
    sTemp = lstAxis(iIndex).List(0)
    If bChildren And bAll Then
        sQuery = "{[" & sTemp & "], [" & sTemp & "]." & _
                sType & "}"
    Else
        sQuery = "[" & sTemp & "]." & sType
    End If
```

If multiple dimensions have been selected we need to construct a CROSSJOIN, so we loop through the selected dimensions. For each individual dimension we use the same syntax as for a single dimension:

```
      Case Else
          sQuery = sQuery & "crossjoin("

          ' loop through the selected items
          For iItem = 0 To lstAxis(iIndex).ListCount - 1
              sTemp = lstAxis(iIndex).List(iItem)
              If bChildren And bAll Then
                  sQuery = sQuery & "{[" & sTemp & "], [" & _
                          sTemp & "]." & sType & "},"
              Else
                  sQuery = sQuery & "[" & sTemp & "]." & _
                          sType & ","
              End If
          Next
```

We explicitly add a comma to separate the members in a crossjoin, so at the end of the loop, we strip off the trailing comma. This saves having to keep track of which item we are on, and only adding the comma if we aren't on the last item.

```
          sQuery = Left(sQuery, Len(sQuery) - 1)
          sQuery = sQuery & ")"
      End Select
```

And finally we return the string containing the `Axis` definition.

```
      QueryBuildIndex = sQuery & sOn
```

There's nothing very complex about this function – it's just building up a set of known options given the user input. So, once the string is built, we need to create a cellset from it.

Running the Query

Earlier in the chapter we showed that using the `Open` method of the `CellSet` object is all that's required to create the data. So, in our example, we need to do the same, using the query we've just built.

First we create a new `CellSet` object, again using a global variable, since we'll be using this in several routines:

```
      m_cstData.Open sQuery, m_catData.ActiveConnection
```

Then we open the cellset, using the `ActiveConnection` property of the existing `Catalog` as our connection details. Assuming the query executed correctly, we run a function to process the results, which fills the grid with the results:

```
      QueryProcess
```

This function simply builds up an HTML table of the data.

Displaying the Results

There are two parts to displaying the results, depending upon which sort of query has been executed. If we're dealing with a three-dimensional query, then we need some way to show the third dimension.

The first two dimensions will be displayed in a simple table. We will add a combo box to allow the user to select the third dimension, or page, and the rows and columns for the selected page will be displayed in the table.

The Pages

Because the third dimension will be stored in a combo box, we simply need to fill this. First we check whether three axes are being used, and if so we start building them:

```
Private Sub QueryProcess()

    Dim iPageMembers    As Integer    ' number of members
    Dim iMember         As Integer    ' current member
    Dim iPositions      As Integer    ' number of poisitions
    Dim iPosition       As Integer    ' current position
    Dim sCaption        As String     ' caption to display
    Dim sPageCaption    As String     ' caption for the page
    Dim posP            As ADOMD.Position

    ' are pages being used
    If m_cstData.Axes.Count = 3 Then
```

Next we clear the existing contents of the `Pages` combo, and set two variables to store the total number of members for the page and the number of positions for the page:

```
        cboPages.Clear
        iPageMembers = m_cstData.Axes(Pages).DimensionCount
        iPositions = m_cstData.Axes(Pages).Positions.Count
```

Now we can loop through the `Positions`. Remember, at this stage we're not looking at the data – just the headings. So, we want to create a heading made up from the various `Members`:

```
        For iPosition = 0 To iPositions - 1
            sPageCaption = ""
            Set posP = m_cstData.Axes(Pages).Positions(iPosition)

            ' and then through the members for each position
            For iMember = 0 To iPageMembers - 1
```

Since the `Member` names have square brackets around them we call a separate function to format the name nicely. We won't describe that function here, but it's well commented in the downloadable code.

```
                sPageCaption = FormatName(posP.Members(iMember).Name)
            Next
```

All this means is that instead of, say:

```
[Store Type].[All].[Deluxe Supermarket]
```

we get:

```
Store Type / All / Deluxe Supermarket
```

It's not a big issue, but it makes the text easier to read.

Next we can use this newly formatted string as the text in pages combo box. Notice that this is only the display text – the actual value is the position number. We'll be using the position number to index into the `Cellset` later.

```
        cboPages.AddItem sPageCaption
    Next
    Set posP = Nothing
End If
```

And finally we can call the routine to fill the grid:

```
BuildTable
```

The Rows and Columns

Filling the grid is quite simple, and I freely admit to a bit of code reuse here. When you install the OLAP Services you get a Visual Basic Sample, and I've used the code from this, with a few minor additions. Why? Well, the code's freely available and it saves having to write it myself. The sample code only handles two axes, so I've added code to make this work. I'm not going to describe the whole function here – just the bits that get the data from the cellset into the grid:

The first piece of code to describe is if there are two axes – that is, Rows and Columns:

```
iGrdRow = iHeaderRowCnt
For iCellRow = 0 To iCellRowCnt - 1
  iGrdCol = iHeaderColCnt
  For iCellCol = 0 To iCellColCnt - 1
    Set clCur = m_cstData(iCellCol, iCellRow)
    .TextMatrix(iGrdRow, iGrdCol) = sGetCellValue(clCur)
    iGrdCol = iGrdCol + 1
  Next
  iGrdRow = iGrdRow + 1
Next
```

This loops through the rows and columns using two standard loops. The index variables of these loops are used to index into the `Cellset`.

The code for three dimensions is not much different:

```
iGrdRow = iHeaderRowCnt
For iCellRow = 0 To iCellRowCnt - 1
    iGrdCol = iHeaderColCnt
    For iCellCol = 0 To iCellColCnt - 1
        Set clCur = m_cstData(iCellCol, iCellRow, m_iPage)
        .TextMatrix(iGrdRow, iGrdCol) = sGetCellValue(clCur)
        iGrdCol = iGrdCol + 1
    Next
    iGrdRow = iGrdRow + 1
Next
```

The difference here is that we add a third dimension to the cellset, since this contains the `Pages` of data.

That's all there is to getting the data from the cellset. The remaining code deals with the user interface side of things.

For a simple query, such as `Product` along the columns, and `Time` along the rows, you get this:

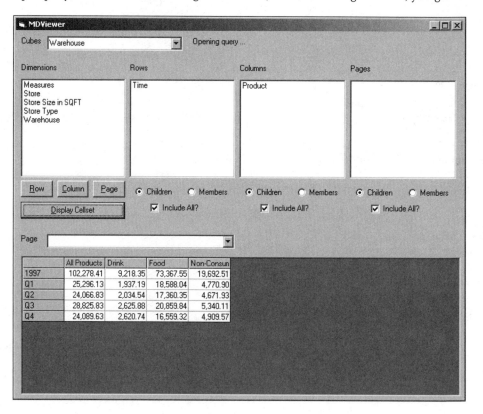

Adding the `Store Type` to the rows gives this output:

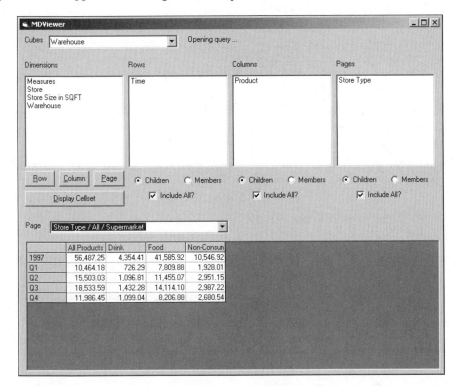

I won't run through any more samples – it's better if you try it out and examine them for yourself. One thing to watch out for is selecting members, especially with more than one item per axis. Depending upon the members, the query could take a little while to run.

Enhancements

This sample is quite simple, and there are plenty of ways in which it could be improved. I kept it simple so that you could learn how ADOMD works, without getting too bogged down. Listed below are some of the things I'd like to do to this and the reasons why:

❑   Add proper column and row spanning for the headings when multiple dimensions are used. This would just make the table look nicer. One of the problems with this is that you have to identify how many inner `Members` there are for each outer `Member`. The information held within the `Cellset` doesn't give you this information directly, so you have to go to the `Catalog` to work it out.

❑   When using `Members` (as opposed to `Children`) in a query, allow the levels to indent. For example, when selecting `Time.Members` it would be good to see something like this:

1997	Total		value
	Q1	Total	value
		1	value
		2	value
		3	value
	Q2	Total	value

Once again we are foiled by the simplicity of the Cellset, because we don't have all of the information. We can identify the depth in the Level hierarchy for each member, but we don't know the total depth. For that we'd have to go to the Catalog.

❑ Allow the selection of Children or Members on a Dimension basis, rather than an Axis basis. This would make the utility more flexible.

There are plenty of others, but that'll do for now.

Quick Solutions

Now that you've spent some time learning how ADOMD works and studying the code to produce simple tabular output, I'll show you some quicker ways to use the OLAP Services. Why didn't I do this at the beginning? Well, this is a chapter about ADOMD, and not about some already supplied components. However, as a developer you might well be under tight deadlines, so it's useful to know what's available, and also if you need to quickly prototype something.

The Sample Visual Basic Project

The OLAP Services come with a sample Visual Basic project, which is quite powerful. It looks like this:

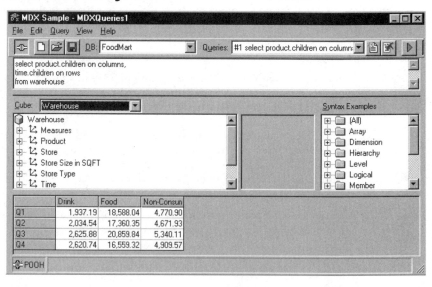

You get a window at the top where you can type in MDX queries, a section in the middle where you can explore the catalog information, and a table at the bottom to show the output of the query. The output produced is pretty much the same as for the scriptlet, except that this Visual Basic sample only handles two axes. It's quite trivial to modify though, if you need to.

The OLAP Manager Cube Browser

As I was trawling through the files installed by the OLAP Services, I found an OCX. Being naturally inquisitive I found out this is the OLAP Manager Cube Browser. Hmm, I thought. Sounds interesting. So, I dropped it into a Visual Basic form and added the following to the form's Load event:

```
CubeBrowser1.ConnectWStr "Pooh", "FoodMart", "Warehouse"
```

I then ran the project and got this:

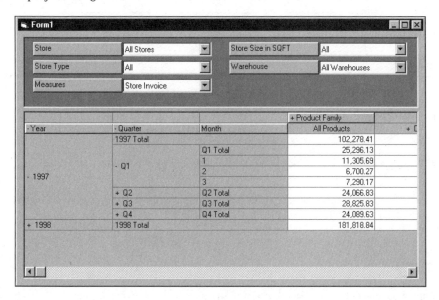

Wow, very cool. All of the dimensions are shown as combo boxes at the top. When you drop down one of these you get a treeview listing the hierarchies, levels, members, and so on. You can drag the dimensions on the grid, where they become part of the structure, automatically performing crossjoins where necessary. You also get expandability built right in.

This OCX works in web pages too, so if you are using IE you could just drop this onto a web page.

Office

The other simple way to use the OLAP Services is to use the PivotTable from Excel. From the <u>D</u>ata menu you can select the <u>P</u>ivotTable and PivotChart Report... option, which will launch a small wizard to help you create the pivot details. You should pick the <u>E</u>xternal Data Source option, and you'll have the option to connect to an OLAP Server. What this gives you is very similar to the control shown above:

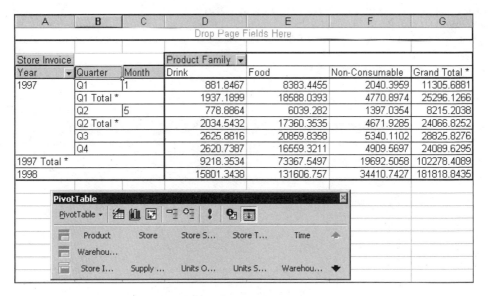

You can drag and drop items onto the rows and columns, drill down, and so on. You can also switch to a graph with just a simple click of a button.

Summary

This chapter has focused on an area that not many people are using (compared to standard ADO, that is). The OLAP services provide a great way to analyze data, especially when there is lots of data that can be viewed in many different ways.

In this chapter we've tried to cover the core requirements for using ADOMD, including:

❑ What exactly OLAP data is, and how it can be viewed.

❑ The basics of the MDX query language, and how you can use it to easily produce table summaries of data.

❑ How to use ADOMD to run those queries, and extract the information.

There is plenty more to learn about ADOMD and OLAP, but to give it the credit it's due would probably require a whole book.

I have no doubt that OLAP is very powerful feature, and that ADOMD gives a simple interface into it. It's a large market and one that is steadily increasing, and provides a great way to analyze complex data. Like ADO though, it is a data manipulation language, and therefore requires work to construct suitable user interfaces, but this definitely isn't a downside. It gives you the flexibility to use a powerful method of data management, and match it to any interface you desire.

ADOX: Data Source Definitions and Security

Introduction to ADOX

ADO 2.1 saw the introduction of two entirely new sets of objects to extend the functionality of ADO still further. We met one of these – ADOMD – in the previous chapter. The second is ADOX, or **ADO Extensions for DDL and Security**. As the name suggests, ADOX in fact provides two new sets of functionality. The ADOX object model contains objects which allow us to manage database security, and also to perform **Data Definition Language** operations.

Data Definition Language (DDL) is the name given to the set of SQL commands which we use to modify the schema of the database. That is, DDL is used to create, drop and alter objects in the database. DDL doesn't actually put any data into the database, do searches, or take out data: it's used strictly to build a framework in which programmers and end users can place their data. Prior to ADO 2.1, these DDL commands had to be performed using SQL statements, which meant that we sometimes had to use code specific to a given data store (such as using Access SQL). This goes against the grain of the UDA strategy.

The ADO Extensions are designed to access the Data Definition Language of the data store, abstracting these features into a simple set of components. This allows us to access metadata, create tables and procedures, etc., without knowing the specific language that the data store uses.

The second aspect of ADOX covers security. The SQL language contains another sub-language, known as **Data Control Language** (DCL), which is used to manage the security of a database. DCL comprises a number of SQL commands for assigning or denying permissions to particular users or groups of users and for assigning users to or removing them from groups. Again, ADOX abstracts these DCL operations so that we don't need to know the SQL syntax used by the data store.

In ADO 2.5, ADOX hasn't changed much and the technology is still quite young and not supported that well by all providers. Access developers used to using DAO will be familiar with defining and manipulating the data store via an object model, and it is the Jet provider that actually has best support for ADOX. Other providers, such as those for SQL Server and Oracle, do not support as many features (such as the ability to create new stored procedures). (If you try to use an unsupported feature for your data provider an error will occur.)

This begs the question, why bother? If Access (Jet) is the only provider that gives full support then why don't Access developers stick with what they know, namely DAO? Well, ADOX support will grow, and many of the limitations of ADOX will hopefully be resolved as new providers are released. This means that we will eventually have a more or less provider-neutral object model (API) for all our Data Definition and Security needs (although there will always be some anomalies, such as data types that are available for some providers and not others). Having an object model that is supported by many data providers is, of course, one of the reasons for the success of ADO, and that success should eventually translate to ADOX. A DAO-to-ADOX object map is provided on MSDN at `http://msdn.microsoft.com/library/officedev/off2000/achowDAOToADOX.htm`, which should prove useful should use you wish to migrate from DAO to ADOX.

This chapter will examine the ADOX object model, giving the strengths and limitations together with lots of relevant examples and code snippets. There is a brief overview of using SQL-DMO – a provider-specific API for performing the same operations as ADOX (and more) that provides a way of overcoming some of the shortcomings of ADOX with the SQL Server 7.0 provider.

Using ADOX

Before you can use ADOX in your project, you will need to reference the type library. This is called Microsoft ADO Ext. 2.5 for DDL and Security, and is located in the file `msadox.dll` (usually installed in the `\Program Files\Common Files\System\Ado` directory). In addition to this, you may want to add a reference to ADO 2.5, although this is not required unless you want to create new procedures and views, in which case you will need to create an ADO `Command` object. If you are developing in VBScript for the Web, you should be aware that constants used in ADOX are not defined in `adovbs.inc` – instead add a reference in `Global.asa`:

```
<!--METADATA TYPE="TypeLib" NAME="Microsoft ADO Ext. 2.5 for DDL and Security"
        UUID="{00000600-0000-0010-8000-00AA006D2EA4}" VERSION="2.5"-->
```

ADOX Object Model

The ADOX object model observes more of a hierarchy than the ADO object model, but that's because of the nature of the objects it contains. This means that there is a parent object and several child objects:

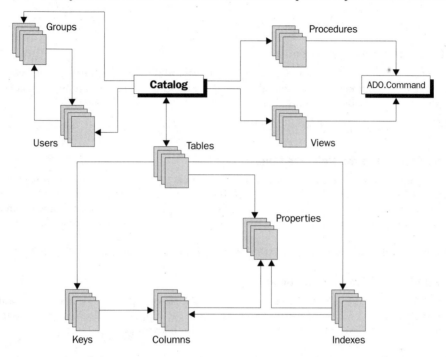

Overview of the ADOX Objects

Before going on to look at the ADOX objects and their methods and properties in detail, we'll have a quick look at each object in turn.

The Catalog Object

The Catalog object is a central repository, and is really just a container for all of the other objects. The Catalog object allows us to connect to a data store and drill-down to the components that it comprises. With the Catalog object we can use the ActiveConnection property to specify the data store that we want to connect to, and then use the collections to obtain more detailed information. It's also possible to obtain and set the owner of various objects without using the collections.

The Table Object and the Tables Collection

A Table object identifies a single table in a catalog, containing information such as the table name and the last change date. It is also a container for the Columns, Indexes and Keys collections (see below).

The Tables collection contains Table objects, one for each table in the catalog.

The Index Object and the Indexes Collection

An Index object contains the details for a single index on a table, identifying attributes such as the index name, whether the index is unique, whether the index allows nulls, etc. Using the Index object's Columns collection (see below), you can see which columns comprise the index.

The Indexes collection contains all of the Index objects for a particular Table.

The Key Object and the Keys Collection

A Key object contains information regarding a table key, identifying such items as its name, whether it is a primary or foreign key, the related table, etc. Like the Index object, the Key object contains a collection of Column objects, identifying the columns that make up the key.

The Keys collection contains a list of keys for a table.

The Column Object and the Columns Collection

A Column object represents an individual column from a Table, Index or Key object. In many respects it is similar to the ADO Field object: but rather than storing the details of a recordset, it holds the details of a stored column, such as its name, its data type, etc. For Key columns it contains details of the related columns, and for Index columns it contains details of the clustering and sorting.

The Columns collection contains all of the columns for a particular Table, Key or Index object.

The Group Object and the Groups Collection

A Group object identifies a security group, containing a list of users in the catalog. Its main role is to allow the retrieval and setting of permission for a named group, or for allowing access to the Users collection, which contains a list of all users belonging to this group.

The Groups collection contains a list of Groups that belong to a particular catalog, or a list of Groups that a particular user belongs to.

The User Object and the Users Collection

A User object contains details of a single user of the data store and contains the user name, the unique ID of the user, and methods to read and write permissions. The User object also contains a Groups collection, which is a list of groups to which the user belongs. You should be careful about writing recursive procedures that traverse the Users and Groups collections, because they point to each other.

The Users collection contains a list of all users in a catalog.

The Procedure Object and the Procedures Collection

A Procedure object identifies a stored procedure in a catalog. The Procedure object has very few properties, mainly because one of these properties represents an ADO Command object. The Procedure object identifies the details about the stored procedure (such as its name and when it was last modified), while the Command object identifies the internal details of the procedure (such as the SQL test, etc.).

The Procedures collection contains a Procedure object for each stored procedure in the Catalog.

The View Object and the Views Collection

A `View` object identifies a single view in a catalog. A view represents a set of records or a virtual table. Like the `Procedure` object, the `View` contains a `Command` object, allowing access to the view command.

The `Views` collection contains a list of `View` objects, one for each view in the catalog.

The Property Object and the Properties Collection

The `Property` object and `Properties` collection are identical to their ADO equivalents.

The Catalog Object

The `Catalog` object is the parent of the `Tables`, `Views`, `Users`, `Groups` and `Procedures` collections, which describe the schema catalog of a data source. The `Catalog` object allows us to connect to a data source, and you can think of this object as representing the database itself. Using the `Catalog` object, we can open or create a database (although not all providers support `Create`), and read or set the ownership of objects.

Create Method

The `Catalog` object's `Create` method creates a new database. This method is not supported in SQL Server or Oracle – for those systems you will need to use another interface; it cannot be done through ADOX. For example, in SQL Server you could use the SQL-DMO `Database` object; we will cover this later in this chapter.

To create a new database using the `Create` method, you can use one of three syntaxes, depending on whether you want to return a connection string, an ADO `Connection` object, or nothing.

The first syntax creates the database but returns nothing. However, after successfully executing, the `ActiveConnection` property of the `Catalog` object will hold an open ADO `Connection` object for the new database:

```
Dim objCat As ADOX.Catalog
Set objCat = New ADOX.Catalog
objCat.Create(strConnectionString)
' The next line displays the version of ADO for the active connection
Msgbox objCat.ActiveConnection.Version
```

In this example, `strConnectionString` is a string variable containing a connection string to an Access database. For example:

```
Provider=Microsoft.Jet.OLEDB.4.0;Data Source=C:\db\mydb.mdb
```

In the second example, the connection string is returned from the `Create` method. This seems a bit pointless, since you have to pass in a connection string in the first place, but the returned string does contain all the default options for the provider, so it may be of some use. Again, the `ActiveConnection` property of the `Catalog` object will hold an ADO `Connection` object.

```
Dim strCon As String
Dim objCat As ADOX.Catalog

Set objCat = New ADOX.Catalog
strCon = objCat.Create(strConnectionString)
```

And after the code is executed `strCon` would equal the complete connection string together with all the default options for the provider:

```
Provider=Microsoft.Jet.OLEDB.4.0; _
Password=""; _
User ID=Admin; _
Data Source=C:\db\mydb.mdb; _
Mode=Share Deny None; _
Extended Properties=""; _
Jet OLEDB:System database=""; _
Jet OLEDB:Registry Path=""; _
Jet OLEDB:Database Password=""; _
Jet OLEDB:Engine Type=5; _
Jet OLEDB:Database Locking Mode=1; _
Jet OLEDB:Global Partial Bulk Ops=2; _
Jet OLEDB:Global Bulk Transactions=1; _
Jet OLEDB:New Database Password=""; _
Jet OLEDB:Create System Database=False; _
Jet OLEDB:Encrypt Database=False; _
Jet OLEDB:Don't Copy Locale on Compact=False; _
Jet OLEDB:Compact Without Replica Repair=False; _
Jet OLEDB:SFP=False
```

The third syntax returns an ADO `Connection` object. Here, I have referenced the ADODB library in my VB project so that I can use early binding to the `Connection` object.

```
Dim objCon As ADODB.Connection
Dim objCat As ADOX.Catalog

Set objCat = New ADOX.Catalog
Set objCon = objCat.Create(strConnectionString)
```

The variable `objCon` now references an open connection to the newly created database, so I can use all of the methods and properties of this ADO object if I want to.

Unsupported Features

If you try to use the `Create` method on a provider that does not support it (such as SQL Server) then you will receive an error such as the following:

-2147467262 – No such interface supported

You can't delete a database in ADOX. For an Access MDB, you would have to use a file system command (such as `kill`) and for SQL Server, you can use the SQL-DMO `Database` object. For other systems, please consult the vendor documentation.

To open an existing database use the `ActiveConnection` property of the `Catalog` object – see below.

GetObjectOwner and SetObjectOwner Methods

These methods return and set the user or group name of the owner of the specified object. Ownership is a security concept within database systems whereby the user who creates a database object is the owner of it. In most cases, the creator of a database object is implicitly granted all permissions, but must then explicitly grant permissions to other users before they can access the object. Setting permissions is discussed in the "Security" section below.

The GetObjectOwner method takes the following syntax:

```
String = Catalog.GetObjectOwner(ObjectName, ObjectType, [ObjectTypeId])
```

The returned string is the name of the user or group which owns the object.

The SetObjectOwner method has:

```
Catalog.SetObjectOwner ObjectName, ObjectType, OwnerName, [ObjectTypeId]
```

Name	Type	Description
ObjectName	String	The name of the object
ObjectType	ObjectTypeEnum	The type of object
ObjectTypeID	Variant	The GUID for the object type. This argument is only required if the ObjectType is argument is set to adPermObjProviderSpecfic
OwnerName	String	The name of the user or group which will be the new owner of the object

The object type is represented by one of the following ObjectTypeEnum constants:

Constant	Value	Description
adPermObjProviderSpecific	-1	The object is of a provider-specific type. If ObjectType is set to adPermObjProviderSpecific, the ObjectTypeId parameter must be supplied.
adPermObjTable	1	The object is a table
adPermObjColumn	2	The object is a column
adPermObjDatabase	3	The object is a database
adPermObjProcedure	4	The object is a stored procedure
adPermObjView	5	The object is a view

So, to retrieve the name of the owner of a table called `authors`:

```
Dim objCat As ADOX.Catalog

Set objCat = New ADOX.Catalog
objCat.ActiveConnection = strConnectionString
strAuthorOwner = objCat.GetObjectOwner("Authors", adPermObjTable)
```

In the case of an Access database, the security database must be explicitly set in the connection string. For example:

```
strConnectionString = "Provider=Microsoft.Jet.OLEDB.4.0; " & _
                       "Data Source=C:\pubs.mdb; " & _
                       "Jet OLEDB:System database=" & _
                       "C:\Program Files\Microsoft Office 2000\Office\system.mdw;"
```

You may also need to ensure that no other users are currently accessing the workgroup file.

For example, to make a user named "Fred" the owner of the Authors table, we would use:

```
objCat.SetObjectOwner "Authors", adPermObjTable, "Fred"
```

Fred must already exist in the `Users` collection and, in the case of an Access database, the security database must be explicitly set in the connection string (as above). If we want to add a user to the `Users` collection, then we can use the `Append` method (we discuss the `Users` collection in more detail below):

```
objCat.Users.Append "Fred", "FredsNewPassword"
```

Unsupported Features

This method returns an error for providers that don't support it. Below is the error from SQL Server:

3251 – Object or provider is not capable of performing requested operation

Usually, every object in a database must have an owner; therefore you can't set the owner to a null value or `Nothing`.

ActiveConnection Property

This read-write property sets or returns an ADO `Connection` object or the corresponding connection string.

To get the current connection string we use:

```
strConn = objCat.ActiveConnection
```

And to get an ADO `Connection` object instead of a string:

```
Set objConn = objCat.ActiveConnection
```

We can also set the active connection with either a string or a `Connection` object. For example, using a string:

```
objCat.ActiveConnection = strConn
```

And to set the active connection using an ADO `Connection` object:

```
Set objCat.ActiveConnection = objConn
```

We can also close the connection by setting the `ActiveConnection` to `Nothing` (although it is better practice first to call the `Close` method):

```
Set objCat.ActiveConnection = nothing
```

Collections of the Catalog Object

As we have seen, the `Catalog` object provides access to all the other objects in the ADOX object model. Each type of individual object is accessed through a collection, and the `Catalog` object has the following five collections. These are dealt with in more detail in the next sections of this chapter:

- ❑ `Tables` –the tables in the database
- ❑ `Groups` – the group accounts in the database
- ❑ `Users` – the user accounts in the database
- ❑ `Procedures` – the stored procedures in the database
- ❑ `Views` – the views in the database

Managing Tables

We can manage the tables in the database using the `Tables` collection and the `Table` object. Each table in the database is represented by a `Table` object, and these individual `Table` objects can be managed through the `Tables` collection. Let's have a look at the collection first. This object – like all the collection objects in ADOX – has `Append`, `Delete` and `Refresh` methods, and `Item` and `Count` properties. This is a pretty standard model for all collection objects everywhere, but let's have a look some examples to demonstrate them.

The Tables Collection

As you will imagine, the `Tables` collection allows us to manage `Table` objects by enumerating through the items in the collection, adding tables to the collection and deleting them from it.

Retrieving a List of Tables

For example, if you want to retrieve a list of tables in your database an add them to a combo box called `cboTables`, you could iterate through the `Tables` collection using a `For` or `For...Each` loop:

```
Dim objTables as ADOX.Tables
Dim i as Integer
Set objTables = objCat.Tables 'objCat is our catalog
For i = 0 To objTables.Count - 1
   cboTables.AddItem objCat.Tables(i).Name
Next
```

If you don't want to show tables of a particular type, you can use the `Type` property of the `Table` object. For example:

```
For Each objTable In objTables
    If objTable.Type <> "SYSTEM TABLE" Then
        cboTables.AddItem objTable.Name & " - " & objTable.Type
    End If
Next
```

In Access, this will still show hidden tables. If you don't want these, you can use the `Properties` collection of a table and look for the `"Jet OLEDB:Table Hidden in Access"` property. For example:

```
For Each objTable In objTables
    If Not objTable.Properties("JET OLEDB:Table Hidden in Access").value Then
        cboTables.AddItem objTable.Name
    End if
Next
```

The `Properties` collection and the `Type` property are discussed in more detail below. In SQL Server, the `Tables` collection also includes all the views! If you want to filter these out, you can use the `Type` property of the `Table` object: the views will have a type of either `"VIEW"` or `"SYSTEM VIEW"`.

Creating and Deleting Tables

You can append and delete tables in your database using the `Append` and `Delete` methods of the `Tables` collection. These methods are not available for the Oracle provider.

To add a new table to the catalog, we simply pass in a predefined `Table` object into the `Append` method of the `Tables` collection:

```
Dim objNewTable As ADOX.Table

Set objNewTable = New ADOX.Table
Set objTables = objCat.Tables                     'objCat is our catalog
objNewTable.Name = "MyNewTable"                   'give the table a name
objNewTable.Columns.Append "Col1",adVarWChar,30   'give it a column
objTables.Append newtable                         'append it
```

Notice that before we append the table to the database, we first add a column to the table by calling the `Append` method of the `Columns` collection (this method should be distinguished from the `Append` method of the `Tables` collection; we will examine it shortly). Although the code would work for an Access database without appending a column, SQL Server needs more information about the table before it will append it. It is best therefore to create the columns and other objects before you append them. In addition, if you want to set provider-specific properties (such as the `"Jet OLEDB:Table Hidden in Access"` one we saw earlier) you'll need to set the `ParentCatalog` property first. We'll expand on this in a little while when looking at the `Table` object. First, though, let's see how we can delete a table. Here you just pass in either the name of the table to delete:

```
Set objTables = objCat.Tables    'objCat is our catalog
objTables.Delete "MyNewTable"    'Delete the table
```

Or the table's index position in the collection:

```
Set objTables = objCat.Tables    'objCat is our catalog
objTables.Delete (0)             'Delete the table in ordinal position 0
```

Refreshing the Tables Collection

We can update the collection to reflect the current database's schema with the `Refresh` method:

```
Set objTables = objCat.Tables  'objCat is our catalog
ObjTables.Refresh
```

The Table Object

The `Table` object represents a single table in the database. You can create a table using the `Append` method of the `Tables` collection (as shown above). A `Table` object has `Columns`, `Keys`, `Indexes` and `Properties` collections, as well as the properties `DateCreated`, `DateModified`, `Name`, `Type`, and `ParentCatalog`.

Referencing a Table

You can refer to a table using either the (zero-based) index of the `Table` object's position in the collection or the table's name. So, if `objCat` is our catalog and we want to refer to the `Authors` table we can use:

```
ObjCat.Tables("Authors")
```

Or:

```
ObjCat.Tables(2)   'if the Authors table has the ordinal position 2
```

The ordinal number is useful if you want to loop through all the tables as in the example of retrieving a list of tables above.

The DateCreated and DateModified Properties

These two read-only properties simply return a variant containing, respectively, the date the table was created and the date the table structure was last modified:

```
DateC = objCat.Tables("Authors").DateCreated
DateM = objCat.Tables("Authors").DateModified
Msgbox "Authors table first created: " & DateC & ". Last modified: " & DateM
```

The Name Property

This sets or returns the name of the table. However, for some providers (including those for SQL Server and Oracle) this property is read-only for existing tables.

```
Dim objTable as ADOX.Table
For Each objTable In objCat.Tables
   lstTables.AddItem objTable.Name 'lstTables is a listbox
Next
```

To set a table name:

```
ObjCat.Tables("Authors").Name = "AuthorsArchive"
```

The Type Property

This is a read-only property (even for a new table) that returns a string value that specifies the type of table. The provider defines the type. To determine the types available in your database consult the documentation or write a test script that loops through the tables and displays the type. For example:

```
Dim objTable as ADOX.Table
For Each objTable In objCat.Tables
    lstTables.AddItem objTable.Name & " = " & objTable.Type
Next
```

For an Access database this gave the following types:

- ❑ TABLE
- ❑ SYSTEM TABLE
- ❑ ACCESS TABLE

For a SQL Server database I had:

- ❑ TABLE
- ❑ SYSTEM TABLE
- ❑ SYSTEM VIEW
- ❑ VIEW

You will also see GLOBAL TEMPORARY for temporary tables.

The ParentCatalog Property

The read-write ParentCatalog property allows us to read or set the catalog for a table. It is useful to set this property before appending a table to the catalog if you want to set provider-specific properties. For example, if you want to create a hidden table in an Access database, you need to set the "Jet OLEDB:Table Hidden in Access" property to True. You might think we could do this with code similar to this:

```
Dim objNewTable As ADOX.Table

Set objNewTable = New ADOX.Table
objNewTable.Name = "MyNewTable"
objNewTable.Columns.Append "FirstName", adVarWChar, 25
objNewTable.Properties("Jet OLEDB:Table Hidden in Access") = True
objCat.Tables.Append objNewTable 'this will fail
```

However, dynamic properties are just that – dynamic. So the "Jet OLEDB:Table Hidden in Access" property only exists in the Properties collection of Jet databases, and if we attempt to access this property before we have specified the Jet provider, we will receive an error:

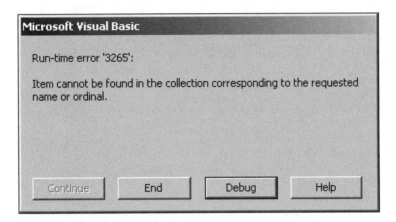

However, if we specify the `ParentCatalog` first, the Jet property we want will be available, since the `objCat Catalog` object is connected to an Access database. This code will therefore work:

```
Dim objNewTable As ADOX.Table

Set objNewTable = New ADOX.Table
objNewTable.Name = "MyNewTable"
objNewTable.Columns.Append "FirstName", adVarWChar, 25
Set objNewTable.ParentCatalog = objCat
objNewTable.Properties("Jet OLEDB:Table Hidden in Access") = True
objCat.Tables.Append objNewTable
```

Reading this property back returns a `Catalog` object.

Working with Dynamic Table Properties

Each `Table` object has a number of dynamic properties which are specific to a particular provider. As with the standard ADO dynamic properties, the ADOX dynamic properties are vital for the extensibility of ADO, as they allow each provider to expose a different set of properties.

The Properties Collection

The `Properties` collection lets us access these provider-specific dynamic table properties through a set of property objects. Since it is a collection, we can loop through it in the usual way. For example the following creates a list of all the provider-specific properties with their values for an Access table called authors, and places the list in a listbox called `lstProps`:

```
Dim objProp As ADOX.Property
For Each objProp In objCat.Tables("Authors").Properties
    lstProps.AddItem objProp.Name & " = " & objProp.Value
Next
```

In this instance this produced the following:

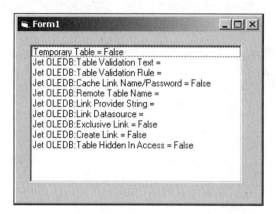

For a SQL Server catalog, the only dynamic property that I received was "temporary table", and this gave an error when trying to retrieve the value of it (3251 – Object or provider is not capable of performing requested operation). We have to assume that SQL Server 7.0 has buggy support for dynamic properties – hopefully it will be fixed in SQL Server 7.5. However, the other properties of the Property object (Attributes, and Type) were available, so the following code did work (even though it's not very useful):

```
For Each objProp In objCat.Tables("Authors").Properties
    lstProps.AddItem objProp.Name & " = " & objProp.Attributes
Next
```

This produced:

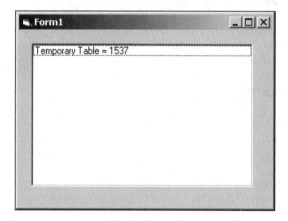

Obviously, the dynamic properties for Access databases are more useful than those for SQL Server. The Attributes and Type properties are discussed in more detail below. In particular, the Attributes property is useful for determining whether a dynamic property is read-only. A list of dynamic properties can be found in Appendix J.

Refreshing the Properties Collection

The Refresh method updates the Property objects in the Properties collection with details from the provider:

```
objCat.Tables("Authors").Properties.Refresh
```

The Count Property of the Properties Collection

The Count property simply returns the number of properties that there are in the collection:

```
Msgbox "There are " & objCat.Tables("Authors").Properties.Count & _
        " dynamic properties in the Authors table."
```

The Property Object

Each dynamic property in the Properties collection is represented by an object with four properties: Name, Type, Attributes and Value. We've seen the Name and Value properties above; they are used simply to return the name of the dynamic property and to retrieve or set the value of that property for the appropriate Table object. Let's have a look at the Attributes and Type properties.

The Attributes property returns information about the dynamic property in the form of a long value that can be one or more of the PropertyAttributesEnum values:

Constant	Value	Description
adPropNotSupported	0	The property is not supported by the provider
adPropRequired	1	The property is a required property
adPropOptional	2	The property is an optional property
adPropRead	512	The property can be read
adPropWrite	1024	The property can be set (written to)

The value is a bitmask value which is computed by adding the relevant values together. For example, for a read-only, required property the value would be $512 + 1$, or 513; and for a read-write required property the value would be $1024 + 512 + 1 = 1537$. However, if we are writing in Visual Basic, we do not need to worry about the numbers, since we can use the constants. In order to determine whether a specific value is set, we use the Boolean AND operator:

```
If objCat.Tables("Authors").Properties _
            ("Jet OLEDB:Table Hidden In Access").Attributes AND adPropWrite Then
        'property can be changed
End If
```

The Type property returns one of the DataTypeEnum that indicates the data type for the property. The ADO DataTypeEnum constants are listed in Appendix B, and a mapping of these data types to native Access and SQL Server data types can be found in Appendix E. For example, the following code will display 11, which is the value for the adBoolean constant:

```
Msgbox objCat.Tables("Authors").Properties _
                            ("Jet OLEDB:Table Hidden In Access").Type
```

Managing Columns

Each column in a database table is represented in the ADOX object model by a `Column` object and, as with the other ADOX objects, all the `Column` objects for a given table are contained within a collection. Therefore, each `Table` object has a `Columns` collection, which contains one `Column` object for each column in the table.

The Columns Collection

As with any other collection, we can loop through the `Columns` collection of a table using a `For...Each` or a `For...Next` loop. For example:

```
Dim objCol As ADOX.Column
For Each objCol In objCat.Tables("Authors").Columns
    lstColumns.AddItem objCol.Name
Next
End Sub
```

The `Columns` collection has the standard `Item` and `Count` properties and the `Refresh` method, which have been covered in other sections of this chapter. It also has the standard `Append` and `Delete` methods, but let's have a look at these in the context of a `Column`.

To create a new column, we can either create a `Column` object and append it to the `Columns` collection, or simply call the `Append` method directly and feed in the name, data type and size. The `Column` object is dealt with in detail below. Here's an example of using the `Append` method without first creating a column object (this will work in Access, but for SQL Server on an existing table you would need to define a new `Column` object first and at a minimum set the `Attributes` property to allow the new column to contain `Null` – see below):

```
objCat.Tables("Authors").Columns.Append "Birthday", adDate
```

The syntax for this method is:

```
Columns.Append Column, [Type], [DefinedSize]
```

Where:

Parameter	Description
Column	Either the `Column` object to be appended to the `Columns` collection or the name of the column to create and append.
Type	Optional. A long value that specifies the data type of the column. The `Type` parameter corresponds to the `Type` property of a `Column` object. See Appendix E for details of ADOX data types.
DefinedSize	Optional. A long value that specifies the size of the column. The `DefinedSize` parameter corresponds to the `DefinedSize` property of a `Column` object.

To delete a column, we use the `Delete` method on the `Columns` collection, passing in either the name of the column or its index position within the `Columns` collection. For example:

```
objCat.Tables("Authors").Columns.Delete "Birthday"
```

The Column Object

The Column object represents a single column (field) in a table. It has no methods, but quite a few properties (as well as a dynamic Properties collection for provider-specific properties) that we will detail below. We can create and delete columns using the Append and Delete methods of the Columns collection (see above).

We can create a Column object in the usual way:

```
Dim objCol As ADOX.Column
Set objCol = New ADOX.Column
```

The Attributes Property

This read-write property determines whether the column is fixed-length, or whether it can contain null values. Its value is comprised of the ColumnAttributesEnum constants:

Constant	Value	Description
adColFixed	1	The column is a fixed-length column, with each row containing exactly the same number of bytes or characters
adColNullable	2	The column can contain Null values

So, to specify a new column as nullable, we would write:

```
Dim objCol As ADOX.Column
Set objCol = New ADOX.Column
objCol.Attributes = adColNullable
```

To specify both of these attributes, we use bitwise operations:

```
Dim objCol As ADOX.Column
Set objCol = New ADOX.Column
objCol.Attributes = adColFixed Or adColNullable
```

Bear in mind that the fixed-length attribute may also be determined by the column's data type (e.g. char is fixed length and varChar is not).

To read an attribute back:

```
For Each objCol In objCat.Tables("Authors").Columns
    lstColumns.AddItem objCol.Name & ", Nullable = " & _
                    ((objCol.Attributes And adColNullable) = adColNullable)
Next
```

If you don't specify a value for the Attributes property, the default value is zero, which indicates that the column is variable-length and may not contain Null values.

The DefinedSize Property

This read-write property sets or retrieves the maximum size of a column as a long integer. This is applicable to variable-length columns only. For example, to set the property:

```
Dim objCol As ADOX.Column
Set objCol = New ADOX.Column
objCol.DefinedSize = 40
```

And to read the property:

```
For Each objCol In objCat.Tables("Authors").Columns
    lstColumns.AddItem objCol.Name & " - " & objCol.DefinedSize
Next
```

This property is read-only for `Column` objects which have already been appended to a collection.

The Name Property

Sets or returns the name of the column as a string. For example:

```
Dim objCol As ADOX.Column
Set objCol = New ADOX.Column
objCol.Name = "Birthday"
```

The NumericScale Property

The `NumericScale` property applies only to columns with a data type of `adNumeric` or `adDecimal`. This property sets or returns a byte value which specifies the scale for the column (the number of digits to the right of the decimal point).

```
Dim objCol As ADOX.Column
Set objCol = New ADOX.Column
objCol.Type = adNumeric
objCol.NumericScale = 4
```

This property is read-only for `Column` objects already appended to a collection.

The Precision Property

This property also applies only to numeric columns. It contains a long which specifies the maximum number of digits allowed.

```
Dim objCol As ADOX.Column
Set objCol = New ADOX.Column
objCol.Type = adNumeric
objCol.NumericScale = 4
objCol.Precision = 10
```

Again, this property is read-only for `Column` objects already appended to a collection.

ParentCatalog Property

Like the ParentCatalog property of the Table object (see above), it is useful to set this property before appending a column to a table if you want to set provider-specific (dynamic) properties. The dynamic properties are dealt with in more detail below, but here is an example of setting the "Jet OLEDB:Allow Zero Length" dynamic column property to True for an Access database. Note that this would fail if the ParentCatalog property were not set before the dynamic property.

```
Dim objCol As ADOX.Column
Set objCol = New ADOX.Column
objCol.Attributes = adColNullable
objCol.Name = "NickName"
objCol.Type = adVarWChar
objCol.DefinedSize = 20
objCol.ParentCatalog = objCat 'this needs to be set before the next line
objCol.Properties("JET OLEDB:Allow Zero Length") = True
objCat.Tables("Authors").Columns.Append objCol
```

This property is read-write and returns a Catalog object.

The RelatedColumn Property

For columns which represent a foreign key, this property specifies the name of the primary key column in the related table. Because this property applies only to key columns, we must refer to this property via a Key object, and not directly from the Table. Attempting to access this from the Table object will produce the error 3210 – Operation not allowed in this context. So the following will fail:

```
MsgBox objCat.Tables("titleauthor").Columns("Au_id").RelatedColumn 'will fail.
```

Instead, you must first create or reference a Key object and set that object's RelatedTable property. You can then set the property by referencing the key you have created:

```
MsgBox objCat.Tables("titleauthor").Keys(0).Columns("Au_id").RelatedColumn
```

This will give you the related column to the first key in the titleauthor table. Details of the Keys collection and Key object are given below.

You can set this property only on columns that haven't yet been appended to the collection.

SortOrder Property

This property specifies whether an index column is to be sorted in ascending or descending order. As with the RelatedColumn property, this property does not apply to all columns in a table and therefore cannot be accessed directly through a Table object. You must refer to this property via an Index object, otherwise you will get the error 3210 – Operation not allowed in this context.

```
MsgBox objCat.Tables("Titleauthor").Indexes(0).Columns("Au_id").SortOrder
```

To set this property, first create an Index object and then set the sort order of one of the columns in the index. Details of the Indexes collection and the Index object are given later on in this chapter.

The property sets or returns a `SortOrderEnum` as shown in the table:

Constant	Value	Description
adSortAscending	1	The column is sorted in ascending order (the default)
adSortDescending	2	The column is sorted in descending order

The Type Property

This property sets or returns a long value that can be one of the `DataTypeEnum` constants. The default value is `adVarWChar`. The `DataTypeEnum` constants are listed in Appendix B. Note that not all data types are supported by different providers, so refer to Appendix E as a guide to the types you can use with different providers (for example, a date field in Access is `adDate` where as in SQL Server it is `adDBTimeStamp`). A list of the ADO `DataTypeEnum` constants with equivalents for Access, SQL Server, Oracle, VB and VC can also be found at `http://www.able-consulting.com/ADODataTypeEnum.htm`.

This property can only be set for columns that have not yet been appended to the `Columns` collection.

Working with Dynamic Column Properties

The dynamic properties of a `Column` object work in much the same way as those for a `Table` object: each `Column` object has a `Properties` collection which contains one `Property` object for each available provider-specific property. Below is an example of the dynamic provider-specific properties for an Access database. Bear in mind that dynamic property support in SQL Server version 7 is not complete. We can iterate through the collection in the usual way:

```
Dim objProp As ADOX.Property
For Each objProp In objCat.Tables("Authors").Columns("Author").Properties
    lstProps.AddItem objProp.Name & " = " & objProp.Value
Next
```

This produces the following:

Managing Indexes

An index is a feature used to speed up searching and sorting in a table when the field that is indexed is used as a search criterion. The flip side is that an index slows down creation of new records. However, you should not simply equate adding indexes with good performance on a query – there are other factors to include too. For example, it is better to have a query that uses a single statement rather than sub queries, and the order of fields used in the index can have an impact on the effectiveness of the query if the order used in the WHERE clause is different. SQL Server 7.0 has an Index Tuning Wizard that can help you produce effective indexes and there is plenty of information in Books Online on designing indexes (search for "Designing an Index" and "Index Tuning Recommendations"). Access 2000, too, has the Performance Analyzer and information on designing indexes in the **Working with Primary Keys and Indexes** section in the online help. For other providers, please consult the vendor documentation.

The Indexes Collection

This is a collection of all the indexes within a specified table. It supports the standard collection methods (Delete and Refresh) and properties (Item and Count) that you should be familiar with by now. As usual, we can iterate through the collection to manipulate each Index object for a given table. For example, this code adds to a listbox the Name of each Index object in a table called Title Author:

```
Dim objIndex As ADOX.Index
For Each objIndex In objCat.Tables("Title Author").Indexes
    lstIndexes.AddItem (objIndex.Name)
Next
```

And to display how many indexes there are on this table:

```
Dim objIndex As ADOX.Index
Msgbox objCat.Tables("Title Author").Indexes.Count
```

To add an Index to a table, we use the Indexes collection's Append method. This takes the syntax:

```
Indexes.Append Index, [Columns]
```

Where:

Parameter	Description
Index	Either the Index object which is to be appended to the Indexes collection, or the name of a new index to be created and appended.
Columns	Optional. A variant value that specifies the name of the column to be indexed. This parameter corresponds to the value of the Name property of a Column object.

So, to create an index on the Au_fname field in the Authors table without creating an Index object first, we would write:

```
objCat.Tables("Authors").Indexes.Append "NewIndex","Au_fname"
```

An array of column names can be passed in the second parameter if you want an index based on more than one column:

```
objCat.Tables("Titles").Indexes.Append "TitleISBN", Array("Title", "ISBN")
```

However, it is preferable to create an Index object first and then specify the columns in that, because this method allows us to specify some important properties of the Index object such as Clustered or Unique. For example (the Index object is dealt with in more detail below):

```
Dim objIndex As ADOX.Index
Set objIndex = New ADOX.Index
objIndex.Name = "AuthorFLName"
objIndex.Unique = False
objIndex.Columns.Append ("Au_fname")
objIndex.Columns.Append ("Au_lname")
objCat.Tables("Authors").Indexes.Append objIndex
```

To delete an index, we use the Delete method, again passing in either the name of the index, or its position in the Indexes collection:

```
objCat.Tables("Authors").Indexes.Delete "AuthorFLName"
```

The Index Object

This represents a single Index in a table. It has no methods and five properties detailed below. In addition, it has Columns and Properties collections.

The Clustered Property

A table can only have one clustered index, and it is this index which determines the storage order of data in a table. You should consider carefully which index you would like clustered in a table. It is not just an obvious choice of the field(s) you query on most often. Bear the following in mind:

❑ A clustered index is very efficient on columns that are often searched on for a **range of values**, because after the first value is found the next values will be physically adjacent to the found one. For example, a clustered index on a date field that was often queried as a range ("between start date and end date") would be efficient.

❑ Clustered indexes are efficient for finding a specific row when the indexed value is **unique.**

❑ A clustered index is not efficient on columns that undergo frequent changes, because this results in the entire row moving as the database resorts the rows so they are in the correct physical order.

❑ Although a clustered index can contain multiple columns, it's better to have as few columns as possible. This limits the IO needed when a value in one of those columns changes.

❑ The primary key (see below) is automatically created as the clustered index unless you specify otherwise.

The Clustered property contains a Boolean value. You can only set it on indexes that have not yet been appended to the Index collection, and it will fail if an existing clustered index already exists in the table – you will need to delete that index first.

```
Dim objIndex As ADOX.Index
Set objIndex = New ADOX.Index
Dim objOldCIndex As ADOX.Index

'First find and delete the existing clustered index
'Ideally you would then recreate this index with the
'clustered property as false
For Each objOldCIndex In objCat.Tables("Authors").Indexes
    If objOldCIndex.Clustered = True Then
        objCat.Tables("Authors").Indexes.Delete objOldCIndex.Name
        'the delete may fail if other contraints in the table deny it.
        Exit For
    End If
Next

'Build the new clustered index
objIndex.Name = "AuthorFLName"
objIndex.Unique = False
objIndex.Columns.Append ("Au_fname")
objIndex.Columns.Append ("Au_lname")
objIndex.Clustered = True
objCat.Tables("Authors").Indexes.Append objIndex
```

The `Clustered` property is read-only for Access databases with a primary key (since the primary key is automatically set as a clustered index).

The IndexNulls Property

This property indicates whether null values will be included in the index. The property can be one of the four `AllowNullsEnum` constants:

Constant	Value	Description
adIndexNullsAllow	0	Entries in which the key columns are `Null` are permitted in the index. If a null value is entered in a key column, the entry is inserted into the index.
adIndexNullsDisallow	1	The index does not allow entries in which the key columns are null. If a null value is entered in a key column, an error will occur. This is the default value.
adIndexNullsIgnore	2	Entries containing null keys are not inserted into the index. If a null value is entered in a key column, the entry is ignored and no error occurs.
adIndexNullsIgnoreAny	4	Entries where some key column has a null value are not inserted into the index. For an index with a multi-column key, if a null value is entered in any column, the entry is ignored and no error occurs. This value is not supported by the Jet provider.

This property is read-only in SQL Server 7.0 and will always return 1. Below is an example of setting the property for the Jet provider:

```
Dim objIndex As ADOX.Index
Set objIndex = New ADOX.Index
objIndex.Name = "AuthorFLName"
objIndex.Unique = False
```

```
objIndex.Columns.Append ("Au_fname")
objIndex.Columns.Append ("Au_lname")
objIndex.IndexNulls = adIndexNullsAllow
objCat.Tables("Authors").Indexes.Append objIndex
```

This property is read-only on Index objects already appended to a collection.

The Name Property

This is simply the name of the index. It is read-write for new indexes and for indexes already appended to the Indexes collection. However, I found that trying to change the name of an existing Index object in SQL Server generated an error (Index Already Exists).

The PrimaryKey Property

Indicates whether the index is the primary key of the table. It is a Boolean value. When choosing which column(s) to use as the primary key, you should bear the following in mind:

❑ The primary key is the index whose values uniquely identify each record in the table, so choose it carefully.

❑ Primary keys are also used to create relationships between tables.

❑ Specifying that an index is the primary key will automatically append it to the Keys collection (see below) of the table with a type of adKeyPrimary.

❑ There can only be one primary key index in each table.

❑ You can't delete a primary key index if it is participating in a relationship – you will need to delete the relationship first – this is done using the Keys collection and Key object (see below).

❑ Setting the PrimaryKey value to True will also set the Unique property to True. You cannot have an index that is not unique and is the primary key.

❑ You can only change the PrimaryKey property on Index objects not yet appended to the Indexes collection.

❑ The default value is False.

The following code creates a new index as the primary key:

```
Dim objIndex As ADOX.Index
Set objIndex = New ADOX.Index
objIndex.Name = "AuthorFLName"
objIndex.Columns.Append ("Au_fname")
objIndex.Columns.Append ("Au_lname")
objIndex.PrimaryKey = True
objCat.Tables("Authors").Indexes.Append objIndex
```

The Unique Property

This specifies that the index must contain unique values: no two rows in the table may have the same value in the index column, or, for a mutli-column index, the same combination of values in the indexed columns. The Unique property is read-write for new indexes, but read-only for indexes that are already appended to the Indexes collection. The default value is False, although primary key indexes are always unique. Specifying that an Index is unique will automatically add it to the Keys collection with a type of adKeyUnique.

Creating an index that is unique is also a good way of removing duplicates from a table. For example, let's say you have bought two mailing lists of names and addresses; you want to merge them together and throw out the duplicates. First, you need to define what is a duplicate for this situation – you may decide that any record with the same Company Name and Postcode constitutes a duplicate. Now create an empty table with an index containing these two fields and make the index unique. If you insert the data from the two mailing lists into this table it will throw out any duplicates as they are inserted.

Here is an example of creating a unique index:

```
Dim objIndex As ADOX.Index
Set objIndex = New ADOX.Index
objIndex.Name = "AuthorFLName"
objIndex.Columns.Append ("Au_fname")
objIndex.Columns.Append ("Au_lname")
objIndex.Unique = True
objCat.Tables("Authors").Indexes.Append objIndex
```

The Columns Collection for Index Objects

As we have seen in the above examples, each `Index` object has a `Columns` collection. This collection represents the columns used in the index. Refer to the section on "Managing Columns" for details of this collection and the `Columns` object. In particular, the `SortOrder` property of a column specifies how an index is sorted.

The Properties Collection for Index Objects

As we have seen for other objects, each provider can supply its own dynamic properties for various objects. An index can also have these dynamic properties. Here is a list of provider-specific properties from an Access database:

```
Dim objProp As ADOX.Property
For Each objProp In objCat.Tables("Authors").Indexes("AuthorFLName").Properties
    lstProps.AddItem objProp.Name
Next
```

This produced the following output:

For a SQL Server database, the same code produced the following list:

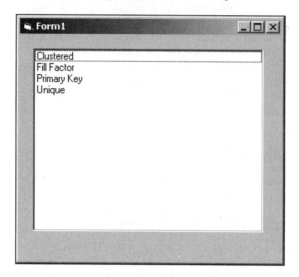

There is obviously some overlap here with these dynamic properties and the ADOX ones. Most of them here, however, are read-only (you can determine which by looking at the Attributes property – see previous sections on dynamic properties for details). You can read the Name, Value, Type and Attributes of the property. For details of these properties, see the section above on "Working with Dynamic Table Properties".

Managing Keys

A key is a special type of index, and there are three types of keys:

- ❑ **Primary Key** – used to identify each record in the table uniquely and to create relationships between tables. This can also be set by changing the PrimaryKey property of the Index object. See that section above for more details on Primary Keys.

- ❑ **Foreign Key** – Relationships between two tables are created by relating a primary key in one table with a matching foreign key in one or more related tables. The foreign key does not need to have the same name as the primary key, but it does need to be the same datatype, and each entry in a foreign key column must be identical to an entry in the primary column in the related table.

- ❑ **Unique Key** – A unique key indicates that only unique values may exist in the column: no two rows may have identical values in this column. Again, this can be set using the Unique property of the Index object; alternatively, we can create a Key object. Primary key fields are always unique.

The type of key is in indicated by the Type property (see below).

In ADOX, every key is represented by a Key object. Just like an Index object, a Key object contains a collection of Column objects. The RelatedColumn property of a column can only be accessed when you examine a column as part of a key. For example, we cannot use this code to access a Column object's RelatedColumn property:

```
MsgBox objCat.Tables("titleauthor").Columns("Au_id").RelatedColumn
```

Instead, we must refer to the Key object thus:

```
MsgBox objCat.Tables("titleauthor").Keys(0).Columns("Au_id").RelatedColumn
```

This will return the related column for the first key in the titleauthor table.

The Keys Collection

This is a collection of all the Key objects within a specified table. It supports the standard collection methods (Delete and Refresh) and properties (Item and Count), which you should be familiar with by now. The Append method is used to add a new Key to the collection and has the following syntax:

```
Keys.Append Key, [KeyType], [Column], [RelatedTable], [RelatedColumn]
```

Where:

Parameter	Description
Key	The Key object which is to be appended to the Keys collection, or the name of the key which is to be created and appended
KeyType	Optional. A long value that specifies whether the key is a primary, foreign or unique key.
Column	Optional. The name of the column to be indexed, or an array of column names. The Column parameter corresponds to the value of the Name property of a Column object.
RelatedTable	Optional. The name of the related table. The RelatedTable parameter corresponds to the value of the Name property of a Table object.
RelatedColumn	Optional. The name of the related column for a foreign key. The RelatedColumn parameter corresponds to the value of the Name property of a Column object.

Creating a New Key

Although you can create a new key in a single line as detailed above, I found more success with creating a Key object first, as in the following example:

```
Dim objKey As ADOX.Key
Set objKey = New ADOX.Key
objKey.Name = "NewKey"
objKey.Columns.Append ("Au_fname")
objKey.Columns.Append ("Au_lname")
objKey.Type = adKeyUnique
objCat.Tables("Authors").Keys.Append objKey
```

To delete the key, use the `Delete` method of the `Keys` collection:

```
objCat.Tables("Authors").Keys.Delete ("NewKey")
```

The Key Object

Each primary, foreign and unique key in a table is represented by a `Key` object in the ADOX object model. This object exposes a number of properties for managing the key and the table relationship that the key represents. We can use this object to create a relationship between two tables in a database (we will see how to do this shortly).

The Name Property

This read-write property contains a string value representing the name of the key. However, it is read-only on `Key` objects already appended to a collection.

```
Dim objKey As ADOX.Key
Set objKey = New ADOX.Key
objKey.Name = "NewKey"
```

The Type Property

Reads or sets the type of key (whether the key is a primary, foreign or unique key) from one of three `KeyTypeEnum` constants:

Constant	Value	Description
adKeyPrimary	1	The key is a primary key (default).
adKeyForeign	2	The key is a foreign key.
adKeyUnique	3	The key is a unique key.

Again, this property is read-only on `Key` objects already appended to a collection:

```
Dim objKey As ADOX.Key
Set objKey = New ADOX.Key
objKey.Type = adKeyUnique
```

The Columns Collection for a Key Object

A `Key` object has a collection of columns that are included in it. For example, to create a new `Unique` key on the au_lname and au_fname columns:

```
Dim objKey As ADOX.Key
Set objKey = New ADOX.Key
objKey.Name = "NewKey"
objKey.Columns.Append ("Au_fname")
objKey.Columns.Append ("Au_lname")
objKey.Type = adKeyUnique
objCat.Tables("Authors").Keys.Append objKey
```

When creating a foreign key, the column(s) in the key will need to have a `RelatedColumn` property indicating the primary key for the related table. See the section on "Creating a Relationship" below for more details on this.

The RelatedTable Property

This property contains a string value which is used to set or return the name of the related table for a foreign key. See the "Creating a Relationship" section for more details on this.

The DeleteRule Property

Deleting an entry in a table with a primary key column could potentially cause data integrity conflicts (because we can be left with foreign keys in other tables which have no corresponding primary key), so we need a way to specify what action to take when this occurs. We can do this with the `DeleteRule` property; this property specifies what is to happen when a a primary key is deleted. This property is read-only for `Key` objects already appended to a collection. Its value can be one of four `RuleEnum` constants:

Constant	Value	Description
adRINone	0	No action is taken; this is the default, but may mean that the delete fails, since referential integrity could be broken.
adRICascade	1	Cascade changes. For example, deleting a record will cause all related records in related tables also to be deleted.
adRISetNull	2	The value of the foreign key column(s) in the related table will be set to null.
adRISetDefault	3	The value of the foreign key column(s) in the related table will be set to the default value for the column.

The following code causes any deletions to be cascaded to all related records in other tables:

```
Dim objKey As ADOX.Key
Set objKey = New ADOX.Key
objKey.Name = "PrimaryKey"
objKey.Columns.Append ("Au_ID")
objKey.Type = adKeyPrimary
objKey.DeleteRule = adRICascade
objCat.Tables("Authors").Keys.Append objKey
```

The UpdateRule Property

This is similar to the `DeleteRule` property, but indicates what will happen when a value in a primary key field is updated rather than deleted. Again, this is read-only on `Key` objects already appended to a collection and can be one of the four `RuleEnum` constants:

Constant	Value	Description
adRINone	0	No action is taken; this is the default, but may mean that the delete fails, since referential integrity could be broken.
adRICascade	1	Cascade changes. For example, deleting a record will cause all related records in related tables also to be deleted.
adRISetNull	2	The value of the foreign key column(s) in the related table will be set to null.
adRISetDefault	3	The value of the foreign key column(s) in the related table will be set to the default value for the column.

Creating a Relationship

To create a relationship between two tables using ADOX, there are two basic steps:

1. Create a primary key in one table

2. Create a foreign key in the related table with the following properties:

- ❑ These keys must contain columns of the same data type as the primary key
- ❑ The `RelatedTable` property must be set to the name of the table for the primary key
- ❑ The `RelatedColumn` property of the column(s) in the key must be set to the name of the primary key column

Let's run through an example from scratch, creating two tables and relating them together. This code first creates a `Company` table with two columns: `CompanyName` and `CompanyID`, which is the primary key. Then we create a `Contacts` table with three columns: `ContactName`, `ContactID` (the primary key) and `lnkCompanyID`, which is the foreign key that links to the `Company` table and the `CompanyID` column. This code assumes that the `objCat` catalog is already pointing to a valid connection to the Jet 4.0 Provider.

```
Dim objTableComps As New ADOX.Table
Dim objTableContacts As New ADOX.Table
Dim objColCompName As New ADOX.Column
Dim objColCompID As New ADOX.Column
Dim objColContName As New ADOX.Column
Dim objColContID As New ADOX.Column
Dim objColContFK As New ADOX.Column
Dim objPKeyComp As New ADOX.Key
Dim objPKeyCont As New ADOX.Key
Dim objFKey As New ADOX.Key

'Create and append the Primary table
objTableComps.Name = "Company"
objCat.Tables.Append objTableComps

'Create and append column 1
objColCompName.Name = "CompanyName"
objColCompName.Type = adVarWChar
objColCompName.DefinedSize = 30
objTableComps.Columns.Append objColCompName

'Create and Append column 2
objColCompID.Name = "CompanyID"
objColCompID.Type = adInteger
objTableComps.Columns.Append objColCompID

'Create and append Primary Key on col2
objPKeyComp.Name = "PKCompany"
objPKeyComp.Type = adKeyPrimary
objPKeyComp.Columns.Append "CompanyID"
objTableComps.Keys.Append objPKeyComp

'Create and Append the Related Table
objTableContacts.Name = "Contacts"
objCat.Tables.Append objTableContacts

'Create and append column 1
objColContName.Name = "ContactName"
objColContName.Type = adVarWChar
objColContName.DefinedSize = 30
objTableContacts.Columns.Append objColContName
```

```
'Create and Append column 2
objColContID.Name = "ContactID"
objColContID.Type = adInteger
objTableContacts.Columns.Append objColContID

'Create and Append column 3
objColContFK.Name = "lnkCompanyID"
objColContFK.Type = adInteger
objTableContacts.Columns.Append objColContFK

'Create and append Primary Key on col2
objPKeyCont.Name = "PKContact"
objPKeyCont.Type = adKeyPrimary
objPKeyCont.Columns.Append "ContactID"
objTableContacts.Keys.Append objPKeyCont

'Create and append Foriegn Key on col 3
objFKey.Name = "FKCompany"
objFKey.Type = adKeyForeign
objFKey.Columns.Append "lnkCompanyID"
objFKey.Columns("lnkCompanyID").RelatedColumn = "CompanyID"
objFKey.RelatedTable = "Company"
objTableContacts.Keys.Append objFKey
```

Viewed in Access 2000, our relationship looks like this:

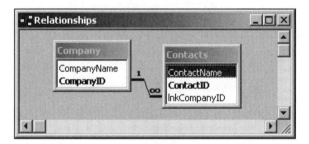

Managing Stored Procedures and Views

The `Procedures` collection represents the stored procedures in the catalog. A stored procedure is a precompiled collection of code such as SQL statements and optional control-of-flow statements that are a feature of SQL Server and Oracle, but not of Access.

The `Views` collection represents the views in a catalog. A view is a filtered set of records or a virtual table. In SQL Server, these are called views; they are similar to Saved Queries in Access. However, they are not exactly the same, as we shall see.

Creating views and stored procedures through ADOX is not supported by the SQL Server Provider, but this can be done through SQL-DMO or through the CREATE PROCEDURE and CREATE VIEW SQL statements. Conversely, you *can* create views and stored procedures in ADOX using the Jet 4.0 Provider, but Access doesn't support them through its usual UI! This is all a bit strange. When you create a stored procedure or view in Access, it actually stores it in the hidden system MSysObjects table with a type of 5, but you won't be able to see it anywhere in the Access Database Window or use it within Access without writing ADO code. You could consider this to be a benefit – an easy way to hide destructive procedures from users, perhaps (but don't think it replaces implementing security properly). The views and stored procedures do, however, show up in the Data View window in the Microsoft Visual Database Tools (supplied with Visual Basic and Visual InterDev).

However, just to confuse things further I found that this **Data View** window could move views and procedures around from one category to the next; that is, if you create a view with a command that has a parameter, it will become a stored procedure, and if you create a stored procedure with no parameters, it shows up in the **Views** folder. I found that this was sometimes reflected in the ADOX collections and sometimes not! All in all, this is a peculiar state of affairs. However, once you are aware that views and procedures within Access are really the same thing, that they can't have the same name, and you get over the fact that they can sometimes appear to move from one collection to another, then they could certainly be useful. So let's get on and have a look at the code.

Creating Views and Procedures

Creating these objects is slightly different to the other ADOX objects we have seen so far. We can't use the `New` keyword to create a new instance of these objects and then append it to the collection thus:

```
Dim objView as New ADOX.View 'this won't work
Dim objProc as New ADOX.Proc 'neither will this
```

This will produce a compile error.

Instead, we must create an ADO `Command` object and use that to create a new `View` or `Procedure` (so you'll need to add a reference to ADO 2.5 in your project):

```
Dim objCommand As ADODB.Command

Set objCommand = New ADODB.Command
objCommand.CommandText = "SELECT * FROM authors ORDER BY au_lname"

objCat.Views.Append "AuthorsByLNameView", objCommand
```

This creates a new view called `AuthorsByLNameView` which we can execute using ADO:

```
Dim objRS As ADODB.Recordset
Dim objCmd As ADODB.Command

Set objCmd = New ADODB.Command
objCmd.ActiveConnection = objCat.ActiveConnection
objCmd.CommandText = "AuthorsByLNameView"
Set objRS = objCmd.Execute
```

Creating a `Procedure` is similar, but of course we use the `Procedures` collection rather than the `Views` collection. Access will accept input parameters in the procedure, but not output parameters.

```
Dim objProc As ADOX.Procedure
Dim objCommand As ADODB.Command
Dim objParam As ADODB.Parameter

Set objCommand = New ADODB.Command
Set objParam = New ADODB.Parameter

objParam.Name = "lastname"
objParam.Type = adVarWChar
objParam.Size = 20
objParam.Direction = adParamInput

objCommand.CommandText = "SELECT * FROM Authors WHERE au_lname = @lname "
objCommand.Parameters.Append objParam

objCat.Procedures.Append "AuthorsByLNameProc", objCommand
```

We could then execute it using ADO as in this example:

```
Dim objRS As ADODB.Recordset
Dim objCmd As ADODB.Command

Set objCmd = New ADODB.Command
objCmd.ActiveConnection = objCat.ActiveConnection
objCmd.CommandText = "AuthorsByLNameProc"
Set objRS = objCmd.Execute(, Array("Dull"))
```

To delete a `View` or `Procedure`, we use the `Delete` method of the appropriate collection:

```
objCat.Views.Delete "AuthorsByLNameView"
```

The Collections

These are standard collection objects as detailed elsewhere in this chapter. SQL Server is capable of showing the `Procedures` collection, but not the `Views`. However, `Views` are displayed as part of the `Tables` collection in SQL Server!

```
Dim objView As ADOX.View
lstViews.Clear
For Each objView In objCat.Views
    lstViews.AddItem objView.Name
Next
```

```
Dim objProc As ADOX.Procedure
lstProcs.Clear
For Each objProc In objCat.Procedures
    lstProcs.AddItem objProc.Name
Next
```

The Procedure and View Objects

These objects have no methods and the same four properties. If you have just appended a new object, then to get true values for the `DateModified` and `DateCreated` properties you will need to call the `Refresh` method on the collection. The four properties are:

❑   `Name` – the name as a string

❑   `DateCreated` (read-only) – the date that the object was created

❑   `DateModified` (read-only) – the date that the object was last modified

❑   `Command` – sets or returns the ADO `Command` object on which the `View` or `Procedure` is based. We saw above how we need to set this property when we create a new stored procedure or view. Reading the `Command` property returns a `Command` object with its `CommandText` set to the SQL statements executed by the view/procedure:

```
Dim objProc As ADOX.Procedure
Dim objCom As ADODB.Command

'get the command object
Set objCom = objCat.Procedures("AuthorsByLNameProc").Command
'show the text of the command
MsgBox objCom.CommandText
```

Managing Security

Security in ADOX is currently only supported by the Jet provider and not by SQL Server or Oracle. Jet security relies on a security database called the **Workgroup Information File**. By default, this is a file called `system.mdw` installed in `C:\Program Files\Microsoft Office\Office\system.mdw` (depending, of course, on the location of your Office installment). However, do not use this file if you want to make your database truly secure; since it is the same file that is distributed with every copy of Access, simply using this file is a security hazard. Instead, create a new `.mdw` file using either the **User-Level Security Wizard** in Access or the **MS Access Workgroup Administrator** utility that ships with Access (and will be installed in your Microsoft Office folder by default). For more information on security in Access, search the Access on-line help for `"Security"`.

This single `.mdw` (workgroup information) file can be used by multiple MDB files and contains the profiles of users and groups of users, together with related SIDs (Security Identifiers). These SIDs then act as keys to unlock objects within the MDBs.

ADOX cannot create the workgroup information file; instead we *must* specify an existing one as part of the connection string for our catalog, if we want to manage security through ADOX:

```
Dim objCat As ADOX.Catalog
Set objCat = New ADOX.Catalog
strcon = "Provider=Microsoft.Jet.OLEDB.4.0;Data Source=C:\pubs.mdb;"
strcon = strcon & "Jet OLEDB:System database=" & _
                "D:\Program Files\Microsoft Office\Office\system.mdw"
objCat.ActiveConnection = strConn
```

We can then use ADOX to manage groups and users in the workgroup file and to manage permissions on the objects in the database we are working with.

Working with Groups and Users

You won't be surprised to learn that each user profile in the workgroup information file is represented in ADOX by a User object, and every group by a Group object, and you'll be even less surprised that these User and Group objects are contained within a Users and a Groups collection. You can view this information from different perspectives. For example, each Group contains a Users collection, which represents the users in that Group, and each User object has a Groups collection to represent the groups to which that user belongs. Because of this circular relationship, you need to be very careful when using recursion on these objects!

The collections are again standard collections with the normal methods and properties. The Append method as usual has a slightly different syntax for each object. Here's how you append a Group to the collection using a string:

```
objCat.Groups.Append "Trainers"
```

Or by creating a Group object first:

```
Dim objGroup As ADOX.Group
Set objGroup = New ADOX.Group
objGroup.Name = "Trainers"
objCat.Groups.Append objGroup
```

And to then add some users to the group:

```
objGroup.Users.Append "Paul"
objGroup.Users.Append "John"
```

Note that you have to append the Users after you have appended the Group, and that "John" and "Paul" must already exist in the Catalog's Users collection.

To create a User, we also use the Append method of the Users collection, but this time we use the Users collection of the Catalog object. We can pass into this either strings containing the user's name and password:

```
objCat.Users.Append "Fred", "password"
```

Or a predefined User object:

```
Dim objUser As ADOX.User
Set objUser = New ADOX.User
objUser.Name = "Paul"
objUser.ChangePassword "", "password"
objCat.Users.Append objUser
```

Notice that to set the password using this syntax, we have to use the ChangePassword method of the User object. The password is an empty string if not explicitly set. To add this User to a Group, we call the Append method of its Groups collection:

```
objUser.Groups.Append "Trainers"
```

We have to do this after we have appended the User to the Users collection, and the Group must already exist in the Catalog's Groups collection.

To delete a Group or User, we call the Delete method of the collection in question. So, to delete a user from the Catalog completely:

```
Objcat.Users.Delete("Paul")
```

But to remove a user from a group, we must delete them from the Group's Users collection:

```
ObjCat.Groups("Trainers").Users.Delete ("Paul")
```

This still leaves "Paul" as a user in the Catalog and any other groups he currently belongs to, but removes him from the "Trainers" group.

Changing a User's Password

To change a user's password, we call the ChangePassword method of the User object:

```
Dim objUser As ADOX.User
Set objUser = objCat.Users("Paul")
objUser.ChangePassword "password", "guitar"
```

Notice that we can't read a password; we can only change it.

User and Group Permissions

We can treat Users and Groups the same programmatically with respect to the permissions we grant and deny them. However, in real terms it is far easier if you can only set group permissions, since once you start setting permissions for individual users it can quickly become hard to manage and keep track of which users have specific permissions. I typically like to keep the smallest number of groups I can and assign permissions only to those groups, not to individuals. This makes it far easier to deal with users that change roles – you just append them to the new group, or delete them from the collection altogether. Both the User and the Group objects have the following methods:

The GetPermissions Method

This method reads the permissions of an object in the database. It returns a bitmask long value consisting of one or more of the RightsEnum constants and indicates the permissions that the user has on the specified object.

```
Long = GroupOrUser.GetPermissions(Name, ObjectType, [ObjectTypeId])
```

Where:

Name	DataType	Description
Name	Variant	The name of the object for which the permissions will be returned. If Name is set to a null value, the permissions for the object container will be returned.
ObjectType	Long	One of the ObjectTypeEnum constants, which specifies the type of the object.
ObjectTypeId	Variant	The GUID for a provider-specific object which is not defined by the OLE DB specification. This parameter is required if ObjectType is set to adPermObjProviderSpecific; otherwise, it is not used.

For example, to get permissions on the Authors table for the Trainers group and then see if they can read and write to the table design:

```
Dim objGroup As ADOX.Group
Dim lngPerm As Long
Set objGroup = objCat.Groups("Trainers")
lngPerm = objGroup.GetPermissions("Authors", adPermObjTable)
If (lngPerm And adRightReadDesign = adRightReadDesign) And _
              (lngPerm And adRightWriteDesign = adRightWriteDesign) Then
   MsgBox "Trainers can read from and write to the design of the authors table"
Else
   MsgBox "Trainers can't modify the design of the authors table"
End If
```

To check for permissions on the Tables container in this example, substitute Null for the name:

```
lngPerm = objGroup.GetPermissions(Null, adPermObjTable)
```

The `RightsEnum` constants are:

Constant	Value	Description
adRightRead	-2147483648 (&H80000000)	The user or group has permission to read data from the object.
adRightNone	0	The user or group has no permissions on the specified object.
adRightReadDesign	1024 (&H400)	The user or group has permission to read the design for the object.
adRightUpdate	1073741824 (&H40000000)	The user or group has permission to perform UPDATEs on the object.
adRightReadPermissions	131072 (&H20000)	The user or group has permission to read the permissions for the specified object in the catalog.
adRightCreate	16384 (&H4000)	The user or group has permission to create new objects of this type.
adRightWriteDesign	2048 (&H800)	The user or group has permission to alter the design for the object.
adRightDrop	256 (&H100)	The user or group has permission to drop the specified object from the catalog.
adRightWritePermissions	262144 (&H40000)	The user or group has permission to set the permissions for the object in the catalog.
adRightFull	268435456 (&H10000000)	The user or group has full permissions on the specified object.
adRightInsert	32768 (&H8000)	The user or group has permission to perform INSERTs on the object.
adRightMaximumAllowed	33554432 (&H2000000)	The user or group has the maximum number of permissions allowed by the provider.
adRightWithGrant	4096 (&H1000)	The user or group has permission to grant permissions to other users or groups on the object.
adRightExclusive	512 (&H200)	The user or group has permission to access the specified object exclusively.
adRightWriteOwner	524288 (&H80000)	The user or group has permission to change the owner of the object.
adRightExecute	536870912 (&H20000000)	The user or group has permission to execute the specified object.
adRightDelete	65536 (&H10000)	The user or group has permission to delete data from the specified object.
adRightReference	8192 (&H2000)	The user or group has permission to reference the object.

The `ObjectTypeEnum` constants are:

Constant	Value	Description
adPermObjProviderSpecific	-1	The object is of a provider-specific type. If the `ObjectType` parameter is set to `adPermObjProviderSpecific`, then the `ObjectTypeId` parameter must also be specified.
adPermObjTable	1	The object is a table.
adPermObjColumn	2	The object is a column.
adPermObjDatabase	3	The object is a database.
adPermObjProcedure	4	The object is a stored procedure.
adPermObjView	5	The object is a view.

The SetPermissions Method

This method also works in exactly the same way for both `User` and `Group` objects:

```
GroupOrUser.SetPermissions Name, ObjectType, Action, Rights, [Inherit], _
                           [ObjectTypeId]
```

Where:

Name	DataType	Description
Name	Variant	The name of the object for which the permissions will be returned. If `Name` is set to a null value, the permissions for the object container will be returned.
ObjectType	Long	One of the `ObjectTypeEnum` constants, which specifies the type of the object.
Action	Long	One of the `ActionEnum` constants; this specifies whether the permissions are to be granted, denied, set or revoked (see below).
Rights	Long	A bitmask of one or more of the `RightsEnum` constants; this indicates the permissions that will be granted or denied.
Inherit	Long	Optional. One of the `InheritTypeEnum` constants; this parameter specifies the inheritence behavior for these permissions. The default is `adInheritNone`.
ObjectTypeId	Variant	The GUID for a provider-specific object which is not defined by the OLE DB specification. This parameter is required if `ObjectType` is set to `adPermObjProviderSpecific`; otherwise, it is not used.

For example, to grant the `Trainers` group permission to read and write to the design of the `Authors` table and leave all other permissions at their ciurrent settings, and to specify that permissions for other objects and containers in the `Authors` table (e.g. columns) will inherit these permissions:

```
Dim objGroup As ADOX.Group
Set objGroup = objCat.Groups("Trainers")
objGroup.SetPermissions "Authors", adPermObjTable, adAccessGrant, _
                    adRightWriteDesign + adRightReadDesign, adInheritBoth
```

Again, we can substitute the name of the object with `Null` if we want to set permissions for the collection.

The `ActionEnum` constants are:

Constant	Value	Description
adAccessGrant	1	Grant the specified permissions to the user or group. This does not affect other permissions.
AdAccessSet	2	Grant exactly the specified permissions to the user or group. This will overwrite any existing permissions.
adAccessDeny	3	Deny the specified permissions to the user or group.
adAccessRevoke	4	Revoke any permissions for the user or group.

The `InheritTypeEnum` constants are:

Constant	Value	Description
adInheritNone	0	The permissions are not inherited (the default).
AdInheritObjects	1	The permissions are inherited by non-container objects.
adInheritContainers	2	The permissions are inherited by other containers.
adInheritBoth	3	The permissions are inherited both by objects and by other containers.
adInheritNoPropagate	4	The `adInheritObjects` and `adInheritContainers` flags are not propagated to an inherited entry.

The Role of SQL-DMO

Because support for ADOX is rather limited in SQL Server 7.0 and earlier, you may wish to examine the possibility of SQL-DMO. Before we leave this chapter, I will simply give you a brief introduction to SQL-DMO and point you to further resources if you need them (this is after all an ADO book!)

What is SQL-DMO?

SQL-DMO stands for SQL Server Distributed Management Objects. It is an object model similar to ADOX, which enables us to manipulate the data store. It has both advantages and disadvantages against ADOX; the major disadvantage being that it is vendor-specific (this is bad because we have to learn a new API for each vendor), and the major advantage is that the whole object model is functional (unlike ADOX, which as we have seen has lots of missing and patchy areas in relation to SQL Server 7.0).

SQL-DMO is a COM server implemented as `sqldmo.dll` and installed as part of the SQL Server client installation.

SQL-DMO goes further than ADOX in what it allows us to automate. Using SQL-DMO, we can automate:

❑ SQL Server administrative tasks, such as configuring memory requirements on the server or setting up remote servers.

❑ SQL Server object creation and administration – this is the area that overlaps with ADOX.

❑ Creation and administration of SQL Server Agent jobs, alerts, and operators. For example, we could create a new backup schedule.

❑ Installation and configuration of SQL Server replication.

SQL-DMO uses stored procedures on the server to perform its work (we don't call them directly, but the API maps to them). These stored procedures can easily be re-installed if they have been removed or changed for some reason. Executing the Transact-SQL script `sqldmo.sql` that is shipped with SQL Server 7.0 will reinstall them automatically.

How Do I Get Started?

The client machines need SQL Server ODBC Driver, version 3.70 or later, which ships with SQL Server version 7.0 and for the client network library to be properly configured. Once that is set up you will be able to add a reference to your project to the **Microsoft SQLDMO Object Library**.

Here's some sample Visual Basic code for connecting to a server and listing the tables in a database:

```
Dim sqlServer As sqldmo.sqlServer
Dim objDatabase As sqldmo.Database
Dim objTable As sqldmo.Table

Set sqlServer = New sqldmo.sqlServer

' Replace with your SQL Server name, username & password
sqlServer.Connect "Vale2000s", "sa", ""

Set objDatabase = sqlServer.Databases("Pubs")
For Each objTable In objDatabase.Tables
    lstTables.AddItem objTable.Name
Next
```

Alternatively, we could use ASP:

```
<%
    Set sqlserver = server.createobject("SQLDMO.SQLServer")
    sqlServer.Connect "Vale2000s", "sa", ""
    Set objDatabase = sqlServer.Databases("Pubs")
    For Each objTable In objDatabase.Tables
        Response.Write objTable.Name & "<BR>"
    Next
%>
```

You can see that this is pretty similar to ADOX so far. Similarly, if we want to create a new table. Here's how in VB:

```
Dim sqlServer As sqldmo.sqlServer
Dim objDatabase As sqldmo.Database
Dim objNewTable As New sqldmo.Table
Dim objCol1 As New sqldmo.Column

Set sqlServer = New sqldmo.sqlServer
sqlServer.Connect "Vale2000s", "sa", ""
Set objDatabase = sqlServer.Databases("Pubs")

objNewTable.Name = "NewTable"

objCol1.Name = "Company"
objCol1.AllowNulls = True
objCol1.Datatype = "varChar"
objCol1.Length = 30
objNewTable.Columns.Add objCol1

objDatabase.Tables.Add objNewTable
```

Compare this to the ADOX examples at the start of the chapter – they are very similar. The main difference is that we can perform operations with SQL-DMO that aren't yet available with ADOX for SQL Server, and that we are using a vendor-specific (rather than a generic) API. For example, we saw earlier that you could not add groups to SQL Server using ADOX. The equivalent to a group in SQL Server is a Database Role. So, to create a new Role for a database we would do this:

```
Dim sqlServer As sqldmo.sqlServer
Dim objDatabase As sqldmo.Database
Dim objDatabaseRole As New sqldmo.DatabaseRole

Set sqlServer = New sqldmo.sqlServer
sqlServer.Connect "Vale2000s", "sa", ""
Set objDatabase = sqlServer.Databases("Pubs")
objDatabaseRole.Name = "Trainers"
objDatabase.DatabaseRoles.Add objDatabaseRole
```

The SQL-DMO object model is a large one and very powerful. However, you must decide whether it is worthwhile learning this object model now to obtain functionality not yet supported by ADOX, or whether to wait for the promise of SQL Server 7.5 providing better ADOX support. But remember that, even then, ADOX will not support all the features of SQL-DMO (such as replication and other administrative tasks), so it may still be worth learning to use this API for those cases.

Where Can I Find Out More?

The SQL Server 7.0 Books online has full documentation for the object model together with many examples and sample code in VB and VC++. You might also like to check out 'Professional SQL Server 7.0 Development Using SQL-DMO, SQL-NS & DTS', ISBN 1-861002-80-7, also from Wrox Press.

Summary

In this chapter, we explored the ADOX object model. ADOX allows us to modify database schemas and security settings through a standard object model. ADOX currently provides most functionality when used in conjunction with the Jet Provider. However, we should see support for ADOX improved in future releases of other providers, such as that for SQL Server. We have seen how you can examine the properties of database tables, and the columns, indexes and keys in them, using ADOX, and how you can create your own in code. We then moved on to looking at Procedures and Views and found confusing support for these both in Access and SQL Server, but discovered that once you have mastered the idiosyncrasies, these objects can be useful too. Next we looked at security, a feature only currently supported by the Jet Provider, and saw how we can use it to create new Users and Groups, and to assign permissions to these objects. Finally we had a brief look at SQL-DMO, as a possible alternative to ADOX for those working with SQL Server which provides functionality that ADOX does not currently support.

11

Performance Tuning ADO

Let's start with a couple of quotes:

> *"Write Better Code"*
> Jon Jenkins (Wrox author)

Hmm, a good tip, but probably not what you want to hear. It would also make a very short chapter, so we need to expand on that a little. Let's try another:

> *"Without measurements, you do not understand your application's performance. You are groping blindly, making half-informed guesses. You have not identified your performance problems and you cannot begin to make any improvements or do capacity planning."*
> George Reilly (IIS development team, and Wrox Author)

That's much better.

There's no doubt that performance is a big issue, so we need to get some things straight. Everything here is my own opinion. It's either something I've formed over my time of using ADO, or it's something the excellent set of technical reviewers metaphorically slapped me around the face with. The conclusions I'll put forward in this chapter are what I've found, under a certain set of scenarios. What I suggest may not work for you, and some of what I say may only be applicable to new development projects. I'm well aware that many people have to retrofit ADO into existing applications, and they can't always implement the best possible solution. It's tough, but that's the way development often goes.

So, the aim of this chapter is to have a look at the performance of ADO under various situations. Don't take the results here as any definitive proof that one method is better than another. What I'm trying to do is show you the sort of problems that can arise, and the ways in which you can identify them. Use this chapter as a guide for your own performance testing.

In particular we are going to look at:

❏ What sort of tools you can use to test ADO.

❏ Some of the basic reasons why performance is a problem.

❏ How you can use ADO to get the best from your data access.

❏ How to put your ADO applications under stress, to simulate many users.

In Chapter 1 you saw how the Microsoft data access strategy has changed over the years, and you've seen why we've got OLE DB and ADO. I'm not going to repeat that – ADO is here, so let's get used to it. Let's use it where it's appropriate and try to get the best from it.

> **All of the tests in this chapter were performed on a Dell PowerEdge 1300, with a Pentium II 400Mhz Processor, 256Mb Memory, and a 9Gb U2W SCSI disk, running Windows 2000 Release Candidate 3.**

Performance Testing Tools

Throughout this chapter I'll be using a few tools to help with the testing of performance. One thing you should really note is there aren't many testing tools available. In the future we'll see Microsoft supplying much better performance analysis tools, and there may also be some third party tools available. If you are working on a big, long-term project, then you might also consider writing your own test tool.

SQL Server Profiler

The SQL Server Profiler is one of my favorite development tools, because it lets me see exactly what's happening during access to SQL Server. It's installed as one of the default options, so you don't even have to do anything special to get hold of it.

The SQL Profiler is similar to the SQL Trace tool that is shipped with SQL Server 6, and its job is to trace the requests and responses between a client and a server. When you start the profiler you will be prompted by a default set of Traces. You can either pick one of these, or create your own:

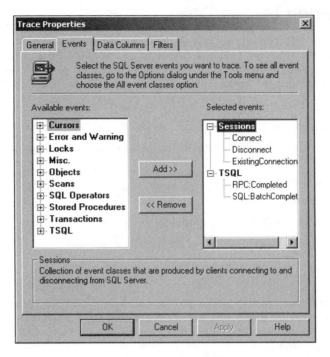

The section on the left is where you can select which events you wish to trace, and the right shows which events you have already selected. If at this point you press OK, you are then taken to the Trace window, with the trace running. Executing a simple query (opening a recordset against a table) you can see what results this trace shows:

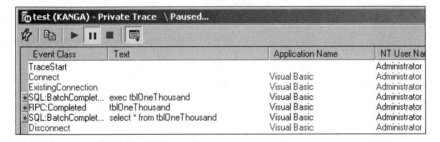

Here you can see that the connections are shown, and the SQL batches, including the text of the batch. There are a whole heap of things you can monitor from the Profiler, including the execution plan of a query, stored procedure executions, and so on.

If you want to see exactly what's happening between your client application and SQL Server, then this is the tool to use. It's really worthwhile spending a little time getting used to how it works and what sort of information it can give you.

Web Application Stress Tool

The Microsoft Web Application Stress Tool (WAST) is, quite simply, fabulous, and replaces the cumbersome WebCAT. The idea behind WAST is that it lets you run web pages (ASP or HTML) for a set length of time, and then it reports exactly how many times that page was served from the web server. There is a huge range of options, available from a simple graphical front end. Here's a simple list of some of them:

- ❏ You can record accesses to a web page, or set of pages, and use that as a test script.

- ❏ You can specify the number of threads to use when accessing pages, to simulate the number of users.

- ❏ You can use other machines to give a more accurate picture of how the server responds to network requests.

- ❏ You can set user profiles for use in multiple accesses to a page.

- ❏ You can run tests for any number of days, hours or minutes.

- ❏ You can specify a bandwidth, to test pages against modems.

The list goes on, and there's really too much to try and explain here. The greatest feature of WAST is the way you can increase the number of threads, thus simulating a number of users. I've used this to perform many of my tests in this chapter, so that I can get a much better idea of how certain ADO features perform under stress.

The picture below shows the script view of WAST:

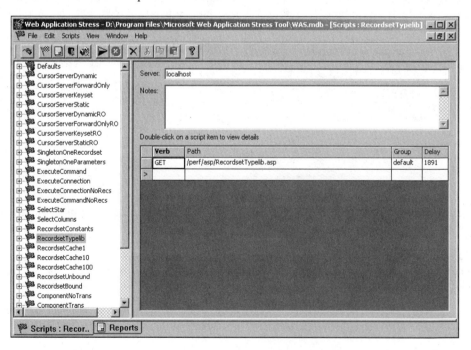

On the left you have a list of scripts, and selecting a script allows you to specify the HTTP verb (in this case a simple GET) and the file to test. You can have multiple files per script, and you can group them together, allowing certain groups to have a set percentage of the hits. This way you can tailor the testing to your particular application.

You can also set different properties for the script, as shown below:

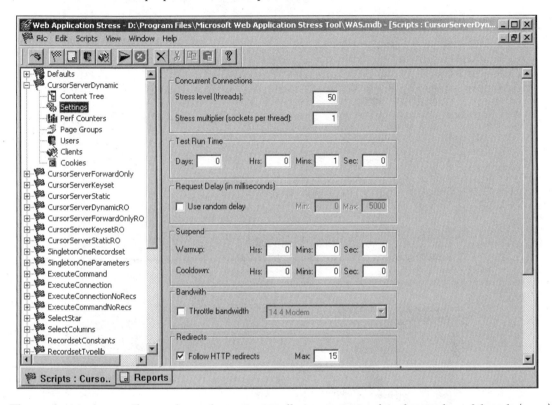

The top box is the one I've used most here, since it allows you to simulate the number of threads (users) that are accessing the page. You can also specify how long the test is to run for, and various other parameters.

Like the SQL Profiler, WAST is really something you should sit down and have a go with. Create a few test scripts, try them out, and get a good feel for how it works. You can get this tool from http://webtool.rte.microsoft.com.

Visual Studio Analyzer

Visual Studio Analyzer (VSA) is a feature that not many people know about, but it's actually a really powerful tool. Like the SQL Analyzer, it's not really a performance tool, but designed to monitor the interaction between COM components. It is supplied with Visual Studio Enterprise Edition.

Starting VSA and selecting the Analyzer Wizard, leads you through a series of dialogs. The first, shown below, allows you to pick a list of machines to monitor. These machines must also have VSA installed.

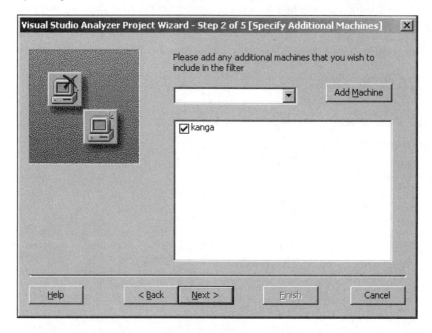

The next dialog allows you to pick the COM components to be monitored:

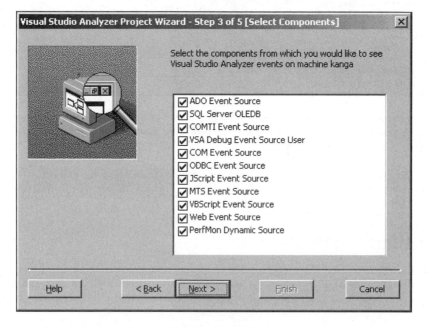

Here you can see that ADO, SQL Server OLEDB, and ODBC are listed.

Next you can pick from a list of filters:

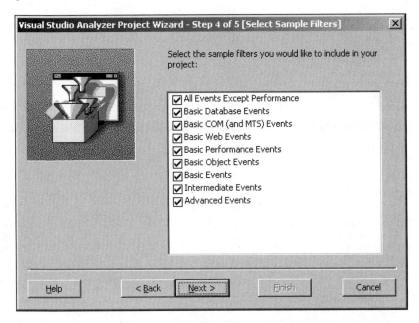

Next, after a summary dialog, you'll be able to press the Finish button, from where the main window is shown. Like Visual Basic, there's a Project Explorer, which in VSA shows the parts that make up the current project:

If you then double-click on the event log, you see the list of COM events:

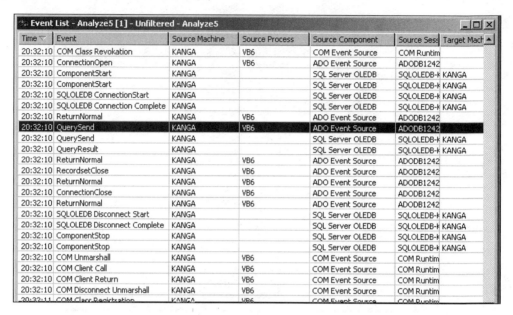

Here I've run a simple Visual Basic program to run an ADO query. You can see the ADO connection opening, which in turn calls the SQLOLEDB provider, and then sends a query to SQL Server.

There's far more to VSA than shown above. Since you can monitor multiple machines, you can use VSA to show the interaction between COM objects acting remotely. Watching the diagram in real time shows the data flow between the machines. This diagram view is also available for components, so you can see the interaction between them. If you are building n-tier systems, this is extremely useful.

Custom Tools

The final tool I've used is a custom tool I built for the ADO 2.0 Programmer's Reference book. This tool simply allows you to connect to a data source and run through a few preset tests, or run SQL commands. The main testing window is shown below:

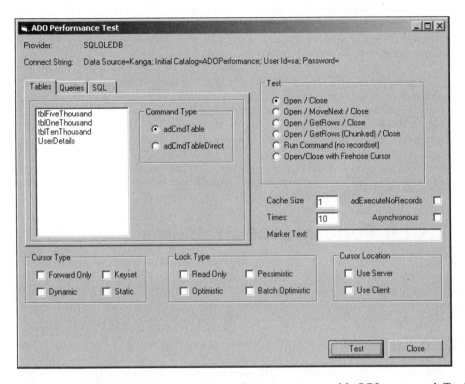

The tabs allow you to pick from tables, stored procedures, or an enterable SQL command. To the right you can select a set of tests to perform, as well as being able to set the `CacheSize` for a `Recordset` and the number of times the test should be performed. The bottom part of the screen allows you to select different cursor types, locations, and lock types. Pressing the Test button then runs the tests, takes the average time, and logs the details to an Access database.

It's a fairly rudimentary tool, but works well enough for a limited set of tests. The code is freely available on the supporting Web site, but remember – you shouldn't use this exclusively for your testing. It doesn't perform stress testing, and it can only test a set number of features. However it could give you some ideas for building your own testing tool.

Art or Science?

There's nothing a programmer hates more than being told the performance of their latest application sucks. Unfortunately data access is one of those areas that tends to get a lot of criticism, not just from users, but also from programmers themselves.

Writing applications that use ADO isn't rocket science, so let's not kid ourselves. OK, sometimes it feels like rocket science would be easier, but I just put that down to teething troubles and the learning curve. By and large, programmers like to learn and deal with new technology, so there are always going to be problems. Although programming tools have become more sophisticated and easier to use, they still can't produce perfect applications for us. That's because we're human. We make mistakes. We write the way we've always written, and we do what the documentation tells us. We have deadlines, so we cut corners, and make compromises all of the time.

You can't lie about it, because it's happened to most of us, but that's no reason to take this as the default way of writing software. Despite the fact that applications are different, the process of writing them is very similar. What's really important is not to focus too narrowly on a particular problem, because this can cloud your judgement in respect to the entire application.

In today's business we have to look at 'the big picture'. We have to design applications which not only respond to the immediate requirements, but which are also flexible enough to cope with the future. It was Benjamin Franklin who said, 'In this world nothing is certain but death and taxes'. However, I feel quite confident when I say that it's certain that the amount of data we have to store and access, and the number of users accessing that data will increase.

So, if I'm correct, we need to look at how to get the best performance out of what we've got today, and how we can make sure that performance doesn't degrade too much as both the data and users increase.

Reasons for Performance Problems

So what is it that causes these performance problems? If there was a simple answer this would be a very short chapter, so it's lucky for me that there are many different reasons. I'm not going to go into a huge amount of depth on each one, because some are beyond the scope of what I'm really trying to achieve here. However, we can look at some simple areas where performance can easily be improved.

Database Server

Perhaps too obvious to include, but it needs to be said. Many people start their database programming life using Microsoft Access, and whilst it's a great workgroup database, it's not designed for the enterprise world. If you are building applications that will either contain a large amount of data, or will be used by a large number of people, then Access is just not going to perform well enough.

If your number of users is going to be 5 or less, then the Microsoft Developer Engine (MSDE) is a good solution. This ships with Office 2000, and is also available for Visual Studio users. MSDE is a version of the SQL Server 7.0 data engine that runs on both the Windows NT and Windows 9x platforms. Since it's SQL Server, you'll gain a great increase in performance over Access. What you don't get is the nice management environment that the full version of SQL Server comes with.

For a larger number of users you'll need to consider larger database systems, such as Microsoft SQL Server, Oracle, Sybase, and so on. These are designed to handle larger numbers of users, as well as larger amounts of data. If you intend your application to grow along with your organization, then you really need to look at one of these as a way to manage your data storage.

Database Design

There are many books devoted to database design, and I'm not going to repeat it here, but it is an important point. Sometimes you'll inherit a database, in which case you either have to stick with it or go through a tedious redesign and data transfer. Not only is this costly, but it also introduces a potential for errors to creep into the data.

Other times you design the perfect database for on-line transactions, but then have to use it for data analysis. Often the two have different requirements on the best way data should be stored. For example, if you have to write an application that takes data from several tables and produce summary analysis of these, then you could speed the application by de-normalizing the data, or perhaps by creating separate tables and performing pre-calculations. The fewer table joins the database has to do, then the faster it can run. The point I'm making here is that sometimes the requirements of your database are different depending upon what sort of access you are doing. If you design your database to cater for two different access schemes, you might compromise the performance of both.

For more information on performance tuning SQL Server, see Professional SQL Server 7.0 Programming, ISBN 1-861002-31-9, also from Wrox. This contains a whole chapter on performance. For other databases you should do the same. Find a book that explains how the database works, and what sort of specific things can be done to help performance.

Application Design

This is yet another of those problems that you might not be able to do much about. A few years ago it was said that 60% of a developer's time was spent on program maintenance, with only 40% going toward new development. The upsurge of the Internet and web applications has, I think, changed this figure. Since the Web is a new medium, new applications had to be written, so the old patch, patch, patch cycle was interrupted.

However, internet time has meant that even after just a year or so, some of these web applications are ready for an overhaul, so perhaps the maintenance figure is creeping back upwards again. That's not to say there was anything wrong with the web sites, but it's just a sign of the times. A web site that stands still is a web site that ultimately will die. The use of components and MTS has also meant that some ASP sites are being re-written quite soon after they were originally written. As technology moves faster, so does the amount of maintenance..

So, when you are thinking about performance, you can build some of it in when the application is designed and constructed. Again there's no simple set of hard and fast rules, but there is a set of common ideas to think about.

Actual versus Perceived Performance

One important point to remember is that the performance of an application lives and dies by the user. It doesn't matter if you think a particular routine is optimized to perfection if the user has to wait too long for a response. This is the **perceived performance**. If the user thinks it's slow, then it's slow, no matter what you think. If they see something happening, they are less inclined to believe performance is poor. Remember, they are the one using the application.

This user perception has been around for many years – it's the reason splash screens were created. They gave the user something to look at whilst the program was loading. It seemed as though something was happening, therefore the user could accept the loading time.

Your data-driven applications can use the same technique. For example, in query-based applications, you may allow users to enter a search criterion to find selected records. The important thing to consider is that the screen size is limited, so the user can only see a certain number of records at once. Therefore, is it worth creating a recordset containing the complete set of records? This is especially important when dealing with n-tier systems and disconnected recordsets, since you'll be using client-based cursors where the entire recordset has to be loaded.

For example, let's consider a user query that matches 500 records. The problem occurs because the user has to wait for all 500 records to be processed before they can see the first batch. There are two common ways around this problem:

❑ **Paging**. – Only return a single page of records at a time. The user gets a quicker response because only the records they are going to view are processed.

❑ **Asynchronous Processing**. – Using the asynchronous flags on recordset processing allows ADO to return the first few rows of the recordset immediately, and then continue returning the rest of the rows in the background.

The asynchronous approach unfortunately doesn't work if you are using middle-tier components, because they can't act as a stream to just feed records through asynchronously from the data source. However, there may be situations where this is appropriate.

The important point to remember is that it's not necessarily your actual code that's providing the bottleneck. The expectations of the user also have to be considered. This is crucial when testing, as it means you must take the interface speed into account.

Data Caching

Caching data locally can be a boon for performance, but there are two things to consider:

❑ It's really only effective if you have data that doesn't change much. There's no point caching the data if it changes frequently and you have to keep refreshing the cache. Data typically considered good for caching is that used for lookups (countries, states, and so on).

❑ You have to perform extra coding to ensure that the cache is kept up-to-date. You can do this either by automatically refreshing the data on the application startup, or by having some sort of flag that indicates when the cache needs to be refreshed.

The extra coding isn't a big issue, and it's pretty easy to do. Depending upon your application you could cache data locally in a database (Access or MSDE) or XML files. The advantage of this is you reduce the load on the server, as well as reducing the network load.

Component Design

Don't think that because you've broken your application into components, your problems are over. The whole area of component design and application architecture using components can sometimes be mind-numbing. There are so many ways of constructing both components and applications, that many developers become confused as to what they should do.

In fact, the design of these components could have an impact on performance, and there are some important issues to think about.

Transactional and Non-Transactional Methods

The first point is you shouldn't mix transactional and non-transactional methods in the same MTS or COM+ component. A fairly standard approach is to put all methods relating to one database object into a single component, mixing both the methods that require transactions and those that don't. The problem is that even when you call the non-transactional method, the component joins (or creates a new) transaction, even when it's not required, because the transactional ability is a feature of the component, not a method. For example, consider the following code:

```
Public Function GetUserDetails(sEmail As String) _
                As ADODB.Recordset

    Dim cmdUser As New ADODB.Command
    Dim rsUser As New ADODB.Recordset

    With cmdUser
        .ActiveConnection = m_sConn
        .CommandText = "usp_GetUserDetails"
        .CommandType = adCmdStoredProc
        .Parameters.Append .CreateParameter("@sEmail", _
                        adVarChar, adParamInput, 255, sEmail)
    End With

    rsUser.CursorLocation = adUseClient
    rsUser.Open cmdUser, , adOpenStatic, adLockReadOnly

    Set rsUser.ActiveConnection = Nothing

    Set GetUserDetails = rsUser

End Function
```

Pretty standard stuff – it accepts a single argument, and uses this for the parameter to a stored procedure. The method then returns a disconnected recordset containing the details for the user. If you put this method into a component and then mark the component as Requires Transaction under MTS or Component Services, then every time you call this method you join a transaction.

It's easy to test this too. I created two identical components, using only the above code, and installed them into the Component Services. I marked one component as Requires Transaction and left the other as having Transactions Not Supported. I then created a simple Visual Basic project that called the components several times, and used the Visual Studio Analyzer to monitor the COM calls. For the transacted component I got this:

Time ▽	Event	Source Machine	Source Process	Source Component
12:32:39	SQLOLEDB Join DTC	KANGA		SQL Server OLEDB
12:32:39	SQLOLEDB Join DTC	KANGA		SQL Server OLEDB
12:32:39	QuerySend	KANGA		SQL Server OLEDB
12:32:39	QueryResult	KANGA		SQL Server OLEDB
12:32:39	SQLOLEDB Join DTC	KANGA		SQL Server OLEDB
12:32:39	SQLOLEDB Join DTC	KANGA		SQL Server OLEDB
12:32:39	QuerySend	KANGA		SQL Server OLEDB
12:32:39	QueryResult	KANGA		SQL Server OLEDB
12:32:39	SQLOLEDB Join DTC	KANGA		SQL Server OLEDB
12:32:39	SQLOLEDB Join DTC	KANGA		SQL Server OLEDB
12:32:39	QuerySend	KANGA		SQL Server OLEDB
12:32:39	QueryResult	KANGA		SQL Server OLEDB
12:32:39	SQLOLEDB Join DTC	KANGA		SQL Server OLEDB
12:32:39	SQLOLEDB Join DTC	KANGA		SQL Server OLEDB
12:32:39	QuerySend	KANGA		SQL Server OLEDB
12:32:39	QueryResult	KANGA		SQL Server OLEDB
12:32:39	SQLOLEDB Join DTC	KANGA		SQL Server OLEDB
12:32:39	SQLOLEDB Join DTC	KANGA		SQL Server OLEDB
12:32:39	QuerySend	KANGA		SQL Server OLEDB
12:32:39	QueryResult	KANGA		SQL Server OLEDB

This shows that for every call to the method the OLEDB Provider for SQL Server (SQLOLEDB) joins a transaction. Now have a look at the un-transacted component:

Time ▽	Event	Source Machine	Source Process	Source Component
12:34:43	QuerySend	KANGA		SQL Server OLEDB
12:34:43	QueryResult	KANGA		SQL Server OLEDB
12:34:43	QuerySend	KANGA		SQL Server OLEDB
12:34:43	QueryResult	KANGA		SQL Server OLEDB
12:34:43	QuerySend	KANGA		SQL Server OLEDB
12:34:43	QueryResult	KANGA		SQL Server OLEDB
12:34:43	QuerySend	KANGA		SQL Server OLEDB
12:34:43	QueryResult	KANGA		SQL Server OLEDB
12:34:43	QuerySend	KANGA		SQL Server OLEDB
12:34:43	QueryResult	KANGA		SQL Server OLEDB
12:34:43	QuerySend	KANGA		SQL Server OLEDB
12:34:43	QueryResult	KANGA		SQL Server OLEDB
12:34:43	QuerySend	KANGA		SQL Server OLEDB
12:34:43	QueryResult	KANGA		SQL Server OLEDB
12:34:43	QuerySend	KANGA		SQL Server OLEDB
12:34:43	QueryResult	KANGA		SQL Server OLEDB
12:34:43	QuerySend	KANGA		SQL Server OLEDB

See. No transactions, and no extraneous COM calls. This means that this second component will be more efficient. And not only is it more efficient for the component layer, but look at the output from the SQL Profiler. The diagram below shows the transacted component:

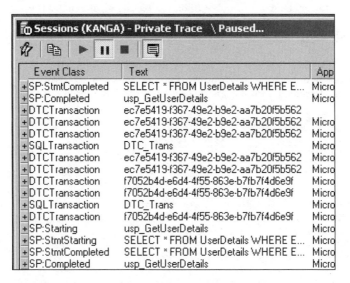

SQL Server is doing lots of work to manage the transaction, even though nothing is actually going to change. Compare this with the output below, showing the non-transacted component:

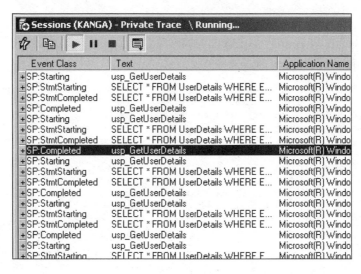

Again, much less work being done. Consider the impact this could have if you have many components and many users.

On their own, the above screenshots show that more work is being done in the transacted case, but my timing tests of this have proved inconclusive, especially under Windows 2000. On a Windows NT 4 machine, the transacted component was marginally faster (in the region of 5 to 10 ASP pages) when simulating 5 or 10 users. For larger numbers of users, the reverse was true, with the transacted component being slower. Under Windows 2000, the results were exactly the same. I would have expected some form of difference, but this isn't anything to worry about. One of the reasons for moving the read-only code into a non-transacted components was so that locking wouldn't take place, and the above only shows what work is being done – not what impact this has on other components.

The splitting of components by transaction is where a difference can really be shown. Along with the above components, I created another that just updated the same table, using code like this:

```
Private Const m_sConn As String = "Provider=SQLOLEDB; " & _
    "Data Source=Kanga; Initial Catalog=ADOPerformance;" & _
    "User ID=sa"


Public Function UpdateUserDetails(sEmail As String, _
        sName As String, sAddress As String, _
        sCity As String, sState As String, _
        sZipCode As String) As Boolean

    On Error GoTo UpdateUserDetails_Err

    Dim cmdUser     As New ADODB.Command
    Dim objContext  As COMSVCSLib.ObjectContext

    Set objContext = GetObjectContext

    With cmdUser
        .ActiveConnection = m_sConn
        .CommandText = "usp_UpdateUserDetails"
        .CommandType = adCmdStoredProc
        .Parameters.Append .CreateParameter("@sEmail", _
            adVarChar, adParamInput, 255, sEmail)
        .Parameters.Append .CreateParameter("@sUserName", _
            adVarChar, adParamInput, 255, sName)
        .Parameters.Append .CreateParameter("@sAddress", _
            adVarChar, adParamInput, 255, sAddress)
        .Parameters.Append .CreateParameter("@sCity", _
            adVarChar, adParamInput, 50, sCity)
        .Parameters.Append .CreateParameter("@sState", _
            adChar, adParamInput, 2, sState)
        .Parameters.Append .CreateParameter("@sZipCode", _
            adVarChar, adParamInput, 15, sZipCode)
        .Execute
    End With

    UpdateUserDetails = True

    objContext.SetComplete
```

```
UpdateUserDetails_Exit:
    Set cmdUser = Nothing
    Set objContext = Nothing
    Exit Function

UpdateUserDetails_Err:
    UpdateUserDetails = False
    objContext.SetAbort
    Resume UpdateUserDetails_Exit


End Function
```

This is a straightforward component that just calls a stored procedure to update a table. Now we can run some more tests, this time calling either the transacted or non-transacted read-only component, followed by this new transacted component. This is a much more realistic scenario, with both data reads and data updates happening at the same time. The results are shown below – the figures are the number of web pages served:

Users	Transacted	Non-Transacted
1	10	16
5	31	26
10	55	66
20	111	125
50	282	298

Here we can clearly see that using the non-transacted component is faster. This is because it's not doing any locking, therefore the update component isn't blocked at all. Another way of getting around this is to use SQL Server lock hints (see below).

If you find the idea of using two components in your client code cumbersome, then you might like to create a third component, to act as a database wrapper. All client calls could call this wrapper component, which would hand off calls to one of the other two components. This makes your client code easier to code and maintain.

SQL Server Lock Hints

If the above solution of splitting your components isn't possible, then you might be able to use SQL Server locking hints to force no locks. This is useful when you know that a particular routine is read-only, but has to be used in a transactional component.

For example, you could add the NOLOCK option to a SELECT statement:

```
SELECT *
FROM authors WITH (NOLOCK)
```

This tells SQL Server not to issue any locks or honor any locks. The caveat is that dirty reads are possible, so you may end up reading data from uncommitted transactions.

Stateless, Stateless, Stateless

Traditional object-oriented design allows the use of properties and methods on components. This is often the most suitable design scenario for two-tier or non-transactional components, but it's not the best way when building n-tier solutions, especially when using MTS or the COM+ Services.

MTS and the COM+ Services on Windows 2000 provide a rich framework for the management of components, including aspects such as transaction management and object pooling (when used with an appropriate language, such as C++). To achieve the best scalability from components managed by these services they should be designed to act in a stateless manner. This means removing properties and using methods only, passing in property values as arguments to the method. Doing this guarantees that the component can be reused more effectively.

Hardware and Money

Yet again this is one option that you may have no control over, but ask yourself one question. Can the performance be improved by upgrading the hardware? Applications such as SQL Server and Exchange perform much better when more memory is available. Hardware is cheap – programmers aren't. Is it more cost-effective to spend a few hundred dollars on more memory, than to have a programmer spend a week trying to tweak an application? Is a thousand dollars for a new server a lot of money when in three months time your users are complaining bitterly about the performance, and you have to have a team of programmers improve the application?

It's easy for me to say these things because it's not my money. It's probably not yours either, but that's no reason why you shouldn't put this forward as a sensible way to improve performance. However, it shouldn't be used as the default option, or as an excuse for bad programming practices. You must look at the long-term plan for your application, and think of the hardware as just one of the factors that can influence performance, remembering that increasing hardware power won't necessarily increase application performance. For example, adding a second CPU won't mean that applications suddenly perform twice as fast. Applications have to be written to take things like multiple CPUs into account.

A Test Plan

Show me a developer who likes testing. Go on. I bet you can't. Let's face facts, testing is pretty dull, but it's a fact of life. As a developer you have a responsibility not only to write good code, but also to test it to its limits. Even if you are lucky enough to have separate test teams, there's no getting away from the fact that you wrote the code. If it doesn't perform well, then you're responsible. So, you have to test.

Now one thing to get straight is that testing isn't a haphazard affair. Some of you probably tend to program by having some fuzzy specification in your head and you just sit down and start coding. You probably do testing the same way (lots of `Debug.Print` and `Response.Write` statements I bet). Well, this is one of those situations where you need to be organized and thorough. Testing, like coding, should be approached in a systematic way, with a proper plan, and there are no short cuts.

As part of that testing plan you should include performance testing. As a developer you *have* to justify this, because you know as the data and users increase, performance will probably drop.

Test Data

If you intend to do any sort of testing, then it's imperative that you have some form of test data. Ideally this should be as similar to your live data as possible, but there are situations where you don't have any live data. In these cases it's always good to create your own test data, making sure you fill the database tables with as many rows as you think necessary.

For my test data I used a table on SQL Server 7.0 with the following definition:

Field	Type	Null
KeyField	int IDENTITY (1, 1)	NOT NULL
Description	varchar (50)	NULL
ForeignKey	int	NULL
TextField1	char (10)	NULL
TextField2	varchar (10)	NULL
TextField3	varchar (20)	NULL
IntegerField	int	NULL
CurrencyField	money	NULL
BitField	bit	NOT NULL

There's nothing particularly special about this. It has a few common fields, and represents an average-to-small row size. Some of the testing I did without any indexes and some I did with indexes. Where appropriate I'll mention which version of the table is used. For your own testing, you'll want to ensure that your test tables are the same as your live tables in structure. This way you'll test not only the data, but things such as table joins.

There are several ways of setting up test data, but the one I like the best is a pretty simple routine. The character fields will be filled with some random plus some less random data. The ForeignKey field is an incrementing number, changing every 10 rows. The IntegerField and CurrencyField both contain the same value – a random number between -9999 and 9999. Finally, BitField toggles its value for every row.

I won't describe this procedure here, but it's downloadable from the support site, and it's pretty well documented. What you end up with is a table that looks like this:

KeyField	Description	ForeignKey	TextField1	TextField2	TextField3	IntegerField	CurrencyField	BitField
1	FVGJAAAAAAAAAA	1	FVGJAAAAAA	FVGJAA	FVGJA	1114	1114	0
2	DDMGCCCCCCCC	1	DDMGCCCCC		DDMGCCCC	-88025	-88025	1
3	ZBJPMMMMMMMMM	1	ZBJPMMMMM	ZBJPMM	ZBJPMMMMMMMM	-2236	-2236	0
4	RFMOPPP	1	RFMOPPP	RFMOP	RFM	-82118	-82118	1
5	COFRDDDDDDDDD	1	COFRDDDDD	COFRDD	COF	-37034	-37034	0
6	JHYJNNNNNNNNNN	1	JHYJNNNNN	J	JHYJN	-22120	-22120	1
7	UQLOPPPP	1	UQLOPPPP	UQLOPPPP	UQLOPPPP	-15623	-15623	0
8	XTAUPPPPPPPPPPP	1	XTAUPPPPP	XTAU	XTAUPPPPPPPPP	804	804	1
9	PRTCKKKKKKK	1	PRTCKKKKK	PRT	PRTCKKKKKKK	-27944	-27944	0
10	SDXKHHHHHHHHH	1	SDXKHHHHH	SDXKHH	SDXKHH	6929	6929	1
11	KFBWQQ	2	KFBWQQ	KFBWQ	KFBWQQ	5193	5193	0
12	JTZGQQQQQQQQQ	2	JTZGQQQQQ	JTZGQQQ	J	6112	6112	1
13	NQAT	2	NQAT	NQAT	NQAT	2881	2881	0
14	NJHMEEEEEEEEEE	2	NJHMEEEEE	NJHMEEE		-23366	-23366	1
15	ONOSIIIIIIIIIIIII	2	ONOSIIIII	ON	O	-7118	-7118	0
16	QVWAQQQQQQQC	2	QVWAQQQQQ	QV	Q	9437	9437	1
17	ZZLDV	2	ZZLDV	ZZLDV	ZZLDV	-9628	-9628	0
18	ITXQHHHHHHHHH	2	ITXQHHHH	ITXQHHHH	ITXQHHHHHH	-91859	-91859	1
19	NULKWWWWWWW	2	NULKWWWWWW	NUL	NULKWWWWWWWW	6824	6824	0
20	LZIBMMMMMMMV	2	LZIBMMMM	LZI	L	5505	5505	1
21	XDJBWWWWWWW	3	XDJBWWWWW	XDJ	XDJBWWW	1865	1865	0
22	JJDZHHHHHHHH	3	JJDZHHHHH	JJDZH	JJDZ	5924	5924	1

I really can't emphasize enough how important it is to produce test data, and enough of it to make your testing worthwhile. It's no good adding 20 rows to your database and testing against that, when in real life you might be dealing with 1000, 10000, or more. As I said at the beginning of the chapter, the amount of data you will be storing is bound to increase, so you might as well include that in your testing plan.

ADO Performance

OK, that's enough about the external factors involved in performance. Now it's time to turn our attention to ADO. Once again I'll emphasis that what's detailed here is guidelines. There are certain details that can definitely improve performance, but these may not be suitable for your particular application. Use these ideas as a guideline.

Listed below is a random set of things you should consider when using ADO. Some give definite performance improvements, and others less definite, but either way they are points you should test yourself.

OLE DB Providers

The first, and most obvious, point to make is that you should use the native OLE DB Providers, and not the OLE DB Provider for ODBC. The native providers have one less layer to go through, are more optimized for ADO, and are therefore faster.

If you have to use ODBC (maybe your data source doesn't have an OLE DB Provider), then using a DSN can be slower than using a DSN-less connection string. The reason is simple – the details of a DSN are stored in the registry, so when you request a connection to the DSN, the registry must be searched. This might only be marginally slower, but every little helps.

Connection Pooling

Another area to knock on the head is that of connection pooling. When you close a connection to a data store, as far as you are concerned the connection is closed. Underneath the covers however, OLE DB keeps the connection open and places it in a pool of unused, matching connections. It keeps a pool for each unique connection string. When a connection is next opened, OLE DB takes one from the matching pool and hands it back to the application. If no connection is available in the pool, then a new one is opened.

This pooling is done because the actual process of connecting to a data store is relatively expensive, so any way it can be minimized is a good thing. It's especially useful in Web situations, where many similar connections to the data store are opened and closed in quick succession.

One important point to note is my highlighting the word *exactly*. When I say exactly the same details, I mean all of the details in the connection string, including the security details and the transaction affinity. If the new connection is not in a transaction and the entire connection string matches, then a pooled connection can be used. If the new connection is in a transaction, then only a pooled connection from the same transaction can be reused.

Connection pooling is applicable whether using the native OLE DB Providers or the OLE DB Provider for ODBC, and is also activated when ADO is used in components under MTS or the COM+ Component Services under Windows 2000. Pooling is enabled by default, so you don't have to do anything to take advantage of it.

> For OBDC this is called **Connection Pooling**, and for OLE DB it's called **Resource Pooling**. These are often used interchangeably, and from the ADO point of view they provide the same facilities. Because OLE DB has resource pooling on by default, when using the OLE DB Provider for ODBC you will be using OLE DB Resource Pooling.

Automatic Disconnection

In previous versions of ADO, if you didn't explicitly close the connection or recordset, then the connection was not pooled. This could easily occur by just letting variables go out of scope. In ADO 2.5 this doesn't happen, and a connection variable that goes out of scope will have its connection closed and pooled.

Outside of MTS or the COM+ Services, if you do not keep a connection open, then the OLE DB resource pool will be closed. Within MTS or COM+, these pools are kept as long as the connections in them have not been released and have not timed out.

Don't let automatic disconnection be an excuse for bad programming practice. If you explicitly open a connection then you should always close it.

Changing the Pool Timeout

Connections are held in the pool for a default of 60 seconds. For ODBC connections you can change this value from the Pooling tab on the ODBC Data Sources Administrator dialog.

For OLE DB, you can change this value from the following registry key:

```
HKEY_CLASSES_ROOT\CLSID\ClassID\SPTimeout
```

For example, for the SQL Server Provider, this would be:

```
HKEY_CLASSES_ROOT\CLSID\{0C7FF16C-38E3-11d0-97AB-00C04FC2AD98}\SPTimeout
```

Note that for OLE DB, it was not possible to change the timeout value prior to OLE DB 2.5. For ODBC the pooling timeout was changeable from version 3.5 onwards.

Pooling and Transactions

As mentioned earlier, one point that's worth noting is that components that use transactions have different pooling requirements than those that don't use transactions. Transactions are applicable at the session level, so if a transacted connection were pooled, it wouldn't be appropriate to serve this to a non-transactional component.

This isn't something you have to worry about, since it's all handled for you, but it's just another of those *exactly* situations. A transacted connection isn't exactly the same as a non-transacted connection. This is easily proved by using the two components created earlier in some code like this:

```
Dim rs As ADODB.Recordset
Dim objNoTrans As New wroxADOTestNoTrans.TestNoTrans
Dim objTrans As New wroxADOTestTrans.TestTrans

Set rs = objNoTrans.GetUserDetails("me@here")
rs.Close

Set rs = objTrans.GetUserDetails("me@here")
rs.Close

Set rs = objNoTrans.GetUserDetails("me@here")
rs.Close

Set rs = objTrans.GetUserDetails("me@here")
rs.Close

Set rs = Nothing
Set objTrans = Nothing
Set objNoTrans = Nothing
```

The output from SQL Profiler is the following:

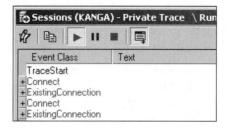

There are two components, with the same connection details. One component is marked as requiring a transaction, and the other as not supporting transactions. Calling a component twice opens and closes a connection twice, but these connections are pooled, so we only see one connection open for each component type. There are two components, therefore we see two connections. If the transacted and non-transacted connections were exactly the same, then we'd have seen only one connection.

Pooling and Temporary Data

Using temporary tables or temporary stored procedures in SQL Server is one area where connection pooling can be a disadvantage. Again, this is because pooling occurs at the session level, and so does use of `tempdb`. If you have a batch of SQL statements that create temporary tables or temporary stored procedures, then these temporary objects exist until the connection is closed.

This isn't a problem if you use stored procedures, since temporary objects created within a stored procedure are removed when the procedure finishes.

Disabling Connection Pooling

Although certainly not recommended, if you do want to disable connection pooling (perhaps for testing), then you can add a value to the end of the connection string. The table below details the OLE DB services that are enabled and disabled by the addition value:

Connection String Addition	OLE DB Services
`OLE DB Services = -1`	All services are enabled. This is the default.
`OLE DB Services = -2`	All services are enabled, except for pooling.
`OLE DB Services = -4`	All services are enabled, except for pooling and automatic transaction enlistment.
`OLE DB Services = -5`	All services are enabled, except for the Client Cursor Engine.
`OLE DB Services = -8`	All services are enabled, except for pooling, automatic transaction enlistment, and the Client Cursor Engine.
`OLE DB Services = 3`	Only pooling and automatic transaction enlistment are enabled, and only at the session level.
`OLE DB Services = 0`	No services are enabled.

For example, to disable OLE DB resource pooling in Visual Basic you could use a connection string like this:

```
Dim sConn   As String
Dim conPubs As New ADODB.Connectin

sConn = "Provider=SQLOLEDB; Data Source=Kanga;" & _
        " Initial Catalog=pubs;" & _
        " User ID=sa; OLE DB Services = -2"

conPubs.Open sConn
```

Cursors: Types, Location and Locking

The issue of cursor types, location and locking modes is always one that arouses a great deal of discussion. So, first, let's refresh our memory as to what the cursor types are, and what the difference is between them:

Cursor Type	Description
Static	A static cursor contains a copy of the data at the time the recordset was created. This means that modifications by other users are not visible.
Forward Only	Similar to a static cursor in that it contains a copy of the data at the time the recordset was created, except that you can only scroll forwards through the records. Only being able to scroll forwards means that once the record pointer has moved past a record, the record can be forgotten about. OLE DB doesn't have to keep track of previous records, therefore performance is improved. MoveFirst can often be used, but this re-runs the query.
Keyset	Contains a copy of the keys of the data at the time the recordset was created. This means that you can see data changes to existing records. New records added by others are not visible because they weren't part of the keyset at the time of creation. Records deleted by others are not deleted from the recordset, although they are not available.
Dynamic	Dynamic cursors point directly at the data, therefore all changes made by other users are visible.
Firehose	For SQL Server only, this is the default cursor type if no other is specified, and is not the same as a forward-only cursor. When this cursor type is requested, SQL Server doesn't wait for the data to be requested, but just streams it directly to the ADO services. It is the fastest and most efficient way to get read-only data from SQL Server.

Which cursor type you use depends on what sort of functionality you require. One important point to note is that although forward-only cursors don't allow moving back through the records, some providers allow you to do a `MoveFirst`. This seems contrary to what you'd expect, but what actually happens is that the query is re-executed. Don't fall into the trap of thinking 'forward only is faster, *and* I can move back to the beginning'. Re-executing the command will always be slower than picking a different cursor type.

Which Type to Use

So, the question remains as to which cursor type to use. Well, if you are using client side cursors (for example, for disconnected recordsets), then it doesn't make much difference, because all of the data is read onto the client cursor service at the time the recordset is opened. This is because client-side cursors are always static cursors.

What you will see, though, is a big difference when using the different server-side cursor types.

Using my custom testing tool (more later) I opened and closed a table containing 1000 rows (but didn't read any data), using all four cursor types, and optimistic and read-only locking. I ran each test 10 times and took the average time (in milliseconds) for each run. The table below lists the results for server-side cursors:

	Cursor Type			
LockType	adOpenDynamic	adOpenForwardOnly	adOpenKeyset	adOpen Static
adLockOptimistic	4.7	4.7	9.4	10.9
adLockReadOnly	3.1	3.1	60.9	54.7

There are two points to note here:

❏ Read-only cursors are faster for dynamic and forward-only cursors, but not for keyset and static, where they are much slower.

❏ Keyset and static cursors, irrespective of locking, are much slower that dynamic and forward-only cursors.

The results may seem odd, but there's one big factor to take into account here – and that's SQL Server. When you use keyset or static cursors with SQL Server, a copy of the data is placed in `tempdb`, and that copy is used as the source of the recordset. So the extra time is the time taken to copy the data from the original table into the temporary table in `tempdb`. Not only can this have a big impact on performance of ADO, but it uses resources on SQL Server, which could become a problem with a large number of users.

To prove that it's not just the cursor types themselves causing the problem, I repeated the test against an Access 2000 database, resulting in the following:

LockType	Cursor Type			
	adOpenDynamic	adOpenForward Only	adOpenKeyset	adOpenStatic
`adLockOptimistic`	7.9	7.8	9.4	9.4
`adLockReadOnly`	7.8	6.2	7.8	9.4

The times here are much more closely matched, so it's not an ADO cursor related issue.

The times for the SQL Server tests don't really prove a great deal, since these are just for a single process. To perform some stress testing with multiple users, I created ASP pages to replicate the tests (just opening and closing the recordset). Using the Web Stress Testing Tool from Microsoft I simulated several threads (users) accessing these pages for a minute. The results are below, showing the average number of page hits in that minute per thread:

Threads	Lock Type	Cursor Type			
		Dynamic	Forward Only	Keyset	Static
1	Optimistic	10	36	43	59
	Read Only	10	36	41	58
5	Optimistic	10	35	41	59
	Read Only	10	35	40	56
10	Optimistic	10	36	42	59
	Read Only	10	35	38	54
20	Optimistic	10	35	42	58
	Read Only	10	35	30	37
50	Optimistic	10	35	41	55
	Read Only	10	35	16	18

Since this measures page hits, the higher the number the better, and this really does show some interesting results. Now we see that dynamic cursors are the slowest, and like forward-only cursors, they don't degrade when under stress. What's particularly noteworthy is that when using keyset and static cursors in read-only mode, the performance degrades noticeably as the number of users increases. The optimistic locking method doesn't show this characteristic. I only wish I could explain this, but I'm just as surprised as you at these results.

What this clearly shows is the value of testing against a large number of users. The pages I used in these tests are available from the supporting web site.

Prepared Statements and Stored Procedures

For most queries, using a stored procedure will nearly always be quicker than using a SQL string as the command text, because SQL Server has precompiled the stored procedure. SQL Server has an execution plan (which can also be cached), and thus it doesn't have to work out table or index details at the time of the command execution.

This isn't always the case though, as it is possible to write stored procedures that aren't efficient. You should use the Query Plan facilities of SQL Server to identify these.

Using the Prepared property on a Command object is useful if you can't use a stored procedure and the command might be executed more than once. This could happen if the user is building up the command details (perhaps from a list of tables and columns). Preparing the command means that SQL takes the command text, compiles it (much like a stored procedure) and then executes it. The compiled command is kept in cache for as long as the connection is active, so any subsequent calls to the command will be faster. It's only the first call that will be marginally slower, since the initial compilation has to take place. For example, the following Visual Basic code prepares the statement before executing it:

```
Dim cmdPubs    As New ADODB.Command
Dim rsAuthors As ADODB.Recordset
Dim sConn      As String

sConn = "Provider=SQLOLEDB; Data Source=Kanga;" & _
        " Initial Catalog=pubs; User ID=sa"

With cmdPubs
    .ActiveConnection = sConn
    .CommandType = adCmdStoredText
    .CommandText = "SELECT * FROM authors"
    .Prepared = True
    Set rsAuthors = .Execute
End With
```

The use of prepared statements is also impacted by pooling, since prepared statements are associated with a connection. These prepared statements will remain until the connection is closed, so tempdb could get large if this isn't managed carefully.

Parameters and Refresh

This should be a fairly obvious point, but don't use the Refresh method of the Command object's Parameters collection in production code. This method call causes the provider to examine the stored procedure and send all of the parameter details back to the client. If this doesn't seem that much, then think about what the database has to do. It has to look up the procedure, then find the parameters, then find the data types for these parameters, then produce a recordset, which ADO interprets and converts into the Parameters collection.

Under SQL Server this is handled by the sp_procedure_params_rowset stored procedure. You might like to have a look at it to see how much work it has to do. Try running it yourself with a stored procedure and look at the Execution Plan – it's doing a lot of work.

There's also something else you should watch for when using parameters. Consider the following Visual Basic code:

```
Dim cmdUserDetauls As New ADODB.Command

sConn = "Provider=SQLOLEDB; Data Source=Kanga;" & _
        " Initial Catalog=ADOPerformance; User ID=sa"

With cmdUserDetails
    .ActiveConnection = sConn
    .CommandText = "usp_GetUserDetailsOutput"
    .CommandType = adCmdStoredProc
    Debug.Print .Parameters(0).Name
End With

Set cmdUserDetails = Nothing
```

You might think that this would fail on the `Debug.Print` line, since no parameters have been defined, but this actually performs a `Refresh`. This could cause problems if you then try to `Append` parameters to the collection, since they will already exist.

Output Parameters Instead of Singletons

When using stored procedures, it's quite common to do something like this:

```
CREATE PROCEDURE usp_GetUserDetails
    @sEmail varchar(255)
AS
    SELECT *
    FROM    UserDetails
    WHERE   Email = @sEmail
```

This is termed a singleton select, since it's only returning a single row (assuming there are no duplicate email addresses in the table). In terms of recordsets, a singleton query is not very efficient, since you will only ever have a single row of data. It's actually more effective to use output parameters instead. For example:

```
CREATE PROCEDURE usp_GetUserDetailsOutput
    @sEmail     varchar(255),
    @iID        int             OUTPUT,
    @sUserName  varchar(255)    OUTPUT,
    @sAddress   varchar(255)    OUTPUT,
    @sCity      varchar(50)     OUTPUT,
    @sState     char(2)         OUTPUT,
    @sZipCode   varchar(15)     OUTPUT
AS
    SELECT @iID = UserID, @sUserName = UserName,
           @sAddress = Address, @sCity = City,
           @sState = State, @sZipCode = ZipCode
    FROM    UserDetails
    WHERE   Email = @sEmail
```

For my test data the performance of the second parameter, as called from an ASP page under stress, was half as fast again as the first page, returning on average 31 pages per minute, as opposed to 19 pages per minute for the recordset.

Execute: Connection versus Command

I read recently that for action queries it was more efficient to use the Execute method of the Connection object, than to use the Execute method of the Command object. So, to test this I used the following two ASP pages:

For the Command I used:

```
Dim cmdUserDetails As New ADODB.Command

sConn = "Provider=SQLOLEDB; Data Source=Kanga;" & _
        " Initial Catalog=ADOPerformance; User ID=sa"

Set cmdUserDetails = Server.CreateObject("ADODB.Command")

cmdUserDetails.CommandText = "usp_UpdateUserDetails"
cmdUserDetails.CommandType = adCmdStoredProc
cmdUserDetails.ActiveConnection = sConn

cmdUserDetails.Execute , Array("me@here", _
                  "Dave Sussman", _
                  "my new address", "here", "qq", "987654")
```

For the Connection I used:

```
Dim conTest As New ADODB.Connection

sConn = "Provider=SQLOLEDB; Data Source=Kanga;" & _
        " Initial Catalog=ADOPerformance; User ID=sa"

Set conTest = Server.CreateObject("ADODB.Connection")

conTest.open sConn
conTest.Execute "usp_UpdateUserDetails ('me@here', _
                  'Dave Sussman', 'my new address', _
                  'here', 'qq', '987654')", ,adCmdStoredProc

conTest.close
```

Testing these under stress did show an improvement for the Connection object, but it was marginal – in the region of 10 pages a minute faster. Still, on a busy site this might help.

Execution Options

Another situation that can be used to improve performance of non-rowset returning action queries, is the use of the `adExecuteNoRecords` constants as part of the `Options` argument for an executed command. This instructs ADO that the command doesn't return any rows, and that no recordset should be built. If you don't specify this then an empty recordset is built and discarded.

Once again the tests show a marginal improvement in using this option.

SELECT *

Another often quoted performance improvement is not to use `SELECT *` when you don't need all of the columns. For example, if you only need two or three columns from a table containing twenty columns, then `SELECT *` will be slower. It's recommended you use the actual column names in your `SELECT` statements. I did a few tests and found there to be very little difference. Sometimes one method was faster, other times the other method. It's another of those options you might like to test yourself, since it depends so much on your data.

Constants in ASP

Some time ago I learned the trick of including the ADO constants by using the METADATA tag instead of including the `adovbs.inc` file. I'd been told it was more efficient, but had never put it to the test. For example, including the constants is generally done like this:

```
<!-- #INCLUDE FILE="adovbs.inc" -->
```

To reference the typelib, you can do this:

```
<!-- METADATA TYPE="typelib" FILE="C:\Program Files\
                Common Files\System\ado\msado15.dll" -->
```

or, if you don't want to specify a physical location of the ADO dll, you can reference the GUID:

```
<!-- METADATA TYPE="typelib"
     UUID="00000200-0000-0010-8000-00AA006D2EA4" -->
```

My tests found that using the `typelib` instead of the `include` file, enabled about 5 to 10 more pages to be served per minute. An alternative would be to include only those constants you need directly in your code. For example:

```
<%
   adStateOpen = 1
   adUseServer = 2

     . . .
%>
```

This method gives results somewhere in between including the constants and using a `typelib`.

ADO Cache Size

One point that many people often forget is the use of the `CacheSize` property of the recordset object. This property dictates the number of records cached in local memory, and the number read into that local memory at any one time. This might not seem as though it could be important, but think about a table with 1000 rows. By default, the cache size is 1, so for each row in the table there will be 1000 reads. Increasing the cache size means fewer data reads, therefore improved performance.

I tested this with the following ASP code:

```
sConn = "Provider=SQLOLEDB; Data Source=Kanga;" & _
        " Initial Catalog=ADOPerformance; User ID=sa"

Set rs = Server.CreateObject("ADODB.Recordset")

rs.CacheSize = 1
rs.Open "tblOneThousand", sConn

If rs.State = adStateOpen Then
    While Not rs.EOF
        rs.MoveNext
    Wend
    rs.Close
End If
Set rs = Nothing
```

OK, it doesn't do much, but it illustrates the point. I ran this three times, increasing the cache size each time.

Cache Size	Pages Served
1	752
10	1003
100	1033

This clearly shows that increasing the cache size improves performance. However, you shouldn't increase this too far, since a larger cache means more resources are used, and you can eventually start to see a performance drop. Since the performance varies, this is one performance feature that you really do have to test yourself.

Caching

Caching data is one obvious way of improving performance, but it's not something that should be done without a great deal of thought and design. I'm not going to go into great depths about caching mechanisms, but there are a few pointers worth thinking about.

It's important to distinguish the idea of explicit data caching from that of the CacheSize, as mentioned above. The CacheSize has to do with the amount of data transferred in one go and implicitly cached by the cursor engine, and not the idea of storing data locally. However, CacheSize can influence things such as scrolling. For example, if the CacheSize is greater than the size of the recordset, then scrolling can be performed entirely within the local cache, without touching the server at all.

Caching Data on the Client

Caching data on the client can take many forms, and depends on your application design. I mentioned earlier in the chapter that using cached tables in a local database can often bring performance benefits. Listed below are a few methods I've successfully employed in the past:

❑   In Visual Basic applications I've cached frequently used data in the program itself. One of the first things the program did was load the data and store it in arrays, hidden listboxes, or disconnected recordsets, where it can quickly be accessed later in the application. This method is generally only useful for small amounts of data.

❑   Using a local Access database for larger amounts of data that don't change very often is also effective. This imposes less strain on the server, as well as reducing network load.

❑   In ASP applications an Application variable can be used with great effect, but again it's best used for small amounts of data. It's fairly easy to do. The page that requires the data first looks in the Application variable. If the data isn't present then the data store can be opened, the data read in, and stored in the Application variable, perhaps as a ready formatted piece of HTML. By the time the page is called, the data will be present, and therefore the database doesn't need to be hit. This can give real improvements in page response times.

Caching Objects in ASP

One thing you should never do is store objects in Application or Session variables. It's often tempting to think that storing an opened ADO Connection object in the Application will save time, because you won't have to open the connection again.

What actually happens is different:

❑   You bypass connection pooling, which is designed to improve connection opening, and to reduce resources used on the database server.

❑   You ruin any chances your ASP application will have of scalability. This is because you lock the user session down to a single thread, which means blocking may take effect.

This is not just a problem with ADO, but with any object marked as Apartment Threaded. If you've looked in the ADO directory, you might have noticed that there are a couple of .reg files, one of which allows you to switch ADO into a Free Threaded mode. Don't be tempted to do this, and then start storing the ADO objects in Session state, because there's no guarantee of a performance improvement, and often you'll see a performance drop. If you want to read more about this, consult *Beginning Components for ASP* or *Professional ASP 3.0*, both published by Wrox Press, where it's explained in great detail.

In Windows 2000, IIS5 and ASP 3.0 don't actually let you store an Apartment Threaded object on an Application level variable.

Binding Columns to Variables

Another fairly simple improvement is one many people don't think of – that of using local variables to bind to members of a collection. For example, consider the following code:

```
rs.Open "tblOneThousand", sConn

If rs.State = adStateOpen Then
    While Not rs.EOF
        Response.Write rs("Description") & "<BR>"
        rs.MoveNext
    Wend
    rs.Close
End If
Set rs = Nothing
```

This simple code loops through a recordset, printing out the `Description` column. The problem here is that every time you go through the loop you are indexing into the recordset. The solution is simple:

```
rs.Open "tblOneThousand", sConn

If rs.State = adStateOpen Then
    Set fldDesc = rs("Description").Value
    While Not rs.EOF
        Response.Write fldDesc & "<BR>"
        rs.MoveNext
    Wend
    rs.Close
End If
Set rs = Nothing
```

This sets a local variable to reference the indexed variable, and then uses the local variable in the loop. Testing the above showed an improvement of approximately 100 pages per minute being served. You could get better improvements if you were referencing many columns.

Further Reading and Tools

If you are serious about getting the best from your application, then there are some books that you might find useful. One I've mentioned before, but the other I haven't:

❑ Inside SQL Server 7.0, by Ron Soukup and Kalen Delaney, Microsoft Press. Both Ron and Kalen wrote parts of SQL Server, so they really know what they are talking about.

❑ Professional SQL Server 7 Programming, published by Wrox Press

There are also some useful tools, some of which I've already mentioned:

- ❑ The Visual Studio Analyzer is supplied as part of Visual Studio 6. It's not optimised to work with COM+ applications (as in Windows 2000), but it's still useful. Future products from Microsoft (such as AppCenter and Visual Studio 7) will have better features for those of you on Windows 2000.

- ❑ The SQL Profiler is supplied as part of SQL Server 7.0. You can use this to monitor all aspects of SQL commands.

- ❑ Web Application Stress Testing Tool (nee Homer), is incredibly easy to use and can help pinpoint slow-running Web pages. At the time of writing this tool was available from `http://homer.ms.rte.com`.

- ❑ Custom Tools. My custom tool is available from the supporting Wrox Web site, but it's fairly crude. It's intended to show some simple areas of performance testing, but the code is available, so customize it to suit your own needs. Or write your own from scratch.

- ❑ System Internals provide a great range of little utilities for monitoring what's really going on. Two I particularly like are Filemon and Regmon, which monitor file system and registry access. System Internals can be found at `http://www.sysinternals.com`.

- ❑ WebHammer, from ServerObjects, tests Web servers and applications. More information is available from `http://www.serverobjects.com/products.htm#WebHammer`.

- ❑ LoadRunner, from MercuryInteractive, is designed to test and predict the behavior of enterprise level applications. More information from `http://www.merc-int.com/products/loadrunguide.html`.

- ❑ AppMetrics from Xtremesoft, which is a COM testing platform. More information from `http://www.xtremesoft.com/`.

Summary

If you've read between the lines in this chapter then you'll realize that planning hasn't been far from the agenda. There really is no point writing an application if you don't plan to test it in a way that's realistic. It's no good testing bits of code, or components, just to see if they work, because that's all that will be proved – they work. You won't prove how well they work, especially under stress.

So, in this chapter I've tried to highlight the areas you should look at when considering performance testing. These have included:

- ❑ The idea that performance is only as bad as its perception.

- ❑ The need to take the whole application into account. How an application works, with a large number of users, is imperative as part of your test plan.

- ❑ The need to create realistic test data.

- ❑ Some specific areas of ADO where performance could be a problem.

- ❑ The sort of tools you can use to pinpoint poorly performing areas of your application.

As I've said several times, these are things you really need to test yourself, in respect to your particular application. That's why I haven't built a large suite of samples, because they probably wouldn't be applicable. All of the ASP pages I used are available for download, along with the custom test tool, so you can use these as a basis for your own test routines.

12

Directory Services

ADO and OLE DB are together very powerful because of their ability to access any data source from any COM-aware language for which an OLE DB provider has been written, and to expose the information via a common set of COM interfaces which are easy to use.

In this chapter we're going to look at how to get to a special category of data sources – Directory Services. For these we will need to learn to use another technology: the Active Directory Services Interfaces (ADSI). This is partly because there is currently no OLE DB provider that gives full access to these sources, and partly because ADSI is more suited than ADO for directory services anyway. This means that we won't see much of ADO in this chapter, though we will bring ADO back in towards the end of the chapter when we come to cover searching, since in this area ADSI itself relies in some ways on OLE DB and ADO.

You may have already encountered directory services – in particular if your domain is controlled by Windows 2000 domain controllers, in which case you will have met Active Directory, the directory service that handles Windows domains in Windows 2000. And if you write code to administer Exchange Server in either Windows 2000 or NT4 you will probably have needed to use the Exchange Directory. We're going to start off by looking at what precisely a directory service is and how it is different from other data sources. Then we'll look at ADSI itself – we'll discover that ADSI is essentially another set of COM interfaces, which like ADO are available to any COM-aware language, including scripting languages, and which are implemented by **ADSI providers**. In fact, we'll discover that ADSI is conceptually quite similar in many ways to OLE DB, but that the interfaces are specifically optimized to access directories.

Later in the chapter we'll look at some VB code samples that show how to browse and search directories and carry out other common tasks using ADSI, and we'll finish up with a section that covers extra considerations you'll need to be aware of if you code up your ADSI clients in C++ rather than VB or VBScript. Along the way we'll meet adsvw.exe, a useful utility supplied by Microsoft that lets you browse or search any directory that is accessible through an ADSI provider, and which is quite convenient to use for browsing round the directories installed on your network.

What is a Directory Service?

This is clearly the first question we need to ask. Unfortunately it's not a question that's easy to answer precisely, since there isn't really a clear definition. Instead, we'll begin by giving a couple of examples of the directory services you might want to access for which you will need to use ADSI, then we'll examine the common properties that tend to characterise these and other directory services.

Directories you're likely to meet include:

❑ **Active Directory**. This is the directory that has been introduced with Windows 2000. It is the directory of all the resources and security permissions for a Windows domain or domain tree or forest. In a real sense, you can think of Active Directory almost as *being* the domain, since it is used to control all access to resources in a domain. Because of the unique importance of Active Directory, we will devote a whole section of this chapter to looking at this topic.

❑ **The Exchange Directory**. That is to say the directory that stores information about mail recipients and configuration information for your Exchange Server installation. We'll look at Exchange Server in chapter 13.

❑ **The IIS Metabase**. This is the directory that stores all the configuration information for Internet Information Server, including such things as details of virtual directories, security permissions and recognised MIME types.

❑ **Novell Directory Services** (**NDS**). These are the equivalent of Active Directory, but for a Novell system. However NDS has been around for a few years.

❑ **The Site Server Membership Directory**. This is the directory of users of your web site which is maintained by Site Server for personalization purposes.

❑ **Netscape Directory Server** and the **openLDAP Directory Server**. These are general-purpose directories that can be used to store any information you want in them.

If you want to access any of the above directories, then you'll find that the main way to do so is through ADSI, rather than ADO. Having said that, ADO does play a role when you request searches against a directory using ADSI – a particular aspect of directories that we'll examine in more detail later in the chapter. So let's look at what characterises a typical directory.

The first point to note is that a directory is a data source. In that regard it is no different from any of the data sources you would normally use ADO or OLE DB to access. Directory services will however often satisfy the following conditions:

❑ They have a hierarchical, tree-like structure, in which each object in the directory may contain other objects (children). This is similar to what you might find in XML and web publishing.

❑ They are used predominantly for looking up information. This means that it is expected that they will be read more often than they are written to – so they will usually be optimized for read access.

❑ They have sophisticated search facilities, and are able to respond to fairly complex queries, such as 'give me all the users who are not administrators and who haven't logged on for two weeks'.

- They do not have any of the sophisticated transaction monitoring that many relational databases – such as SQL server – have. They will obviously have all the inbuilt protection necessary to ensure that they are unlikely to get corrupted, and that new data written to them is sensible, but that is all.

- They are scaleable. To this end, they will often be replicated – that is to say, multiple copies of the directory stored on different computers. If they are replicated then it is tolerable for the replicas to get out of sync for a short period. In other words, if some data gets updated in one of the replicas, there will be a noticeable wait before the updates get propagated to all the other replicas.

- They are open. That is to say they are accessed by standard methods rather than custom APIs that are specific to each directory. Hence one piece of client software should be able to access any of a number of different directories using a standard API.

- The objects about which information is stored in directories often corresponds closely to things that can be associated with real world objects – for example a directory may be a directory of users or computers. Each object in the directory has a number of associated properties (or attributes) – such as name, time of last login, etc., which describe that object.

Reading through that list the first thing that may strike you is that many of these characteristics could equally well describe many other data sources, which you would not identify as being directories. For example, almost any relational database will also have sophisticated search facilities – probably using the SQL language. Similarly it is arguable that *any* data source for which an OLE DB provider is available is already automatically open, since it is accessible through the ADO and OLE DB APIs! And that's why I emphasized that the above list is a list of typical directory characteristics rather than a firm definition. Of the earlier list of directories that I gave, all of those directories will satisfy *most* of the directory characteristics (the main exception is that the IIS metabase and earlier versions of Novell Netware directories do not support complex search queries). Other data sources may also satisfy many of those characteristics.

Having said that, the most important characteristics of directories are the first two from the above list – that a directory is mostly there for the lookup of information, and that it usually has a hierarchical structure.

Incidentally, you may have noticed I've swapped a bit between the terms **directory** and **directory service**. To some extent these terms are interchangeable in everyday use. The full term *Directory Service* emphasizes that we are dealing not just with the information store but also with the related APIs and other software that allows clients to access the data. Often this software will take the form of an NT service whose main function is to listen out for requests for data and respond to them.

Example: The Telephone Directory

The good old-fashioned paper-based telephone directory is often quoted as an example of a directory – and with good reason. It is in many ways the perfect example. Let's consider how well it matches up to six of the seven criteria I listed above for a directory (the one I've omitted is transaction monitoring, which isn't so relevant here):

Hierarchical Structure

Within any country you will usually find a number of books, each covering a particular geographical area. Within any one book are contained a large number of entries (phone numbers) corresponding to that area. There aren't that many levels of the hierarchy there, but it's definitely somewhat like a hierarchical structure – and it's certainly nothing like the structure of a relational database.

Used Mainly for Lookup

What else do you use your telephone directory for? Phone books are definitely optimized for more frequent reading than writing. Writing updates generally involves a huge printing and distribution operation to produce new phone books – which is why it will normally be done perhaps once a year at most. Reading an entry from the phone book is a lot quicker (and cheaper!)

Search Facilities

Search facilities are limited simply because this is a paper-based medium rather than a computer-based one. But in many countries, there will be an extra book, the yellow pages, which lists companies and other organizations ordered according to the type of trade they are in. This means that users can perform simple searches for all entries of a certain category. Admittedly this is nothing like the sophisticated search facilities you'd get from a computer-based directory, but in principle the option to search is there. (Looking up in the white pages doesn't by the way count as a search, because to do that you have to already know the name of the entry you are interested in).

Scaleable/Replicated

The phone directory is extremely scaleable – it is well adapted to having millions of people looking up numbers at the same time. The way the phone companies achieve this is generally very simple: they print millions of phone books! So the scaleability is achieved by pure replication.

In this category I also mentioned the fact that replicas are allowed to get out of sync for short periods. For phone directories, the periods are rather longer – I've lived in several houses where the phone book was as much as a couple of years out of date! Our replica of the directory has been allowed to become out of sync with the more up-to-date replicas. But it doesn't matter too much, since if I do need a number that there's a problem with, all I need to do is ring directory enquiries to ask for the up-to-date phone number.

Open

I think the format of phone directories issued by the various companies and in the different countries is fairly standard. You usually see something like two columns – a column with the name and address of the person and another column with their phone number in. The entries are arranged in alphabetical order by their names. I've never picked up a phone book, either in my home country of the UK or while travelling abroad, and thought 'Heck, I don't understand this format. The information's arranged all funny. Where's the phone numbers?' And believe me, there's a *lot* of different companies that produce phone directories in the UK so I've seen a fair few different companies' directories.

Corresponds to Real World Objects

The phone books store information about people and organizations (specifically their addresses and phone numbers). You can't get much more 'real' than a person.

Introducing ADSI

Now we've got a rough idea of what makes a directory, we'll have a look at the ADSI set of interfaces defined for accessing them.

ADSI is in many ways quite similar to OLE DB. Where OLE DB defines a set of COM interfaces which can be used to access a data source, ADSI defines another set of COM interfaces which can be used to access a directory. In OLE DB these interfaces are backed up by a number of **providers** – each provider is able to provide access to one data source. Similarly, in ADSI, the ADSI interfaces are implemented by ADSI providers – that is to say, sets of COM components which are designed to interact with particular directories. In fact, ADSI is the set of interfaces Microsoft have defined for this purpose, together with a number of standard providers to allow access to commonly used directory services and a few extra runtime COM components that smooth the whole process out.

Why ADSI?

You may be wondering what the point of ADSI is. Why have another set of interfaces to do what – when it comes down to it – is nothing more than access a specialized data source? What's wrong with ADO? Why don't we just write more OLE DB providers to allow ADO to access these directories.

There are a couple of answers to this question. Perhaps the most obvious one is that ADO is a general-purpose technology. It is there to access *any* data source, no matter what the structure of that data source is. It is inevitable that in order to achieve this generality there is going to be some sacrifice in terms of the ADO and OLE DB interfaces not being optimally designed to take full advantage of certain specialized data sources. This is the case for hierarchical directories. Although ADO is perfectly able to handle hierarchical directories, that isn't its primary purpose. It was really designed with relational databases in mind – the kind of databases where you can get a query answered by issuing an SQL command – which ADO often does not attempt to interpret but simply hands over to the appropriate database to figure out. ADO does not support interfaces that are designed to allow easy browsing of a treelike structure. ADSI does. ADSI allows you very easily to navigate around a tree, examining the children of an object or locating an object's parent.

Another factor is that part of Microsoft's motivation for developing the ADSI interfaces was almost certainly a desire to provide an easy way of accessing Active Directory. Make no doubt about it, Active Directory is *the* flagship technology that comes with Windows 2000. The lack of an open and sophisticated directory service was widely regarded as one of the main reasons for the failure of NT4 to achieve the same market domination for computer networks in large enterprises as it and its smaller relative Windows 9x did in the home and small business market. Microsoft wants Active Directory to be a success, which means they need Active Directory to be easy to use. So they really needed a set of COM interfaces that provided a very well-matched wrapper around Active Directory.

The problem with ADO in this regard is that you have to do quite a bit of translation between Active Directory's hierarchical view of the world and ADO's command-based view of the world. Once again ADSI excels here since its interfaces, while designed to allow access to any directory, are particularly well matched to the structure of Active Directory. This also means that when used to access Active Directory (or for that matter quite a large number of other directories), ADSI can get away with providing only a very thin wrapper around the directory service while still being convenient for scripting and VB clients to use. There are the obvious performance advantages here.

Most of the ADSI interfaces are dual interfaces, which means they can be used by clients written in any COM-aware language, ranging from C++ to VB to J++ to scripting languages. However we're going to present most of the code samples in this chapter in VB, since in our view this is the language which leads to the clearest samples that demonstrate how to use the ADSI interfaces. Converting samples from VB to VBScript is fairly trivial. For the most part we'll also assume that C++ programmers are able to convert COM method calls from VB to C++ without extra instruction. However, we will finish off the chapter with a quick look at some of the extra facilities available to clients written in C++, who are able to use ADSI's few custom interfaces as well as a range of helper API functions that are available for ADSI.

ADSI in Action

Here's where we come to our first code sample. I'm going to demonstrate ADSI by listing all the user accounts on my local computer, a domain controller running Windows 2000 Server named BiggyBiggy. (Don't ask... it's a long story. I liked the name when I picked it). This code is in VB, and it will work on any machine, whether running Windows 2000, Windows NT, or Windows 9x, provided that computer has ADSI installed. The code is a standard VB executable project, containing a listbox called List1. Note that in order to use ADSI from VB, we need to include the ActiveDS type library in the project references.

The code for our sample reads as follows:

```
Option Explicit

Private Sub Form_Load()

' bind to the local computer
Dim oComputer As IADsContainer
Set oComputer = GetObject("WinNT://BiggyBiggy")

' list all the users
oComputer.Filter = Array("user")
Dim oUser As IADs
For Each oUser In oComputer
    List1.AddItem oUser.Name
Next

Set oComputer = Nothing
Set oUser = Nothing

End Sub
```

I'm not expecting you to understand all the code just yet – I just want you to notice how simple and relatively intuitive it is. We first bind to (that is to say, instantiate) the COM ADSI component that represents the local computer using VB's GetObject function. We then use a For...Each loop to list all the objects in that computer that happen to be users. Immediately prior to the loop, we set a filter that indicates we only want the For...Each loop to return users, not any other objects (if we didn't do this, we'd get groups, NT Services and the odd print queue back as well). The code refers to two interfaces, IADs and IADsContainer. These are standard ADSI interfaces, which we will describe soon.

And just to demonstrate that that code did work, here are the results of running it:

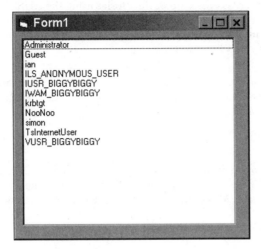

ADSI Provider Architecture

ADSI is based on providers in much the same way as ADO and OLE DB are. The idea is that Microsoft has defined a standard set of COM interfaces. For each directory service an ADSI provider is available. The ADSI provider consists of COM components which expose the ADSI interfaces. So the client application needs to make sure that it hooks up to the appropriate ADSI provider for the directory service it requires, but this is very easy to do. In the code sample that lists users, you probably scarcely even noticed the line in which we made sure we'd hooked up to the correct provider (it was the line

```
Set oComputer = GetObject("WinNT://BiggyBiggy")
```

which connected us up to a provider known as the WinNT provider.)

When you install ADSI, you get several providers written by Microsoft automatically, these are known as system providers. To some extent, which providers you get depend on the system you are running, but in general you will normally find you have these providers:

- ❑ **LDAP:** Lets you access *any* directory which meets the LDAP standard (we'll explain LDAP soon; it's a general protocol that governs communication with directories). Active Directory does meet the LDAP standard, so this is the provider you will use to talk to Active Directory.

- ❑ **WinNT:** Gives access to data concerning your local network. It lets you identify which domains are on it, and access user and group accounts and other information concerning the computers on your network.

- ❑ **NWCompat:** and **NDS:** Give access to Novell Netware directories.

In addition if you have IIS installed, you'll probably have this provider:

- ❑ **IIS:** Lets you access the IIS Metabase.

However, those aren't necessarily the only providers around. It is quite possible for third parties to write their own providers to allow access to any other directories using the ADSI standard. However writing ADSI providers is beyond the scope of this book: here we will concentrate on writing ADSI clients, although it is worth bearing in mind that you may come across third party providers not covered here, which have been written for your clients to use.

If you want to learn how to write an ADSI provider, you might want to check out Professional ADSI Programming (ISBN 1-861002-26-2), by Simon Robinson, also published by Wrox Press, which explains how to do this.

Installing ADSI

If you are running any version of Windows 2000, then you will have ADSI installed as part of the operating system. If you are running Windows 9x or Windows NT4 then you will need to download ADSI from Microsoft's web site. At the time of writing, the current version of ADSI is 2.5.

When you install ADSI you will get the following:

❑ The Microsoft System Providers

❑ The ADSI router – a component which allows browsing of the various ADSI providers on your system

❑ Some COM components that are shared between all ADSI providers

❑ Some registry entries under the `HKLM/Software/Microsoft/ADs` key, mostly to do with the providers registering their presence as ADSI providers

In order to develop software that uses ADSI, you will also need the ADSI SDK, which is downloadable from Microsoft's web site, at `http://www.microsoft.com/ntserver/nts/downloads/other/ADSI25/sdk.asp`. The ADSI SDK gives you various header files as well as a copy of the MSDN ADSI documentation and a large number of samples. It also gives you a very useful tool called `adsvw.exe`, which you can use to browse around the installed ADSI providers and which we will demonstrate in soon in this chapter.

Exploring the ADSI Providers

As with any technology, the best way to find out about it is to start poking around in it. Microsoft has provided a very useful tool that enables you to do exactly that with ADSI. It's the Active Directory Browser, `adsvw.exe`, which presents a simple user interface that lets you look around and even modify the information in any directory that is exposed through an ADSI provider.

If you start up `adsvw.exe`, you first get a dialog box asking if you want to **browse** the directories (Object Viewer) or **search** for objects that satisfy certain criteria (Query).

For now we're going to do some exploring, so we'll select **Object Viewer**.

You'll then get another dialog box that essentially asks you whereabouts you want to start browsing (**New ADsPath**), as well as inviting you to supply a username and password. We want to look around everywhere so we'll put in ADs: as the ADsPath. (An **ADsPath** is basically just a pathname to an object):

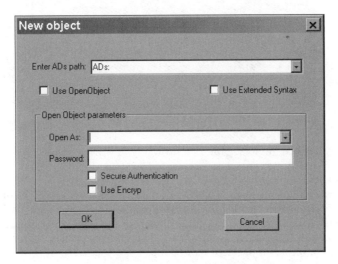

We're not bothering with a username and password here, so we'll leave the other fields blank (Note that the **Use OpenObject** checkbox is blank. This is normally checked by default, and instructs adsvw.exe to use the supplied username and password – so you'll need either to uncheck it, or type the username and password of a valid user account). If this checkbox is unchecked, ADSI uses what is known as default authentication, which for most providers means assuming you are the user you are logged in to NT as.

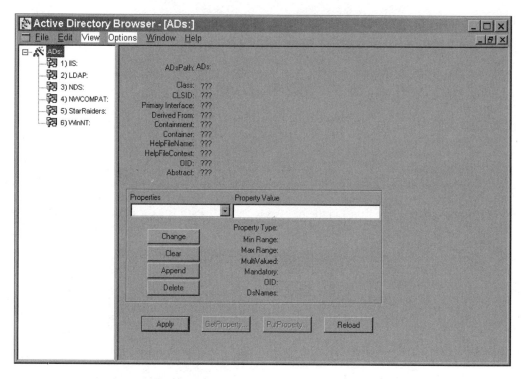

Once you've got this far, you get to see the real browsing at work:

From the screenshot you can see that adsvw.exe gives you two panes in its window. The left hand pane is a standard tree view, and so gives you a good idea of the tree structure of the directories available, while the right hand pane displays various properties of the currently selected object, along with some controls that allow you to modify that object. In the screenshot, the selected object is the ADSI router, ADs:, and it happens that many standard ADSI properties are not defined for the router – hence all the question marks in the right hand pane.

In this screenshot, we've just opened up one level of the tree below the ADSI router. The main purpose of the router is to allow enumeration over the providers on your system, so its children are objects that represent the ADSI providers which are installed – these are known as **namespace objects**. You can see all the normal system providers here, as well as StarRaiders, which is a provider that I wrote as part of the samples for *Professional ADSI Programming* – just to reinforce the point that you can write your own providers if you want to!

> *This is probably a good point to emphasize the distinction between ADSI (the set of interfaces that allows you to access any directory service) and Active Directory (a particular directory that stores information needed to manage domains in Windows 2000). It's easy to get the two names confused. Even Microsoft has confused the names on occasions, as shown by these adsvw.exe screenshots. The title bar in the Windows incorrectly displays the text Active Directory Browser, when in fact the tool is an ADSI browser, not an Active Directory browser – adsvw.exe can be used to examine any directory, not just Active Directory.*

If we look inside the namespace object, `LDAP:`, we'll see our Active Directory installation, as shown in the following screenshot. This particular screenshot will only work if your computer is in a domain controlled by Windows 2000 domain controllers:

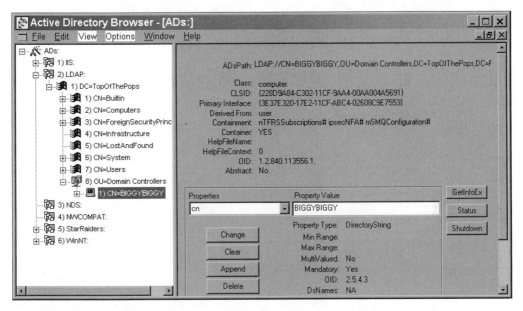

Inside Active Directory, we start off by seeing my domain, `TopOfThePops`, immediately below the `LDAP:` object. (The node named LDAP: is roughly speaking just a placeholder that indicates that everything under it is made available through the LDAP provider. It's often called a **namespace** object). Inside the domain are various containers for different types of object stored in Active Directory: users, computers (member workstations), domain controllers (the rest of the computers) and various nodes containing system related objects. I've opened up the Domain Controllers node to expose my one domain controller, BiggyBiggy.

The WinNT provider exposes some similar information, though this provider will work on NT4 as well as Windows 2000: WinNT doesn't need an installation of Active Directory.

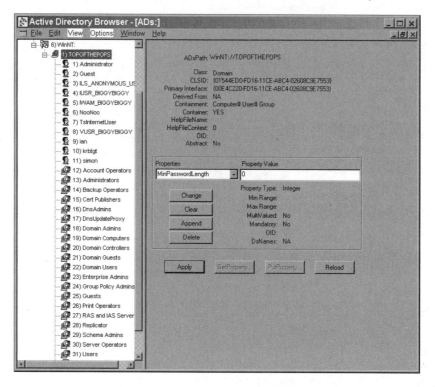

The directory structure viewed through WinNT isn't quite as well organized – you tend to find more objects mixed up under the same node. Thus, here, under the domain object, you find all the user and group accounts, mixed up with computers, rather than having each type of object separated in its own node. On the other hand, you can easily replicate this screenshot using any Windows operating system, not just Windows 2000.

Introducing LDAP

We've mentioned that Active Directory and certain other directories meet the LDAP standard. LDAP is the **Lightweight Directory Access Protocol**. It's a standard that defines how communication with directories takes place over a network or over the Internet. It differs from ADSI in that it is in many ways a lower level standard. Where ADSI defines certain COM interfaces, LDAP defines the actual structure of messages passed back and forward over the network, and what operations may be performed against a directory service. Also, ADSI works much more on the client side. What I mean by this is that ADSI providers are all in-process COM servers, so all the action as far as ADSI is concerned takes place on the local machine that your client process is running on. If an LDAP directory is located somewhere else on the network or the Internet, then getting a query from your machine to the directory and returning the information from the query back to your machine in a suitable format is the province of the LDAP protocol. The ADSI LDAP provider then takes over and translates the information from the LDAP format to or from the usual COM method calls that your ADSI client uses. You could say that all ADSI essentially defines is a component-based client-side API for talking to directories. ADSI does not specify how the providers should be implemented internally, or what protocols they should use to contact the directory service over the network.

It should also be pointed out that ADSI is Microsoft-specific, whereas LDAP is an industry-wide recognized standard.

What this all means is that if a directory service complies with the LDAP specifications, then it should be possible to write one program that sits on a client computer and is able to talk to any such directory service. Such a program is the ADSI LDAP provider. The LDAP provider can be thought of as a set of components that are able to understand the LDAP protocol and so translate LDAP operations to and from COM method calls as defined by ADSI. So the LDAP provider is the one that an ADSI client will use to communicate with any LDAP based directory service. All the other ADSI providers are there to communicate with particular directories that do not meet the LDAP requirements.

Of the directories we've discussed, the ones that meet the LDAP specifications include

- ❑   Active Directory
- ❑   The Microsoft Exchange Directory
- ❑   The Microsoft Site Server Directory
- ❑   Netscape Directory Server
- ❑   The openLDAP Directory Service

This means that any of those directories will be accessed through the LDAP provider if you are using ADSI.

WinNT and Active Directory Compared

The two ADSI providers that are likely to be in most common use are the WinNT provider and the LDAP provider connected to Active Directory. This is because both of these providers allow you to examine and modify many of your network settings. In addition, Microsoft has promised that future releases of Site Server and Exchange Server will allow the Site Server Membership directory and the Exchange Directory to be merged into Active Directory.

Active Directory is a very advanced directory service which is only available in Windows 2000. Because it is intended as the directory that controls Windows domains, it will by default only store information that is related to the domain as a whole. This information includes:

- ❑   Global domain user and group accounts
- ❑   Computer accounts
- ❑   Information related to security policies
- ❑   Security information – security descriptors and access control lists etc. for the objects stored within Active Directory
- ❑   Configuration information for the domain. The structure of domain trees and trust relationships.

However it should be stressed that Active Directory is simultaneously intended as a general purpose directory – which means that it is possible to store any other information you want in it – as long as you (or some systems administrator) is willing to do the work involved in getting the extra information stored in Active Directory – either adding it manually using a tool like adsvw.exe, or, more likely, writing an application that uses ADSI to add the required information).

The WinNT provider can in some ways be thought of as providing some of the facilities offered by Active Directory for networks running NT4. In Windows NT4 there is no centralized directory of resources similar to Active Directory. The WinNT provider, however, queries round the registries etc. of the various machines on the network, as well as looking at NT4 Server's (more restricted) domain database, and presents this information to the ADSI client *as if* it were a unified directory. This means that the facilities offered by the WinNT provider are not restricted to Windows 2000, but it does mean that all of the new features of domains that are introduced with Windows 2000 cannot be accessed using the WinNT provider. It will only let you get to functionality that was available in NT4 as well. For example, with Windows 2000, it became possible to form hierarchical trees of domains. The structure of such trees cannot be examined with the WinNT provider, which sees only lots of isolated domains – as was the situation in NT4.

Another restriction of the WinNT provider is that the information it makes available is fixed. Whereas in Active Directory it is possible to add any information you want to the directory (details of employees of a company, for example, or even – if you're so inclined – something like cookery recipes!) Any such information added to Active Directory will not be viewable through the WinNT provider, which is designed to expose a fixed, standard, set of information. Having said that, the information that WinNT: does expose does include some stuff that is not by default stored in Active Directory. This means that even on machines running Windows 2000, the WinNT provider can play an important role.

Information exposed by the WinNT provider, which is also stored in Active Directory, includes:

❑ Global domain user and group accounts

❑ Domain computer accounts

Objects that can, by default, only be accessing through the WinNT provider include:

❑ Local machine user and group accounts

❑ NT services running on individual machines

❑ Active file shares and details of who is currently using them and which folders are being accessed via file shares

❑ Print queues on machines, and the print jobs currently being processed or waiting in the queues

Note that when I talk about accessing objects through the WinNT provider, I actually mean more than just getting and setting data. Besides accessing data, ADSI includes some interfaces that allow you to perform some elementary operations to control some objects within the directories. This means, for example, that it is possible to use the WinNT provider to start and stop services, and to suspend processing of print jobs. Some such operations can in principle also be done through LDAP, but the WinNT provider tends to expose more objects that allow these types of operation.

Programming with ADSI

We're now at the point where we've got all the necessary background to start looking in more detail at how to write ADSI clients. We're going to concentrate on Active Directory and the WinNT provider in our samples, though the same general principles apply to all other ADSI providers.

Binding to Directory Objects

ADSI works on the principle that whenever you want to access a particular object in a directory, you do so by instantiating a COM object that provides a wrapper around the corresponding directory object. The COM component in effect pretends to be the directory object. It takes its own copy of all the data that describes the directory object (the properties of the directory object) and sits in the same process space as the client, so calling methods on the component is very fast. To the client it appears for the most part as if it really is talking to the directory object when in reality it is talking to the ADSI COM component. Internally, the component handles all the actual communication with the directory service, including, if necessary, calling out over the network if the directory service is hosted on a different computer. The only point where the distinction between the COM component and the directory object becomes apparent to the client is in the need to occasionally call methods to either load the component with all the data from the underlying directory object or to write any changes made to the data in the component back to the directory service.

Binding to directory objects in VB or VBScript is made using VB's GetObject function, as illustrated in the earlier example:

```
Set oComputer = GetObject("WinNT://BiggyBiggy")
```

What you need to pass to GetObject is a string that uniquely identifies the directory object you are interested in. This string is known as the **ADsPath**. We can get an idea of how ADsPaths work if we modify our sample code that displays user accounts so that it displays the ADsPaths as well.

```
Option Explicit

Private Sub Form_Load()

' bind to the local computer
Dim oComputer As IADsContainer
Set oComputer = GetObject("WinNT://BiggyBiggy")
Dim oComputerADs As IADs
Set oComputerADs = oComputer

List1.AddItem "Bound to computer " & oComputer.ADsPath
List1.AddItem ""

' list all the users
oComputer.Filter = Array("user")
Dim oUser As IADs
For Each oUser In oComputer
    List1.AddItem "User Name: " & oUser.Name
    List1.AddItem "ADsPath: " & oUser.ADsPath
    List1.AddItem ""
Next

Set oComputer = Nothing
Set oUser = Nothing

End Sub
```

Again for the time being don't worry if bits of the code aren't yet that clear – we'll go over that soon. The only changes we've made to the previous sample is to display the ADsPaths of the computer object and the users returned. We've also had to define a new variable. This is because we are using two interfaces here. The interface IADs is the interface that exposes automation properties such as the object's name and ADsPath, whereas IADsContainer is the interface that allows you to enumerate over other objects contained within an object – in other words objects that lie beneath it in the tree. Previously we only needed the IADsContainer interface on the computer object, whereas now we need the IADs interface on the same object in order to get to the ADsPath.

This code produces these results:

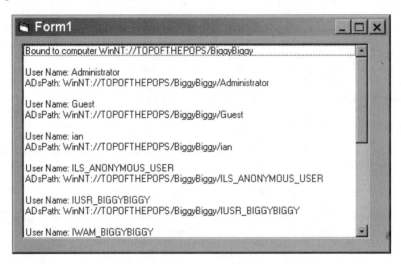

Referring back to the screenshot we presented of adsvw.exe being used to explore the WinNT directory, we can see this screenshot shows that in WinNT the user objects exist as children of the computer object on which the user accounts are registered. So our code really is listing the children of the computer object. And the results of our sample show that the ADsPaths of these children are formed by adding the user names on to the ADsPath of the computer object.

> *You'll notice an apparent discrepancy in the ADsPath of the computer: We bound to the computer object by naming the ADsPath as WinNT://BiggyBiggy, but this object has declared its own ADsPath as WinNT://TOPOFTHEPOPS/BiggyBiggy. TOPOFTHEPOPS is the name of the domain – the discrepancy is not a problem. It occurs because the WinNT provider allows you to omit the name of the local domain from an ADsPath when binding to an object – something I've taken advantage of in the code.*

This roughly shows us that ADsPaths really are pathnames that work in much the same way that file system paths to files work. They consist of the names of objects in the directory tree that you meet as you work down the hierarchy to get to the object in question. This is not however always the case – we'll look at the exceptions to this principle in a moment, but it's a good first approximation.

In more detail, the first part of the ADsPath is the name of the ADSI provider that exposes the object. We're using the WinNT provider, so our ADsPaths start with WinNT. There then follows a colon followed by two forward slashes, then we are into the part of the ADsPath that determines where within the particular directory that object is located. The WinNT provider uses the objects working down the directory tree from left to right, and with each name in the ADsPath separated by slashes. However, it is important to understand that this part of the ADsPath is provider-specific. For example, the LDAP provider uses a completely different format, which reads bottom-up rather than top-down, as we can see if we modify the sample to examine the children of the LDAP domain object instead.

To do this, all we need to do is modify the ADsPath of the object that we initially bind to, so our GetObject call becomes:

```
Set oComputer = GetObject("LDAP://dc=TopOfThePops,dc=Fame,dc=com")
Dim oComputerADs As IADs
Set oComputerADs = oComputer
```

```
List1.AddItem "Bound to domain " & oComputer.ADsPath
```

Note that we are now binding to a domain object rather than a computer object. I guess for code readability I really ought to change that variable name oComputer to something like oDomain as well, but I'll leave that for now. I will however remove the line that sets the filter to users, since we are now going to list all child objects, whatever their type:

```
'oComputer.Filter = Array("user")
```

Using the LDAP provider allows me to use the full domain name recognized by Windows 2000 – I've called my domain TopOfThePops.Fame.com, which the LDAP provider requires to be written in LDAP format, as dc=TopOfThePops,dc=Fame,dc=com. (dc here stands for domain component). However, NT4 is unable to cope with domain names made of multiple components, and will only recognize TOPOFTHEPOPS – so this is the name the WinNT provider, which must remain compatible with NT4, uses.

Now the code produces these results:

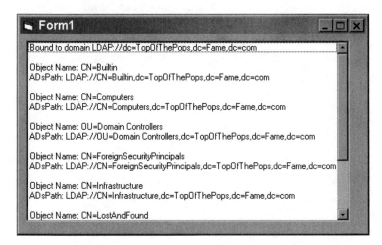

So as not to be misleading I've changed user name to object name in the text displayed. The information displayed here corresponds to the screenshot earlier of adsvw.exe being used to explore Active Directory. Here we can see that the ADsPath is formed differently: LDAP uses commas rather than slashes to separate the components in the ADsPath. It also uses prefixes to denote the type of object (CN=Computers rather than just Computers). But most importantly, it lists the objects working *up* the tree instead of down it. Reading from left to right, after the initial LDAP: we see the name of the object furthest down the tree first.

This is important because it means you cannot always rely on being able to form ADsPaths by concatenating the name of an object on to the ADsPath of the parent, with some suitable separator symbol. That trick will work for WinNT but it won't work for the LDAP provider.

A Note About Classes

I've hinted at the fact that there are different types of directory object. For example, we've just been discussing objects that represent computers and domains. Active Directory also contains users and groups, while other providers contain other objects – for example WinNT: allows access to Services and print queues. The type of object is represented by something called a **class**. In directories, all objects are of a certain class – for example 'User' or 'Computer'. The class is the thing that indicates what properties a particular object can have ('Username' makes sense for a user but not for a print queue!). Most directories have a special area in the directory known as the **schema container**, which contains information that defines what properties are allowed for each class. Detailed study of the schema container is a bit beyond the scope of this chapter, but we will touch on how to access it programmatically as we need to in the samples.

The ADSI Interfaces

Before we can go much further, we need to get familiar with the two core ADSI interfaces that we've been using, IADs and IADsContainer.

IADs is exposed by *all* ADSI directory objects so you can always count on this interface being present. However, IADsContainer is only exposed by those ADSI objects where the underlying directory object is able to contain other objects – in other words to act as a parent in the directory tree to other objects. For example, in WinNT, computers expose IADsContainer since they can contain users, groups and other objects. Users, on the other hand, cannot contain anything else, so they do not expose IADsContainer.

IADs

IADs exposes the following automation properties:

Property	Description
Name	The name of the object
ADsPath	The ADsPath of the object
Class	The name of the type (class) of the object, eg. computer, user
Schema	The ADsPath of a special object, known as the **schema object**, which describes what can be stored in objects of this class
Parent	The ADsPath of the parent to this object – that is the object above this object in the directory hierarchy
Guid	A GUID that uniquely identifies this class of object. Not implemented in all providers.

These properties all return strings (for C++ developers: BSTR), and are all read-only.

IADs also exposes these methods:

Method	Description
Get	Retrieves the value of a property from the cache
GetEx	Similar to Get but retrieves the value in a different format
Put	Sets the value of a property in the cache
PutEx	Similar to Put but has a couple of extra options that describe how you are setting the property (eg. are you replacing a value or appending new values). Put always replaces a value.
GetInfo	Updates the cache from the underlying directory object
SetInfo	Updates the underlying directory object from the cache
GetInfoEx	Similar to GetInfo but allows optimization of network access by allowing you to specify which properties should be loaded instead of loading the entire cache.

These methods refer to something called the **cache** or the **property cache**. This is just the local copy of the information in the underlying directory object that we mentioned the ADSI component maintains. Note that there's normally no need for ADSI clients to call GetInfo explicitly since it is called automatically when the ADSI provider detects that it is required (that is, the cache is uninitialized and you attempt to read a property in it.) You only need to call it explicitly if for some reason you believe the cache may have become out of date. SetInfo, by contrast, must always be called whenever you have any changes that need to be written to the directory – otherwise your changes will be lost as soon as the ADSI component gets released.

From these tables we can see that, roughly speaking, the IADs properties are there to retrieve standard data that you need available to be able to manipulate the object, while the IADs methods are concerned with getting and setting the rest of the data stored in the object.

In order to use the IADs methods we need to be familiar with the concept of a schema. The directory schema is in some ways similar to a database schema. The purpose of it can be understood by taking as an example computer objects. With the WinNT provider, ADSI can be used to store a fair amount of information about computers, such as their operating system, who the person responsible for the computer is, and the processor type. So the directory needs some way of indicating that this information is allowed to be stored in the object. Or, to put it in more technical language, that the **properties** or **attributes** of a computer object include these items. The way that this is done is through a **schema object**. Somewhere in the directory will be an object named Computer which exposes the special interface IADsClass (as well as IADs) and which is able to describe what a computer object is. We won't go into the IADsClass interface in detail here. What we need to know is that the automation properties it exposes include these:

Property	Description
MandatoryProperties	List of the names of the properties which *must* be present on all objects of class Computer
OptionalProperties	List of the names of the properties which *may* optionally be present on all objects of class Computer

Both of these automation properties return an array of strings (if coding clients in C++ you will need to know that this is actually a VARIANT containing a SAFEARRAY of VARIANTs, each inner VARIANT containing a BSTR).

One point that is important to understand is that conceptually a directory object is really no more than the set of all its attributes – in other words, it is the set of attributes that define the object.

Putting IADs Into Practice

So if you want to display a known property of an object, you will simply use either the Get or GetEx methods. Say you want to retrieve the value of the property OperatingSystem. In VB you could do it like this:

```
Dim strOS As String
strOS = oComputerADs.Get("OperatingSystem")
```

The difference between Get and GetEx is to do with the fact that some properties can have more than one value. If more than one value is present, then Get will return the results in an array. Since OperatingSystem has only one value, Get returns a simple string here. GetEx will *always* return the results in an array. So GetEx is more useful if you don't know how many values are going to be returned and want to be sure of what format the values are going to turn up in. So our above code snippet would if you preferred to use GetEx look something more like:

```
Dim strOS
For Each strOS In oComputerADs.GetEx("OperatingSystem")
    ' process strOS
Next
```

That's easy enough but it relies on your knowing the name of the property you are interested in. If you don't know the name of the property it's a bit harder, and you will most likely need to use the schema. The following code sample illustrates this process. It's a VB sample which binds to an ADSI computer object in WinNT, lists all its automation properties, then uses the schema to list all the other properties available for the object. The process involves binding to the schema object that describes Computers and using its MandatoryProperties and OptionalProperties automation properties exposed by IADsClass to find out the names of the properties exposed by computer objects.

Here's the code. First we bind to the computer object and list all its IADs automation properties:

```
Option Explicit

Private Sub Form_Load()

' bind to the local computer
Dim oComputer As IADs
Set oComputer = GetObject("WinNT://BiggyBiggy")

List1.AddItem "Bound to this object"
List1.AddItem "Name: " & oComputer.Name
List1.AddItem "ADsPath: " & oComputer.ADsPath
List1.AddItem "Class: " & oComputer.Class
List1.AddItem "Schema: " & oComputer.Schema
List1.AddItem "Parent: " & oComputer.Parent
List1.AddItem "Guid: " & oComputer.Guid
```

Now we bind to the class schema object:

```
'bind to the schema object
Dim oSchema As IADsClass
Set oSchema = GetObject(oComputer.Schema)

Dim strPropName
Dim strPropValue
```

Then we enumerate through all the mandatory properties of the Computer, and for each one display all the values. Note that we use GetEx here to guard against the fact that we don't know how many values will be returned for each property. Finally we do the same for the optional properties:

```
List1.AddItem ""
List1.AddItem "MANDATORY PROPERTIES"
For Each strPropName In oSchema.MandatoryProperties
   List1.AddItem strPropName & ":"
   For Each strPropValue In oComputer.GetEx(strPropName)
      List1.AddItem "   " & strPropValue
   Next
Next
List1.AddItem ""
List1.AddItem "OPTIONAL PROPERTIES"
```

```
For Each strPropName In oSchema.OptionalProperties
   List1.AddItem strPropName & ":"
   For Each strPropValue In oComputer.GetEx(strPropName)
       List1.AddItem "   " & strPropValue
   Next
Next

Set oComputer = Nothing
Set oSchema = Nothing

End Sub
```

And here are the results (you can even spot the typo I made when I first installed Windows and told Windows who the owner of the computer was!):

This shows that `Computer` objects in WinNT do not have any mandatory properties, but do have a number of optional properties.

IADsContainer

IADsContainer exposes the following properties:

Property	Description
_NewEnum	Returns a standard COM enumerator object that exposes the IEnumVARIANT interface, which can be used to enumerate the children of this object
Filter	Restricts the children enumerated over to those of certain classes
Hints	Optimizes network access by indicating that only certain properties are required to be returned to the property cache of children enumerated
Count	Returns the number of children of the object that satisfy the filter. Not often used because you can just find out the children by enumerating anyway – and some providers don't implement this property.

And the following methods:

Method	Description
GetObject	Returns an interface pointer to the named child object
MoveHere	Moves an object from elsewhere in the directory tree to be a child of this container. Can also be used to rename directory objects.
CopyHere	Similar to MoveHere but takes a copy of the directory object instead
Create	Creates a new object which is a child of this container
Delete	Deletes the specified child object

So IADsContainer is responsible for both enumerating through children and for creating, deleting and moving directory objects. Note that if you want to create or move, etc. an object, you always do so by calling the appropriate IADsContainer method on its *parent*.

We're not going to go into moving, copying, creating or deleting objects in this chapter. We're mainly interested in the use of IADsContainer to navigate around the tree. For this all we really need are the _NewEnum and Filter properties. And we've already seen these properties in action, in the first sample in which we enumerated the users on a computer:

```
' list all the users
oComputer.Filter = Array("user")
Dim oUser As IADs
For Each oUser In oComputer
   List1.AddItem "User Name: " & oUser.Name
   List1.AddItem "ADsPath: " & oUser.ADsPath
   List1.AddItem ""
Next
```

The technique of exposing a collection of objects via a property called _NewEnum which exposes an enumerator object that implements the IEnumVARIANT interface is a standard one in COM – and a technique that VB is aware of. Which is why VB is able to handle the processing of the COM enumerator object automatically inside a For...Each loop. If you are coding in C++, you will need to be more explicit about the use of the enumerator.

The main point to notice here is that what is returned from the enumerator is an actual interface pointer. In other words if you use a For...Each loop on an IADsContainer interface, the provider will actually instantiate and bind to the COM components that represent each of the children. That is the standard way in ADSI of navigating down a directory tree.

In order to navigate up the tree, you will use the IADs::Parent property. Note however that in this case you just get the ADsPath of the parent – if you want to actually bind to the parent object then you will need to use the ADsPath to do so explicitly using GetObject.

Authenticating to an ADSI Object

In all the work we've done so far we haven't bothered to actually authenticate to the object. We've just relied on having permissions to do what we want by default.

If we use GetObject to bind to an ADSI object, then default authentication will be used. What this means is up to the individual ADSI provider to determine, but for both the WinNT provider and Active Directory it means you will be bound to the object as whatever user you are logged in as. If that account doesn't have the appropriate permissions to access the directory (and the most obvious case in which it probably won't is if the ADSI client is an ASP page running under the Internet guest account) then you will need to supply some alternative credentials.

It is not possible to do this with one single method call. Rather, in ADSI, supplying credentials is a two-stage process. First of all you must bind using default credentials (in other words, using GetObject) to the namespace object for the provider you are interested in. Recall that this is simply the object that is at the top of the directory tree for the ADSI provider in question. So if you want to supply credentials to bind to an object exposed by the WinNT provider, you'll first bind to the namespace object with ADsPath WinNT:. If you want to supply a username and password to an object in Active Directory, you must first bind to the namespace object with ADsPath LDAP:.

Namespace objects expose another interface, IADsOpenDSObject. IADsOpenDSObject implements a single method, OpenDSObject. OpenDSObject is the method you need to bind to an object supplying credentials. It takes four parameters:

❏ The ADsPath of the object you wish to bind to

❏ Your username

❏ Your password

❏ A flag that indicates exactly how the authentication is to be carried out – e.g. whether encryption schemes are to be used when transmitting your password over the network. For this chapter we will simply set this flag to 1, which indicates that normal NT authentication should be used.

So to authenticate, for example, to a computer object using the WinNT provider, the code would look something like this:

```
Dim oNamespace As IADsOpenDSObject
Dim oObj As IADs
Set oNamespace = GetObject("WinNT:")
Set oObj = oNamespace.OpenDSObject("WinNT://BiggyBiggy", "Simon", _
                               "MyPassword", 1)
```

Searching

So far what we've shown you how to do involves binding to an ADSI object and browsing around the directory tree. That is to say, exploring the tree by binding to an object then moving either up or down from that object in the hierarchy of the tree. However, I've also indicated that it is also important that directories support searching – that is to say, identifying all instances of an object which satisfy certain criteria, no matter where it might be in the directory. This is the subject of this section.

Searching in ADSI is a fairly large topic – and there are quite a few concepts to understand, which means we're going to need to spend a few pages exploring the ideas behind searching in ADSI, before we demonstrate how to write ADSI clients that can request searches to be executed. We'll mostly demonstrate searching in practice by using the user interface provided by the adsvw.exe utility.

Although this is a chapter about ADSI, most of what we are actually going to learn about the concepts behind searching actually comes from LDAP rather than ADSI. This is because the only Windows-centric ADSI provider that supports searching is the ADSI LDAP provider. The LDAP provider itself doesn't really do that much processing on search requests – it essentially just passes the request on to the underlying LDAP-compliant directory service. Which means that the requests we need to send to the LDAP provider are really LDAP requests.

Basic LDAP Searching Concepts

The nearest telephone analogy to searching is, as we've remarked, looking in the yellow pages. For example, if I look under the 'Florists' section of my Cumbria and North Lancashire Yellow Pages, then I am effectively performing a search for objects which have three properties: they are businesses (rather than private homes), they are florists, and they are based in my local area. Unfortunately, for telephone directories printed on paper, that's about as sophisticated as searching can get.

SQL also provides a facility to do searches, via the SELECT statement. For example, if I'm running a cinema with a database of films, and I want to identify the times of all the showings of Star Wars Episode 1, I might type in something like

```
SELECT Showings.Time
FROM Showings INNER JOIN
Films ON Showings.FilmID = Films.FilmID
WHERE (Films.Name = 'Starwars')
```

This statement picks up all the required showings, but notice that it does require some knowledge of the structure of the database: implicit in this statement is the assumption that the database contains two tables, Films and Showings, and that they are joined by a FilmID key. We also assume there is a column in the Showings table that gives the time and a column in the Films table that gives the name of the film. Clearly, in order to perform a query that isn't particularly complex, a fairly detailed understanding of the particular database is required.

Searching in directories is more powerful than this, since it does not require any prior knowledge of the directory structure (though if you do have any such knowledge you may be able to make the search more efficient). There are no tables to specify – all you need to indicate is what conditions the entries you require must satisfy. We've already indicated that an object in a directory is really no more than a set of properties. And accordingly the way you indicate what you are looking for in a search is to indicate the required values of the properties. For example, if we imagine that our telephone directory example is stored in a computer directory, and write down our criteria in our search for a florist, we might come up with:

```
(&(Location=Lancashire)(Category=Business)(BusinessType=Florist))
```

This syntax may look unfamiliar. I've written this request using a formal search request syntax defined by LDAP, and which I'll explain later in the chapter.

Notice that this criterion does not make any assumptions about directory structure. In fact, it's even more general than that that. It might look from the query that we've assumed that directory objects have the three attributes Location, Category and BusinessType – but we haven't. We've simply said, in effect, that *if* there are any objects in the directory that have these attributes and *if* those attributes have the specified values, then we want details of those objects to be returned. So what I've just written down is a precise statement of what I'm looking for, but it doesn't make any assumptions either about what sorts of object are stored where in the directory, or what properties objects in the directory might have. All we've assumed is that the directory is able to understand the syntax we've written our criteria in.

In fact that last assumption isn't too restrictive. I've rather jumped the gun here by writing my criteria in a format that is defined by LDAP version 3 (the current version of LDAP) and therefore recognized by all LDAP v3 directories. The criteria is more formally known as an **LDAP Search Filter**, since it specifies what objects I want. In other words, the search filter effectively filters out all the other objects in the directory. We'll look at the precise syntax used in the search filters soon. At this point the real things I want you to notice at this stage are these:

❑ It is possible to express the filter entirely by setting conditions for the values of properties.

❑ Searching doesn't necessarily imply any element of browsing around the tree. You don't need to know anything about the structure of the directory.

This last point is significant because we earlier argued that one of the reasons for defining ADSI as a separate set of interfaces was that ADO doesn't allow any convenient way of browsing around a directory tree, whereas ADSI does. So we just seem to have argued ourselves into a position where there's no point in having ADSI at all as far as searching is concerned! In fact, as we'll see later, this is correct. It is possible to carry out searches by using ADO, with a special OLE DB provider that connects to ADSI. In fact, in VB and scripting languages, that is the only way that client applications can request searches. But that's starting to get into programming details – before we do that, we're going to have a closer look at how searching works in practise, by using Microsoft's adsvw.exe tool again.

Using adsvw.exe to Perform Searches

We can request a search in `adsvw.exe` by selecting Query from the New dialog box that appears when we start the application:

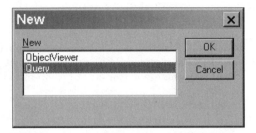

This brings up a dialog box asking for details of the search request. For this example, I'm going to request a search for all users stored in my installation of Active Directory:

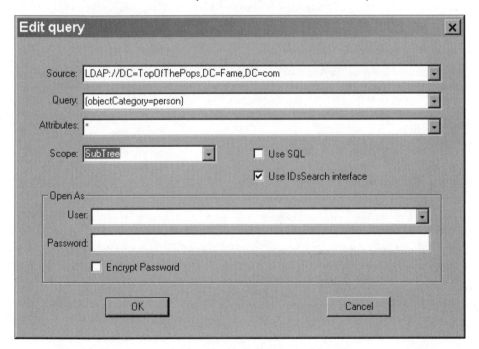

This dialog box indicates there are a fair few parameters that need to be set. We'll ignore the settings at the bottom of the dialog box, the ones grouped together as Open As – these settings just allow you to enter authentication credentials for an account on whose behalf you want the search to be conducted. If you leave these blank, default credentials will be used. We'll also ignore the Use SQL and Use IDsSearch Interface check boxes, since these only effect certain internal details of ADSI searching which are beyond the scope of this chapter and don't affect the search results. The four parameters we are interested in are the ones listed in this dialog box as Source, Query, Attributes and Scope.

Query is the LDAP search filter that we've already mentioned. It's a string that indicates precisely what objects we are interested in – what conditions these objects must satisfy. I've said this is to be a search for user accounts in Active Directory. As it happens, all objects in Active Directory have an attribute called `objectCategory`, which contains a string that describes the nature of the object. User accounts all have the value `'Person'` stored in this attribute, which means that a search filter of `(objectCategory=Person)` will serve our needs – at least for Active Directory.

The `Query` (search filter) is what defines the search – the other parameters all allow some optimization to take place – as we'll see in a moment – by imposing restrictions at the outset on where in the directory to look for the information and what information to return

The **Source** (often also called the **search base**) is the `ADsPath` of an object. It is used, in conjunction with the **scope**, to define the portion of the directory in which the search will be conducted. So if you happen to know roughly where in the directory the objects you are interested in are located, you can make the search more efficient by a suitable choice of these parameters. How they work is this:

❏ If the `scope` is set to `base` then only the object whose `ADsPath` is given as the search base will be searched. In other words, that one single object will be returned if it satisfies the criteria, no objects will be returned if it doesn't. This may not sound particularly useful as far as ADSI is concerned, but it does have some uses in the context of the LDAP protocols.

❏ If the `scope` is set to `onelevel` then only immediate children of the search base will be searched. This gives an effect similar to browsing the children of an object using the `IADsContainer` interface, but potentially allows more complex search filters. (When using `IADsContainer` the only filter you can set is to indicate the classes of object you want returned).

❏ If the `scope` is set to `subtree` then the base object will be checked to see if it satisfies the search filter, and all objects lying anywhere below it in the directory hierarchy will also be searched.

In this example, I've set the scope to `subtree` and the search base to the `ADsPath` of the LDAP namespace object, `LDAP:`. This will cause the whole of Active Directory to be searched, and is what you would do if you have no idea where in the directory the objects you are interested in might be.

Finally the remaining parameter, `Attributes`, allows us to optimize network access by specifying which properties we are interested in. Where the search filter narrows down which objects we are interested in, the `Attributes` parameter narrows down what data should be returned for those objects. In the screenshot, I've entered a `*` here, to indicate that the values of all attributes should be returned.

When we hit **OK** on the **Edit Query** dialog, we will get presented with another dialog, which asks us to select certain more advanced search criteria:

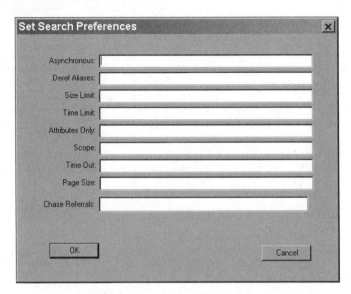

There's no need to enter any data here. This dialog box is asking you to set certain advanced search preferences, such as whether the search should be carried out asynchronously and what the maximum time you want the server to spend on the search is. However, the default values for all these preferences are fine.

When you click **OK** to the **Set Search Preferences** dialog, the search is executed and the results displayed:

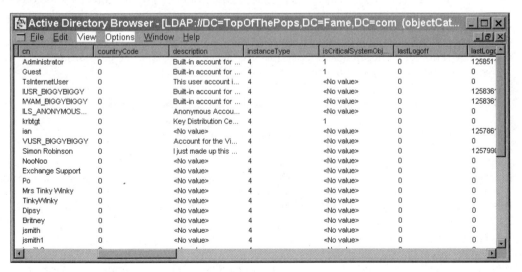

The format of these results is quite reminiscent of a table in a relational database. The results are divided into rows and columns – each row corresponds to a directory object which was found to satisfy the search criteria. Each column gives the value of a certain named property, from the properties requested. Recall that in this example, I requested *all* attributes – which means that there are a lot of columns!

One vital point to understand is that the search does not actually return any interface pointers to any ADSI objects. All you get back are the values of certain properties. If you will subsequently wish to manipulate one of the objects you have found, you must normally make sure you include the ADsPath as one of the requested attributes – then you can use the ADsPath to bind to the object in question using VB's GetObject function in the normal way. You request the ADsPath via the list of attributes required – with the adsvw.exe user interface it's the edit box in the first search request dialog, that we added * to. adsvw.exe is quite sophisticated in this regard and will ask for the ADsPath if you haven't explicitly specified it, but when writing your own code you will need to explicitly ask for the ADsPath.

LDAP Search Filters

Before we finally go on to see how to code up search requests programmatically, we need to take a quick look at the syntax for LDAP search filters. This syntax, like the rest of the LDAP protocols, is formally defined on the Internet in a Request for Comments. Specifically, search filters are defined in RFC 2254. The RFCs are available at http://www.ietf.org/rfc.html The syntax allows for some quite sophisticated subtleties, but we'll just quickly cover the basics here.

A search filter is a set of conditions that indicate that certain attributes should be present and have certain values. For example, the search filter that we used earlier was

```
(&(Location=Lancashire)(Category=Business)(BusinessType=Florist))
```

This contains three conditions. The attribute Location should be present and contain the value Lancashire. Similarly, the attribute Category should be present and contain the value Business, while the attribute BusinessType should contain Florist. Each condition is placed in round brackets, and the & (indicating a logical AND operation) before all these conditions indicates that they must all be satisfied. Notice that such operators are placed before all the conditions to which they apply, rather than between them. The more intuitive-looking filter

```
(Location=Lancashire)&(Category=Business)&(BusinessType=Florist)
```

would not be understood, and would most likely produce an error.

Other than & (AND) the operators | (OR) and ! (NOT) may be used. Conditions contained in round brackets can be nested to any level of depth – the brackets being used to indicate the order with which logical expressions should be evaluated. Finally, the entire search filter should be contained in round brackets. These principles are probably easiest to understand with a few examples:

```
(&(objectCategory=person)(cn=s*))
```

requests all users (objects with objectCategory of person) whose common name property begins with s. Note the use of the wildcard character * here, to indicate any string.

```
(&(objectCategory=person)(|(cn=s*)(cn=a*))
```

The brackets here indicate that the OR condition should be evaluated first. This filter requests all users whose common name property begins with either s or a.

```
(!(objectCategory=person))
```

This filter requests all directory objects that are not users.

One final point to note is the absence of quote marks. This means that we need a way of representing special characters, such as spaces or brackets that are intended to be part of strings in the search filters rather than part of the search filter syntax. The way this is done is by using a hexadecimal escape sequence based on the character's ASCII value. For example, the hexadecimal ASCII value of the opening bracket, (, is 0x28. So if we wanted to search for an object with a common name of (left, the request would be (cn=\28left).

Requesting Searches Programmatically

Now we've had a chance to understand how searching ADSI directories works in principle, we are in a position to see how to write code that requests searches using ADSI.

We've already mentioned that if you are programming in VB or scripting languages, you won't directly use ADSI to carry out searches – you will use ADO in conjunction with an OLE DB ADSI provider. The situation is shown in the figure:

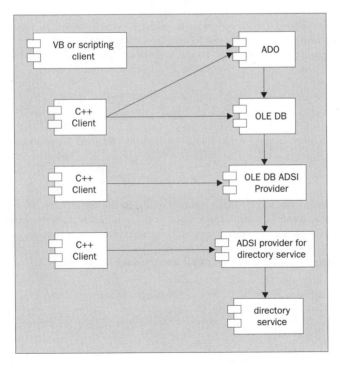

Down the right hand side of the diagram lies the chain of components that a search request passes through. The chain is based on an OLE DB provider that is designed to allow access to any ADSI directory – a provider which in effect translates from ADSI to OLE DB. We haven't encountered this provider before because it has only very restricted functionality at present – in fact the only thing it can do is request searches. The existence of this provider means that it is possible to request a search using ADO – the request passing through OLE DB, the OLE DB ADSI provider, and finally the ADSI interfaces implemented by the relevant ADSI provider (usually the LDAP provider) before it reaches the directory service.

The relevant interface in the ADSI provider is an interface called IDirectorySearch, which contains methods to set up a search filter and the various other preferences involved with a search, to carry out the search, and to enumerate through the results. However we will not be examining IDirectorySearch in this chapter. In fact, IDirectorySearch is not a dual interface (for people not familiar with the terminology: a dual interface is a COM interface that satisfies certain extra requirements that must be met if the interface is to be used by clients written in scripting languages). and it is not described by the ADSI type library, ActiveDS.tlb, which means it cannot be accessed from clients written in VB or scripting languages – it is really intended for use by C++ clients. So the only point at which VB and scripting clients can pass a request into the chain shown in the figure is by using ADO. By contrast, C++ clients can use the ADSI provider directly by calling up methods of IDirectorySearch, or can alternatively use either OLE DB or ADO directly.

What all this means in practise is that if you want to carry out a search on a directory exposed through ADSI using VB or VBScript, then you simply need to create the usual ADO objects, pass in a command string that indicates that the provider you're interested in is the ADSI provider, then pass in your search request as an ADO command string.

So after all that discussion there's actually very little in the way of new programming to explain – if you've got this far in the book then you already know how to use ADO! The only bits of information you still need are the string you pass to ADO to indicate you wish to use the OLE DB ADSI provider – that string is ADsDSOObject – and the precise syntax of the command string.

The command string needs to convey the four search parameters we discussed earlier – the scope, search base, search filter and attributes required. There are two formats that are recognized by the OLE DB ADSI provider – a SQL-based format, and a format known as the LDAP format (a somewhat misleading name since the format has little to do with LDAP beyond containing an LDAP search filter).

The LDAP format

In this format, the four parameters are simply concatenated in the order base, filter, attributes, scope. The search base must be enclosed in angled brackets, and the four parameters should be separated by semicolons. (Any attributes in the attribute list should be separated by commas).

In this format our earlier request for a search of all users would be written:

```
<LDAP://DC=TopOfThePops,DC=Fame,DC=Com>;(objectCategory=person);*;subtree
```

The SQL format

This format is based on the SQL SELECT statement. A search request is written as:

```
SELECT attribute-list FROM 'search-base' WHERE search-filter
```

The search base will normally be enclosed in single quotes. So for example our earlier request for users would be written:

```
SELECT * FROM 'LDAP://DC=TopOfThePops,DC=Fame,DC=Com' WHERE
(objectCategory=person)
```

This is more readable, though doesn't allow specification of the search scope. This must be specified separately as the Scope property of the Command object when using this syntax – if it is not set then it will default to subtree. There are some other options that it is possible to add to the SELECT query – notably it is possible to append ORDER BY in order to request that the results appear in a certain sequence. It's not the purpose of this chapter to go into full details of the various options in the command syntaxes, but details are in the MSDN ADSI documentation.

We are now in a position to demonstrate some sample code. The VB Basic Search sample performs roughly the search for users that we attempted using adsvw.exe. The main difference is that instead of asking for all properties, it requests just one property, the common name – requesting one property saves us from having to write a complex user interface to display all the properties in tabular form! We've also used the ORDER BY SQL statement to ensure the results are displayed in alphabetical order. The project is a standard VB project, with a list box called list1, and the code to request the search is as follows. Note that since this code doesn't use ADSI directly, there is no need to reference the ActiveDS type library. However, we do need to reference the ADO type library.

```
Option Explicit

Private Sub Form_Load()

On Error Resume Next

Dim oConnection As New Connection
Dim oRecordset As New Recordset

oConnection.Provider = "ADsDSOObject"
oConnection.Open "Active Directory Provider"

Dim strCommand As String

strCommand = _
    "SELECT cn FROM 'LDAP://dc=TopOfThePops,dc=Fame,dc=com' WHERE" & _
    "objectCategory='person' ORDER BY cn"

Set oRecordset = oConnection.Execute(strCommand)

While Not oRecordset.EOF
   List1.AddItem oRecordset.Fields(0).Value
   oRecordset.MoveNext
Wend

End Sub
```

Note that I've used the name of my own domain in this code – obviously if trying it out you'll need to substitute the name of your own domain!

Running this code produces these results:

Using ADSI from C++

So far we've presented all our examples in VB on the basis that that makes for simpler code in which it is easy to understand what is going on. For the most part, converting ADSI client code from VB to C++ is no different to converting any other code that uses COM components. For example, the VB code that obtains the class of an object

```
dim strClass as String
strClass = oObject.Class
```

translates in C++ to:

```
BSTR bstrClass
hr = pObject->get_Class(&bstrClass);
```

However there are a couple of extra differences in the case of ADSI:

❑ When carrying out searching, C++ clients can use the ADSI `IDirectorySearch` interface directly instead of going through ADO. (Though it should be noted that this does not change which providers you can carry out searching through – searches are always carried out using `IDirectorySearch`, even if this is done indirectly using ADO). Similarly there is an extra interface, `IDirectoryObject`, which reproduces most of the methods of `IADs` and `IADsContainer`, but in a way that is sometimes more efficient (it uses some low level techniques to by-pass the property cache), and which is only available to C++ clients.

❑ There are a number of API functions supplied designed to make certain tasks easier in C++. These API functions are often termed **helper functions**.

❑   ADSI extensively uses VARIANTs – which VB is able to handle automatically, but which need to be dealt with explicitly in C++.

We won't be looking at the IDirectorySearch or IDirectoryObject interfaces in this chapter, but we will briefly go over some of the more important helper functions. The format of this section is that we will first introduce the two most important helper functions that are used to bind to objects, with short 2 or 3 line code snippets to show how to use them, then we will go over a longer code sample, the C++ ListProperties sample, which will list the properties of a computer object – in fact doing exactly what our earlier VB ListProperties sample did, but in C++. The C++ ListProperties sample will demonstrate how to manipulate the VARIANTs that frequently occur in ADSI.

Before we begin, though, a quick note about the header files etc. that you need to include in C++ projects. You will need the header file ActiveDS.h:

```
#include "ActiveDS.h"
```

An out-of-date version of this file, which covers ADSI 2.0, is supplied with Visual Studio 6. You will need to obtain the up to date version, and ensure that the paths in your project are set to ensure the correct version of the header file is #included. The easiest way is to download the latest version of the ADSI SDK (currently the ADSI 2.5 SDK) from Microsoft's web site. This is the same SDK that you will need in order to obtain the adsvw.exe browsing and searching utility.

You will need to link to two libraries, ActiveDS.lib and ADsIID.lib – again these are supplied with the ADSI SDK, though Visual Studio 6 has out-of-date versions of them.

ActiveDS.h is a general header file that simply includes all the other header files in which definitions of interfaces, helper functions, error codes and other useful constants are defined. ActiveDS.lib is the equivalent library, while ADsIID.lib defines all the ADSI CLSIDs and IIDs. Note that if you are using ADSI from an ATL 3.0 or later project you will need to add the symbol _ATL_NO_UUIDOF to the preprocessor symbols for this library to work correctly.

Binding to an ADSI Object

In VB we do this using the GetObject function, which instantiates a particular identifiable instance of a component. This should be contrasted with the situation in ADO, in which CreateObject, or the equivalent, but more efficient, New keyword is used to instantiate ADO components:

ADSI:

```
Dim oObj As IADs
Set oObj = GetObject("WinNT://BiggyBiggy")
```

ADO:

```
Dim oConnection As New Connection
```

or:

461

```
Dim oConnection
Set oConnection = CreateObject("ADODB.Connection")
```

This causes a problem in C++, since while the C++ API function CoCreateInstance() corresponds to VB's CreateObject or New, in C++ there was until recently no direct equivalent command to GetObject, although Windows 2000 has introduced the new CoGetObject() API function which does the work of VB's GetObject(). GetObject encapsulates a fair amount of behind-the-scenes functionality involving COM monikers, which would normally need to be explicitly coded in C++. Since binding to an ADSI object is quite a fundamental process, it's clearly essential for there to be a quick and easy way of doing this in any language. For this reason, ADSI provides the API function, ADsGetObject(), which provides identical functionality to VB's GetObject. ADsGetObject() is used like this:

```
HRESULT hr;
IADs *pComputer;
hr = ADsGetObject(L"WinNT://BiggyBiggy",IID_IADs,(void**)&pComputer);
```

In other words, it takes as parameters the required ADsPath, the interface IID and a pointer to the memory location that should receive the interface pointer. And as with COM method calls, it returns an HRESULT to indicate the success or failure of the operation.

With the new CoGetObject() function, ADsGetObject() will no longer strictly be necessary on W2K machines, but you'll probably prefer to use ADsGetObject() to ensure backwards compatibility with NT4 and Windows 9x computers.

Authenticating to an ADSI Object

Somewhat unusually, this is an operation that is simpler in C++ than in VB and VBScript. There is no need to explicitly separately bind to the namespace object and use the IADsOpenDSObject::OpenDSObject() method on it. This is all handled automatically for you by another helper function, ADsOpenObject().

ADsOpenObject() is used like this:

```
HRESULT hr;
IADs *pComputer;
hr = ADsOpenObject(L"WinNT://BiggyBiggy",L"UserName",L"Password",1
IID_IADs,(void**)&pComputer);
```

In other words, it takes the same parameters as for ADsGetObject, with the addition of the username and password you want to use to authenticate, as the second and third parameters. The fourth parameter is an integer that indicates how you wish to authenticate. It is one of the same values used as authentication flags in IADsOpenDSObject::OpenDSObject(), so in the above code snippet we've used the value 1 to indicate normal NT authentication.

Other Helper Functions

ADsGetObject() and ADsOpenObject() are the helper functions you will encounter most often, since you will normally use one of them to bind to an ADSI object in the first place. (The alternative to using one of these functions is some fairly complex code that explicitly manipulates COM monikers to identify the ADSI object from the ADsPath – which is what VB's GetObject and the helper function ADsGetObject() do internally anyway). Other tasks for which helper functions are available are:

❑ Memory allocation and deallocation (for certain method calls where memory should be allocated by the provider and freed by the client)

❑ Converting arrays of strings and integers into the VARIANT format used by many ADSI methods.

❑ Building enumerators and using them to enumerate through collections

❑ Returning extended error messages.

Since this is only an introductory chapter, we don't have space to go into all these helper functions here, but the details are in MSDN.

The C++ ListProperties Sample

Finally we come to the C++ ListProperties sample, which demonstrates how to list properties in C++. This sample does exactly the same thing as our earlier VB-based ListProperties sample – that is to say, it binds to a computer object using the WinNT provider and lists its mandatory and optional properties – except it is coded in C++. This means that we will see a lot of the stuff that was going on under the scenes in VB explicitly coded.

Here's what the C++ ListProperties sample looks like when it is run. It's a console application:

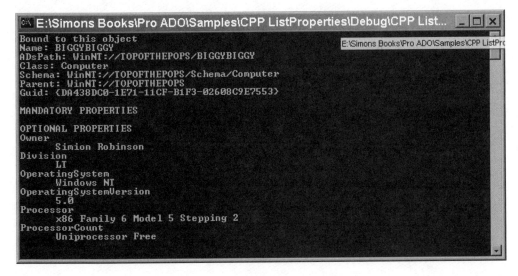

We'll check out the code now. Although this application is a console application, we have made use of ATL's CComPtr<> template and CComVariant and CComBSTR classes to make our manipulation of interface pointers, variants and BSTRs easier. This means that the stdafx.h precompiled header file needs to include the following:

```
#include <iostream.h>
#include "windows.h"
#include "ActiveDS.h"
#include "atlbase.h"
```

The main body of the code contains the main() function, as well as a function DisplayProps(), which handles the displaying of the property names and values.

The main() function is long but reasonably straight forward:

```
int main(int argc, char* argv[])
{
#define TESTFAIL if (FAILED(hr)) { cout << "Failed " << hr << endl;
MessageBox(NULL, "Done", "Done", MB_OK); return 1;}

    USES_CONVERSION;
    CoInitialize(NULL);
    CComPtr<IADs> spComputer;
    HRESULT hr;

    hr = ADsGetObject(L"WinNT://BiggyBiggy",IID_IADs,(void**)&spComputer);
    TESTFAIL;
    cout << "Bound to this object" << endl;
    CComBSTR bstrName, bstrADsPath, bstrClass, bstrSchema, bstrParent,
            bstrGuid;

    hr = spComputer->get_Name(&bstrName); TESTFAIL;
    cout << "Name: " << W2A(bstrName) << endl;
    hr = spComputer->get_ADsPath(&bstrADsPath); TESTFAIL;
    cout << "ADsPath: " << W2A(bstrADsPath) << endl;
    hr = spComputer->get_Class(&bstrClass); TESTFAIL;
    cout << "Class: " << W2A(bstrClass) << endl;
    hr = spComputer->get_Schema(&bstrSchema); TESTFAIL;
    cout << "Schema: "<< W2A(bstrSchema) << endl;
    hr = spComputer->get_Parent(&bstrParent); TESTFAIL;
    cout << "Parent: " << W2A(bstrParent) << endl;
    hr = spComputer->get_GUID(&bstrGuid); TESTFAIL;
    cout << "Guid: " << W2A(bstrGuid) << endl;

    // bind to the schema object
    CComPtr<IADsClass> spSchema;
    hr = ADsGetObject(bstrSchema, IID_IADsClass, (void**)&spSchema); TESTFAIL;
    CComVariant varMandProps, varOptProps;
    hr = spSchema->get_MandatoryProperties(&varMandProps); TESTFAIL;
    cout << endl << "MANDATORY PROPERTIES" << endl;
    DisplayProps(varMandProps, spComputer);
```

```
      hr = spSchema->get_OptionalProperties(&varOptProps); TESTFAIL;
      cout << endl << "OPTIONAL PROPERTIES" << endl;
      DisplayProps(varOptProps, spComputer);

      MessageBox(NULL, "Done", "Done", MB_OK);
      return 0;
  }
```

We start off by initializing COM and declaring some variables etc. The USES_CONVERSION macro is needed because we will be using the ATL conversion macro, W2A, to convert BSTRs to ASCII strings to be displayed using the C++ output stream. Error checking is fairly restricted – we've defined a TESTFAIL macro which checks an HRESULT and, if the HRESULT indicates a failure, terminates the main() function, and hence the program:

```
#define TESTFAIL if (FAILED(hr)) { cout << "Failed " << hr << endl;
MessageBox(NULL, "Done", "Done", MB_OK); return 1;}
```

In a production environment, we would check all HRESULTs returned from method calls, but since I don't want to clutter up the sample code with error checking, I've only checked those method calls where failures are most likely to occur (e.g. binding to an ADSI object, but not when merely retrieving a property).

We bind to the computer object using the ADsGetObject() helper function:

```
      hr = ADsGetObject(L"WinNT://BiggyBiggy",IID_IADs,(void**)&spComputer);
```

and display its IADs automation properties. Then we bind to the schema object and retrieve the IADsClass automation properties, MandatoryProperties and OptionalProperties, which give us the lists of property names. These lists are passed to the function DisplayProps(), to actually display the property names and values. DisplayProps() is where we really start to notice the difference between VB and C++. Whereas in VB a simple For...Each loop was sufficient to display the properties, in C++ we need to be aware of and explicitly code around the actual data structures used by ADSI.

For any multi-valued property, ADSI will return the property as a VARIANT containing a SAFEARRAY of VARIANTs. These inner VARIANTs are what contain the actual values – one VARIANT per value. Having understood this, we should be able to see what's going on in the DisplayProps() function:

```
  void DisplayProps(CComVariant &varProps, CComPtr<IADs> spComputer)
  {
    USES_CONVERSION;

    _ASSERTE(varProps.vt == (VT_VARIANT | VT_ARRAY));
    SAFEARRAY *psa = varProps.parray;
    HRESULT hr;
    CComVariant *pvarData;
    hr = SafeArrayAccessData(psa, (void**)&pvarData);
    for (unsigned i=0 ; i< psa->rgsabound->cElements ; i++)
    {
      CComBSTR bstrPropName;
      bstrPropName = (pvarData+i)->bstrVal;
      cout << W2A(bstrPropName) << endl;
```

```
        // now return and display the values of these properties
        CComVariant varVals;
        hr = spComputer->GetEx(bstrPropName, &varVals);
        _ASSERTE(varVals.vt == (VT_VARIANT | VT_ARRAY));
        SAFEARRAY *psaVals = varVals.parray;
        CComVariant *pvarValues;
        hr = SafeArrayAccessData(psaVals, (void**)&pvarValues);
        for (unsigned j=0 ; j<psaVals->rgsabound->cElements ; j++)
        {
            CComVariant varValue = pvarValues[j];
            hr = varValue.ChangeType(VT_BSTR);
            cout << "          " << W2A(varValue.bstrVal) << endl;
        }
        hr = SafeArrayUnaccessData(psaVals);
    }
    hr = SafeArrayUnaccessData(psa);
}
```

`DisplayProps()` is handed a `CComVariant` – and it first checks that this does indeed contain a `SAFEARRAY` of VARIANTs. Having done this, it iterates through the elements of the `SAFEARRAY` in a for loop. Since we are dealing with an array of mandatory or optional properties here, we can be certain that the inner VARIANTs contain BSTR, which is why we are able to extract the property name using:

```
        CComBSTR bstrPropName;
        bstrPropName = (pvarData+i)->bstrVal;
```

Once we have the name, we obtain the corresponding value by passing the name to the `IADs::GetEx()` method:

```
        hr = spComputer->GetEx(bstrPropName, &varVals);
```

As usual, this method appears to have an extra parameter when called from C++, as compared to its VB version, since what in VB is the return value (in this case the array of values) is in C++ another parameter.

Once again, the result, is returned in varVals as a VARIANT of SAFEARRAYs of VARIANTs – but in this case we cannot be sure what the data type of the inner VARIANTs is, so we need to convert it to a BSTR before displaying – which we do using the `CComVariant::ChangeType()` member function, which will handle all the same data types that VB can handle:

```
        CComVariant *pvarValues;
        hr = SafeArrayAccessData(psaVals, (void**)&pvarValues);
        for (unsigned j=0 ; j<psaVals->rgsabound->cElements ; j++)
        {
            CComVariant varValue = pvarValues[j];
            hr = varValue.ChangeType(VT_BSTR);
            cout << "          " << W2A(varValue.bstrVal) << endl;
        }
        hr = SafeArrayUnaccessData(psaVals);

    }
    hr = SafeArrayUnaccessData(psa);
```

Summary

We've now gone through a quick tour of the facilities offered by ADSI. We've seen how the ADSI interfaces are better suited than the ADO ones for accessing a certain category of data sources, known as directory services. We've briefly explored a few of these interfaces, notably IADs and IADsContainer, and shown how we can use these interfaces to browse directories. We've also seen how we can use the OLE DB ADSI provider to carry out searches.

Inevitably in one chapter we've only been able to cover the very basics of ADSI. There are a large number of other ADSI interfaces designed to handle specialist tasks such as controlling print queues and NT services. There are also a large number of other directory services that can be accessed using ADSI, which we've not had space to explore, such as the IIS Metabase and Netscape Directory Server. However, since ADSI is designed as a generic standard for accessing directories, in principle the way we use ADSI to access these directories is no different to the code we've presented that accesses the WinNT provider.

13

Exchange Server

This chapter will be a brief introduction to the use of ADO and Exchange 2000. Why a 'brief introduction'? Well, there are several reasons:

❑ At the time of writing Exchange 2000 was at Beta 3, running on Windows 2000 RC2. As with all beta code, it's not guaranteed to stay the same for the released product.

❑ Some of the techniques ADO uses to access Exchange have already been introduced, in Chapter 8.

❑ ADO doesn't give us everything we'd really need to interact fully with Exchange.

This last point is an interesting one. In the ADO world, we have been clamouring for access to Exchange for some time now, and what we've been given is access to the data store. That's fine for many purposes, but it's worth thinking about what we really need to achieve. Are we trying to write an email-enabled application, or are we just trying to get access to the information held in Exchange? Whether we use ADO or not will depend upon our answer, and we'll see why as we go through the chapter.

So, in this chapter we are going to look at:

❑ How to connect to Exchange 2000 with ADO

❑ What facilities ADO and Exchange 2000 provide

❑ Other methods of accessing Exchange 2000

It's important to note that the features described in this chapter will only work against Exchange 2000, which in turn only runs on Windows 2000. The ADO client features will work on any platform, so long as ADO 2.5 is being used.

Exchange 2000

If we consider the Holy Grail of Universal Data Access, then we must consider every form of data storage, and email systems are certainly a form of that. The amount of email sent every day is too large even to estimate, and this isn't the only thing that mail systems do. They manage newsgroups, mailing lists, document stores, and so on. It therefore seems sensible to allow access to this data, using a familiar method.

The question is, therefore, what can an ADO connection to Exchange actually give us? Well, it can give us access to pretty much everything held in the Information Store, in a similar way to the way we used the Internet Publishing Provider. But, before we go into the details of this, you need to know a little about Exchange 2000, and in particular about its Web Store.

The Web Store

The Web Store is an integral part of Exchange 2000, and provides many of the features of a web server and a file system, mapping onto the Exchange Information Store. In effect, it's a virtual directory giving access to mailboxes and public folders. It is set up automatically when we install Exchange, and appears like this in the Internet Services Manager:

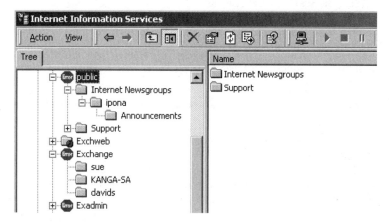

It creates several virtual directories, but the one that really interests us is the Exchange one. If you've used previous version of Exchange and Outlook Web Access, then you'll be familiar with this concept. Typing the URL into a browser gives you a version of Outlook, constructed for web usage.

What's particularly interesting is that the local path for this virtual directory points to a directory under M:, which is a standard drive letter mapping that Exchange sets up upon installation. For my setup, it looks like this in Explorer:

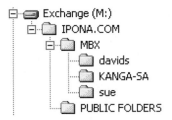

At the top of this hierarchy, there is a directory for the Exchange domain, and under that two more folders. One, MBX, contains sub-directories for each Exchange mailbox, and the other maps to the Public Folders in Exchange.

Connecting to Exchange 2000

So, if the Exchange Information Store is exposed as a URL, we can use the Record and Recordset objects to access it. In fact, the method is pretty much the same as with the Internet Publishing Provider. Here's some Visual Basic code as an example:

```
Dim conExchange As New ADODB.Connection
Dim recMailbox  As New ADODB.Record
Dim sSrc        As String

sSrc = "file://./backofficestorage/ipona.com/MBX/sue/"

conExchange.Open "Provider=Exoledb.DataSource; " & _
                 "Data Source=" & sSrc & _
                 "; User ID=sue@ipona.com; Password=vroom"
```

The connection string is what you won't have seen before, although it doesn't really differ that much from previous examples. The OLE DB Provider for Exchange is called Exoledb.DataSource, and the User ID and Password options work in much the same was as for database connections, although we need to put in the fully qualified Exchange name for the user name – this is in the form user_name@domain_name. The Data Source identifies the mailbox or folder hierarchy to be opened. At the beginning of this we have:

```
file://./backofficestorage/ipona.com/
```

In this example ipona.com is the name of the Exchange domain, and the directory preceding it just identifies the Web Store. After the domain name we then put one of two things:

❏   MBX/user_name to get access to a user mailbox

❏   Public Folders to get access to the public folders.

Once the connection is open, we can open a Record:

```
recMailbox.Open , conExchange
```

And then we can traverse through the contents (we will look at the code for the Traverse function shortly):

```
Traverse recMailbox

recMailbox.Close
conExchange.Close
Set recMailbox = Nothing
Set conExchange = Nothing
```

Examining the Message Store

The Traverse routine is pretty simple – this example just prints the files and folders to the debug window:

```
Private Sub Traverse(recFolder As ADODB.Record)

    Dim rsChildren As ADODB.Recordset
    Dim recChild   As New ADODB.Record
    Static iLevel  As Integer

    Debug.Print Space(iLevel * 2) & recFolder("DAV:displayname")

    iLevel = iLevel + 1
    Set rsChildren = recFolder.GetChildren

    While Not rsChildren.EOF
        If rsChildren("DAV:iscollection") Then
            recChild.Open rsChildren
            Traverse recChild
            recChild.Close
            Set recChild = Nothing
        Else
            Debug.Print Space(iLevel * 2) & rsChildren("DAV:displayname")
        End If
        rsChildren.MoveNext
    Wend
    iLevel = iLevel - 1

    rsChildren.Close
    Set rsChildren = Nothing

End Sub
```

You've seen this routine before, in Chapter 8. It simply starts at a node in a tree, and then creates a recordset of the children of that node. It loops through those children, and for any folders it finds, it repeats the process; otherwise it just prints the name.

What you'll notice is that when accessing the fields, we use fields with a DAV prefix. For the Internet Publishing Provider we had RESOURCE_ISCOLLECTION and RESOURCE_DISPLAYNAME to identify the collection flag and the displayable name, whereas now we use DAV:iscollection and DAV:displayname. We'll look at the fields is a moment.

The result of all of this is:

```
Tasks
  Make Christmas Pudding.EML
Notes
  Defrost the turkey.EML
Journal
Drafts
Contacts
  No Subject.EML
Calendar
  {C847C19A-A3B2-495A-8AC2-BCBA1633A8D6}.EML
Deleted Items
Sent Items
  Remember....EML
  RE%3A Racing.EML
Outbox
Inbox
```

You can see a list of folders with the mailbox, and under each folder, a list of items. Notice that the mail items are suffixed with EML, which identifies them as MIME-encoded items. Appointments aren't given a name, which is why the item in the Calendar folder has a GUID as its name.

The Fields of an Item

OK, so it's pretty easy to loop through the items, but what can we do with them? When we looked at the Internet Publishing Provider, we used the Stream object to access the contents of a file. This isn't so useful when dealing with Exchange because the contents of an item (a mail message for example) contain all the information about that item. So all the various parts of a message – the address, subject lines, contents and so on – can't easily be distinguished by reading the contents.

To access the items individually, we have to use the Fields collection of the Record or Recordset. So, how do you know what the fields are? Well, the fields differ depending upon what sort of item we're looking at. There are three basic types:

❑   A folder, as identified by a Record object.

❑   A folder item, as identified by a Record object.

❑   A folder or folder item, as identified by a row in a Recordset object.

Many of these are the same, and a `Recordset` doesn't have any fields that are not in a `Record`, but the two `Record` types can have different fields.

DAV Fields

Let's look at the DAV fields first. These are shared between all three types of items:

Field	Data Type	Description
DAV:abstract	adVarWChar	A brief abstract of the resource
DAV:autoversion	adBoolean	Indicates whether or not the server automatically performs a checkin/checkout when a resource is modified
DAV:checkintime	adFileTime	The date and time the resource was last checked in
DAV:childautoversioning	adBoolean	Indicates whether or not the server automatically performs a checkin/checkout on child resources, when a collection resource is modified
DAV:childcount	adInteger	The number of resources contained by this resource, including child collections
DAV:childversioning	adBoolean	Indicates whether or not child resources support versioning
DAV:comment	adVarWChar	A brief comment about the resource
DAV:contentclass	adVarWChar	Identifies the content class of the resource
DAV:creationdate	adFileTime	Data and time the resource was created
DAV:defaultdocument	adVarWChar	Identifies the default document for a collection; this is more applicable to Web sites
DAV:displayname	adVarWChar	The resource name used for displaying to users
DAV:getcontentlanguage	adVarWChar	The Content-Language header, as returned by an HTTP GET
DAV:getcontentlength	adInteger	The Content-Length header, as returned by an HTTP GET
DAV:getcontenttype	adVarWChar	The Content-Type header, as returned by an HTTP GET

Field	Data Type	Description
DAV:getetag	adVarWChar	The ETag header, as returned by an HTTP GET
DAV:getlastmodified	adFileTime	The Last-Modified header, as returned by an HTTP GET
DAV:haschildren	adBoolean	Indicates whether or not the resource has children
DAV:hassubs	adBoolean	Indicates whether or not the collection contains other collections that are folders
DAV:href	adVarWChar	The URL of the resource
DAV:id	adVarWChar	The unique identifier
DAV:iscollection	adBoolean	Indicates whether or not the resource is a collection resource – that is, whether it contains other resources
DAV:isfolder	adBoolean	Indicates whether or not the resource should appear as a folder; an absent value should be taken as true
DAV:ishidden	adBoolean	Indicates whether or not the resource is hidden, and is not a form of protection, more of a UI hint. If absent the resource is not hidden.
DAV:isreadonly	adBoolean	Indicates whether or not the resource is read-only
DAV:isroot	adBoolean	Indicates whether or not the resource is the root resource for the current namespace
DAV:isstructureddocument	adBoolean	Indicates whether or not the resource is a structured document; an example of this could be an HTML page containing images
DAV:isversioned	adBoolean	Indicates whether or not the resource is controlled by a version control system
DAV:lastaccessed	adFileTime	The date and time the resource was last accessed
DAV:lockdiscovery	adVarWChar	Describes, as an XML stream, the active locks on the resource
DAV:mergedfrom	adVarWChar	Describes the resources from which this resource was merged

Table Continued on Following Page

Field	Data Type	Description
DAV:nosubs	adBoolean	Indicates whether or not a collection allows child collections to be created
DAV:objectcount	adInteger	The number of non-folder resources in the collection
DAV:parentname	adVarWChar	The name of the resource's parent
DAV:resourcetype	adVarWChar	Describes the type of the resource
DAV:reserved	adBoolean	Indicates whether or not the collection is reserved, and therefore managed by the server
DAV:revisioncomment	adVarWChar	The comment associated with the current resource revision
DAV:revisionid	adVarWChar	The server-assigned revision identifier
DAV:revisionlabel	adVarWChar	The label associated with the current revision of the resource
DAV:revisionuri	adVarWChar	The unique resource indicator for the resource
DAV:searchrequest	adVarWChar	The query used when searching
DAV:searchtype	adVarWChar	The type of query used
DAV:supportedlock	Array of adVariant	A list of the types of locks supported by the server
DAV:uid	adVarWChar	A unique ID given to the version of the resource; each version of each resource will have a unique identifier
DAV:uri	adVarWChar	The URI for the resource
DAV:visiblecount	adInteger	The number of visible, non-folder resources in the collection
DAV:vresourceid	adVarWChar	The unique identifier for the version

One interesting thing to notice is that the facilities for version control are already built in. Since the Information Store is accessible through IIS, you can use the basic version control (FrontPage Server Extensions) that IIS supports. What you will also notice is that all of these are really related to the metadata of the resource – that is, what it is and what properties it has. They don't contain the contents, and this is where the other fields come in.

Other Fields

I'm not going to list all of the other fields, because there are too many, but I will give you a list of a few, just so you can get the idea of what they contain. I'll then tell you where you can find out more about these, as well as getting the complete list.

Field	Data Type	Description
`urn:schemas:contacts:email1`	`adVarWChar`	Email address of a contact
`urn:schemas:httpmail:from`	`adVarWChar`	Contents of the From field in a mail message
`urn:schemas:httpmail:fromemail`	`adVarWChar`	Email address of the From field in a mail message
`urn:schemas:httpmail:hasattachement`	`adBoolean`	Indicates whether or not the mail message has an attachement
`urn:schemas:httpmail:read`	`adBoolean`	Indicates whether or not the item has been read
`urn:schemas:mailheader:newsgroups`	`adVarChar`	The newsgroups to which the item was posted

I don't think I need to show any more – you get the idea. All of these fields are fully documented in the CDO documentation, and anything that can be set as a property through an email client is accessible through a field.

Namespaces

These above fields all belong to **namespaces** – that's the part of the field that uniquely identifies a set of common properties. At the time of writing, not all of these are fully documented, but the list below should explain what they are and where you can find out more information about them.

Namespace	Description	More Information
`DAV:`	The WebDAV properties	`http://www.webdav.org`
`http://schemas.microsoft.com/exchange`	Properties for resources managed by Microsoft Exchange Server 2000	CDO for Windows 2000 documentation
`http://schemas.microsoft.com/mapi`	Properties for MAPI resources	MAPI documentation
`http://schemas.microsoft.com/repl`	Properties for Microsoft Exchange Server Replication	Exchange Server documentation

Table Continued on Following Page

Namespace	Description	More Information
`urn:schemas:calendar`	Properties for the Calendar folder	CDO for Windows 2000 documentation
`urn:schemas:contacts`	Properties for the Contacts folder	CDO for Windows 2000 documentation
`urn:schemas:httpmail`	Properties for mail messages	CDO for Windows 2000 documentation
`urn:schemas:mailheader`	Properties for the SMTP mail header	CDO for Windows 2000 documentation
`urn:schemas-microsoft.com:exch-data`	Additional Exchange data	Exchange Server documentation
`microsoft.com:office`	Properties for Microsoft Office documents	Office 2000 Resource Kit

As you can see, the properties for resources come from many different places. There are several properties that appear in more than one namespace, in particular in the `httpmail` and `mailheader` namespaces. The main difference is the way some of the data is formatted – see the documentation for more details.

Using the Fields

Using the fields is no different to using fields in any other ADO application, so you could quite easily build your own email client. You could use the traversing method to get only folders, and then add them to some form of treeview control. When the user clicks on a node of the treeview, you could open that item as a `Record` and use the `GetChildren` method to get the items in the folder, perhaps displaying them in a list of some sort.

When an item is selected, you could open it as a `Record`, and use the fields to display the contents – such as the message details and who it's from. All of this is fairly easy – in fact, you could modify the scriptlet from Chapter 8 quite easily. I did a quick hack and got this result:

The left of the screen just displays the folders; when one of these is selected, we run the following code in the browser to display the items in the selected folder:

```
var recFolder = new ActiveXObject("ADODB.Record");
var recItem = new ActiveXObject("ADODB.Record");
var rsFiles = new ActiveXObject("ADODB.Recordset");
var sTable = '';

// open the selected folder
recFolder.open('', m_sConnStub + m_sItemURL, adModeRead,
               adOpenIfExists, adOpenRecordUnspecified,
               m_sUserName, m_sPassword);

// get a recordset containing the items
rsFiles = recFolder.getChildren();

// build an HTML table, starting with the heading
sTable = '<TABLE BORDER="1"><TR>' +
         '<TD>From</TD>' +
         '<TD>Subject</TD>' +
         '<TD>Received</TD></TR>';

// loop through the items
while (!rsFiles.EOF)
{
    // open the item as a record, so we can get the
    // item specific fields
    recItem.open(rsFiles);
    sTable += '<TR>' +
              '<TD>' + recItem("urn:schemas:httpmail:from") + '</TD>' +
              '<TD>' + recItem("urn:schemas:httpmail:subject") + '</TD>' +
              '<TD>' + recItem("urn:schemas:httpmail:datereceived") + '</TD>' +
              '</TR>';
    recItem.close();
    rsFiles.moveNext();
}
sTable += '</TABLE>';

// display the contents
spanContents.innerHTML = sTable;

// tidy up
rsFiles.close();
rsFiles = null;
recFolders = null;
recItem = null;
```

The most important thing to note about this code is that for each row in the recordset, we open a new `Record` object, using that row item as the source. This is because the `Recordset` contains the common properties for all items held by a folder. To get access to the details of the message, we have to open the message individually.

This code is fairly easy, and not very different to the samples we saw earlier in the book. The real problem I have with this code is whether there's any real reason for doing it this way. There are plenty of excellent email clients already, and Outlook Web Access in Exchange 2000 is also excellent. About the only reason that comes to mind is if you need to build a customized email client, or want to build email facilities into an existing application. If that's the case, then I suspect that ADO won't be the main technology you would use – CDO would be much more appropriate.

Non-ADO Access to Exchange

So, why won't ADO be the only way of accessing Exchange data? It's simple really: ADO doesn't give you everything you'd need, and is not always suitable for everybody and every occasion. Collaboration Data Objects (CDO), for example, is a set of COM components that provide access to all aspects of Exchange Server. This may appeal to programmers who aren't familiar with ADO, or who simply want easy access to mail facilities.

One of the features that ADO doesn't provide is the ability to search through the Exchange message store. For me this is a particularly important point, since not only does Exchange control my email, but also a large set of newsgroups. Being able to provide a customized search facility through all newsgroup messages would be extremely useful, but it's not possible with ADO. However, there are other ways to do this, and one of those is described below.

Using the XMLHTTP Object to Search Exchange

Whilst this isn't an ADO task, I think it's useful enough to warrant inclusion. The XMLHTTP object is part of the Microsoft XML support provided with Internet Explorer 5, and it gives us access to HTTP through a COM object, using XML as the format for data transport. I mentioned this object in Chapter 7, but it's also useful for talking to Exchange.

Using this object is pretty simple – there are only a few properties and methods:

Name	Type	Description
abort	Method	Cancels the current HTTP request
getAllResponseHeaders	Method	Retrieves the HTTP headers
getResponseHeader	Method	Retrieves an individual HTTP header
onReadyStateChange	Event	Fired when the state of the object changes
open	Method	Opens an HTTP request to a specific URL
readyState	Property	Identifies the state of the object
responseBody	Property	Identifies the body of the response, as a stream of bytes

Name	Type	Description
responseStream	Property	Identifies the body of the response, as a Stream object
responseText	Property	Identifies the body of the response, as a string
responseXML	Property	Identifies the body of the response, as an XML DOM object
send	Method	Sends an HTTP request, and receives the response
setRequestHeader	Method	Sets an HTTP header
status	Property	Identifies the HTTP status code of the request
statusText	Property	Identifies the HTTP response status

You may not think this relevant, but bear with me. I've previously mentioned that DAV is based on HTTP, and extends the number of available HTTP commands. This means that you can perform DAV commands through the XMLHTTP object. So, what's this got to do with searching? Well, read on...

DAV Searching and Locating

DAV Searching and Locating (DASL) is, like WebDAV, a specification from the W3C, this time dealing specifically with the protocol for searching WebDAV servers. At the time of writing, this is still under discussion, and exists only as an Internet Draft.

Although the DASL specification isn't finished, Microsoft has implemented a version that allows us to search through IIS5 using HTTP requests and the Index Server search format. It's likely that IIS5 will be updated to cater for the DASL query language once it's been approved. They won't throw away the Index Server format, but will probably support both query methods.

So, if DASL is implemented in IIS5, that means we can perform searches using it. For example, imagine that you wanted a list of the folders for a particular mailbox. The Index Server query string would look like this:

```
SELECT    "DAV:displayname" AS displayname
FROM      Scope(' DEEP TRAVERSAL OF "" ')
WHERE     "DAV:isfolder" = true
AND       "DAV:ishidden" = false
ORDER BY  "DAV:displayname" ASC
```

This would search for folders that aren't hidden, and return the displayname of the folder (assuming you are authorized to view this information). You could use this query through ADO, using the OLE DB Provider for Index Server, but it's much more sensible to go directly to the DAV server. It's also extremely simple to do, as the following Visual Basic code shows:

```
Dim httpDAV As New MSXML.XMLHTTPRequest
Dim sURL    As String
Dim sQuery  As String

sURL - "http://www.ipona.com/exchange/sue"

sQuery = "<searchrequest xmlns=""DAV:"">" & _
         "<sql>" & _
         "SELECT ""DAV:displayname"" AS DisplayName" & _
         " FROM SCOPE (' DEEP TRAVERSAL OF """" ')" & _
         " WHERE ""DAV:isfolder"" = true" & _
         " AND ""DAV:ishidden"" = false" & _
         " ORDER BY ""DAV:displayname"" ASC" & _
         "</>" & _
         "</>"

httpDAV.Open "SEARCH", sURL, False, "IPONA\sue", "vroom"
httpDAV.setRequestHeader "Content-type", "text/xml"

httpDAV.send Text1.Text
Debug.Print httpDAV.responseText
Set httpDAV = Nothing
```

Note that we can't just fire off this query directly – it has to be formatted correctly as a DAV query, which consits of two XML elements. The first is the root element, identifying the stream of XML as a search request:

```
<searchrequest xmlns="DAV:">
```

The second element identifies the type of search request – in this case, the SQL form of querying:

```
<sql>
```

Then, within the search type element, we can place the query, and send this to the DAV server. A stream of XML is returned, which when viewed in IE looks like this:

```
  <?xml version="1.0" ?>
- <a:multistatus xmlns:b="urn:uuid:c2f41010-65b3-11d1-a29f-00aa00c14882/" xmlns:c="xml:" xmlns:d="urn:schemas-microsoft-
    com:office:office" xmlns:a="DAV:">
- <a:response>
    <a:href>http://www.ipona.com/exchange/sue/Calendar/</a:href>
  - <a:propstat>
      <a:status>HTTP/1.1 200 OK</a:status>
    - <a:prop>
        <DisplayName>Calendar</DisplayName>
      </a:prop>
    </a:propstat>
  </a:response>
- <a:response>
    <a:href>http://www.ipona.com/exchange/sue/Contacts/</a:href>
  - <a:propstat>
      <a:status>HTTP/1.1 200 OK</a:status>
    - <a:prop>
        <DisplayName>Contacts</DisplayName>
      </a:prop>
    </a:propstat>
  </a:response>
- <a:response>
    <a:href>http://www.ipona.com/exchange/sue/Deleted%20Items/</a:href>
  - <a:propstat>
      <a:status>HTTP/1.1 200 OK</a:status>
    - <a:prop>
        <DisplayName>Deleted Items</DisplayName>
      </a:prop>
    </a:propstat>
  </a:response>
- <a:response>
    <a:href>http://www.ipona.com/exchange/sue/Drafts/</a:href>
      <a:propstat>
```

Here you can see that the root element is called `<multistatus>`, indicating that the response contains multiple items of data, represented by `<response>` elements. Each of these contains the details of the requested items from the search.

If we were using this from within IE, we could simply run this through an XSL stylesheet to turn it into an HTML table and display the results. In Visual Basic, you might want to assign the XML string to an XML DOM object, and process the results that way, perhaps putting them into a grid of some sort.

You might wonder why I've made a point of showing how this is done. Well firstly, it's useful. It's never been easy to search through Exchange before, but now it is. I've also mentioned this because, as you are probably aware, I'm a big fan of WebDAV, and I think it has huge potential. The fact the Outlook Web Access in Exchange 2000 is based entirely on XML and DAV shows just how powerful it can be.

Summary

I've deliberately made this a short chapter for two reasons:

❑ At the time of writing, Exchange 2000 (and indeed ADO 2.5) is still in beta. ADO 2.5 is supposed to be complete, but Exchange definitely isn't, so I didn't want to risk leading you down a path that might change.

❑ I wanted to concentrate on the ADO features as much as possible, and in many cases, these are very similar to those covered in the Internet Publishing chapter.

For these reasons, I've concentrated on the areas that are really applicable to this book. We saw that the Web Store provides the new interface to Exchange data, and that we use this as the access method from ADO. Since the Web Store is exposed as a web site, the standard URL access mechanism works, as does the method of navigating through the message store.

It's important to remember that ADO isn't the only access mechanism, and that other methods might provide a more suitable way to perform a task. Just because we've been clamoring for ADO access, doesn't mean to say it's the most suitable for all occasions. Just use ADO where and when appropriate, such as when you need recordset access to the Exchange store. Otherwise, you should consider using other technologies, such as CDO.

14

RDS: Remoting Your Data

Remote Data Services (RDS) is a technology developed by Microsoft that extends the capabilities of ADO to work on the client, remote from a server. The heart of most business-critical applications is its data. While ADO solves many of the server-side data manipulation needs, it cannot cross the boundaries of the Internet; at least not without a little help. That is where RDS steps in. In this chapter, we will discuss how we can employ RDS to bring the features of the ADO `Recordset` to the client. What we won't discuss is a line-by-line syntactic reference of each object. We'll leave that to the appendices in this book. Instead, we'll show you how to use RDS to implement real-world business solutions.

In this chapter we will discuss the following topics:

- ❑ The goods on RDS
- ❑ Querying for data using the `DataFactory`
- ❑ Using the `DataSpace` to invoke the `DataFactory`
- ❑ Using the `DataSpace` to invoke custom business objects
- ❑ Data binding with the `DataControl`
- ❑ Where do we go from here?

The Goods on RDS

Traditional web application implementations allow you to retrieve data from a database server via ASP on the web server. But once the data has been retrieved, it is formatted into a static HTML page that is sent to the client's browser. If the data needs to be manipulated in any way, we are extremely limited on the client to the point where we can merely view the output as we formatted it back in the ASP. RDS, along with the help of DHTML, addresses the limitation of static data in web pages.

Breaking Away from Static Client-Side Data

With the help of RDS, we can now remote an ADO `Recordset` to the client computer. We are no longer limited to static data on the client side. The client requests the `Recordset` from the web server using RDS. The `Recordset` is generated on the server and transported back to the client to be used in the browser (for our examples). This technology works across the Web (using HTTP and HTTPS), over a LAN using DCOM, or on the same physical computer. The remote `Recordset` returned to the client stays active while the client page is active in the browser. This allows the data to be manipulated in the client without being connected to the web server or the database. You may have heard the term 'Disconnected Recordset' to describe this process as RDS is used to marshal the ADO `Recordset` from the server to the client.

RDS works disconnected through HTTP over your intranet, extranet or the Internet. It enables client applications to work with a disconnected `Recordset` remoted from a web server using a completely stateless model. This means the server could shut down and restart between RDS client requests without affecting the client. This provides for better scalability of server applications and fits well with the MTS and n-tiered programming models.

So now that we know we can remote a disconnected `Recordset` to the client, let's think about why we would do this. What does this buy us in the grand scheme of things? For starters, we can now make the interface on a web browser much more user-friendly and interactive. Now that we can bring the data right to the browser, we can display a limited (and manageable) number of records on a page and allow the user to navigate forwards and backwards through the data pages. We can also allow the user to update the data in the browser's `Recordset`, then send (marshal) the data changes back to the server to update the database. RDS, combined with DHTML, brings a whole new world of interactivity to the web user that was previously unavailable to them.

Before we continue, it is important to point out that RDS is a feature that is embedded within Internet Explorer version 4 and up. It is part of the MDAC and, along with the lightweight ADOR `Recordset`, is installed as part of Internet Explorer. The good side of this is that your Internet Explorer users already have RDS capabilities without any additional installation requirements. The bad side of this is that RDS only works within the Internet Explorer browser, meaning that it will not work in Netscape. So for an Internet technology, RDS is only good for web applications for which you can guarantee that your users will be using Internet Explorer 4 or greater. The most typical applications for RDS are in corporate intranets and extranets, where often there is a company-wide mandate of the browser type and version.

Aside from the Internet, where RDS is seldom thought of being used on the client end of a LAN application, on a LAN you can implement a front end using Visual Basic or Visual C++ and utilize RDS on a client to retrieve recordsets from a centralized server. This way you can use the `Recordset` in the client application to validate data entry using the metadata from the `Recordset`, fill the Recordset with inputted data, and more!

The RDS Model

The RDS data flow model (shown in the following figure) demonstrates how data can be remoted to the client. Keep in mind that this is an overview of this entire chapter and that we'll go over all of these objects in the upcoming pages.

The data consumer (the web browser, in our case) uses the `RDS.DataControl` to request a `Recordset` from the database. The `DataControl` uses the `RDS.DataSpace` (built into the `DataControl`) to locate the web server and invoke the server-side business object known as the `RDSServer.DataFactory`. The `DataFactory` is used to query the database and create an ADO `Recordset` which is then transported back across the Internet using the HTTP protocol in the Microsoft proprietary format known as ADTG (Advanced Data TableGram). This format allows the `Recordset` to be dematerialized on the server and then rematerialized on the client:

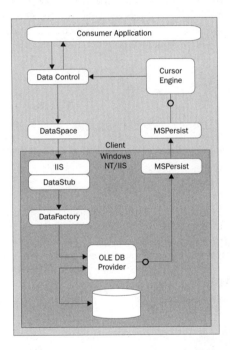

Phew! I'm sure there are a lot of questions brewing in your mind from this quick overview. So where do we start to explain how to use this model? Let's begin by going through the `DataFactory`'s features and how it grabs the data from the database and generates a recordset. Then, we'll see how we can use the `DataSpace` to invoke the `DataFactory` to create the `Recordset` and return it to the client. We'll walk through all of this starting now as we go over the `DataFactory`. But for now, simply know that `DataFactory` is a server-side ActiveX server (also known as a Business Object) and that the `DataControl` and the `DataSpace` are client-side objects.

So enough with theory and concepts. Most developers, like myself, live and learn through the tangibles. So without further delay, let's dive into the examples demonstrating the features of the RDS objects.

Querying for Data Using the DataFactory

The DataFactory is an ActiveX server, inherent to RDS, that can be used to create a disconnected ADO Recordset. That is, the DataFactory generates a Recordset that can then be completely disconnected from a data source. In fact, you could create your own ActiveX server to do exactly what the DataFactory does for us. We wouldn't want to do this, however, unless we needed something more than what the DataFactory offers us (we'll discuss this topic more in the upcoming section on the RDS.DataSpace).

Generating a Disconnected Recordset

So what does the DataFactory offer us? Given the database connection string and the SQL query to retrieve the data, the DataFactory generates an ADO Recordset object then disconnects itself from the database server. Keep in mind that all of this happens on the web server. For example, we can create the DataFactory from a Visual Basic project and call the Query method of the DataFactory to create the Recordset. Let's take a look at this:

```
Dim objDF As RDSServer.DataFactory
Dim objRS As ADOR.Recordset
Dim strConn As String
Dim strSQL As String

strConn = "Provider=SQLOLEDB.1;Initial Catalog=pubs;Data Source=dimaggio;"
strConn = strConn & "User ID=sa;Password=;"
strSQL = "SELECT au_fname, au_lname, city, state FROM authors"

Set objDF = New RDSServer.DataFactory
Set objRS = objDF.Query(strConn, strSQL)
```

Notice that we create the DataFactory, set its connection string to a valid SQL Server database and specify a valid SQL query to retrieve a list of the authors from the pubs database. Then, we pass these two parameters (connection string and SQL) to the Query method of the DataFactory. The Query method then returns an ADOR Recordset object back. As you can see, this is a simple implementation of an ActiveX server (the RDSServer.DataFactory). We probably wouldn't use the DataFactory to create an ADO Recordset on its own as the ADODB library creates a Recordset just the same and has vastly more functionality.

Query Syntax

Below is the syntax of the Query method of the DataFactory. The Query method uses a valid SQL query string to return a Recordset. The query should use the SQL dialect that is native to the database server.

```
set recordset = DataFactory.Query(Connection, Query)
```

Recordset	An object variable that represents a recordset.
DataFactory	An object variable that represents an RDSServer.DataFactory object.
Connection	A string containing the server connection information. This is similar to the Connect property.
Query	A string containing the SQL query.

Here is an example:

```
set objRS = objDataFactory.Query("dsn=pubs;UID=sa;PWD=saturn;", _
                                 "SELECT * FROM authors")
```

Marshaling

However, the `DataFactory` has one major advantage that we can reap the rewards of: we can marshal the generated `Recordset` across the web or a LAN (Local Area Network) to a client PC. Normally, an object cannot be passed across a LAN or the Internet by value as it is automatically passed by reference. But RDS breaks this barrier by allowing us to pass a specific object (the `ADOR.Recordset`) across a LAN or the Internet by breaking the `Recordset` down into the ADTG Microsoft proprietary format. The `Recordset` can then be reconstructed on the client, thus simulating passing the `Recordset` by value. But to accomplish this task, we need more than the `DataFactory`; we must call upon the services of the `RDS.DataSpace`.

Using the DataSpace to Invoke the DataFactory

The question is, 'How do we get the `Recordset` that the `DataFactory` generates from the server to the client?'. By now you've probably guessed that the answer lies within the `RDS.DataSpace`. We learned in the last section that we can use the `DataFactory` to generate a disconnected `Recordset` on the server; in this section we'll see how we can transport this `Recordset` to the client over HTTP. The implementation is almost exactly the same for HTTP, HTTPS, DCOM and in-process servers; we only change a single parameter in the call to the `DataSpace` object to specify the transport protocol. But for our examples, we'll use HTTP, as this is often the protocol used for many RDS programmers.

Remotely Invoking the DataFactory

OK, so let's see how we can invoke the `DataFactory` ActiveX server from a client using the `DataSpace`. To accomplish this, the `DataSpace` can invoke an ActiveX server remotely by creating a client-side proxy of the `DataFactory` that is on the server. But before it can do this, we need to give the `DataSpace` directions to the web server and the ActiveX server. These directions are specified by using the `CreateObject` method of the `DataSpace`. Let's take a look at its syntax, shown below.

CreateObject Syntax

The `CreateObject` method creates a proxy for the target business object and returns a pointer to it. The proxy packages and marshals data to the server-side stub for communications with the business object to send requests and data over the Internet.

HTTP Syntax:
```
set object = DataSpace.CreateObject("ProgID", "http://MyWebServer")
```

HTTPS Syntax:
```
set object = DataSpace.CreateObject("ProgID", "https://MyWebServer ")
```

DCOM Syntax:
```
set object = DataSpace.CreateObject("ProgID", "network_machine_name")
```

HTTP Example:

```
set objMyObject = objDataSpace.CreateObject("MyBusinessRules.MyBusinessObject", _
                                            "http://www.bluesand.com")
```

HTTPS Example:

```
set objMyObject = objDataSpace.CreateObject("MyBusinessRules.MyBusinessObject", _
                                            "https://www.bluesand.com")
```

DCOM Example:

```
set objMyObject = objDataSpace.CreateObject("MyBusinessRules.MyBusinessObject", _
                                            "MyServer")
```

Remoting the DataFactory

To invoke the `DataFactory` remotely and return a `Recordset` to the client, we first need to create the `DataSpace` in an HTML file. We'll use VBScript for our examples as RDS only works in Internet Explorer.

```
Set objDS = CreateObject("RDS.DataSpace")
```

Alternatively, you can create the `DataSpace` object by using the standard <OBJECT> HTML tag, as shown here.

```
<OBJECT CLASSID="clsid:BD96C556-65A3-11D0-983A-00C04FC29E36" ID="objDS">

</OBJECT>
```

Notice that within client-side VBScript, we can create objects using the `CreateObject` method. Here we create an instance of the `RDS.DataSpace` object that we will use to remotely invoke the `DataFactory` on the web server. To do this, we can issue the following line of code:

```
set objDF = objDS.CreateObject("RDSServer.DataFactory", _
                               "http://www.MyWebServer.com")
```

This line of code instructs the `DataSpace` to create a client-side proxy to the server-side ActiveX server (the `DataFactory`) that resides on the web server located at `http://www.MyWebServer.com`. The net result is that the `DataSpace`'s `CreateObject` method creates a proxy object on the client which represents the `DataFactory` object on the server in the `objDF` variable. We can now use this `objDF` variable to refer to the remote ActiveX server and issue its methods.

For example, we can issue the `Query` method of the `DataFactory`, just as we did a few examples ago. Just like last time, the `DataFactory` is used to create a disconnected `Recordset` on the server of all of the authors in the `pubs` database. However, what is different this time is that we will return that `Recordset` to the client application (the browser in our example) where we can navigate and manipulate the data.

```
<SCRIPT Language="VBScript">
strConn = "Provider=SQLOLEDB.1;Initial Catalog=pubs;Data Source=dimaggio;"
strConn = strConn & "User ID=sa;Password=;"
strSQL = "SELECT au_fname, au_lname, city, state FROM authors"
```

```
Set objDS = CreateObject("RDS.DataSpace")
Set objDF = objDS.CreateObject("RDSServer.DataFactory", _
                              "http://www.MyWebServer.com")
Set objRS = objDF.Query(strConn, strSQL)
</SCRIPT>
```

Security Issues

At this point, you might be wondering what would prevent anyone from remotely invoking the `DataFactory` on your IIS web server. Well, if you're not careful, nothing will stop them. But thankfully, there is a way to filter out which ActiveX servers can be remotely invoked. Otherwise, anyone could query or update our data across the Internet.

Securing Your Web Server

Since, by default, RDS allows implicit remoting of the `DataFactory`, we need to decide whether this is the appropriate setting for our IIS web server. Normally, we would want to disable this feature as it opens our databases to the possibility of unauthorized usage. This is especially true with the `DataFactory` as it is a standard RDS component; that is, all a third party would need to know to invoke it is the name or IP of the web server.

For example, a web client could issue a SQL command along with the name or IP address of a remote SQL Server system, a SQL account and password, database name, and a SQL query string. If the request is valid (the remote server is reachable by the IIS server, the user account and password are correct, and the database name is valid), the query results will be sent through HTTP back to the client. Although it is true that this requires significant inside information, the potential accessibility of this information should not be underestimated; organizations that don't practice good computing practices could have blank or easy-to-guess passwords on their SQL administrator accounts. The `DataFactory`, along with other installed ODBC drivers opens other possibilities, including possible access to non-published files on the IIS server. So where is this key located? Take a look at the following figure, as it depicts where the registry keys of custom business objects that can be remotely invoked using RDS are located:

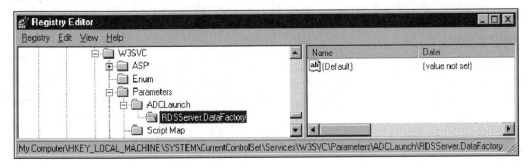

> If you don't intentionally use the implicit remoting functionality in the DataFactory
> object, you should disable it on your web server. You can still use RDS to invoke
> custom business objects on the server (as we will discuss soon), but you must explicitly
> enable access to these ActiveX servers by creating registry keys for them on the web
> server.

Removing Implicit DataFactory Functionality

If the following registry entry is removed from the IIS server, then the implicit remoting functionality of
the RDSServer.DataFactory will also be disabled.

This registry key can be removed using the Registry Editor (REGEDT32.exe), or other tools for
manipulating the registry.

HKEY_LOCAL_MACHINE\SYSTEM\CurrentControlSet\Services\W3SVC\
Parameters\ADCLaunch\RDSServer.DataFactory

You can also use the REGDEL.exe command-line utility to disable remoting of the DataFactory.
REGDEL.exe is a device available as part of the Windows NT Resource Kit utilities that can be used to
delete registry entries from the command line. Copy the following text into a .bat file (such as,
c:\RemoveIt.bat) and process the batch file on machines on which you want to do away with the
DataFactory components:

```
@ECHO OFF
REM This is a batch file that will remove RDS components from the Registry
REM REGDEL.EXE from the Resource Kit must be in your PATH
set Mykey=HKEY_LOCAL_MACHINE\SYSTEM\CurrentControlSet\Services\W3SVC
REGDEL %Mykey%\Parameters\ADCLaunch\RDSServer.DataFactory
```

Using the DataSpace to Invoke Custom Business Objects

So the DataFactory just doesn't excite you. You aren't impressed with a simple ActiveX server that
returns a Recordset, as you need much more out of your ActiveX server. Well, there's your answer:
use your own ActiveX server remotely. You can invoke any ActiveX server from a client application
using RDS, as long as you create the registry key on the web server to allow its creation.

When to Remotely Invoke Custom Business Objects

Before we continue with the code samples, let's review why we would want to invoke an ActiveX server from the client. In fact, there are several reasons for creating an instance of a custom business object using the `DataSpace` on the client rather than by using an Active Server Page (ASP) on the web server. For starters, the `DataSpace` provides the following advantages:

❏ The capability to request numerous business objects from a single web page without retrieving new web pages or refreshing the current web page. This permits more flexibility and usability in the design of a web page. For example, the user can enter a zip code in an HTML text box and we can remotely invoke an ActiveX server on a web server to retrieve the corresponding city and state.

❏ The ability to use the `DataSpace` to retrieve the data and cache it on the client. This improves the client interface's performance by reducing the load on the server, and is especially useful if custom business objects return a large amount of data. There is a hit up front in transporting the data across the Internet if the connection is slow and is running synchronously. But once the data has completely transported to the client, the data can easily and rapidly be navigated.

But there are times when it is more appropriate to use an ASP instead of the `DataSpace`. Here are some of these typical situations:

❏ Business objects that must perform secure transactions and must not be allowed to be invoked remotely.

❏ The client browser does not allow ActiveX controls.

The latter stipulation exists because the `DataSpace` cannot be used in Internet Explorer unless it allows ActiveX controls to be downloaded to it. So if you want to use the `DataSpace`, you must instruct your users to lower their security settings for your web site (via a Local Intranet Zone) to enable ActiveX controls to be downloaded.

> You may get a security violation error when you try to invoke a custom business object using the `DataSpace` from a browser. To avoid this, make sure that you use the IP of the default web site for the server parameter of the `DataSpace` object's `CreateObject` method. If you are using virtual directories, the ASP `server.servervariables` SERVER_NAME and LOCAL_ADDR may not resolve to the correct IP and will yield the error 'Internet Server Error.'

Enabling Your Custom Business Object for Remoting

There are some crucial requirements for a custom business object to be invoked remotely from a client using RDS. First of all, to successfully launch a custom business object on the web server from a client, the custom business object's `ProgID` must be entered into the registry properly. This requirement protects the security of your web server by running only sanctioned executables. To enter your custom business object in the appropriate place in the system's registry, follow these steps:

❑   From the Start menu, click Run.

❑   Type RegEdit and click OK.

❑   In the Registry Editor, navigate to the HKEY_LOCAL_MACHINE\System\CurrentControlSet\ Services\W3SVC\Parameters\ADCLaunch registry key.

❑   Select the ADCLaunch key, and then on the Edit menu, point to New, and click Key.

Type the `ProgID` of your custom business object and click *Enter*. Leave the Value entry blank. For example, you could type (without the quotation marks) 'ADODB.Command' to allow remoting of the ADO Command object ActiveX server.

Automatic Registration

Alternatively, the text below can be copied into a text file and given a `.reg` extension, such as `EnableRemoting.Reg`. By double-clicking the .reg file on the server these specified changes will be made to the server registry automatically. Instead, you can also use the `regedit` utility to navigate to the registry hive named below and add the name of the business object as a new key. Be sure to use the name of your object and not the sample name (`MyObject.MyClass`) listed here.

```
REGEDIT4

[HKEY_LOCAL_MACHINE\SYSTEM\CurrentControlSet\Services\W3SVC\
Parameters\ADCLaunch\MyObject.MyClass]
```

Remotely Invoking a Custom Business Object

So we've discussed when to create custom business objects for remote invocation, when ASP is a better solution, and how to be aware of the security implications. Now let's take a look at a sample custom business object written in Visual Basic (although we could have used any COM-compliant language) that we'll remotely invoke from a web client.

We'll walk through creating an ActiveX server that retrieves all of the book titles for a given author. We'll call this method `RetrieveTitles` and use it on a web page that, in ASP, loads a combo box with all of the valid author names. Then, when the user changes the current author selection in the HTML combo box, we fire some RDS code that invokes the `RetrieveTitles` method in our ActiveX server back on the web server. This method will return the valid titles to the client so we can display them on the current page of the browser. The figure overleaf shows what the web page looks like when it first appears to the user:

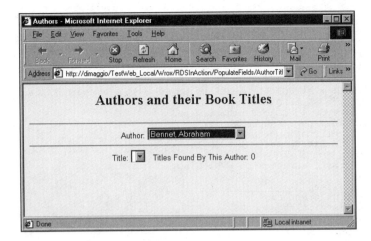

When the user selects an author, our code retrieves the list of titles the author has written to the second combo box. The result is shown here, and we see that Marjorie Green has written 2 titles:

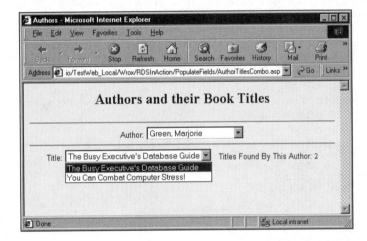

Show 'em How it's Done

Now that we've seen the results, let's take a look under the covers to see how this is accomplished. First, we need to create the Visual Basic ActiveX DLL project that will become our ActiveX server. I called mine `RDSTest` but you should call yours something appropriate to your project. Then, I created a class that I called `Author` as it will be used to retrieve information about an author. In our example, this information will be the author's titles. Within the `Author` class, we create the `RetrieveTitles` method, as shown below:

```
Public Function RetrieveTitles(strAuthorID As String) As ADOR.Recordset
    Dim objConn As ADODB.Connection
    Dim objRS As ADODB.Recordset
    Dim strSQL As String
    Dim strConn As String

    Set objConn = New ADODB.Connection
    strConn = "Provider=SQLOLEDB.1;Initial Catalog=pubs;Data Source=dimaggio;"
    strConn = strConn & "User ID=sa;Password=;"
    objConn.CursorLocation = adUseClient
```

```
    objConn.Open strConn
    Set objRS = New ADODB.Recordset
    With objRS
        strSQL = "SELECT t.title_id, t.title"
        strSQL = strSQL & " FROM titleauthor ta INNER JOIN titles t"
        strSQL = strSQL & " ON ta.title_id = t.title_id"
        strSQL = strSQL & " WHERE ta.au_id = '" & strAuthorID & "'"
        .Source = strSQL
        .LockType = adLockBatchOptimistic
        .CursorType = adOpenStatic
        .CursorLocation = adUseClient
        Set .ActiveConnection = objConn
        .Open
        Set .ActiveConnection = Nothing
    End With
    objConn.Close
    Set objConn = Nothing
    Set RetrieveTitles = objRS
End Function
```

This method connects to the pubs database using an appropriate connection string (make sure you customize your connection string according to your database server settings). Then we set the Recordset's properties and open the Recordset. But notice that before we open the Recordset, we set the cursor location to be adUseClient. This is in preparation for disconnecting the Recordset after we open it. Once we open the Recordset, we do just that: we disconnect the Recordset from the ADO Connection by setting the ActiveConnection property of the Recordset to the keyword Nothing. Finally, we close out this method by returning our disconnected Recordset to the calling application (which in our case will be the web page).

We also need a method to retrieve the name and Social Security Number of each author from the authors table of the pubs database:

```
Public Function RetrieveNames() As ADOR.Recordset
    Dim objConn As ADODB.Connection
    Dim objRS As ADODB.Recordset
    Dim strSQL As String
    Dim strConn As String

    Set objConn = New ADODB.Connection
    strConn = "Provider=SQLOLEDB;Initial Catalog=pubs;Data Source=dimaggio;"
    strConn = strConn & "User ID=sa;Password=;"
    objConn.CursorLocation = adUseClient
    objConn.Open strConn
    Set objRS = New ADODB.Recordset
    With objRS
        strSQL = "SELECT DISTINCT au_id AS SSN, au_fname + ' ' + " & _
                    "au_lname AS FullName FROM authors"
        .Source = strSQL
        .LockType = adLockBatchOptimistic
        .CursorType = adOpenStatic
        .CursorLocation = adUseClient
        Set .ActiveConnection = objConn
        .Open
        Set .ActiveConnection = Nothing
    End With
    objConn.Close
    Set objConn = Nothing
    Set RetrieveNames = objRS
End Function
```

This method is essentially the same as the RetrieveTitles function, except for the SQL command executed against the database. Here we select the au_id column as the SSN field, and we combine the au_fname and au_lname columns into the FullName field.

Registering the DLL in the Hive

Once we compile and make this ActiveX server into a DLL, we need to make sure that we register the DLL properly (VB does this part for us) and that we register the DLL in the ADCLaunch hive, as discussed earlier in this chapter. We can do that by creating the key in the hive shown below:

```
\HKEY_LOCAL_MACHINE
   \SYSTEM
      \CurrentControlSet
         \Services
            \W3SVC
               \Parameters
                  \ADCLaunch
```

Be sure to name your key RDSTest.Author or whatever you named your ActiveX project and class. This is crucial to making the DataSpace work. Your key entry can also be made by copying this section of code into a .reg file and running it.

```
REGEDIT4

[HKEY_LOCAL_MACHINE\SYSTEM\CurrentControlSet\Services\W3SVC\Parameters\ADCLaunch\RDSTest.Author]
```

Now we are ready to use our ActiveX server in a web page!

Coding the Web Page

The code below contains the ASP code and the HTML contained within the AuthorTitlesCombo.asp. This code is used to render the page as it appears when the user first requests this page. However, conspicuously omitted from the listing below is the client-side code that uses RDS to retrieve the author's titles when an author is selected. We'll add that code later.

```asp
<%@LANGUAGE=VBSCRIPT%>
<%Option Explicit%>
<%
dim objRS_Authors
dim objAuthor

set objAuthor = Server.CreateObject("RDSTest.Author")
set objRS_Authors = objAuthor.RetrieveNames
%>
<HTML>
<HEAD>
<TITLE>Authors</TITLE>
</HEAD>
<BODY bgcolor=#fafad2>
<CENTER>

<H2>Authors and their Book Titles</H2>
<HR>
<FONT>Author: </FONT>
<SELECT id="cboFullName" size=1>
   <%do while not objRS_Authors.EOF%>
      <OPTION value="<%=objRS_Authors("SSN")%>">
                  <%=objRS_Authors("FullName")%>
      <%objRS_Authors.MoveNext
   loop%>
</SELECT>
<HR>
<FONT>Title: </FONT>
<SELECT id="cboTitles" size=1></SELECT>
```

```
  <FONT>Titles Found By This Author: </FONT>
<SPAN id="spnTitleCount">0</SPAN>

</CENTER>
```

The client-side code that we'll use is listed below. Looking at the `window_onload` event, notice that the web server variable is set to my web server's name. Make sure you change this to point to your web server's IP address. Once we set the web server location variable, we create the `DataSpace` object in the variable `mobjDS`. This event fires when the window first loads and creates the `DataSpace` in a global (to this web page) variable that we can use for the life of this page.

Running on DCOM:

We can change the following code to make this work over a LAN by altering the server name from "http://dimaggio" (in my example) to the name of the remote machine. This will tell the DataSpace that the business object is an in-process DLL on the named machine. We can also change the server name to an empty string, which indicates that DLL is running on the local machine.

Then we need to write the code that retrieves the titles for the selected author. The appropriate place to do this is in the `cboFullName_onChange` event, as it fires when the author combo box's currently selected item changes. This event's responsibility is to:

❑ Retrieve the titles from the database via our ActiveX server

❑ Load the titles into the `cboTitles` HTML combo box

```
<SCRIPT LANGUAGE="VBSCRIPT">

dim mstrWebServer
dim mobjDS
dim mobjRS_Titles

sub window_onload()
    mstrWebServer = "http://dimaggio"
    set mobjDS = CreateObject("RDS.DataSpace")
    cboFullName.focus
end sub

sub cboFullName_onChange()
    RetrieveTitles
    LoadTitles
    mobjRS_Titles.Close
end sub

sub RetrieveTitles()
    dim objAuthor
    dim strAuthorID

    strAuthorID = cboFullName.value
    set objAuthor = mobjDS.CreateObject("RDSTest.Author", mstrWebServer)
    set mobjRS_Titles = objAuthor.RetrieveTitles(strAuthorID)
end sub

sub LoadTitles()
    dim objOption

    do while cboTitles.options.length
        cboTitles.options.remove 0
    loop
```

```
    if mobjRS_Titles.EOF then
        set objOption = document.createElement("<OPTION>")
        objOption.text = "<None>"
        objOption.value = "None"
        cboTitles.add objOption
        spnTitleCount.innerText = "0"
    else
        do while not mobjRS_Titles.EOF
            set objOption = document.createElement("<OPTION>")
            objOption.text = mobjRS_Titles("Title")
            objOption.value = mobjRS_Titles("Title_id")
            cboTitles.add objOption
            mobjRS_Titles.MoveNext
        loop
        spnTitleCount.innerHTML = "<FONT>" & mobjRS_Titles.Recordcount & "</FONT>"
    end if
end sub
</SCRIPT>
</BODY>
</HTML>
```

We retrieve the titles through the `RetrieveTitles` subroutine. In this routine, we first grab the SSN of the currently selected author using the code: `strAuthorID = cboFullName.value`. Then, we create the client-side proxy to our `RDSTest.Author` object using the `DataSpace`. To do this, we pass the web server location and the `ProgID` of the custom business object (same `ProgID` that is in the web server's registry in the `ADCLaunch` hive). This returns to us a client-side reference to the `Author` object and gives us access to its methods, such as the `RetrieveTitles` method. To this, we pass the author's SSN that we just grabbed and the `RetrieveTitles` method generates a `Recordset`, on the server, of the author's titles. Then the `Recordset` is marshaled to the client (using Microsoft's ADTG format) and is reconstructed in our web page. Now we can use this `Recordset` to populate the `cboTitles` HTML combo box (this code is shown in the subroutine `LoadTitles`).

Taking a Visual Basic ActiveX component and making it run with RDS is really not that difficult. However, there are a few issues to keep in mind, such as:

❑   Make sure the IP address of the web server where the custom business object resides is specified in the `DataSpace`'s `CreateObject` method.

❑   Make sure that the ActiveX server component is registered in the Windows Registry of the system on which that component will run. If the component is not registered on that machine, use `RegSvr32` to register the server DLL on the web machine.

You need to enter the following key in the web server's registry to allow the ActiveX server to be remotely invoked through RDS, if you have not already:

```
HKEY_LOCAL_MACHINE\SYSTEM\CurrentControlSet\Services\W3SVC\Parameters\ADCLaunch\My
Object.MyClass
```

You can expand on this technique for such applications where a user selects a customer and their full address is retrieved to the client page, as well. This is a better technique than retrieving all addresses of all customers as this could take a long time for a lot of data that we will never display or make use of. In our example above, we would not want to grab all the titles for all authors as this list has the potential to be huge. So instead, we grab the data on demand thus making the application much more user-friendly.

But what if we want to display an entire `Recordset` (or at least most of it) on the web page, how do we accomplish this? We could use the `DataSpace` to invoke the `RDSServer.DataFactory` or a custom business object on the web server to retrieve the `Recordset` to the client, but what then? How do we get the data on the web page easily? This is where the `RDS.DataControl` steps in.

Data Binding with the DataControl

The `DataControl` is the third of the RDS objects. It uses the `DataSpace` to create the `DataFactory` back on the web server to generate and return a `Recordset` to the client. But that's not all; the `DataControl` also can be bound to HTML elements to display the data in its underlying `Recordset` automatically. We can bind the `DataControl` to the `<INPUT>`, `<DIV>`, `<SPAN>`, `<SELECT>`, `<TABLE>` and many other HTML tags. For example, we can bind a list of all of the authors in the pubs database to an HTML table using the `DataControl`, as shown here:

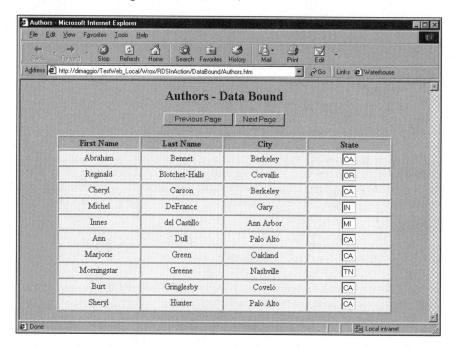

The example shown above binds the `DataControl` to the HTML table and has each field bound individually to a `<SPAN>` within the table's columns. Notice the HTML for this page, shown below. There is very little more than basic HTML going on in here.

```
<html>
<head>

<script language="vbscript">
sub window_onload()
   objDC.Server = "http://dimaggio"
   objDC.Connect = "Provider=SQLOLEDB.1;User ID=sa;Password=;Initial
Catalog=pubs;Data Source=dimaggio"
   objDC.SQL = "select au_fname, au_lname, city, state from authors order by
au_lname, au_fname"
   objDC.Refresh
end sub

sub btnNextPage_OnClick()
   tblAuthor.nextPage
end sub
```

```
sub btnPreviousPage_OnClick()
   tblAuthor.previousPage
end sub
</script>

<!-- RDS DataControl -->
<object classid="clsid:bd96c556-65a3-11d0-983a-00c04fc29e33" id="objDC" width="0"
      height="0">
</object>

<title>Authors</title>
</head>
<body>
<center>

<h2>Authors - Data Bound</h2>

<input id="btnPreviousPage" name="btnPreviousPage" type="button"
      value="Previous Page">
<input id="btnNextPage" name="btnNextPage" type="button" value="Next Page">
<br>
<br>
<table id="tblAuthor" border="1" datasrc="#objDC" width="640" datapagesize="10">
   <thead align="CENTER">
      <td width="25%" nowrap><b>First Name</b></td>
      <td width="25%" nowrap><b>Last Name</b></td>
      <td width="25%" nowrap><b>City</b></td>
      <td width="25%" nowrap><b>State</b></td>
   </thead>
   <tr align="CENTER">
      <td bgcolor="LightGoldenRodYellow"><span id="spnFirstName"
         datafld="au_fname"></span></td>
      <td bgcolor="LightGoldenRodYellow"><span id="spnLastName"
         datafld="au_lname"></span></td>
      <td bgcolor="LightGoldenRodYellow"><span id="spnCity"
         datafld="city"></span></td>
      <td bgcolor="LightGoldenRodYellow"><input type=text id="spnState"
         datafld="state"></td>
   </tr>
</table>

</center>
</body>
</html>
```

First of all, you probably noticed the HTML <OBJECT> tag with the long class ID. This represents the RDS.DataControl object which we'll refer to by its ID of objDC:

```
<!-- RDS DataControl -->
<object classid="clsid:bd96c556-65a3-11d0-983a-00c04fc29e33"
      id="objDC" width="0" height="0">
</object>
```

> **You need to make the height and width of the DataControl to 0. Otherwise, the DataControl, which has no visible aspects, will take up real estate on the web page. In effect, it would display a large blank area on the web page. To avoid this, we simply set its height and width to 0.**

Take a look at the `window_onload` event. Here we set the `Server`, `Connect` and `SQL` properties of the `DataControl` object to the web server's location, the database connection string and a valid SQL query. Once these key properties are set, we issue the `Refresh` method of the `DataControl` to:

❑   Go to the web server and invoke the `DataFactory` (using the `DataSpace`)

❑   Have the `DataFactory` connect to the database and query it using the SQL

❑   Then generate an `ADOR.Recordset` and return it to the client and the `DataControl`

Binding Data to an HTML <TABLE> Using the DataControl

So how did we bind the `Recordset` to the table? Notice the HTML table (`tblAuthor`) in the last figure has an attribute called `datasrc` set to the ID of the `DataControl` preceded by the # character. This tells the `DataControl` that the `tblAuthor` HTML table will utilize its `Recordset`. But now we have to tell the `DataControl` where to bind its columns to. The first 4 columns in the figure are bound to <SPAN> tags embedded within the table's cells. This produces a read-only effect for the data. The last column is bound to an <INPUT> tag of type `text`, which produces a field that can be updated directly in the client-side `Recordset`.

Now let's take a look at the navigational buttons on this web page. You might think there was a lot of code behind these buttons. If so, you'd be surprised that all it took was a single line of code for each to work. By simply using the HTML table's inherent `nextPage` and `previousPage` methods, we can make a fully navigable table of data. But of course we need to specify how many records we want to show on the page at a time. We indicate this by setting the HTML table's `datapagesize` attribute to 10 (in our example). This means that when we press the button to navigate to the next page, we will go to records 11 through 20 (or whatever is left) of the `Recordset`. The greatest aspect of these navigational methods is that the error handling is done for us. For example, you will not receive an error when you are on the first page of the `Recordset` and you repeatedly click the button to go to the previous page.

Updating the Data

You may have noticed that in the last section I alluded that the data could be bound to an HTML element so that it could be updateable. This is another key feature of RDS which allows us to create a page that allows us to easily update multiple records of a recordset and then send all of the changes back to the database. We can accomplish this by issuing the `DataControl`'s `SubmitChanges` method. This method only marshals back the records that have changed to reduce network traffic and reduce inefficiency.

Let's take a look at another web page that builds off of the last example to produce a fully updateable `Recordset` using the `DataControl` bound to an HTML table. The following figure shows this updateable `Recordset` as its columns are bound to <INPUT> elements within an HTML table.

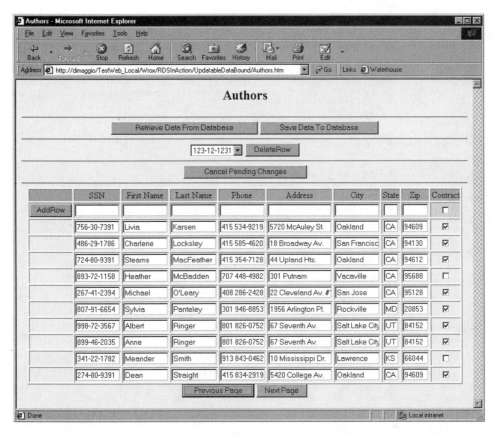

We've also added a few extra features to this page, as I am sure you have noticed. For starters, we created a **Save Data to Database** button that issues the `SubmitChanges` method of the `DataControl`, thus saving all data changes made to the `DataControl`'s `Recordset` to the database. We also added a **Cancel Pending Changes** button, which cancels all changes we made to the `Recordset` on this page since the last `SubmitChanges` was issued or the page as loaded. As you might have been able to guess, this button issues the `DataControl`'s `CancelChanges` method.

I also added a button to refresh the `Recordset` from the database, just to be complete. This button invokes the `DataControl`'s `Refresh` method. Then, to make it a bit more interesting and to leave you with a working example of a fully updateable data bound HTML table, I added buttons to add a row and delete a row. These buttons invoke the `DataControl`'s `Recordset`'s methods that add a new row and delete the current row, respectively. These features are simple to implement once you realize that the `DataControl` contains a valid `ADOR.Recordset` object.

I included all of the HTML and code below for you to chew on, as shown below:

```
<HTML>
<HEAD>
<SCRIPT language=vbscript>
option explicit

dim mstrSQL
```

```
'--- Put your web server IP here
'---********************************
'---***CHANGE THIS AS PER YOUR PROJECT
const cstrServer = "http://dimaggio"
const cConnectString = "Provider=SQLOLEDB.1;User ID=sa;Password=;" & _
                       "Initial Catalog=pubs;Data Source=dimaggio"
'---********************************

const adStateClosed = 0
const adStateOpen = 1
const adFilterNone = 0
const adFilterPendingRecords = 1
Const adMarshalAll = 0
Const adMarshalModifiedOnly = 1

const adcReadyStateComplete = 4
const adcExecSync = 1
const adcFetchUpFront = 1

sub RetrieveData()
   if mobjDC.ReadyState = adcReadyStateComplete and _
      mobjDC.Recordset.State = adStateOpen then
        mobjDC.CancelUpdate
   end if
   mobjDC.Refresh
end sub

sub window_onload()
    mstrSQL = "SELECT au_id AS SSN, au_lname AS 'Last Name',"
    mstrSQL = mstrSQL & " au_fname AS 'First Name', phone AS Phone, "
    mstrSQL = mstrSQL & " address AS Address, city AS City, state AS State, "
    mstrSQL = mstrSQL & " zip As Zip, contract As Contract "
    mstrSQL = mstrSQL & " FROM authors "
    mstrSQL = mstrSQL & " ORDER BY au_lname, au_fname"

    mobjDC.Server = cstrServer
    mobjDC.Connect = cConnectString
    mobjDC.SQL = mstrSQL
    mobjDC.FetchOptions = adcFetchUpFront
    mobjDC.ExecuteOptions = adcExecSync

    RetrieveData
    LoadComboList
end sub

sub btnNextPage_OnClick()
   tblAuthor.nextPage
end sub

sub btnPreviousPage_OnClick()
   tblAuthor.previousPage
end sub

sub btnSave_OnClick()
   on error resume next
   mobjDC.SubmitChanges
end sub

sub btnCancel_OnClick()
   mobjDC.CancelUpdate
end sub
```

```
sub btnRetrieve_OnClick()
   if mobjDC.Recordset.State = adStateOpen then
      mobjDC.Recordset.Close
   end if
   RetrieveData
   LoadComboList
end sub

sub btnDeleteRow_OnClick()
   mobjDC.Recordset.Find "SSN = '" & frmAuthor.cboSSN.value & "'"
   if not mobjDC.Recordset.EOF then
      mobjDC.Recordset.Delete
   end if
   mobjDC.Recordset.MoveFirst
   LoadComboList
end sub

sub btnAddRow_OnClick()
   if MsgBox("Are you sure you want to add this row?", vbYesNo, _
            "Save Authors") = vbYes then
      mobjDC.Recordset.AddNew
      mobjDC.Recordset("SSN") = frmAuthor.SSN.value
      mobjDC.Recordset("First Name") = frmAuthor.[First Name].value
      mobjDC.Recordset("Last Name") = frmAuthor.[Last Name].value
      mobjDC.Recordset("Phone") = frmAuthor.Phone.value
      mobjDC.Recordset("Address") = frmAuthor.Address.value
      mobjDC.Recordset("City") = frmAuthor.City.value
      mobjDC.Recordset("State") = frmAuthor.State.value
      mobjDC.Recordset("Zip") = frmAuthor.Zip.value
      mobjDC.Recordset("Contract") = frmAuthor.Contract.checked
      mobjDC.Recordset.Update
      ClearNewRow
      LoadComboList
   end if
end sub

sub ClearList()
   do while frmAuthor.cboSSN.options.length
      frmAuthor.cboSSN.options.remove 0
   loop
end sub

sub ClearNewRow()
   frmAuthor.[Address].value = ""
   frmAuthor.[City].value = ""
   frmAuthor.[First Name].value = ""
   frmAuthor.[Last Name].value = ""
   frmAuthor.[Phone].value = ""
   frmAuthor.[SSN].value = ""
   frmAuthor.[State].value = ""
   frmAuthor.[Zip].value = ""
   frmAuthor.[Contract].checked = false
end sub

sub LoadComboList()
   dim objOption

   ClearList
   mobjDC.Recordset.Filter = adFilterNone
   mobjDC.Recordset.Sort = "SSN ASC"
   mobjDC.Recordset.MoveFirst
   do while not mobjDC.Recordset.EOF
      set objOption = document.createElement("OPTION")
      objOption.text = mobjDC.Recordset("SSN")
      objOption.value = mobjDC.Recordset("SSN")
      frmAuthor.cboSSN.add objOption
      mobjDC.Recordset.MoveNext
   loop
```

```
        mobjDC.Recordset.Sort = ""
        mobjDC.Recordset.MoveFirst
    end sub


    sub mobjDC_onError(SCode, Description, Source, CancelDisplay)
        MsgBox "Record changes could not be saved due to" & _
            " 1 or more data integrity violations."
        CancelDisplay = True
    end sub
</SCRIPT>

<!-- RDS DataControl -->
<OBJECT classid="clsid:bd96c556-65a3-11d0-983a-00c04fc29e33"
        id="mobjDC" width="0" height="0">
</OBJECT>

<TITLE>Authors</TITLE>
</HEAD>
<BODY bgcolor=AliceBlue>
<CENTER>

<H2>Authors</H2>
<FORM id="frmAuthor" action="" method="post">
<HR>
<INPUT id=btnRetrieve type=button value="Retrieve Data From Database">
<INPUT id=btnSave type=button value="Save Data To Database">
<HR>
<SELECT id="cboSSN" size="1">
</SELECT>
<INPUT id=btnDeleteRow type=button value=DeleteRow>
<HR>
<INPUT id=btnCancel type=button value="Cancel Pending Changes">
<HR>
<TABLE id="tblAuthor" border="1" datasrc="#mobjDC" width="640" datapagesize="10">
    <THEAD align="middle" bgcolor=#c0c0c0>
    <TR>
        <TD nowrap> </TD>
        <TD nowrap>SSN</TD>
        <TD nowrap>First Name</TD>
        <TD nowrap>Last Name</TD>
        <TD nowrap>Phone</TD>
        <TD nowrap>Address</TD>
        <TD nowrap>City</TD>
        <TD nowrap>State</TD>
        <TD nowrap>Zip</TD>
        <TD nowrap>Contract</TD>
    </TR>
    <TR align="middle" bgcolor=#ffff00>
        <TD nowrap><INPUT id=btnAddRow name=btnAddRow type=button value=AddRow></TD>
        <TD nowrap><INPUT type="textbox" id="SSN" size=10></TD>
        <TD nowrap><INPUT type="textbox" id="First Name" size=10></TD>
        <TD nowrap><INPUT type="textbox" id="Last Name" size=10></TD>
        <TD nowrap><INPUT type="textbox" id="Phone" size=10></TD>
        <TD nowrap><INPUT type="textbox" id="Address" size=15></TD>
        <TD nowrap><INPUT type="textbox" id="City" size=10></TD>
        <TD nowrap><INPUT type="textbox" id="State" size=2></TD>
        <TD nowrap><INPUT type="textbox" id="Zip" size=5></TD>
        <TD nowrap><INPUT type="checkbox" id="Contract"></TD>
    </TR>
    </THEAD>
    <TR align="middle" bgcolor=#fafad2>
        <TD nowrap> </TD>
        <TD nowrap><INPUT id="txtSSN" type="text" datafld="SSN" size="10"></TD>
        <TD nowrap><INPUT id="txtFirstName" type="text" datafld="First Name"
            size="10"></TD>
        <td nowrap><input id="txtLastName" type="text" datafld="Last Name"
            size="10"></TD>
```

```
        <TD nowrap><INPUT id="txtPhone" type="text" datafld="Phone" size="10"></TD>
        <TD nowrap><INPUT id="txtAddress" type="text" datafld="Address"
           size="15"></TD>
        <TD nowrap><INPUT id="txtCity" type="text" datafld="City" size="10"></TD>
        <TD nowrap><INPUT id="txtState" type="text" datafld="State" size="2"></TD>
        <TD nowrap><INPUT id="txtZip" type="text" datafld="Zip" size="5"></TD>
        <TD nowrap><INPUT id="chkContract" type="checkbox" datafld="Contract"></TD>
    </TR>
</TABLE>
<INPUT id=btnPreviousPage type=button value="Previous Page">
<INPUT id=btnNextPage type=button value="Next Page"> 

</FORM>
</CENTER>

</BODY>
</HTML>
```

Where Do We Go From Here?

RDS is a great technology that can be built upon to achieve a more interactive and user-friendly interface. We showed how we can implement these features in an Internet Explorer browser, but we could easily adapt many of these examples to the LAN world as RDS lends itself to stateless n-tiered architectures. Other ideas that logically sprout from RDS include using the DataSpace to invoke a custom business object that returns a Recordset back to the web page (as we did in this chapter); but then we use the returned Recordset as the source of the DataControl. We can do this by setting the DataControl's SourceRecordset property to the returned Recordset. This gives us more flexibility than simply making a simple SQL query via the DataFactory, as the DataControl does inherently. Another more complex idea could involve using the DataSpace to retrieve an empty Recordset and to use its metadata (Fields collection) to validate the web page's HTML fields. Think about it: this is very possible as we have all of the information we need right in the Recordset (datatypes, lengths, nullability, etc.). Your users will love you for validating their data automatically before submitting their page with errors. But whatever your idea is, the basic truth is that RDS is just another door that has been opened to internet developers that allows us to brainstorm new ideas on how to use the data that we can now get on a web page.

15

Developing OLE DB Providers

In Chapter 2, we briefly introduced the concept of creating custom OLE DB providers to expose non-standard data sources or provide extended features on top of existing OLE DB data providers. The main benefit of doing so is that data can be accessed through the standard ADO object model, without requiring developers to learn yet another data access technology. In this chapter, we will look at some of the theory behind developing custom providers, and in the next chapter, we will go on to look at how this works in practice, developing an OLE DB provider for the Registry. So, in this chapter, we will discuss:

❑ A few of the virtually endless list of data sources that can be exposed by custom OLE DB Providers

❑ Why and when you should expose data through custom OLE DB Providers

❑ How custom OLE DB providers compare to data-exposing COM components

❑ The two types of custom OLE DB Providers

❑ The OLE DB Simple Provider (OSP) architecture

❑ How the OSP architecture fits within the architecture of OLE DB

Before you begin casually reading through this chapter, you should first be warned. Developing custom OLE DB Providers is not a task for the novice or intermediate ADO programmer. Instead, this task should be left up to the ADO professionals who have a solid understanding of ADO and COM. Are you up to the challenge? If you think so, then grab a highly caffeinated drink, a new highlighter and read on!

Custom OLE DB Providers

The powerful ability to develop custom OLE DB data and OLE DB service providers is the key to the Universal Data Access strategy. Developers no longer have to wait and rely on Microsoft or another third party vendor to supply OLE DB providers. Instead, developers can create their own COM components that function as OLE DB providers by exposing any type of data through the standard OLE DB interfaces. Consequently, a custom OLE DB Provider can be used from ADO just like any other OLE DB Provider. A few examples of the virtually endless list of possible data sources that could be exposed by custom OLE DB data providers include:

- ❑ Microsoft Repository
- ❑ Personal Address Book
- ❑ Windows Registry
- ❑ Scheduled Tasks
- ❑ Windows Media content
- ❑ Shared Memory
- ❑ Windows Installer Packages
- ❑ MS DTC Log
- ❑ IIS Activity Logs
- ❑ Temporary Internet Files
- ❑ Type Libraries
- ❑ MTS/COM+ Catalog
- ❑ Performance Monitor
- ❑ Word documents
- ❑ PowerPoint presentations
- ❑ Excel Spreadsheets

In addition to these existing data sources, OLE DB providers could also be developed for industry-specific or application-specific data sources such as custom file formats, stock feeds and search engines.

> **OLE DB should change the way you look at data. In particular, the ability to create custom OLE DB data providers should make you reconsider what is and what isn't a data source.**

Faster, more reliable and more scalable OLE DB data providers can also be developed as alternatives to the existing providers supplied by Microsoft. For example, we could develop a custom OLE DB data provider for Oracle Databases that would be an alternative to the Microsoft OLE DB provider for Oracle. Since all OLE DB providers expose their functionality through the standard OLE DB interfaces, the data providers could easily be interchanged without requiring code changes on the part of the OLE DB consumer.

As I mentioned earlier, a custom OLE DB provider can also take on the role of an OLE DB service provider by both consuming and producing OLE DB data. For example, an OLE DB service provider could be developed to provide heterogeneous join capabilities by using existing OLE DB data providers to retrieve data from various data sources, joining the data together and finally returning the joined data to the OLE DB consumer:

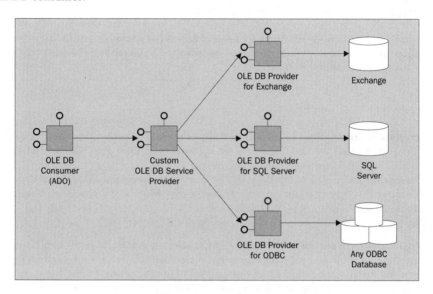

Why (*Not*) Expose Data Through OLE DB?

We've already touched on some of the many benefits of developing custom OLE DB providers, but how does exposing data through custom OLE DB providers compare to other techniques? If you're like most developers, chances are you've been developing custom data access routines and encapsulating them in reusable COM components.

For example, many developers have at some time created or used COM components for accessing and manipulating data stored in the Windows Registry. These components typically encapsulate complex Win32 API function calls and expose the Registry Data through a custom COM interface. One example of such a component might expose a single interface with two methods: GetRegValue and SetRegValue. The GetRegValue method could allow the client to retrieve the data associated with a specified Registry value and the SetRegValue method could change a Registry value's data and create a Registry value if necessary.

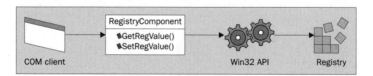

Exposing data through COM components, like in this example, provides binary component reusability and a simplified programming model because custom data access functionality is separated from other aspects of the application. Almost every one of the data sources we discussed in the last section currently supplies a set of COM components and interfaces to expose their data. So what's the problem with this approach?

> **The problem with encapsulating custom data access functionality within normal COM components is that each component exposes a separate custom interface for providing data access and manipulation.**

There are two aspects to this problem:

❑ **Developers are required to learn a new object model for each data source.** To access the Microsoft Repository you might use the complex Microsoft Repository Interfaces, to read records from the Internet Information Server (IIS) activity logs you might use the IIS Logging Utility component (`IISLog.LogScripting`), to retrieve and manipulate data in the Windows Registry you can choose between either Microsoft's simplified Registration Manipulation Classes (`RegObj`), our custom COM component, or one of the hundreds of third-party COM components for accessing the Registry.

❑ **Applications are committed to one set of COM components.** After an application has been developed against one set of components, a significant amount of re-coding will usually be required for an application to take advantage of another component. For example, we might decide that we need the ability to enumerate through Registry keys, a feature that is not provided by our custom Registry component (`RegComponent`). We discover that another developer has created a set of COM components for the Registry that provides this required functionality, but since the interfaces for these components are significantly different to our `RegComponent`, switching would require major changes to our client application.

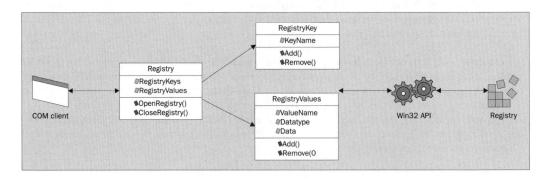

> The solution to these problems is to develop components as OLE DB providers. OLE DB providers feature the same benefits as normal COM components such as reusability and encapsulation. The only difference between OLE DB providers and normal COM components is that OLE DB providers expose their data access functionality through a set of standard OLE DB interfaces rather than through custom interfaces. By implementing the standard OLE DB interfaces, developers can leverage the functionality provided by OLE DB providers without learning a proprietary API or object model. Instead, developers can utilize the features and flexibility of the simplistic ADO object model. Additionally, OLE DB providers can be interchanged based on their performance, scalability and reliability advantages without requiring major code revisions to client applications. Understanding that an OLE DB provider is simply a COM component that implements a subset of the pre-defined OLE DB interfaces is fundamental to developing custom OLE DB providers.

Since all OLE DB providers expose their functionality in a standard way, not only can we use ADO to access various data sources without any significant code changes, but we can also enhance the functionality of custom OLE DB providers through the use of existing OLE DB service providers and service components such as:

❑ Transaction enlistment

❑ Session pooling

❑ Persistence Service

❑ Client Cursor Engine

❑ (Data) Shape Service

❑ (Data) Remoting Provider

Before you create another COM component and define yet another custom interface, step back for a moment and consider the purpose of the component. Will it be responsible for exposing some sort of data? Or will it perform generic operations such as calculations or summarizations on any type of data? If you answered 'yes' to either of these previous questions, then the final question is not 'Why expose data through OLE DB?', but rather, 'Why *not* expose data through OLE DB?' OLE DB providers are not an alternative to developing normal COM components in all situations. However, when you're considering implementing a COM component to encapsulate custom data access or data manipulation, you should *first* consider developing the COM component as an OLE DB provider. If all data were exposed through OLE DB and thus accessible from the simple ADO components, we as developers would spend a lot less time learning new object models and have more time to focus on the business aspects of software development.

Types of Custom OLE DB Providers

Custom OLE DB data providers and custom service providers can be classified into two additional categories: full OLE DB providers and simple OLE DB providers.

Full OLE DB Providers

Full (or standard) OLE DB providers are COM components that can implement and expose data through *any* of the OLE DB interfaces. As a result, they are unlimited in functionality. Due to the complexity of the OLE DB interfaces, 'full' OLE DB providers can only be developed using C++.

All of the OLE DB data providers and OLE DB service providers we've discussed thus far in this book are considered full OLE DB providers. For example, the OLE DB provider for SQL Server (SQLOLEDB), the OLE DB provider for Internet Publishing and the OLE DB provider for Active Directory Services, just to name a few, can all be referred to as 'full' OLE DB providers.

However, it's important to note that this terminology is usually only used when trying to differentiate between a simple provider from a standard provider which is implemented in C++.

Simple OLE DB Providers

Simple OLE DB providers are COM components that implement and expose data through the OLE DB Simple Provider (OSP) interfaces. Unlike the standard OLE DB interfaces, the OSP interfaces are COM-automation interfaces so they can be implemented in any language that supports the development of COM components including Visual Basic, Visual J++, and of course Visual C++. The OSP interfaces are invoked by the OLE DB Simple Provider (MSDAOSP), an in-process COM server that acts as a translator between the standard OLE DB interfaces and the OSP interfaces. The OLE DB Simple Provider and the OSP interfaces are collectively known as the OSP Toolkit.

It's important to understand that the OSP Toolkit was designed to allow developers to create simple but robust providers that require minimal effort to expose data through OLE DB. A provider based on the OSP interfaces can support asynchronous or synchronous data retrieval, inserting, updating and deleting data, and searching within a data set. With these features, simple providers are sufficient for exposing most data sources that can be represented in a tabular format, however they are limited in functionality when compared to full OLE DB providers. Specifically, providers built with the OSP interfaces have the following limitations:

❑   Simple providers do not support commands, transactions or batch updates.

❑   They can not provide any metadata about the rowset other than the column name.

❑   All data is exposed as variants.

❑   RDS and the OLE DB Remoting Provider cannot be used with a simple provider.

❑   Simple providers cannot be used from SQL Server's Data Transformation Services (DTS).

❑   They also cannot be used with Visual Basic's Data Environment Designer (DED) when performing data binding, because Simple providers do not support commands.

❑   Simple providers cannot be extended to support any additional OLE DB interfaces.

Before you create an OLE DB Provider using the OLE DB Simple Provider Interfaces, consider these limitations and make sure your custom data access and manipulation needs can be solved with a simple provider implementation. If you require greater functionality in your custom provider than can be achieved through the OSP Toolkit, the only alternative is to develop a Full OLE DB provider using C++.

> **Developing Full OLE DB providers requires a mastery of the Component Object Model, C++, and the OLE DB interfaces. This topic is a book in its own right. For these reasons, in this chapter we will focus solely on 'simple' OLE DB providers. Even with their limitations, you will find that the OLE DB Simple Provider interfaces can be used to satisfy almost any custom data access requirements. For more information about developing a Full OLE DB provider, please consult the Platform SDK.**

OLE DB Simple Provider (OSP) Architecture

To develop simple OLE DB providers effectively, you must first understand the underlying OLE DB Simple Provider (OSP) architecture. At the center of the OSP architecture is a multi-threaded COM server called the Microsoft OLE DB Simple Provider (MSDAOSP). MSDAOSP effectively acts as a mediator between the OLE DB consumer and a simple provider, translating method calls on the complex OLE DB interfaces to method calls on the COM-automation OLEDBSimpleProvider interface.

> **The terminology used to describe the OLE DB Simple Provider architecture can easily become confusing. When we use the terms 'OLE DB Simple Provider' or 'OSP', we are not referring to a custom provider, but instead we are referring to the set of components contained in the MSDAOSP.dll in-process COM server. To distinguish this from the in-process COM server that contains the OSP implementation and the OSP Data Object, we will use the term 'simple OLE DB provider' (or just 'simple provider') to refer to the latter.**

In this chapter, we are going to focus on using a simple OLE DB provider from ADO. However, a simple provider can be also be leveraged from Internet Explorer, where it acts as a Data Source Object (DSO) by supplying data for DHTML data binding. In this environment, the OSP architecture is slightly different.

OLE DB Simple Provider (MSDAOSP)

The OLE DB Simple Provider, also known as MSDAOSP, implements the standard OLE DB interfaces necessary to support the base level of functionality, known as Level 0 OLE DB conformance, that is required of every OLE DB Provider. As the following diagram illustrates, when OLE DB consumers such as ADO call methods on these OLE DB interfaces, the OLE DB Simple Provider either processes the method call itself or invokes the appropriate method(s) on a simple provider through the OLEDBSimpleProvider interface:

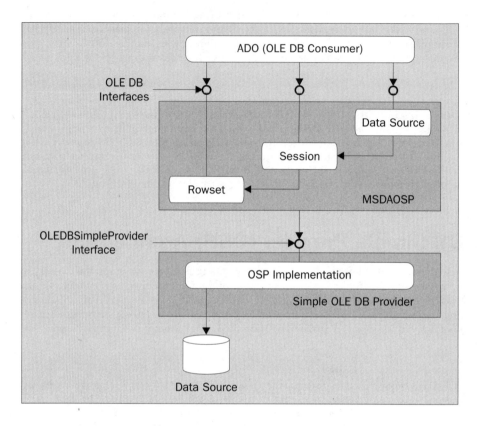

OLEDBSimpleProvider Interface

The OLEDBSimpleProvider interface is used by MSDAOSP to retrieve and perform operations on data managed by a simple provider. The simple provider's component that implements the OLEDBSimpleProvider interface is called the **OSP implementation**. The OLEDBSimpleProvider interface defines 14 methods, which can be divided into the following six categories:

- ❑ Schema methods
- ❑ Variant methods
- ❑ Insertion and deletion methods
- ❑ Asynchronous data retrieval methods
- ❑ Listener methods
- ❑ Miscellaneous methods

Let's discuss each of these categories and analyze the 14 methods defined by the OLEDBSimpleProvider interface that fall in these categories.

Schema Methods

The schema methods are responsible for providing metadata information about the rows and columns of the set of data, or dataset, exposed by the OSP implementation. Unfortunately, the `OLEDBSimpleProvider` interface is limited to exposing basic metadata information such as the number of rows and columns in the dataset and the read/write status of individual cells, entire rows, entire columns or the entire dataset. This metadata information is exposed through the following methods:

getRowCount

Visual Basic Definition

```
Function getRowCount() As Long
```

Visual C++ Definition

```
HRESULT getRowCount([out, retval] LONG *pcRows)
```

When the `getRowCount` method is invoked, an OSP implementation should return the number of rows in the dataset. This value is exposed through the ADO `Recordset`'s `RecordCount` property. The row count returned should not include row header or column name information.

getColumnCount

Visual Basic Definition

```
Function getColumnCount() As Long
```

Visual C++ Definition

```
HRESULT getColumnCount([out,retval] LONG *pcColumns)
```

The `getColumnCount` method should return the number of columns in the dataset. This value is used by ADO when a `Recordset` is opened to determine the number of `Field` objects in the recordset's `Fields` collection.

getRWStatus

Visual Basic Definition

```
Function getRWStatus(ByVal iRow As Long, ByVal iColumn As Long) As MSDAOSP.OSPRW
```

Visual C++ Definition

```
HRESULT getRWStatus([in] LONG iRow, [in] LONG iColumn,
                    [out, retval] OSPRW *prwStatus)
```

The `getRWStatus` method should return the read/write status for the entire dataset, an entire column, an entire row or an individual cell depending on the combination of values in the `iRow` and `iColumn` parameters. Here's how the combination of these parameters work:

Applies To	Condition
Cell	The iColumn parameter specifies a valid column number and iRow specifies a valid row number
Column	The iRow parameter is −1 and iColumn specifies a valid column number
Row	The iColumn parameter is −1 and the iRow parameter specifies a valid row number
Dataset	Both the iRow parameter and the iColumn parameter are −1

The getRWStatus method can return one of the following three possible values:

Value	Description
OSPRW_READONLY	The cell, row, column or dataset is read-only.
OSPRW_READWRITE *or* OSPRW_DEFAULT	The cell, row, column or dataset can be modified, added to or deleted.
OSPRW_MIXED	The read-write status of the cell, row, column or dataset is unknown *or* is a combination of read-only and read/write.

Variant Methods

The variant methods are responsible for retrieving and setting values in the dataset exposed by the OSP implementation. As the category name suggests, all data is retrieved and set using variants. Consequently, there is no need for schema methods to expose the datatype of each column. The variant methods include:

getVariant

Visual Basic Definition

```
Function getVariant(ByVal iRow As Long, ByVal iColumn As Long, _
                    ByVal format As MSDAOSP.OSPFORMAT) As Variant
```

Visual C++ Definition

```
HRESULT getVariant([in] LONG iRow, [in] LONG iColumn, [in] OSPFORMAT format,
                   [out, retval] VARIANT *pVar)
```

The getVariant method should return the value for the cell specified by the iRow and iColumn parameters. When MSDAOSP wants the names of the columns/fields, the getVariant method will be invoked and passed a value of 0 for the iRow parameter. The format parameter indicates the format in which the data should be returned. This parameter can have one of the following values:

Value	Description
OSPFORMAT_RAW	The cell's actual, unformatted value should be returned.
or	
OSPFORMAT_DEFAULT	
OSPFORMAT_HTML	The cell's value should be converted to an HTML string before it is returned, although a provider can optionally return a plain string without any HTML tags or attributes.
OSPFORMAT_FORMATTED	The cell's value should be converted to a string before it is returned. OSP implementations are expected to support the OSPFORMAT_FORMATTED option.

setVariant

Visual Basic Definition

```
Sub setVariant(ByVal iRow As Long, ByVal iColumn As Long, _
            ByVal format As MSDAOSP.OSPFORMAT, ByVal Var As Variant)
```

Visual C++ Definition

```
HRESULT setVariant([in] LONG iRow, [in] LONG iColumn, [in] OSPFORMAT format,
                [in, retval] VARIANT Var)
```

When the setVariant method is invoked, an OSP implementation should set the value for the specified cell with the new value in the Var parameter. Read-only provider's aren't required to support any functionality behind this method. The format parameter can have the same values with the setVariant method as it could with the getVariant method. However, with the setVariant method, the format parameter indicates the current format of the data in the Var parameter.

Insertion and Deletion Methods

The insertion and deletion methods are responsible for inserting or deleting rows in the dataset exposed by the OSP implementation. As you might guess, two methods fall in this category:

deleteRows

Visual Basic Definition

```
Function deleteRows(ByVal iRow As Long, ByVal cRows As Long) As Long
```

Visual C++ Definition

```
HRESULT deleteRows([in] LONG iRow, [in] LONG cRows,
                [out, retval] LONG *pcRowsDeleted)
```

The deleteRows method should cause the OSP implementation to delete the number of rows specified in the cRows parameter, starting at the row specified in the iRow parameter. A value of –1 in the iRow parameter indicates that all rows should be deleted. This method should return the actual number of rows that were deleted.

insertRows

Visual Basic Definition

```
Function insertRows(ByVal iRow As Long, ByVal cRows As Long) As Long
```

Visual C++ Definition

```
HRESULT insertRows([in] LONG iRow, [in] LONG cRows,
                   [out, retval] LONG *pcRowsInserted)
```

When the `insertRows` method is called, an OSP Implementation should insert the number of empty rows specified by the `cRows` parameter, starting at the location in the dataset specified by the `iRow` parameter. The values for individual cells in the new row(s) are set through calls to the `setVariant` method.

Asynchronous Data Retrieval Methods

The asynchronous data retrieval methods are responsible for allowing `MSDAOSP` to check an OSP implementation's asynchronous status and control the progress of asynchronous data retrieval. The asynchronous data retrieval methods include:

isAsync

Visual Basic Definition

```
Function isAsync() As Long
```

Visual C++ Definition

```
HRESULT isAsync([out, retval] BOOL *pbAsynch)
```

The `isAsync` method should return a value of `1` if the OSP implementation supports asynchronous data retrieval, or `0` if asynchronous data retrieval is not supported.

getEstimatedRows

Visual Basic Definition

```
Function getEstimatedRows() As Long
```

Visual C++ Definition

```
HRESULT getEstimatedRows([out, retval] LONG *piRows)
```

The `getEstimatedRows` method should return the estimated number of rows in the dataset if the OSP implementation supports asynchronous data retrieval. If for some reason the number of rows cannot be estimated, this method should return a value of `-1`. Synchronous providers should return either `-1` or the actual row count, which should match the value returned from the `getRowCount` method.

stopTransfer

Visual Basic Definition

```
Sub stopTransfer()
```

Visual C++ Definition

```
HRESULT stopTransfer()
```

When the `stopTransfer` method is called, an OSP implementation should stop asynchronous data retrieval. An OSP implementation should attempt to expose any data and schema information about the data transferred before receiving this cancellation request. However, if this is not possible, the OSP implementation should return an error on all subsequent calls on the `OLEDBSimpleProvider` interface.

Listener Methods

The listener methods are responsible for allowing MSDAOSP to register and unregister as a listener of callback methods or events that will be raised by the OSP implementation. We'll discuss listeners in more detail later in this chapter, but first let's look at the two listener methods defined by the `OLEDBSimpleProvider` interface:

addOLEDBSimpleProviderListener

Visual Basic Definition

```
Sub addOLEDBSimpleProviderListener(ByVal pospIListener As _
                            MSDAOSP.OLEDBSimpleProviderListener)
```

Visual C++ Definition

```
HRESULT addOLEDBSimpleProviderListener([in] OLEDBSimpleProviderListener
                            *posplListener)
```

The `addOLEDBSimpleProviderListener` should cause the OSP implementation to register or add the reference to the OSP listener specified in the `pospIListener` argument into an array or collection. Later, an OSP implementation can call methods on all the references in the collection or array.

removeOLEDBSimpleProviderListener

Visual Basic Definition

```
Sub removeOLEDBSimpleProviderListener(ByVal pospIListener As _
                            MSDAOSP.OLEDBSimpleProviderListener)
```

Visual C++ Definition

```
HRESULT removeOLEDBSimpleProviderListener([in] OLEDBSimpleProviderListener
                            *posplListener)
```

When the `removeOLEDBSimpleProviderListener` method is invoked, an OSP implementation should unregister or remove all references to the OSP listener specified in the `pospIListener` variable. This method is called when a listener is no longer interested in receiving callbacks issued by the OSP implementation.

Miscellaneous Methods

The `OLEDBSimpleProvider` interface also defines two methods that don't really fall into any of the other categories. These two methods are:

getLocale

Visual Basic Definition

```
Function getLocale() As String
```

Visual C++ Definition

```
HRESULT getLocale([out,retval] BSTR *pbstrLocale)
```

The `getLocale` method should return a string value that indicates the **locale** or country of origin of the dataset. This method is provided so that the consumer can perform conversions or special operations on the dataset exposed by the OSP implementation when the data is in another language. Alternatively, an OSP implementation could determine the default locale of the operating system and perform the necessary conversions internally.

Find

Visual Basic Definition

```
Function find(ByVal iRowStart As Long, ByVal iColumn As Long, _
            ByVal val As Variant, ByVal findFlags As MSDAOSP.OSPFIND, _
            ByVal compType As MSDAOSP.OSPCOMP) As Long
```

Visual C++ Definition

```
HRESULT find([in] LONG iRowStart, [in] LONG iColumn, [in] VARIANT val,
            [in] OSPFIND findFlags, [in] OSPCOMP compType,
            [out, retval] LONG *piRowFound)
```

The `find` method should cause the OSP implementation to search through the dataset, comparing the value specified in the `val` parameter against the value in the column specified by the `iColumn` parameter. The search should start at the row specified in the `iRowStart` parameter. The `findflags` parameter specifies the additional search options through the following supported values:

Value	Description
OSPFIND_CASESENSITIVE	The search should be case sensitive.
OSPFIND_UP	The search should be in descending order.
OSPFIND_UPCASESENSITIVE	The search should be case-sensitive in descending order.
OSPFIND_DEFAULT	The search should be case-insensitive in ascending order.

The type of comparsion perfomed against the value specified in the `val` parameter and the actual column's value should vary based on the value of the `compType` parameter. The supported values for this parameter are:

Value	Description
OSPCOMP_EQ	Search for the first value equal to the value in the `val` parameter.
or	
OSPCOMP_DEFAULT	

Value	Description
OSPCOMP_GE	Search for the first value greater than or equal to the value in the val parameter.
OSPCOMP_GT	Search for the first value greater than the value in the val parameter.
OSPCOMP_LE	Search for the first value less than or equal to the value in the val parameter.
OSPCOMP_LT	Search for the first value less than the value in the val parameter.
OSPCOMP_NE	Search for the first value not equal to the value in the val parameter.

The find method should immediately return the row number where the first match is found. If no rows meet the criterion passed in, the find method should return -1, indicating that no match was made.

OSP Data Object

Before an OLE DB consumer can retrieve and manipulate data exposed by an OSP implementation, the consumer must establish a connection to the OLE DB Simple Provider (MSDAOSP) and open an OLE DB Rowset – the OLE DB equivalent of an ADO Recordset. OLE DB providers do not always expose exactly the same rowset, but instead an OLE DB provider supplies the infrastructure for accessing a certain type or format of data in a standard way through the OLE DB interfaces. The actual rows and columns that should be included in a rowset are usually specified by the OLE DB consumer through the use of a **text command**, such as a SQL statement. Most OLE DB providers can expose multiple rowsets over the same data source, with each rowset having varying contents. The OLE DB Provider for SQL Server, for example, simply defines a model for accessing SQL Server data. The contents of the rowset returned by the provider vary based on the SQL statement specified by the OLE DB consumer.

OLE DB consumers specify the rowset they desire by calling the OpenRowset method of the IOpenRowset OLE DB interface which is implemented by the OLE DB Simple Provider. With ADO, this is accomplished through an ADO Recordset object's Open method, or through a Connection object's Execute method. As the mediator between the OLE DB consumer and the OSP implementation, when MSDAOSP processes an OpenRowset method call, it must inform the OSP implementation which dataset it should load and expose through the OLEDBSimpleProvider interface. In other words, when MSDAOSP's IOpenRowset::OpenRowset method is invoked, MSDAOSP must forward the rowset request to the OSP implementation which supplies the actual data. However, you might have noticed that not one of the 14 methods defined by the OLEDBSimpleProvider interface is responsible for allowing MSDAOSP to specify the dataset that the OSP implementation should load and expose. Instead this functionality is performed through an additional COM component called an OSP Data Object (ODO).

An OSP Data Object acts as an abstraction layer between the OLE DB Simple Provider and the OSP implementation. When an OLE DB consumer establishes a connection to MSDAOSP, MSDAOSP creates a single instance of the simple provider's ODO component. MSDAOSP can then use the new OSP Data Object as a factory for creating instances of components that implement the OLEDBSimpleProvider interface, with each instance exposing a different set of data.

When MSDAOSP receives a request for an OLE DB Rowset, it forwards the request to a simple provider's OSP Data Object by invoking either the GetDataMember method of the IDataSource interface or a method named msDataSourceObject on the ODO's default, IDispatch, interface. Both of these methods accept a text command such as a SQL statement as a parameter, and return a reference to a new instance of a simple provider's OSP implementation. This text command, sometimes called a **DataMember**, is what we specify in the Source parameter of an ADO Recordset's Open method or the CommandText parameter of a Connection's Execute method. When the reference to the new instance of the OSP implementation has been returned to MSDAOSP, the OSP Data Object steps out of the way and methods can be invoked on the new instance of the OSP implementation directly through its OLEDBSimpleProvider interface. These methods are invoked as a result of method calls by the OLE DB consumer to MSDAOSP through the OLE DB interfaces:

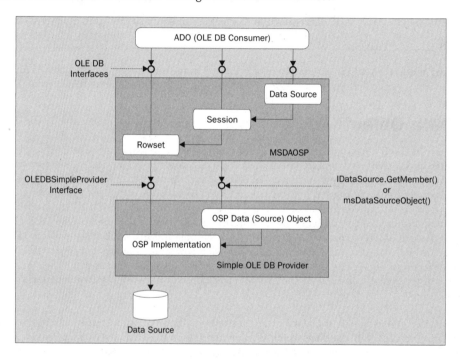

There is one important exception when MSDAOSP will not call the IDataSource::GetDataMember method to request a new instance of the OSP implementation. MSDAOSP will simply share an existing instance of the OSP implementation when the OLE DB consumer (e.g. ADO) requests a new recordset/rowset with the same text command as one requested previously against the same instance of the OSP Data Object. In other words, if you attempt to open an ADO Recordset using the same text command that was used to open a previous Recordset, MSDAOSP will not involve the OSP Data Object, but instead MSDAOSP will share the existing OSP implementation instance. This behavior is only true when the OSP Data Object implements the IDataSource interface. If the ODO implements the msDataSourceObject method instead, then a new instance of the OSP Implementation will *always* be requested by MSDAOSP, regardless of the text command.

The OSP Data Object *could* actually be the same component that implements the OLEDBSimpleProvider interface, simply returning a reference to itself whenever its IDataSource::GetDataMember method or msDataSourceObject method is called. If a simple provider always exposed the same dataset through the OLEDBSimpleProvider interface, this approach would not cause any problems. However, this approach is not recommended because an ODO should be able to expose multiple instances of a simple provider's OSP implementation. Remember, each OSP implementation represents a unique dataset from an exclusive or a shared data source. A single OSP Data Object will return a new instance of the OSP implementation for each unique data member specified by the OLE DB consumer.

Within the OSP architecture, each OLE DB consumer's connection to the OLE DB Simple Provider (MSDAOSP) represents an instance of a simple provider's OSP Data Object. Likewise, each open recordset/rowset represents an instance of a simple provider's OSP implementation, with one exception. If the OLE DB consumer opens a recordset/rowset with the same text command as a recordset/rowset opened previously on the same connection and the ODO implements the IDataSource interface then MSDAOSP will share an instance of a simple provider's OSP implementation.

The one-to-many relationship of OSP Data Objects to OSP implementation instances is depicted in the following diagram. Notice that once the OSP Data Object has created an instance of the OSP implementation and returned a reference to the new instance to MSDAOSP, the OSP Data Object steps aside and MSDAOSP calls methods on the OSP implementation directly through the OLEDBSimpleProvider interface:

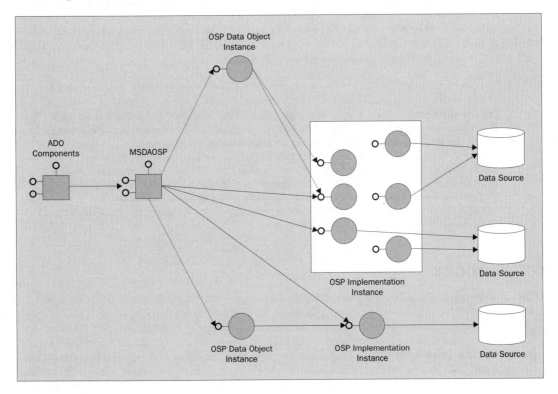

Why Two Methods?

As we saw above, an OSP Data Object is required to implement *either* the GetDataMember method of the IDataSource interface *or* a method named msDataSourceObject on the ODO's default, IDispatch, interface. While both the GetDataMember and the msDataSourceObject methods serve the same purpose, there are some subtle differences. As a result, both methods are supported by the OSP architecture to enable the development of ODOs in various development languages. Let's briefly look at the differences between these two methods.

GetDataMember

The GetDataMember method is one of five methods defined by the IDataSource interface. While we're currently only concerned with the GetDataMember method, COM specifies that we must implement either all or none of the methods defined by an interface. The GetDataMember method is defined with the RESTRICTED attribute in the Microsoft Data Source Interface's type library (MSDATSRC.TLB). Consequently, only OSP Data Objects developed in Visual C++ can implement the IDataSource interface.

msDataSourceObject()

OSP Data Objects that support the msDataSourceObject method can be developed in any lanaguage that supports the development of COM components, including Visual Basic, Visual J++ and of course Visual C++. The msDataSourceObject method must be defined on an ODO component's default, IDispatch, interface. If you want your simple provider to act as a Data Source Object (DSO) within the DHTML data binding architecture, your ODO must implement the msDataSourceObject method rather than the IDataSource::GetDataMember method. Additionally, when a simple provider is going to be used in this environment, the msDataSourceObject method must be assigned a dispatch ID (DISPID) of −3900 and it must expose only one data set.

> If you're developing simple OLE DB providers in Visual Basic 6.0, instead of implementing the msDataSourceObject method on your OSP Data Object's default interface, you can change your ODO's DataSourceBehavior design-time property to 1 − vbDataSource. When you do so, an additional method named GetDataMember will be added to the class object for your component. However, behind the scenes Visual Basic actually implements the IDataSouce interface. When the IDataSource::GetDataMember method is called by MSDAOSP, Visual Basic secretly forwards the method call to the class's GetDataMember method (Class_GetDataMember) and converts the parameters to automation-compatible datatypes.

Notifications

So far we've been discussing the communication within the OSP architecture as if it were one-directional, with all method calls coming from the OLE DB Simple Provider (MSDAOSP). MSDAOSP calls either the msDataSourceObject method or the IDataSource::GetDataMember method on the OSP Data Object to request an instance of the OSP implementation. MSDAOSP then performs data retrieval and manipulation by invoking methods on the new instance of the OSP implementation through the OLEDBSimpleProvider interface. However, on certain occasions a simple provider's OSP Data Object or OSP implementation may need to perform call-backs to MSDAOSP. These call-backs are known as **notifications**.

Notifications are simply method calls performed within the OSP architecture that notify all interested objects about changes to data exposed by a simple provider. Why is this important? Imagine a common scenario where two ADO recordsets share the same instance of an OLE DB simple provider's OSP implementation, and therefore the recordsets share the same set of data. We saw in the last section that this scenario can occur when a recordset is opened with the same text command as one opened previously through the same ADO connection. In this case, one recordset could modify, delete or insert data and as a result, the other recordset would have a view of the data that is actually inconsistent with the actual dataset managed by the simple provider. However, notifications allow a simple provider to inform all objects that register an interest in receiving notifications (called **listeners**) that changes have occurred within a dataset, so that they can resynchronize their copy of the dataset with the simple provider's dataset.

For example, in the following diagram, the OSP implementation provides data access to the Favorites list in Internet Explorer. Both `Recordset1` and `Recordset2` share the same instance of the OSP implementation and so they also share the same dataset. When the last record is deleted in `Recordset1`, the OSP implementation performs the operation on the dataset and sends back a notification to `MSDAOSP`, which forwards the notification to all interested listeners (in this example the `Recordset1` and `Recordset2` objects). When the `Recordset2` object is notified that a record has been deleted it automatically adjusts its view of the dataset to be in sync with the underlying data source:

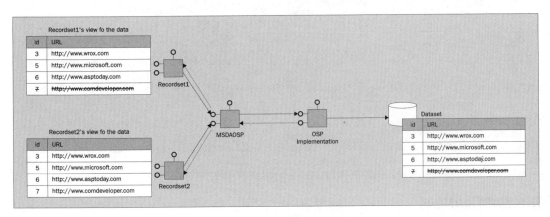

There are three levels or types of notifications that occur within the OSP Architecture:

❑   OSP Notifications

❑   Data Source Notifications

❑   OLE DB Notifications

The following diagram illustrates the place of these types of notifications within the OLE DB architecture. It also shows the interfaces through which these notifications are performed:

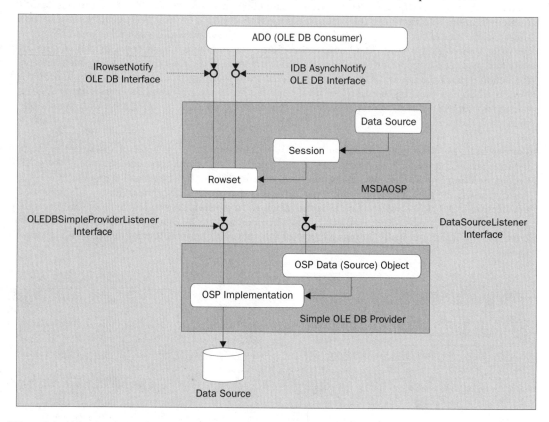

We will now look at OSP, Data Source, and OLE DB notifications in more detail.

OSP Notifications

OSP notifications are methods invoked by a simple provider's OSP implementation as a result of asynchronous data retrieval or dataset manipulation requests through the OLEDBSimpleProvider interface. These methods are defined by the OLEDBSimpleProviderListener interface, which is implemented by MSDAOSP. MSDAOSP registers and unregisters itself as a listener for OSP notifications by calling the addOLEDBSimpleProviderListener and removeOLEDBSimpleProviderListener methods of an OSP implementation's OLEDBSimpleProvider interface. The OSP implementation should maintain a collection of references to OSP listeners (objects implementing the OLEDBSimpleProviderListener interface) and adjust the inventory of this collection as appropriate when the addOLEDBSimpleProviderListener and removeOLEDBSimpleProviderListener methods are invoked.

> The only time an OSP implementation will have references to multiple listeners is when multiple ADO recordsets are opened against the same ADO connection with the same text command and the provider's ODO implements the `IDataSource` interface. If a recordset is opened with a different text command or against a new ADO connection, `MSDAOSP` will request a new instance of the simple provider's OSP implementation. `MSDAOSP` will always request a new instance of the OSP implementation when the ODO implements the `msDataSourceObject` method instead of the `IDataSource` interface. However, with some intelligent coding, you can work around this issue and return a reference to an existing OSP implementation when the `msDataSourceObject` method is called.

The methods defined by the `OLEDBSimpleProviderListener` interface include two methods related to asynchronous data retrieval and three pairs of pre- and post-notifications for the standard data manipulation Insert, Update and Delete events. If an OSP implementation does not support functionality that requires a notification then the OSP implementation should not call the corresponding methods on the `OLEDBSimpleProviderListener` interface. For example, if an OSP implementation is read-only, there is no reason why it should call any of the methods of the `OLEDBSimpleProviderListener` interface related to data being inserted, updated or deleted. The eight methods defined by the `OLEDBSimpleProviderListener` interface are:

aboutToChangeCell

Visual Basic Definition

```
Sub aboutToChangeCell(iRow As Long, iColumn As Long)
```

Visual C++ Definition

```
HRESULT aboutToChangeCell([in] LONG iRow, [in] LONG iColumn)
```

The `aboutToChangeCell` method notifies the listener that the cell specified by the `iRow` and `iColumn` parameters is about to be modifed. This method should be called before the OSP implementation changes a cell's value as a result of the `setVariant` method of the `OLEDBSimpleProvider` interface being invoked by `MSDAOSP`.

cellChanged

Visual Basic Definition

```
Sub cellChanged (iRow As Long, iColumn As Long)
```

Visual C++ Definition

```
HRESULT cellChanged([in] LONG iRow, [in] LONG iColumn)
```

The `cellChanged` method notifies the listener that the cell specified by the `iRow` and `iColumn` parameters has been modified. This method should be called after the OSP implementation has changed a cell's value as a result of a call to the `setVariant` method of the `OLEDBSimpleProvider` interface. All subsequent calls by `MSDAOSP` to the `getVariant` method should return the new value(s).

aboutToDeleteRows

Visual Basic Definition

```
Sub aboutToDeleteRows (iRow As Long, cRows As Long)
```

Visual C++ Definition

```
HRESULT aboutToDeleteRows([in] LONG iRow, [in] LONG cRows)
```

The aboutToDeleteRows method notifies the listener that a number of rows as specified in the cRows parameter are about to be deleted, beginning at the row specified in the iRow parameter. This method should be called before the OSP implementation deletes rows as a result of the deleteRows method of the OLEDBSimpleProvider interface being invoked by MSDAOSP.

deletedRows

Visual Basic Definition

```
Sub deletedRows (iRow As Long, cRows As Long)
```

Visual C++ Definition

```
HRESULT deletedRows ([in] LONG iRow, [in] LONG cRows)
```

The deleteRows method notifies the listener that the number of rows specified in the cRows parameter, beginning at the row specified in the iRow parameter, have been deleted. This method should be called after the OSP implementation has deleted rows from the dataset due to a deleteRows method call. All subsequent calls by MSDAOSP to the getRowCount method should return the adjusted number of rows.

aboutToInsertRows

Visual Basic Definition

```
Sub aboutToInsertRows (iRow As Long, cRows As Long)
```

Visual C++ Definition

```
HRESULT aboutToInsertRows ([in] LONG iRow, [in] LONG cRows)
```

The aboutToInsertRows method notifies the listener that the number of rows specified in the cRows parameter and beginning at the row specified in the iRow parameter have been inserted. This method should be called before the any rows are inserted into the dataset due to the insertRows method of the OLEDBSimpleProvider interface is invoked by MSDAOSP.

insertedRows

Visual Basic Definition

```
Sub insertedRows (iRow As Long, cRows As Long)
```

Visual C++ Definition

```
HRESULT insertedRows ([in] LONG iRow, [in] LONG cRows)
```

The insertedRows method notifies the listener that the number of rows specified in the cRows parameter are about to be inserted beginning at the row specified in the iRow parameter. This method should be called after the OSP implementation has inserted rows into the dataset as a result of the insertRows method of the OLEDBSimpleProvider interface being invoked by MSDAOSP. All subsequent calls by MSDAOSP to the getRowCount method should return the adjusted number of rows.

rowsAvailable

Visual Basic Definition

```
Sub rowsAvailable (iRow As Long, cRows As Long)
```

Visual C++ Definition

```
HRESULT rowsAvailable ([in] LONG iRow, [in] LONG cRows)
```

The `rowsAvailable` method notifies the listener that the number of rows specified in the `cRows` parameter and beginning at the row specified in the `iRow` parameter are now available. This method is used by asychronous OSP implementations to notify `MSDAOSP` that it can now retrieve the data for the spceified records by calling the `getVariant` method of the `OLEDBSimpleProvider` interface.

transferComplete

Visual Basic Definition

```
Sub transferComplete (xfer As OSPXFER)
```

Visual C++ Definition

```
HRESULT transferComplete([in] OSPXFER doneReason)
```

The `transferComplete` method notifies the listener that asynchronous loading of the dataset is complete. The `xfer` parameter indicates that the dataset is completely loaded without errors and is now available (`OSPXFER_COMPLETE`), that an error has occurred loading the dataset (`OSPXFER_ABORT`), or that loading the dataset has been canceled (`OSPXFER_ERROR`) because of a call by `MSDAOSP` to the `stopTransfer` method of the `OLEDBSimpleProvider` interface.

Data Source Notifications

Where OSP notifications are methods invoked by a simple provider's OSP implementation, Data Source notifications are methods invoked by a simple provider's OSP Data Object (ODO). Data Source notifications should be called when the structure of a dataset has changed and as a result, the listener should request a new instance of the OSP implementation. For example, dataset structure changes would include: changes to the number of columns in the dataset, column name changes, changes to the type of a column in the dataset, or resorting of the dataset.

MSDAOSP registers and unregisters itself as a listener for Data Source notifications by calling the `addDataSourceListener` and `removeDataSourceListener` methods of the `IDataSource` interface. If the ODO chooses to support the `msDataSourceObject` method instead of the `IDataSource` interface, the ODO can also implement the `addDataSourceListener` method on the ODO's default, `IDispatch`, interface.

Data Source notifications consist of three methods defined by the `IDataSourceListener` interface:

dataMemberChanged

Visual Basic Definition

```
Sub dataMemberChanged(bstrDM As DataMember)
```

Visual C++ Definition

```
HRESULT dataMemberRemoved ([in] BSTR qualifier)
```

533

The dataMemberChanged method notifies the listener that the structure of a dataset has changed. The qualifier parameter specifies the data member (or text command) that identifies the dataset that was changed. When MSDAOSP receives this notification, it should request a new instance of the OSP implementation by calling either the IDataSource interface's GetDataMember method or the msDataSourceObject method of the ODO.

dataMemberAdded

Visual Basic Definition

```
Sub dataMemberAdded(bstrDM As DataMember)
```

Visual C++ Definition

```
HRESULT dataMemberAdded ([in] BSTR qualifier)
```

The dataMemberAdded method notifies the listener that a new dataset is available. The qualifier parameter specifies the data member (or text command) that identifies the dataset that is now available.

dataMemberRemoved

Visual Basic Definition

```
Sub dataMemberRemoved(bstrDM As DataMember)
```

Visual C++ Definition

```
HRESULT dataMemberChanged ([in] BSTR qualifier)
```

The dataMemberRemoved method notifies the listener that a dataset has been removed. The qualifier parameter specifies the data member (or text command) that identifies the dataset that is no longer available.

Unlike OSP notifications, Data Source notifications are typically not needed because most simple providers don't change the structure of the dataset after an instance of the OSP implementation has been created and returned to MSDAOSP. However, if an ODO does issue Data Source notifications, it must broadcast them to every registered listener.

OLE DB Notifications

When MSDAOSP receives OSP notifications and Data Source notifications through the OLEDBSimpleProviderListener and IDataSourceListener interfaces, it forwards them to the OLE DB consumer by calling methods on OLE DB callback interfaces implemented by the consumer. Two OLE DB interfaces are used by MSDAOSP for issuing notifications to the OLE DB consumer:

IDBAsynchNotify

The IDBAsynchNotify interface is implemented by an OLE DB consumer such as ADO that wants to receive notifications about the progress of asynchronous operations. The IDBAsynchNotify interface defines three methods: OnLowResource, OnProgress and OnStop. MSDAOSP calls these methods when it receives corresponding notifications from an OSP implementation. For example, MSDAOSP calls the OnProgress method to notify the consumer of the current progress of the asynchronous operation when an OSP implementation issues the rowsAvailable notification. Likewise, the OnStop method is called by MSDAOSP when it receives a transferComplete notification with a status of OSPXFER_ABORT or OSPXFER_ERROR from the OSP implementation.

IRowsetNotify

The `IRowsetNotify` interface is implemented by an OLE DB consumer (such as ADO) that wants to receive notifications about changes within a column or row, or within the entire dataset. The `IRowsetNotify` interface defines three methods: `OnFieldChange`, `OnRowChange` and `OnRowsetChange`. These methods are also called by `MSDAOSP` when it receives corresponding notifications from an OSP implementation. However, these methods are a little more difficult to trace back to the originating OSP notification because there is not a one-to-one relationship between an OSP notification and an OLE DB notification. Instead, the methods defined by the `IRowsetNotify` interface accept a `DBREASON` parameter and a `DBEVENTPHASE` parameter. The `DBREASON` parameter indicates the reason for the notification, such as `DBREASON_ROW_DELETED` and `DBREASON_ROW_UPDATED`, while the `DBEVENTPHASE` parameter indicates the phase of the event, such as `DBEVENTPHASE_ABOUTTODO` and `DBEVENTPHASE_DIDEVENT`.

> **For more information about the** `IDBAsynchNotify` **and the** `IRowsetNotify` **OLE DB interfaces, please consult the Platform SDK.**

Simple OLE DB Provider Lifecycle

Perhaps the best way to understand how the OSP Data Object (ODO) and the OSP implementation components work together with the OLE DB Simple Provider (`MSDAOSP`) is to look at a simple ADO code sample. We will use the following five simple lines of ADO pseudo-code:

```
Connection.Open connection_string
Recordset.Open text_command
Recordset.Fields(field_name).value = "test"
Recordset.Close
Connection.Close
```

The diagram below shows the interaction between the components:

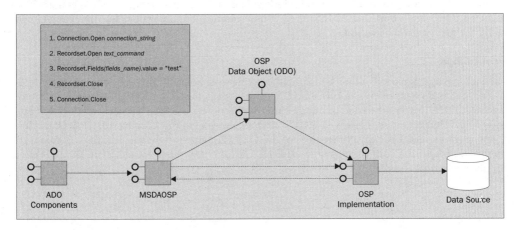

Let's break this simple code example down one line at a time and examine what's going on behind the scenes within the OSP architecture.

Connection.Open connection_string

When an ADO connection is opened against the OLE DB Simple Provider (MSDAOSP), MSDAOSP creates a single instance of the OSP Data Object (ODO) that was specified in the connection string or in the Registry.

Recordset.Open text_command

When a recordset is requested as the result of either a Recordset.Open method call or a Connection.Execute method call, MSDAOSP calls either the msDataSourceObject method on the OSP Data Object's default interface or the GetDataMember method on the ODO's implementation of the IDataSource interface. The *text_command* specified in the Recordset.Open or Connection.Execute method call is forwarded as a parameter to the msDataSourceObject or GetDataMember method. Both the msDataSourceObject and the GetDataMember methods should return a new instance of the OSP implementation to MSDAOSP. MSDAOSP can then construct an OLE DB Rowset by calling the schema methods on the OSP implementation through the OLEDBSimpleProvider interface. Finally, ADO translates the OLE DB Rowset into a scrollable ADO Recordset object. This process is repeated for each recordset request, unless both the recordset requested has the same text command as one already opened on the same connection, and the provider's OSP Data Object implements the IDataSource interface. In this case, MSDAOSP bypasses the OSP Data Object and shares the existing instance of the OSP implementation. Every recordset request also results in MSDAOSP calling the OLEDBSimpleProvider interface's addOLEDBSimpleProviderListener method to increment the OSP listener count.

Recordset.Fields(field_name).value = "test"

Almost any operations can be performed against a Recordset opened from a simple provider. In this example, the consumer is requesting that the value of a named field be changed to "test". ADO sends the request to MSDAOSP, which forwards it to the OSP implementation by calling the setVariant method of the OLEDBSimpleProvider interface. The OSP implementation is then responsible for updating the actual data source. Since data will be modified, the OSP implementation should fire a notification to each registered listener both before and after the data is modified. When a listener receives a notification that data has changed, it may request the new values for the changed cell by calling the getVariant method.

Recordset.Close

When a recordset is closed, either by explicitly calling a Recordset object's Close method, or when the Recordset object reference is released, MSDAOSP calls the OLEDBSimpleProvider interface's removeOLEDBSimpleProviderListener method to notify the OSP implementation that an OSP listener has been removed. However, MSDAOSP does *not* release the instance of the OSP implementation as you might expect. Instead, all instances of the OSP implementation will continue to remain in memory until *after* the connection to the OLE DB Simple Provider is closed, even though the number of OSP listeners might be zero.

Connection.Close

When a connection is closed, either by explicitly calling a Connection object's Close method, or when the Connection object reference is released, MSDAOSP turns on its garbage collection mechanism and immediately returns control to the OLE DB consumer. After a few seconds, MSDAOSP first destroys any instances of the OSP implementation associated with the connection and finally it destroys the single instance of the OSP Data Object that represents the connection.

Summary

In this chapter we scratched under the surface of ADO into the territory of OLE DB. In particular, we learned that:

- ❏ A custom OLE DB data provider can be developed to expose virtually any data source

- ❏ Custom OLE DB providers are simply COM components that expose data access and manipulation through the OLE DB interfaces instead of custom COM interfaces.

- ❏ There are two types of custom OLE DB providers: full OLE DB providers and simple OLE DB providers.

- ❏ A simple OLE DB provider is composed of at least two COM components: an OSP implementation and an OSP Data Object.

- ❏ The Microsoft OLE DB Simple Provider (MSDAOSP) acts as a mediator between the OLE DB consumer and a simple provider.

- ❏ As a mediator, MSDAOSP translates method calls on the complex OLE DB interfaces to method calls on the COM-automation OLEDBSimpleProvider interface.

- ❏ Notifications are essentially callbacks that are used to communicate data changes and the status of asynchronous operations.

A thorough understanding of these complex concepts and intricate details of simple providers is essential before we can successfully go on to develop one. Armed with this knowledge, we're now ready to implement a custom OLE DB provider using the OSP interfaces – which is exactly what we'll do in the next chapter!

Creating an OLE DB Provider for the Windows NT/2000 Registry

In the previous chapter, we looked at the theory behind developing a custom OLE DB provider using the OLE DB Simple Provider (OSP) toolkit. The multi-layered OSP architecture can easily become confusing. If you're thoroughly confused about simple OLE DB providers and the OSP architecture, don't worry. The best way to understand the OSP architecture is to create our own simple OLE DB provider, so now we're going to do just that! In this chapter we're going to apply what we have learned and develop a fully functional OLE DB data provider for the Windows NT/2000 Registry, appropriately called REGOLEDB. Our REGOLEDB Provider will support retrieving, inserting, updating and deleting registry keys and values. But we'll discuss all these details shortly, so let's get started!

Developing the REGOLEDB Provider

Developing a simple OLE DB provider can be broken down into a six-step process:

1. Designing and planning the provider

2. Establishing the project

3. Creating the OSP Data Object

4. Creating the OSP implementation

5. Registering the simple OLE DB provider

6. Testing, debugging and distributing the provider

> **Both the source code and compiled version of the** REGOLEDB **Provider are available from Wrox Press's web site located at** http://www.wrox.com.

While we're going to focus on the development of a simple provider for the Windows NT/2000 Registry, most all of the concepts we'll discuss during each of these steps can be applied to the development of any simple OLE DB provider, regardless of the data source.

Design and Planning

Undoubtedly, the most important stage in the development of an OLE DB provider is the design and planning stage. OLE DB providers are different to independent COM components or applications, in that they must integrate within a sophisticated component-based architecture, the OLE DB architecture, and interact with OLE DB consumers and existing OLE DB service providers. The decisions made during the design of an OLE DB provider will have a direct impact on the performance, scalability, and reliability not only of the provider itself, but also of any application which uses it. Additionally, there is nothing worse than spending hours or even days developing an OLE DB provider (or any type of software for that matter), only to discover a problem or limitation that cannot be worked around without rewriting major portions of code. For these reasons and from personal experience, I cannot stress enough the importance of carefully considering and analyzing every aspect of an OLE DB provider before you proceed with the actual development.

This design and planning stage can actually be broken down into several inter-related phases:

- ❑ Analyzing the requirements of the consumer
- ❑ Understanding the data source
- ❑ Deciding on a tabular data format
- ❑ Defining the text command
- ❑ Choosing a development tool/language
- ❑ Defining the physical implementation
- ❑ Defining how errors will be handled

Let's discuss each of these phases.

Analyzing the Requirements of the Consumer

Before thinking about building a custom OLE DB provider, it's important to understand the consumer. It's helpful to ask yourself questions such as:

- ❑ Who is the consumer?
- ❑ What data does the consumer need to access?
- ❑ Does the consumer need the ability to update, insert or delete data?
- ❑ Does the consumer require support for commands or transactions?
- ❑ Is there an existing OLE DB provider that can provide the required functionality?
- ❑ Do these requirements warrant a simple OLE DB provider or a full OLE DB provider?

As I have already mentioned, we will be developing an OLE DB provider for the Windows NT/2000 Registry, appropriately named REGOLEDB. The *base consumers* for REGOLEDB will be applications and components that need to retrieve, update, insert and delete data in the Windows NT/2000 Registry through ADO. At the time of writing, there are no other OLE DB providers available for the Windows NT/2000 Registry. However, even if there were an available provider, depending on the requirements of the consumer it might be advantageous to develop a custom OLE DB provider that effectively acts as an OLE DB service provider by performing custom data access or data manipulation on top of data exposed by an existing OLE DB data provider for the Registry.

While support for commands and transactions would be a nice feature, it is not typically a strict requirement of most consumers. Therefore, we should be able to leverage the OSP architecture to develop a "simple" OLE DB provider. However, before we make a final decision on this issue, we need to analyze the Windows NT/2000 Registry as a data source and determine how we should present registry data in a tabular format to the consumer.

Understanding the Data Source

It is essential to understand all the details about the data source which our OLE DB provider will expose. These details include: the data format/structure of the data source, the read/write attributes of the data source, and the existing APIs or COM interfaces available for accessing the data source.

The Windows NT or Windows 2000 Registry is a data source used to store all types hardware and software configuration information. For example, within the Registry you can find information such as:

- ❑ The version of Internet Explorer
- ❑ The applications associated with text (.txt) files
- ❑ The threading model of an ADODB.Recordset
- ❑ The ODBC drivers installed on the system
- ❑ The shared components and the clients that depend on them
- ❑ The type and speed of the processor(s)
- ❑ The network adapters, protocols and services installed

The Registry is organized as a hierarchical set of **keys** and **values**, which work in a similar way to the set of directories and files in which a file system is organized. A registry key is an organization unit or node in the registry hierarchy that can contain one or more registry values and other keys, sometimes called sub-keys. A registry value is a data entry stored under a registry key that consists of a name and associated data.

The hierarchical Windows NT/2000 Registry can be viewed and manipulated with a graphical utility called the Registry Editor (RegEdit.exe). As you can see from the following screenshot, one piece of information stored in the Registry is the version of Internet Explorer which is installed on the machine.

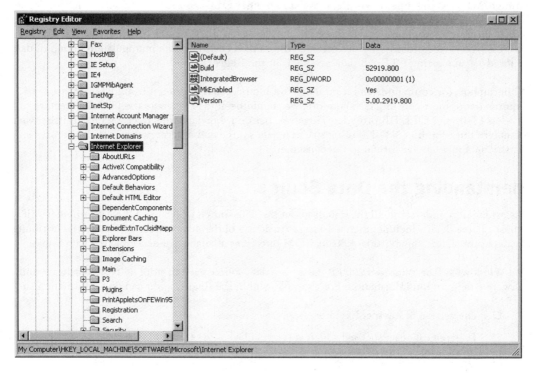

Every registry value is assigned one of ten specific data types. Of these, the three most common are:

❑ REG_SZ – A value of the type REG_SZ contains a null-terminated string. This is the most widely used data type. Every key has a default value of the REG_SZ data type.

❑ REG_BINARY – A value of the type REG_BINARY contains binary data stored in any form.

❑ REG_DWORD – A value of the type REG_DWORD contains a 32-bit number. This is the most common data type for storing numeric data.

There are five predefined Registry keys, called root keys, which are used to organize data in the Registry. While root-keys cannot be modified, deleted or created, keys and values can be created under them. The five root-keys in the Windows NT/2000 Registry are:

❑ HKEY_LOCAL_MACHINE. This key stores computer-specific hardware, software and operating system configuration information. The HKEY_CLASSES_ROOT and HKEY_CURRENT_CONFIG root keys are actually just subsets of the HKEY_LOCAL_MACHINE root key.

❑ HKEY_USERS. The HKEY_USERS key stores profiles for each user who has logged onto the machine. A user profile includes user-specific information such as window positions, desktop configurations, color schemes and the mouse and keyboard behavior.

❏ HKEY_CLASSES_ROOT. This key is simply a pointer or reference to the HKEY_LOCAL_MACHINE\SOFTWARE\Classes key. Both of the keys contain information about file associations, shortcuts and registered COM components.

❏ HKEY_CURRENT_USER. A pointer or reference to the appropriate sub-key under HKEY_USERS for the user currently logged on. For example, if the default user is logged on, HKEY_CURRENT_USER will show the same sub-keys and values as the HKEY_USERS\.DEFAULT key.

❏ HKEY_CURRENT_CONFIG. A pointer or reference to the HKEY_LOCAL_MACHINE\SYSTEM\CurrentControlSet\Hardware Profiles\Current key. Both of these keys store configuration information that about the machines hardware configuration.

The lowest-level and most complex technique for accessing and manipulating the Windows NT/2000 Registry programmatically is through the use of the Win32 API functions. All registry operations are exposed through these functions. The most common Win32 API functions for accessing and manipulating the Registry include:

❏ RegOpenKeyEx. Opens and returns a handle to a specified key.

❏ RegCloseKey. Closes an open key specified by the key's handle.

❏ RegSetValueEx. Changes the data associated with a specified registry value or creates the registry value if it doesn't already exist.

❏ RegQueryValueEx. Retrieves the data associated with a specified registry value.

Due to the complexity of these functions, there have been many COM components developed, both third-party components and custom components, that encapsulate the Win32 API function calls and expose data and functionality through custom COM interfaces. While our REGOLEDB Provider could leverage one of these simpler COM components instead of calling the Win32 API functions directly, most of the time there are major performance advantages if an OLE DB provider utilizes the lowest-level data access technique available. To maximize performance and scalability, our REGOLEDB provider will use the Win32 API functions for accessing and manipulating registry data.

Choosing a Tabular Data Format

Once we are familiar with the data source(s), we need to devise an approach for exposing data in a tabular (row and column) format. Full OLE DB providers are not restricted to a fixed tabular format, but instead can leverage the OLE DB interfaces for semi-structured data to expose each row as an independent unit with a variable number of columns. We saw in chapter 13 that these semi-structured OLE DB interfaces, which are accessible in ADO through the Record and Stream objects, are ideal for exposing hierarchical data sources such as Microsoft Exchange folders.

Even though the Windows NT/2000 Registry is a hierarchical data source, we're going to expose registry data in a tabular format so we can leverage the OSP Toolkit. There are actually a number of ways we could flatten a hierarchy down into a two-dimensional (tabular) dataset.

One possibility would be to load and expose a dataset containing *all* of the registry items below a specified sub-key. For example, the consumer would be able specify a text command of `"HKEY_LOCAL_MACHINE\SOFTWARE"` that would return a dataset similar to the following:

FullName	ItemType	Data
HKEY_LOCAL_MACHINE\SOFTWARE\ (Default)	REG_SZ	Null
HKEY_LOCAL_MACHINE\SOFTWARE\Classes\	KEY	N/A
HKEY_LOCAL_MACHINE\SOFTWARE\Classes\ (Default)	REG_SZ	Null
HKEY_LOCAL_MACHINE\SOFTWARE\Classes*\	KEY	N/A
HKEY_LOCAL_MACHINE\SOFTWARE\Classes*\ (Default)	REG_SZ	Null
HKEY_LOCAL_MACHINE\SOFTWARE\Classes*\ AlwaysShowExt	REG_SZ	Null
HKEY_LOCAL_MACHINE\SOFTWARE\Classes*\InfoTip	REG_SZ	prop:Type; Author;Title ;Subject;Com ment;Size
HKEY_LOCAL_MACHINE\SOFTWARE\Classes\.asa\	KEY	N/A
HKEY_LOCAL_MACHINE\SOFTWARE\Classes\.asa\ (Default)	REG_SZ	Asafile
HKEY_LOCAL_MACHINE\SOFTWARE\Classes\.asa\Content Type	REG_SZ	text/asa
HKEY_LOCAL_MACHINE\SOFTWARE\Classes\.asp\	KEY	N/A
HKEY_LOCAL_MACHINE\SOFTWARE\Classes\.class\ (Default)	REG_SZ	Null
HKEY_LOCAL_MACHINE\SOFTWARE\Classes\.class\Content Type	REG_SZ	Java/*
...	...	...
HKEY_LOCAL_MACHINE\SOFTWARE\Clients\	KEY	N/A
HKEY_LOCAL_MACHINE\SOFTWARE\Clients\ (Default)	REG_SZ	Null
HKEY_LOCAL_MACHINE\SOFTWARE\Clients\Calendar\	KEY	N/A
...	...	...

This dataset contains a row for each registry key or registry value, called a **registry item**. If the registry item is a value then the value's datatype is returned in the ItemType column and the value's data is accessible from the Data column. If the registry item is a key then "Key" is returned in the ItemType column and the value of the Data column is not applicable (N/A). This dataset structure itself has no obvious flaws and it is fairly simple; however, let's look at the contents of the dataset. In this scenario *all* of the registry keys and values below HKEY_LOCAL_MACHINE\SOFTWARE would be loaded into the dataset. As you can imagine, this "top-down" approach would severely limit scalability and performance because most of the time the consumer will typically be looking for a particular key or value. If the consumer specified a text command of `"HKEY_CLASSES_ROOT"` the dataset would probably contain thousands of rows.

Another possibility would be to keep the same dataset structure, but limit the dataset to only the *immediate* sub-keys and values under the registry key specified by the consumer. If the consumer specified a text command of "HKEY_LOCAL_MACHINE\SOFTWARE", as in the last scenario, a dataset similar to the following would be returned:

FullName	ItemType	Data
HKEY_LOCAL_MACHINE\SOFTWARE\ (Default)	REG_SZ	Null
HKEY_LOCAL_MACHINE\SOFTWARE\Classes\	KEY	N/A
HKEY_LOCAL_MACHINE\SOFTWARE\Clients\	KEY	N/A
HKEY_LOCAL_MACHINE\SOFTWARE\Excell Data Corporation\	KEY	N/A
HKEY_LOCAL_MACHINE\SOFTWARE\INTEL\	KEY	N/A
HKEY_LOCAL_MACHINE\SOFTWARE\Jetstream\	KEY	N/A
HKEY_LOCAL_MACHINE\SOFTWARE\KasperskyLab\	KEY	N/A
HKEY_LOCAL_MACHINE\SOFTWARE\McAfee\	KEY	N/A
HKEY_LOCAL_MACHINE\SOFTWARE\Microsoft\	KEY	N/A
HKEY_LOCAL_MACHINE\SOFTWARE\NEC\	KEY	N/A
HKEY_LOCAL_MACHINE\SOFTWARE\Nico Mak Computing\	KEY	N/A
HKEY_LOCAL_MACHINE\SOFTWARE\ODBC\	KEY	N/A
HKEY_LOCAL_MACHINE\SOFTWARE\Policies\	KEY	N/A
HKEY_LOCAL_MACHINE\SOFTWARE\Program Groups\	KEY	N/A
HKEY_LOCAL_MACHINE\SOFTWARE\Secure\	KEY	N/A
HKEY_LOCAL_MACHINE\SOFTWARE\SimTech\	KEY	N/A
HKEY_LOCAL_MACHINE\SOFTWARE\Voice\	KEY	N/A
HKEY_LOCAL_MACHINE\SOFTWARE\Windows 3.1 Migration Status\	KEY	N/A
...	...	...

In this scenerio, the dataset only contains the values and *immediate* sub-keys under HKEY_LOCAL_MACHINE\SOFTWARE, and not the entire "top-down" hierarchy beginning at this location. This approach would result in much smaller datasets, and this would improve the scalability and performance of the provider. However, there is much less flexibility with this narrowly focused dataset. If the consumer decides it needs a registry value or key under the Microsoft sub-key, the consumer would be required to open a new recordset, specifying a text command of "HKEY_LOCAL_MACHINE\SOFTWARE\Microsoft".

In Chapter 6, we looked at the powerful technique of data shaping and hierarchical recordsets. Hierarchical recordsets are a perfect solution for exposing registry keys and values in a tabular format. Our dataset's structure could be modified to support an additional column named `Children` that returns a reference to an ADO recordset containing all of the registry items for the registry key represented by the current row. For example, the text command of `"HKEY_LOCAL_MACHINE\SOFTWARE"` that we've discussed in the previous scenarios would initially return a **parent** dataset similar to the following:

FullName	ItemType	Data	Children
HKEY_LOCAL_MACHINE\SOFTWARE\(Default)	REG_SZ	Null	N/A
HKEY_LOCAL_MACHINE\SOFTWARE\Classes\	KEY	N/A	Recordset object
HKEY_LOCAL_MACHINE\SOFTWARE\Clients\	KEY	N/A	Recordset object
HKEY_LOCAL_MACHINE\SOFTWARE\ Excell Data Corporation\	KEY	N/A	Recordset object
HKEY_LOCAL_MACHINE\SOFTWARE\INTEL\	KEY	N/A	Recordset object
HKEY_LOCAL_MACHINE\SOFTWARE\Jetstream\	KEY	N/A	Recordset object
HKEY_LOCAL_MACHINE\SOFTWARE\KasperskyLab\	KEY	N/A	Recordset object
HKEY_LOCAL_MACHINE\SOFTWARE\McAfee\	KEY	N/A	Recordset object
HKEY_LOCAL_MACHINE\SOFTWARE\Microsoft\	KEY	N/A	Recordset object
HKEY_LOCAL_MACHINE\SOFTWARE\NEC\	KEY	N/A	Recordset object
HKEY_LOCAL_MACHINE\SOFTWARE\ Nico Mak Computing\	KEY	N/A	Recordset object
HKEY_LOCAL_MACHINE\SOFTWARE\ODBC\	KEY	N/A	Recordset object
HKEY_LOCAL_MACHINE\SOFTWARE\Policies\	KEY	N/A	Recordset object
HKEY_LOCAL_MACHINE\SOFTWARE\Program Groups\	KEY	N/A	Recordset object
HKEY_LOCAL_MACHINE\SOFTWARE\Secure\	KEY	N/A	Recordset object
HKEY_LOCAL_MACHINE\SOFTWARE\SimTech\	KEY	N/A	Recordset object
HKEY_LOCAL_MACHINE\SOFTWARE\Voice\	KEY	N/A	Recordset object
HKEY_LOCAL_MACHINE\SOFTWARE\ Windows 3.1 Migration Status\	KEY	N/A	Recordset object
...	...	...	...

For registry items with a type of "KEY" the Children column can contain a valid reference to the values and immediate sub-keys for the current row. For example, the Recordset object in the Children column for the "HKEY_LOCAL_MACHINE\SOFTWARE\Microsoft" row in the above dataset might have the following contents:

FullName	ItemType	Data	Children
HKEY_LOCAL_MACHINE\SOFTWARE\Microsoft\ (Default)	REG_SZ	Null	N/A
HKEY_LOCAL_MACHINE\SOFTWARE\Microsoft\ACS\	KEY	N/A	Recordset object
HKEY_LOCAL_MACHINE\SOFTWARE\Microsoft\ Active Setup\	KEY	N/A	Recordset object
HKEY_LOCAL_MACHINE\SOFTWARE\Microsoft\Ads\	KEY	N/A	Recordset object
HKEY_LOCAL_MACHINE\SOFTWARE\Microsoft\ Advanced INF Setup\	KEY	N/A	Recordset object
HKEY_LOCAL_MACHINE\SOFTWARE\Microsoft\ Automation Manager\	KEY	N/A	Recordset object
HKEY_LOCAL_MACHINE\SOFTWARE\Microsoft\ BOOTPMibAgent\	KEY	N/A	Recordset object
HKEY_LOCAL_MACHINE\SOFTWARE\Microsoft\ Code Store Database\	KEY	N/A	Recordset object
HKEY_LOCAL_MACHINE\SOFTWARE\Microsoft\COM3\	KEY	N/A	Recordset object
HKEY_LOCAL_MACHINE\SOFTWARE\Microsoft\ Command Processor\	KEY	N/A	Recordset object
HKEY_LOCAL_MACHINE\SOFTWARE\Microsoft\ Conferencing\	KEY	N/A	Recordset object
HKEY_LOCAL_MACHINE\SOFTWARE\Microsoft\ Cryptography\	KEY	N/A	Recordset object
HKEY_LOCAL_MACHINE\SOFTWARE\Microsoft\ DataAccess\	KEY	N/A	Recordset object
HKEY_LOCAL_MACHINE\SOFTWARE\Microsoft\ DataFactory\	KEY	N/A	Recordset object
HKEY_LOCAL_MACHINE\SOFTWARE\Microsoft\ DeviceManager\	KEY	N/A	Recordset object
HKEY_LOCAL_MACHINE\SOFTWARE\Microsoft\ DevStudio\	KEY	N/A	Recordset object
HKEY_LOCAL_MACHINE\SOFTWARE\Microsoft\Dfrg\	KEY	N/A	Recordset object
HKEY_LOCAL_MACHINE\SOFTWARE\Microsoft\ Direct3D\	KEY	N/A	Recordset object
...	...	...	...

Notice that both the parent and child recordsets/datasets have the same structure and both define a `Children` column. For this reason, the hierarchical recordset can be nested to any depth, just like the registry keys it represents. A row in a child recordset can contain a grandchild recordset, which can contain a great-grandchild recordset, and so on.

The following diagram illustrates the use of hierarchial recordsets for exposing the registry keys and values. Notice that a row's `Children` column effectively acts as a pointer to another dataset within exactly the same structure. This hierarchical recordset approach allows a consumer effectively to "zoom-in" on certain areas of the Registry without the overhead of loading unneeded registry items:

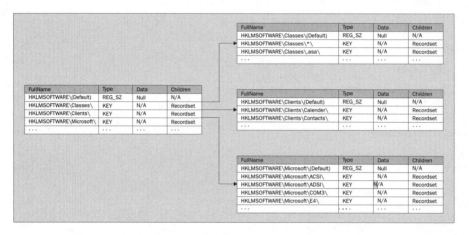

To maximize the performance and scalability while minimizing memory requirements, our REGOLEDB Provider will only initially return the parent records of the hierarchical recordset. When the value of the `Children` column/field is requested, the REGOLEDB Provider will then load and return the child recordset. Only the parent recordset and the child recordsets that are requested by the consumer will ever be loaded, not the entire hierarchy. This behavior is similar to a parameterized command using the MSDATASHAPE OLE DB Service Provider; however we'll implement this functionality within our REGOLEDB Provider's OSP implementation.

In the following diagram, a recordset is opened against the "HKEY_LOCAL_MACHINE\SOFTWARE" key. When the current record in this recordset is "HKEY_LOCAL_MACHINE\SOFTWARE\CLIENTS", the `Children` field will return an open recordset that contains the registry items immediately under this key. However, this child recordset is not created and opened until the value of the `Children` column is requested for the "HKEY_LOCAL_MACHINE\SOFTWARE\CLIENTS" row:

Defining the Text Command

We mentioned earlier that when a recordset is opened, a text command is passed to the OSP Data Object. This text command can be specified in the Source parameter of an ADO Recordset object's Open method or in the CommandText parameter of an ADO Connection object's Execute method. The OSP Data Object and the OSP implementation can use this text command to determine which dataset should be exposed. Therefore, the provider dictates the format and syntax of the text command. With our REGOLEDB Provider the text command could be as simple as a single value that specifies a registry key. For example, the following code could cause an ADO Recordset to be opened that contains the immediate registry items under the HKEY_LOCAL_MACHINE\SOFTWARE registry key:

```
Recordset.Open "HKEY_LOCAL_MACHINE\SOFTWARE"
```

This simple text command syntax would work fine if the only piece of data we want to specify in the text command is the registry key the provider should open. However, most custom OLE DB providers will need to allow the consumer to provide several pieces of data when opening a recordset. For example, what if the consumer wants to specify which fields should be included in the recordset, or what if the consumer wants the recordset only to include registry values and not registry keys? In either of these cases, we must devise a technique for specifying multiple items or pieces of data within the single text command string. There are actually an unlimited number of different approaches we could take in this situation.

One frequently used technique is to separate each item within the text command with a pre-defined separating character. For example, in the following code we specify in the text command that the recordset should be opened against the `"HKEY_LOCAL_MACHINE\SOFTWARE"` registry key and that it should include only the `FullName` and the `ItemType` columns. Notice that the data items within the text command are named and separated by semi-colons (`;`). This syntax is similar to the syntax used for the `ConnectionString` parameter of the ADO `Connection` object's `Open` method:

```
Recordset.Open _
    "KEY=HKEY_LOCAL_MACHINE\SOFTWARE;Fields=FullName,ItemType"
```

Another possible technique would be to format the text command as a Structured Query Language (SQL) `SELECT` statement:

```
Recordset.Open _
    "SELECT FullName, ItemType WHERE KEY=HKEY_LOCAL_MACHINE\SOFTWARE"
```

The major problem with both of these tactics is that they require the `REGOLEDB` Provider to perform complex string parsing. Instead of using these proprietary techniques for the text command format, why not format the text command as XML? This is a perfect scenario for using XML for two reasons:

- ❑ XML is extensible. The Extensible Markup Language provides a model for describing, exchanging and processing any kind of data. After an initial set of elements and attributes have been defined, any number of additional elements and attributes can easily be added.

- ❑ XML doesn't require manual parsing. Since XML allows data to be described in a standard format, applications can leverage existing components, such as the Microsoft XML Document Object Model (DOM), to parse XML data. The DOM can then expose this parsed data through its simple object model. By relying on the DOM to parse and extract pieces of data from the text command, we can save lots of development time that would otherwise have to be spent writing error-prone string parsing code.

For these reasons our `REGOLEDB` Provider will only support XML-based text commands. These XML-based text commands must contain the following elements:

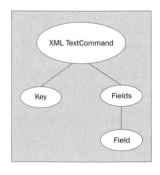

XMLTextCommand

`<XMLTextCommand>` is the root element that contains both the `<Key>` and `<Fields>` elements. There should only be one `<XMLTextCommand>` element within the text command submitted to the REGOLEDB Provider.

Key

The `<Key>` element contains the full registry key which the consumer wants to open. There should only be one `<Key>` element within an `<XMLTextCommand>` element.

Fields

The `<Fields>` element is a parent element for any number of `<Field>` elements. The `<Fields>` element also supports an optional attribute named `All`. If a value of `"True"` is specified for the `All` attribute, the REGOLEDB Provider will expose all of the fields. If the `All` attribute is not specified or if it contains a value of `"False"`, the REGOLEDB provider will require the text command to list each field individually using the `<Field>` element. There should only be one `<Fields>` element within an `<XMLTextCommand>` element.

Field

The `<Field>` element contains as a value the name of the field the REGOLEDB Provider should include in the recordset. Unlike the other elements, there can be multiple `<Field>` elements – one for each field that should be included in the recordset. With the first version of our REGOLEDB Provider there are five unique fields, and thus five possible values for the `<Field>` element. These five fields are: `ItemName`, `FullName`, `ItemType`, `Data` and `Children`. If a value of `"True"` is specified for the `All` attribute of the `Fields` element then any `<Field>` elements in the text command will simply be ignored.

Based on the definition of these elements, a consumer could specify the following text command to open a recordset exposing all of the fields and containing all of the immediate registry keys and values under the HKEY_LOCAL_MACHINE\SOFTWARE key:

```
<XMLTextCommand>
    <Key>HKEY_LOCAL_MACHINE\SOFTWARE</Key>
    <Fields>
        <Field>ItemName</Field>
        <Field>FullName</Field>
        <Field>ItemType</Field>
        <Field>Data</Field>
        <Field>Children</Field>
    </Fields>
</XMLTextCommand>
```

The same command text could be condensed to four lines by using the `All` attribute of the `<Fields>` element:

```
<XMLTextCommand>
    <Key>HKEY_LOCAL_MACHINE\SOFTWARE</Key>
    <Fields All="True"/>
</XMLTextCommand>
```

As you can see, by using XML as the syntax for text commands, our REGOLEDB Provider can easily expose additional functionality simply by supporting additional attributes or elements. Additionally, we'll have an easier time implementing our REGOLEDB Provider since we can rely on the XML Document Object Model (DOM) for parsing the text command.

Choosing a Development Tool/Language

Any development tool or language that supports the development of custom COM components that can implement pre-defined interfaces can be used to develop simple OLE DB providers. This includes Visual Basic, Visual J++ and Visual C++. Since all three of these development languages meet the requirements, choosing a development language for implementing a simple OLE DB provider is more of a personal preference than it is a crucial design decision. However, if you are well experienced with COM component development in C++, this might be the best route because it allows you to leverage existing code should you ever decide to convert your simple provider into a full OLE DB provider. For the development of our REGOLEDB Provider, we will use Visual Basic 6 Service Pack 3 because of its simplicity and large user-base.

Defining the Physical Implementation

All simple OLE DB providers should be implemented with at least two COM components. One component acts as the OSP Data Object and is responsible for implementing either the IDataSource interface or the msDataSourceObject method on the component's default, IDispatch, interface. The other component will play the role of the OSP implementation, implementing the OLEDBSimpleProvider interface. With our REGOLEDB Provider, the OSP Data Object will be named DataSource and the OSP implementation will be named "Provider". To simplify the development of the REGOLEDB Provider so that we can focus on the provider-specific aspects, I've encapsulated complex registry API calls within a Private class module named RegistryItems:

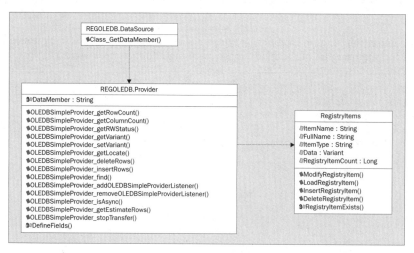

The RegistryItems class is responsible for maintaining an in-memory array containing the information about the registry keys and values which the provider component will expose through the OLEDBSimpleProvider interface. When the provider component receives data retrieval requests, data manipulation requests or schema information requests, it simply calls the appropriate method(s) and/or properties on an instance of the RegistryItems class module. The methods and properties implemented by the RegistryItems class are defined as follows:

LoadRegistryItems

```
Public Sub LoadRegistryItems(ByVal sKey As String)
```

The `LoadRegistryItems` method loads all of the immediate registry keys and values under the key specified by the `sKey` parameter into a private array. This array is a temporary cache for registry items and it is used for all subsequent method calls to the `RegistryItems` class module. Every item within the array represents a row that is exposed by the provider component. The index of the row corresponds with the index of the registry item in the array.

ModifyRegistryItem

```
Public Sub ModifyRegistryItem(ByVal lRow As Long)
```

The `ModifyRegistryItem` method either creates or modifies a key or value in the Registry based on the values of the `RegistryItem` specified by the `lRow` parameter.

InsertRegistryItem

```
Public Sub InsertRegistryItem()
```

The `InsertRegistryItem` method allocates a new item in the in-memory array of registry items maintained by the `RegistryItems` class module. The values for the new item are specified in the `ItemName`, `ItemType` and `Data` properties. The new registry item only exists in memory and is not created in the Registry until the values have been specified and the `ModifyRegistryItem` method is called.

DeleteRegistryItem

```
Public Sub DeleteRegistryItem(ByVal lRow As Long)
```

The `DeleteRegistryItem` method removes the `RegistryItem` specified by the `lRow` parameter both from the in-memory array and from the actual Registry.

RegistryItemExists

```
Private Function RegistryItemExists(ByVal sItemName As String, _
                    ByVal enumType As RegistryDataTypesEnum) As Boolean]
```

The `RegistryItemExists` method checks to see whether a value or key exists in the Registry with the name specified by the `sItemName` parameter. This method is used internally by the `RegistryItems` class to maintain synchronization between the in-memory array of registry items and the actual Registry.

ItemName

```
Public Property ItemName(ByVal lRow As Long)
```

The `ItemName` property returns or sets the name of the registry item (key or value) specified by the `lRow` parameter using the in-memory array of `RegistryItems`. Any changes to a registry item's `ItemName` will not be applied to the Registry until the `ModifyRegistryItem` method is called.

FullName

```
Public Property FullName(ByVal lRow As Long)
```

The FullName read-only property returns the full path and name of the registry item (key or value) specified by the lRow parameter by retrieving it from the in-memory array of registry items.

ItemType

```
Public Property ItemType(ByVal lRow As Long) As String
```

The ItemType property returns or sets the type of the registry item specified by the lRow parameter using the in-memory array of registry items. Any changes to a registry item's ItemType will not be applied to the Registry until the ModifyRegistryItem method is called. Only the "String", "DWORD" and "Key" types are supported.

Data

```
Public Property Data(ByVal lRow As Long)
```

The Data property returns or sets the data of the registry item specified by the lRow parameter using the in-memory array of registry items. Any changes to a registry item's Data will not be applied to the Registry until the ModifyRegistryItem method is called. The Data property is only valid with registry items that represent values.

RegistryItemCount

```
Public Property RegistryItemCount As Long
```

The RegistryItemCount read-only property returns the number of registry items loaded in the in-memory array maintained by the RegistryItems class.

Error Handling

During the design phase of an OLE DB provider, it is important to define how run-time errors will be handled when they occur. When defining error handling for any COM component, including OLE DB providers, we must first identify the client of the component. In the case of a simple OLE DB provider the client is not the OLE DB consumer (ADO), but instead the client is the OLE DB Simple Provider (MSDAOSP). As a result, we should avoid any error handling techniques that require any user interaction. Instead, any "show-stopper" errors that prevent a simple OLE DB provider from carrying out a method call should be raised to MSDAOSP, which will raise the error back to the OLE DB consumer. If the OLE DB consumer is ADO then the error will be added to the ActiveConnection's Errors collection. The Microsoft OLE DB Error Library (OLEDB32.dll) defines an enumeration named OLEDBErr which contains constants for standard OLE DB error numbers. Four of the general errors that you'll encounter are:

❑ DB_E_NOTSUPPORTED. This constant is used to indicate that a particular feature or behavior is not supported by the OLE DB provider.

❑ DB_E_ERRORSOCCURRED. Indicates that some type of error occurred in the OLE DB provider.

❑ DB_E_READONLY. Indicates that the cell being updated is read-only.

❑ DB_E_ERRORSINCOMMAND. Indicates that the format or contents of the text command was invalid.

With our REGOLEDB Provider, we'll simply raise all errors back to MSDAOSP. If you are developing a provider for use in a production environment, it is advisable also to log the error with a descriptive error message to a database, a text file or the Windows NT/2000 Event Log so that the error can later be examined and the appropriate action can be taken to prevent it from recurring. We'll discuss more about detecting and handling errors in the section on "Testing, Debugging and Deploying the Simple OLE DB Provider."

REGOLEDB Design Summary

In summary, the first version of the REGOLEDB Provider will:

❑   Allow consumers to retrieve, update, delete and insert keys and values in the Registry

❑   Use the Win32 API Registry functions for physically implementing this functionality

❑   Provide a flexible and efficient hierarchical recordset model for exposing registry items

❑   Use Visual Basic 6 as the development language

❑   Support XML as the text command syntax

That's not a bad list of features for a "simple" OLE DB provider. However, if you want to implement enhancements to the REGOLEDB Provider, I have a few suggestions:

❑   Allow consumers to perform data modifications without opening a recordset

❑   Include support for all the Registry datatypes

❑   Support Distributed Transactions through the use of COM+ Compensating Resource Managers or by developing REGOLEDB as a full OLE DB provider

❑   Provide more flexibility with the XML-based text command syntax

❑   Support a read-only mode that restricts inserts, updates and deletes of registry items

Now we've looked at the details for the design and planning stage, let's move on to the implementation. I'm sure you will find that now all of the important decisions are out of the way, developing our OLE DB provider for the Windows NT/2000 Registry will be a piece of cake.

Establishing the Project

Before we can begin writing code for our
REGOLEDB Provider, we need to setup our Visual
Basic project by establishing the appropriate
references and adding the DataSource,
Provider and RegistryItems class modules.
First, create a new **ActiveX DLL** project in Visual
Basic 6.0. Rename the project to the name of our
simple OLE DB provider, in this case REGOLEDB.

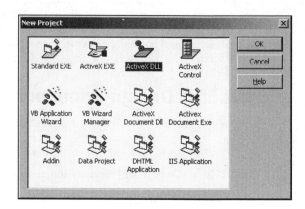

Next, we need to add references to the following COM servers and type libraries:

❑ **Microsoft OLE DB Error Library** (OLEDB32.dll) – The OLE DB Error Library defines
several standard OLE DB Error numbers that REGOLEDB can raise back to consumers when
something goes wrong.

❑ **Microsoft OLE DB Simple Provider 1.5 Library** (SIMPDATA.tlb) – The OLE DB Simple
Provider 1.5 Type Library defines the OLEDBSimpleProvider and
OLEDBSimpleProviderListener interfaces that we need to create a simple OLE DB
provider.

❑ **Microsoft ActiveX Data Objects 2.5 Library** (MSADO15.dll) – ADO is used internally by our
REGOLEDB Provider to support the hierarchical recordset feature we discussed earlier.

❑ **Microsoft XML, version 2.0** (MSXML.dll) – The Microsoft XML Document Object Model is
used to parse the text command that is specified by the consumer.

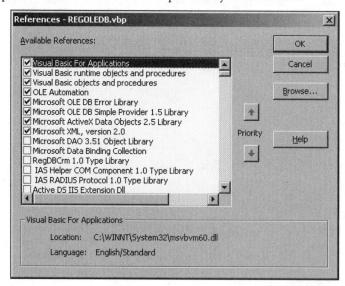

When an ActiveX DLL project is created, Visual Basic includes one class module named `Class1`. Rename this existing class module to "RegistryItems", change the instancing property to `1 – Private` and add the code for accessing and manipulating the Windows NT/2000 Registry through the Win32 API calls. Since this code is long, the complete code listings for the RegistryItems class module have been ommitted from this chapter and instead can be downloaded from the Wrox web site..

After the `RegistryItems` class module has been created, add two more class modules to the `REGOLEDB` project. Rename one of the class modules to "Provider" and make sure the instancing property is set to `5 – MultiUse`. Rename the other class module to "DataSource" and verify that its instancing property also has a value of `5 – MultiUse`.

When you have completed this stage you should have an ActiveX DLL project with three class modules: `RegistryItems`, `Provider` and `DataSource`. Don't worry about implementing any code in the `Provider` or `DataSource` components; we'll accomplish these tasks in the next two steps.

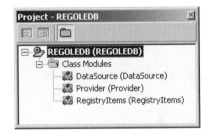

> If you want to save some time, a Visual Basic 6.0 project template for developing simple OLE DB providers is available from the Wrox Press web site at
> `http://www.wrox.com`.

Creating the OSP Data Object

Creating the OSP Data Object is probably the easiest stage in the development of a simple OLE DB provider. Remember, an OSP Data Object is simply a COM component that implements either the `IDataSource` interface or the `msDataSourceObject` method. Visual Basic 6.0 provides a design-time property named "DataSourceBehavior" that makes creating the OSP Data Object even easier.

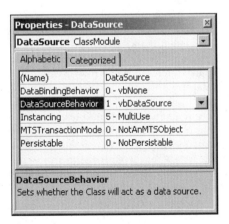

When our `DataSource` component's `DataSourceBehavior` property is changed to 1 – vbDataSource, Visual Basic automatically adds a reference to the Microsoft Data Source Interfaces (`MSDATSRC.tlb`) if there wasn't one already:

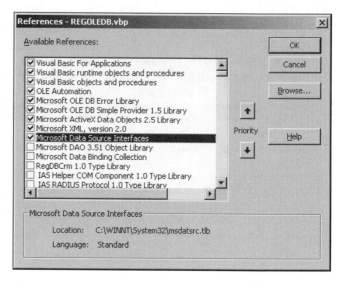

Visual Basic also adds a method/event to the class object called `GetDataMember` when a class module's `DataSourceBehavior` property is changed to **1 – vbDataSource**. Unlike the `IDataSource` interface's `GetDataMember` method, the class object's `GetDataMember` method uses COM-automation compatible datatypes. Behind the scenes, Visual Basic implements the `IDataSource` interface and forwards method calls on `IDataSource::GetDataMember` to the class object's `GetDataMember` method. The class object's `GetDataMember` method is defined as follows:

```
Private Sub Class_GetDataMember(DataMember As String, Data As Object)
```

The class object's `GetDataMember` method, just like the `IDataSource::GetDataMember` and the `msDataSourceObject` methods, is invoked when an ADO Recordset is opened against a connection to the simple OLE DB provider. This method should be treated as an event for initializing the loading of data. The `DataMember` parameter contains the text command that was specified in the `Source` parameter of an ADO `Recordset` object's `Open` method or as the `CommandText` parameter of an ADO `Connection` object's `Execute` method. The `Data` parameter passed by reference should be used to return a reference to a new instance of the component that implements the `OLEDBSimpleProvider` interface.

In our `DataSource` component, when the `GetDataMember` method is invoked we'll create an instance of our `Provider` component, pass it the `DataMember` value and return the reference to the new instance in the `Data` parameter. Once this method completes and the OLE DB Simple Provider (`MSDAOSP`) has a reference to an instance of the `Provider` component, it will begin calling the appropriate methods using the `OLEDBSimpleProvider` interface.

```
Private Sub Class_GetDataMember(DataMember As String, Data As Object)

    Dim objProvider As Provider

    On Error GoTo ErrorHandler
```

```
        'create a new instance of the Provider component
        Set objProvider = New Provider

        'pass our instance of the Provider component the
        '...DataMember parameter via the Provider's DataMember Friend Property
        objProvider.DataMember = DataMember

        'return a reference to the new instance of the Provider component
        '...in the byref Data parameter
        Set Data = objProvider

ExitProcedure:
        'Release our temporary reference to the Provider component
        Set objProvider = Nothing

        'exit this procedure
        Exit Sub

ErrorHandler:
        'an error occured, raise it error back to MSDAOSP
        Err.Raise Err.Number, Source:=App.Title, Description:=Err.Description

        'exit this procedure
        Resume ExitProcedure
End Sub
```

Notice that we don't perform any parsing or interpretation of the DataMember parameter here. Instead, we simply pass it to our new instance of the Provider component through its DataMember property. The Provider component validates, parses (with the help of the XML Document Object Model) and interprets and loads the appropriate registry items based on the value of the DataMember. If an error should occur in the Class_GetDataMember method we simply raise the error back to MSDAOSP.

Well that's all for the REGOLEDB Provider's OSP Data Object. I told you it was simple! I hope this builds up your confidence before we move on to the creation of the OSP implementation.

Creating the OSP Implementation

Creating the OSP implementation is usually where the bulk of the work is involved for developing a simple OLE DB provider, and our REGOLEDB Provider is no exception. So, without further delay, let's get started.

Implementing the OLEDBSimpleProvider Interface

Our first task in creating an OSP implementation is to implement the OLEDBSimpleProvider interface. This is accomplished using the Implements statement in our Provider component's General Declarations section:

```
    'we must implement the OLEDBSimpleProvider interface
    '...so this component can act as the OSP Implementation
    Implements OLEDBSimpleProvider
```

559

OLEDBSimpleProvider will now be listed as an object in our **Object** list. COM states that we are required to support every method defined by the interface we are implementing, with no exceptions. We'll implement and provide functionality behind each of these methods in just a moment, but first we need to define some initialization code for our Provider component.

Instantiating the RegistryItems Class

Since the RegistryItems private class module encapsulates *all* of the Win32 API calls to retrieve, create, modify and delete registry keys and values, we will be using this class frequently during the life of the Provider component. For this reason, let's declare a private (member) variable named m_objRegistryItems in the **General Declarations** section of the Provider component:

```
Private m_objRegistryItems As RegistryItems
```

When our Provider component is instantiated, we will create an instance of the RegistryItems private class module, storing the reference in our private variable and releasing the instance when our Provider component is destroyed:

```
Private Sub Class_Initialize()
    'create a new instance of our RegistryItems class
    Set m_objRegistryItems = New RegistryItems
End Sub
```

```
Private Sub Class_Terminate()
    'release our instance of the RegistryItems class module
    Set m_objRegistryItems = Nothing
End Sub
```

Other Member Variables

While we're in the **General Declarations** section, let's also define some other member variables that we'll use during the lifetime of our Provider component:

```
'dim a member variable for each column to store the index
'...of the column within the m_asColumnNames array
Private m_lColIndex_ItemName As Long
Private m_lColIndex_FullName As Long
Private m_lColIndex_ItemType As Long
Private m_lColIndex_Data As Long
Private m_lColIndex_Children As Long

'dim a member variable for storing the number of columns exposed
Private m_lColumnCount As Long

'declare an array of strings to hold the names of the fields in order
'...with the indexes of the items in the array corresponding to their
'...enum values above (also to their column numbers)
Private m_asColumnNames() As String

'dim a member variable to hold a reference to the IXMLDOMElement
'...that represents the XMLTextCommand element in the Text Command
Private m_elmXMLTextCommand As MSXML.IXMLDOMElement
```

Interpreting the Text Command and Loading the Dataset

We've already seen how the DataSource component calls the Provider component's `DataMember` property, forwarding it the text command that was specified as a parameter to the DataSource's `GetDataMember` method, now let's implement that `DataMember` property.

Let's declare our error handler for the `DataMember` property and dimension some procedural variables that we'll need to parse the text command specified in the `sDataMember` parameter:

```
Public Property Let DataMember(ByVal sDataMember As String)
    Dim lCharAt As Long
    Dim sKey As String
    Dim sTemp_SupportChildren As String
    Dim domXMLDataMember As MSXML.DOMDocument
    Dim elmFields As MSXML.IXMLDOMElement
    Dim elmKey As MSXML.IXMLDOMElement
    Dim sHKEY As String

    On Error GoTo ErrorHandler
```

Before we leverage the XML Document Object Model for parsing the XML-based text command passed in the `sDataMember` parameter, we need to validate that a text command has been specified. If none has been specified, our REGOLEDB Provider's OSP implementation will raise an error back to MSDAOSP and exit the property procedure:

```
    If Len(Trim$(sDataMember)) = 0 Then
        'invalid datamember, first turn off this method's ErrorHandler
        On Error GoTo 0

        'raise an OLEDB general fail error back to the calling procedure
        Err.Raise OLEDBError.DB_E_ERRORSINCOMMAND, Source:=App.Title, _
                Description:="No text command specified!"

        'exit this procedure
        GoTo ExitProcedure
    End If
```

Parsing the Text Command

After we have performed that simple validation test, we need to create an instance of the `MSXML.DOMDocument` object and use the new instance to load the XML-based text command specified in the `sDataMember` parameter. If an error occurs during parsing and loading the `sDataMember` parameter's value, we return a descriptive error to the `DataSource` component:

```
    'create an instance of the MSXML.DOMDocument component
    Set domXMLDataMember = New MSXML.DOMDocument

    'load the XML passed in the sDataMember variable
    domXMLDataMember.loadXML sDataMember

    If domXMLDataMember.parseError.errorCode <> 0 Then
        'an error occured parsing the XML-based query string
```

```
        'turn off our ErrorHandler
        On Error GoTo 0

        '...raise an error back to MSDAOSP
        Err.Raise OLEDBERROR.DB_E_ERRORSINCOMMAND, Source:=App.Title, _
            Description:="The following error occured loading the text command:" & _
                         vbCrLf & domXMLDataMember.parseError.reason & _
                         vbCrLf & domXMLDataMember.parseError.Line & _
                         vbCrLf & domXMLDataMember.parseError.srcText

        'exit this procedure
        GoTo ExitProcedure
    End If
```

Checking for the Root Element

Now let's get a reference to an `IXMLDOMElement` object that represents the root `<XMLTextCommand>` element, using our instance of `MSXML.DOMDocument`. If the `<XMLTextCommand>` element does not exist, our `REGOLEDB` Provider will simply raise an error back to the `DataSource` component and exit the `DataMember` property:

```
    'get a reference to the XMLTextCommand root element into our member variable
    Set m_elmXMLTextCommand = domXMLDataMember.selectSingleNode("XMLTextCommand")

    If m_elmXMLTextCommand Is Nothing = True Then
        'the XMLTextCommand element doesn't exist

        'turn off our ErrorHandler
        On Error GoTo 0

        '...raise an error back to MSDAOSP
        Err.Raise OLEDBERROR.DB_E_ERRORSINCOMMAND, Source:=App.Title, _
            Description:="The text command must have one root element named" & _
                         "'XMLTextCommand'"

        'exit this procedure
        GoTo ExitProcedure
    End If
```

Checking for the <Key> and <Fields> Elements

Now we need to get references to the `IXMLDOMElement` objects that represent the `<Key>` and `<Fields>` elements that are under the `<XMLTextCommmand>` element. Again, if either the `<Key>` or the `<Fields>` element doesn't exist, we raise an error back to the `DataSource` component and exit this procedure:

```
    'get a reference to the Key element
    Set elmKey = m_elmXMLTextCommand.selectSingleNode("Key")

    If elmKey Is Nothing = True Then
        'the Key element doesn't exist

        'turn off our ErrorHandler
        On Error GoTo 0
```

```
         '...raise an error back to the DataSource component
         Err.Raise OLEDBERROR.DB_E_ERRORSINCOMMAND, Source:=App.Title, _
            Description:="The text command must have one element named 'Key'"

         'exit this procedure
         GoTo ExitProcedure
      End If

      'get a reference to the Fields element
      Set elmFields = m_elmXMLTextCommand.selectSingleNode("Fields")

      If elmFields Is Nothing = True Then
         'the Fields element doesn't exist

         'turn off our ErrorHandler
         On Error GoTo 0

         '...raise an error back to the DataSource component
         Err.Raise OLEDBERROR.DB_E_ERRORSINCOMMAND, Source:=App.Title, _
            Description:="The text command must have one element named 'Fields'"

         'exit this procedure
         GoTo ExitProcedure
      End If
```

Now that we have a reference an `IXMLDOMElement` object representing the `Fields` element, let's call a private method named `DefineFields` and pass it the reference. The `DefineFields` method is responsible for defining the columns/fields that are included in the dataset/recordset based on the attributes and child elements of the `<Fields>` element. We'll discuss the `DefineFields` method in more detail in just a moment:

```
      'interpret the Fields element and expose the appropriate fields
      DefineFields elmFields
```

Finally, let's retrieve all of the registry keys and values immediately under the registry key specified in the `<Key>` element's value. The `RegistryItems` class module encapsulates all of this functionality within its `LoadRegistryItems` method:

```
      'now retrieve the Registry key's and values
      '...under the key specified in the Key element's value
      m_objRegistryItems.LoadRegistryItems elmKey.nodeTypedValue
```

Don't forget to implement the `ExitProcedure` label where we perform clean up by releasing all our interface references before exiting the `DataMember` property:

```
ExitProcedure:
    'release our references to the XML elements
    Set elmKey = Nothing
    Set elmFields = Nothing

    'release our instance of the MSXML.DOMDocument component
    Set domXMLDataMember = Nothing

    'exit this procedure
    Exit Property
```

Fianlly, we'll also implement some very simple error handling; we just raise any errors that occur back to the caller, which is the `DataSource` component:

```
ErrorHandler:
    'an error occured, raise it back to the caller
    Err.Raise Err.Number, Source:=App.Title, Description:=Err.Description

    'exit this procedure
    GoTo ExitProcedure
End Property
```

We saw that the `DataMember` property relies on two other methods: the `DefineFields` private method and the `LoadRegistryItems` method of the `RegistryItems` class module. I won't bore you here with the details about the `LoadRegistryItems` method. Instead, you can download the source for the `RegistryItems` class module from the Wrox Press web site. However, let's implement the `DefineFields` method.

Defining the Selected Fields

The `DefineFields` method is a `Private` subroutine that accepts a single parameter named `elmFields` of the type `MSXML.IXMLDOMElement`:

```
Private Sub DefineFields(ByRef elmFields As MSXML.IXMLDOMElement)
```

Let's declare our error handler for the `DefineFields` method and dimension some procedural variables that we'll need in this method to interpret the attributes and child elements under the `<Fields>` element in the text command:

```
Dim attAll As MSXML.IXMLDOMAttribute
Dim nod As MSXML.IXMLDOMNode
Dim bAllFields As Boolean

On Error GoTo ErrorHandler
```

Remember, our REGOLEDB Provider will expose all of the fields/columns in the dataset if the <Fields> element's All attribute is set to "True". We therefore set a reference to the IXMLDOMAttribute object that represents the All attribute for the passed reference to the <Fields> element:

```
'get a reference to the All attribute of the Elements node
Set attAll = elmFields.Attributes.getNamedItem("All")
```

Now we check whether the All attribute is missing, and if it is missing, we set our procedural variable named bAllFields to False. Otherwise, we convert the value of the All attribute to a Boolean and store it in our bAllFields variable:

```
If attAll Is Nothing = True Then
    'the All attribute was not specified, default to false
    bAllFields = False

Else
    'the All attribute was specified, get it's value in a boolean
    bAllFields = CBool(attAll.Value)
End If
```

Now let's evaluate the value of our bAllFields procedural variable. If it has a value of True, we want to expose all of the fields/columns in the dataset. However, we don't actually notify MSDAOSP of the field/column names yet. Instead, we'll simply initialize our member variables to store the column count, the index of each column in the dataset, and each column name. The column names will be stored in an array named m_asColumnNames with the column's index used as the index into the array. MSDAOSP will later request the number of columns and each column's name by calling the getColumnCount and the getVariant methods of the OLEDBSimpleProvider interface.

```
If bAllFields = True Then
    'the consumer wants all the fields to be exposed in the dataset/Recordset
    m_lColumnCount = 5

    'store the indexes of our Columns/Fields in member variables
    '...this will speed data retrieval and modifications later
    m_lColIndex_ItemName = 1
    m_lColIndex_FullName = 2
    m_lColIndex_ItemType = 3
    m_lColIndex_Data = 4
    m_lColIndex_Children = 5

    'load our Column Names array with the names of each Field/Column
    '...in the correct order so their index in the array corresponds
    '...with the columns member variable
    ReDim m_asColumnNames(1 To m_lColumnCount) As String

    'now load the array
    m_asColumnNames(m_lColIndex_ItemName) = "ItemName"
    m_asColumnNames(m_lColIndex_FullName) = "FullName"
    m_asColumnNames(m_lColIndex_ItemType) = "ItemType"
    m_asColumnNames(m_lColIndex_Data) = "Data"
    m_asColumnNames(m_lColIndex_Children) = "Children"
```

If the `bAllFields` procedural variable is not `True`, then the consumer did not want to include all the fields/columns in the dataset and individual `<Field>` elements are probably specified under the `<Fields>` element. So we verify that the `<Fields>` element has child nodes and then begin looping through the collection of child nodes:

```
Else
    'the consumer only wants specific fields in the Recordset
    '...check for Field elements under the Fields element that has the
    '...field name as a value.  For each one that is found, add it to
    '...our array of fields names.

    If elmFields.hasChildNodes = True Then
        For Each nod In elmFields.childNodes
```

Since we used the Visual Basic For...Each syntax to loop through the child nodes collection, our procedural variable nod represents the current child node. If the node's name is "Field" then this is a `<Field>` element. We increment our column count stored in the member variable `m_ColumnCount` and increase the size of our `m_asColumnNames` array:

```
If StrComp(nod.nodeName, "Field", vbBinaryCompare) = 0 Then
    'increment our counter that stores the number of columns
    m_lColumnCount = m_lColumnCount + 1

    'redim our array to hold the additional column name
    ReDim Preserve m_asColumnNames(1 To m_lColumnCount) As String
```

We extract the field's name from the content of the `<Field>` element and add it to the new location in the `m_asColumnNames` array and set the column's index equal to its location in the array. If the `<Field>` element's value is anything other than one the accepted field/column names, we must raise a descriptive error back to the caller:

```
Select Case UCase$(Trim$(nod.nodeTypedValue))
    Case "ITEMNAME"
        m_asColumnNames(m_lColumnCount) = "ItemName"

        '...store the index of the column
        m_lColIndex_ItemName = m_lColumnCount

    Case "FULLNAME"
        m_asColumnNames(m_lColumnCount) = "FullName"

        '...store the index of the column
        m_lColIndex_FullName = m_lColumnCount

    Case "ITEMTYPE"
        m_asColumnNames(m_lColumnCount) = "ItemType"

        '...store the index of the column
        m_lColIndex_ItemType = m_lColumnCount

    Case "DATA"
        m_asColumnNames(m_lColumnCount) = "Data"
```

```
                            '...store the index of the column
                            m_lColIndex_Data = m_lColumnCount

                        Case "CHILDREN"
                            m_asColumnNames(m_lColumnCount) = "Children"

                            '...store the index of the column
                            m_lColIndex_Children = m_lColumnCount

                        Case Else
                            'the specified column name doesn't exist

                            'turn off our error handler
                            On Error GoTo 0

                            '...and raise back an error to the caller
                            Err.Raise OLEDBErr.DB_E_ERRORSINCOMMAND, _
                                    Source:=App.Title, _
                                    Description:="Invalid Field/Column Name!"
                        Exit Sub
                    End Select
                End If
            Next
        End If
    End If
```

Finally, the column names should exist in the `m_asColumnNames` array and the `m_lColumnCount` member variable should contain the number of items in this array. However, if the `<Fields>` element's `All` attribute was `False` or not specified and no `<Field>` elements were specified, then no fields/columns have been defined. In this case, we need to raise an error back to the caller because the text command was invalid:

```
    If m_lColumnCount = 0 Then

        'turn off our error handler
        On Error GoTo 0

        '...and raise back an error to the caller
        Err.Raise OLEDBErr.DB_E_ERRORSINCOMMAND, Source:=App.Title, _
            Description:="The Fields element's All atribute or individual Field" & _
                        " Elements must be specified in the text command!"

        'exit this procedure
        GoTo ExitProcedure
    End If
```

Finally, let's not forget to implement our standard `ExitProcedure` and `ErrorHandler` labels for the `DefineFields` subroutine:

```
ExitProcedure:
    'exit this procedure
    Exit Sub

ErrorHandler:
    'an error occured, raise it back to the caller
    Err.Raise Err.Number, Source:=App.Title, Description:=Err.Description

    'exit this procedure
    Resume ExitProcedure
End Sub
```

You can now breathe a sigh of relief because we've implemented all of the custom methods defined by our `Provider` component. Next, we need to begin implementing each of the methods defined by the `OLEDBSimpleProvider` interface. Don't worry, most of the complex functionality is encapsulated in the `RegistryItems` class module so implementing most of the `OLEDBSimpleProvider` interface's methods simply involves calling a few methods on our instance of the `RegistryItems` class module.

Implementing the Listener Methods

We saw earlier that `MSDAOSP` registers and unregisters itself as a listener for OSP notifications by calling the `addOLEDBSimpleProviderListener` and `removeOLEDBSimpleProviderListener` methods through an OSP Implementations `OLEDBSimpleProvider` interface. Before we implement these methods in our `Provider` component, let's define another member variable (in the **General Declarations** section) of the type `VBA`. This is the collection that will be responsible for holding references to the OSP listeners:

```
Private m_colOSPListeners As VBA.Collection
```

We also need to create a new instance of a `VBA.Collection` when our `Provider` component is instantiated and release the instance when our `Provider` component is destroyed:

```
Private Sub Class_Initialize()

    'create a new instance of a Collection component to
    '...store references to registered OSPListeners
    Set m_colOSPListeners = New VBA.Collection

    'create a new instance of our RegistryItems class
    Set m_objRegistryItems = New RegistryItems
End Sub
```

```
Private Sub Class_Terminate()

    'release our instance of the VBA.Collection component that
    '...stores references to registered OSPListeners
    Set m_colOSPListeners = Nothing

    'release our instance of the RegistryItems class module
    Set m_objRegistryItems = Nothing
End Sub
```

addOLEDBSimpleProviderListener Method

The addOLEDBSimpleProviderListener method receives a reference to an object implementing the OLEDBSimpleProviderListener interface in the pospIListener parameter. When this method is called, we check that the passed reference is valid, and then our Provider component should simply add the reference to our collection of OSP listeners:

```
Private Sub OLEDBSimpleProvider_addOLEDBSimpleProviderListener( _
            ByVal pospIListener As OLEDBSimpleProviderListener)

    On Error GoTo ErrorHandler

    'Add the passed listener to the collection of listeners

    If pospIListener Is Nothing = False Then
        'the passed OLEDBSimpleProviderListener object is valid
        '...now add it to our collection of OSP Listeners
        m_colOSPListeners.Add pospIListener
    End If


ExitProcedure:
    'exit this procedure
    Exit Sub

ErrorHandler:
    'an error occured, raise it back to the caller
    Err.Raise OLEDBError.DB_E_ERRORSOCCURRED, Source:=App.Title, _
            Description:="An error occured adding the specified OSP Listener!"

    'exit this procedure
    Resume ExitProcedure
End Sub
```

removeOLEDBSimpleProviderListener Method

The removeOLEDBSimpleProviderListener method also receives a reference to an object implementing the OLEDBSimpleProviderListener interface in the pospIListener parameter. As you can probably guess, the removeOLEDBSimpleProviderListener method should simply remove the passed reference from our collection of OSP listeners:

```
Private Sub OLEDBSimpleProvider_removeOLEDBSimpleProviderListener( _
            ByVal pospIListener As OLEDBSimpleProviderListener)

    Dim lOSPListenerCounter As Long
    Dim lOSPListenerCount As Long

    On Error GoTo ErrorHandler

    'get the count of OSP Listeners into a variable
    lOSPListenerCount = m_colOSPListeners.Count


    For lOSPListenerCounter = 1 To lOSPListenerCount
        If m_colOSPListeners(lOSPListenerCounter) Is pospIListener Then
            'the OSP Listener in the collection is the same as the parameter

            'Remove it from our collection
            m_colOSPListeners.Remove lOSPListenerCounter
            Exit For
        End If
    Next lOSPListenerCounter

ExitProcedure:
    'exit this procedure
    Exit Sub

ErrorHandler:
    'an error occured, raise the error back to the caller
    Err.Raise OLEDBError.DB_E_ERRORSOCCURRED, Source:=App.Title, _
            Description:="An error occured removing the specified OSP Listener!"

    'exit this procedure
    Resume ExitProcedure
End Sub
```

In this method, we have to loop through each item in our collection of OSP listeners until we find a reference that is the same as the reference specified in the pospIListener parameter. When we find a match, we can remove the reference from the collection by calling the Collection object's Remove method and specifying the index of the item as a parameter. Unfortunately, we can't use the more friendly For...Each syntax for looping through the collection of OSP listeners because the OLEDBSimpleProviderListener interface is derived from IUnknown and not from IDispatch.

Implementing the Schema Methods

Now we're ready to implement the functionality behind the schema methods defined by the OLEDBSimpleProvider interface. When an ADO Recordset is opened against MSDAOSP, one of the first items of data MSDAOSP requests from the OSP implementation is the column count and row count of the dataset. These requests are made through the schema methods getColumnCount and getRowCount which are defined by the OLEDBSimpleProvider interface.

getColumnCount Method

When the getColumnCount method is called on our Provider component, it should return our member variable m_lColumnCount which contains the number of columns in the dataset:

```
Private Function OLEDBSimpleProvider_getColumnCount() As Long
   On Error GoTo ErrorHandler

   'return the number of fields this instance of the
   '...Provider component is exposing
   OLEDBSimpleProvider_getColumnCount = m_lColumnCount

ExitProcedure:
   'exit this procedure
   Exit Function

ErrorHandler:
   'an error occured, raise it back to the caller
   Err.Raise OLEDBError.DB_E_ERRORSOCCURRED, Source:=App.Title, _
            Description:="An error occured returning the column/field count!"

   'exit this procedure
   Resume ExitProcedure
End Function
```

getRowCount method

Implementing the getRowCount method is almost as simple. However, instead of storing the row count in a member variable we simply call the RegistryItemsCount read-only property of our instance of the RegistryItems class to request the number of rows in the dataset:

```
Private Function OLEDBSimpleProvider_getRowCount() As Long
   On Error GoTo ErrorHandler

   'return the exact number of Registry Items in the dataset
   OLEDBSimpleProvider_getRowCount = m_objRegistryItems.RegistryItemCount

ExitProcedure:
   'exit this procedure
   Exit Function

ErrorHandler:
```

```
      'an error occured, raise it back to the caller
      Err.Raise OLEDBError.DB_E_ERRORSOCCURRED, Source:=App.Title, _
            Description:="An error occured returning the row/record count!"

      'exit this procedure
      Resume ExitProcedure
End Function
```

getRWStatus Method

The last schema method we need to implement is the getRWStatus function, which should return the read/write status for an individual cell, a particular column, a particular row or the entire dataset, depending on the combination of values in the iRow and iColumn parameters.

Our Provider component supports modifications to all rows with no exceptions. It also supports modifications to all columns except the FullName and Children columns that are always read-only. Consequently, whenever the read/write status is requested for the FullName or Children columns, our Provider component should return an enum value of OSPRW_READONLY. If the wildcard value of −1 is specified for the iColumn parameter, indicating that the request is for the read/write status of all the columns or the entire dataset, then our provider component should return an enum value of OSPRW_MIXED because some columns are read-only and some are read-write. Finally, for any other value specified in the iColumn parameter, our Provider component should return an enum value of OSPRW_READWRITE. We can simply ignore the value of the iRow parameter because all rows can be modified:

```
    Private Function OLEDBSimpleProvider_getRWStatus(ByVal iRow As Long, _
                                        ByVal iColumn As Long) As OSPRW

    On Error GoTo ErrorHandler

    Select Case iColumn
        Case m_lColIndex_Children, m_lColIndex_FullName
            'the read/write status of the Children and the
            '...FullName column is always read-only
            OLEDBSimpleProvider_getRWStatus = OSPRW_READONLY

        Case -1
            'the read/write status is mixed for all the
            '...columns and the entire dataset
            OLEDBSimpleProvider_getRWStatus = OSPRW_MIXED

        Case Else
            'the read/write status is read & write for all other columns
            '...regardless of the row
            OLEDBSimpleProvider_getRWStatus = OSPRW_READWRITE
    End Select

ExitProcedure:
    'exit this procedure
    Exit Function
```

```
ErrorHandler:
    'an error occured, raise it back to the caller
    Err.Raise OLEDBERROR.DB_E_ERRORSOCCURRED, Source:=App.Title, _
            Description:="An error occured returning the read/write status!"

    'exit this procedure
    Resume ExitProcedure
End Function
```

Implementing Asynchronous Data Retrieval Methods

Next we shall implement the asynchronous data retrieval methods defined by the
OLEDBSimpleProvider interface. The asynchronous data retrieval methods include isAsync and
StopTransfer.

isAsync Method

The isAsync method is called by MSDAOSP to request whether or not a simple OLE DB provider
supports loading data asynchronously. Asynchronous data retrieval is ideal for situations where data is
being transferred across inconsistent or slow networks, such as the Internet, or in situations where you
might be exposing thousands of records. Since our REGOLEDB Provider does not support asynchronous
data retrieval, the isAsync method should return a value of 0 when it is invoked on the Provider
component:

```
Private Function OLEDBSimpleProvider_isAsync() As Long
    On Error GoTo ErrorHandler

    'this OSP implementation does not support Asynchronous operations so return 0
    OLEDBSimpleProvider_isAsync = 0

ExitProcedure:
    'exit this procedure
    Exit Function

ErrorHandler:
    'an error occured, raise the error back to the caller
    Err.Raise OLEDBError.DB_E_ERRORSOCCURRED, Source:=App.Title, _
            Description:="An error occured returning the Async status!"

    'exit this procedure
    Resume ExitProcedure
End Function
```

getEstimatedRows Method

Simple OLE DB providers that support asynchronous data retrieval are required to return the estimated number of rows when the getEstimatedRows function is invoked on the OSP implementation. If the provider is unable to provide an estimated row count then it should return a value of -1. Our REGOLEDB Provider is synchronous, so it should return the exact number of rows in the dataset just as the getRowCount method does:

```
Private Function OLEDBSimpleProvider_getEstimatedRows() As Long
    On Error GoTo ErrorHandler

    'return the exact number of RegistryItems in the dataset
    '...since this OSP implementation doesn't support asynchronous data retrieval
    OLEDBSimpleProvider_getEstimatedRows = m_objRegistryItems.RegistryItemCount

ExitProcedure:
    'exit this procedure
    Exit Function

ErrorHandler:
    'an error occured, raise it back to the caller
    Err.Raise OLEDBError.DB_E_ERRORSOCCURRED, Source:=App.Title, _
        Description:="An error occured returning the estimated row/record count!"

    'exit this procedure
    Resume ExitProcedure
End Function
```

stopTransfer Method

The final asynchronous data retrieval method we have to implement is the stopTransfer method. This method is called by MSDAOSP to notify asynchronous providers that the consumer has canceled the asynchronous data retrieval. Synchronous providers should do nothing when this method is called because their data is already loaded:

```
Private Sub OLEDBSimpleProvider_stopTransfer()
    'Do nothing because we are already populated
End Sub
```

Implementing Insertion and Deletion methods

The fourth category of methods defined by the OLEDBSimpleProvider interface that we need to implement contains the insertion and deletion methods. The insertion and deletion methods include insertRows and deleteRows.

insertRows Method

The insertRows method is called when the MSDAOSP receives a request to insert a record into the dataset. However, the insertRows method does not accept the data to insert as parameters, as you might expect. Instead, the insertRows method only accepts two parameters named iRow and cRows. The iRow parameter specifies the starting location in the dataset where the row(s) should be inserted and the cRows parameter specifies the number of rows that should be inserted.

We can ignore the `iRow` parameter because when the `AddNew` method is called on an ADO Recordset, the `iRow` parameter always specifies the last position in the dataset. It is also not currently possible to insert multiple rows with one statement using ADO so our `Provider` component won't support multi-row inserts. Therefore, if the `cRows` parameter is greater than 1 our `Provider` component will raise an error back to `MSDAOSP`:

```
Private Function OLEDBSimpleProvider_insertRows(ByVal iRow As Long, _
                                                ByVal cRows As Long) As Long

    Dim lOSPListenerCounter As Long
    Dim lOSPListenerCount As Long
    Dim objOSPListener As OLEDBSimpleProviderListener

    On Error GoTo ErrorHandler

    If (cRows > 1) Then
        'The consumer indicates it wants to insert several rows

        'turn off our error handler
        On Error GoTo 0

        'now raise the error
        Err.Raise OLEDBError.DB_E_NOTSUPPORTED, Source:=App.Title, _
                Description:="Multi-row insertions are not supported!"

        'exit this procedure
        GoTo ExitProcedure
    End If
```

Since we will be inserting a row into and thus changing the dataset, we must first pre-notify all registered OSP listeners. This involves looping through our collection of references to objects implementing the `OLEDBSimpleProviderListener` interface and calling the `aboutToInsertRows` method on each reference. The `aboutToInsertRows` method should be forwarded the `iRow` and `cRows` parameters, which indicate the starting location and the number of rows that are about to be inserted:

```
    'get the number of OSPListeners into a variable
    lOSPListenerCount = m_colOSPListeners.Count

    'Pre-Notify the OSP Listeners that we are about insert row(s)
    For lOSPListenerCounter = 1 To lOSPListenerCount
        'loop through our collection of subscribed OSP Listener objects
        '...and notify each one of them that we are ABOUT to insert row(s)

        'place the reference to the OSPListener into a temporary reference
        Set objOSPListener = m_colOSPListeners(lOSPListenerCounter)

        'make the necessary method call
        objOSPListener.aboutToInsertRows iRow, cRows

        'release the temporary reference
        Set objOSPListener = Nothing
    Next lOSPListenerCounter
```

Now it's time to actually insert the row into our dataset. This involves calling the InsertRegistryItem method of our instance of the RegistryItems class, which simply allocates a location for a new row and updates the row count. Notice that the actual registry key or value represented by the row is not created until both the ItemName and ItemType fields have been set to valid values through calls to the setVariant method:

```
m_objRegistryItems.InsertRegistryItem
```

After a new row has been allocated in the dataset and the row count has been updated, we need to post-notify all registered OSP listeners. This involves calling the insertedRows method on each reference in our collection of OSP listeners. The insertedRows method should also be forwarded the iRow and cRows parameters, which indicate the starting location and the number of rows that were inserted:

```
'Post-Notify the OSP Listeners that we have inserted new row(s)
For lOSPListenerCounter = 1 To lOSPListenerCount
    'loop through our collection of subscribed OSP Listener objects
    '...and notify each one of them that we HAVE inserted new Row(s)

    'place the reference to the OSPListener into a temporary reference
    Set objOSPListener = m_colOSPListeners(lOSPListenerCounter)

    'make the necessary method call
    objOSPListener.insertedRows iRow, cRows

    'release the temporary reference
    Set objOSPListener = Nothing
Next lOSPListenerCounter
```

The OLEDBSimpleProvider interface's insertRows method should always return the number of rows that have been inserted. With our Provider component, we'll simply return the cRows parameter, which will always have a value of 1:

```
'Return number of inserted rows
'...with this provider this value will always be 1
OLEDBSimpleProvider_insertRows = cRows
```

Finally, to complete the insertRows method we need to implement our standard ExitProcedure and ErrorHandler labels. Should an error occur, our Provider component will simply raise an error back to MSDAOSP and return a value of 0, indicating that now rows were inserted.

```
ExitProcedure:
    'exit this procedure
    Exit Function

ErrorHandler:
    'an error occured, return 0 for the number of Rows inserted
    OLEDBSimpleProvider_insertRows = 0

    'raise the error back to the caller
```

```
      Err.Raise OLEDBError.DB_E_ERRORSOCCURRED, Source:=App.Title, _
              Description:="An error occured inserting rows/records " & _
                          "into the dataset/recordset!"


   'exit this procedure
   Resume ExitProcedure
End Function
```

deleteRows Method

The deleteRows method is called when MSDAOSP receives a request to delete a record into the dataset. The deleteRows method also accepts two parameters named iRow and cRows. The iRow parameter specifies the starting location in the dataset where the row(s) should be deleted and the cRows parameter specifies the number of rows that should be deleted. If the iRow parameter has a value of –1, MSDAOSP is requesting that all rows be deleted. Our REGOLEDB Provider does not support multi-row deletes, so if the cRows parameter is greater than 1 or the iRow parameter equals –1 then the Provider component will raise an error back to MSDAOSP:

```
Private Function OLEDBSimpleProvider_deleteRows(ByVal iRow As Long, _
                                               ByVal cRows As Long) As Long

   Dim lOSPListenerCounter As Long
   Dim lOSPListenerCount As Long
   Dim objOSPListener As OLEDBSimpleProviderListener


   On Error GoTo ErrorHandler

   If (cRows > 1) Or (iRow = -1) Then
      'The consumer indicates they want to delete several rows (cRows > 1)
      '...or they want to delete all rows (iRow = -1)

      'turn off our error handler
      On Error GoTo 0

      'now raise the error
      Err.Raise OLEDBError.DB_E_NOTSUPPORTED, Source:=App.Title, _
              Description:="Multi-row deletions are not supported!"

      'exit this procedure
      GoTo ExitProcedure
   End If
```

Since we will be deleting a row and thus changing the dataset, we must first pre-notify all registered OSP listeners. This involves looping through our collection of references to objects implementing the OLEDBSimpleProviderListener interface and calling the aboutToDeleteRows method on each reference. The aboutToDeleteRows method should be forwarded the iRow and cRows parameters, which indicate the starting location and the number of rows that are about to be deleted:

```
   'get the number of OSPListeners into a variable
   lOSPListenerCount = m_colOSPListeners.Count

   'Pre-Notify the OSP Listeners that we are about Delete row(s)
   For lOSPListenerCounter = 1 To lOSPListenerCount
      'loop through our collection of subscribed OSP Listener objects
```

```
                 '...and notify each one of them that we are ABOUT to delete row(s)

              'place the reference to the OSPListener into a temporary reference
              Set objOSPListener = m_colOSPListeners(lOSPListenerCounter)

              'make the necessary method call
              objOSPListener.aboutToDeleteRows iRow, cRows

              'release the temporary reference
              Set objOSPListener = Nothing
        Next lOSPListenerCounter
```

Now it's time actually to delete the row from our dataset. This involves calling the
DeleteRegistryItem method of our instance of the RegistryItems class. The
DeleteRegistryItems method deletes the row from the dataset (the in-memory array), adjusts the
row count of the dataset and deletes the actual registry key or value from the Registry:

```
       m_objRegistryItems.DeleteRegistryItem iRow
```

After a row has been deleted from the dataset and the row count has been updated, we need to post-
notify all registered OSP listeners. This involves calling the deletedRows method on each reference in
our collection of OSP Listeners. The deletedRows method should also be forwarded the iRow and
cRows parameters, which indicate the starting location and the number of rows that were deleted:

```
       'Post-Notify the OSP Listeners that we have Deleted existing row(s)
       For lOSPListenerCounter = 1 To lOSPListenerCount
           'loop through our collection of subscribed OSP Listener objects
           '...and notify each one of them that we HAVE deleted new Row(s)

           'place the reference to the OSPListener into a temporary reference
           Set objOSPListener = m_colOSPListeners(lOSPListenerCounter)

           'make the necessary method call
           objOSPListener.deletedRows iRow, cRows

           'release the temporary reference
           Set objOSPListener = Nothing
       Next lOSPListenerCounter
```

The OLEDBSimpleProvider interface's deleteRows method should always return the number of
rows that have been deleted. With our Provider component, we'll simply return the cRows parameter,
which will always have a value of 1:

```
       'Return number of Deleted rows
       '...with this provider this value will always be 1
       OLEDBSimpleProvider_deleteRows = cRows
```

Finally, to complete the `deleteRows` method we need to implement our standard `ExitProcedure` and `ErrorHandler` labels. Should an error occur, our `Provider` component will simply raise an error back to `MSDAOSP` and return a value of 0, indicating that now rows were deleted.

```
ExitProcedure:
    'exit this procedure
    Exit Function

ErrorHandler:
    'an error occured, return 0 for the number of Rows deleted
    OLEDBSimpleProvider_deleteRows = 0

    'raise the error back to the caller
    Err.Raise OLEDBError.DB_E_ERRORSOCCURRED, Source:=App.Title, _
            Description:="An error occured deleting the specified " & _
                         "rows/records into the dataset/recordset!"

    'exit this procedure
    Resume ExitProcedure
End Function
```

Implementing the Variant Methods

The variant methods category, which includes `getVariant` and `setVariant`, are the core methods of the `OLEDBSimpleProvider` interface. As we saw in the previous chapter, these methods are called to retrieve or set the value of a particular cell.

getVariant Method

We'll begin implementing the `getVariant` method by defining the error handler for the method and the procedural variables we'll use:

```
Private Function OLEDBSimpleProvider_getVariant(ByVal iRow As Long, _
                                    ByVal iColumn As Long, _
                                    ByVal format As OSPFORMAT) _
                                As Variant

    Dim rsChildren As ADODB.Recordset

    On Error GoTo ErrorHandler
```

The `getVariant` method accepts two parameters named `iRow` and `iColumn`, which specify the cell for which the OSP implementation should return data. When the `iRow` parameter has a value of 0, `MSDAOSP` is not requesting data from the dataset, but instead is requesting the name of the column/field specified by the `iColumn` parameter. In the `DefineFields` private method, we loaded a member array with each column name using the column's index as the index in the array. When a column name is requested in the `getVariant` method, we can simply use the passed `iColumn` parameter as the index in our array of column names:

```
    If iRow = 0 Then
        'this is a non-data row, return the name for the specified column
        OLEDBSimpleProvider_getVariant = m_asColumnNames(iColumn)
```

If the `iRow` parameter has a value greater than 0 then `MSDAOSP` is requesting data for a particular cell in the dataset. Based on the column specified by the `iColumn` parameter, let's call the appropriate property on our instance of the `RegistryItems` class module passing the row index as a parameter:

```
    Else
        'the OLE DB Consumer wants data.  Reach into our instance of the
        '...RegistryItems class module and return the appropriate data based
        '...on the passed column number

        Select Case iColumn
            Case m_lColIndex_ItemName
                OLEDBSimpleProvider_getVariant = m_objRegistryItems.ItemName(iRow)

            Case m_lColIndex_FullName
                OLEDBSimpleProvider_getVariant = m_objRegistryItems.FullName(iRow)

            Case m_lColIndex_ItemType
                OLEDBSimpleProvider_getVariant = m_objRegistryItems.ItemType(iRow)

            Case m_lColIndex_Data
                OLEDBSimpleProvider_getVariant = m_objRegistryItems.Data(iRow)
```

Requests for data in the `Children` column must be handled differently because the `Children` column returns an open ADO `Recordset` containing the child registry items below the specified row. This involves opening a new ADO `Connection` and `Recordset` against ourselves, but specifying a different registry key in the XML-based text command. But first we need to make sure that the row specified represents a registry key and not a registry value. If the row specified by the `iRow` parameter does represent a registry value, we must return an error to `MSDAOSP` and exit the `getVariant` method:

```
            Case m_lColIndex_Children
                'Verify that this RegistryItem is a key and not a value

                If StrComp(m_objRegistryItems.ItemType(iRow), "Key", _
                        vbTextCompare) <> 0 Then

                    'Only registry keys have child items, values do not.

                    'turn off our error handler
                    On Error GoTo 0

                    '...Raise an error back to MSDAOSP
                    Err.Raise OLEDBError.DB_E_NOTSUPPORTED, Source:=App.Title, _
                            Description:="The children column is only supported " & _
                                    " for rows with an ItemType of 'Key'!"

                    'return nothing, or a null reference
                    Set OLEDBSimpleProvider_getVariant = Nothing

                    'exit this procedure
                    GoTo ExitProcedure
                End If
```

Before we open a new recordset against ourselves (i.e., against the REGOLEDB Provider), we need to modify the XML-based text command. We can accomplish this task by simply changing the `<Key>` element's value to the current row's FullName column using our reference to the IXMLDOMElement object that we established in the DefineFields method:

```
m_elmXMLTextCommand.selectSingleNode("Key").Text = _
                                m_objRegistryItems.FullName(iRow)
```

Now we can finally establish a new ADO Connection against ourselves and open and return an ADO Recordset containing the child registry keys and values. We'll use the XML that we just modified as the Source parameter of the Recordset's Open method:

```
            'create a new Children Recordset
            Set rsChildren = New ADODB.Recordset

            'open a recordset and a connection against this OLE DB provider
            rsChildren.Open Source:=m_elmXMLTextCommand.xml, ActiveConnection:= _
                    "Data Source=REGOLEDB.DataSource;Provider=MSDAOSP;"

            'return a reference to this open Children Recordset
            Set OLEDBSimpleProvider_getVariant = rsChildren

            'release our temporary variable reference
            Set rsChildren = Nothing

    End Select
End If
```

Finally, let's define our standard ExitProcedure and ErrorHandler labels for the getVariant method:

```
ExitProcedure:
    'exit this procedure
    Exit Function

ErrorHandler:
    'an error occured, raise it back to the caller
    Err.Raise OLEDBError.DB_E_ERRORSOCCURRED, Source:=App.Title, _
            Description:="An error occured retrieving the data for " & _
                    "the specified cell!"

    'exit this procedure
    Resume ExitProcedure
End Function
```

setVariant Method

The setVariant method is one of the more complex methods we have to implement for the Provider component. Let's begin by defining our error handler for the method and defining our procedural variables:

```
Private Sub OLEDBSimpleProvider_setVariant(ByVal iRow As Long, _
                                    ByVal iColumn As Long, _
                                    ByVal format As OSPFORMAT, _
                                    ByVal Var As Variant)

    Dim lOSPListenerCounter As Long
    Dim lOSPListenerCount As Long
    Dim objOSPListener As OLEDBSimpleProviderListener

    On Error GoTo ErrorHandler
```

Since we will be modifying the value in a cell, we must first pre-notify all registered OSP listeners. This involves looping through our collection of references to objects implementing the OLEDBSimpleProviderListener interface and calling the aboutToChangeCell method on each reference. The aboutToChangeCell method should be forwarded the iRow and iColumn parameters, which indicate the cell whose value is to be modified:

```
    'get the number of OSPListeners into a variable
    lOSPListenerCount = m_colOSPListeners.Count

    'Pre-Notify the OSP Listeners that we are about to change a value
    For lOSPListenerCounter = 1 To lOSPListenerCount
        'loop through our collection of subscribed OSP Listener objects
        '...and notify each one of them that we are about to change a field value

        'place the reference to the OSPListener into a temporary reference
        Set objOSPListener = m_colOSPListeners(lOSPListenerCounter)

        'make the necessary method call
        objOSPListener.aboutToChangeCell iRow, iColumn

        'release the temporary reference
        Set objOSPListener = Nothing
    Next lOSPListenerCounter
```

Now let's modify the data in the specified cell by calling the appropriate property on our instance of the RegistryItems class module and passing it the new value which is specified in the Var parameter. Remember, the FullName and Children columns are read-only. If the iColumn parameter specifies the index for either of these columns, we will raise an error back to MSDAOSP and exit the setVariant method:

```
    Select Case iColumn
        Case m_lColIndex_ItemName
            .ItemName(iRow) = Var

        Case m_lColIndex_FullName
            'This field is Read-Only
```

```
                    'turn off our error handler
                    On Error GoTo 0

                    'raise an error back to MSDAOSP
                    Err.Raise OLEDBError.DB_E_READONLY, Source:=App.Title, _
                            Description:="The FullName column/field is read-only!"

                    'exit this procedure
                    GoTo ExitProcedure

            Case m_lColIndex_ItemType
                .ItemType(iRow) = Var

            Case m_lColIndex_Data
                .Data(iRow) = Var

            Case m_lColIndex_Children
                'This field is Read-Only

                    'turn off our error handler
                    On Error GoTo 0

                    'raise an error back to MSDAOSP
                    Err.Raise OLEDBError.DB_E_READONLY, Source:=App.Title, _
                            Description:="The Children column/field is read-only!"

                    'exit this procedure
                    GoTo ExitProcedure
        End Select
```

The properties `ItemName`, `ItemType` and `Data` properties only modify the values in the internal dataset managed by the `RegistryItems` class and not in the actual Registry. After we have made our changes to the data using any of these properties, we need to call the `ModifyRegistryItem` method on our instance of the `RegistryItems` class. The `ModifyRegistryItem` method will call the appropriate Win32 API functions to apply the changes to the Registry by changing an existing registry key or value, or by inserting the registry key or value if it hasn't been created yet:

```
'modify the actual key or value in the Registry if it already exist
'...or force it to be created if it doesn't exist already
m_objRegistryItems.ModifyRegistryItem iRow
```

After a row in the dataset has been modified, we need to post-notify all registered OSP listeners. This involves calling the `cellChanged` method on each reference in our collection of OSP listeners. The `cellChanged` method should also be forwarded the `iRow` and `iColumn` parameters, which indicate the cell whose value has been modified:

```
'Post-Notify the OSP Listeners that we have changed a value
For lOSPListenerCounter = 1 To lOSPListenerCount
    'loop through our collection of subscribed OSP Listener objects
    '...and notify each one of them that we HAVE changed a field value
```

```
        'place the reference to the OSPListener into a temporary reference
        Set objOSPListener = m_colOSPListeners(lOSPListenerCounter)

        'make the necessary method call
        objOSPListener.cellChanged iRow, iColumn

        'release the temporary reference
        Set objOSPListener = Nothing
    Next lOSPListenerCounter
```

Finally, to complete the `setVariant` method we need to implement our standard `ExitProcedure` and `ErrorHandler` labels:

```
ExitProcedure:
    'exit this procedure
    Exit Sub

ErrorHandler:
    'an error occured, raise the error back to the caller
    Err.Raise OLEDBError.DB_E_ERRORSOCCURRED, Source:=App.Title, _
            Description:="An error occurred changing or inserting " & _
                         "the value into the specified cell!"

    'exit this procedure
    Resume ExitProcedure
End Sub
```

Implementing Miscellaneous Methods

The final category of methods defined by the `OLEDBSimpleProvider` interface that we need to implement contains two miscellaneous methods. The miscellaneous methods category, as we've defined it, consists of the `getLocale` and the `find` methods.

As we saw in the previous chapter, the `getLocale` function is responsible for returning the **locale** or country of origin for the data. Our REGOLEDB provider will return the locale of `"en-us"`, which stands for English-United States. A complete list of locales can be found, ironically, under the registry key HKEY_CLASSES_ROOT\MIME\Database\Rfc1766.

```
Private Function OLEDBSimpleProvider_getLocale() As String
    On Error GoTo ErrorHandler

    OLEDBSimpleProvider_getLocale = "en-us"

ExitProcedure:
    'exit this procedure
    Exit Function

ErrorHandler:
    'an error occured, raise it back to the caller
```

```
        Err.Raise OLEDBError.DB_E_ERRORSOCCURRED, Source:=App.Title, _
                Description:="An error occured returning the locale " & _
                            "for the dataset/recordset!"

    'exit this procedure
    Resume ExitProcedure
End Function
```

While the `find` method only provides *basic* search functionality within a dataset, it is probably the most complicated method to support. In fact, it's tempting simply to raise the OLE DB error `DB_E_NOTSUPPORTED` when the `find` method is invoked! However, even basic searching functionality is a powerful feature to expose to consumers. It enables ADO clients simply to call the single `find` method of an ADO `Recordset` object to search for a particular row within the recordset.

Let's begin implementing the `find` method in our `Provider` component by defining our error handler for the method and the procedural variables we'll use to search through the dataset:

```
Private Function OLEDBSimpleProvider_find(ByVal iRowStart As Long, _
                                          ByVal iColumn As Long, _
                                          ByVal val As Variant, _
                                          ByVal findFlags As OSPFIND, _
                                          ByVal compType As OSPCOMP) As Long

    Dim enumComparisonType As VbCompareMethod
    Dim lStartRegistryItem As Long
    Dim lStopRegistryItem As Long
    Dim lStepValue As Long
    Dim lFindResult As Long
    Dim vComparisonValue As Variant
    Dim lStrCompResult As Long
    Dim lRegistryItemCounter As Long

    On Error GoTo ErrorHandler
```

Next let's perform some simple validations before proceeding. Our `Provider` component does not support searching against the `Children` column that contains an ADO `Recordset`. If the value of the `iColumn` parameter, which specifies the column to search against, is equal to our `Children` column's index, we raise an error back to `MSDAOSP`:

```
    If iColumn = m_lColIndex_Children Then
        'turn off our error handler
        On Error GoTo 0

        'raise an error back to MSDAOSP
        Err.Raise OLEDBErr.DB_E_NOTSUPPORTED, Source:=App.Title, _
                Description:="Searching against the Children column " & _
                            "is not supported!"

        'exit this procedure
        GoTo ExitProcedure
    End If
```

Now let's initialize some of our procedural variables based on the value of the findFlags parameter. The findFlags parameter indicates the order and case-sensitivity of the search. Based on the value of this parameter, we'll initialize four procedural variables that we'll later use to perform the search:

- ❑ enumComparisonType. The enumComparisonType variable stores information about the case-sensitivity of the search. If the search is case-sensitive, this variable should have a value of vbBinaryCompare. With case-insensitive searches, this variable should have a value of vbTextCompare.

- ❑ lStartRegistryItem. The lStartRegistryItem variable should contain the index of the row where we'll begin the search.

- ❑ lStopRegistryItem. The lStopRegistryItem variable should contain the index of the last row that will be searched.

- ❑ lStepValue. The lStepValue variable stores an integer value indicating the direction of the search. For ascending searches, this variable will have a value of 1. With descending searches, this variable will have a value of -1.

```
Select Case findFlags
   Case OSPFIND_DEFAULT
       'the consumer want's to use the default search options
       '...In-casesensitive and Ascending
       enumComparisonType = vbTextCompare
       lStartRegistryItem = iRowStart
       lStopRegistryItem = m_objRegistryItems.RegistryItemCount
       lStepValue = 1

   Case OSPFIND_CASESENSITIVE
       'the consumer want's the search to be Case Sensitive
       '...assume Ascending order
       enumComparisonType = vbBinaryCompare
       lStartRegistryItem = iRowStart
       lStopRegistryItem = m_objRegistryItems.RegistryItemCount
       lStepValue = 1

   Case OSPFIND_UP
       'the consumer wants to search descending
       '...assume case-insensitive
       enumComparisonType = vbTextCompare
       lStartRegistryItem = m_objRegistryItems.RegistryItemCount
       lStopRegistryItem = iRowStart
       lStepValue = -1

   Case OSPFIND_UPCASESENSITIVE
       'the consumer wants to search descending, case-sensitive
       enumComparisonType = vbBinaryCompare
       lStartRegistryItem = m_objRegistryItems.RegistryItemCount
       lStopRegistryItem = iRowStart
       lStepValue = -1
End Select
```

The last procedural variable we need to initialize is that named lFindResult. The lFindResult variable stores the index of the row where the first match is found. This variable is used as the return value for the find method. We'll default the lFindResult procedural variable to –1, indicating that no rows were found:

```
lFindResult = -1
```

Now we can finally begin our search through the dataset by starting a loop beginning at the location specified in our lStartRegistryItem variable, going to the value specified in our lStopRegistryItem variable and incrementing or decrementing based on the value of the lStepValue variable. Now you can see why we set the values of these procedural variables earlier based on the value of the findFlags parameter:

```
For lRegistryItemCounter = lStartRegistryItem To lStopRegistryItem _
                                             Step lStepValue
```

Within our loop, the first task we need to perform is to get the value for the current row into a variable. This involves calling the appropriate property on our instance of the RegistryItems class module based on the value of the iColumn parameter:

```
Select Case iColumn
    Case m_lColIndex_ItemName
        vComparisonValue = m_objRegistryItems.ItemName(lRegistryItemCounter)

    Case m_lColIndex_FullName
        vComparisonValue = m_objRegistryItems.FullName(lRegistryItemCounter)

    Case m_lColIndex_ItemType
        vComparisonValue = m_objRegistryItems.ItemType(lRegistryItemCounter)

    Case m_lColIndex_Data
        vComparisonValue = m_objRegistryItems.Data(lRegistryItemCounter)
End Select
```

The next task within the for loop will be actually to perform the comparison, but first we must determine whether this will be a string-based, alphanumeric comparison or whether this will be a numeric comparison. We can determine the type of comparison that will should be performed by checking the type of the value we will be searching for, which is stored in the val variant parameter. If we're performing a string-based comparison (most likely), then we can perform the actual comparison using the StrComp function.

```
If VarType(val) = vbString Then
    'we're performing comparisons against string-based data
    '...use the StrComp function

    lStrCompResult = StrComp(vComparisonValue, val, enumComparisonType)
```

Based on the value of the `compType` parameter, which specifies the comparison criterion, let's evaluate the return value from the `StrComp` function. Once we have found the first match where the comparison criterion is compatible with the `StrComp` return value, we store the index of the current row into the `lFindResult` procedural variable and exit the `For...Next` loop. For example if the `compType` parameter has a value of `OSPCOM_DEFAULT` or `OSPCOMP_EQ`, indicating that we are searching for the first value that *equals* the `val` parameter, and if the return value from the `StrComp` function is 0, indicating that the `val` parameter was equal to the current row's value, then we store the index of the current row and exit the loop:

```
Select Case compType
    Case OSPCOMP_DEFAULT, OSPCOMP_EQ:
        'searching for the first value = to the val parameter

        If lStrCompResult = 0 Then
            lFindResult = lRegistryItemCounter
            Exit For
        End If

    Case OSPCOMP_GE
        'searching for the first value >= to the val parameter

        If lStrCompResult >= 0 Then
            lFindResult = lRegistryItemCounter
            Exit For
        End If

    Case OSPCOMP_GT
        'searching for the first value > than the val parameter

        If lStrCompResult > 0 Then
            lFindResult = lRegistryItemCounter
            Exit For
        End If

    Case OSPCOMP_LE
        'searching for the first value <= to the val parameter

        If lStrCompResult <= 0 Then
            lFindResult = lRegistryItemCounter
            Exit For
        End If

    Case OSPCOMP_LT
        'searching for the first value < than the val parameter

        If lStrCompResult < 0 Then
            lFindResult = lRegistryItemCounter
            Exit For
        End If

    Case OSPCOMP_NE
        'searching for the first value <> than the val parameter
```

```
              · If lStrCompResult <> 0 Then
                    lFindResult = lRegistryItemCounter
                    Exit For
              End If
         End Select
```

Thankfully, numeric comparisons are a little simpler, especially after we have implemented the alphanumeric comparsions. Numeric comparisons simply involve comparing the integer value of the passed `val` parameter against the integer value of our `vComparisonValue` procedural variable which stores the value for the specified column in the current row. Since this comparison is numeric, the `StrComp` function is not involved. However, we still have to perform the comparison of the two values differently based on the comparison type specified in the `compType` parameter. For example, if the `compType` parameter has a value of `OSPCOMP_DEFAULT` or `OSPCOMP_EQ`, indicating that we are searching for the first match that *equals* the `val` parameter, then the comparison checks if the integer values of the `val` parameter and the `vComparisonValue` variable are *equal*. When we find a match based on the specified criterion, we store the index of the current row in the `lFindResult` parameter and exit the `For...Next` loop:

```
     Else
         'this is a numeric comparison, based on the comparison info specified
         '...by the consumer in the compType variable, compare the specified
         '... columns value for the current row against the searched value

         Select Case compType
            Case OSPCOMP_DEFAULT, OSPCOMP_EQ:
               'searching for the first value = to the val parameter

               If CLng(vComparisonValue) = CLng(val) Then
                  lFindResult = lRegistryItemCounter
                  Exit For
               End If

            Case OSPCOMP_GE
               'searching for the first value >= to the val parameter

               If CLng(vComparisonValue) >= CLng(val) Then
                  lFindResult = lRegistryItemCounter
                  Exit For
               End If

            Case OSPCOMP_GT
               'searching for the first value > than the val parameter

               If CLng(vComparisonValue) > CLng(val) Then
                  lFindResult = lRegistryItemCounter
                  Exit For
               End If

            Case OSPCOMP_LE
               'searching for the first value <= to the val parameter
```

```
                    If CLng(vComparisonValue) <= CLng(val) Then
                        lFindResult = lRegistryItemCounter
                        Exit For
                    End If

                Case OSPCOMP_LT
                    'searching for the first value < than the val parameter

                    If CLng(vComparisonValue) < CLng(val) Then
                        lFindResult = lRegistryItemCounter
                        Exit For
                    End If

                Case OSPCOMP_NE
                    'searching for the first value <> than the val parameter

                    If CLng(vComparisonValue) <> CLng(val) Then
                        lFindResult = lRegistryItemCounter
                        Exit For
                    End If
            End Select
        End If
    Next lRegistryItemCounter
```

Finally, we return the value of the lFindResult procedural variable to MSDAOSP. If we found a row then the lFindResult variable will contain the index of the first row found. If we didn't find a row, the lFindResult variable will contain the default value of −1, indicating that no rows were found:

```
    OLEDBSimpleProvider_find = lFindResult
```

Of course, we don't want to forget our standard ExitProcedure and ErrorHandler labels in the find method:

```
ExitProcedure:
    'exit this procedure
    Exit Function

ErrorHandler:
    'an error occured

    'return a -1 indicating that now rows were found
    OLEDBSimpleProvider_find = -1

    'raise an error back to the caller
    Err.Raise OLEDBError.DB_E_ERRORSOCCURRED, Source:=App.Title, _
        Description:="An error occured searching through the dataset/recordset!"

    'exit this procedure
    Resume ExitProcedure
End Function
```

Building the REGOLEDB Provider

Once the `Provider` component has been created, we can perform a build of the REGOLEDB provider just like we would with any other COM component. But before you do, you should verify that the `Threading Model` for the project is set to **Apartment Threaded**. Let's also change the `Project Description` to "REGOLEDB - OLE DB Provider for the Windows NT/2000 Registry". If you don't select a `Threading Model` of **Apartment Threaded**, this won't cause any errors when using the simple provider. However, performance will suffer when multiple recordsets are opened against the provider because all instances of the same component will be serialized to a single thread of execution.

Since this component doesn't depend on user interaction, we can check the `Unattended Execution` option. This will cause any message boxes to be written to the Windows NT/2000 Event Log. However, do not select the `Retained In Memory` option, because MSDAOSP should have complete control over the lifetime of a simple OLE DB provider's OSP implementation.

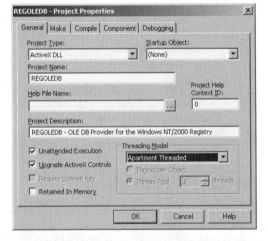

After the initial build has been created it is also recommended that you change the component compatibility settings to **Binary Compatibility** to ensure that you preserve backwards compatiblity with previous builds. Otherwise, Visual Basic will automatically change the Class ID and Interface ID when you rebuild the provider.

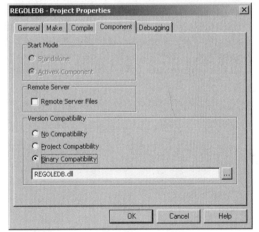

Registering the Provider

Before we can begin using our REGOLEDB Provider, it must be registered. There are two types of registration for simple OLE DB providers:

❑ Partial registration

❑ Full registration

Although there is no functional difference between these two types of registration, the approach you choose effects how ADO connections are established to your simple provider. Both types of registration require the OLE DB Simple Provider (MSDAOSP.DLL) also to be registered. Let's discuss the differences between these two registration techniques.

> **Visual Basic actually registers a COM server (simple OLE DB provider) automatically when you perform a build. However, if you want to deploy the provider to another machine(s), it will require registration before it can be used.**

Partial Registration

Partial registration simply involves registering a simple OLE DB provider using the Regsvr32.exe application, just like you would any other in-process COM server. No additional registry keys or values are created beyond those required by COM. As a result, connections to simple OLE DB providers that are "partially" registered must be established differently to connections to typical OLE DB providers. In particular, when an ADO Connection is established, MSDAOSP must be specified as the Provider, and the Programmatic ID (ProgID) of the simple OLE DB provider's OSP Data Object must be specified in the Data Source dynamic property. In the following example, we specify values for both of these properties before opening a connection to our REGOLEDB Provider:

```
Dim conDataSource As ADODB.Connection

'create a new instance of an ADODB.Connection
Set conDataSource = New ADODB.Connection

conDataSource.Provider = "MSDAOSP"
conDataSource.Properties("Data Source").Value = "REGOLEDB.DataSource"
conDataSource.Open

'close & release our instance of the ADODB.Connection
conDataSource.Close
Set conDataSource = Nothing
```

Alternatively, the `Provider` and `Data Source` properties can both be specified in the `ConnectionString` property or in the `ConnectionString` parameter of an ADO `Connection` object's `Open` method:

```
Dim conDataSource As ADODB.Connection

'create a new instance of an ADODB.Connection
Set conDataSource = New ADODB.Connection

conDataSource.Open ConnectionString:= _
                    "Data Source=REGOLEDB.DataSource;Provider=MSDAOSP;"


'close & release our instance of the ADODB.Connection
conDataSource.Close
Set conDataSource = Nothing
```

While I prefer to use the `ConnectionString` approach, it doesn't really matter how you specify the `Provider` and the `Data Source` properties when establishing a connection to a simple OLE DB provider. What's important to remember is that with partial registration the provider specified must always be `MSDAOSP` and the `Data Source` specified must be the `ProgID` of the simple OLE DB provider's OSP Data Object.

Full Registration

With full registration, all the provider-specific information is specified in the registry in addition to the standard in-process COM server registration entries. As a result, full registration allows connections to be established to the simple OLE DB provider simply by specifying the name of the provider for an ADO `Connection` object's `Provider` property. For example, if our `REGOLEDB` Provider is "fully" registered, the following code will open an ADO Connection to the provider:

```
Dim conDataSource As ADODB.Connection

'create a new instance of an ADODB.Connection
Set conDataSource = New ADODB.Connection

'Specify the name of the Simple OLE DB Provider
conDataSource.Provider = "REGOLEDB"
conDataSource.Open

'close & release our instance of the ADODB.Connection
conDataSource.Close
Set conDataSource = Nothing
```

We can also connect to a fully registered provider the same way as partially registred provider:

```
Dim conDataSource As ADODB.Connection

'create a new instance of an ADODB.Connection
Set conDataSource = New ADODB.Connection

conDataSource.Provider = "MSDAOSP"
conDataSource.Properties("Data Source").Value = "REGOLEDB.DataSource"
conDataSource.Open

'close & release our instance of the ADODB.Connection
conDataSource.Close
Set conDataSource = Nothing
```

Where partial registration required MSDAOSP to be specified as the Provider when establishing a connection, full registration uses a trick called **registry redirection** to redirect request for a simple OLE DB provider to MSDAOSP. To understand better how this "registry redirection" trick works, let's take a look at the registry keys and values for our REGOLEDB Provider when it is fully registered:

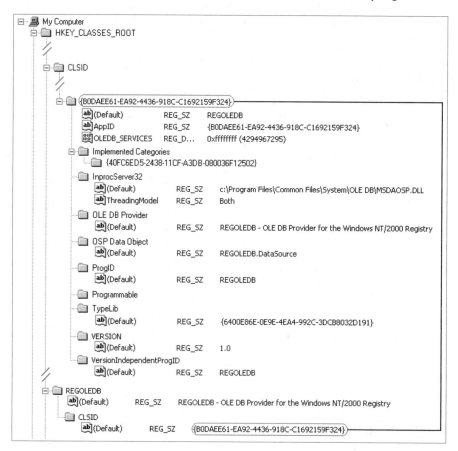

Notice that under the CLSID key, instead of storing the location and threading model of our REGOLEDB.Provider component, the values store the location and threading model of the OLE DB Simple Provider (MSDAOSP). This registry redirection causes MSDAOSP to be loaded whenever a connection is opened agaіnst the REGOLEDB Provider.

Some of the other registry differences between full and partial registration include:

OLE DB Provider

The presence of the OLE DB Provider key identifies this COM component as an OLE DB provider. This registry key's default value is the descriptive name of the provider.

OSP Data Object

The OSP Data Object key's default value stores the ProgID of a simple OLE DB provider's OSP Data Object. When MSDAOSP is loaded, as a result of registry redirection, it retrieves this key's default value. MSDAOSP then instantiates the OSP Data Object whose ProgID is specified in this registry value. This is different to the partial registration technique where we were required to specify the OSP Data Object's ProgID in a Connection object's Data Source dynamic property.

OLEDB_SERVICES

The OLEDB_Services registry value, located under an OSP implementation component's CLSID key, determines the OLE DB services supported by the simple provider.

Since the only OLE DB service a simple provider can support is MSDAOSP and it *must* support this service, a simple provider's OLEDB_Services value should be the same as the as MSDAOSP's OLEDB_Services value, which is hex ffffffff.

Performing Full Registration of a Simple Provider

To utilize full registration with a simple OLE DB provider, we must perform these two operations:

❑ Register the simple provider just as you would register any in-process COM component, using regsrv32.exe. If you only want to perform partial registration, this is the only operation you need to perform.

❑ Add the appropriate keys and values we just described to the Registry for your simple provider's OSP Data Object. Instead of performing this operation manually, you can download a template registration file from the Wrox Press web site and fill in the template with your provider-specific values.

A data link (.udl) file can be used to verify quickly that a simple provider is registered correctly. When a simple OLE DB provider is fully registered, it will appear as an entry in the OLE DB Providers list in the Data Links window. After selecting your provider from this list, simply click the Test Connection button on the Connection tab:

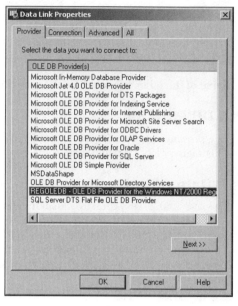

Partially Registering the REGOLEDB Provider

Since full registration requires additional registry entries, which results in more complexity during deployment, I recommend using the partial registration technique. Most installation utilities will automatically register in-process COM servers (DLLs) automatically, which satisfies the requirements for paritial registration without any additional work. For this reason, let's go ahead and partially register our REGOLEDB Provider by executing Regsvr32.exe specifying the path to the provider as a parameter. For example:

```
regsvr32.exe "C:\Professional ADO 2.5\REGOLEDB\Provider\REGOLEDB.dll"
```

To verify that our REGOLEDB Provider has been registered correctly, first create a new file with the extension .udl and run this file. This will cause the Data Link Properties dialog to be displayed. From here, select the Microsoft OLE DB Simple Provider from the OLE DB Providers list on the first tab:

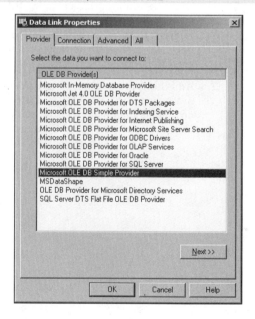

Finally, since we used the partial registration technique, we must specify the `ProgID` of the REGOLEDB Provider's OSP Data Object in the **Data Source** field on the **Connection** tab. After this step has been completed, simply click the **Test Connection** button to verify that a connection can be established to our REGOLEDB Provider:

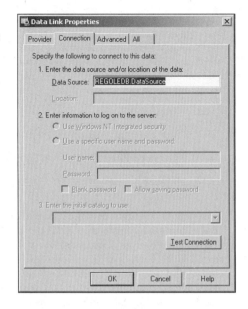

Testing, Debugging and Deploying the Provider

Phew! We're done with the hard part – creating and registering the components that compose the REGOLEDB Provider. However, no provider is complete without proper testing, debugging and packaging for deployment.

Testing the REGOLEDB Provider

A thorough and well-planned testing process is essential to the development of any successful COM components. However, OLE DB providers warrant additional testing because of their required integration within the OLE DB architecture. Where normal COM or MTS/COM+ components are typically invoked directly by the client requesting the functionality, OLE DB providers must interact with existing OLE DB consumers, such as ADO, and OLE DB service providers, such as the Client Cursor Engine and the OLE DB Persistence Provider (`MSPersist`). Simple providers further add to the complexity by introducing the multi-layered OSP architecture. Typically, the more layers of abstraction between the client and the data, the more possibilities there are for things to go wrong. However, thorough testing can eliminate these issues before they become costly problems.

Probably the easiest and fastest way to test a simple OLE DB provider with ADO is to blindly load up an instance of Visual Basic and write a few lines of simple code that tests every feature supported by the Provider. But, instead of just creating meaningless test scenarios, I like to create a useful application(s) to test components. This makes the testing process less tedious and more of a fun, thought-provoking exercise. Additionally, testing OLE DB providers by using them in a sample application quickly exposes a provider's shortcomings and problems by most accurately simulating how they might be used in the real world.

To test our `REGOLEDB` Provider we'll create an Active Server Page (ASP) named `odbcdsn.asp` that displays information about each ODBC System DSN configured on a machine. A Data Source Name (DSN) is a logical name assigned to all the information required to establish a connection to an ODBC database. This information might include:

- ❑ The ODBC driver to use
- ❑ The database name
- ❑ The name of the server
- ❑ The type of security to use
- ❑ Network addresses or server names

DSNs allow connections to be established to an ODBC database simply by specifying the DSN in the connection string, instead of all of the connection information. ODBC DSNs can be managed using the ODBC Data Source Administrator application or the ODBC API. However, ODBC DSNs are actually stored in the Registry. As you can see in the following diagram, a list of System DSNs (DSNs visible to every login account) are stored as Registry values under the Registry key `HKEY_LOCAL_MACHINE\SOFTWARE\ODBC\ODBC.INI\ODBC Data Sources`. Each of these System DSNs also has a sub-key located under `HKEY_LOCAL_MACHINE\SOFTWARE\ODBC\ODBC.INI\`. Under this sub-key you can find all of the connection information that composes a System DSN:

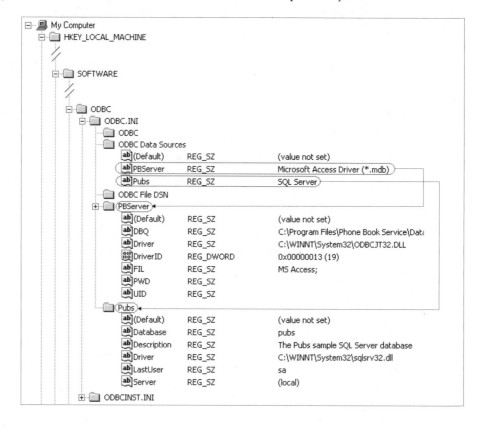

Our `odbcdsn.asp` Active Server Page will test our REGOLEDB Provider by retrieving and displaying the list of System DSNs and all of their connection information. Let's start implementing it by importing the ADODB type library using the <METADATA> tag so that we can use the ADO constants:

```
<%@ Language=VBScript %>
<% Option Explicit %>

<!-- import the ADODB type library -->
<!-- METADATA TYPE="typelib" uuid="{00000205-0000-0010-8000-00AA006D2EA4}" -->
```

Next, let's create a function named BuildTextCommand that uses the XML Document Object Model and the passed sKey parameter to build an XML-based text command which we can use to open a recordset against our REGOLEDB Provider:

```
<%
    Function BuildTextCommand(sKey)
        'this function Builds an XML-based text command using the value
        '...specified in the sKey parameter as the Key elements value

        dim domXMLDataMember
        dim elmXMLTextCommand
        dim elmFields
        dim elmKey

        'create an instance of the MSXML.DOMDocument
        set domXMLDataMember = Server.CreateObject("MSXML.DOMDocument")

        'create the XMLTextCommand, Fields, and Key elemements
        set elmXMLTextCommand = domXMLDataMember.createElement("XMLTextCommand")
        set elmFields = domXMLDataMember.createElement("Fields")
        set elmKey = domXMLDataMember.createElement("Key")

        'set the value of the Key element
        elmKey.Text = sKey

        'create the All attribute for the Fields element with a value of "True"
        elmFields.setAttribute "All", "True"

        'append the XMLTextCommand root element to the document
        domXMLDataMember.appendChild elmXMLTextCommand

        'append the Fields and Key elements to the root XMLTextCommand elements
        elmXMLTextCommand.appendChild elmFields
        elmXMLTextCommand.appendChild elmKey

        'return the XML to the caller
        BuildTextCommand = domXMLDataMember.xml

        'release our interface references
        set elmFields = Nothing
        set elmKey = Nothing
        Set elmXMLTextCommand = Nothing
        Set domXMLDataMember = Nothing
    End Function
%>
```

When the page is loaded, we need to create and establish an ADO connection to our REGOLEDB Provider. Then we need to create and open two ADO recordsets. One recordset, named rsODBCDSNList, will contain a list of the System DSNs which are stored as registry values under the key HKEY_LOCAL_MACHINE\SOFTWARE\ODBC\ODBC.INI\ODBC Data Sources. The other recordset is named rsODBCINI and will contain the registry keys and values under the key HKEY_LOCAL_MACHINE\SOFTWARE\ODBC\ODBC.INI. The keys within this recordset contain the attributes of the System DSN. We'll call our BuildTextCommand function to build the XML-based text commands used to open these recordsets:

```asp
<%
    'dimension our page-level variables
    dim rsODBCDSNList
    dim rsODBCINI
    dim rsODBCDSNInfo
    dim conDataSource
    dim sTextCommand


    'create an instance of an ADODB.Connection
    set conDataSource = Server.CreateObject("ADODB.Connection")

    'open a connection to the REGOLEDB Provider
    conDataSource.Open "Provider=MSDAOSP;Data Source=REGOLEDB.DataSource;"

    'build the text command for the ...ODBC.INI\ODBC Data Sources key
    '...and open a Recordset containing the keys and values under this key
    sTextCommand = BuildTextCommand( _
                "HKEY_LOCAL_MACHINE\SOFTWARE\ODBC\ODBC.INI\ODBC Data Sources")
    set rsODBCDSNList = conDataSource.Execute(sTextCommand)


    'build the text command for the ...ODBC.INI key
    '...and open a Recordset containing the keys and values under this key
    sTextCommand = BuildTextCommand("HKEY_LOCAL_MACHINE\SOFTWARE\ODBC\ODBC.INI")
    set rsODBCINI = conDataSource.Execute(sTextCommand)
%>
```

Before we start displaying the list of ODBC System DSNs, we will insert some standard HTML tags and define a table containing two columns named **DSN Name** and **Driver Name**. Notice that we rely on a Cascading Style Sheet (CSS) named odbcdsn.css for the formatting of this page. This style sheet and this entire example are available online from the Wrox web-site.

```html
<HTML>
<HEAD>
    <LINK REL="stylesheet" TYPE="text/css" HREF="odbcdsn.css">
    <TITLE>ODBC System DSNs</TITLE>
</HEAD>
<BODY>
    <TABLE CLASS="cls_tblODBCDSNs">
        <THEAD CLASS="cls_thdODBCDSN">
```

```
        <TR>
          <TH CLASS="cls_tdHeading_DSNName" COLSPAN=2> DSN Name</TH>
          <TH CLASS="cls_tdHeading_DriverName"> Driver Name</TH>
        </TR>
      </THEAD>
      <TBODY ID="tbdyODBCDSNs">
```

Now we can create a row in our HTML table for each ODBC System DSN by looping through every record in the `rsODBCDSNList` recordset and placing the registry value's `ItemName` in the **DSN Name** column and the registry value's data in the **Driver Name** column. But we only create the table row if the current record represents a registry value and not a registry key:

```
<%
    do while rsODBCDSNList.eof = false
    'loop through each record display the information about each System DSN

        'make sure this Registry Item is a value with a valid name
        if rsODBCDSNList.fields("ItemType").value <> "Key" then
%>
          <TR ONBLUR="window.status='';" CLASS="cls_trODBCDSN">
            <TD>                            
            </TD>
            <TD CLASS="cls_tdRecord_DSNName">
              <%=rsODBCDSNList.fields("ItemName").value%>
            </TD>
            <TD CLASS="cls_tdRecord_DriverName">
              <%=rsODBCDSNList.fields("Data").value%>
            </TD>
          </TR>
```

After we've created a row containing the DSN name and the driver name, we search within our `rsODBCINI` recordset for a key with the same name as the DSN. If we find a match (the `Bof` and `Eof` properties both equal false), we make sure that the found record represents a registry key. If it does, we get a reference to a recordset containing records that represent its registry keys and values by retrieving the value from the `Children` column into the `rsODBCDSNInfo` variable:

```
<%
            'search for the corresponding key under the ODBC.INI key
            rsODBCINI.find "ItemName='" & _
                        rsODBCDSNList.fields("ItemName").value & "'", , _
                        adSearchForward, 1

            if rsODBCINI.eof = false and rsODBCINI.bof = false then
               'a record was found for the ODBC DSN under the ODBC.INI key

                'make sure the item is a key
                if rsODBCINI.fields("ItemType").value = "Key" then

                    'get a reference to this Registry Key's Children Recordset
                    '...which contains the extended ODBC DSN's information
                    set rsODBCDSNInfo = rsODBCINI.fields("Children").value
%>
```

If the child recordset contains records, we create another HTML table with Field and Value columns. Then we create a row in this new table for each attribute of the DSN by looping through every record in the rsODBCDSNInfo recordset and placing the registry value's ItemName in the Field column and the registry value's Data in the Value column. After we've displayed each record in the rsODBCDSNInfo recordset, close and release it:

```
<%
                            if rsODBCDSNInfo.eof = false then
%>
                        <TR>
                            <TD>
                                <DIV STYLE="display:visible"> </DIV>
                            </TD>
                            <TD COLSPAN=2>
                                <DIV ID="tblODBCDSNInfo" STYLE="display:visible">
                                    <TABLE CLASS="cls_tblODBCDSNInfo">
                                        <THEAD>
                                            <TH CLASS="cls_tdHeading_Field">
                                                 Field
                                            </TH>
                                            <TH CLASS="cls_tdHeading_Value">
                                                 Value
                                            </TH>
                                        </THEAD>
                                        <TBODY>
<%
                            do while rsODBCDSNInfo.eof = false
%>
                                        <TR>
                                            <TD CLASS="cls_tdRecord_Field">
                                            <%=rsODBCDSNInfo.fields("ItemName").value%>
                                            </TD>
                                            <TD class="cls_tdRecord_Value">
                                            <%=rsODBCDSNInfo.fields("Data").value%>
                                            </TD>
                                        </TR>
<%
                            rsODBCDSNInfo.movenext
                        loop
%>
                                        </TBODY>
                                    </TABLE>
                                </DIV>
                                <BR>
                            </TD>
                        </TR>
<%
                        end if

                        'release our reference to this ODBC DSN's extended information
                        rsODBCDSNInfo.close
                        set rsODBCDSNInfo = nothing
                    end if
                end if
```

Once we have completed all of the processing for finding and displaying an ODBC System DSN's attributes, we move to the next DSN in our recordset:

```
        end if

        'move to the next record
        rsODBCDSNList.movenext
    loop
%>

    </TBODY>
  </TABLE>

</BODY>
</HTML>
```

Finally, we close and release all references to our `Recordset` and `Connection` objects:

```
<%
    'close and release our Recordset containing the DSN keys
    rsODBCINI.close
    set rsODBCINI = nothing

    'close and release our Recordset containing the list of DSN's
    rsODBCDSNList.close
    set rsODBCDSNList = nothing

    'close and release the connection to the REGOLEDB provider
    conDataSource.Close
    set conDataSource = nothing
%>
```

Our `odbcdsn.asp` Active Server Page is now complete. When you load this page in Internet Explorer you should see all the ODBC System DSNs configured on the machine in the parent table and every attribute about each DSN in a child table:

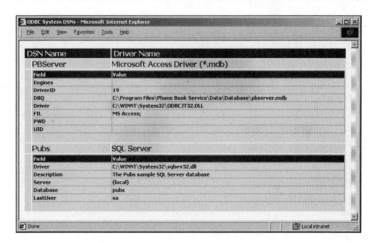

This simple ASP page isn't a bad start for testing our REGOLEDB Provider. In this example, we tested basic data retrieval, searching and the hierarchial recordset feature provided through the Children column. We also created a generic function naned BuildTextCommand that leveraged the XML Document Object Model to build XML-based text commands that can be used to open recordsets against our provider. However, we didn't test updating, inserting or deleting records in this example. I'll leave this exercise up to you. Perhaps you could test this base functionality by extending our ODBC System DSN example to support the creation, modification and deletion of System DSNs. Or perhaps you want to retrieve and manipulate some other data such as:

- ❑ The shared components and their clients installed on the system: each shared component is assigned a sub-key under HKEY_LOCAL_MACHINE\SOFTWARE\Microsoft\Shared Tools. Under each component's sub-key is a key named Clients that contains a registry value for each client of the shared component.

- ❑ Visual Studio Analyzer events, event categories and event sources: located under the HKEY_LOCAL_MACHINE\SOFTWARE\Microsoft\VisualStudio\Analyzer are four sub-keys: Dynamic Event Sources, Event Categories, Event Sources and Events. Under each of these sub-keys are keys for each respective item. For example, a sub-key exists for each registered VSA event under the key HKEY_LOCAL_MACHINE\SOFTWARE\Microsoft\VisualStudio\Analyzer\Events.

- ❑ Custom registry data: you can retrieve, create, update or delete registry keys and values in almost any location in the Registry. For example, you might want to store software configuration information such as window positions, help files and file locations using a custom sub-key and values under HKEY_LOCAL_MACHINE\SOFTWARE. However, if the data is user-specific then it belongs somewhere under the HKEY_CURRENT_USER or the HKEY_USERS root keys.

These are just a few examples of the wealth of data found in the Windows NT/2000 Registry which you can now access and manipulate through the simple and familiar ADO object model!

> **Microsoft has a tendency to change the registry keys and values used to store product configuration data between product versions. In fact, sometimes product configuration data disappears from the Registry completely with new product releases. For this reason, I do not recommend accessing and manipulating product configuration data in the Registry for *production* systems, *unless* there is no API available for accessing and manipulating the data programmatically. This is not an issue with custom configuration data because you are in control of what registry keys and values are used.**

Once the basic functionality of your components is working, you should also test the components with OLE DB services and OLE DB service providers such as the Client Cursor Engine and the Persistence Service.

Debugging our REGOLEDB Provider

Testing not only verifies that a Simple OLE DB Provider supports the required functionality, but it also exposes bugs in the provider. Any experienced developer knows that no matter what you want to call them, bugs, issues or problems do occur. No software is perfect because software is built by imperfect humans. Good coding practices and a thorough design can reduce the number of initial bugs in a simple OLE DB provider; however, sometimes unforeseen issues arise. Since there is no way to avoid all bugs totally, it is important to understand how to resolve them when they do occur. There are three techniques that you can easily apply to debug and resolve problems with simple OLE DB providers:

- ❑ Source code debugging
- ❑ Layer elimination
- ❑ Run-time monitoring

Source Code Debugging

Source code debugging involves debugging software at the source-code level. Debugging a simple OLE DB provider's source code is just like debugging any in-process COM Server. Since we developed our REGOLEDB Provider in Visual Basic, we can simply create a Visual Basic project group containing the REGOLEDB project and another project that tests our REGOLEDB Provider. When the test project is executed, you can step through code, watch the values of variables, and view the call stack between both projects.

> If you are creating simple OLE DB providers in Visual Basic, you might find it extremely helpful to set up a project group and perform testing and debugging *while* you are developing your custom OLE DB Provider.

Layer Elimination

We've seen how a simple OLE DB provider is one in-process COM Server within the sophisticated OSP and OLE DB architectures. Generally, the more layers of components involved, the more likely it is that problems will occur. Layer elimination involves eliminating or removing component layers within a software architecture to track down the source of a problem.

We can apply this layer elimination technique to simple OLE DB providers by eliminating the ADO and MSDAOSP layers between the consumer application and the provider's OSP implementation. As a result, an application would invoke methods on an OSP implementation directly, through the OLEDBSimpleProvider interface and the application could receive notifications by implementing the OLEDBSimpleProviderListener interface. This simplified architecture is depicted in the following diagram:

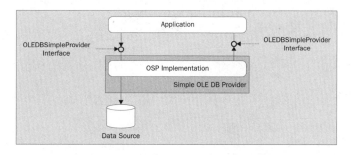

Let's try this layer elimination technique with our REGOLEDB Provider. First start a new **Standard EXE** project in Visual Basic and establish references to the following type libraries and COM servers:

❑ Microsoft OLE DB Simple Provider 1.5 Library (SIMPDATA.tlb)

❑ REGOLEDB – OLE DB Provider for the Windows NT/2000 Registry (REGOLEDB.dll)

Remember, there's no need to establish a reference to the ADODB library because we're going to bypass ADO and the OLE DB Simple Provider (MSDAOSP).

Next let's implement the OLEDBSimpleProviderListener interface in the default form's **General Declarations** section:

```
Implements OLEDBSimpleProviderListener
```

In the form's Load event, declare some procedural variables and create an instance of our REGOLEDB provider's OSP implementation (REGOLEDB.Provider component):

```
Dim objREGOLEDBProvider As REGOLEDB.Provider
Dim objOLEDBSimpleProvider As MSDAOSP.OLEDBSimpleProvider

Dim sSource As String

'create an instance of the REGOLEDB Provider's OSP Implementation
Set objREGOLEDBProvider = New REGOLEDB.Provider
```

Now let's construct an XML-based text command and pass it to our instance of the REGOLEDB.Provider component by calling the DataMember property. This will cause our REGOLEDB Provider to load the dataset containing the registry items found at the location specified in the text command:

```
'build the XML-based text command it's a little easier
'...to construct a string instead of using the MSXML DSO
sSource = "<XMLTextCommand>" & vbCrLf & _
          "<Key>HKEY_LOCAL_MACHINE\SOFTWARE</Key>" & vbCrLf & _
          "<Fields>" & vbCrLf & _
          "<Field>ItemName</Field>" & vbCrLf & _
          "<Field>FullName</Field>" & vbCrLf &_
          "<Field>ItemType</Field>" & vbCrLf & _
          "<Field>Data</Field>" & vbCrLf & _
          "</Fields>" & vbCrLf & "</XMLTextCommand>"

'load the dataset by passing the text command to our
'...Provider component's DataMember property
objREGOLEDBProvider.DataMember = sSource
```

Now w set a reference to the `OLEDBSimpleProvider` interface from our existing instance of the `REGOLEDB.Provider` component and, since this form implemented the `OLEDBSimpleProviderListener` interface, register this form as an OSP listener by calling the `addOLEDBSimpleProviderListener` method:

```
'now acquire a reference to the OLEDBSimpleProvider interface
Set objOLEDBSimpleProvider = objREGOLEDBProvider

'register ourselves as a listener
objOLEDBSimpleProvider.addOLEDBSimpleProviderListener Me
```

From here we can test any operations on our `REGOLEDB` Provider by calling methods on our instance of the `Provider` component through the `OLEDBSimpleProvider` interface, which we have a reference to in the `objOLEDBSimpleProvider` variable. For example, the following code will loop through every column for every record in the dataset and print the row to the debug window:

```
Dim lColumnCount As Long
Dim lRowCount As Long

Dim lColumnCounter As Long
Dim lRowCounter As Long

Dim sTempRow As String

With objOLEDBSimpleProvider
    'get the RowCount and ColumnCount into variables
    lRowCount = .getRowCount
    lColumnCount = .getColumnCount

    For lRowCounter = 0 To lRowCount Step 1
        'loop through each row in the dataset

        'clear the value in our temporary variable
        sTempRow = ""

        For lColumnCounter = 1 To lColumnCount Step 1
            'loop through each column and construct our Row string
            sTempRow = sTempRow & vbTab & _
                        .getVariant(lRowCounter, lColumnCounter, OSPFORMAT_DEFAULT)
        Next lColumnCounter

        'print a string containing the current row's data to the debug window
        Debug.Print sTempRow
    Next lRowCounter
End With

'release our references to the OLEDBSimpleProvider and the default
'...interfaces on our instance of the REGOLEDB.Provider component
Set objOLEDBSimpleProvider = Nothing
Set objREGOLEDBProvider = Nothing
```

Or perhaps you would like to test row insertion and the `aboutToInsertRows` and `insertedRows` notifications by calling the `insertRows` method on the `Provider` component through the `OLEDBSimpleProvider` interface:

```
Dim lRowCount As Long

With objOLEDBSimpleProvider
    'get the RowCount and ColumnCount into variables
    lRowCount = .getRowCount

    'insert a new row in the last location in the dataset
    .insertRows lRowCount + 1, 1
End With

'release our references to the OLEDBSimpleProvider and the default
'...interfaces on our instance of the REGOLEDB.Provider component
Set objOLEDBSimpleProvider = Nothing
Set objREGOLEDBProvider = Nothing
End Sub
```

```
Private Sub OLEDBSimpleProviderListener_aboutToInsertRows(ByVal iRow As Long, _
                                                ByVal cRows As Long)
    MsgBox "aboutToInsertRows" & vbCrLf & _
           "iRow = " & iRow & vbCrLf & _
           "cRows = " & cRows
End Sub
```

```
Private Sub OLEDBSimpleProviderListener_insertedRows(ByVal iRow As Long, _
                                                ByVal cRows As Long)
    MsgBox "insertedRows" & vbCrLf & _
           "iRow = " & iRow & vbCrLf & _
           "crows = " & cRows
End Sub
```

If our application can successfully peform operations on the OSP implementation through the `OLEDBSimpleProvider` interface then the problem might be within ADO or `MSDAOSP`. While problems with ADO and `MSDAOSP` are unlikely, they are always a possiblity. However, if an application cannot successfully perform operations on the OSP implementation then the problem is most likely caused by our simple provider. Either way, the layer elimination debugging technique can direct you to the general source of the problem.

Run-time Monitoring

I like to refer to run-time monitoring as "duck-duck-goose" debugging. Run-time monitoring involves using logging mechanisms to monitor or watch the operations performed by a software application or component at run-time. This debugging technique is particularly useful for troubleshooting in situations in which a debugger is not available, source code is not available, or problems occur that don't appear when the code is run in the debugger. Based on the information logged, you must make an educated guess as to what the problem is and the source of the problem.

In Chapter 11, we saw that Visual Studio Analyzer (VSA), included with Microsoft Visual Studio 6.0, is a powerful tool for monitoring the performance of ADO and SQLOLEDB. However, we can also fire existing and custom VSA events from our REGOLEDB provider. An in-depth discussion about registering and raising VSA events and the VSA programming model is out of the scope of this book; however, included with the REGOLEDB Provider that's available for download from our web site, is a component named VSAnalyzer. The VSAnalyzer component encapsulates all of the required functionality to raise custom VSA events and support registration and unregistration of our REGOLEDB Provider as an event source. Currently, the VSAnalyzer component supports an event for each method defined by the OLEDBSimpleProvider and the IDataSource interfaces. However, the events supported by the VSAnalyzer component can easily be modified. Our Provider component can simply create an instance of the VSAnalyzer component and raise an event by calling a single method on that instance whenever a method is invoked through the OLEDBSimpleProvider interface. For example, the following code calls the FireEvent method on an existing instance of the VSAnalyzer component to raise a VSA event named getColumnCount whenever the getColumnCount method is invoked:

```
Private Function OLEDBSimpleProvider_getColumnCount() As Long
    On Error GoTo ErrorHandler


    'return the number of fields this instance of the
    '...Provider component is exposing
    OLEDBSimpleProvider_getColumnCount = m_lColumnCount

    'raise an VSA Event for this method
    m_objVSAnalyzer.FireEvent "getColumnCount", Array("Return Value"), _
                            Array(CStr(m_lColumnCount))

ExitProcedure:
    'exit this procedure
    Exit Function

ErrorHandler:
    'an error occured, raise it back to the caller
    Err.Raise OLEDBError.DB_E_ERRORSOCCURRED, Source:=App.Title, _
            Description:="An error occured returning the column/field count!"

    'exit this procedure
    Resume ExitProcedure
End Function
```

If the event or the OSP implementation is not registered with VSA, the VSAnalyzer component will gracefully handle any errors when the FireEvent method is called and it will simply continue execution. In production code it is not likely that you would want the overhead of raising a VSA event simply to trace method calls on the OLEDBSimpleProvider interface. However, in some cases, the minimal overhead of raising a VSA event is acceptable, even in production code when you consider the awesome run-time debugging features VSA events provide.

When raising VSA events, we can specify data for any existing or custom fields. All of the data associated with a VSA event is accessible from Visual Studio Analyzer, where it can be sorted, filtered and archived:

Field	Value
Arguments	
Category	REGOLEDB - All Events
Causality ID	{81384953-A1E0-4997-84F8-EFB87468AFAD}
Correlation ID	
Duration	0
Duration (ms)	0
Dynamic Event Data	0
Event	getColumnCount
Exception	
Full Category	REGOLEDB - All Events
Return Value	
Security Identity	Administrator
Source	REGOLEDB
Source Component	REGOLEDB
Source Handle	
Source Machine	JCONARD
Source Process	VB6
Source Process ID	1904
Source Session	REGOLEDB
Source Thread	3d8
Target Component	
Target Handle	
Target Machine	
Target Process	
Target Process ID	0
Target Session	
Target Thread	
Time	1:11:25.473 10/15/99
Type	Outbound

While most of the time information is logged to a file, a database or the Windows NT/2000 Event Log, Visual Studio Analyzer is a very powerful alternative that can aid the debugging of a simple OLE DB provider, or for that matter, of any application or component.

Deploying our REGOLEDB Provider

Now that our REGOLEDB Provider has been tested and debugged, it's time to package it for deployment. We won't start a discussion on using any one particular installation building tool. Almost any utility can satisfy the requirements for deploying a simple OLE DB provider – after all it's just another in-process COM server. However, you do need to be aware of what files should be deployed with a simple provider and where those files are available.

Since we developed our REGOLEDB Provider with Visual Basic 6.0, we must deploy core OLE Automation files and Visual Basic 6.0 run-time files. Although most setup tools will package these files automatically, they are also available as a self-extracting executable from Microsoft's support web-site at http://support.microsoft.com. Please refer to the following Knowledge Base articles for more details:

- ❑ #Q190130 – INFO: Description of VB 6.0 Run Time and OLE Automation Files
- ❑ #Q192461 – FILE: VBRun60.exe Installs Visual Basic 6.0 Run-Time Files
- ❑ #Q235420 – FILE: VBRun60sp3.exe Installs Visual Basic 6.0 Run-Time Files

In addition to the standard Visual Basic 6.0 run-time and OLE Automation files, our REGOLEDB Provider also requires the following files:

Filename	Install location	Description
msdaosp.dll	\Program Files\Common Files\System\OLE DB	OLE DB Simple Provider
msdatsrc.tlb	\WinNT\System32 or \Windows\System	Type library that defines the IDataSource and IDataSourceListener interfaces.
simpdata.tlb	\WinNT\System32 or \Windows\System	Type library that defines the IOLEDBSimpleProvider and IOLEDBSimpleProviderListener interfaces.
msxml.dll	\WinNT\System32 or \Windows\System	The Microsoft XML Parser and Document Object Model (DOM).
msado15.dll	\Program Files\Common Files\System\ADO	The ADODB library that contains all of the ADO components.
oledb32.dll	\Program Files\Common Files\System\OLE DB	The OLE DB Core Services, which also define the standard OLE DB error numbers.

With the exception of msxml.dll and simpdata.tlb, all of these files are included with MDAC 2.5. Version 2.0 of the Microsoft XML Parser (msxml.dll) is installed with Internet Explorer 5.0. An upgrade to version 2.0 is available as a separate download from Microsoft's XML Developer Center located at http://msdn.microsoft.com/downloads/tools/xmlparser/xmlparser.asp. The type library that defines the OSP interfaces (simpdata.tlb) can be downloaded from the Wrox web site. All type libraries and COM servers require registration before they can be used; however, most installation utilities perform registration automatically.

> **If you chose full registration for your simple OLE DB provider, you must also include a registration file with your provider. It's also a good idea always to include a ReadMe file with your component that documents known problems and the provider's behavior and currently supported functionality.**

Summary

In this chapter we turned our knowledge of custom OLE DB providers into wisdom by implementing a fully-functional and quite sophisticated "simple" OLE DB provider for the Windows NT/2000 Registry. Granted, not every custom OLE DB provider requires as much work as our REGOLEDB Provider did. This is especially true with read-only providers, which don't require functionality behind the insertRows, deleteRows and setVariant methods of the OLEDBSimpleProvider interface. However, our REGOLEDB Provider demonstrated almost every feature available to simple OLE DB providers, including data retrieval, data manipulation (insert, update and delete), searching and notifications. During the six steps of the REGOLEDB Provider's development cycle we learned:

❏   Careful design and planning is critical for successfully developing a custom OLE DB provider

❏   XML is ideal for situations in which you need to store or transfer multiple pieces of data within a single string

❏   How to implement hierarchical recordsets with a simple OLE DB provider

❏   The two different registration techniques for simple OLE DB providers – full and partial registration – and the benefits of each

❏   How to establish an ADO connection and open a recordset against a simple OLE DB provider

❏   Three valuable debugging techniques that can be applied to the development of any COM components – source code debugging, layer elimination, and run-time monitoring

Now you're ready to develop your own "simple" OLE DB provider for almost any data source from Excel Spreadsheets or Windows Media content to custom file formats or internet search engines. The possible data sources that can be exposed by custom OLE DB providers are virtually endless. But best of all, by exposing data through OLE DB, you can use the familiar ADO object model to access these data sources regardless of the format, location or structure of the data!

ADO In Action

Working with ADO

There are many things that you can do with ADO – you have read about most of them already. What we are doing in this chapter is providing you with some small samples that you can use in some of your applications as templates or just to give you some ideas during development. We will be putting together a small application that uses several of the aspects of ADO to query and update different type of data. We will try to build on other code examples where possible.

We're going to try to touch a lot of the cool features of ADO here. We will start off with disconnected recordsets and then move to using Index Server and Exchange Server at the end of the chapter.

Disconnected Recordsets

One of the features of ADO that makes it a very useful technology is the concept of a disconnected recordset. As you have seen in previous chapters, a disconnected recordset has several advantages:

❑   You do not hold on to any connections to the database

❑   The recordsets can be passed between objects over the network or through layers of business objects

❑   Small recordsets can be placed in a message queue with MSMQ (recordsets under 2MB in size)

❑   You can persist the data to your disk for later retrieval

The key idea here is that disconnecting a recordset frees up valuable database connections. Connecting to and maintaining connections to a database is a very expensive task. Each connection requires additional resources on the database server, that could be better used with data access such as stored procedures and queries. Keeping connections open unnecessarily also reduces the number of connections allowed depending on current access licenses.

Creating a Middle-Tier Component

We will be creating a middle tier COM component that simply returns a disconnected recordset. While this is not a difficult task, this is a nice piece of code that can be used for templates functions.

Our COM component is being created as an out of process DLL since we may be calling the function over DCOM or out of MTS. All of the code samples in this chapter will be functions within our component.

In order to get started we need to create our base project. Open Visual Basic and select an **ActiveX DLL** project. You will have a project named **Project1** with a class called **Class1**. Obviously these are not very descriptive names, so we need to change them to reflect the purpose of our object. When you are writing COM components you want to get into the habit of creating meaningful names. This will help you to organize your code, and will assist other developers in properly using your components. We will rename the project from **Project1** to **ADOLibrary**. Rename **Class1** to **ADOFunctions**. This gives us a fairly descriptive progID of `ADOLibrary.ADOFunctions`. This is how we will refer to our object when we use the `CreateObject` method to instantiate a component.

Let's take a look at the code needed to create this component.

First, we need to declare some local variables to hold the connection information. This will be used later when we are creating the recordset. Note the first line of code is `OPTION EXPLICIT`. This forces us to declare any variables that we use. It is good programming practice to implement this since Visual Basic will generate an error if you try to use an undeclared function. This is very handy for catching those little spelling errors that you would otherwise miss.

```
OPTION EXPLICIT

'local variable(s) to hold property value(s)
Private m_sConnectionString As String
Private m_sUserName As String 'local copy
Private m_sPassword As String 'local copy
```

These should be pretty clear at this point. We need to know the connection string, username, and password in order to create an ADO `Connection` object. We set these variables though a few basic properties.

```
Public Property Let ConnectionString(ByVal sConnectionString As String)
 m_sConnectionString = sConnectionString
End Property

Public Property Get ConnectionString() As String
 ConnectionString = m_sConnectionString
End Property

Public Property Let Password(ByVal sPassword As String)
 m_sPassword = sPassword
End Property
```

```
Public Property Let UserName(ByVal sUserName As String)
m_sUserName = sUserName
End Property
```

We could have made the variables public and left the property let/get pairs out, but it is good to get in the habit of creating property access methods within COM objects. This makes the code much clearer, and you can later process the data that comes in and goes out of the properties.

The code above should be standard COM that (hopefully) you have seen before. Now we get into the code function in our class module: `ReturnRS`.

We declare the function and our local variables. We need variables for a `Recordset` and a `Connection`.

```
Public Function ReturnRS(sConnectionString as String, sUserName as string, sPassword
as String, sSQL As String) As ADODB.Recordset

Dim cn As ADODB.Connection
Dim rs As ADODB.Recordset
```

Set up an error handler. Some errors that we can anticipate happening are invalid SQL strings and invalid connection strings. We will raise an error in the error handler, and let the client application handle the errors.

```
On Error GoTo ReturnRS_Error
```

Once we have our variables then we need to set them to the appropriate objects.

```
Set cn = New ADODB.Connection
Set rs = New ADODB.Recordset
```

I am often asked why I do not declare my objects with the `New` keyword in the `Dim` statement as such:

```
Dim cn as New ADODB.Connection
```

Generally when you are testing objects you may check to see if the object is set to nothing (meaning that the object has not been created). When you are declaring a `Recordset` object with this syntax and you check to see if the object is set to nothing, ADO will create the object for you, so the object will always be set to a valid object reference and you may run incorrect code. In order to eliminate any issues such as this I prefer to `Dim` my variable on one line and `Set` it on another. This is a documented issue with ADO, and you can find more information in the Microsoft Knowledge Base:

Q189838 – PRB: Next Recordset Never Returns Null or Nothing

If the connection string is blank then we cannot make a connection and we need to exit the function before we do cause an error.

```
If Len(Trim$(sConnectionString)) = 0 Then
 'We need a connection string in order to work
 Err.Raise vbObjectError + 512, "ADOLibrary.ADOFunctions", "You must supply a
connection string"
Exit Function
```

If there is something in the connection string then we will try to create the connection. The first item we need to feed the connection is the `CursorLocation`. We need to set this to `adUseClient`, otherwise we cannot disconnect the recordset.

```
Else
'We need a client cursor in order to disconnect the recordset
cn.CursorLocation = adUseClient

'Open the connection
cn.Open sConnectionString, sUserName, sPassword
```

We can now create the recordset. There are several ways to create a recordset in ADO, but for the example we will use the `Open` method of the recordset. I prefer to use `Open` here since it makes the code a little easier to read. Note that we are setting the locking to `adLockBatchOptimistic` so we can later update the changes we make on the disconnected recordset. We will see an example of updated disconnected data in the next section.

```
'If we set the lock type to adLockBatchOptimistic then we can later
'reconnect the recordset and update the changes that we made offline
rs.Open sSQL, cn, adOpenStatic, adLockBatchOptimistic, adCmdText
```

Since we are disconnecting the recordset, we need to set the `ActiveConnection` property to nothing. This completely disconnects the recordset from the database and allows us to send it to other applications or components.

```
'We are disconnecting the recordset, so we need to disconnect the
'connection to the database
Set rs.ActiveConnection = Nothing
```

All is well so far, so we will return the recordset back to the client.

```
'Return the recordset
Set ReturnRS = rs
End If
```

It is always a good programming practice to clean up after ourselves. Although Visual Basic does a good job of garbage collection, sometimes it needs a little help. Destroying our objects will prevent any problems with resource or memory leaks.

```
'Clean up after ourselves
rs.Close
cn.Close

Set rs = Nothing
Set cn = Nothing

Exit Function
```

If we run into an error then we jump to our error handler. We simply send the error back to the client since we cannot try to fix a problem with the connection string or SQL statement. Any other error would be with the database server being offline or some other problem beyond our control. If there were any errors that we could trap and fix, then we would do so here and issue a resume or resume next statement.

```
ReturnRS_Error:
 Set cn = Nothing
 Err.Raise Err.Number, Err.Source, Err.Description

 End Function
```

This gives you a fairly generic COM component for returning disconnected recordsets. There is a lot more that you can do with this function, but the base functionality exists to use this as-is.

Updating Disconnected Data

In our previous example, we sent back a disconnected recordset that could be updated. If we want to send the changes back to the database then we need to take a few specific steps. We need to verify that we are not generating a conflict between records. As you have seen in earlier chapters, a disconnected recordset has three properties when it is reconnected and resynched with the database: `OriginalValue`, `UnderlyingValue`, and `Value`. We need to be sure that the `UnderlyingValue` and `OriginalValue` are the same, or we have a conflict with the record. We can add this to the COM object that we created in the previous example. If we put this into a new object then we need to copy the local variables and the property declarations.

We start by declaring our function and local variables. We are returning to the client an array of bookmarks for the records that have conflicts. If we were writing a custom business or data object then we would be able to handle certain conflicts (such as a `StockOnHand` field), but since this is generic we need to send the information back to the client so the client can handle the details. The `ArrConflicts()` parameter is set as a variant so we can return a safe array back to the client. We are also declaring a variable of type `ADODB.Field`. We are using this to loop through each field (remember this is a generic function) when we check for conflicts.

```
Public Sub ResyncRecordset (ByVal rsResync As ADODB.Recordset, ByRef ArrConflicts() As
Variant, sConnectionString As String, sUserName As String, sPassword As String)
```

We declare our local variables and counters

```
Dim cn As ADODB.Connection
Dim lConflicts As Long
Dim i As Integer
```

Don't forget to add your error handler to the function. This is always a good programming practice, and you should now be getting into the habit of setting an error handler in your routines.

```
On Error GoTo ResyncRecordset _Error
```

We will instantiate our connection object and open it. This connection is then used to reconnect the recordset back to the database.

```
Set cn = New ADODB.Connection
cn.Open sConnectionString, suserid, sPassword

'Reconnect the recordset
Set rsResync.ActiveConnection = cn
```

First we will see if there are any pending changes, by checking for pending records. If the RecordCount is 0 then we know that there are no pending records, and we can skip over the update code to save processing time.

```
'Filter the recordset for only pending updates
rsResync.Filter = adFilterPendingRecords

'Determine if there are any pending records
If rsResync.RecordCount > 0 Then
```

If there are pending records then we need to update all of the records and check for any errors. We are changing the error handler here so we do not fall into our standard error trapping. We need to check this error and handle it accordingly.

```
'We add this for our UpdateBatch statement
'to check for conflicts
On Error Resume Next

'Update all of the pending records as one batch
rsResync.UpdateBatch adAffectGroup
```

If we get an error then we know that there were some conflicts when updating the records. We will then loop through the conflicts and add the bookmark into our conflict array parameter.

```
If Err Then
  'Filter the recordset for those records that could
  'not be updated due to conflicts
  rsResync.Filter = adFilterConflictingRecords

  'Redim our array to hold the bookmarks of the
  'conflicing records
  ReDim ArrConflicts(rsResync.RecordCount)
```

Loop though each conflicting record and add a bookmark to that record.

```
For i = 0 To rsResync.RecordCount - 1
  'Add the bookmark of each conflict to the array
  ArrConflicts(i) = rsResync.Bookmark
  rsResync.MoveNext
Next

End If
```

Reset our error handler since we now want it to trap further errors.

```
On Error Goto ResyncRecordset_Error

End If
```

We need to disconnect the recordset again since this is the way that it came into us.

```
Set rsResync.ActiveConnection = Nothing
```

Close our connection and set it to nothing so that we are able to clean up after ourselves.

```
   cn.Close

   Set cn = Nothing

   Exit Sub

ResyncRecordset _Error:

   'Re-raise the error if we have one
   Err.Raise Err.Number, Err.Source, Err.Description
```

If we have an error then we will re-raise it back to the client and close the connection. We first need to see if the connection is open. If it is then we close it, otherwise we just destroy the connection object.

```
   'If the connection is open then we want to close it
   If cn.State = adStateOpen Then
     cn.Close
   End If

   Set cn = Nothing

End Sub
```

This now adds a generic function to your object, that allows you to update records or catch conflicts so you can resolve them.

Persisting Recordsets

You may notice that the code sample in this section is very similar to that of the ReturnRS example that we just looked at. This is due to the fact that you need to disconnect a recordset before you persist the recordset to the disk. The beginning of this function is nothing new except for the addition of the sPath, sFile, and OutputFormat parameters.

```
Public Function PersistSQL(ByVal sSQL As String, ByVal sPath As String, ByVal sFileName
As String, OutputFormat As PersistFormatEnum, sConnectionString as String, sUserName
as String, sPassword as String) As Boolean

Dim cn As ADODB.Connection
Dim rs As ADODB.Recordset

Set cn = New ADODB.Connection
Set rs = New ADODB.Recordset

On Error GoTo PersistSQL_Error

If Len(Trim$(sConnectionString)) = 0 Then
'We need a connection string in order to work
PersistSQL = False
Exit Function
Else
'Open the connection
cn.Open sConnectionString, sUserName, sPassword

'We need a client cursor in order to disconnect the recordset
cn.CursorLocation = adUseClient

'If we set the lock type to adLockBatchOptimistic then we can later
'reconnect the recordset and update the changes that we made offline
rs.Open sSQL, cn, adOpenStatic, adLockBatchOptimistic, adCmdText
```

```
'We are disconnecting the recordset, so we need to disconnect the
'connection to the database
Set rs.ActiveConnection = Nothing
If Right$(sPath, 1) <> "\" Then 'Append a \ if necessary
sPath = sPath & "\"
End If
If Len(Dir(sPath & sFileName)) Then
'The file exists. We need to delete it
Kill sPath & sFileName
End If
rs.Save sPath & sFileName, OutputFormat
End If

'Clean up after ourselves
rs.Close
cn.Close

Set rs = Nothing
Set cn = Nothing

PersistSQL = True

Exit Function

PersistSQL_Error:
Err.Raise vbObjectError + 512, Err.Source, Err.Description
PersistSQL = False

End Function
```

There are very few changes to this code overall. We simply build a path and filename from our input parameters and call the `Save` method. The `OutputFormat` parameter is using the ADO constant of `adPersistADTG` (the Microsoft recordset format) or `adPersistXML`, which will persist the data as an XML recordset. The format that you choose really does not make a difference since either type of persisted recordset can be used as a valid data source. Keep in mind that XML stores more information about the actual data, so all XML recordsets will be larger than the ADTG format. Unless you are saving huge resultsets then this should not be a big problem, but if you are sending these over slow connections or over the Internet then you may want to consider the size difference of the two formats.

Dynamically Creating Recordsets

There are times where a recordset is the object that we need, but we do not need the overhead of a database server. ADO allows you to build a recordset without a data provider. This gives you the flexibility and power of a recordset without the need to tie the recordset to a database.

We return an ADO recordset to the client. Within the function we need to declare a variable of type `ADODB.Recordset` to build the recordset.

```
Public Function CreateOfflineRS as ADODB.Recordset

Dim rsDynamic As ADODB.Recordset
```

Always trap for errors.

```
On Error GoTo CreateOfflineRS_Error
```

Set our recordset object, and set the `CursorLocation` property to `adUseClient` since we do not use a data provider.

```
Set rsDynamic = New ADODB.Recordset

rsDynamic.CursorLocation = adUseClient
```

We then use the `Append` method of the `Fields` collection to build the structure of the recordset.

```
'Add all of the fields that you like.
rsDynamic.Fields.Append "FirstName", adVarChar, 50
rsDynamic.Fields.Append "MiddleName", adVarChar, 50
rsDynamic.Fields.Append "LastName", adVarChar, 50
rsDynamic.Fields.Append "Age", adInteger
rsDynamic.Fields.Append "Birthdate", adDate
```

We don't need an active connection. This is overkill since you never set a connection in the first place, but it is consistent with our other code and does not present any problems.

```
Set rsDynamic.ActiveConnection = nothing

Exit Sub
```

Just in case we run into an error, we need to trap it.

```
CreateOfflineRS_Error:

Call Err.Raise(vbObjectError + 512, Err.Source, Err.Description)

End Sub
```

There is a lot you can do with recordsets that do not use a data store. You can still persist the data with the `Save` method, filter the records with the `Filter` property, or add and delete records like you would with a normal recordset. One limitation to offline recordsets is that you are unable to create a recordset that is identical to a database table, and then try to connect the created recordset to the actual table. If you need this ability then you will need to create the recordset based on a connection to the database. Combining the ability to add and update with the ability to persist the data lets you build in client side data storage without resorting to low level file functions.

Data Shaping

In Chapter 6 we built a sample application that displays the data that we retrieve in a `SHAPE` command. It would be very handy to be able to create a function that walks the structure and shows us what the `SHAPE` command looks like from a design perspective. This sample function will do just that. You send in the connection information and the `SHAPE` command, and the `DisplayShapeFormat` function returns a string that is an outline of the `SHAPE` command on a field-by-field basis.

```
Function DisplayShapeFormat (sShapeCommand As String, sConnectionString As String, _
                    sUserName As String, sPassword As String) As String
```

In order for this function to work, we need to get from the user the connection string, username, and password to build the connection and the `SHAPE` command that they want to display. We will return a formatted string with the `SHAPE` outline.

```
Dim cn As ADODB.Connection
Dim rs As ADODB.Recordset
```

We need both a connection and a recordset to get the SHAPE information.

```
Dim sShapeString As String
```

This is a local variable that will be used with our recursive function that 'walks' the recordset. Since we are using recursion in this series of functions, we need to pass the data items as parameters rather than getting a return variable from a function. This string will be passed by reference so we can modify the actual string within the functions.

```
On Error GoTo DisplayShapeFormat_Error
```

As with every other function, we need to set up error handling.

```
sShapeString = ""

Set cn = New ADODB.Connection
Set rs = New ADODB.Recordset
cn.Provider = "MSDataShape"
cn.Open sConnectionString, sUserName, sPassword
```

We connect to our data source. We have added the call to the Provider property just in case the user is not fully aware that data shaping requires two providers. If the user does specify a proper connection string for data shaping then this property is ignored. See Chapter 6 for more information on building a connection string for data shaping.

```
rs.Open sShapeCommand, cn, adOpenStatic, adLockReadOnly, adCmdText
```

We open our recordset with the SHAPE command that was sent into the function. There is a good possibility that we can run into an error here with an invalid SHAPE command. If we do then we will fall into our error handling routine.

```
RecurseShapeRS rs, 0, sShapeString
```

This makes the first call to our recursive function. We are sending the recordset, the level to be used for indentation of our return string, and the string that will be modified within the function.

```
rs.Close
cn.Close
Set rs = Nothing
Set cn = Nothing

DisplayShapeFormat = sShapeString
```

We clean up and release the memory that our objects used, and we close our recordset and connection. We then return the local string that we passed into our recursive function as the return value.

```
    Exit Function

    DisplayShapeFormat_Error:

    Err.Raise Err.Number, Err.Source, Err.Description

    If rs.State = adStateOpen Then
    rs.Close
    End If

    If cn.State = adStateOpen Then
    cn.Close
    End If

    Set rs = Nothing
    Set cn = Nothing

    End Function
```

If we happen to run into an error then we will go through the error trapping above.

The next function is the recursive function that walks the recordset and draws the shape of the recordset.

```
    Sub RecurseShapeRS(ByVal rs As ADODB.Recordset, ByVal Level As Long, _
                                        ByRef sFormat As String)
```

We need the shaped recordset, the level (used for indentation of the string), and the string that we will be populating.

```
    Dim I As Integer

    For I = 0 To rs.Fields.Count - 1
```

We will loop though each field in the recordset.

```
    If sFormat = "" Then
    sFormat = Space$(Level * 3) & rs(I).Name
    Else
    sFormat = sFormat & vbCrLf & Space$(Level * 3) & rs(I).Name
    End If
```

We append the name of the field with the string along with the indentation level. If we have a child recordset then the field names will be indented three spaces for clarity. We indent three additional spaces for each level of our recordset.

```
    If rs(I).Type = adChapter Then
    RecurseShapeRS rs(I).Value, Level + 1, sFormat
```

If the field type is `adChapter` then we have a child recordset. All child recordsets within a shaped recordset are of the chapter data type, so we need to call our function again since we are now displaying another recordset. We add one to the level since we are entering a new level in the hierarchy of the recordset. We continue to pass out formatting strings to the functions ,so that we will be able to populate the string with all of the field values.

```
End If
Next I
```

We continue to loop through the fields in the current recordset. When we finish the last recursive call then our string will display all of the data for our `SHAPE` command. We could expand this by adding the data types of each field (which would make this function even more useful) or generate a nicer report of the `shape` of the recordset using some graphical images.

```
End Sub
```

Combining this function with the sample shaping application that we built in Chapter 6 will be very handy tools for you to use when utilizing shaped recordsets within your application.

ADOX – ActiveX Data Objects Extensions for DDL

The ADOX library gives a developer the ability to programmatically create and modify databases. This base function can be used with an application to create a database if it does not exist. You can also use these libraries to convert from one database to another. For instance, you can use the ADOX library to open a DB2 database and convert each object to a SQL Server object. This library is also handy for listing items such as users (which we will be building a function for) and querying other objects within the database other than tables and data-centric objects.

Our first set of functions can be used to build a table within a database.

```
Option Explicit

Private objCatalog As ADOX.Catalog

Public Function CreateDatabase(strConnectionString As String) As Boolean

On Error GoTo CreateDatabase_Error

'Create an empty catalog object
Set objCatalog = New ADOX.Catalog
```

This creates the catalog object that is the main container object for the database which we will be utilizing. Not all providers support the full ADOX extensions, so you need to be careful when writing generic ADOX functions. Currently only the OLEDB Provider for Jet databases supports all of the ADOX extensions, but look for more providers to add this ability as ADO continues to grow in importance.

```
'Call the method on ADOX.Catalog
Call objCatalog.Create(strConnectionString)
```

We create the catalog object from the connection string that is passed into our function.

```
CreateDatabase = True
```

If there are no errors then we return a `True` value otherwise we fall into our error handling and raise the appropriate error:

```
Exit Function

CreateDatabase_Error:

CreateDatabase = False
Call Err.Raise(vbObjectError + 512, Err.Source, Err.Description)

End Function
```

Our first utility function lists the users in a database. These ADOX function can be used to build an administrative toolkit for your databases. It is easy to see the tables, views, and stored procedures within a database. It is much more difficult to get a list of the valid users within a database. If you are upsizing or converting a database then you will want to convert the security information as well or you will be spending a lot of time adding the users back into the system. You can access the `GetPermissions` and `SetPermissions` methods to create a security upsizing wizard for your databases. We will look at getting the list of users in a group, and then reading the permissions for the user for each table in the database.

```
Public Function CreateTable(strTableName As String) As Boolean

Dim tbl As ADOX.Table
Dim col As ADOX.Column
Dim indx As ADOX.Index

On Error GoTo CreateTable_Error:

Set tbl = New ADOX.Table
tbl.Name = strTableName

'Add the newly created method to the tables collection.
objCatalog.Tables.Append tbl

'Add all of the columns that you like.
Call tbl.Columns.Append("FirstName", adVarChar, 255)
Call tbl.Columns.Append("MiddleName", adVarChar, 255)
Call tbl.Columns.Append("LastName", adVarChar, 255)
Call tbl.Columns.Append("Age", adInteger, 255)
Call tbl.Columns.Append("Birthdate", adDate)

'Create an index.
Set indx = New ADOX.Index

indx.Clustered = False
indx.Columns.Append "LastName"
indx.Name = "LastNameIndex"
'Make the index the primary key of the table.
indx.PrimaryKey = True

tbl.Indexes.Append indx

CreateTable = True
```

```
Exit Function

CreateTable_Error:

CreateTable = False
Call Err.Raise(vbObjectError + 512, Err.Source, Err.Description)

End Function
```

We have demonstrated how ADOX can operate on the internal structure of a database, now let's look at how ADOX can be used to look at the security within a database. Our next function will list all the groups, users, and permissions for a database. This will give you a base report that cannot easily be extracted from SQL Server or Microsoft Access.

```
Private Function GetRights(sConnectionString As String, sUserName As String, sPassword
As String) As String

Dim oCatalog As ADOX.Catalog
```

The catalog object is the base object for using ADOX. This will expose the internal database information to us.

```
Dim oConnection As ADODB.Connection
```

We need a connection to the database in order to access the internal structure.

```
Dim oUser As ADOX.User
Dim oGroup As ADOX.Group
Dim oTable As ADOX.Table
```

We will be looping through the tables, groups, and users in the database. These will be used in For...Each loops to run though the collections.

```
Dim lRights As Long
Dim sRights As String
Dim sOutput As String
```

These are the additional temporary variables that we will be using to store information during the processing of our function. The names should be self-explanatory.

```
On Error GoTo GetRights_Error
```

We enable error handling since we do not know if the provider will expose all of the ADOX functionality, or if the connection string is valid.

```
Set oConnection = New ADODB.Connection

oConnection.Open sConnectionString, sUserName, sPassword

Set oCatalog = New ADOX.Catalog
oCatalog.ActiveConnection = oConnection
```

We open our connection and our catalog.

```
With oCatalog
For Each oGroup In .Groups
```

We will loop through the groups, then the users, and finally the tables. We will be displaying this information in an indented format so that it is easier to see.

```
sOutput = sOutput & "GROUP:" & oGroup.Name & vbCrLf
For Each oUser In .Users
```

The users collection contains all of the users (or logins) within the database.

```
sOutput = sOutput & Space$(1) & "USER:" & oUser.Name & vbCrLf
For Each oTable In .Tables
```

Once we have drilled down to the user level, we can start looping through the tables in the database, and get the security information for each user. We could also go through the views, stored procedures, and other objects, but we are just going to loop though the tables since our function is already fairly long.

```
sOutput = sOutput & Space$(2) & "TABLE:" & oTable.Name & vbCrLf
lRights = oUser.GetPermissions(oTable.Name, adPermObjTable)
```

The `GetPermissions` method will return a long integer with the user rights information. The user rights are ANDable values such that we need to see if the returned value contains a specific right. The next set of code will look at the value returned by the `GetPermissions` method and build the string of rights that the user has. You could easily build a function for each right and check it individually.

```
If lRights = adRightNone Then
sRights = "No rights"
Else
If lRights And adRightExecute = adRightExecute Then
sRights = sRights & "Execute" & ","
End If
If lRights And adRightRead = adRightRead Then
sRights = sRights & "Read" & ","
End If
If lRights And adRightUpdate = adRightUpdate Then
sRights = sRights & "Update" & ","
End If
If lRights And adRightInsert = adRightInsert Then
sRights = sRights & "Insert" & ","
End If
If lRights And adRightDelete = adRightDelete Then
sRights = sRights & "Delete" & ","
End If
If lRights And adRightReference = adRightReference Then
sRights = sRights & "Reference" & ","
End If
If lRights And adRightCreate = adRightCreate Then
sRights = sRights & "Rights-Create" & ","
End If
If lRights And adRightWithGrant = adRightWithGrant Then
sRights = sRights & "Rights-Grant" & ","
End If
If lRights And adRightReadDesign = adRightReadDesign Then
sRights = sRights & "Design-Read" & ","
End If
```

```
If lRights And adRightWriteDesign = adRightWriteDesign Then
sRights = sRights & "Design-Write" & ","
End If
If lRights And adRightWriteOwner = adRightWriteOwner Then
sRights = sRights & "Change Owner" & ","
End If
If lRights And adRightFull = adRightFull Then
sRights = sRights & "Full Rights" & ","
End If
If lRights And adRightExclusive = adRightExclusive Then
sRights = sRights & "Exclusive" & ","
End If
If lRights And adRightMaximumAllowed = adRightMaximumAllowed Then
sRights = sRights & "Maximum Rights" & ","
End If
If lRights And adRightDrop = adRightDrop Then
sRights = sRights & "Drop" & ","
End If
If lRights And adRightReadPermissions = adRightReadPermissions Then
sRights = sRights & "Permissions-View" & ","
End If
If lRights And adRightWritePermissions = adRightWritePermissions Then
sRights = sRights & "Permissions-Modify" & ","
End If
End If

If Right$(sRights, 1) = "," Then
sRights = Left$(sRights, Len(sRights) - 1)
End If
```

This long series of code individually ANDs a value with the current permission settings. When writing a function you may find it to be important to know if the user has full access, or no access, or any combination. Any section of code above can be used to check if a specific permission setting for a user had been set.

```
sOutput = sOutput & Space$(3) & sRights & vbCrLf & vbCrLf
sRights = ""
Next
Next
Next
End With

GetRights = sOutput
```

We finish concatenating the output string and send the value back to the calling application. Once that is complete we can then use the following code to clean up and release the memory that was in use.

```
oConnection.Close

Set oCatalog = Nothing
Set oConnection = Nothing

Exit Function
```

If we happen to hit an error, we fall into our error trapping and simply re-raise the error and release the memory for the objects.

```
GetRights_Error:
Err.Raise Err.Number, Err.Source, Err.Description
Set oCatalog = Nothing
Set oConnection = Nothing

End Function
```

There is obviously a lot more to ADOX than we've covered here, but you have an example of modifying a structure as well as querying the security of a system. These can get you started on creating your own specific functions to manipulate and interrogate your database.

ADO and LDAP

LDAP or the Lightweight Directory Access Protocol is an Internet standard for an interface to a directory service. Microsoft Exchange and Windows 2000 are Active Directory providers. These providers allow you to look up user and object information within a data store. In Exchange, for example, you can use ADO to query for a user or in Windows 2000 (or Windows NT 4.0 with ADSI installed), you can query for a user in a domain, a printer, or a computer.

We will look at some code samples that demonstrate how you would look up this information. Our first example will look up users in Exchange, and the second example will demonstrate a search for a network resource.

Querying Microsoft Exchange

Microsoft Exchange can be queried though ADO by using the ADsDSOObject provider. This is the generic ADSI provider that can be used with Exchange, Site Server, or any other LDAP aware system. We are going to put together a simple function that returns the Exchange data for a specific user. Keep in mind that this code can also be used for the other Microsoft LDAP systems. In order for our function to work, we need to pass in an LDAP path (LDAP://<Server>/o=<organization>) and the user that we are getting information on. In return we get back an ADO Recordset with the user's information.

> Whenever you use any LDAP provider you need to be sure that the LDAP port is open. Your system administrator can assist you with configuring this along with the appropriate security settings.

Our first code sample is the function that will actually query Microsoft Exchange for the user information. We will follow this up with a sample function that calls the first function.

```
Function GetExchangeInfo(sLDAPPath As String, sUserName As String) As ADODB.Recordset

On Error GoTo GetExchangeInfo_Error
```

As always, we need to have some error trapping in our code.

```
Const ADS_SCOPE_SUBTREE = 2
```

631

We define this constant to be used later. This lets ADO know the physical scope of the search. There are three valid constants that are declared in the ADO library:

- ☐ ADS_SCOPE_BASE

- ☐ ADS_SCOPE_ONELEVEL

- ☐ ADS_SCOPE_SUBTREE

```
Set cn = CreateObject("ADODB.Connection")
Set cmd = CreateObject("ADODB.Command")
```

Since we are using ADO we will need a connection object. We will also be using a command object to return the results.

```
cn.Provider = "ADsDSOObject"
```

The `ADsDSOObject` is the data provider for ADSI.

```
cn.Open "Active Directory Provider"
```

We open the ADO connection to the active directory.

```
Set cmd.ActiveConnection = cn
```

Our command needs an active connection. We will use the connection object that we just built.

```
cmd.CommandText = "select ADsPath, uid, title, givenName, sn,
physicalDeliveryOfficeName,telephoneNumber from '" & sLDAPPath & "' where uid='" &
sUserName & "'"
```

The `sLDAPPath` must be a valid LDAP syntax. We will see an example of valid syntax in the next function, but you may want to refer to your LDAP provider documentation since the organizational structure of the LDAP server will dictate the full length of the path. One important note about the LDAP syntax: the recordset is in the reverse order of the select list. Our recordset will have `telephoneNumber`, `physicalDeliveryOfficeName`, `sn`, `givenName`, `title`, `uid`, and `AdsPath` as the recordset field order.

```
cmd.Properties("Page Size") = 100
cmd.Properties("Timeout") = 60
```

We set the timeout to 60 seconds.

```
cmd.Properties("searchscope") = ADS_SCOPE_SUBTREE
```

Here is where we set the scope of the search of the active directory.

```
cmd.Properties("Cache Results") = False
```

You typically do not want to cache the results of the query since this will decrease overall performance, and there is usually little likelihood of the cache being utilized. This may come in handy if you query the same user many times.

```
Set GetExchangeInfo = cmd.Execute
```

We execute the command and return the results to the calling application.

```
Set cmd = Nothing
Set cn = Nothing
```

We clean up after ourselves and exit the function.

```
Exit Sub
```

If we happen to get an error, (an invalid LDAP path and invalid user will be the most common errors) then we fall into the error trapping where we re-raise the error to the calling application.

```
GetExchangeInfo_Error:

Err.Raise Err.Number, Err.Source, Err.Description

If cn.state = adStateOpen then
 cn.close
End if

Set cmd = Nothing
Set cn = Nothing

End Function
```

We have a handy application for looking up the user, now let's look at an example of calling our function:

```
Dim rs As ADODB.Recordset
Dim fld As ADODB.Field

Set rs = New ADODB.Recordset
```

The above lines should be easy for you to understand at this point.

```
Set rs = GetExchangeInfo("LDAP://Screamer/o=OOCS", "BrianMat")
```

We call our function and pass in the information about the LDAP path, (Screamer is the Exchange Server and o=OOCS is the organization that I am looking up), the next function is the username (Exchange alias name) that we would like to see. All we want to do at this point is loop through the resulting recordset and see the fields and values that are returned. We do this though a standard for each loop.

```
Do While Not rs.EOF
For Each fld In rs.Fields
Debug.Print fld.Name & " : " & fld.Value
Next
rs.MoveNext
Loop
```

The output in the debug window on my machine is as follows:

```
telephoneNumber : 704-763-8633
physicalDeliveryOfficeName :
sn : Matsik
givenName : Brian
title : Senior Consultant
uid : BrianMat
ADsPath : LDAP://Screamer/cn=BrianMat,cn=Recipients,ou=CHARLOTTE,o=OOCS
```

We can use this base functionality to query any LDAP provider as long as we are asking for columns that are valid to the LDAP provider (see your documentation for a list of valid fields) and the user is in the correct format for the LDAP provider.

Index Server

Microsoft Index Server comes with Internet Information Server in the Windows NT Option Pack and with IIS 5.0 as part of Windows 2000. Index Server is used to index the contents of a site (similar to Yahoo, Lycos, Excite, etc.). Microsoft has released an OLEDB provider for Index Server that allows developers to search for content using a more friendly SELECT style syntax. We have put together an example ASP page that lets a user search the Index Server database for pages that contain specific content.

```
<%@ Language=VBScript %>
<%
OPTION EXPLICIT

on error resume next

dim cn
dim rs
dim sSQL
dim sSearchString
dim iPos
```

We do not need to declare our variables, but it is always good practice to do so. If you want to be sure that all of your variables are declared before the page can use them then add the OPTION EXPLICIT declaration at the beginning of your ASP code. An error will be generated if you try to use a variable that has not been declared.

```
set cn = server.CreateObject("adodb.connection")
set rs = server.CreateObject("adodb.recordset")

cn.ConnectionString = "provider=msidxs;"
cn.Open
```

We use the same connection and recordset types that we would in any other ADO application. The main difference is the provider that we use. Microsoft Index Server uses the `msidxs` provider for accessing the data store.

```
sSearchString = Request.Form("txtQueryString")
```

We use `sSearchString` as a temporary variable to store the search criteria. We do this for two reasons. The first is that it is much less typing to use a shorter name, and we do not continue to make calls to objects for the static property information. At this point the `sSearchString` variable contains the data that was fed to our page through the form. In an ideal world you would like to create a full featured parser function that would format the user's search string to allow them to put quotation marks or parentheses for grouped names (such as 'Windows NT' AND 'Index Server' versus Windows AND NT AND Index AND Server'). If the user sends us a string that has spaces and no Boolean operators then the page will fail when we query the string. This is the reason for the ON ERROR RESUME NEXT statement in the code. We do check for the OLEDB error of –2147217900.

```
if sSearchString <> "" then
sSQL = "SELECT FileName, Rank, DocTitle, Size, vPath "
sSQL = sSQL & "from SCOPE() WHERE CONTAINS "
sSQL = sSQL & " ('" & Replace(sSearchString, "'", """") & "') > 0 "
sSQL = sSQL & "ORDER BY Rank DESC"
rs.Open sSQL, cn
end if
```

There are several items we can add in our SELECT statement (note that * is not one of them). Here is a list of some of the more common items that can be used in the SELECT statement with an Index Server query:

Attribute or Property	Meaning
Contents	Words or phrases in the document. This is the default if no other attribute or property is specified.
Create	The date and time that the file was originally created.
DocAuthor	The Author property for the document.
DocComments	The value of the Comments property for that document
DocKeywords	The keywords specified for that document.
DocPageCount	The number of pages in the document.
DocSubject	The Subject property for that document.
DocTitle	The Title property for the document.
Filename	The name of the file.
HitCount	The number of hits for the content search in the document.
Path	The actual path and file name of the document.
Rank	The relative matching score for the query, from 0 to 1000.

Table Continued on Following Page

Attribute or Property	Meaning
Size	The size of the file in bytes.
Vpath	The server's virtual path and file name for the document.
Write	The date and time that the file was last updated.

```
if err.number = -2147217900 then
'We have an improperly formatted search string.
end if

%>
```

We are using a form that posts back to itself. This is a fairly common practice in ASP coding where the page is not very complex. We reduce the time required to load a second page, and we reduce the overall number of pages in our application.

```
<HTML>
<HEAD>
<META NAME="GENERATOR" Content="Microsoft Visual Studio 6.0">
</HEAD>
<BODY>
```

We have our standard HTML header information here.

```
<form method=post action=QueryIndexServer.asp>
<INPUT type="text" id=txtQueryString name=txtQueryString>
<INPUT type="submit" value="Submit" id=submit1 name=submit1>
<INPUT type="reset" value="Reset" id=reset1 name=reset1>
</form>
```

This is the form that we will use for our query. We have simply added a textbox for the query, a submit button, and a reset button. You could easily add an advanced search page that lets the user build complex queries.

```
<%

if sSearchString <> "" and err.number = 0 then
```

If we have entered something in the search box and we have not received an error due to a syntax issue, then we need to proceed into creating our output information.

```
Response.Write("<BR><HR><BR>")
Response.Write("Searching for: " & sSearchString & "<BR>")
Response.Write("<table border=1>")
Response.Write("<TR><THEAD>")
Response.Write("<TD>" & "File" & "</TD>")
Response.Write("<TD>" & "Rank" & "</TD>")
Response.Write("<TD>" & "Title" & "</TD>")
Response.Write("<TD>" & "Size" & "</TD>")
Response.Write("</TR></THEAD>")
do while not rs.EOF
Response.Write("<TR>")
Response.Write("<TD>" & "<A HREF=" & rs("vPath").value & ">" & rs("FileName").value &
"</A>" & "</TD>")
```

Here we are building a link where the user can navigate to the page directly from the results table. The vPath field contains a relative URL to the page on our site.

```
Response.Write("<TD>" & rs("Rank").value & "</TD>")
```

The rank field gives us a relative hit percentage that we can use to determine how relevant the page is to our search. Users like to know if this page just happened to get a hit, but is almost guaranteed to be irrelevant, or if a page has enough hits to be a sure bet.

```
Response.Write("<TD>" & rs("DocTitle").value & "</TD>")
Response.Write("<TD>" & round((cdbl(rs("Size").value) / 1000), 1) & "kb" & "</TD>")
```

Here we determine the file size. We should always let the user know how big the page is so they know what to expect. There is little that is more frustrating than to wait for a huge page to download just to find out that the contents are irrelevant to our intended search.

```
rs.MoveNext
Response.Write("</TR>")
loop
Response.Write("</table>")

rs.Close
cn.Close
end if

set rs=nothing
set cn=nothing
```

We always like to clean up our variable to avoid potential memory leaks.

```
%>

</BODY>
</HTML>
```

And finally we close our HTML and ASP tags for the page.

This example is still lacking some key functionality, especially that of formatting a user's query. But, you can see that this example exposes to you the base functionality required to access Index Server and start working toward a full-featured search page.

Putting It All Together

It is very difficult to come up with an ADO sample that displays most of the functionality that ADO has to offer. What we will do is take the functions that we put together in the previous part of this chapter, and build an application that will let us query several ADO data sources. A generic tool such as this can be very handy for a developer since there are many times when we need to get to data to verify connections or the underlying data in our data store.

The application that we will be putting together will let us query LDAP (Exchange), IIS Index Server, any SQL database, and will also allow for data shaping. We will be able to persist our data to the hard drive and later open the data file and view it within the grid on the main form. All of this is very useful from a development and testing standpoint. My web applications rely on data shaping for reporting and displaying data and it is critical to be able to view and retrieve my test data easily. Other times I need to see before and after snapshots of my data. We will be able to address those issues here. I will also show you how to get that handy connection builder wizard from Visual Studio integrated into your applications. You will be surprised how easy it is to be able to do this.

First, let's take a look at the main window of the application. There is not a lot there initially:

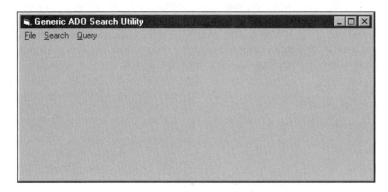

We do have several key items under the menus though.

First, the File menu:

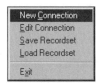

The New Connection and Edit Connection choices will invoke the connection builder wizard. This will allow you to dynamically create a connection within your application without manually typing the connection string or using another tool such as the Visual Basic data environment to do so for you.

Save Recordset and Load Recordset will let us persist the recordset and load it from the disk. This lets us look at before and after pictures of our data or lets us look at the data when we are not connected to the database system. These are items that you may use more and more, with client/server systems where the workforce is often offline, such as a traveling sales force. ADO can persist any type of recordset, so you could persist all of the sales information for a specific client or even download information from the Exchange server before you go on the road. There are many practical uses for persisted data.

Under the Search menu we have LDAP and IIS. LDAP will actually query the Exchange data store. You could adapt this to call a generic LDAP provider simply by utilizing only the commonly named fields between the different LDAP providers or adding an additional list of LDAP provider information. We have limited ourselves to Exchange only for simplicity. There are some great examples of generic ADSI/LDAP queries as well as Exchange and Site Server specific queries in the ADSI SDK. Many of these do not yet use ADO – they use the ADSI interface. The ADSI provider for ADO is still new on the scene and has not yet gained the wide acceptance of all developers since the LDAP provider is currently read-only with all recordsets. As Microsoft enhances the LDAP OLEDB provider you should see more developers moving to ADO for these queries if for no other reason than consistency with data access which is all part of the Universal Data Access initiative from Microsoft. UDA gives developers a common and very familiar data access mechanism, and more developers are moving to ADO for just that reason – simplicity and uniformity.

Finally, we have the Query menu. We can use the choices here to take our recordset offline (disconnect) and reconnect the recordset later. This is different to persisting the data since disconnecting the recordset simply frees the data connection but still keeps the recordset in memory. The Normal SQL Provider item is for accessing traditional data stores with a read/write data grid. The Data Shape option is specifically designed to handle shaped recordsets and utilize the hierarchical FlexGrid control, which is read-only. You can access a standard Select query from the Data Shape option, but you cannot execute a SHAPE command from the Normal SQL Provider option.

If we call a shaped recordset then the HFlexGrid will be populated with the records

If we call the following SHAPE command using the Northwind sample database available with Access or SQL Server:

```
SHAPE {SELECT * FROM "dbo"."Customers"} AS rsCustomers APPEND (( SHAPE {SELECT * FROM
"dbo"."Orders"} AS rsOrders APPEND ({SELECT OrderID, ProductID, UnitPrice * Quantity AS
LineTotal FROM [Order Details]} AS rsOrderDetails RELATE 'OrderID' TO 'OrderID') AS
rsOrderDetails, SUM(rsOrderDetails.'LineTotal') AS OrderTotal) AS rsOrders RELATE
'CustomerID' TO 'CustomerID') AS rsOrders, SUM(rsOrders.'OrderTotal') AS TotalSales
```

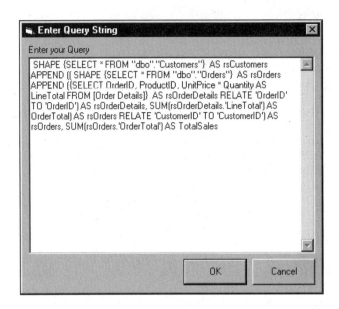

Our main form will populate with the SHAPE command recordsets in the FlexGrid control.

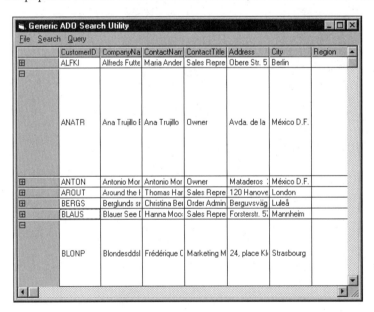

If we attempt to execute the SHAPE command without setting the connection information then we are immediately greeted by the connection builder wizard:

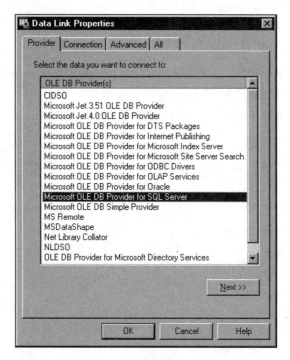

Neat, huh? No more fumbling with connection strings or trying to manually loop though a shaped recordset. The code behind the menu option is rather simple and very similar to that from the sample application in our earlier Data Shaping chapter.

```
Private Sub mnuQueryDataShape_Click()
```

Our SQL string is declared as static so we can send it to the query input form for later modification. This allows us to maintain different SQL statements for the many different ADO functions that we can have. Since some of the syntax for generating a recordset is different, we want to have a quick way to pull in the existing text without fumbling around with the slight syntax variations that we may need to deal with.

```
Static sSQL As String

Me.MousePointer = vbHourglass

On Error Resume Next
```

If our ConnectionString is blank (we have initialized this variable in the Form_Load event), then we need to build the connection object. The easiest way to do this is to invoke the connection wizard. We call the code that is in the File | New Connection menu to do this.

```
If cn.ConnectionString = "" Then
Call mnuFileNewConnection_Click
cn.ConnectionString = "Provider=MSDataShape;Data " & cn.ConnectionString
End If
```

Once we have the connection string set up we need to append the data shaping specific information on the beginning of the string. Remember that a data shape connection needs a provider and a data provider entry. The code for `mnuFileNewConnection` follows this code listing.

```
sSQL = frmDataShape.GetQueryString(sSQL)
```

The `GetQueryString` method calls the input form we use for all SQL commands. We have created this method to allow us to pass back the SQL information for processing. The `sSQL` parameter is optional and is only used if we want the query textbox to be populated with the last query string that we used (hence the need for static variables).

```
If sSQL <> "" Then
If cn.State = adStateClosed Then
cn.Open
End If
```

If the `GetQueryString` returns a string then we will process the rest of the function, otherwise we drop to the end of the function. We do this because the user may not enter a string or may cancel the form without inputting a string. Note that we are not verifying the syntax before we execute, simply because it is easier to trap the error for an invalid SQL string than it is to write our own data shape parser.

If the recordset object is open (the recordset is global to the application), then we need to close it and re-open with our new SQL statement.

```
If rs.State = adStateOpen Then
rs.Close
End If

rs.Open sSQL, cn, adOpenStatic, adLockBatchOptimistic, adCmdText
```

The most common error we will get is an invalid SHAPE command. If we entered an invalid command then we will send the error to the user.

```
If Err Then
MsgBox "Error - " & Err.Number & ":" & Err.Description
Err.Clear
End If
```

If we go through the check then we will set the FlexGrid `DataSource` property to the recordset object. Note that I use `hfg` for hierarchical FlexGrid, so the notation may be a bit confusing in the beginning.

```
Set hfgRSShape.DataSource = rs
```

If there are any problems then we will let the user know here. Otherwise we need to show the FlexGrid and hide the data grid.

```
If Err Then
MsgBox "Error - " & Err.Number & ":" & Err.Description
Err.Clear
End If

hfgRSShape.Visible = True
dgRSGrid.Visible = False
End If

Me.MousePointer = vbNormal

End Sub
```

That is all we need to do to display the contents of a shaped recordset, and create a connection object for building the connection object if it does not exist. Remember that we simply called the menu code to generate the connection wizard. Let's look at the actual code behind the menu option.

```
Private Sub mnuFileNewConnection_Click()

Dim oDataLink As MSDASC.DataLinks
Set oDataLink = New MSDASC.DataLinks

On Error Resume Next

Set cn = oDataLink.PromptNew

Set oDataLink = Nothing

End Sub
```

I told you that you would be surprised by how easy it is to display the wizard. Just be sure that you have included the Microsoft OLE DB Service Component 1.0 Type Library, or just late bind the object. I prefer the early bound method especially in a development application, or when using a library that I am unfamiliar with. Early binding gives you the Intellesense on the actual objects. This is a big time saver on new libraries. If I am writing an application that should utilize late binding then I will write the code early bound and simply change the object creation code with the late binding `CreateObject` method.

There is a cool trick that you can use to impress the other developers on your team. I like to add this code into test applications just so I can quickly create or modify a connection object. If you want to modify an existing connection object then just change the `PromptNew` method. As you see in the `mnuFileEditConnection` code we are modifying the active connection object:

```
Private Sub mnuFileEditConnection_Click()

Dim oDataLink As MSDASC.DataLinks
Set oDataLink = New MSDASC.DataLinks

On Error Resume Next

oDataLink.PromptEdit cn

Set oDataLink = Nothing

End Sub
```

This is essentially the same code as the `mnuFileNewConnection` code with the exception that we are calling `PromptEdit` rather than `PromptNew`.

The function to generate a regular recordset from a traditional relational database is almost identical to the data `shape` code except that we use a standard data grid to display the data so we can make modifications.

```
Static sSQL As String

Me.MousePointer = vbHourglass

On Error Resume Next

If cn.ConnectionString = "" Then
Call mnuFileNewConnection_Click
End If

sSQL = frmDataShape.GetQueryString(sSQL)

If sSQL <> "" Then
If cn.State = adStateClosed Then
cn.Open
End If

If rs.State = adStateOpen Then
rs.Close
End If

If Err Then
MsgBox "Error - " & Err.Number & ":" & Err.Description
Err.Clear
End If
```

We are using an ADO data control for some additional flexibility. We also need to call the `Rebind` method of the data grid to rebind all of the columns to the new data source.

```
Adodc1.ConnectionString = cn.ConnectionString
Adodc1.RecordSource = sSQL
Adodc1.Refresh
dgRSGrid.ReBind
```

```
dgRSGrid.Visible = True
hfgRSShape.Visible = False
End If

Me.MousePointer = vbNormal

End Sub
```

I cheated a bit here by using an ADO data control as an intermediate step to populating the data grid, but I typically do this just out of old habit. You could skip this step and assign the recordset to the grid, but I always feel that I can use a data control to expose most of the connection and recordset objects that would require an ADO recordset and connection object. This also eliminates another global variable and additional setup code for the connection and recordset objects that I would otherwise have to use.

Our menu choices give us the ability to persist and load a recordset as well. If we want to persist the recordset then we simple select the File | Save Recordset menu choice and it executes its code:

```
Private Sub mnuFileSaveRecordset_Click()

On Error Resume Next
```

Before we save a recordset we need to be sure it is disconnected. We disconnect the recordset by setting the `ActiveConnection` property to nothing.

```
rs.ActiveConnection = Nothing
```

We are calling the common dialog control and executing the `ShowSave` method to get the Windows standard save dialog.

```
CommonDialog1.ShowSave
```

If the filename property is blank then the user canceled the dialog, so we do not want to call any of the other save code. If they did provide a filename then we call the `Save` method of the recordset.

```
If CommonDialog1.FileName = "" Then
Else
```

We need to delete the file before we call `Save` if it exists on the system. If not, the `Save` method will generate an error since it does not automatically overwrite the file. We are saving the format as the ADTG format, but we could have easily modified this function to save in XML format by modifying the second parameter to be `adPersistXML`.

```
Kill CommonDialog1.FileName
rs.Save CommonDialog1.FileName, adPersistADTG
End If

End Sub
```

When we want to load a recordset we call the code behind the File | Load Recordset method.

```
Private Sub mnuFileLoadRecordset_Click()

CommonDialog1.ShowOpen
```

If the recordset is open then we need to close it.

```
If rs.State = adStateOpen Then
rs.Close
End If
```

Just in case there is an active connection on the recordset then we need to close it.

```
rs.ActiveConnection = Nothing
rs.Open CommonDialog1.FileName
```

We then redisplay the results in the FlexGrid. Why the FlexGrid? Well, we do not know what kind of recordset we are dealing with. There is no way to tell (upon opening the file), if this is a shaped recordset or a normal single item recordset unless you search the field list for any field of type `adChapter` (which is the data type of a child recordset). For example, the following code would achieve this if you desire:

```
Dim fld As adodb.Field
For Each fld In rs.Fields
  If fld.Type = adChapter Then
   'This is a shaped recordset
  Else
   'This is a standard recordset
  End If
Next
```

We err on the side of caution and display this in the FlexGrid. An alternative we could have used would be to try to display the recordset in the normal ADO grid and fall back to the FlexGrid if there is an error, but this falls closer to a kludge since there are other reasons why an error would generate besides the fact that the recordset could have been shaped.

```
dgRSGrid.Visible = False
hfgRSShape.Visible = True
Set hfgRSShape.DataSource = rs
End If

End Sub
```

The full source code of this sample can be downloaded from the Wrox Press site. The sample application is fully functional and will be updated from time to time to add additional functionality.

Summary

In this chapter we've looked at some samples that you can use as templates to build on or as useful background to give ideas when you're developing your own applications. We've seen samples which have done the following:

- ❑ Created a middle-tier COM component that returns a disconnected recordset
- ❑ Looked at code which will persist a recordset to disk
- ❑ Built a recordset without a data provider
- ❑ Created a function that displays the shape of a recordset
- ❑ Demonstrated how ADOX can operate on the internal structure of a database
- ❑ Examined how ADOX can be used to look at the security within a database
- ❑ Coded a function that queries Exchange for data on a specific user
- ❑ Put together an ASP page that searches the Index Server database for pages containing specific content

To finish the chapter we used what we'd learnt to build an application capable of querying a variety of ADO data sources, such as Index Server, LDAP or a SQL database, and which also allowed for data shaping.

Overall, these are fairly simple functions that expose a lot of the functionality of ADO. You can use some of the functions as a base for your custom ADO libraries. As you continue to use ADO you will find more functions that may be missing from the providers that you need to build functions for, or you may find that there are functions specific to your application or business that you feel would assist your development efforts. In either case you can use ADO to query many types of data and provide added flexibility for offline applications that previous data access technologies could not.

Data Transfer: A Business-to-Business Case Study

We have already seen what role XML is going to play as a data transfer mechanism, and now we are going to look at a practical example of how to use ADO and XML to build an application to interact with product suppliers. Typically, most e-commerce sites do not stock the products displayed on the site themselves. Instead, they usually develop relationships with several different product suppliers, and they simply take an order that was placed by a customer from the e-commerce site, and send the order information to the product supplier to fulfill the order. This case study will address a common problem for most e-commerce sites, namely how to fulfill those orders that have been placed from the web storefront utilizing several different product suppliers without having to re-write everything for each new product supplier.

This case study will tackle the problem of transferring data to and from product suppliers for an e-commerce site. In this chapter, we will cover:

❏   How to build complex hierarchical recordsets based upon stored procedures.

❏   How to leverage the XML capabilities of ADO 2.5.

❏   How to integrate ADO 2.5 features with IIS 5.0, SQL Server 7.0, Active Server Pages 3.0 and COM+.

Background

The scenario for this case study will be centered on a large e-commerce flower web site. The company will be referred to as XYZ Flowers. XYZ Flowers does not physically maintain any flower arrangements at their office. Instead, they have several suppliers that they work with to fulfill all of the orders that are placed on their web site. In this scenario, we will be looking at the infrastructure of the web site, not the web site itself. We are concerned with the business-to-business processes, not the business-to-consumer processes.

XYZ Flowers maintains a centralized database of all products and orders, and they have agreements in place with all of their suppliers that state that each supplier will maintain a condensed version of this database containing only the products and orders specific to the respective supplier. Each supplier is responsible for updating the following data:

❑   Inventory of products they are stocking.

❑   Supplier settings (such as contact name, phone number, etc.).

❑   Order status for all orders assigned to them.

XYZ Flowers is responsible for giving suppliers access to the following data:

❑   Supplier-specific product catalog.

❑   Supplier settings.

❑   Supplier orders.

The Business Problem

All of the data that XYZ Flowers is responsible for making available to suppliers is **hierarchical** in nature. The XYZ Flowers server must be able to send and receive data updates at any time upon request. Each supplier may or may not have the same application to retrieve and update data from XYZ Flowers.

The main obstacle we have to overcome in this scenario is how to get the data to and from suppliers in a format that is independent from both the supplier's and XYZ Flowers' existing systems. This is important because we want this system to be as flexible as possible. The other challenge is to ensure that the XYZ Flowers server can perform data transfers without any user intervention and always be available.

The Solution

The simplest solution to the first obstacle is to use ADO's XML capabilities to communicate with the suppliers. By using XML as the data format, we have a very flexible, elegant way of both sending and receiving the data. XYZ Flowers does not need to know anything about the supplier's application architecture, and the suppliers do not need to know any underlying details about XYZ Flowers' application architecture.

> *We could have just used a simple ASCII text format, but our data is hierarchical, and we would have had to denormalize it in order to put it into flat ASCII text files.*

In order to use XML as the data format, both sides must agree on the definition of the data structure. In this case, we are going to assume that XYZ Flowers has convinced all of its suppliers to use the Microsoft rowset schema (covered in Chapter 7). By using the rowset schema, we do not have to write any extra code converting the data to and from XML, because ADO uses the rowset schema and it will do the conversion work for us.

The solution to the availability issue is to make use of Active Server Pages (ASP) technology. This will allow IIS to process all of the data transfers, and if we wanted to, we could then take advantage of IIS's security. In this case, I recommend using **Secure Sockets Layer** (**SSL**). When using SSL, the browser must send the proper certificate to the server in order to be authenticated. Using SSL, all requests made to the web server will be done via an HTTPS connection. Since the data being sent is also encrypted by SSL, we are reasonably assured that all of the data will be transferred securely.

For more info on SSL, see Chapter 25 of Professional Active Server Pages 3.0, also by Wrox Press.

> *A better solution is to integrate the application with MSMQ; so if the database server is offline, updates can still be made to the database. The ability to queue requests will be Phase II of the application, and will not be covered in this case study.*

Another argument for using ASP in our solution is that ADO 2.5 integrates very well with ASP 3.0. Specifically, ADO 2.5 integrates with the ASP `Request` and `Response` objects. You will see this integration take place later when we build the COM objects. For the database, we will be using SQL Server 7.0.

Data Architecture

Before we start writing ADO code to access the database, we must first build the database. This section will focus on doing just that, building the tables, relationships, and stored procedures for our database.

There are three main groups of data that we will be using in this example:

❑ Supplier

❑ Product

❑ Order

Within these three groups of data, there are one or more supporting data tables. The name of our database will be `supplier_case`. All data structures and stored procedures will be represented as SQL scripts, which will be available for download.

In order to best take advantage of SQL Server's engine (or MSDE's), all data retrievals, updates, inserts, and deletes in the application will be carried out by stored procedures. In my opinion, this is the fastest, most scalable, and the most efficient way of retrieving, updating, inserting, and deleting data.

Supplier Data

The supplier data is used to identify the particular supplier that XYZ is trading with. The fields in this table are mainly standard address data. Every supplier will be assigned a unique `supplier_id`, which will be an auto-incrementing `IDENTITY` field and will act as the table's primary key.

To support the supplier data needs in the application, the database will contain a supplier table. This table will have the following data structure:

```
CREATE TABLE [dbo].[supplier] (
    [supplier_id] [int] IDENTITY(1,1)
        CONSTRAINT [PK_supplier] PRIMARY KEY NONCLUSTERED
        NOT NULL,
    [supplier_name] [varchar] (50) NOT NULL,
    [contact_first_name] [varchar] (50) NULL,
    [contact_last_name] [varchar] (50) NULL,
    [address_line_1] [varchar] (50) NOT NULL,
    [address_line_2] [varchar] (50) NULL,
    [city] [varchar] (30) NOT NULL,
    [state] [varchar] (20) NOT NULL,
    [postal_code] [varchar] (15) NOT NULL,
    [country] [varchar] (20) NULL,
    [email_address] [varchar] (100) NULL,
    [phone] [varchar] (20) NOT NULL,
    [fax] [varchar] (20) NULL,
    [fedex_account_number] [varchar] (12) NULL,
    [fedex_meter_number] [varchar] (10) NULL,
    [comments] [varchar] (6000) NULL)
ON [PRIMARY]
```

Supplier Stored Procedures

We will utilize two stored procedures for the supplier data: `usp_get_supplier` and `usp_update_supplier`.

Here is the code for `usp_get_supplier`:

```
IF EXISTS (SELECT * FROM sysobjects
        WHERE id = object_id(N'[usp_get_supplier]')
        AND OBJECTPROPERTY(id, N'IsProcedure') = 1)
DROP PROCEDURE [usp_get_supplier]
GO
CREATE PROCEDURE usp_get_supplier
    @supplier_id int
```

```
AS
SELECT
    supplier_id,
    supplier_name,
    contact_first_name,
    contact_last_name,
    address_line_1,
    address_line_2,
    city,
    state,
    postal_code,
    country,
    email_address,
    phone,
    fax,
    fedex_account_number,
    fedex_meter_number,
    comments
FROM
    Supplier
WHERE
    supplier_id = @supplier_id

RETURN(@@ERROR)
```

This stored procedure returns all of the fields for a particular supplier. When building the stored procedure, we first test to see if the stored procedure exists in the database or not. If it does exist, we simply delete it, since we are going to create it on the next line of code. This same test will be repeated in every single stored procedure that we write. We then select all of the fields we need from the supplier table based upon the supplier_id that we input to the stored procedure. We then finish by returning the SQL Server global variable @@ERROR, which will be zero if no errors occurred, or the SQL Server error number if there was an error. Similar to how we drop the stored procedure every time it is created, we will return @@ERROR in every single stored procedure as well.

Here is the code for usp_update_supplier:

```
IF EXISTS (SELECT * FROM sysobjects WHERE
            id = object_id(N'[usp_update_supplier]')
            AND OBJECTPROPERTY(id, N'IsProcedure') = 1)
DROP PROCEDURE [usp_update_supplier]
GO
CREATE PROCEDURE usp_update_supplier
    @supplier_id            int,
    @supplier_name          varchar(50),
    @contact_first_name     varchar(50),
    @contact_last_name      varchar(50),
    @address_line_1         varchar(50),
    @address_line_2         varchar(50),
    @city                   varchar(30),
    @state                  varchar(20),
    @postal_code            varchar(15),
```

```
        @country                    varchar(20),
        @email_address              varchar(100),
        @phone                      varchar(20),
        @fax                        varchar(20),
        @fedex_account_number       varchar(12),
        @fedex_meter_number         varchar(10),
        @comments                   varchar(6000)
AS
UPDATE
    supplier
SET
    supplier_name = @supplier_name,
    contact_first_name = @contact_first_name,
    contact_last_name = @contact_last_name,
    address_line_1 = @address_line_1,
    address_line_2 = @address_line_2,
    city = @city,
    state = @state,
    postal_code = @postal_code,
    country = @country,
    email_address = @email_address,
    phone= @phone,
    fax= @fax,
    fedex_account_number = @fedex_account_number,
    fedex_meter_number = @fedex_meter_number,
    comments= @comments
WHERE
    supplier_id = @supplier_id

RETURN(@@ERROR)
```

This stored procedure takes all of the fields from the supplier table as its input parameters, and then updates the record of the given `supplier_id` with all of the input parameter values.

Product Data

The product data is used to identify the products that XYZ Flowers is selling. The data for the products is slightly more complex than the supplier data. For products, there will be products that also have accessories. For example, some flowers will have vases. The flower is the main product, and the vase is the accessory product. Inventory will be tracked by allowing the suppliers to enter their predictions of how many of each product will be available on each day. The system uses this information to decide whether or not to display a particular product. If multiple suppliers can provide the same product, the system will first use availability and then cost to choose a supplier. The inventory of accessories will not be addressed in this case study.

To support the accessory product data needs in the application, the database will contain a `product` table. This table will have the following data structure:

```
CREATE TABLE [dbo].[product] (
    [product_id] [int] IDENTITY(1,1)
    CONSTRAINT [PK_product] PRIMARY KEY NONCLUSTERED NOT NULL ,
    [sku] [varchar] (100) NOT NULL ,
    [product_name] [varchar] (50) NOT NULL ,
    [display_order] [int] NOT NULL ,
    [sale_price] [money] NOT NULL ,
    [compare_price] [money] NOT NULL ,
    [small_image_file] [varchar] (255) NULL ,
    [small_image_width] [int] NULL ,
    [small_image_height] [int] NULL ,
    [medium_image_file] [varchar] (255) NULL ,
    [medium_image_width] [int] NULL ,
    [medium_image_height] [int] NULL ,
    [large_image_file] [varchar] (255) NULL ,
    [large_image_width] [int] NULL ,
    [large_image_height] [int] NULL ,
    [flower_care] [varchar] (6000) NULL ,
    [date_available] [datetime] NOT NULL ,
    [end_date_available] [datetime] NOT NULL ,
    [is_accessory] [bit] DEFAULT (0) NOT NULL ,
    [product_weight] [real] NOT NULL)
ON [PRIMARY]
```

To support the accessory product data needs in the application, the database will contain a product_accessory table. This table will have the following data structure:

```
CREATE TABLE [dbo].[product_accessory] (
    [product_accessory_id] [int] IDENTITY(1,1)
        CONSTRAINT [PK_product_accessory] PRIMARY KEY NONCLUSTERED
        NOT NULL,
    [main_product_id] [int] NOT NULL
        CONSTRAINT [FK_main_product_id_product_id]
        FOREIGN KEY ([main_product_id]) REFERENCES
        [product]([product_id]),
    [accessory_product_id] [int] NOT NULL
        CONSTRAINT [FK_accessory_product_id_product_id]
        FOREIGN KEY ([accessory_product_id]) REFERENCES
        [product]([product_id]))
ON [PRIMARY]
```

You might have noticed that there is no supplier_id field in the product table. That is because one supplier can have many products, and some suppliers can potentially supply the same products. This is called a many-to-many relationship. In order to account for this relationship, we simply create a separate table that links suppliers and products, and it will have this structure:

```
CREATE TABLE [dbo].[product_supplier] (
    [product_supplier_id] [int] IDENTITY(1,1)
        CONSTRAINT [PK_product_supplier] PRIMARY KEY NONCLUSTERED
        NOT NULL,
    [product_id] [int] NOT NULL
        CONSTRAINT [FK_product_supplier_product_id]
        FOREIGN KEY ([product_id]) REFERENCES
        [product]([product_id]),
    [supplier_id] [int] NOT NULL
        CONSTRAINT [FK_product_supplier_supplier_id]
        FOREIGN KEY ([supplier_id]) REFERENCES
        [supplier]([supplier_id]),
    [cost] [money] NOT NULL)
ON [PRIMARY]
```

The database will contain an `Inventory` table in order to keep track of inventory. This table will have the following data structure:

```
CREATE TABLE [dbo].[Inventory] (
    [inventory_id] [uniqueidentifier] DEFAULT (NEWID())
        CONSTRAINT [PK_inventory] PRIMARY KEY NONCLUSTERED
        NOT NULL,
    [product_supplier_id] [int] NOT NULL
        CONSTRAINT [FK_inventory_product_supplier_id]
        FOREIGN KEY ([product_supplier_id]) REFERENCES
        [product_supplier]([product_supplier_id]),
    [inventory_date] [datetime] NOT NULL,
    [quantity] [int] NOT NULL)
ON [PRIMARY]
```

Product Stored Procedures

We will utilize three stored procedures for the supplier data: `usp_get_supplier_products`, `usp_get_product_accessory`, and `usp_update_inventory_from_supplier`. Here is the code for `usp_get_supplier_products`:

```
IF EXISTS (SELECT * FROM sysobjects
            WHERE id = object_id(N'[usp_get_supplier_products]')
            AND OBJECTPROPERTY(id, N'IsProcedure') = 1)
DROP PROCEDURE [usp_get_supplier_products]
GO
CREATE PROCEDURE usp_get_supplier_products
    @supplier_id int
AS
SELECT DISTINCT
    p.product_id,
    p.sku,
    p.product_name,
    p.flower_care,
    p.date_available,
```

```
        p.end_date_available,
        p.product_weight,
        ps.product_supplier_id,
        ps.cost
FROM
    product AS p INNER JOIN product_supplier AS ps ON
    p.product_id = ps.product_id
WHERE
    ps.supplier_id = @supplier_id
```

```
RETURN(@@ERROR)
```

This stored procedure takes a `supplier_id` as its input parameter, and then returns product data for all of the products that a particular supplier carries.

Here is the code for `usp_get_product_accessory`:

```
IF EXISTS (SELECT * FROM sysobjects
            WHERE id = object_id(N'[usp_get_product_accessory]')
            AND OBJECTPROPERTY(id, N'IsProcedure') = 1)
DROP PROCEDURE [usp_get_product_accessory]
GO
CREATE PROCEDURE usp_get_product_accessory
AS
SELECT
    product_accessory_id,
    main_product_id,
    accessory_product_id
FROM
    product_accessory
```

```
RETURN(@@ERROR)
```

This stored procedure simply returns a `Recordset` of the selected fields for all rows in the table. Normally, we would put a `WHERE` clause here to restrict the number of rows returned. Due to a limitation with saving parameterized-hierarchical recordsets as XML, we will return all rows. This decision will be discussed later in this case study.

In order for suppliers to update their inventory, we must first check to see if there is an inventory record for the particular day that the supplier is reporting on. If there is, then we update it. If there is not, then we insert a new inventory record for the product and supplier combination. Here is the code for the `usp_update_inventory_from_supplier` procedure:

```
IF EXISTS (SELECT * FROM sysobjects WHERE
    id = object_id(N'[usp_update_inventory_from_supplier]')
    AND OBJECTPROPERTY(id, N'IsProcedure') = 1)
DROP PROCEDURE [usp_update_inventory_from_supplier]
GO
```

```
CREATE PROCEDURE usp_update_inventory_from_supplier
    @supplier_id     int,
    @product_id      int,
    @quantity        int,
    @inventory_date  datetime
AS
DECLARE
    @product_supplier_id int,
    @new_inventory_date varchar(10)

SET @new_inventory_date = CAST(MONTH(@inventory_date) AS varchar(2)) + '/'
                        + CAST(DAY(@inventory_date) AS varchar(2)) + '/'
                        + CAST(YEAR(@inventory_date) AS char(4))

IF (
    SELECT
        COUNT(*)
    FROM
        inventory AS inv INNER JOIN
        product_supplier AS ps ON
        ps.product_supplier_id = inv.product_supplier_id
    WHERE
        ps.product_id = @product_id AND
        ps.supplier_id = @supplier_id AND
        CAST(MONTH(inv.inventory_date) AS varchar(2)) + '/'
            + CAST(DAY(inv.inventory_date) AS varchar(2)) + '/'
            + CAST(YEAR(inv.inventory_date) AS char(4)) = @new_inventory_date) > 0
    BEGIN
        UPDATE
            inventory
        SET
            quantity = @quantity,
            inventory_date = @inventory_date
        FROM
            inventory AS inv INNER JOIN
            product_supplier AS ps ON
            inv.product_supplier_id = ps.product_supplier_id
        WHERE
            ps.product_id = @product_id AND
            ps.supplier_id = @supplier_id AND
            CAST(MONTH(inv.inventory_date) AS varchar(2)) + '/'
                + CAST(DAY(inv.inventory_date) AS varchar(2)) + '/'
                + CAST(YEAR(inv.inventory_date) AS char(4)) = @new_inventory_date
    END
ELSE
```

```
        BEGIN
            SET @product_supplier_id = (
                SELECT
                    product_supplier_id
                FROM
                    product_supplier
                WHERE
                    product_id = @product_id AND
                    supplier_id = @supplier_id)
                INSERT INTO inventory (
                    product_supplier_id,
                    inventory_date,
                    quantity)
                VALUES (
                    @product_supplier_id,
                    @inventory_date,
                    @quantity)
        END
```

```
RETURN(@@ERROR)
```

This stored procedure first tests to see if there is a matching record in the inventory table. If there is, then the record is updated with the values of the input parameters. If there is no matching record, then a new record is inserted into the inventory table.

Order Data

The order data is used to identify the products that XYZ has sold. The data for the orders is the most complex data that we will deal with. An order can be comprised of one or more products shipped in one or more boxes to one or more locations. Order data will consist of an order header record, which has one or more order boxes associated with it, and each order box has one or more order details associated with it. For example, an order can have multiple flowers, and each different flower will be in its own box with its respective accessories.

To support the order header data needs in the application, the database will contain an order_header table. This table serves as the header record for each order, and has the following data structure:

```
CREATE TABLE [dbo].[order_header] (
    [order_header_id] [uniqueidentifier] DEFAULT (NEWID())
        CONSTRAINT [PK_order_header] PRIMARY KEY NONCLUSTERED NOT NULL ,
    [remark] [varchar] (255) NULL ,
    [order_number] [varchar] (36) NOT NULL ,
    [language] [varchar] (50) NULL ,
    [current_status] [varchar] (16) NOT NULL ,
    [occasion] [varchar] (50) NULL ,
    [delivery_date] [smalldatetime] NOT NULL ,
    [ship_date] [smalldatetime] NOT NULL ,
    [order_sub_total] [smallmoney] NOT NULL ,
    [discount_amount] [smallmoney] NOT NULL ,
    [shipping_charge] [smallmoney] NULL ,
```

```
    [sales_tax] [smallmoney] NULL ,
    [credit_card_type] [char] (4) NULL ,
    [credit_card_number] [varchar] (50) NOT NULL ,
    [credit_card_exp_month] [char] (2) NULL ,
    [credit_card_exp_year] [char] (4) NULL ,
    [credit_card_first_name] [varchar] (30) NOT NULL ,
    [credit_card_last_name] [varchar] (40) NOT NULL ,
    [credit_card_auth_code] [varchar] (36) NULL ,
    [completed_date] [smalldatetime] NULL ,
    [order_total] AS ([order_sub_total] + [shipping_charge] + [sales_tax] -
        [discount_amount]))
ON [PRIMARY]
```

To support the order box data needs in the application, the database will contain an `order_box` table. This table is used to track different boxes that are part of the same order. Each 'box' can be tracked separately because it has its own tracking number. The `order_box` table has the following data structure:

```
CREATE TABLE [dbo].[order_box] (
    [order_box_id] [uniqueidentifier] DEFAULT (NEWID())
        CONSTRAINT [PK_order_box] PRIMARY KEY  NONCLUSTERED NOT NULL ,
    [order_header_id] [uniqueidentifier] NOT NULL
        CONSTRAINT [FK_order_box_order_header_id]
        FOREIGN KEY ([order_header_id])
        REFERENCES [order_header]([order_header_id]),
    [supplier_id] [int] NULL
        CONSTRAINT [FK_order_box_supplier_id]
        FOREIGN KEY ([supplier_id]) REFERENCES [supplier]([supplier_id]),
    [shipper] [char] (10) NULL ,
    [shipping_number] [varchar] (36) NULL ,
    [bill_first_name] [varchar] (50) NOT NULL ,
    [bill_last_name] [varchar] (50) NOT NULL ,
    [bill_addr_1] [varchar] (50) NOT NULL ,
    [bill_addr_2] [varchar] (50) NULL ,
    [bill_city] [varchar] (30) NOT NULL ,
    [bill_state] [varchar] (20) NOT NULL ,
    [bill_postal_code] [varchar] (10) NOT NULL ,
    [bill_country_code] [char] (3) DEFAULT ('USA') NOT NULL ,
    [bill_phone] [varchar] (30) NULL ,
    [bill_email] [varchar] (100) NULL ,
    [ship_first_name] [varchar] (50) NOT NULL ,
    [ship_last_name] [varchar] (50) NOT NULL ,
    [ship_company] [varchar] (50) NULL ,
    [ship_title] [varchar] (40) NULL ,
    [ship_addr_1] [varchar] (50) NOT NULL ,
    [ship_addr_2] [varchar] (50) NULL ,
    [ship_city] [varchar] (30) NOT NULL ,
    [ship_state] [varchar] (20) NOT NULL ,
    [ship_postal_code] [varchar] (10) NOT NULL ,
```

```
    [ship_country_code] [char] (3) DEFAULT ('USA') NOT NULL ,
    [ship_phone] [varchar] (30) NULL ,
    [gift_message] [varchar] (4000) NULL ,
    [fedex_shipping_charge] [smallmoney] NULL ,
    [ship_date] [datetime] NULL ,
    [delivery_date] [datetime] NULL)
ON [PRIMARY]
```

To support the order detail data needs in the application, the database will contain an order_detail table. This table holds the details for the products that comprise an order. The order_detail table has the following data structure:

```
CREATE TABLE [dbo].[order_detail] (
    [order_detail_id] [uniqueidentifier] DEFAULT (NEWID())
        CONSTRAINT [PK_order_detail] PRIMARY KEY  NONCLUSTERED NOT NULL ,
    [order_box_id] [uniqueidentifier] NOT NULL
        CONSTRAINT [FK_order_detail_order_box_id]
        FOREIGN KEY ([order_box_id]) REFERENCES [order_box]([order_box_id]),
    [product_id] [int] NOT NULL
        CONSTRAINT [FK_order_detail_product_id]
        FOREIGN KEY ([product_id]) REFERENCES [product]([product_id]),
    [quantity] [int] DEFAULT (1) NOT NULL ,
    [price_each] [money] NOT NULL ,
    [cost_each] [money] NULL)
ON [PRIMARY]
```

Order Stored Procedures

We will utilize four stored procedures for the supplier data: usp_get_order_header, usp_get_order_box, usp_get_order_detail, and usp_update_order_header. Here is the code for usp_get_order_header:

```
IF EXISTS (SELECT * FROM sysobjects WHERE
    id = object_id(N'[usp_get_order_header]')
    AND OBJECTPROPERTY(id, N'IsProcedure') = 1)
DROP PROCEDURE [usp_get_order_header]
GO
CREATE PROCEDURE usp_get_order_header
    @supplier_id  int
AS
SELECT DISTINCT
    oh.order_header_id,
    ob.supplier_id,
    oh.order_number,
    oh.language,
    oh.current_status,
    oh.delivery_date,
    oh.ship_date
FROM
```

```
        order_header AS oh INNER JOIN order_box AS ob
        ON oh.order_header_id = ob.order_header_id
    WHERE
        ob.supplier_id = @supplier_id
```

```
    RETURN (@@ERROR)
```

This stored procedure retrieves the pertinent fields of all records from the order_header table for whatever supplier_id is submitted.

Here is the code for usp_get_order_box:

```
IF EXISTS (SELECT * FROM sysobjects WHERE
    id = object_id(N'[usp_get_order_box]')
    AND OBJECTPROPERTY(id, N'IsProcedure') = 1)
DROP PROCEDURE [usp_get_order_box]
GO
CREATE PROCEDURE usp_get_order_box
AS
SELECT
    order_box_id,
    order_header_id,
    supplier_id,
    shipper,
    shipping_number,
    ship_first_name,
    ship_last_name,
    ship_company,
    ship_title,
    ship_addr_1,
    ship_addr_2,
    ship_city,
    ship_state,
    ship_postal_code,
    ship_country_code,
    ship_phone,
    gift_message,
    ship_date,
    delivery_date
FROM
    order_box
```

```
    RETURN(@@Error)
```

This stored procedure retrieves the selected fields for all rows of the order_box table, similar to usp_get_product_accessory.

Here is the code for usp_get_order_detail:

```
IF EXISTS (SELECT * FROM sysobjects WHERE
    id = object_id(N'[usp_get_order_detail]')
    AND OBJECTPROPERTY(id, N'IsProcedure') = 1)
DROP PROCEDURE [usp_get_order_detail]
GO
CREATE PROCEDURE usp_get_order_detail
AS
SELECT
    order_detail_id,
    order_box_id,
    product_id,
    quantity,
    price_each,
    cost_each
FROM
    order_detail

RETURN(@@Error)
```

Again, similar to usp_get_order_box, this stored procedure returns all rows from the order_detail table.

When suppliers are updating the status of orders, we will be checking the status that they are sending. If the supplier is not capable of fulfilling the order, then we will remove the supplier association from the order box. Here is the code for usp_update_order_header:

```
IF EXISTS (SELECT * FROM sysobjects WHERE
    id = object_id(N'[usp_update_order_header]')
    AND OBJECTPROPERTY(id, N'IsProcedure') = 1)
DROP PROCEDURE [usp_update_order_header]
GO
CREATE PROCEDURE usp_update_order_header
    @order_header_id  varchar(36),
    @current_status   varchar(16)
AS
IF @current_status = 'UNABLE TO SEND'
    BEGIN
        --Remove the supplier association for the order
        UPDATE
            order_box
        SET
            supplier_id = NULL
        FROM
            order_header AS oh INNER JOIN
            order_box AS ob ON
            ob.order_header_id = oh.order_header_id
        WHERE
            oh.order_header_id = @order_header_id
    END
```

```
--Update the current status
UPDATE
    order_header
SET
    current_status = @current_status
WHERE
    order_header.order_header_id = @order_header_id
```

RETURN(@@ERROR)

This stored procedure checks the current_status input parameter. If the current_status is 'UNABLE TO SEND', then the supplier relationship is set to NULL, i.e. removed. It then updates the current_status of the order based upon the value of the order_header_id input parameter.

All of the database scripts have been combined into three script files titled initialize_supplier_case.sql, create_sp_supplier_case.sql, and populate_supplier_case.sql. All of the scripts will be available from the Wrox website. The last script, populate_supplier_case.sql, will actually populate the tables with sample data for testing purposes. Again, the name of the database that initialize_supplier_case.sql creates is called supplier_case. After running the scripts in the SQL Server Query Analyzer, your database tables and relationships should resemble this diagram:

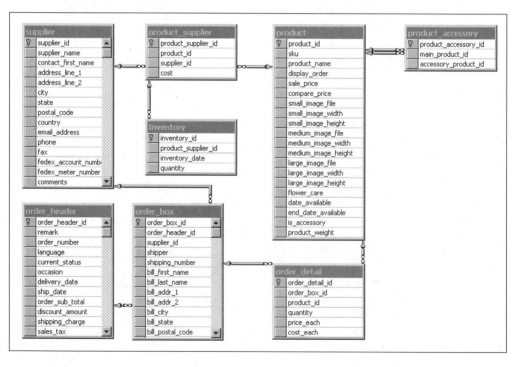

In order to re-create this diagram, you need to select Diagrams *under the* supplier_case *database in SQL Server Enterprise Manager, and then specify* New Database Diagram. *Then just add all of the tables that were created from the* initialize_supplier_case *script, and arrange them in a way that is easy to view. When you save the diagram, you will get the following warning:* Column 'order_total' in table 'order_header' is a computed column. If you make changes that require a table recreate, it will be converted to a non-computed column. *This just means that if you try to change structure of the table, you need to make sure that* order_total *is still a computed column.*

Application Architecture

The application architecture for this case study is pretty straightforward. The suppliers will only be able to update their inventory levels, orders status, and their settings. XYZ Flowers will provide settings by supplier, orders by supplier, and products by supplier. The interface, or glue, between our business objects and the suppliers will be ASP pages. HTTP will be the data transfer mechanism across the Internet and the ASP pages will call one of the business objects to either retrieve or update data. Here is a diagram of the architecture and data-flow:

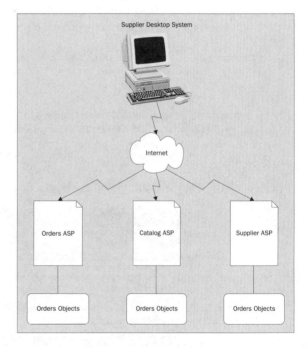

The Business Objects

The application will consist of six business objects. It will consist of one Visual Basic ActiveX DLL, SupplierServer.dll, and the DLL will have the following classes (objects): Catalog, CatalogTx, Orders, OrdersTx, Settings, and SettingsTx. We really only need three objects: Catalog, Orders, and Settings. We have created six objects instead of three objects in order to separate the transactional operations from the non-transactional operations. For example, retrieving orders does not require a transaction, but updating the status of orders does require a transaction. I use the suffix Tx when naming the objects that require a transaction. Their MTSTransactionMode property will always be 2-Requires Transaction. The classes that do not require a transaction will have their MTSTransactionMode property set to 1-No Transactions. By organizing our objects in this manner, all objects created can take advantage of COM+ services, and the objects that do not need to be transactional will not incur the additional overhead of a COM+ transactional context.

Normally, it is good practice to separate your business objects from your data access layer, but in this case we are going to combine the two into the same DLL because there is not much business logic that needs to be applied. The objects are mostly doing data access only, and if we did split the application into business objects and a data access layer, the business objects would just be passing recordsets through from the data access layer. My intention here is to avoid having the application have to create another object during a data retrieval or update.

All of the business objects, whether they use transactions or not, will be run under the context of COM+. The COM+ `ObjectContext` object provides the ability to utilize the context of all of IIS's ASP objects. As you will see later, this context will prove useful in exchanging XML data with ADO.

To allow for flexible error handling, we will be using a custom error-handler COM object written in Visual Basic (`ErrorHandler.dll`). This DLL and its source code will be available for download from `www.wrox.com`. The error handler will have only one method, `SetError`, with the following syntax:

```
SetError(AppPath As String, AppName As String, ModuleName As String, _
         ProcedureName As String, ErrNumber As Long, ErrSource As String, _
         ErrDescription As String)
```

This method will generate a self-appending text file titled `AppName_errors.txt` in the same directory as your application or COM object. In a production environment, you may to change the output of the `ErrorHandler` object to the Windows NT Application Event Log. We will also be using the `DOMDocument` object to verify that the incoming XML files are well formed.

The screenshot below points out all references that this project requires:

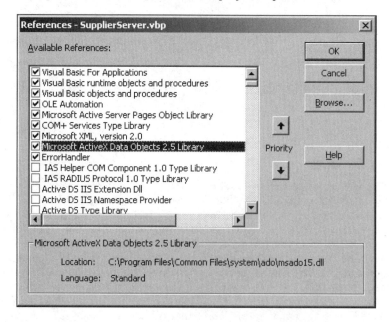

The `SupplierServer` DLL will have a `Public Sub Main()` as its startup object. The purpose of `Sub Main()` is to initialize the database connection string for the DLL. `Sub Main()` is located inside a standard module titled `basMain`. Here is the code for `basMain`:

```
Option Explicit

Private mstrConnection As String

Public Sub Main()

    'Change the Dat Source to match
    'whatever machine name you are
    'connecting to
    mstrConnection = "Provider=SQLOLEDB;Data Source=MCCLAPTOP;" _
                    & "Initial Catalog=supplier_case;User Id=sa;Password=;"

End Sub

Public Function DataConnectionH() As String

    DataConnectionH = "Provider=MSDataShape;Data " & mstrConnection

End Function

Public Function DataConnectionR() As String

    DataConnectionR = mstrConnection

End Function
```

Note how we encapsulate the connection strings with a public function. This protects any data from being inappropriately accessed and is a good practice to follow with all ActiveX DLLs that you build. Something in this module that may look strange is that we have two different connection strings. This is because hierarchical data must use the `MSDataShape` provider, but also need to have a data provider as well. Some of our functions will return hierarchical data, and others will not. The functions that do not return hierarchical data will just use the regular OLEDB connection string for the SQL Server OLEDB Provider. You will need to change the machine name in the connection string for this code to work correctly.

Below is code that is common to every one of the public classes that we will be building:

```
Option Explicit

Implements ObjectControl

Private mobjContext As ObjectContext
Private Const MODULE_NAME = "Orders"

Private Sub ObjectControl_Activate()

    Set mobjContext = GetObjectContext
```

```
    End Sub

    Private Function ObjectControl_CanBePooled() As Boolean

        ObjectControl_CanBePooled = True

    End Function

    Private Sub ObjectControl_Deactivate()

        Set mobjContext = Nothing

    End Sub
```

If you have worked with MTS or COM+ before, the code above should look familiar. If you have not, this code first implements the IobjectControl interface, then simply sets a private, module-level variable equal to the current ObjectContext of COM+ in ObjectControl_Activate. This means as soon as this class is instantiated, it will be running under the context of COM+. We then go ahead and set the CanBePooled property to TRUE, although COM+ will not pool COM objects written in VB6. Maybe VB7! Finally, in ObjectControl_Deactivate, we release the resources of the ObjectContext variable when the class is destroyed.

Orders Objects

The orders objects are responsible for retrieving supplier orders from the database, and also allowing the suppliers to update the status of their orders. The Orders class is responsible for retrieving the supplier orders from the database, and the OrdersTx class is responsible for allowing the suppliers to update the status of their orders. The Orders class will have only one method, appropriately titled GetOrders. The GetOrders method will build a hierarchical recordset, transform it into an XML type response, and then use the web server (IIS) to send the XML response back to the calling client.

Here is the code for GetOrders:

```
Public Function GetOrders(Supplier As Variant) As Variant

On Error GoTo ErrorHandler

    Dim cmd As ADODB.Command
    Dim cn As ADODB.Connection
    Dim rst As ADODB.Recordset
    Dim objResponse As ASPTypeLibrary.Response
    Dim objError As ErrorHandler.Errors
    Dim strDescription As String
    Dim strSQL As String

    Set objResponse = mobjContext("Response")
    Set cmd = New ADODB.Command
    Set cn = New ADODB.Connection
    Set rst = New ADODB.Recordset

    'Open with the hierarchical connection stringcn.Open DataConnectionH()
```

```
        strSQL = "SHAPE {{? = CALL dbo.usp_get_order_header(?)}}" & _
                 " AS OrderHeader APPEND ((SHAPE {{CALL dbo.usp_get_order_box}}" & _
                 " AS OrderBox APPEND ({{CALL dbo.usp_get_order_detail}}" & _
                 " AS OrderDetail RELATE 'order_box_id' TO 'order_box_id')" & _
                 " AS OrderDetail)" & _
                 " AS OrderBox RELATE 'order_header_id' TO 'order_header_id')" & _
                 " AS OrderBox"

    With cmd
        .ActiveConnection = cn
        .CommandType = adCmdText
        .CommandText = strSQL
        .Parameters.Append .CreateParameter("RETURN_VALUE", adInteger, _
                                            adParamReturnValue, 4)
        .Parameters.Append .CreateParameter("@supplier_id", adInteger, _
                                            adParamInput, 4, CLng(Supplier))
        .Execute
    End With

    With rst
        .CursorLocation = adUseClient
        .Open cmd
        If .EOF Or .BOF Then
            objResponse.Write "There are no orders to view at this time."
        Else
            'Save the contents of this recordset
            'as XML and return it to the browser.
            objResponse.ContentType = "text/xml"
            .save objResponse, adPersistXML
        End If
        .Close
    End With
    cn.Close
    mobjContext.SetComplete

ExitProc:
    Set cmd = Nothing
    Set cn = Nothing
    Set rst = Nothing
    Set objError = Nothing
    Set objResponse = Nothing
    Exit Function

ErrorHandler:
    mobjContext.SetAbort
    Set objError = New ErrorHandler.Errors
    strDescription = Err.Description
    objError.SetError App.Path, App.EXEName, MODULE_NAME, _
    "GetOrders", Err.Number, Err.Source, strDescription
    objResponse.Write "<B>Error = " & strDescription & "</B>"
    Resume ExitProc

End Function
```

Note how we are using ADO to build and persist a hierarchical recordset to XML. It was not possible before ADO 2.5 to save hierarchical recordsets as XML. Previously, we were able to build hierarchical recordsets, but we could not save them as XML. The technique of building and saving hierarchical recordsets is an extremely powerful one; however, there are some performance issues that you must consider. The way that we are building the recordset in this case is to pass in an input parameter to the first stored procedure, usp_get_order_header. The input parameter is the supplier_id of the supplier whose orders are to be retrieved. Notice how the other two stored procedures, usp_get_order_box and usp_get_order_detail, do not have any input parameters at all.

We have two choices to evaluate in this situation. We can either create our hierarchical recordset as we have done, with only the parent recordset stored procedure being able to accept parameters, or we can allow all of the stored child recordset stored procedures to accept parameters. When we choose option one, we may be potentially bringing in several thousand unnecessary child records (the order_box and order_detail tables). However, if we choose option 2 and build the hierarchical recordset utilizing parameters for the order_box and order_detail stored procedures, then we will only be retrieving the data that we really need. When building the recordset in this manner, the child recordset's stored procedures may potentially be executed several times, but that is still better than retrieving potentially thousands of unnecessary records.

> *ADO 2.5 does not support saving a hierarchical recordset as XML in the case where the child stored procedures have one or more input parameters.*

The solution is either to wait for another release of ADO, or to build your own function to save the parameterized hierarchical recordset as XML.

In this case study, we will not be building our own XML file. We will let ADO do the work for us, especially since it is very likely that someone on the receiving end of our XML file transfer will be using ADO to open the XML file and read its contents. Remember, ADO uses the Microsoft Rowset schema and cannot open XML files that are using any other schema. We have also agreed on the Rowset schema with all of our suppliers as well, so if we were to build a function to save the parameterized hierarchical recordset as XML, we would need to conform to this schema. Probably by the time you are reading this, either Microsoft, myself, or someone else may have already posted the code to do this. That will probably be my first mission after this writing!

It is also important to note how we are taking advantage of ASP 3.0's Response object streaming capability (**NOTE: This is only possible with IIS 5.0**). This saves us the intermediate steps of having to save the ADO-generated XML to a file and then read in the text for the Response object. Instead we just save the recordset directly to the ASP Response object.

The OrdersTx class will have one public function, titled ProcessOrders, and one private function called UpdateOrders. This code will receive an incoming XML text stream, open it with an ADO Stream object, and then and open the Stream as an ADO recordset. It will then proceed to loop through the recordset and process the order status for every record. Remember, the MTSTransactionMode property for thisclass is 2-RequiresTransaction. Here is the code for ProcessOrders:

```
Public Function ProcessOrders() As Variant

    On Error GoTo ErrorHandler

    Dim objXMLDom As MSXML.DOMDocument
    Dim objRequest As ASPTypeLibrary.Request
    Dim objResponse As ASPTypeLibrary.Response
    Dim rstOrders As ADODB.Recordset
    Dim stm As ADODB.Stream
    Dim objError As ErrorHandler.Errors
    Dim strDescription As String

    Set objRequest = mobjContext("Request")
    Set objResponse = mobjContext("Response")

    'See if anything has been posted to IIS
    If objRequest.ServerVariables("REQUEST_METHOD") = "POST" Then

        'Instantiate a DOMDocument object
        Set objXMLDom = New MSXML.DOMDocument

        'Make sure we get the whole text stream
        objXMLDom.async = False

        'Test to see if the XML is well-formed
        If objXMLDom.Load(objRequest) = False Then
            Err.Raise vbObjectError + 1001, Err.Source, _
                        "The XML document is not properly formatted."
        Else
            'Open the XML as a recordset
            Set rstOrders = New ADODB.Recordset
            Set stm = New ADODB.Stream


            'Write the XML to the stream
            stm.WriteText objXMLDom.xml

            'Set the end of the stream
            stm.SetEOS

            'Go back to the start of the stream
            stm.Position = 0

            'Open the recordset from the stream
            rstOrders.Open stm

            'Make call to process the order updates
            If UpdateOrders(rstOrders) = False Then
                Err.Raise vbObjectError + 1002, Err.Source, _
                            "There was an error updating the orders."
            Else
                objResponse.Write "All orders have been successfully updated."
            End If
```

```
        End If
    Else

        'Nothing was posted
        objResponse.Write "No data has been posted."

    End If

    'Commit transaction, release objects
    mobjContext.SetComplete

ExitProc:
    Set objRequest = Nothing
    Set objResponse = Nothing
    Set objXMLDom = Nothing
    Set rstOrders = Nothing
    Set stm = Nothing
    Set objError = Nothing
    Exit Function

ErrorHandler:
    mobjContext.SetAbort
    strDescription = Err.Description
    Set objError = New ErrorHandler.Errors
    objError.SetError App.Path, App.EXEName, MODULE_NAME, _
                    "ProcessOrders", Err.Number, Err.Source, strDescription
    objResponse.Write "<B>Error = " & strDescription & "</B>"
    Resume ExitProc

End Function
```

Similar to the code from GetOrders, this code first gets the context of the ASP Response object. It also gets the context of the ASP Request object. The next thing we must do is check to see whether or not someone is posting data to the page. If they are not, then we simply return a message stating that there was no data posted. If the request is a post, then we must check to see whether the XML is well-formed or not. If it is not, then we raise an error. If the XML is well-formed, then we proceed to open the XML text stream with an ADO Stream object. We then open the ADO Recordset from the ADO Stream, and loop through and process the status of all of the orders in the Recordset. It seems like you should be able to open the ADO Recordset directly from the ASP Request object, but when trying to do exactly as mentioned I received an error. This bug will most likely be fixed by the time you are reading this. Try it out and test to see if it produces an error or not.

Here is the code for the UpdateOrders private function:

```
Private Function UpdateOrders(rstOrders As ADODB.Recordset) As Boolean

    Dim cmd As ADODB.Command

    Set cmd = New ADODB.Command
    With cmd
        .ActiveConnection = DataConnectionR()
        .CommandType = adCmdStoredProc
        .CommandText = "usp_update_order_header"
        .Parameters.Append .CreateParameter("@order_header_id", _
                        adVarchar, adParamInput, 36)
        .Parameters.Append .CreateParameter("@current_status", _
                        adVarChar, adParamInput, 16)
        Do Until rstOrders.EOF
            .Parameters("@order_header_id").Value = _
                        rstOrders.Fields("order_header_id").Value
            .Parameters("@current_status").Value = _
                        rstOrders.Fields("current_status").Value
            .Execute
            rstOrders.MoveNext
        Loop
    End With
    Set cmd = Nothing
    UpdateOrders = True

End Function
```

This code simply loops through the incoming recordset and executes the usp_update_order_header stored procedure to update the status of each order in the recordset.

The code for the remaining objects is very similar to the code for the Orders and OrdersTx classes. They all need to receive and transfer XML, and they all use the exact same techniques illustrated previously to get and update their respective data. Below is the code for the GetCatalog, ProcessInventory, UpdateInventory, GetSettings, ProcessSettings and UpdateSettings methods.

Catalog Objects

Here is the code for the GetCatalog function in the Catalog class:

```
Public Function GetCatalog(Supplier As Variant) As Variant

On Error GoTo ErrorHandler

    Dim cn As ADODB.Connection
    Dim cmd As ADODB.Command
    Dim rst As ADODB.Recordset
    Dim objResponse As ASPTypeLibrary.Response
    Dim objError As ErrorHandler.Errors
    Dim strDescription As String
    Dim strSQL As String
```

```
    Set objResponse = mobjContext("Response")
    Set cmd = New ADODB.Command
    Set cn = New ADODB.Connection
    Set rst = New ADODB.Recordset

    'Open with the hierarchical connection string
    cn.Open DataConnectionH()


    strSQL = "SHAPE {{? = CALL usp_get_supplier_products(?) }}  " & _
             " AS Catalog APPEND ({{CALL usp_get_product_accessory }} " & _
             " AS Accessories RELATE 'product_id' TO 'main_product_id')" & _
             " AS Accessories"

    With cmd
        .ActiveConnection = cn
        .CommandType = adCmdText
        .CommandText = strSQL
        .Parameters.Append .CreateParameter("RETURN_VALUE", _
                        adInteger, adParamReturnValue, 4)
        .Parameters.Append .CreateParameter("@supplier_id", _
                        adInteger, adParamInput, 4, CLng(Supplier))
        .Execute
    End With

    With rst
        .CursorLocation = adUseClient
        .Open cmd
        If .EOF Or .BOF Then
           objResponse.Write "There are no catalog items to view at this time."
        Else
           objResponse.ContentType = "text/xml"
           .save objResponse, adPersistXML
        End If
           .Close
    End With
    cn.Close
    mobjContext.SetComplete

ExitProc:
    Set cmd = Nothing
    Set cn = Nothing
    Set rst = Nothing
    Set objResponse = Nothing
    Set objError = Nothing
    Exit Function
```

```
ErrorHandler:
    mobjContext.SetAbort
    Set objError = New ErrorHandler.Errors
    strDescription = Err.Description
    objError.SetError App.Path, App.EXEName, MODULE_NAME, _
                    "GetCatalog", Err.Number, Err.Source, strDescription
    objResponse.Write "<B>Error = " & strDescription & "</B>"
    Resume ExitProc

End Function
```

This function is similar to the `GetOrders` function from the `Orders` class. The function is expecting a `supplier_id` as its argument, and then uses the `supplier_id` to call the stored procedures to build a hierarchical recordset of the supplier's products. This recordset is then saved as an XML stream, and then the XML stream is sent back to the calling client via the ASP `Response` object.

Here is the code for the `ProcessInventory` function in the `CatalogTx` class:

```
Public Function ProcessInventory() As Variant

On Error GoTo ErrorHandler

    Dim objXMLDom As MSXML.DOMDocument
    Dim objRequest As ASPTypeLibrary.Request
    Dim objResponse As ASPTypeLibrary.Response
    Dim rstInventory As ADODB.Recordset
    Dim stm As ADODB.Stream
    Dim objError As ErrorHandler.Errors
    Dim strDescription As String

    Set objRequest = mobjContext("Request")
    Set objResponse = mobjContext("Response")

     'See if anything has been posted to IIS
    If objRequest.ServerVariables("REQUEST_METHOD") = "POST" Then

        'Instantiate a DOMDocument object
        Set objXMLDom = New MSXML.DOMDocument

        'Make sure we get the entire text stream
        objXMLDom.async = False

        'Test to see if the XML is well formatted
        If objXMLDom.Load(objRequest) = False Then
            Err.Raise vbObjectError + 1001, Err.Source, _
                    "The XML document is not properly formatted."
        Else

            'Open the XML as a recordset
            Set rstInventory = New ADODB.Recordset
            Set stm = New ADODB.Stream
```

```
            'Write the XML to the stream
            stm.WriteText objXMLDom.xml

            'Set the end of the stream
            stm.SetEOS

            'Go back to the start of the stream
            stm.Position = 0

            'Open the recordset from the stream
            rstInventory.Open stm
            'Make call to update the inventory
            If UpdateInventory(rstInventory) = False Then
                Err.Raise vbObjectError + 1002, Err.Source, _
                        "There was an error updating the inventory."
            Else
                objResponse.Write "The catalog has been successfully updated."
            End If

        End If
    Else
        objResponse.Write "No data posted."
    End If

    'Commit transaction, release objects
    mobjContext.SetComplete

ExitProc:
    Set objXMLDom = Nothing
    Set rstInventory = Nothing
    Set stm = Nothing
    Set objRequest = Nothing
    Set objResponse = Nothing
    Set objError = Nothing
    Exit Function

ErrorHandler:
    mobjContext.SetAbort
    strDescription = Err.Description
    Set objError = New ErrorHandler.Errors
    objError.SetError App.Path, App.EXEName, MODULE_NAME, _
                    "ProcessInventory", Err.Number, Err.Source, strDescription
    objResponse.Write "<B>Error = " & strDescription & "</B>"
    Resume ExitProc

End Function
```

Similar to the ProcessOrders function in the OrdersTx class, this function receives an XML text stream, opens the stream with an ADO Stream object, then opens the ADO Recordset from the ADO Stream, and then loops through and processes all of the records in the Recordset.

Here is the code for the `UpdateInventory` private function in the `CatalogTx` class:

```
Private Function UpdateInventory(rstInventory As ADODB.Recordset) As Boolean

    Dim cmd As ADODB.Command

    Set cmd = New ADODB.Command
    With cmd
        .ActiveConnection = DataConnectionR()
        .CommandType = adCmdStoredProc
        .CommandText = "usp_update_inventory_from_supplier"
        .Parameters.Append .CreateParameter("@supplier_id", adInteger, _
                                    adParamInput, 4)
        .Parameters.Append .CreateParameter("@product_id", adInteger, _
                                    adParamInput, 4)
        .Parameters.Append .CreateParameter("@quantity", adInteger, _
                                    adParamInput, 4)
        .Parameters.Append .CreateParameter("@inventory_date", adDBDate, _
                                    adParamInput)
        Do Until rstInventory.EOF
            .Parameters("@supplier_id").Value = _
                            rstInventory.Fields("supplier_id").Value
            .Parameters("@product_id").Value = _
                            rstInventory.Fields("product_id").Value
            .Parameters("@quantity").Value = rstInventory.Fields("quantity").Value
            .Parameters("@inventory_date").Value = _
                            rstInventory.Fields("inventory_date").Value

            .Execute
            rstInventory.MoveNext
        Loop
    End With
    Set cmd = Nothing
    UpdateInventory = True

End Function
```

This code simply loops through the incoming recordset and executes the
`usp_update_inventory_from_supplier` stored procedure to update the inventory level of each
record in the recordset.

Settings Objects

Here is the code for the `GetSettings` public function in the `Settings` class:

```
Public Function GetSettings(Supplier As Variant) As Variant

On Error GoTo ErrorHandler

    Dim cmd As ADODB.Command
    Dim rst As ADODB.Recordset
    Dim objResponse As ASPTypeLibrary.Response
    Dim objError As ErrorHandler.Errors
    Dim strDescription As String
```

```
            Set objResponse = mobjContext("Response")
            Set cmd = New ADODB.Command
            Set rst = New ADODB.Recordset

            With cmd
                .ActiveConnection = DataConnectionR()
                .CommandType = adCmdStoredProc
                .CommandText = "usp_get_supplier"
                .Parameters.Append .CreateParameter("RETURN_VALUE", adInteger, _
                                        adParamReturnValue, 4)
                .Parameters.Append .CreateParameter("@supplier_id", adInteger, _
                                        adParamInput, 4, CLng(Supplier))
                .Execute
            End With

            With rst
                .CursorLocation = adUseClient
                .Open cmd
                If .EOF Or .BOF Then
                    objResponse.Write "There are no settings to view at this time."
                Else
                    objResponse.ContentType = "text/xml"
                    .save objResponse, adPersistXML
                End If
                .Close
            End With
            mobjContext.SetComplete

ExitProc:
            Set cmd = Nothing
            Set rst = Nothing
            Set objResponse = Nothing
            Set objError = Nothing
            Exit Function

ErrorHandler:
            mobjContext.SetAbort
            Set objError = New ErrorHandler.Errors
            strDescription = Err.Description
            objError.SetError App.Path, App.EXEName, MODULE_NAME, "GetSettings", _
                            Err.Number, Err.Source, strDescription
            objResponse.Write "<B>Error = " & strDescription & "</B>"
            Resume ExitProc

End Function
```

Here is the code for the `ProcessSettings` public function in the `SettingsTx` class:

```
Public Function ProcessSettings() As Variant

On Error GoTo ErrorHandler

    Dim objXMLDom As MSXML.DOMDocument
    Dim objResponse As ASPTypeLibrary.Response
    Dim objRequest As ASPTypeLibrary.Request
    Dim rstSettings As ADODB.Recordset
    Dim stm As ADODB.Stream
    Dim objError As ErrorHandler.Errors
    Dim strDescription As String

    Set objResponse = mobjContext("Response")
    Set objRequest = mobjContext("Request")

    'See if anything has been posted to IIS
    If objRequest.ServerVariables("REQUEST_METHOD") = "POST" Then

        'Instantiate a DOMDocument object
        Set objXMLDom = New MSXML.DOMDocument

        'Make sure we get the entire text stream
        objXMLDom.async = False

        'Test to see if the XML is well formatted
        If objXMLDom.Load(objRequest) = False Then
            Err.Raise vbObjectError + 1001, Err.Source, _
                    "The XML document is not properly formatted."
        Else

            'Open the XML as a recordset
            Set rstSettings = New ADODB.Recordset
            Set stm = New ADODB.Stream

            'Write the XML to the stream
            stm.WriteText objXMLDom.xml

            'Set the end of the stream
            stm.SetEOS

            'Go back to the start of the stream
            stm.Position = 0

            'Open the recordset from the stream
            rstSettings.Open stm
            'Make call to update the settings
            If UpdateSettings(rstSettings) = False Then
                Err.Raise vbObjectError + 1002, Err.Source, _
                        "There was an error updating the settings."
            Else
                objResponse.Write "The supplier settings have been " & _
                        "successfully updated."
            End If
```

```
        End If
    Else
        objResponse.Write "No data posted."
    End If

    'Commit transaction, release objects
    mobjContext.SetComplete

ExitProc:
    Set rstSettings = Nothing
    Set stm = Nothing
    Set objRequest = Nothing
    Set objResponse = Nothing
    Set objXMLDom = Nothing
    Set objError = Nothing
    Exit Function

ErrorHandler:
    mobjContext.SetAbort
    strDescription = Err.Description
    Set objError = New ErrorHandler.Errors
    objError.SetError App.Path, App.EXEName, MODULE_NAME, "ProcessSettings", _
                    Err.Number, Err.Source, strDescription
    objResponse.Write "<B>Error = " & strDescription & "</B>"
    Resume ExitProc

End Function
```

This function is similar to the `ProcessOrders` and `ProcessInventory` functions.
`ProcessSettings` receives an XML text stream, opens it with an ADO `Stream` object, then opens an
ADO `Recordset` from the ADO `Stream`, and then sends the recordset to the `UpdateSettings`
private function to update the database.

Here is the code for the `UpdateSettings` private function in the `SettingsTx` class:

```
Private Function UpdateSettings(rstSettings As ADODB.Recordset) As Boolean

    Dim cmd As ADODB.Command
    Dim fld As ADODB.Field

    Set cmd = New ADODB.Command
    With cmd
        .ActiveConnection = DataConnectionR()
        .CommandType = adCmdStoredProc
        .CommandText = "usp_update_supplier"
        For Each fld In rstSettings.Fields
            .Parameters.Append .CreateParameter(fld.Name, fld.Type, adParamInput, _
                                        fld.DefinedSize, fld.Value)
        Next
        .Execute
    End With
```

```
        Set cmd = Nothing
        Set fld = Nothing
        UpdateSettings = True

End Function
```

This code simply takes the metadata from the incoming recordset to execute the usp_update_supplier stored procedure to update the settings for a particular supplier.

Once the code is finished for the SupplierServer.dll object, we then need to make sure it compiles correctly. Once it is compiled, the next step is to register it with COM+. I am not going to go through the steps to do that here, but I do want to make sure that when the object is registered into COM+, it is set as a Server Application (this is the default).

> *See Professional Active Server Pages 3.0 for more information on registering components with COM+.*

The Active Server Pages

The active server pages in this application are set up to go hand-in-hand with every one of the public functions that our classes have. To recap, we have the following public functions: GetOrders, ProcessOrders, GetCatalog, ProcessInventory, GetSettings, and ProcessSettings. Naturally our ASP pages are as follows: GetOrders.asp, ProcessOrders.asp, GetCatalog.asp, ProcessInventory.asp, GetSettings.asp, and ProcessSettings.asp. We also have an additional ASP page titled TestPage.asp, which acts as our test harness for all of the data retrieval or 'get' actions. All ASP pages must go into the same directory, and you should create a new virtual directory on IIS to run them. I am using the virtual directory Supplier. I also recommend that you select High (Isolated) in the Application Protection dropdown box for the properties of the Supplier virtual directory. This will allow you to easily unload SupplierServer.dll from memory if you need to recompile the DLL while testing it.

Here is the code for GetOrders.asp:

```
<%@ LANGUAGE=VBScript %>
<%Option Explicit%>

<%

Dim objSupplier
Dim lngSupplier
Dim blnReturn

lngSupplier = Request.QueryString("supplier_id")

If CLng(lngSupplier) > 0 Then
    Set objSupplier = Server.CreateObject("SupplierServer.Orders")
    blnReturn = objSupplier.GetOrders(lngSupplier)
    Set objSupplier = Nothing
Else
```

```
        Response.Write "A QueryString is needed to identify the Supplier"
    End If

%>
```

This page takes a `supplier_id` passed in through a request, and then passes the `supplier_id` as an argument to the `GetOrders` method of the `Orders` class.

Here is the code for `ProcessOrders.asp`:

```
<%@ Language=VBScript %>
<%Option Explicit%>

<%

Dim objSupplierServer
Dim blnReturn

Set objSupplierServer = Server.CreateObject("SupplierServer.OrdersTx")
blnReturn = objSupplierServer.ProcessOrders()
Set objSupplierServer = Nothing

%>
```

`ProcessOrders.asp` requires an XML stream to be passed in. It then calls the `ProcessOrders` function of the `OrdersTx` class to update the order status of all of the orders in the XML file.

The rest of the ASP code for the other data retrievals and updates follows the same pattern as the previous two ASP files above. Here is the code for `GetCatalog.asp`:

```
<%@ Language=VBScript %>
<%Option Explicit%>

<%

Dim objSupplier
Dim lngSupplier
dim blnReturn

lngSupplier = Request.QueryString("supplier_id")

If CLng(lngSupplier) > 0 Then
    Set objSupplier = Server.CreateObject("SupplierServer.Catalog")
    blnReturn = objSupplier.GetCatalog(lngSupplier)
    Set objSupplier = Nothing
Else
    Response.Write "A QueryString is needed to identify the Supplier"
End If

%>
```

Again, this is similar to `GetOrders.asp`. This page expects a `supplier_id` to be passed in, and then passes the `supplier_id` value as an argument to the `GetCatalog` function of the `Catalog` class.

Here is the code for `ProcessInventory.asp`:

```
<%@ Language=VBScript %>
<%Option Explicit%>

<%

Dim objSupplier
Dim blnReturn

Set objSupplier = Server.CreateObject("SupplierServer.CatalogTx")
blnReturn = objSupplier.ProcessInventory()
Set objSupplier = Nothing

%>
```

`ProcessInventory.asp` is very similar to `ProcessOrders.asp` in that it too requires an XML stream to be passed in. It then calls the `ProcessInventory` function of the `CatalogTx` class to update the supplier's inventory levels.

Here is the code for `GetSettings.asp`:

```
<%@ Language=VBScript %>
<%Option Explicit%>

<%

Dim objSupplier
Dim lngSupplier
Dim blnReturn

lngSupplier = Request.QueryString("supplier_id")

If CLng(lngSupplier) > 0 Then
    Set objSupplier = Server.CreateObject("SupplierServer.Settings")
    blnReturn = objSupplier.GetSettings(lngSupplier)
    Set objSupplier = Nothing
Else
    Response.Write "A QueryString is needed to identify the supplier"
End if

%>
```

Similar to `GetOrders.asp` and `GetCatalog.asp`, `GetSettings.asp` expects a `supplier_id` to be passed in through a query string, and passes this to the `GetSettings` method of the `Settings` class.

Here is the code for `ProcessSettings.asp`:

```
<%@ Language=VBScript %>
<%Option Explicit%>


<%

Dim objSupplier
Dim blnReturn

Set objSupplier = Server.CreateObject("SupplierServer.SettingsTx")
blnReturn = objSupplier.ProcessSettings()
Set objSupplier = Nothing

%>
```

`TestPage.asp` is our test harness for all of the data retrieval operations for the application. It simply gives us a list of all suppliers in the supplier table and provides hyperlinks to each of the data retrieval operations for each supplier. Here is the code for `TestPage.asp`:

```
<%@ Language=VBScript %>
<%Option Explicit%>
<%

Dim rst
Dim strConnection

Set rst = CreateObject("ADODB.Recordset")
strConnection = "PROVIDER=SQLOLEDB;Data Source=MCCLAPTOP;" & _
                "Initial Catalog=supplier_case;User Id=sa;Password=;"
rst.Open "SELECT * FROM supplier", strConnection

%>

<HTML>
<HEAD>
<TITLE>Supplier Server Test Page</TITLE>
</HEAD>
<BODY>
<H1 ALIGN=CENTER>ADO 2.5 Case Study Test Page</H1>
<P> </P>
<%
Do Until rst.EOF
%>
    <P><A HREF="GetOrders.asp?supplier_id=<%=rst("supplier_id")%>&days_out=5">
       GetOrders for '<%=rst("supplier_name")%>'</A></P>
    <P><A HREF="GetCatalog.asp?supplier_id=<%=rst("supplier_id")%>">
       GetProducts for '<%=rst("supplier_name")%>'</A></P>
    <P><A HREF="GetSettings.asp?supplier_id=<%=rst("supplier_id")%>">
       GetSettings for '<%=rst("supplier_name")%>'</A></P>
    <P> </P>
<%
```

```
     rst.MoveNext
Loop
Set rst = Nothing

%>

</BODY>
</HTML>
```

Here is what the TestPage.asp should look like in IE5:

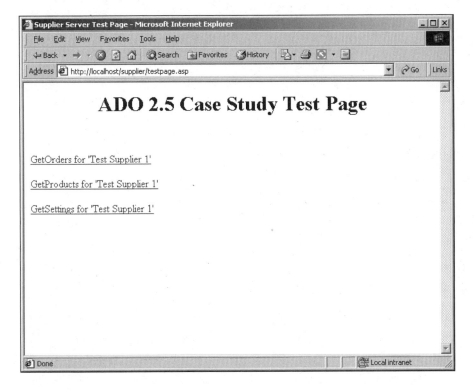

In order to test all of the data update operations for the application, I have built a
small Visual Basic client which will generate the required XML data for each type of
update by supplier, allow you to make changes to the XML files, and then allow you to
post the changes to the web server for processing. This client application will be
available for download as part of the source code for this book.

Summary

In this case study, we saw how ADO, XML, and ASP can help us overcome the problem of transferring data to and from businesses in a format that is not dependent on any existing systems. We were also able to complete these data transfers without any user intervention on the server side.

In the process of solving the business problem for this case study, we practiced how to use Visual Basic and ADO 2.5 to effectively build complex hierarchical recordsets based upon stored procedures, and how to persist them as XML. We also demonstrated how to tightly integrate ASP with ADO through the use of the ASP Response and the Request objects.

ADO Object Summary

Microsoft ActiveX Data Objects 2.5 Library Reference

Properties or methods new to version 2.5 are shown *italicized*.

> **All properties are read/write unless otherwise stated.**

Objects

Name	Description
Command	A Command object is a definition of a specific command that you intend to execute against a data source.
Connection	A Connection object represents an open connection to a data store.
Error	An Error object contains the details about data access errors pertaining to a single operation involving the provider.

Table Continued On Following Page

Name	Description
Errors	The Errors collection contains all of the Error objects created in response to a single failure involving the provider.
Field	A Field object represents a column of data within a common data type.
Fields	A Fields collection contains all of the Field objects of a Recordset object.
Parameter	A Parameter object represents a parameter or argument associated with a Command object based on a parameterized query or stored procedure.
Parameters	A Parameters collection contains all the Parameter objects of a Command object.
Properties	A Properties collection contains all the Property objects for a specific instance of an object.
Property	A Property object represents a dynamic characteristic of an ADO object that is defined by the provider.
Record	A Record object represents a row in a recordset, or a file or directory in a file system or web resource.
Recordset	A Recordset object represents the entire set of records from a base table or the results of an executed command. At any time, the Recordset object only refers to a single record within the set as the current record.
Stream	A Stream object represents a stream of text or binary data.

Command Object

Methods

Name	Returns	Description
Cancel		Cancels execution of a pending Execute or Open call.
CreateParameter	Parameter	Creates a new Parameter object.
Execute	Recordset	Executes the query, SQL statement, or stored procedure specified in the CommandText property.

Properties

Name	Returns	Description
ActiveConnection	Variant	Indicates to which Connection object the command currently belongs.
CommandText	String	Contains the text of a command to be issued against a data provider.
CommandTimeout	Long	Indicates how long to wait, in seconds, while executing a command before terminating the command and generating an error. Default is 30.
CommandType	CommandTypeEnum	Indicates the type of Command object.
Name	String	Indicates the name of the Command object.
Parameters	Parameters	Contains all of the Parameter objects for a Command object.
Prepared	Boolean	Indicates whether or not to save a compiled version of a command before execution.
Properties	Properties	Contains all of the Property objects for a Command object.
State	Long	Describes whether the Command object is open or closed. Read only.

Connection Object

Methods

Name	Returns	Description
BeginTrans	Integer	Begins a new transaction.
Cancel		Cancels the execution of a pending, asynchronous Execute or Open operation.
Close		Closes an open connection and any dependant objects.
CommitTrans		Saves any changes and ends the current transaction.
Execute	Recordset	Executes the query, SQL statement, stored procedure, or provider specific text.

Table Continued On Following Page

Name	Returns	Description
Open		Opens a connection to a data source, so that commands can be executed against it.
OpenSchema	Recordset	Obtains database schema information from the provider.
RollbackTrans		Cancels any changes made during the current transaction and ends the transaction.

Properties

Name	Returns	Description
Attributes	Long	Indicates one or more characteristics of a Connection object. Default is 0.
CommandTimeout	Long	Indicates how long, in seconds, to wait while executing a command before terminating the command and generating an error. The default is 30.
ConnectionString	String	Contains the information used to establish a connection to a data source.
ConnectionTimeout	Long	Indicates how long, in seconds, to wait while establishing a connection before terminating the attempt and generating an error. Default is 15.
CursorLocation	CursorLocationEnum	Sets or returns the location of the cursor engine.
DefaultDatabase	String	Indicates the default database for a Connection object.
Errors	Errors	Contains all of the Error objects created in response to a single failure involving the provider.
IsolationLevel	IsolationLevelEnum	Indicates the level of transaction isolation for a Connection object. Write only.
Mode	ConnectModeEnum	Indicates the available permissions for modifying data in a Connection.
Properties	Properties	Contains all of the Property objects for a Connection object.
Provider	String	Indicates the name of the provider for a Connection object.

Name	Returns	Description
State	Long	Describes whether the Connection object is open or closed. Read only.
Version	String	Indicates the ADO version number. Read only.

Events

Name	Description
BeginTransComplete	Fired after a BeginTrans operation finishes executing.
CommitTransComplete	Fired after a CommitTrans operation finishes executing.
ConnectComplete	Fired after a connection starts.
Disconnect	Fired after a connection ends.
ExecuteComplete	Fired after a command has finished executing.
InfoMessage	Fired whenever a ConnectionEvent operation completes successfully and additional information is returned by the provider.
RollbackTransComplete	Fired after a RollbackTrans operation finished executing.
WillConnect	Fired before a connection starts.
WillExecute	Fired before a pending command executes on the connection.

Error Object

Properties

Name	Returns	Description
Description	String	A description string associated with the error. Read only.
HelpContextID	Long	Indicates the ContextID in the help file for the associated error. Read only.
HelpFile	String	Indicates the name of the help file. Read only.
NativeError	Long	Indicates the provider-specific error code for the associated error. Read only.
Number	Long	Indicates the number that uniquely identifies an Error object. Read only.

Table Continued On Following Page

Name	Returns	Description
Source	String	Indicates the name of the object or application that originally generated the error. Read only.
SQLState	String	Indicates the SQL state for a given Error object. It is a five-character string that follows the ANSI SQL standard. Read only.

Errors Collection

Methods

Name	Returns	Description
Clear		Removes all of the Error objects from the Errors collection.
Refresh		Updates the Error objects with information from the provider.

Properties

Name	Returns	Description
Count	Long	Indicates the number of Error objects in the Errors collection. Read only.
Item	Error	Allows indexing into the Errors collection to reference a specific Error object. Read only.

Field Object

Methods

Name	Returns	Description
AppendChunk		Appends data to a large or binary Field object.
GetChunk	Variant	Returns all or a portion of the contents of a large or binary Field object.

Properties

Name	Returns	Description
ActualSize	Long	Indicates the actual length of a field's value. Read only.
Attributes	Long	Indicates one or more characteristics of a Field object.
DataFormat	Variant	Identifies the format that the data should be displayed in.
DefinedSize	Long	Indicates the defined size of the Field object. Write only.
Name	String	Indicates the name of the Field object.
NumericScale	Byte	Indicates the scale of numeric values for the Field object. Write only.
OriginalValue	Variant	Indicates the value of a Field object that existed in the record before any changes were made. Read only.
Precision	Byte	Indicates the degree of precision for numeric values in the Field object. Read only.
Properties	Properties	Contains all of the Property objects for a Field object.
Status	FieldStatusEnum	Indicates whether a Field object has been added to or delete from the Fields collection (these are cached until Update is called).
Type	DataTypeEnum	Indicates the data type of the Field object. Read only
UnderlyingValue	Variant	Indicates a Field object's current value in the database. Read only.
Value	Variant	Indicates the value assigned to the Field object.

Fields Collection

Methods

Name	Returns	Description
Append		Appends a Field object to the Fields collection.
CancelUpdate		Cancels any changes made to the Fields collection.

Table Continued On Following Page

Name	Returns	Description
Delete		Deletes a Field object from the Fields collection.
Refresh		Updates the Field objects in the Fields collection.
Resync		Resynchronizes the data in the Field objects.
Update		Saves any changes made to the Fields collection.

Properties

Name	Returns	Description
Count	Long	Indicates the number of Field objects in the Fields collection. Read only.
Item	Field	Allows indexing into the Fields collection to reference a specific Field object. Read only.

Parameter Object

Methods

Name	Returns	Description
AppendChunk		Appends data to a large or binary Parameter object.

Properties

Name	Returns	Description
Attributes	Long	Indicates one or more characteristics of a Parameter object.
Direction	ParameterDirectionEnum	Indicates whether the Parameter object represents an input parameter, an output parameter, or both, or if the parameter is a return value from a stored procedure.
Name	String	Indicates the name of the Parameter object.
NumericScale	Byte	Indicates the scale of numeric values for the Parameter object.
Precision	Byte	Indicates the degree of precision for numeric values in the Parameter object.

Name	Returns	Description
Properties	Properties	Contains all of the Property objects for a Parameter object.
Size	Long	Indicates the maximum size, in bytes or characters, of a Parameter object.
Type	DataTypeEnum	Indicates the data type of the Parameter object.
Value	Variant	Indicates the value assigned to the Parameter object.

Parameters Collection

Methods

Name	Returns	Description
Append		Appends a Parameter object to the Parameters collection.
Delete		Deletes a Parameter object from the Parameters collection.
Refresh		Updates the Parameter objects in the Parameters collection.

Properties

Name	Returns	Description
Count	Long	Indicates the number of Parameter objects in the Parameters collection. Read only.
Item	Parameter	Allows indexing into the Parameters collection to reference a specific Parameter object. Read only.

Properties Collection

Methods

Name	Returns	Description
Refresh		Updates the Property objects in the Properties collection with the details from the provider.

Properties

Name	Returns	Description
Count	Long	Indicates the number of Property objects in the Properties collection. Read only.
Item	Property	Allows indexing into the Properties collection to reference a specific Property object. Read only.

Property Object

Properties

Name	Returns	Description
Attributes	Long	Indicates one or more characteristics of a Property object.
Name	String	Indicates the name of the Property object. Read only.
Type	DataTypeEnum	Indicates the data type of the Property object.
Value	Variant	Indicates the value assigned to the Property object.

Record Object

Methods

Name	Returns	Description
Cancel		Cancels the execution of an asynchronous Execute or Open.

Name	Returns	Description
Close		Closes the open record.
CopyRecord	String	Copies the object the Record represents, or a file or directory, from one location to another.
DeleteRecord		Deletes the object the Record represents, or a file or directory.
GetChildren	Recordset	Returns a Recordset containing the files and folders in the directory that the Record represents.
MoveRecord	String	Moves the object the Record represents, or a file or directory, from one location to another.
Open		Opens, or creates a new, existing file or directory.

Properties

Name	Returns	Description
ActiveConnection	Variant	Indicates to which Connection object the specified Recordset object currently belongs.
Fields	Fields	Contains all of the Field objects for the current Recordset object. Read only
Mode	ConnectModeEnum	Indicates the available permissions for modifying data in a Connection.
ParentURL	String	Indicates the absolute URL of the parent Record of the current Record. Read only
Properties	Properties	Contains all of the Property objects for the current Recordset object. Read only
RecordType	RecordTypeEnum	Indicates whether the record is a simple record, a structured document, or a collection. Read only
Source	Variant	Indicates what the Record represents – a URL or a reference to an open Recordset.
State	ObjectStateEnum	Indicates whether the Record is open or closed, and if open the state of asynchronous actions. Read only

Recordset Object

Methods

Name	Returns	Description
AddNew		Creates a new record for an updateable Recordset object.
Cancel		Cancels execution of a pending asynchronous Open operation.
CancelBatch		Cancels a pending batch update.
CancelUpdate		Cancels any changes made to the current record, or to a new record prior to calling the Update method.
Clone	Recordset	Creates a duplicate Recordset object from and existing Recordset object.
Close		Closes the Recordset object and any dependent objects.
CompareBookmarks	CompareEnum	Compares two bookmarks and returns an indication of the relative values.
Delete		Deletes the current record or group of records.
Find		Searches the Recordset for a record that matches the specified criteria.
GetRows	Variant	Retrieves multiple records of a Recordset object into an array.
GetString	String	Returns a Recordset as a string.
Move		Moves the position of the current record in a Recordset.
MoveFirst		Moves the position of the current record to the first record in the Recordset.
MoveLast		Moves the position of the current record to the last record in the Recordset.
MoveNext		Moves the position of the current record to the next record in the Recordset.
MovePrevious		Moves the position of the current record to the previous record in the Recordset.

Name	Returns	Description
NextRecordset	Recordset	Clears the current Recordset object and returns the next Recordset by advancing through a series of commands.
Open		Opens a Recordset.
Requery		Updates the data in a Recordset object by re-executing the query on which the object is based.
Resync		Refreshes the data in the current Recordset object from the underlying database.
Save		Saves the Recordset to a file.
Seek		Searches the recordset index to locate a value
Supports	Boolean	Determines whether a specified Recordset object supports particular functionality.
Update		Saves any changes made to the current Recordset object.
UpdateBatch		Writes all pending batch updates to disk.

Properties

Name	Returns	Description
AbsolutePage	PositionEnum	Specifies in which page the current record resides.
AbsolutePosition	PositionEnum	Specifies the ordinal position of a Recordset object's current record.
ActiveCommand	Object	Indicates the Command object that created the associated Recordset object. Read only.
ActiveConnection	Variant	Indicates to which Connection object the specified Recordset object currently belongs.
BOF	Boolean	Indicates whether the current record is before the first record in a Recordset object. Read only.
Bookmark	Variant	Returns a bookmark that uniquely identifies the current record in a Recordset object, or sets the current record to the record identified by a valid bookmark.

Table Continued On Following Page

Name	Returns	Description
CacheSize	Long	Indicates the number of records from a Recordset object that are cached locally in memory.
CursorLocation	CursorLocationEnum	Sets or returns the location of the cursor engine.
CursorType	CursorTypeEnum	Indicates the type of cursor used in a Recordset object.
DataMember	String	Specifies the name of the data member to retrieve from the object referenced by the DataSource property. Write only.
DataSource	Object	Specifies an object containing data to be represented as a Recordset object. Write only.
EditMode	EditModeEnum	Indicates the editing status of the current record. Read only.
EOF	Boolean	Indicates whether the current record is after the last record in a Recordset object. Read only.
Fields	Fields	Contains all of the Field objects for the current Recordset object.
Filter	Variant	Indicates a filter for data in the Recordset.
Index	String	Identifies the name of the index currently being used.
LockType	LockTypeEnum	Indicates the type of locks placed on records during editing.
MarshalOptions	MarshalOptionsEnum	Indicates which records are to be marshaled back to the server.
MaxRecords	Long	Indicates the maximum number of records to return to a Recordset object from a query. Default is zero (no limit).
PageCount	Long	Indicates how many pages of data the Recordset object contains. Read only.
PageSize	Long	Indicates how many records constitute one page in the Recordset.
Properties	Properties	Contains all of the Property objects for the current Recordset object.

Name	Returns	Description
RecordCount	Long	Indicates the current number of records in the Recordset object. Read only.
Sort	String	Specifies one or more field names the Recordset is sorted on, and the direction of the sort.
Source	String	Indicates the source for the data in a Recordset object.
State	Long	Indicates whether the recordset is open, closed, or whether it is executing an asynchronous operation. Read only.
Status	Integer	Indicates the status of the current record with respect to match updates or other bulk operations. Read only.
StayInSync	Boolean	Indicates, in a hierarchical Recordset object, whether the parent row should change when the set of underlying child records changes. Read only.

Events

Name	Description
EndOfRecordset	Fired when there is an attempt to move to a row past the end of the Recordset.
FetchComplete	Fired after all the records in an asynchronous operation have been retrieved into the Recordset.
FetchProgress	Fired periodically during a length asynchronous operation, to report how many rows have currently been retrieved.
FieldChangeComplete	Fired after the value of one or more Field objects has been changed.
MoveComplete	Fired after the current position in the Recordset changes.
RecordChangeComplete	Fired after one or more records change.
RecordsetChangeComplete	Fired after the Recordset has changed.
WillChangeField	Fired before a pending operation changes the value of one or more Field objects.
WillChangeRecord	Fired before one or more rows in the Recordset change.

Table Continued On Following Page

Name	Description
WillChangeRecordset	Fired before a pending operation changes the Recordset.
WillMove	Fired before a pending operation changes the current position in the Recordset.

Stream Object

Methods

Name	Returns	Description
Cancel		Cancels execution of a pending asynchronous Open operation.
Close		Closes an open Stream.
CopyTo		Copies characters or bytes from one Stream to another.
Flush		Flushes the contents of the Stream to the underlying object.
LoadFromFile		Loads a Stream from a file.
Open		Opens a Stream object from a URL or an existing Record, or creates a blank Stream.
Read	Variant	Reads a number of bytes from the Stream.
ReadText	String	Reads a number of characters from a text Stream.
SaveToFile		Saves an open Stream to a file.
SetEOS		Sets the current position to be the end of the Stream.
SkipLine		Skips a line when reading from a text Stream.
Write		Writes binary data to a Stream.
WriteText		Writes text data to a Stream.

Properties

Name	Returns	Description
Charset	String	Identifies the character set used by the Stream.
EOS	Boolean	Is set to True if the current position is the end of the Stream. Read only
LineSeparator	LineSeparatorEnum	Indicates the character used to separate lines in a text Stream. The default is vbCrLf.

Name	Returns	Description
Mode	ConnectModeEnum	Indicates the available permissions for modifying data in a `Connection`.
Position	Long	Specifies the current position in the `Stream`.
Size	Long	Indicates the length, in bytes, of the `Stream`. Read only
State	ObjectStateEnum	Indicates whether the `Stream` is open or closed, and if open the state of asynchronous actions. Read only
Type	StreamTypeEnum	Indicates whether the Stream contains text or binary data.

Method Calls

Command

Command.Cancel
Parameter = *Command*.CreateParameter(*[Name As String], [Type As DataTypeEnum],* _
    [Direction As ParameterDirectionEnum], [Size As Long], [Value As Variant])
Recordset = *Command*.Execute(*[RecordsAffected As Variant], [Parameters As Variant],* _
    [Options As Long])

Connection

Long = *Connection*.BeginTrans
Connection.Cancel
Connection.Close
Connection.CommitTrans
Recordset = *Connection*.Execute(*CommandText As String, [RecordsAffected As Variant],* _
    [Options As Long])
Connection.Open(*[ConnectionString As String], [UserID As String], [Password As String],* _
    [Options As Long])
Recordset = *Connection*.OpenSchema(*Schema As SchemaEnum, [Restrictions As Variant],* _
    [SchemaID As Variant])
Connection.RollbackTrans

Errors

Errors.Clear
Errors.Refresh

Field

Field.AppendChunk(*Data As Variant*)
Variant = *Field*.GetChunk(*Length As Long*)

705

Fields

*Fields.*Append(*Name As String, Type As DataTypeEnum, [DefinedSize As Long], _*
    [Attrib As FieldAttributeEnum], [FieldValue As Variant])
*Fields.*CancelUpdate
*Fields.*Delete(*Index As Variant*)
*Fields.*Refresh
*Fields.*Resync(*ResyncValues As ResyncEnum*)
*Fields.*Update

Parameter

*Parameter.*AppendChunk(*Val As Variant*)

Parameters

*Parameters.*Append(*Object As Object*)
*Parameters.*Delete(*Index As Variant*)
*Parameters.*Refresh

Properties

*Properties.*Refresh

Record

*Record.*Cancel
*Record.*Close
*String = Record.*CopyRecord(*[Source As String], Destination As String, [UserName As String], _*
    [Password As String], [Options As CopyRecordOptionsEnum], [Async As Boolean])
*Record.*DeleteRecord(*Source As String, Async As Boolean*)
*Recordset = Record.*GetChildren
*String = Record.*MoveRecord([*Source As String], Destination As String, [UserName As String], _*
    [Password As String], [Options As MoveRecordOptionsEnum], [Async As Boolean])
*Record.*Open([*Source As Variant], [ActiveConnection As Variant], [Mode As ConnectModeEnum], _*
    [CreateOptions As RecordCreateOptionsEnum], [Options As RecordOpenOptionsEnum], _
    [UserName As String], [Password As String])

Recordset

*Recordset.*AddNew(*[FieldList As Variant], [Values As Variant]*)
*Recordset.*Cancel
*Recordset.*CancelBatch(*[AffectRecords As AffectEnum]*)
*Recordset.*CancelUpdate
*Recordset = Recordset.*Clone(*[LockType As LockTypeEnum]*)
*Recordset.*Close
*CompareEnum = Recordset.*CompareBookmarks(*Bookmark1 As Variant, Bookmark2 As Variant*)
*Recordset.*Delete(*AffectRecords As AffectEnum*)
*Recordset.*Find(*Criteria As String, [SkipRecords As Long], -*
    [SearchDirection As SearchDirectionEnum], [Start As Variant])
*Variant = Recordset.*GetRows(*Rows As Long, [Start As Variant], [Fields As Variant]*)

String = *Recordset.*GetString(*StringFormat As StringFormatEnum, [NumRows As Long]*, _
    [ColumnDelimeter As String], [RowDelimeter As String], [NullExpr As String])
*Recordset.*Move(*NumRecords As Long, [Start As Variant]*)
*Recordset.*MoveFirst
*Recordset.*MoveLast
*Recordset.*MoveNext
*Recordset.*MovePrevious
Recordset = *Recordset.*NextRecordset(*[RecordsAffected As Variant]*)
*Recordset.*Open(*[Source As Variant], [ActiveConnection As Variant]*,_
    [CursorType As CursorTypeEnum], [LockType As LockTypeEnum], [Options As Long])
*Recordset.*Requery(*[Options As Long]*)
*Recordset.*Resync(*[AffectRecords As AffectEnum], [ResyncValues As ResyncEnum]*)
*Recordset.*Save(*[Destination As Variant], [PersistFormat As PersistFormatEnum]*)
*Recordset.*Seek(*KeyValues As Variant, SeekOption As SeekEnum*)
Boolean = *Recordset.*Supports(*CursorOptions As CursorOptionEnum*)
*Recordset.*Update(*[Fields As Variant], [Values As Variant]*)
*Recordset.*UpdateBatch(*[AffectRecords As AffectEnum]*)

Stream

*Stream.*Cancel
*Stream.*Close
*Stream.*CopyTo(*DestStream As Stream, [CharNumber As Long]*)
*Stream.*Flush
*Stream.*LoadFromFile(*FileName As String*)
*Stream.*Open(*[Source As Variant], [Mode As ConnectModeEnum]*,_
    [Options As StreamOpenOptionsEnum], [UserName As String], [Password As String])
Variant = *Stream.*Read(*[NumBytes As Long]*)
String = *Stream.*ReadText(*[NumChars As Long]*)
*Stream.*SaveToFile(*FileName As String, Options As SaveOptionsEnum*)
*Stream.*SetEOS
*Stream.*SkipLine
*Stream.*Write(*Buffer As Variant*)
*Stream.*WriteText(*Data As String, [Options As StreamWriteEnum]*)

B

ADO Constants

Standard Constants

The following constants are predefined by ADO. For scripting languages these are included in `adovbs.inc` or `adojava.inc`, which can be found in the `Program Files\Common Files\System\ado` directory. For ASP you can either include the `.inc` file, or set a reference to the type library with a `METADATA` tag:

```
<!-- METADATA TYPE="typelib"
          FILE="C:\Program Files\Common Files\System\ADO\msado15.dll" -->
```

For Visual Basic these constants are automatically included when you reference the ADO library.

Constants new to ADO 2.5 are shown *italicized*.

AffectEnum

Name	Value	Description
adAffectAll	3	Operation affects all records in the recordset.
adAffectAllChapters	4	Operation affects all child (chapter) records.
adAffectCurrent	1	Operation affects only the current record.
adAffectGroup	2	Operation affects records that satisfy the current Filter property.

BookmarkEnum

Name	Value	Description
adBookmarkCurrent	0	Default. Start at the current record.
adBookmarkFirst	1	Start at the first record.
adBookmarkLast	2	Start at the last record.

CEResyncEnum

Name	Value	Description
adResyncAll	15	Resynchronizes the data for each pending row.
adResyncAutoIncrement	1	Resynchronizes the auto-increment values for all successfully inserted rows. This is the default.
adResyncConflicts	2	Resynchronizes all rows for which an update or delete operation failed due to concurrency conflicts.
adResyncInserts	8	Resynchronizes all successfully inserted rows, including the values of their identity columns.
adResyncNone	0	No resynchronization is performed.
adResyncUpdates	4	Resynchronizes all successfully updated rows.

CommandTypeEnum

Name	Value	Description
adCmdFile	256	Indicates that the provider should evaluate CommandText as a previously persisted file.
adCmdStoredProc	4	Indicates that the provider should evaluate CommandText as a stored procedure.
adCmdTable	2	Indicates that the provider should generate a SQL query to return all rows from the table named in CommandText.
adCmdTableDirect	512	Indicates that the provider should return all rows from the table named in CommandText.
adCmdText	1	Indicates that the provider should evaluate CommandText as textual definition of a command, such as a SQL statement.
adCmdUnknown	8	Indicates that the type of command in CommandText unknown.
adCmdUnspecified	-1	The command type is unspecified.

CompareEnum

Name	Value	Description
adCompareEqual	1	The bookmarks are equal.
adCompareGreaterThan	2	The first bookmark is after the second.
adCompareLessThan	0	The first bookmark is before the second.
adCompareNotComparable	4	The bookmarks cannot be compared.
adCompareNotEqual	3	The bookmarks are not equal and not ordered.

ConnectModeEnum

Name	Value	Description
adModeRead	1	Indicates read-only permissions.
adModeReadWrite	3	Indicates read/write permissions.
adModeRecursive	32	Used in conjunction with the ShareDeny values to propogate sharing restrictions.
adModeShareDenyNone	16	Prevents others from opening connection with any permissions.
adModeShareDenyRead	4	Prevents others from opening connection with read permissions.
adModeShareDenyWrite	8	Prevents others from opening connection with write permissions.
adModeShareExclusive	12	Prevents others from opening connection.
adModeUnknown	0	Default. Indicates that the permissions have not yet been set or cannot be determined.
adModeWrite	2	Indicates write-only permissions.

ConnectOptionEnum

Name	Value	Description
adAsyncConnect	16	Open the connection asynchronously
adConnectUnspecified	-1	The connection mode is unspecified.

ConnectPromptEnum

Name	Value	Description
adPromptAlways	1	Always prompt for connection information.
adPromptComplete	2	Only prompt if not enough information was supplied.

Table Continued on Following Page

Name	Value	Description
adPromptComplete Required	3	Only prompt if not enough information was supplied, but disable any options not directly applicable to the connection.
adPromptNever	4	Default. Never prompt for connection information.

CopyRecordOptionsEnum

Name	Value	Description
adCopyAllowEmulation	4	If the CopyRecord method fails, simulate it using a file download and upload mechanism.
adCopyNonRecursive	2	Copy the current directory, but not sub-directories.
adCopyOverWrite	1	Overwrite the existing file or directory.
adCopyUnspecified	-1	No copy behavior specified.

CursorLocationEnum

Name	Value	Description
adUseClient	3	Use client-side cursors supplied by the local cursor library.
adUseClientBatch	3	Use client-side cursors supplied by the local cursor library.
adUseNone	1	No cursor services are used.
adUseServer	2	Default. Uses data provider driver supplied cursors.

CursorOptionEnum

Name	Value	Description
adAddNew	16778240	You can use the AddNew method to add new records.
adApproxPosition	16384	You can read and set the AbsolutePosition and AbsolutePage properties.
adBookmark	8192	You can use the Bookmark property to access specific records.
adDelete	16779264	You can use the Delete method to delete records.
adFind	524288	You can use the Find method to find records.
adHoldRecords	256	You can retrieve more records or change the next retrieve position without committing all pending changes.

Name	Value	Description
adIndex	8388608	You can use the Index property to set the current index.
adMovePrevious	512	You can use the ModeFirst, MovePrevious, Move and GetRows methods.
adNotify	262144	The recordset supports Notifications.
adResync	131072	You can update the cursor with the data visible in the underlying database with the Resync method.
adSeek	4194304	You can use the Seek method to find records by an index.
adUpdate	16809984	You can use the Update method to modify existing records.
adUpdateBatch	65536	You can use the UpdateBatch or CancelBatch methods to transfer changes to the provider in groups.

CursorTypeEnum

Name	Value	Description
adOpenDynamic	2	Opens a dynamic type cursor.
adOpenForwardOnly	0	Default. Opens a forward-only type cursor
adOpenKeyset	1	Opens a keyset type cursor.
adOpenStatic	3	Opens a static type cursor.
adOpenUnspecified	-1	Indicates as unspecified value for cursor type.

DataTypeEnum

Name	Value	Description
adBigInt	20	An 8-byte signed integer.
adBinary	128	A binary value.
adBoolean	11	A Boolean value.
adBSTR	8	A null-terminated character string.
adChapter	136	A chapter type, indicating a child recordset.
adChar	129	A string value.
adCurrency	6	A currency value. An 8-byte signed integer scaled by 10,000, with 4 digits to the right of the decimal point.

Table Continued on Following Page

Name	Value	Description
adDate	7	A date value. A double where the whole part is the number of days since December 30 1899, and the fractional part is a fraction of the day.
adDBDate	133	A date value (yyyymmdd).
adDBFileTime	137	A database file time.
adDBTime	134	A time value (hhmmss).
adDBTimeStamp	135	A date-time stamp (yyyymmddhhmmss plus a fraction in billionths).
adDecimal	14	An exact numeric value with fixed precision and scale.
adDouble	5	A double-precision floating point value.
adEmpty	0	No value was specified.
adError	10	A 32-bit error code.
adFileTime	64	A DOS/Win32 file time. The number of 100 nanosecond intervals since Jan 1 1601.
adGUID	72	A globally unique identifier.
adIDispatch	9	A pointer to an IDispatch interface on an OLE object.
adInteger	3	A 4-byte signed integer.
adIUnknown	13	A pointer to an IUnknown interface on an OLE object.
adLongVarBinary	205	A long binary value.
adLongVarChar	201	A long string value.
adLongVarWChar	203	A long null-terminated string value.
adNumeric	131	An exact numeric value with a fixed precision and scale.
adPropVariant	138	A variant that is not equivalent to an Automation variant.
adSingle	4	A single-precision floating point value.
adSmallInt	2	A 2-byte signed integer.
adTinyInt	16	A 1-byte signed integer.
adUnsignedBigInt	21	An 8-byte unsigned integer.
adUnsignedInt	19	An 4-byte unsigned integer.
adUnsignedSmallInt	18	An 2-byte unsigned integer.

Name	Value	Description
adUnsignedTinyInt	17	An 1-byte unsigned integer.
adUserDefined	132	A user-defined variable.
adVarBinary	204	A binary value.
adVarChar	200	A string value.
adVariant	12	An Automation Variant.
adVarNumeric	139	A variable width exact numeric, with a signed scale value.
adVarWChar	202	A null-terminated Unicode character string.
adWChar	130	A null-terminated Unicode character string.

EditModeEnum

Name	Value	Description
adEditAdd	2	Indicates that the AddNew method has been invoked and the current record in the buffer is a new record that hasn't been saved to the database.
adEditDelete	4	Indicates that the Delete method has been invoked.
adEditInProgress	1	Indicates that data in the current record has been modified but not saved.
adEditNone	0	Indicates that no editing is in progress.

ErrorValueEnum

Name	Value	Description
adErrProviderFailed	3000	The provider failed to perform the operation.
adErrInvalidArgument	3001	The application is using arguments that are the wrong type, are out of the acceptable range, or are in conflict with one another.
adErrOpeningFile	3002	An error occurred whilst opening the requested file.
adErrReadFile	3003	An error occurred whilst trying to read from the file.
adErrWriteFile	3004	An error occurred whilst trying to write to the file.
adErrNoCurrentRecord	3021	Either BOF or EOF is True, or the current record has been deleted. The operation requested by the application requires a current record.

Table Continued on Following Page

Name	Value	Description
adErrIllegalOperation	3219	The operation requested by the application is not allowed in this context.
adErrCantChangeProvider	3220	The provider cannot be changed during the operation.
adErrInTransaction	3246	The application cannot explicitly close a Connection object while in the middle of a transaction.
adErrFeatureNotAvailable	3251	The provider does not support the operation requested by the application.
adErrItemNotFound	3265	ADO could not find the object in the collection.
adErrObjectInCollection	3367	Can't append. Object already in collection.
adErrObjectNotSet	3420	The object referenced by the application no longer points to a valid object.
adErrDataConversion	3421	The application is using a value of the wrong type for the current application.
adErrObjectClosed	3704	The operation requested by the application is not allowed if the object is closed.
adErrObjectOpen	3705	The operation requested by the application is not allowed if the object is open.
adErrProviderNotFound	3706	ADO could not find the specified provider.
adErrBoundToCommand	3707	The application cannot change the ActiveConnection property of a Recordset object with a Command object as its source.
adErrInvalidParamInfo	3708	The application has improperly defined a Parameter object.
adErrInvalidConnection	3709	The application requested an operation on an object with a reference to a closed or invalid Connection object.
adErrNotReentrant	3710	The operation is not re-entrant - you cannot perform the operation whilst processing an event.
adErrStillExecuting	3711	The operation cannot be performed during an asynchronous operation.
adErrOperationCancelled	3712	The operation was cancelled by the user.
adErrStillConnecting	3713	The operation cannot be performed during an asynchronous connection.

Name	Value	Description
adErrInvalidTransaction	3714	The transaction is invalid.
adErrNotExecuting	3715	The operation is not executing.
adErrUnsafeOperation	3716	The operation is unsafe under these circumstances. The safety settings of the computer prohibit access data from another domain.
adwrnSecurityDialog	3717	This page is accessing data on another domain. Do you want to allow this?
adwrnSecurityDialogHeader	3718	This page is accessing data on another domain. Do you want to allow this?
adErrIntegrityViolation	3719	The action failed due to a violation of data integrity.
adErrPermissionDenied	3720	The action failed because you do not have sufficient permission to complete the operation.
adErrDataOverflow	3721	The data was too large for the supplied data type.
adErrSchemaViolation	3722	The data conflicts with the data type or the field constraints.
adErrSignMismatch	3723	Data type conversion failed because the value was signed and the field data type is unsigned.
adErrCantConvertvalue	3724	The value cannot be converted for reasons other that a sign mismatch of a data overflow. Data truncation is an example of this.
adErrCantCreate	3725	The field data type is unknown therefore the value cannot be set or retrieved, or the provider had insufficient resources to perform the operation.
adErrColumnNotOnThisRow	3726	The requested field is not contained on this row.
adErrURLDoesNotExist	3727	The URL does not exist.
adErrTreePermissionDenied	3728	You do not have sufficient permissions to access the tree or subtree.
adErrInvalidURL	3729	The supplied URL contains invalid characters.
adErrResourceLocked	3730	The resource identified by the URL is locked by another process.

Table Continued on Following Page

Name	Value	Description
adErrResourceExists	3731	The resource identified by the URL already exists. Specify adCopyOverwrite to replace the resource.
adErrCannotComplete	3732	The action could not be completed.
adErrVolumeNotFound	3733	The provider cannot find the storage device associated with the URL.
adErrOutOfSpace	3734	The operation failed because the server could not obtain enough space to complete the operation.
adErrResourceOutOfScope	3735	The resource URL is outside the scope of the current Record.
adErrUnavailable	3736	The operation failed to complete and the status is unavailable.
adErrURLNamedRowDoesNotExist	3737	The URL in the named Record does not exists.
adErrDelResOutOfScope	3738	The resource URL cannot be deleted because it is out of the allowed scope of the current Record.
adErrPropInvalidColumn	3739	The property cannot be applied to the specified field.
adErrPropInvalidOption	3740	The property attribute is invalid.
adErrPropInvalidValue	3741	The property value is invalid.
adErrPropConflicting	3742	The property value conflicts with another property.
adErrPropNotAllSettable	3743	The property is read-only, or it cannot be set.
adErrPropNotSet	3744	The optional property value was not set.
adErrPropNotSettable	3745	The property is read-only and the value was not set.
adErrPropNotSupported	3746	The property is not supported by the provider.
adErrCatalogNotSet	3747	The action could not be completed because the ParentCatalog is not set.
adErrCantChangeConnection	3748	The connection cannot be changed.
adErrFieldsUpdateFailed	3749	The Update method of the Fields collection failed.
adErrDenyNotSupported	3750	The provider does not support sharing restrictions.
adErrDenyTypeNotSupported	3751	The provider does not support the requested type of sharing restriction.

EventReasonEnum

Name	Value	Description
adRsnAddNew	1	A new record is to be added.
adRsnClose	9	The object is being closed.
adRsnDelete	2	The record is being deleted.
adRsnFirstChange	11	The record has been changed for the first time.
adRsnMove	10	A Move has been invoked and the current record pointer is being moved.
adRsnMoveFirst	12	A MoveFirst has been invoked and the current record pointer is being moved.
adRsnMoveLast	15	A MoveLast has been invoked and the current record pointer is being moved.
adRsnMoveNext	13	A MoveNext has been invoked and the current record pointer is being moved.
adRsnMovePrevious	14	A MovePrevious has been invoked and the current record pointer is being moved.
adRsnRequery	7	The recordset was requeried.
adRsnResynch	8	The recordset was resynchronized.
adRsnUndoAddNew	5	The addition of a new record has been cancelled.
adRsnUndoDelete	6	The deletion of a record has been cancelled.
adRsnUndoUpdate	4	The update of a record has been cancelled.
adRsnUpdate	3	The record is being updated.

EventStatusEnum

Name	Value	Description
adStatusCancel	4	Request cancellation of the operation that is about to occur.
adStatusCantDeny	3	A Will event cannot request cancellation of the operation about to occur.
adStatusErrorsOccurred	2	The operation completed unsuccessfully, or a Will event cancelled the operation.
adStatusOK	1	The operation completed successfully.
adStatusUnwantedEvent	5	Events for this operation are no longer required.

ExecuteOptionEnum

Name	Value	Description
adAsyncExecute	16	The operation is executed asynchronously.
adAsyncFetch	32	The records are fetched asynchronously.
adAsyncFetchNonBlocking	64	The records are fetched asynchronously without blocking subsequent operations.
adExecuteNoRecords	128	Indicates CommandText is a command or stored procedure that does not return rows. Always combined with adCmdText or adCmdStoreProc.
adOptionUnspecified	-1	The command is unspecified.

FieldAttributeEnum

Name	Value	Description
adFldCacheDeferred	4096	Indicates that the provider caches field values and that subsequent reads are done from the cache.
adFldFixed	16	Indicates that the field contains fixed-length data.
adFldIsChapter	8192	The field is a chapter field, and contains a rowset.
adFldIsCollection	262144	The field is a collection.
adFldIsDefaultStream	131072	The field is the default Stream.
adFldIsNullable	32	Indicates that the field accepts Null values.
adFldIsRowURL	65536	The field is a URL.
adFldKeyColumn	32768	The field is part of a key column.
adFldLong	128	Indicates that the field is a long binary field, and that the AppendChunk and GetChunk methods can be used.
adFldMayBeNull	64	Indicates that you can read Null values from the field.
adFldMayDefer	2	Indicates that the field is deferred, that is, the field values are not retrieved from the data source with the whole record, but only when you access them.
adFldNegativeScale	16384	The field has a negative scale.
adFldRowID	256	Indicates that the field some kind of record ID.
adFldRowVersion	512	Indicates that the field time or date stamp used to track updates.
adFldUnknownUpdatable	8	Indicates that the provider cannot determine if you can write to the field.
adFldUnspecified	-1	Attributes of the field are unspecified.
adFldUpdatable	4	Indicates that you can write to the field.

FieldEnum

Name	Value	Description
adDefaultStream	-1	When used as the index into the Fields collection of a record, returns the default Stream for the Record.
adRecordURL	-2	When used as the index into the Fields collection of a record, returns the absolute URL for the Record.

FieldStatusEnum

Name	Value	Description
adFieldAlreadyExists	26	The field already exists.
adFieldBadStatus	12	An invalid status value has been send from the OLE DB provider. This could be related to a an OLE DB 1.0 or 1.1 provider.
adFieldCannotComplete	20	The action cannot be completed by the server of the URL specified in the Source.
adFieldCannotDeleteSource	23	The field cannot delete the source of the field, after a move operation.
adFieldCantConvertValue	2	The field cannot convert the value with data loss.
adFieldCantCreate	7	The field cannot be created because the provider exceeded its limitation.
adFieldDataOverflow	6	The data is too long to fit in the field.
adFieldDefault	13	The default value of the field was used.
adFieldDoesNotExist	16	The field does not exist.
adFieldIgnore	15	The field was skipped when setting values, and no value was set by the provider.
adFieldIntegrityViolation	10	The field update failed because it is a calculated or derived field.
adFieldInvalidURL	17	The field contains invalid URL characters.
adFieldIsNull	3	The provider returned a null value.
adFieldOK	0	The field was successfully added or deleted.
adFieldOutOfSpace	22	The field ran out of space for storage.
adFieldPendingChange	262144	The field has been deleted from and then added to the Fields collection, but the provider has not yet been updated.

Table Continued on Following Page

Name	Value	Description
adFieldPendingDelete	131072	The field has been deleted from the Fields collection, but the provider has not yet been updated.
adFieldPendingInsert	65536	The field has been inserted into the Fields collection, but the provider has not yet been updated.
adFieldPendingUnknown	524288	The provider cannot determine the operation that caused the Status to be set.
adFieldPendingUnknownDelete	1048576	The provider cannot determine the operation that caused the Status to be set, and the field will be deleted from the Fields collection.
adFieldPermissionDenied	9	Permission to modify the field failed because it is read-only.
adFieldReadOnly	24	The field in the data source is read only.
adFieldResourceExists	19	The resource URL specified by the field already exists.
adFieldResourceLocked	18	The resource URL specified by the field is locked by another process.
adFieldResourceOutOfScope	25	The resource specified by the field is outside the scope of the current Record.
adFieldSchemaViolation	11	The field update failed due to a schema violation.
adFieldSignMismatch	5	The value returned by the provider was signed but the ADO field data type was unsigned.
adFieldTruncated	4	The field value was truncated.
adFieldUnavailable	8	The provider could not determine the value of the field.
adFieldVolumeNotFound	21	The volume specified by the URL was not found.

FilterGroupEnum

Name	Value	Description
adFilterAffectedRecords	2	Allows you to view only records affected by the last Delete, Resync, UpdateBatch, or CancelBatch method.
adFilterConflictingRecords	5	Allows you to view the records that failed the last batch update attempt.
adFilterFetchedRecords	3	Allows you to view records in the current cache.

Name	Value	Description
adFilterNone	0	Removes the current filter and restores all records to view.
adFilterPendingRecords	1	Allows you to view only the records that have changed but have not been sent to the server. Only applicable for batch update mode.
adFilterPredicate	4	Allows you to view records that failed the last batch update attempt.

GetRowsOptionEnum

Name	Value	Description
adGetRowsRest	-1	Retrieves the remainder of the rows in the recordset.

IsolationLevelEnum

Name	Value	Description
adXactBrowse	256	Indicates that from one transaction you can view uncommitted changes in other transactions.
adXactChaos	16	Default. Indicates that you cannot overwrite pending changes from more highly isolated transactions.
adXactCursorStability	4096	Default. Indicates that from one transaction you can view changes in other transactions only after they have been committed.
adXactIsolated	1048576	Indicates that transactions are conducted in isolation of other transactions.
adXactReadCommitted	4096	Same as adXactCursorStability.
adXactReadUncommitted	256	Same as adXactBrowse.
adXactRepeatableRead	65536	Indicates that from one transaction you cannot see changes made in other transactions, but that requerying can bring new recordsets.
adXactSerializable	1048576	Same as adXactIsolated.
adXactUnspecified	-1	Indicates that the provider is using a different IsolationLevel than specified, but that the level cannot be identified.

LineSeparatorEnum

Name	Value	Description
adCR	13	The carriage return character.
adCRLF	-1	The carriage return and line feed characters.
adLF	10	The line feed character.

LockTypeEnum

Name	Value	Description
adLockBatchOptimistic	4	Optimistic batch updates.
adLockOptimistic	3	Optimistic locking, record by record. The provider locks records when Update is called.
adLockPessimistic	2	Pessimistic locking, record by record. The provider locks the record immediately upon editing.
adLockReadOnly	1	Default. Read only, data cannot be modified.
adLockUnspecified	-1	The clone is created with the same lock type as the original.

MarshalOptionsEnum

Name	Value	Description
adMarshalAll	0	Default. Indicates that all rows are returned to the server.
adMarshalModifiedOnly	1	Indicates that only modified rows are returned to the server.

MoveRecordOptionsEnum

Name	Value	Description
adMoveAllowEmulation	4	If the attempt to move the record fails, allow the move to be performed using a download, upload and delete set of operations.
adMoveDontUpdateLinks	2	Do not update hyperlinks of the source Record.
adMoveOverWrite	1	Overwrite the target if it already exists.

ObjectStateEnum

Name	Value	Description
adStateClosed	0	Default. Indicates that the object is closed.
adStateConnecting	2	Indicates that the object is connecting.
adStateExecuting	4	Indicates that the object is executing a command.
adStateFetching	8	Indicates that the rows of the recordset are being fetched.
adStateOpen	1	Indicates that the object is open.

ParameterAttributesEnum

Name	Value	Description
adParamLong	128	Indicates that the parameter accepts long binary data.
adParamNullable	64	Indicates that the parameter accepts Null values.
adParamSigned	16	Default. Indicates that the parameter accepts signed values.

ParameterDirectionEnum

Name	Value	Description
adParamInput	1	Default. Indicates an input parameter.
adParamInputOutput	3	Indicates both an input and output parameter.
adParamOutput	2	Indicates an output parameter.
adParamReturnValue	4	Indicates a return value.
adParamUnknown	0	Indicates parameter direction is unknown.

PersistFormatEnum

Name	Value	Description
adPersistADTG	0	Default. Persist data in Advanced Data TableGram format.
adPersistXML	1	Persist data in XML format.

PositionEnum

Name	Value	Description
adPosBOF	-2	The current record pointer is at BOF.
adPosEOF	-3	The current record pointer is at EOF.
adPosUnknown	-1	The Recordset is empty, the current position is unknown, or the provider does not support the AbsolutePage property.

PropertyAttributesEnum

Name	Value	Description
adPropNotSupported	0	Indicates that the property is not supported by the provider.
adPropOptional	2	Indicates that the user does not need to specify a value for this property before the data source is initialized.
adPropRead	512	Indicates that the user can read the property.
adPropRequired	1	Indicates that the user must specify a value for this property before the data source is initialized.
adPropWrite	1024	Indicates that the user can set the property.

RecordCreateOptionsEnum

Name	Value	Description
adCreateCollection	8192	Create a new collection record (directory) at the specified URL.
adCreateNonCollection	0	Create a new record at the specified URL.
adCreateOverwrite	67108864	Overwrite any existing record at the specified URL.
adCreateStructDoc	-2147483648	Create a new structured document record at the specified URL.
adFailIfNotExists	-1	Fail if the URL does not exist.
adOpenIfExists	33554432	Open the record at the specified URL if it exists.

RecordOpenOptionsEnum

Name	Value	Description
adDelayFetchFields	32768	Delay fetching fields until they are requested.
adDelayFetchStream	16384	Delay fetching the Stream until it is requested.

Name	Value	Description
adOpenAsync	4096	Open the Record asynchronously.
adOpenSource	8388608	Open the source document at the URL, rather than the executed contents.
adOpenURLBind	1024	Indicates the connection string contains a URL.

RecordStatusEnum

Name	Value	Description
adRecCanceled	256	The record was not saved because the operation was cancelled.
adRecCantRelease	1024	The new record was not saved because of existing record locks.
adRecConcurrencyViolation	2048	The record was not saved because optimistic concurrency was in use.
adRecDBDeleted	262144	The record has already been deleted from the data source.
adRecDeleted	4	The record was deleted.
adRecIntegrityViolation	4096	The record was not saved because the user violated integrity constraints.
adRecInvalid	16	The record was not saved because its bookmark is invalid.
adRecMaxChangesExceeded	8192	The record was not saved because there were too many pending changes.
adRecModified	2	The record was modified.
adRecMultipleChanges	64	The record was not saved because it would have affected multiple records.
adRecNew	1	The record is new.
adRecObjectOpen	16384	The record was not saved because of a conflict with an open storage object.
adRecOK	0	The record was successfully updated.
adRecOutOfMemory	32768	The record was not saved because the computer has run out of memory.
adRecPendingChanges	128	The record was not saved because it refers to a pending insert.
adRecPermissionDenied	65536	The record was not saved because the user has insufficient permissions.
adRecSchemaViolation	131072	The record was not saved because it violates the structure of the underlying database.
adRecUnmodified	8	The record was not modified.

RecordTypeEnum

Name	Value	Description
adCollectionRecord	1	The record is a collection type (directory)
adSimpleRecord	0	The record is a simple file.
adStructDoc	2	The record is a structured document.

ResyncEnum

Name	Value	Description
adResyncAllValues	2	Default. Data is overwritten and pending updates are cancelled.
adResyncUnderlyingValues	1	Data is not overwritten and pending updates are not cancelled.

SaveOptionsEnum

Name	Value	Description
adSaveCreateNotExist	1	Create a new file if the file does not already exist.
adSaveCreateOverWrite	2	Overwrite any existing file if it exists.

SchemaEnum

Name	Value	Description
adSchemaAsserts	0	Request assert information.
adSchemaCatalogs	1	Request catalog information.
adSchemaCharacterSets	2	Request character set information.
adSchemaCheckConstraints	5	Request check constraint information.
adSchemaCollations	3	Request collation information.
adSchemaColumnPrivileges	13	Request column privilege information.
adSchemaColumns	4	Request column information.
adSchemaColumnsDomainUsage	11	Request column domain usage information.
adSchemaConstraintColumnUsage	6	Request column constraint usage information.
adSchemaConstraintTableUsage	7	Request table constraint usage information.

Name	Value	Description
adSchemaCubes	32	For multi-dimensional data, view the Cubes schema.
adSchemaDBInfoKeywords	30	Request the keywords from the provider.
adSchemaDBInfoLiterals	31	Request the literals from the provider.
adSchemaDimensions	33	For multi-dimensional data, view the Dimensions schema.
adSchemaForeignKeys	27	Request foreign key information.
adSchemaHierarchies	34	For multi-dimensional data, view the Hierarchies schema.
adSchemaIndexes	12	Request index information.
adSchemaKeyColumnUsage	8	Request key column usage information.
adSchemaLevels	35	For multi-dimensional data, view the Levels schema.
adSchemaMeasures	36	For multi-dimensional data, view the Measures schema.
adSchemaMembers	38	For multi-dimensional data, view the Members schema.
adSchemaPrimaryKeys	28	Request primary key information.
adSchemaProcedureColumns	29	Request stored procedure column information.
adSchemaProcedureParameters	26	Request stored procedure parameter information.
adSchemaProcedures	16	Request stored procedure information.
adSchemaProperties	37	For multi-dimensional data, view the Properties schema.
adSchemaProviderSpecific	-1	Request provider specific information.
adSchemaProviderTypes	22	Request provider type information.
adSchemaReferentialContraints	9	Request referential constraint information.
adSchemaReferentialConstraints	9	Request referential constraint information.
adSchemaSchemata	17	Request schema information.
adSchemaSQLLanguages	18	Request SQL language support information.
adSchemaStatistics	19	Request statistics information.

Table Continued on Following Page

Name	Value	Description
adSchemaTableConstraints	10	Request table constraint information.
adSchemaTablePrivileges	14	Request table privilege information.
adSchemaTables	20	Request information about the tables.
adSchemaTranslations	21	Request character set translation information.
adSchemaTrustees	39	Request trustee information.
adSchemaUsagePrivileges	15	Request user privilege information.
adSchemaViewColumnUsage	24	Request column usage in views information.
adSchemaViews	23	Request view information.
adSchemaViewTableUsage	25	Request table usage in views information.

Due to a misspelling in the type library **adSchemaReferentialConstraints** is included twice - once for the original spelling and once for the corrected spelling.

SearchDirectionEnum

Name	Value	Description
adSearchBackward	-1	Search backward from the current record.
adSearchForward	1	Search forward from the current record.

SeekEnum

Name	Value	Description
adSeekAfter	8	Seek the key just after the match.
adSeekAfterEQ	4	Seek the key equal to or just after the match.
adSeekBefore	32	See the key just before the match.
adSeekBeforeEQ	16	Seek the key equal to or just before the match.
adSeekFirstEQ	1	Seek the first key equal to the match.
adSeekLastEQ	2	Seek the last key equal to the match.

StreamOpenOptionsEnum

Name	Value	Description
adOpenStreamAsync	1	Opens the Stream asynchronously.
adOpenStreamFromRecord	4	Opens the Stream using an existing Record as the source.
adOpenStreamUnspecified	-1	Opens the Stream with default options.

StreamReadEnum

Name	Value	Description
adReadAll	-1	Reads all bytes from the Stream, from the current position to the end of the stream.
adReadLine	-2	Reads the next line from the Stream. Uses the LineSeparator property to identify the end of the line.

StreamTypeEnum

Name	Value	Description
adTypeBinary	1	The Stream contains binary data.
adTypeText	2	The Stream contains text data.

StreamWriteEnum

Name	Value	Description
adWriteChar	0	Writes the specified string to the Stream.
adWriteLine	1	Writes the specified string and a line separator to the Stream.
stWriteChar	0	Writes the specified string to the Stream.
stWriteLine	1	Writes the specified string and a line separator to the Stream.

StringFormatEnum

Name	Value	Description
adClipString	2	Rows are delimited by user defined values.

XactAttributeEnum

Name	Value	Description
adXactAbortRetaining	262144	The provider will automatically start a new transaction after a RollbackTrans method call.
adXactAsyncPhaseOne	524288	Perform an asynchronous commit.
adXactCommitRetaining	131072	The provider will automatically start a new transaction after a CommitTrans method call.
adXactSyncPhaseOne	1048576	Performs an synchronous commit.

Miscellaneous Constants

These values are not included in the standard adovbs.inc include file (and are not automatically supplied when using Visual Basic), but can be found in adocon.inc (for ASP) and adocon.bas (for Visual Basic) from the supporting web site, http://www.wrox.com

Many of these may not be necessary to you as an ADO programmer, but they are included here for completeness, and are only really useful as bitmask values for entries in the Properties collection.

DB_COLLATION

Name	Value	Description
DB_COLLATION_ASC	1	The sort sequence for the column is ascending.
DB_COLLATION_DESC	2	The sort sequence for the column is descending.

DB_IMP_LEVEL

Name	Value	Description
DB_IMP_LEVEL_ANONYMOUS	0	The client is anonymous to the server, and the server process cannot obtain identification information about the client and cannot impersonate the client.
DB_IMP_LEVEL_DELEGATE	3	The process can impersonate the client's security context while acting on behalf of the client. The server process can also make outgoing calls to other servers while acting on behalf of the client.
DB_IMP_LEVEL_IDENTIFY	1	The server can obtain the client's identity, and can impersonate the client for ACL checking, but cannot access system objects as the client.
DB_IMP_LEVEL_IMPERSONATE	2	The server process can impersonate the client's security context whilst acting on behalf of the client. This information is obtained upon connection and not on every call.

DB_MODE

Name	Value	Description
DB_MODE_READ	1	Read only.
DB_MODE_READWRITE	3	Read/Write (DB_MODE_READ + DB_MODE_WRITE).
DB_MODE_SHARE_DENY_NONE	16	Neither read nor write access can be denied to others.
DB_MODE_SHARE_DENY_READ	4	Prevents others from opening in read mode.

Name	Value	Description
DB_MODE_SHARE_DENY_WRITE	8	Prevents others from opening in write mode.
DB_MODE_SHARE_EXCLUSIVE	12	Prevents others from opening in read/write mode (DB_MODE_SHARE_DENY_WRITE + DB_MODE_SHARE_DENY_WRITE).
DB_MODE_WRITE	2	Write only.

DB_PROT_LEVEL

Name	Value	Description
DB_PROT_LEVEL_CALL	2	Authenticates the source of the data at the beginning of each request from the client to the server.
DB_PROT_LEVEL_CONNECT	1	Authenticates only when the client establishes the connection with the server.
DB_PROT_LEVEL_NONE	0	Performs no authentication of data sent to the server.
DB_PROT_LEVEL_PKT	3	Authenticates that all data received is from the client.
DB_PROT_LEVEL_PKT_INTEGRITY	4	Authenticates that all data received is from the client and that it has not been changed in transit.
DB_PROT_LEVEL_PKT_PRIVACY	5	Authenticates that all data received is from the client, that it has not been changed in transit, and protects the privacy of the data by encrypting it.

DB_PT

Name	Value	Description
DB_PT_FUNCTION	3	Function; there is a returned value.
DB_PT_PROCEDURE	2	Procedure; there is no returned value.
DB_PT_UNKNOWN	1	It is not known whether there is a returned value.

DB_SEARCHABLE

Name	Value	Description
DB_ALL_EXCEPT_LIKE	3	The data type can be used in a WHERE clause with all comparison operators except LIKE.
DB_LIKE_ONLY	2	The data type can be used in a WHERE clause only with the LIKE predicate.

Table Continued on Following Page

Name	Value	Description
DB_SEARCHABLE	4	The data type can be used in a WHERE clause with any comparison operator.
DB_UNSEARCHABLE	1	The data type cannot be used in a WHERE clause.

DBCOLUMNDESCFLAG

Name	Value	Description
DBCOLUMNDESCFLAG_CLSID	8	The CLSID portion of the column description can be changed when altering the column.
DBCOLUMNDESCFLAG_COLSIZE	16	The column size portion of the column description can be changed when altering the column.
DBCOLUMNDESCFLAG_DBCID	32	The DBCID portion of the column description can be changed when altering the column.
DBCOLUMNDESCFLAG_ITYPEINFO	2	The type information portion of the column description can be changed when altering the column.
DBCOLUMNDESCFLAG_PRECISION	128	The precision portion of the column description can be changed when altering the column.
DBCOLUMNDESCFLAG_PROPERTIES	4	The property sets portion of the column description can be changed when altering the column.
DBCOLUMNDESCFLAG_SCALE	256	The numeric scale portion of the column description can be changed when altering the column.
DBCOLUMNDESCFLAG_TYPENAME	1	The type name portion of the column description can be changed when altering the column.
DBCOLUMNDESCFLAG_WTYPE	64	The data type portion of the column description can be changed when altering the column.

DBCOLUMNFLAGS

Name	Value	Description
DBCOLUMNFLAGS_CACHEDEFERRED	4096	Indicates that the value of a deferred column is cached when it is first read.
DBCOLUMNFLAGS_ISCHAPTER	8192	The column contains a Chapter value.
DBCOLUMNFLAGS_ISFIXEDLENGTH	16	All of the data in the column is of a fixed length.

Name	Value	Description
DBCOLUMNFLAGS_ISLONG	128	The column contains a BLOB value that contains long data.
DBCOLUMNFLAGS_ISNULLABLE	32	The column can be set to NULL, or the provider cannot determine whether the column can be set to NULL.
DBCOLUMNFLAGS_ISROWID	256	The column contains a persistent row identifier.
DBCOLUMNFLAGS_ISROWVER	512	The column contains a timestamp or other row versioning data type.
DBCOLUMNFLAGS_MAYBENULL	64	NULLs can be got from the column.
DBCOLUMNFLAGS_MAYDEFER	2	The column is deferred.
DBCOLUMNFLAGS_WRITE	4	The column may be updated.
DBCOLUMNFLAGS_WRITEUNKNOWN	8	It is not know if the column can be updated.

DBCOMPUTEMODE

Name	Value	Description
DBCOMPUTEMODE_COMPUTED	1	The column is a computed column.
DBCOMPUTEMODE_DYNAMIC	2	The column is computed and always returns the value based upon the computation.
DBCOMPUTEMODE_NOTCOMPUTED	3	The column is not a computed column.

DBLITERAL

Name	Value	Description
DBLITERAL_INVALID	0	An invalid value.
DBLITERAL_BINARY_LITERAL	1	A binary literal in a text command.
DBLITERAL_CATALOG_NAME	2	A catalog name in a text command.
DBLITERAL_CATALOG_SEPARATOR	3	The character that separates the catalog name from the rest of the identifier in a text command.
DBLITERAL_CHAR_LITERAL	4	A character literal in a text command.
DBLITERAL_COLUMN_ALIAS	5	A column alias in a text command.
DBLITERAL_COLUMN_NAME	6	A column name used in a text command or in a data-definition interface.

Table Continued on Following Page

Name	Value	Description
DBLITERAL_CORRELATION_NAME	7	A correlation name (table alias) in a text command.
DBLITERAL_CURSOR_NAME	8	A cursor name in a text command.
DBLITERAL_ESCAPE_PERCENT DBLITERAL_ESCAPE_PERCENT_PREFIX	9	The character used in a LIKE clause to escape the character returned for the DBLITERAL_LIKE_PERCENT literal.
DBLITERAL_ESCAPE_PERCENT_SUFFIX	29	The escape character, if any, used to suffix the character returned for the DBLITERAL_LIKE_PERCENT literal.
DBLITERAL_ESCAPE_UNDERSCORE DBLITERAL_ESCAPE_UNDERSCORE_PREFIX	10	The character used in a LIKE clause to escape the character returned for the DBLITERAL_LIKE_UNDERSCORE literal.
DBLITERAL_ESCAPE_UNDERSCORE_SUFFIX	30	The escape character, if any, used to suffix the character returned for the DBLITERAL_LIKE_UNDERSCORE literal.
DBLITERAL_INDEX_NAME	11	An index name used in a text command or in a data-definition interface.
DBLITERAL_LIKE_PERCENT	12	The character used in a LIKE clause to match zero or more characters.
DBLITERAL_LIKE_UNDERSCORE	13	The character used in a LIKE clause to match exactly one character.
DBLITERAL_PROCEDURE_NAME	14	A procedure name in a text command.
DBLITERAL_SCHEMA_NAME	16	A schema name in a text command.
DBLITERAL_SCHEMA_SEPARATOR	27	The character that separates the schema name from the rest of the identifier in a text command.
DBLITERAL_TABLE_NAME	17	A table name used in a text command or in a data-definition interface.
DBLITERAL_TEXT_COMMAND	18	A text command, such as an SQL statement.
DBLITERAL_USER_NAME	19	A user name in a text command.
DBLITERAL_VIEW_NAME	20	A view name in a text command.
DBLITERAL_QUOTE DBLITERAL_QUOTE_PREFIX	15	The character used in a text command as the opening quote for quoting identifiers that contain special characters.

Name	Value	Description
DBLITERAL_QUOTE_SUFFIX	28	The character used in a text command as the closing quote for quoting identifiers that contain special characters.

DBPARAMTYPE

Name	Value	Description
DBPARAMTYPE_INPUT	1	The parameter is an input parameter.
DBPARAMTYPE_INPUTOUTPUT	2	The parameter is both an input and an output parameter.
DBPARAMTYPE_OUTPUT	3	The parameter is an output parameter.
DBPARAMTYPE_RETURNVALUE	4	The parameter is a return value.

DBPROMPT

Name	Value	Description
DBPROMPT_COMPLETE	2	Prompt the user only if more information is needed.
DBPROMPT_COMPLETEREQUIRED	3	Prompt the user only if more information is required. Do not allow the user to enter optional information.
DBPROMPT_NOPROMPT	4	Do not prompt the user.
DBPROMPT_PROMPT	1	Always prompt the user for initialization information.

DBPROPVAL_AO

Name	Value	Description
DBPROPVAL_AO_RANDOM	2	Columns can be accessed in any order.
DBPROPVAL_AO_SEQUENTIAL	0	All columns must be accessed in sequential order determined by the column ordinal.
DBPROPVAL_AO_ SEQUENTIALSTORAGEOBJECTS	1	Columns bound as storage objects can only be accessed in sequential order as determined by the column ordinal.

DBPROPVAL_ASYNCH

Name	Value	Description
DBPROPVAL_ASYNCH_BACKGROUNDPOPULATION	8	The rowset is populated asynchronously in the background.
DBPROPVAL_ASYNCH_INITIALIZE	1	Initialization is performed asynchronously.
DBPROPVAL_ASYNCH_POPULATEONDEMAND	32	The consumer prefers to optimize for getting each individual request for data returned as quickly as possible.
DBPROPVAL_ASYNCH_PREPOPULATE	16	The consumer prefers to optimize for retrieving all data when the row set is materialized.
DBPROPVAL_ASYNCH_RANDOMPOPULATION	4	Rowset population is performed asynchronously in a random manner.
DBPROPVAL_ASYNCH_SEQUENTIALPOPULATION	2	Rowset population is performed asynchronously in a sequential manner.

DBPROPVAL_BG

Name	Value	Description
DBPROPVAL_GB_COLLATE	16	A COLLATE clause can be specified at the end of each grouping column.
DBPROPVAL_GB_CONTAINS_SELECT	4	The GROUP BY clause must contain all non-aggregated columns in the select list. It can contain columns that are not in the select list.
DBPROPVAL_GB_EQUALS_SELECT	2	The GROUP BY clause must contain all non-aggregated columns in the select list. It cannot contain any other columns.
DBPROPVAL_GB_NO_RELATION	8	The columns in the GROUP BY clause and the select list are not related. The meaning on non-grouped, non-aggregated columns in the select list is data source dependent.
DBPROPVAL_GB_NOT_SUPPORTED	1	GROUP BY clauses are not supported.

DBPROPVAL_BI

Name	Value	Description
DBPROPVAL_BI_CROSSROWSET	1	Bookmark values are valid across all rowsets generated on this table.

DBPROPVAL_BMK

Name	Value	Description
DBPROPVAL_BMK_KEY	2	The bookmark type is key.
DBPROPVAL_BMK_NUMERIC	1	The bookmark type is numeric.

DBPROPVAL_BO

Name	Value	Description
DBPROPVAL_BO_NOINDEXUPDATE	1	The provider is not required to update indexes based on inserts or changes to the rowset. Any indexes need to be re-created following changes made through the rowset.
DBPROPVAL_BO_NOLOG	0	The provider is not required to log inserts or changes to the rowset.
DBPROPVAL_BO_REFINTEGRITY	2	Referential integrity constraints do not need to be checked or enforced for changes made through the rowset.

DBPROPVAL_BT

Name	Value	Description
DBPROPVAL_BT_DEFAULT	0	Use the value defined in the dynamic property Jet OLEDB:Global Bulk Transactions
DBPROPVAL_BT_NOBULKTRANSACTIONS	1	Bulk operations are not transacted.
DBPROPVAL_BT_BULKTRANSACTION	2	Bulk operations are transacted.

DBPROPVAL_CB

Name	Value	Description
DBPROPVAL_CB_NON_NULL	2	The result is the concatenation of the non-NULL valued column or columns.
DBPROPVAL_CB_NULL	1	The result is NULL valued.

DBPROPVAL_CB

Name	Value	Description
DBPROPVAL_CB_DELETE	1	Aborting a transaction deletes prepared commands.
DBPROPVAL_CB_PRESERVE	2	Aborting a transaction preserves prepared commands.

DBPROPVAL_CD

Name	Value	Description
DBPROPVAL_CD_NOTNULL	1	Columns can be created non-nullable.

DBPROPVAL_CL

Name	Value	Description
DBPROPVAL_CL_END	2	The catalog name appears at the end of the fully qualified name.
DBPROPVAL_CL_START	1	The catalog name appears at the start of the fully qualified name.

DBPROPVAL_CM

Name	Value	Description
DBPROPVAL_CM_TRANSACTIONS	1	The provider enlists in COM+ transactions directly.

DBPROPVAL_CO

Name	Value	Description
DBPROPVAL_CO_BEGINSWITH	32	Provider supports the BEGINSWITH and NOTBEGINSWITH operators.
DBPROPVAL_CO_CASEINSENSITIVE	8	Provider supports the CASEINSENSITIVE operator.
DBPROPVAL_CO_CASESENSITIVE	4	Provider supports the CASESENSITIVE operator.
DBPROPVAL_CO_CONTAINS	16	Provider supports the CONTAINS and NOTCONTAINS operators.
DBPROPVAL_CO_EQUALITY	1	Provider supports the following operators: LT, LE, EQ, GE, GT, NE.
DBPROPVAL_CO_STRING	2	Provider supports the BEGINSWITH operator.

DBPROPVAL_CS

Name	Value	Description
DBPROPVAL_CS_COMMUNICATIONFAILURE	2	The DSO is unable to communicate wit the data store.
DBPROPVAL_CS_INITIALIZED	1	The DSO is in an initialized state and able to communicate with the data store.
DBPROPVAL_CS_UNINITIALIZED	0	The DSO is in an uninitialized state.

DBPROPVAL_CU

Name	Value	Description
DBPROPVAL_CU_DML_STATEMENTS	1	Catalog names are supported in all Data Manipulation Language statements.
DBPROPVAL_CU_INDEX_DEFINITION	4	Catalog names are supported in all index definition statements.
DBPROPVAL_CU_PRIVILEGE_DEFINITION	8	Catalog names are supported in all privilege definition statements.
DBPROPVAL_CU_TABLE_DEFINITION	2	Catalog names are supported in all table definition statements.

DBPROPVAL_DF

Name	Value	Description
DBPROPVAL_DF_INITIALLY_DEFERRED	1	The foreign key is initially deferred.
DBPROPVAL_DF_INITIALLY_IMMEDIATE	2	The foreign key is initially immediate.
DBPROPVAL_DF_NOT_DEFERRABLE	3	The foreign key is not deferrable.

DBPROPVAL_DL

Name	Value	Description
DBPROPVAL_DL_OLDMODE	0	Mode used in previous versions of the Jet database.
DBPROPVAL_DL_ALCATRAZ	1	Use new method, allowing row level locking.

DBPROPVAL_DST

Name	Value	Description
DBPROPVAL_DST_MDP	2	The provider is a multidimensional provider (MD).
DBPROPVAL_DST_TDP	1	The provider is a tabular data provider (TDP).
DBPROPVAL_DST_TDPANDMDP	3	The provider is both a TDP and a MD provider.
DBPROPVAL_DST_DOCSOURCE	4	The provider is a document source (Internet Publishing Provider).

DBPROPVAL_GB

Name	Value	Description
DBPROPVAL_GB_EQUALS_SELECT	2	The GROUP BY clause must contain all non-aggregated columns in the select list, and no other columns.
DBPROPVAL_GB_COLLATE	16	A COLLATE clause can be used at the end of each grouping column.
DBPROPVAL_GB_CONTAINS_SELECT	4	The GROUP BY clause must contain all non-aggregated columns in the select list, and it can contain other columns.
DBPROPVAL_GB_NO_RELATION	8	There is no relationship between the columns in the select list and the GROUP BY list.
DBPROPVAL_GB_NOT_SUPPORTED	1	GROUP BY is not supported.

DBPROPVAL_GU

Name	Value	Description
DBPROPVAL_GU_NOTSUPPORTED	1	URL suffixes are not supported. This is the only option supported by the Internet Publishing Provider in this version of ADO.
DBPROPVAL_GU_SUFFIX	2	URL suffixes are generated by the Internet Publishing Provider.

DBPROPVAL_HT

Name	Value	Description
DBPROPVAL_HT_DIFFERENT_CATALOGS	1	The provider supports heterogeneous joins between catalogs.
DBPROPVAL_HT_DIFFERENT_PROVIDERS	2	The provider supports heterogeneous joins between providers.

DBPROPVAL_IC

Name	Value	Description
DBPROPVAL_IC_LOWER	2	Identifiers in SQL are case insensitive and are stored in lower case in system catalog.
DBPROPVAL_IC_MIXED	8	Identifiers in SQL are case insensitive and are stored in mixed case in system catalog.
DBPROPVAL_IC_SENSITIVE	4	Identifiers in SQL are case sensitive and are stored in mixed case in system catalog.
DBPROPVAL_IC_UPPER	1	Identifiers in SQL are case insensitive and are stored in upper case in system catalog.

DBPROPVAL_IN

Name	*Value*	*Description*
DBPROPVAL_IN_ALLOWNULL	0	The index allows NULL values to be inserted.
DBPROPVAL_IN_DISALLOWNULL	1	The index does not allow entries where the key columns are NULL. An error will be generated if the consumer attempts to insert a NULL value into a key column.
DBPROPVAL_IN_IGNOREANYNULL	4	The index does not insert entries containing NULL keys.
DBPROPVAL_IN_IGNORENULL	2	The index does not insert entries where some column key has a NULL value.

DBPROPVAL_IT

Name	*Value*	*Description*
DBPROPVAL_IT_BTREE	1	The index is a B+ tree.
DBPROPVAL_IT_CONTENT	3	The index is a content index.
DBPROPVAL_IT_HASH	2	The index is a hash file using linear or extensible hashing.
DBPROPVAL_IT_OTHER	4	The index is some other type of index.

DBPROPVAL_JCC

Name	*Value*	*Description*
DBPROPVAL_JCC_PASSIVESHUTDOWN	1	New connections to the database are disallowed.
DBPROPVAL_JCC_NORMAL	2	Users are allowed to connect to the database.

DBPROPVAL_LG

Name	*Value*	*Description*
DBPROPVAL_LG_PAGE	1	Use page locking.
DBPROPVAL_LG_ALCATRAZ	2	Use row-level locking.

DBPROPVAL_LM

Name	Value	Description
DBPROPVAL_LM_INTENT	4	The provider uses the maximum level of locking to ensure that changes will not fail due to a concurrency violation.
DBPROPVAL_LM_NONE	1	The provider is not required to lock rows at any time to ensure successful updates.
DBPROPVAL_LM_READ	2	The provider uses the minimum level of locking to ensure that changes will not fail due to a concurrency violation.
DBPROPVAL_LM_WRITE	8	
DBPROPVAL_LM_SINGLEROW	2	The provider uses the minimum level of locking to ensure that changes will not fail due to a concurrency violation.

DBPROPVAL_MR

Name	Value	Description
DBPROPVAL_MR_CONCURRENT	2	More than one rowset create by the same multiple results object can exist concurrently.
DBPROPVAL_MR_NOTSUPPORTED	0	Multiple results objects are not supported.
DBPROPVAL_MR_SUPPORTED	1	The provider supports multiple results objects.

DBPROPVAL_NC

Name	Value	Description
DBPROPVAL_NC_END	1	NULLs are sorted at the end of the list, regardless of the sort order.
DBPROPVAL_NC_HIGH	2	NULLs are sorted at the high end of the list.
DBPROPVAL_NC_LOW	4	NULLs are sorted at the low end of the list.
DBPROPVAL_NC_START	8	NULLs are sorted at the start of the list, regardless of the sort order.

DBPROPVAL_NP

Name	Value	Description
DBPROPVAL_NP_ABOUTTODO	2	The consumer will be notified before an action (ie the Will event).
DBPROPVAL_NP_DIDEVENT	16	The consumer will be notified after an action (ie the Complete event).

Name	Value	Description
DBPROPVAL_NP_FAILEDTODO	8	The consumer will be notified if an action failed (ie a Will or Complete event).
DBPROPVAL_NP_OKTODO	1	The consumer will be notified of events.
DBPROPVAL_NP_SYNCHAFTER	4	The consumer will be notified when the rowset is resynchronized.

DBPROPVAL_NT

Name	Value	Description
DBPROPVAL_NT_MULTIPLEROWS	2	For methods that operate on multiple rows, and generate multiphased notifications (events), then the provider calls OnRowChange once for all rows that succeed and once for all rows that fail.
DBPROPVAL_NT_SINGLEROW	1	For methods that operate on multiple rows, and generate multiphased notifications (events), then the provider calls OnRowChange separately for each phase for each row.

DBPROPVAL_OA

Name	Value	Description
DBPROPVAL_OA_ATEXECUTE	2	Output parameter data is available immediately after the Command.Execute returns.
DBPROPVAL_OA_ATROWRELEASE	4	Output parameter data is available when the rowset is release. For a single rowset operation this is when the rowset is completely released (closed) and for a multiple rowset operation this is when the next rowset if fetched. The consumer's bound memory is in an indeterminate state before the parameter data becomes available.
DBPROPVAL_OA_NOTSUPPORTED	1	Output parameters are not supported.

DBPROPVAL_OO

Name	Value	Description
DBPROPVAL_OO_BLOB	1	The provider supports access to BLOBs as structured storage objects.
DBPROPVAL_OO_DIRECTBIND	16	The provider supports direct binding to BLOBs.

Table Continued on Following Page

Name	Value	Description
DBPROPVAL_OO_IPERSIST	2	The provider supports access to OLE objects through OLE.
DBPROPVAL OO ROWOBJECT	4	The provider supports row objects.
DBPROPVAL_OO_SCOPED	8	The provider supports objects that have scoped operations.
DBPROPVAL_OO_SINGLETON	32	The provider supports singleton operations

DBPROPVAL_ORS

Name	Value	Description
DBPROPVAL_ORS_TABLE	1	The provider supports opening tables.
DBPROPVAL_ORS_INDEX	2	The provider supports opening indexes.
DBPROPVAL_ORS_ INTEGRATEDINDEX	16	The provider supports both the table and index in the same open method.
DBPROPVAL_ORS_ STOREDPROC	4	The provider supports opening rowsets over stored procedures.

DBPROPVAL_OS

Name	Value	Description
DBPROPVAL_OS_ENABLEALL	-1	All services should be invoked. This is the default.
DBPROPVAL_OS_ RESOURCEPOOLING	1	Resources should be pooled.
DBPROPVAL_OS_TXNENLISTMENT	2	Sessions in an MTS environment should automatically be enlisted in a global transaction where required.
DBPROPVAL_OS_CLIENT_CURSOR	4	Disable client cursor.
DBPROPVAL_OS_DISABLEALL	0	All services should be disabled.
DBPROPVAL_OS_AGR_ AFTERSESSION	8	Support for services beyond session level.

DBPROPVAL_PT

Name	Value	Description
DBPROPVAL_PT_GUID	8	The GUID is used as the persistent ID type.
DBPROPVAL_PT_GUID_NAME	1	The GUID Name is used as the persistent ID type.

Name	Value	Description
DBPROPVAL_PT_GUID_PROPID	2	The GUID Property ID is used as the persistent ID type.
DBPROPVAL_PT_NAME	4	The Name is used as the persistent ID type.
DBPROPVAL_PT_PGUID_NAME	32	The Property GUID name is used as the persistent ID type.
DBPROPVAL_PT_PGUID_PROPID	64	The Property GUID Property ID is used as the persistent ID type.
DBPROPVAL_PT_PROPID	16	The Property ID is used as the persistent ID type.

DBPROPVAL_RD

Name	Value	Description
DBPROPVAL_RD_RESETALL	-1	The provider should reset all state associated with the data source, with the exception that any open object is not released.

DBPROPVAL_RT

Name	Value	Description
DBPROPVAL_RT_APTMTTHREAD	2	The DSO is apartment threaded.
DBPROPVAL_RT_FREETHREAD	1	The DSO is free threaded.
DBPROPVAL_RT_SINGLETHREAD	4	The DSO is single threaded.

DBPROPVAL_SQ

Name	Value	Description
DBPROPVAL_SQ_COMPARISON	2	All predicates that support subqueries support comparison subqueries.
DBPROPVAL_SQ_CORRELATEDSUBQUERIES	1	All predicates that support subqueries support correlated subqueries.
DBPROPVAL_SQ_EXISTS	4	All predicates that support subqueries support EXISTS subqueries.
DBPROPVAL_SQ_IN	8	All predicates that support subqueries support IN subqueries.
DBPROPVAL_SQ_QUANTIFIED	16	All predicates that support subqueries support quantified subqueries.
DBPROPVAL_SQ_TABLE	32	Subqueries are supported in place of tables.

DBPROPVAL_SQL

Name	Value	Description
DBPROPVAL_SQL_ANDI89_IEF	8	The provider supports the ANSI SQL89 IEF level.
DBPROPVAL_SQL_ANSI92_ENTRY	16	The provider supports the ANSI SQL92 Entry level.
DBPROPVAL_SQL_ANSI92_FULL	128	The provider supports the ANSI SQL92 Full level.
DBPROPVAL_SQL_ANSI92_ INTERMEDIATE	64	The provider supports the ANSI SQL92 Intermediate level.
DBPROPVAL_SQL_CORE	2	The provider supports the ODBC 2.5 Core SQL level.
DBPROPVAL_SQL_ESCAPECLAUSES	256	The provider supports the ODBC escape clauses syntax.
DBPROPVAL_SQL_EXTENDED	4	The provider supports the ODBC 2.5 EXTENDED SQL level.
DBPROPVAL_SQL_FIPS_ TRANSITIONAL	32	The provider supports the ANSI SQL92 Transitional level.
DBPROPVAL_SQL_MINIMUM	1	The provider supports the ODBC 2.5 EXTENDED SQL level.
DBPROPVAL_SQL_NONE	0	SQL is not supported.
DBPROPVAL_SQL_ODBC_CORE	2	The provider supports the ODBC 2.5 Core SQL level.
DBPROPVAL_SQL_ODBC_EXTENDED	4	The provider supports the ODBC 2.5 EXTENDED SQL level.
DBPROPVAL_SQL_ODBC_MINIMUM	1	The provider supports the ODBC 2.5 EXTENDED SQL level.
DBPROPVAL_SQL_SUBMINIMUM	512	The provider supports the DBGUID_SQL dialect and parses the command text according to SQL rules, but does not support wither the minimum ODBC level nor the ANSI SQL92 Entry level.

DBPROPVAL_SS

Name	Value	Description
DBPROPVAL_SS_ILOCKBYTES	8	The provider supports IlockBytes.
DBPROPVAL_SS_ISEQUENTIALSTREAM	1	The provider supports IsequentialStream.
DBPROPVAL_SS_ISTORAGE	4	The provider supports Istorage.
DBPROPVAL_SS_ISTREAM	2	The provider supports IStream.

DBPROPVAL_SU

Name	Value	Description
DBPROPVAL_SU_DML_STATEMENTS	1	Schema names are supported in all Data Manipulation Language statements.
DBPROPVAL_SU_INDEX_DEFINITION	4	Schema names are supported in all index definition statements.
DBPROPVAL_SU_PRIIVILEGE_ DEFINITION	8	Schema names are supported in all privilege definition statements.
DBPROPVAL_SU_TABLE_DEFINITION	2	Schema names are supported in all table definition statements.

DBPROPVAL_TC

Name	Value	Description
DBPROPVAL_TC_ALL	8	Transactions can contain DDL and DML statements in any order.
DBPROPVAL_TC_DDL_COMMIT	2	Transactions can contain DML statements. DDL statements within a transaction cause the transaction to be committed.
DBPROPVAL_TC_DDL_IGNORE	4	Transactions can only contain DML statements. DDL statements within a transaction are ignored.
DBPROPVAL_TC_DDL_LOCK	16	Transactions can contain both DML and table or index modifications, but the table or index will be locked until the transaction completes.
DBPROPVAL_TC_DML	1	Transactions can only contain Data Manipulation (DML) statements. DDL statements within a transaction cause an error.
DBPROPVAL_TC_NONE	0	Transactions are not supported.

DBPROPVAL_TI

Name	Value	Description
DBPROPVAL_TI_BROWSE	256	Changes made by other transactions are visible before they are committed.
DBPROPVAL_TI_CHAOS	16	Transactions cannot overwrite pending changes from more highly isolated transactions. This is the default.
DBPROPVAL_TI_ CURSORSTABILITY	4096	Changes made by other transactions are not visible until those transactions are committed.

Table Continued on Following Page

Name	Value	Description
DBPROPVAL_TI_ ISOLATED	1048576	All concurrent transactions will interact only in ways that produce the same effect as if each transaction were entirely executed one after the other.
DBPROPVAL_TI_ READCOMMITTED	4096	Changes made by other transactions are not visible until those transactions are committed.
DBPROPVAL_TI_ READUNCOMMITTED	256	Changes made by other transactions are visible before they are committed.
DBPROPVAL_TI_ REPEATABLEREAD	65536	Changes made by other transactions are not visible.
DBPROPVAL_TI_ SERIALIZABLE	1048576	All concurrent transactions will interact only in ways that produce the same effect as if each transaction were entirely executed one after the other.

DBPROPVAL_TR

Name	Value	Description
DBPROPVAL_TR_ABORT	16	The transaction preserves its isolation context (ie, it preserves its locks if that is how isolation is implemented) across the retaining abort.
DBPROPVAL_TR_ABORT_DC	8	The transaction may either preserve or dispose of isolation context across a retaining abort.
DBPROPVAL_TR_ABORT_NO	32	The transaction is explicitly not to preserve its isolation across a retaining abort.
DBPROPVAL_TR_BOTH	128	Isolation is preserved across both a retaining commit and a retaining abort.
DBPROPVAL_TR_COMMIT	2	The transaction preserves its isolation context (ie, it preserves its locks if that is how isolation is implemented) across the retaining commit.
DBPROPVAL_TR_COMMIT_DC	1	The transaction may either preserve or dispose of isolation context across a retaining commit.
DBPROPVAL_TR_COMMIT_NO	4	The transaction is explicitly not to preserve its isolation across a retaining commit.
DBPROPVAL_TR_DONTCARE	64	The transaction may either preserve or dispose of isolation context across a retaining commit or abort. This is the default.
DBPROPVAL_TR_NONE	256	Isolation is explicitly not to be retained across either a retaining commit or abort.
DBPROPVAL_TR_OPTIMISTIC	512	Optimistic concurrency control is to be used.

DBPROPVAL_UP

Name	Value	Description
DBPROPVAL_UP_CHANGE	1	Indicates that SetData is supported.
DBPROPVAL_UP_DELETE	2	Indicates that DeleteRows is supported.
DBPROPVAL_UP_INSERT	4	Indicates that InsertRow is supported.

DBPROPVAL_BP

Name	Value	Description
DBPROPVAL_BP_NOPARTIAL	2	Fail the bulk operation if there is a single error.
DBPROPVAL_BP_PARTIAL	1	Allow the bulk operation to partially complete, possibly resulting in inconsistent data.

JET_ENGINETYPE

Name	Value	Description
JET_ENGINETYPE_UNKNOWN	0	The database type is unknown.
JET_ENGINETYPE_JET10	1	Jet 1.0
JET_ENGINETYPE_JET11	2	Jet 1.1
JET_ENGINETYPE_JET2X	3	Jet 2.x
JET_ENGINETYPE_JET3X	4	Jet 3.x
JET_ENGINETYPE_JET4X	5	Jet 4.x
JET_ENGINETYPE_DBASE3	10	DBase III
JET_ENGINETYPE_DBASE4	11	DBase IV
JET_ENGINETYPE_DBASE5	12	DBase V
JET_ENGINETYPE_EXCEL30	20	Excel 3
JET_ENGINETYPE_EXCEL40	21	Excel 4
JET_ENGINETYPE_EXCEL50	22	Excel 5 (Excel 95)
JET_ENGINETYPE_EXCEL80	23	Excel 8 (Excel 97)
JET_ENGINETYPE_EXCEL90	24	Excel 9 (Excel 2000)
JET_ENGINETYPE_EXCHANGE4	30	Exchange Server
JET_ENGINETYPE_LOTUSWK1	40	Lotus 1

Table Continued on Following Page

Name	Value	Description
JET_ENGINETYPE_LOTUSWK3	41	Lotus 3
JET_ENGINETYPE_LOTUSWK4	42	Lotus 4
JET_ENGINETYPE_PARADOX3X	50	Paradox 3.x
JET_ENGINETYPE_PARADOX4X	51	Paradox 4.5
JET_ENGINETYPE_PARADOX5X	52	Paradox 5.x
JET_ENGINETYPE_PARADOX7X	53	Paradox 7.x
JET_ENGINETYPE_TEXT1X	60	Text
JET_ENGINETYPE_HTML1X	70	HTML

MD_DIMTYPE

Name	Value	Description
MD_DIMTYPE_MEASURE	2	A measure dimension.
MD_DIMTYPE_OTHER	3	The dimension is neither a time nor a measure dimension.
MD_DIMTYPE_TIME	1	A time dimension.
MD_DIMTYPE_UNKNOWN	0	The provider is unable to classify the dimension.

SQL_FN_NUM

Name	Value	Description
SQL_FN_NUM_ABS	1	The ABS function is supported by the data source.
SQL_FN_NUM_ACOS	2	The ACOS function is supported by the data source.
SQL_FN_NUM_ASIN	4	The ASIN function is supported by the data source.
SQL_FN_NUM_ATAN	8	The ATAN function is supported by the data source.
SQL_FN_NUM_ATAN2	16	The ATAN2 function is supported by the data source.
SQL_FN_NUM_CEILING	32	The CEILING function is supported by the data source.
SQL_FN_NUM_COS	64	The COS function is supported by the data source.
SQL_FN_NUM_COT	128	The COT function is supported by the data source.
SQL_FN_NUM_DEGREES	262144	The DEGREES function is supported by the data source.
SQL_FN_NUM_EXP	256	The EXP function is supported by the data source.
SQL_FN_NUM_FLOOR	512	The FLOOR function is supported by the data source.

Name	Value	Description
SQL_FN_NUM_LOG	1024	The LOG function is supported by the data source.
SQL_FN_NUM_LOG10	524288	The LOG10 function is supported by the data source.
SQL_FN_NUM_MOD	2048	The MOD function is supported by the data source.
SQL_FN_NUM_PI	65536	The PI function is supported by the data source.
SQL_FN_NUM_POWER	1048576	The POWER function is supported by the data source.
SQL_FN_NUM_RADIANS	2097152	The RADIANS function is supported by the data source.
SQL_FN_NUM_RAND	131072	The RAND function is supported by the data source.
SQL_FN_NUM_ROUND	4194304	The ROUND function is supported by the data source.
SQL_FN_NUM_SIGN	4096	The SIGN function is supported by the data source.
SQL_FN_NUM_SIN	8192	The SIN function is supported by the data source.
SQL_FN_NUM_SQRT	10384	The SQRT function is supported by the data source.
SQL_FN_NUM_TAN	32768	The TAN function is supported by the data source.
SQL_FN_NUM_TRUNCATE	8388608	The TRUNCATE function is supported by the data source.

SQL_FN_STR

Name	Value	Description
SQL_FN_STR_ASCII	8192	The ASCII function is supported by the data source.
SQL_FN_STR_BIT_LENGTH	524288	The BIT_LENGTH function is supported by the data source.
SQL_FN_STR_CHAR	16384	The CHAR function is supported by the data source.
SQL_FN_STR_CHAR_LENGTH	1048576	The CHAR_LENGTH function is supported by the data source.
SQL_FN_STR_CHARACTER_LENGTH	2097152	The CHARACTER_LENGTH function is supported by the data source.
SQL_FN_STR_CONCAT	1	The CONCAT function is supported by the data source.
SQL_FN_STR_DIFFERENCE	32768	The DIFFERENCE function is supported by the data source.
SQL_FN_STR_INSERT	2	The INSERT function is supported by the data source.
SQL_FN_STR_LCASE	64	The LCASE function is supported by the data source.

Table Continued on Following Page

Name	Value	Description
SQL_FN_STR_LEFT	4	The LEFT function is supported by the data source.
SQL_FN_STR_LENGTH	16	The LENGTH function is supported by the data source.
SQL_FN_STR_LOCATE	32	The LOCATE function is supported by the data source.
SQL_FN_STR_LOCATE_2	65536	The LOCATE_2 function is supported by the data source.
SQL_FN_STR_LTRIM	8	The LTRIM function is supported by the data source.
SQL_FN_STR_OCTET_LENGTH	4194304	The OCTET_LENGTH function is supported by the data source.
SQL_FN_STR_POSITION	8388608	The POSITION function is supported by the data source.
SQL_FN_STR_REPEAT	128	The REPEAT function is supported by the data source.
SQL_FN_STR_REPLACE	256	The REPLACE function is supported by the data source.
SQL_FN_STR_RIGHT	512	The RIGHT function is supported by the data source.
SQL_FN_STR_RTRIM	1024	The RTRIM function is supported by the data source.
SQL_FN_STR_SOUNDEX	131072	The SOUNDEX function is supported by the data source.
SQL_FN_STR_SPACE	262144	The SPACE function is supported by the data source.
SQL_FN_STR_SUBSTRING	2048	The SUBSTRING function is supported by the data source.
SQL_FN_STR_UCASE	4096	The UCASE function is supported by the data source.

SQL_FN_SYS

Name	Value	Description
SQL_FN_SYS_DBNAME	2	The DBNAME system function is supported.
SQL_FN_SYS_IFNULL	4	The IFNULL system function is supported.
SQL_FN_SYS_USERNAME	1	The USERNAME system function is supported.

SQL_OJ

Name	Value	Description
SQL_OJ_ALL_COMPARISON_OPS	64	The comparison operator in the ON clause can be any of the ODBC comparison operators. If this is not set, only the equals (=) comparison operator can be used in an outer join.
SQL_OJ_FULL	4	Full outer joins are supported.
SQL_OJ_INNER	32	The inner table (the right table in a left outer join or the left table in a right outer join) can also be used in an inner join. This does not apply to full out joins, which do not have an inner table.
SQL_OJ_LEFT	1	Left outer joins are supported.
SQL_OJ_NESTED	8	Nested outer joins are supported.
SQL_OJ_NOT_ORDERED	16	The column names in the ON clause of the outer join do not have to be in the same order as their respective table names in the OUTER JOIN clause.
SQL_OJ_RIGHT	2	Right outer joins are supported.

SQL_SDF_CURRENT

Name	Value	Description
SQL_SDF_CURRENT_DATE	1	The CURRENT_DATE system function is supported.
SQL_SDF_CURRENT_TIME	2	The CURRENT_TIME system function is supported.
SQL_SDF_CURRENT_TIMESTAMP	4	The CURRENT_TIMESTAMP system function is supported.

SSPROP_CONCUR

Name	Value	Description
SSPROP_CONCUR_LOCK	4	Use row locking to prevent concurrent access.
SSPROP_CONCUR_READ_ONLY	8	The rowset is read-only. Full concurrency is supported.
SSPROP_CONCUR_ROWVER	1	Use row versioning to determining concurrent access violations. The SQL Table or tables must contain a timestamp column.
SSPROP_CONCUR_VALUES	2	Use the values in of columns in the rowset row.

SSPROPVAL_USEPROCFORPREP

Name	Value	Description
SSPROPVAL_USEPROCFORPREP_OFF	0	A temporary stored procedure is not created when a command is prepared.
SSPROPVAL_USEPROCFORPREP_ON	1	A temporary stored procedure is created when a command is prepared. Temporary stored procedures are dropped when the session is released.
SSPROPVAL_USEPROCFORPREP_ON_DROP	2	A temporary stored procedure is created when a command is prepared. The procedure is dropped when the command is unprepared, or a new command text is set, or when all application references to the command are released.

ADO Properties Collection

The Properties collection deals with dynamic properties that are specific to the provider. All ADO objects have a fixed set of properties (such as Name), but since ADO is designed for use with different providers, a way was needed to allow providers to specify their own properties. The Properties collection contains these properties, and this appendix deals with which properties are supported by which providers, and what these properties actually do.

Some of the properties refer to Rowsets. This is just the OLE DB term for Recordsets.

Property Usage

As you can see from the tables in this appendix, there are very many properties – however, using them is actually quite simple. You simply index into Properties collection, by using the property name itself. For example, to find out the name the provider gives to procedures you could do this:

```
Print objConn.Properties("Procedure Term")
```

For SQL Server, this returns stored procedure and for Access this returns STORED QUERY.

You can iterate through the entire set of properties very simply:

```
For Each objProp In objConn.Properties
   Print objProp.Name
   Print objProp.Value
Next
```

This will print out the property name and value.

For those properties that return custom types, you need to identify whether these return a bitmask or a simple value – the property description identifies this, as it says 'one of' or 'one or more of'. In its simplest forms, these properties will just return a single value. For example, to find out whether your provider supports output parameters on stored procedures you can query the Output Parameter Availability property. This is defined as returning values of type DBPROPVAL_OA, which are as follows:

Constant	Value
DBPROPVAL_OA_ATEXECUTE	2
DBPROPVAL_OA_ATROWRELEASE	4
DBPROPVAL_OA_NOTSUPPORTED	1

Examining this property when connected to SQL Server gives you a value of 4, indicating that output parameters are available when the recordset is closed. Access, on the other hand, returns a value of 1, indicating that output parameters are not supported.

For those properties that return bitmask, you'll need to use Boolean logic to identify which values are set. For example, to query the provider and examine what features of SQL are supported, you can use the SQL Support property. For Access this returns 512, which corresponds to DBPROPVAL_SQL_SUBMINIMUM, indicating that not even the ANSI SQL92 Entry level SQL facilities are provided. On the other hand, SQL Server returns 283, but there isn't a single value for this, so it must be a combination of values. In fact, it corresponds to the sum of the following:

Constant	Value
DBPROPVAL_SQL_ESCAPECLAUSES	256
DBPROPVAL_SQL_ANSI92_ENTRY	16
DBPROPVAL_SQL_ANDI89_IEF	8
DBPROPVAL_SQL_CORE	2
DBPROPVAL_SQL_MINIMUM	1

In order to see whether a specific value is set, use the Boolean AND operator. For example:

```
lngSQLSupport = oConn.Properties("SQL Support")
If (lngSQLSupport AND DBPROPVAL_SQL_CORE) = DBPROPVAL_SQL_CORE Then
    'core facilities are supported
End If
```

A full description of the constants is given in Appendix B.

Property Support

The following table shows a list of all OLEDB properties, and indicates which of them are supported by three widely used drivers: the Microsoft OLEDB driver for Jet, the Microsoft OLEDB driver for ODBC, and the Microsoft OLEDB driver for SQL Server. Since this list contains dynamic properties, not every property may show up under all circumstances. Other providers may also implement properties not listed in this table.

A tick (✓) indicates that the property is supported, and a blank space indicates it is not supported. Note that support for recordset properties may depend upon the locking type, cursor type and cursor location.

Note. This list doesn't include the `Iproperty` *(such as* `IRowset`, *etc) properties. Although these are part of the collection they are not particularly useful for the ADO programmer.*

For the *Object Type* column, the following applies:

RS = `Recordset`

R = `Record`

C = `Connection`

F = `Field`

Property Name	Object Type (RS/R/F/C)	ODBC	Jet	SQL Server	Internet Publishing (IIS5)	MSDataShape	Persist	Remote	Indexing Service	Directory Services	Exchange
Access Order	RS	✓	✓	✓		✓	✓	✓	✓	✓	
Accessible Procedures	C	✓									
Accessible Tables	C	✓									
Active Sessions	C	✓	✓	✓					✓	✓	✓
Active Statements	C	✓									
ADSI Flag										✓	
Alter Column Support	C		✓								
Always use content index	RS								✓		
Append-Only Rowset	RS	✓	✓	✓		✓	✓	✓	✓	✓	
Application Name	C			✓							
Asynchable Abort	C	✓	✓	✓							✓
Asynchable Commit	C	✓	✓	✓							✓
Asynchronous Processing	C					✓					
Asynchronous Rowset Processing	RS	✓	✓	✓		✓	✓	✓	✓	✓	✓
Auto Recalc	RS	✓	✓	✓		✓	✓	✓	✓	✓	
Auto Translate	C			✓							
Autocommit Isolation Levels	C	✓	✓	✓		✓	✓	✓	✓	✓	✓
Background Fetch Size	RS	✓	✓	✓	✓	✓	✓	✓	✓	✓	
Background thread Priority	RS	✓	✓	✓	✓	✓	✓	✓	✓	✓	
BASECATALOGNAME	F	✓	✓	✓	✓	✓	✓	✓	✓	✓	
BASECOLUMNNAME	F	✓	✓	✓	✓	✓	✓	✓	✓	✓	
BASESCHEMANAME	F	✓	✓	✓	✓	✓	✓	✓	✓	✓	
BASETABLENAME	F	✓	✓	✓	✓	✓	✓	✓	✓	✓	
Batch Size	RS	✓	✓	✓	✓	✓	✓	✓	✓	✓	

Property Name	Object Type (RS/R/F/C)	ODBC	Jet	SQL Server	Internet Publishing (IIS5)	MSDataShape	Persist	Remote	Indexing Service	Directory Services	Exchange
Bind Flags	C				✓	✓					
BLOB accessibility on Forward-Only cursor	RS	✓									
Blocking Storage Objects	RS	✓	✓	✓		✓	✓	✓	✓	✓	
Bookmark Information	RS	✓		✓							
Bookmark Type	RS	✓	✓	✓		✓	✓	✓	✓	✓	✓
Bookmarkable	RS	✓	✓	✓	✓	✓	✓	✓	✓	✓	✓
Bookmarks Ordered	RS	✓	✓	✓		✓	✓	✓	✓	✓	✓
Cache Aggressively	C				✓						
Cache Authentication	C		✓			✓		✓			
Cache Child Rows	RS	✓	✓	✓		✓	✓	✓	✓	✓	
Cache Deferred Columns	RS	✓	✓	✓		✓	✓	✓	✓	✓	✓
CALCULATIONINFO	F	✓	✓	✓		✓	✓	✓	✓	✓	
Catalog Location	C	✓	✓	✓					✓	✓	
Catalog Term	C	✓	✓	✓					✓	✓	
Catalog Usage	C	✓		✓					✓	✓	
Change Inserted Rows	RS	✓	✓	✓		✓	✓	✓			✓
Chapter	C						✓				
CLSID	F	✓									
COLLATINGSEQUENCE	F	✓	✓								
Column Definition	C	✓	✓	✓					✓		
Column Privileges	RS	✓	✓	✓		✓	✓	✓	✓	✓	✓
Column Set Notification	RS	✓	✓	✓		✓	✓	✓	✓	✓	
Column Writable	RS	✓	✓	✓		✓	✓	✓	✓	✓	
Command Properties	C						✓				
Command Time Out	RS	✓	✓	✓	✓	✓	✓	✓	✓	✓	

Table Continued on Following Page

Property Name	Object Type (RS/R/F/C)	ODBC	Jet	SQL Server	Internet Publishing (IIS5)	MSDataShape	Persist	Remote	Indexing Service	Directory Services	Exchange
COMPUTEMODE	F	✓									
Connect Timeout	C	✓		✓	✓	✓	✓	✓		✓	
Connection Status	C	✓		✓							
Current Catalog	C	✓	✓	✓					✓		
Current DFMode	C							✓			
Current Language	C			✓							
Cursor Engine Version	RS	✓	✓	✓		✓	✓	✓	✓	✓	
Data Provider	C					✓					
Data Source	C	✓	✓	✓	✓	✓		✓	✓	✓	✓
Data Source Name	C	✓	✓	✓						✓	✓
Data Source Object Threading Model	C	✓	✓	✓		✓		✓	✓	✓	✓
Datasource Type	C				✓						✓
DATETIMEPRECISION	F	✓		✓							
DBMS Name	C	✓	✓	✓					✓		✓
DBMS Version	C	✓	✓	✓					✓		✓
DEFAULTVALUE	F	✓									
Defer Column	RS	✓	✓	✓		✓	✓	✓	✓	✓	✓
Defer scope and security testing	RS							✓			
Delay Storage Object Updates	RS	✓	✓	✓		✓	✓	✓	✓	✓	
DFMode	C							✓			
DOMAINCATALOG	F	✓									
DOMAINNAME	F	✓									
DOMAINSCHEMA	F	✓									
Driver Name	C	✓									

Property Name	Object Type (RS/R/F/C)	ODBC	Jet	SQL Server	Internet Publishing (IIS5)	MSDataShape	Persist	Remote	Indexing Service	Directory Services	Exchange
Driver ODBC Version	C	✓									
Driver Version	C	✓									
Enable Fastload	C			✓							
Encrypt Password	C		✓		✓		✓			✓	
Extended Properties	C	✓	✓	✓		✓		✓		✓	
Fastload Options	RS			✓							
Fetch Backwards	RS	✓	✓	✓	✓	✓	✓	✓	✓	✓	✓
File Usage	C	✓									
Filter Operations	RS	✓	✓	✓		✓	✓	✓	✓	✓	
Find Operations	RS	✓	✓	✓		✓	✓	✓	✓	✓	
Force no command preparation when executing a parameterized command	RS	✓									
Force no command reexecution when failure to satisfy all required properties	RS	✓									
Force no parameter rebinding when executing a command	RS	✓									
Force SQL Server Firehose Mode cursor	RS	✓									
Generate a Rowset that can be marshalled	RS	✓									
General Timeout	C	✓		✓							
Generate URL	C				✓						
GROUP BY Support	C	✓	✓	✓					✓		
Handler	C							✓			

Table Continued on Following Page

Property Name	Object Type (RS/R/F/C)	ODBC	Jet	SQL Server	Internet Publishing (IIS5)	MSDataShape	Persist	Remote	Indexing Service	Directory Services	Exchange
HASDEFAULT	F	✓									
Heterogeneous Table Support	C	✓	✓	✓					✓		
Hidden Columns	RS	✓	✓	✓		✓	✓	✓	✓	✓	
Hold Rows	RS	✓	✓	✓	✓	✓	✓	✓	✓	✓	✓
Identifier Case Sensitivity	C	✓	✓	✓							
Ignore Cached Data	C				✓						
Immobile Rows	RS	✓	✓	✓		✓	✓	✓	✓	✓	✓
Impersonation Level	C					✓		✓			
Include SQL_FLOAT, SQL_DOUBLE, and SQL_REAL in QBU where clauses	RS	✓									
Initial Catalog	C	✓		✓		✓		✓			
Initial Fetch Size	RS	✓	✓	✓		✓	✓	✓	✓	✓	
Initial File Name	C			✓							
Integrated Security	C			✓		✓		✓		*	
Integrity Enhancement Facility	C	✓									
Internet Timeout	C							✓			
ISAUTOINCREMENT	F	✓	✓	✓		✓	✓	✓	✓		
ISCASESENSITIVE	F	✓	✓	✓							
Isolation Levels	C	✓	✓	✓					✓		✓
Isolation Retention	C	✓	✓	✓					✓		✓
ISSEARCHABLE	F	✓		✓							
ISUNIQUE	F	✓									
Jet OLEDB:Bulk Transactions	RS		✓								

Property Name	Object Type (RS/R/F/C)	ODBC	Jet	SQL Server	Internet Publishing (IIS5)	MSDataShape	Persist	Remote	Indexing Service	Directory Services	Exchange
Jet OLEDB:Compact Reclaimed Space Amount	C		✓								
Jet OLEDB:Compact Without Replica Repair	C		✓								
Jet OLEDB:Connection Control	C		✓								
Jet OLEDB:Create System Database	C		✓								
Jet OLEDB:Database Locking Mode	C		✓								
Jet OLEDB:Database Password	C		✓								
Jet OLEDB:Don't Copy Locale on Compact	C		✓								
Jet OLEDB:Enable Fat Cursors	RS		✓								
Jet OLEDB:Encrypt Database	C		✓								
Jet OLEDB:Engine Type	C		✓								
Jet OLEDB:Exclusive Async Delay	C		✓								
Jet OLEDB:Fat Cursor Cache Size	RS		✓								
Jet OLEDB:Flush Transaction Timeout	C		✓								
Jet OLEDB:Global Bulk Transactions	C		✓								
Jet OLEDB:Global Partial Bulk Ops	C		✓								
Jet OLEDB:Grbit Value	RS		✓								
Jet OLEDB:Implicit Commit Sync	C		✓								

Table Continued on Following Page

Property Name	Object Type (RS/R/F/C)	ODBC	Jet	SQL Server	Internet Publishing (IIS5)	MSDataShape	Persist	Remote	Indexing Service	Directory Services	Exchange
Jet OLEDB:Inconsistent	RS		✓								
Jet OLEDB:Lock Delay	C		✓								
Jet OLEDB:Lock Retry	C		✓								
Jet OLEDB:Locking Granularity	RS		✓								
Jet OLEDB:Max Buffer Size	C		✓								
Jet OLEDB:Max Locks Per File	C		✓								
Jet OLEDB:New Database Password	C		✓								
Jet OLEDB:ODBC Command Time Out	C		✓								
Jet OLEDB:ODBC Parsing	C		✓								
Jet OLEDB:ODBC Pass-Through Statement	RS		✓								
Jet OLEDB:Page Locks to Table Lock	C		✓								
Jet OLEDB:Page Timeout	C		✓								
Jet OLEDB:Partial Bulk Ops	RS		✓								
Jet OLEDB:Pass Through Query Bulk-Op	RS		✓								
Jet OLEDB:Pass Through Query Connect String	RS		✓								
Jet OLEDB:Recycle Long-Valued Pages	C		✓								
Jet OLEDB:Registry Path	C		✓								
Jet OLEDB:Reset ISAM Stats	C		✓								

Property Name	Object Type (RS/R/F/C)	ODBC	Jet	SQL Server	Internet Publishing (IIS5)	MSDataShape	Persist	Remote	Indexing Service	Directory Services	Exchange
Jet OLEDB:Sandbox Mode	C		✓								
Jet OLEDB:SFP	C		✓								
Jet OLEDB:Shared Async Delay	C		✓								
Jet OLEDB:Stored Query	RS		✓								
Jet OLEDB:System database	C		✓								
Jet OLEDB:Transaction Commit Mode	C		✓								
Jet OLEDB:Use Grbit	RS		✓								
Jet OLEDB:User Commit Sync	C		✓								
Jet OLEDB:Validate Rules On Set	RS		✓								
Keep Identity	RS			✓							
Keep Nulls	RS			✓							
KEYCOLUMN	F	✓	✓	✓		✓	✓	✓	✓	✓	
Like Escape Clause	C	✓									
Literal Bookmarks	RS	✓	✓	✓		✓	✓	✓	✓	✓	✓
Literal Row Identity	RS	✓	✓	✓		✓	✓	✓	✓	✓	✓
Locale Identifier	C	✓	✓	✓	✓	✓		✓	✓	✓	✓
Location	C	✓				✓		✓	✓	✓	
Lock Mode	RS		✓	✓							
Lock Owner	C				✓						
Maintain Change Status	RS	✓	✓	✓	✓	✓	✓	✓	✓	✓	
Maintain Property Values	C						✓				
Mark For Offline	C				✓						

Table Continued on Following Page

769

Property Name	Object Type (RS/R/F/C)	ODBC	Jet	SQL Server	Internet Publishing (IIS5)	MSDataShape	Persist	Remote	Indexing Service	Directory Services	Exchange
Mask Password	C		✓			✓		✓			
Max Columns in Group By	C	✓									
Max Columns in Index	C	✓									
Max Columns in Order By	C	✓									
Max Columns in Select	C	✓									
Max Columns in Table	C	✓									
Maximum BLOB Length	RS			✓							
Maximum Index Size	C	✓	✓	✓							
Maximum Open Chapters	C			✓					✓		
Maximum Open Rows	RS	✓	✓	✓		✓	✓	✓	✓	✓	✓
Maximum Pending Rows	RS	✓	✓	✓		✓	✓	✓	✓	✓	
Maximum Row Size	C	✓	✓	✓					✓	✓	✓
Maximum Row Size Includes BLOB	C	✓	✓	✓							
Maximum Rows	RS	✓	✓	✓		✓	✓	✓	✓	✓	✓
Maximum Tables in SELECT	C	✓	✓	✓					✓		
Memory Usage	RS	✓	✓	✓		✓	✓	✓	✓	✓	
Mode	C	✓	✓		✓	✓		✓		✓	✓
Multi-Table Update	C	✓	✓	✓							
Multiple Connections	C			✓							
Multiple Parameter Sets	C	✓	✓	✓					✓	✓	
Multiple Results	C	✓	✓	✓		✓		✓		✓	✓
Multiple Storage Objects	C	✓	✓	✓					✓		✓
Network Address	C			✓							
Network Library	C			✓							
Notification Granularity	RS	✓	✓	✓		✓	✓	✓	✓	✓	

Property Name	Object Type (RS/R/F/C)	ODBC	Jet	SQL Server	Internet Publishing (IIS5)	MSDataShape	Persist	Remote	Indexing Service	Directory Services	Exchange
Notification Phases	RS	✓	✓	✓		✓	✓	✓	✓	✓	
NULL Collation Order	C	✓	✓	✓					✓		
NULL Concatenation Behavior	C	✓	✓	✓							
Numeric Functions	C	✓									
Objects Transacted	RS	✓	✓	✓		✓	✓	✓	✓	✓	
OCTETLENGTH	F	✓		✓							
ODBC Concurrency Type	RS	✓									
ODBC Cursor Type	RS	✓									
OLE DB Services	C	✓							✓		
OLE DB Version	C	✓	✓	✓	✓			✓	✓	✓	✓
OLE Object Support	C	✓	✓	✓					✓	✓	✓
OLE Objects	C				✓						
Open Rowset Support	C	✓	✓	✓							
OPTIMIZE	F	✓	✓	✓		✓	✓	✓	✓	✓	
ORDER BY Columns in Select List	C	✓	✓	✓					✓		
Others' Changes Visible	RS	✓	✓	✓		✓	✓	✓	✓	✓	✓
Others' Inserts Visible	RS	✓	✓	✓		✓	✓	✓	✓	✓	✓
Outer Join Capabilities	C	✓									
Outer Joins	C	✓									
Output Parameter Availability	C	✓	✓	✓				✓	✓		
Own Changes Visible	RS	✓	✓	✓		✓	✓	✓	✓	✓	✓
Own Inserts Visible	RS	✓	✓	✓		✓	✓	✓	✓	✓	✓
Packet Size	C			✓							
Pass By Ref Accessors	C	✓	✓	✓					✓	✓	✓

Table Continued on Following Page

Property Name	Object Type (RS/R/F/C)	ODBC	Jet	SQL Server	Internet Publishing (IIS5)	MSDataShape	Persist	Remote	Indexing Service	Directory Services	Exchange
Password	C	✓	✓	✓	✓	✓		✓		✓	✓
Persist Encrypted	C					✓					
Persist Format	C						✓				
Persist Schema	C						✓				
Persist Security Info	C	✓		✓		✓		✓			
Persistent ID Type	C	✓	✓	✓					✓	✓	✓
Position on the last row after insert	RS	✓									
Prepare Abort Behavior	C	✓	✓	✓							✓
Prepare Commit Behavior	C	✓	✓	✓							✓
Preserve on Abort	RS	✓	✓	✓		✓	✓	✓	✓	✓	✓
Preserve on Commit	RS	✓	✓	✓		✓	✓	✓	✓	✓	✓
Procedure Term	C	✓	✓	✓							
Prompt	C	✓	✓	✓	✓	✓		✓	✓	✓	
Protection Level	C					✓		✓			
Protocol Provider	C				✓						
Provider Friendly Name	C	✓	✓	✓					✓	✓	✓
Provider Name	C	✓	✓	✓	✓				✓	✓	✓
Provider Version	C	✓	✓	✓	✓				✓	✓	✓
Query Based Updates/Deletes/Inserts	RS	✓									
Query Restriction	RS							✓			
Quick Restart	RS	✓	✓	✓		✓	✓	✓	✓	✓	✓
Quoted Catalog Names	C			✓							
Quoted Identifier Sensitivity	C	✓		✓							
Read-Only Data Source	C	✓	✓	✓					✓	✓	✓

Property Name	Object Type (RS/R/F/C)	ODBC	Jet	SQL Server	Internet Publishing (IIS5)	MSDataShape	Persist	Remote	Indexing Service	Directory Services	Exchange
Reentrant Events	RS	✓	✓	✓		✓	✓	✓	✓	✓	✓
RELATIONCONDITIONS	F	✓	✓	✓		✓	✓	✓	✓	✓	
Remote Provider	C							✓			
Remote Server	C							✓			
Remove Deleted Rows	RS	✓	✓	✓		✓	✓	✓	✓	✓	✓
Report Multiple Changes	RS	✓	✓	✓		✓	✓	✓	✓	✓	✓
Reshape Name	RS	✓	✓	✓	✓	✓	✓	✓			
Reset Datasource	C	✓		✓					✓		
Resync Command	RS	✓	✓	✓		✓	✓	✓	✓	✓	
Return Pending Inserts	RS	✓	✓	✓		✓	✓	✓	✓	✓	
Return PROPVARIANTs in variant binding	RS								✓		
Row Delete Notification	RS	✓	✓	✓		✓	✓	✓	✓	✓	
Row First Change Notification	RS	✓	✓	✓		✓	✓	✓	✓	✓	
Row Insert Notification	RS	✓	✓	✓		✓	✓	✓	✓	✓	
Row Privileges	RS	✓	✓	✓		✓	✓	✓	✓	✓	✓
Row Resynchronization Notification	RS	✓	✓	✓		✓	✓	✓	✓	✓	
Row Threading Model	RS	✓	✓	✓		✓	✓	✓	✓	✓	✓
Row Undo Change Notification	RS	✓	✓	✓		✓	✓	✓	✓	✓	
Row Undo Delete Notification	RS	✓	✓	✓		✓	✓	✓	✓	✓	
Row Undo Insert Notification	RS	✓	✓	✓		✓	✓	✓	✓	✓	
Row Update Notification	RS	✓	✓	✓		✓	✓	✓	✓	✓	

Table Continued on Following Page

Property Name	Object Type (RS/R/F/C)	ODBC	Jet	SQL Server	Internet Publishing (IIS5)	MSDataShape	Persist	Remote	Indexing Service	Directory Services	Exchange
Rowset Conversions on Command	C	✓	✓	✓					✓	✓	
Rowset Fetch Position Change Notification	RS	✓	✓	✓		✓	✓	✓	✓	✓	
Rowset Query Status	RS								✓		
Rowset Release Notification	RS	✓	✓	✓		✓	✓	✓	✓	✓	
Schema Term	C	✓	✓	✓							
Schema Usage	C	✓	✓	✓							
Scroll Backwards	RS	✓	✓	✓		✓	✓	✓	✓	✓	✓
Server Cursor	RS	✓	✓	✓		✓	✓	✓	✓	✓	✓
Server Data on Insert	RS		✓	✓							
Server Name	C	✓		✓							
Skip Deleted Bookmarks	RS	✓	✓	✓		✓	✓	✓	✓	✓	✓
Special Characters	C	✓									
SQL Content Query Locale String	RS								✓		
SQL Grammar Support	C	✓									
SQL Support	C	✓	✓	✓					✓	✓	✓
Stored Procedures	C	✓									
String Functions	C	✓									
Strong Row Identity	RS	✓	✓	✓		✓	✓	✓	✓	✓	✓
Structured Storage	C	✓	✓	✓					✓		✓
Subquery Support	C	✓	✓	✓					✓		
System Functions	C	✓									
Table Term	C	✓	✓	✓							✓
Time/Date Functions	C	✓									

Table Continued on Following Page

Property Name	Object Type (RS/R/F/C)	ODBC	Jet	SQL Server	Internet Publishing (IIS5)	MSDataShape	Persist	Remote	Indexing Service	Directory Services	Exchange
Transact Updates	C							✓			
Transaction DDL	C	✓	✓	✓					✓		✓
Treat As Offline	C				✓						
Unicode Comparison Style	C			✓							
Unicode Locale Id	C			✓							
Unique Catalog	RS	✓	✓	✓		✓	✓	✓	✓	✓	
Unique Reshape Names	C					✓					
Unique Rows	RS	✓	✓	✓		✓	✓	✓	✓	✓	
Unique Schema	RS	✓	✓	✓		✓	✓	✓	✓	✓	
Unique Table	RS	✓	✓	✓		✓	✓	✓	✓	✓	
Updatability	RS	✓	✓	✓	✓	✓	✓	✓	✓	✓	✓
Update Criteria	RS	✓	✓	✓		✓	✓	✓	✓	✓	
Update Resync	RS	✓	✓	✓		✓	✓	✓	✓	✓	
URL Generation	C										✓
Use Bookmarks	RS	✓	✓	✓	✓	✓	✓	✓	✓	✓	✓
Use Procedure for Prepare	C			✓							
User ID	C	✓	✓	✓	✓	✓		✓		✓	✓
User Name	C	✓	✓	✓						✓	
Window Handle	C	✓	✓	✓	✓	✓		✓	✓	✓	
Workstation ID	C			✓							

✱ For the RC3 beta of Windows 2000 this was reported as 'Integrated Security .'
This has an additional space and point mark at the end of the property name. The final release may have cured this.

Object Properties

This section details the properties by object type, including the enumerated values that they support. These values are not included in the standard `adovbs.inc` include file (and are not automatically supplied when using Visual Basic), but can be found in `adoconvb.inc` and `adoconjs.inc` (for ASP, in VBScript and JScript format) and `adocon.bas` (for Visual Basic) from the supporting web site.

Some properties in this list are undocumented, and I've had to make an educated guess as to their purpose. I've marked these properties with a * *symbol in their description field.*

The Connection Object's Properties

Property Name	Description	DataType
Access Permissions	Identifies the permissions used to access the data source. Read/Write.	ConnectModeEnum
Accessible Procedures	Identifies accessible procedures. Read-only.	Boolean
Accessible Tables	Identifies accessible tables. Read-only.	Boolean
Active Sessions	The maximum number of sessions that can exist at the same time. A value of 0 indicates no limit. Read-only.	Long
Active Statements	The maximum number of statements that can exist at the same time. Read-only.	Long
Alter Column Support	Identifies which portions of the column can be altered.	DBCOLUMNDESCFLAG
Application Name	Identifies the client application name. Read/Write.	String
Asynchable Abort	Whether transactions can be aborted asynchronously. Read-only.	Boolean
Asynchable Commit	Whether transactions can be committed asynchronously. Read-only.	Boolean
Asynchronous Processing	Specifies the asynchronous processing performed on the rowset. Read/Write.	DBPROPVAL_ASYNCH
Auto Translate	Indicates whether OEM/ANSI character conversion is used. Read/Write.	Boolean
Autocommit Isolation Level	Identifies the transaction isolation level while in auto-commit mode. Read/Write.	DBPROPVAL_OS

Property Name	Description	DataType
Bind Flags	Identifies the binding behaviour for resources. Allows binding to the results of a resource rather than the resource itself.	DBBINDURLFLAG
Cache Aggressively	Identifies whether or not the provider will download and cache all properties of the resource, and its stream.	Boolean
Cache Authentication	Whether or not the data source object can cache sensitive authentication information, such as passwords, in an internal cache. Read/Write.	Boolean
Catalog Location	The position of the catalog name in a table name in a text command. Returns 1 (DBPROPVAL_CL_START) if the catalog is at the start of the name (such as Access with \Temp\Database.mdb), and 2 (DBPROPVAL_CL_END) if the catalog is at the end of name (such as Oracle with ADMIN.EMP@EMPDATA). Read/Write.	DBPROPVAL_CL
Catalog Term	The name the data source uses for a catalog, e.g. 'catalog' or 'database'. Read/Write.	String
Catalog Usage	Specifies how catalog names can be used in text commands. A combination of zero or more of DBPROPVAL_CU constants. Read/Write.	DBPROPVAL_CU
Column Definition	Defines the valid clauses for the definition of a column. Read/Write.	DBPROPVAL_CD
Command Properties	The dynamic properties of the Command. [*]	String
Connect Timeout	The amount of time, in seconds, to wait for the initialization to complete. Read/Write.	Long
Connection Status	The status of the current connection. Read-only.	DBPROPVAL_CS
Current Catalog	The name of the current catalog. Read/Write.	String
Current DFMode	Identifies the actual version of the Data Factory on the server. Can be: "21" (the default) for version 2.1 "20" for version 2.0 "15" for version 1.5	String

Table Continued on Following Page

Property Name	Description	DataType
Current Language	Identifies the language used for system messages selection and formatting. The language must be installed on the SQL Server or initialization of the data source fails. Read/Write.	Boolean
Data Provider	For a shaped (hierarchical) recordset, this identifies the provider who supplies the data.	String
Data Source	The name of the data source to connect to. Read/Write.	String
Data Source Name	The name of the data source. Read-only.	String
Data Source Object Threading Model	Specifies the threading models supported by the data source object. Read-only.	DBPROPVAL_RT
Datasource Type	The type of data source.	DBPROPVAL_DST
DBMS Name	The name of the product accessed by the provider. Read-only.	String
DBMS Version	The version of the product accessed by the provider. Read-only.	String
DFMode	Identifies the Data Factory mode. Can be: "21" (the default) for version 2.1 "20" for version 2.0 "15" for version 1.5	String
Driver Name	Identifies the ODBC Driver name. Read-only.	String
Driver ODBC Version	Identifies the ODBC Driver version. Read-only.	String
Driver Version	Identifies the Driver ODBC version. Read-only.	String
Enable Fastload	Indicates whether bulk-copy operations can be used between the SQL Server and the consumer.	Boolean
Encrypt Password	Whether the consumer required that the password be sent to the data source in an encrypted form. Read/Write.	Boolean
Extended Properties	Contains provider specific, extended connection information. Read/Write.	String
File Usage	Identifies the usage count of the ODBC driver. Read-only.	Long

Property Name	Description	DataType
Generate URL	Identifies the level of support of the Internet Server for generating URL suffixes.	DBPROPVAL_GU
General Timeout	The number of seconds before a request times out. This applies to requests other than the connection opening or a command execution.	Long
GROUP BY Support	The relationship between the columns in a GROUP BY clause and the non-aggregated columns in the select list. Read-only.	DBPROPVAL_BG
Handler	The name of the server-side customization program, and any parameters the program uses.	String
Heterogeneous Table Support	Specifies whether the provider can join tables from different catalogs or providers. Read-only.	DBPROPVAL_HT
Identifier Case Sensitivity	How identifiers treats case. Read-only.	DBPROPVAL_IC
Ignore Cached Data	Identifies whether the provider should ignore any cached data for this resource.	Boolean
Impersonation Level	Identifies the level of client impersonation the server can take whilst performing actions on behalf of the client.	DB_IMP_LEVEL
Initial Catalog	The name of the initial, or default, catalog to use when connecting to the data source. If the provider supports changing the catalog for an initialized data source, a different catalog name can be specified in the Current Catalog property. Read/Write.	String
Initial File Name	The primary file name of an attachable database. *	String
Integrated Security	Contains the name of the authentication service used by the server to identify the user. Read/Write.	String
Integrity Enhancement Facility	Indicates whether the data source supports the optional Integrity Enhancement Facility. Read-only.	Boolean
Internet Timeout	The maximum number of milliseconds to wait before generating an error.	Long
Isolation Levels	Identifies the supported transaction isolation levels. Read-only.	DBPROPVAL_TI

Table Continued on Following Page

Property Name	Description	DataType
Isolation Retention	Identifies the supported transaction isolation retention levels. Read-only.	DBPROPVAL_TR
Jet OLEDB:Compact Reclaimed Space Amount	The approximate amount of space that would be reclaimed by a compaction. This is not guaranteed to be exact.	Long
Jet OLEDB:Compact Without Replica Repair	Indicates whether or not to find and repair damaged replicas.	Boolean
Jet OLEDB:Compact Without Relationships	Indicates whether or not to copy relationships to the new database.	Boolean
Jet OLEDB:Connection Control	Identifies the state of the connection, indicating whether other users are allowed to connect to the database or not.	DBPROPVAL_JCC
Jet OLEDB:Create System Database	Indicates whether or not a system database is generated when creating a new data source.	Boolean
Jet OLEDB:Database Locking Mode	Identifies the mode to use when locking the database. The first person to open a database identifies the mode.	DBPROPVAL_DL
Jet OLEDB:Database Password	The database password. Read/Write.	String
Jet OLEDB:Don't Copy Locale on Compact	Indicates that the database sort order should be used when compacting, rather that the locale.	Boolean
Jet OLEDB:Encrypt Database	Indicates whether or not to encrypt the new database.	Boolean
Jet OLEDB:Engine Type	Identifies the version of the database to open, of the version of the database to create.	JET_ENGINETYPE
Jet OLEDB:Exclusive Async Delay	The maximum time (in milliseconds) that Jet will delay asynchronous writes to disk, when the database is open in exclusive mode.	Long
Jet OLEDB:Flush Transaction Timeout	Amount of time of inactivity before the asynchronous write cache is written to the disk.	Long

Property Name	Description	DataType
Jet OLEDB:Global Bulk Transactions	Identifies whether bulk operations are transacted.	DBPROPVAL_BT
Jet OLEDB:Global Partial Bulk Ops	Identifies whether Bulk operations are allowed with partial values. Read/Write.	DBPROPVAL_BP
Jet OLEDB:Implicit Commit Sync	Indicates whether or not implicit transactions are written synchronously.	Boolean
Jet OLEDB:Lock Delay	The number of times to repeat attempts to access a locked page.	Long
Jet OLEDB:Lock Retry	The number of attempts made to access a locked page.	Long
Jet OLEDB:Max Buffer Size	The largest amount of memory (in Kb) that can be used before it starts flushing changes to disk.	Long
Jet OLEDB:Max Locks Per File	The maximum number of locks that can be placed on a database. This defaults to 9500.	Long
Jet OLEDB:New Database Password	Sets the database password.	String
Jet OLEDB:ODBC Command Time Out	The number of seconds before remote ODBC queries timeout.	Long
Jet OLEDB:ODBC Parsing	Indicates whether or not Jet should attempt parsing of ODBC SQL syntax, or only use native Jet syntax.	Boolean
Jet OLEDB:Page Locks to Table Lock	The number of page locks to apply to a table before escalating the lock to a table lock. 0 means the lock will never be promoted.	Long
Jet OLEDB:Page Timeout	The amount of time (in milliseconds) that are waited before Jet checks to see if the cache is out of date with the database.	Long
Jet OLEDB:Recycle Long-Valued Pages	Indicates whether or not Jet aggressively tries to reclaim BLOB pages when they are freed.	Boolean
Jet OLEDB:Registry Path	The registry key that contains values for the Jet database engine. Read/Write.	String
Jet OLEDB:Reset ISAM Stats	Determines whether or not the ISAM statistics should be reset after the information has been returned.	Boolean

Table Continued on Following Page

Property Name	Description	DataType
Jet OLEDB:Sandbox Mode	Indicates whether the database is in Sandbox mode. [*]	Boolean
Jet OLEDB:Shared Async Delay	The maximum time (in milliseconds) to delay asynchronous writes when in multi-user mode.	Long
Jet OLEDB:System database	The path and file name for the workgroup file. Read/Write.	String
Jet OLEDB:Transactio n Commit Mode	A value if 1 indicates that the database commits updates immediately, rather than caching them.	Long
Jet OLEDB:User Commit Sync	Indicates whether or not explicit user transactions are written synchronously.	Boolean
Like Escape Clause	Identifies the LIKE escape clause. Read-only.	String
Locale Identifier	The locale ID of preference for the consumer. Read/Write.	Long
Location	The location of the data source to connect to. Typically this will be the server name. Read/Write.	String
Lock Owner	The string to show when you lock a resource and other users attempt to access that resource. Ignored for the WEC protocol, used with FrontPage Server Extensions. Read/Write.	String
Log text and image writes	Identifies whether writes to text and images fields are logged in the transaction log. Read/Write.	Boolean
Maintain Property Values	Indicates whether or not the property values are persisted along with the data when saving a recordset. Defaults to True. [*]	Boolean
Mark For Offline	Indicates that the URL can be marked for offline use. [*]	Integer
Mask Password	The consumer requires that the password be sent to the data source in masked form. Read/Write.	Boolean
Max Columns in Group By	Identifies the maximum number of columns in a GROUP BY clause. Read-only.	Long

Property Name	Description	DataType
Max Columns in Index	Identifies the maximum number of columns in an index. Read-only.	Long
Max Columns in Order By	Identifies the maximum number of columns in an ORDER BY clause. Read-only.	Long
Max Columns in Select	Identifies the maximum number of columns in a SELECT statement. Read-only.	Long
Max Columns in Table	Identifies the maximum number of columns in a table. Read-only.	Long
Maximum Index Size	The maximum number of bytes allowed in the combined columns of an index. This is 0 if there is no specified limit or the limit is unknown. Read-only.	Long
Maximum Open Chapters	The maximum number of chapters that can be open at any one time. If a chapter must be released before a new chapter can be opened, the value is 1. If the provider does not support chapters, the value is 0. Read-only.	Long
Maximum OR Conditions	The maximum number of disjunct conditions that can be supported in a view filter. Multiple conditions of a view filter are joined in a logical OR. Providers that do not support joining multiple conditions return a value of 1, and providers that do not support view filters return a value of 0. Read-only.	Long
Maximum Row Size	The maximum length of a single row in a table. This is 0 if there is no specified limit or the limit is unknown. Read-only.	Long
Maximum Row Size Includes BLOB	Identifies whether Maximum Row Size includes the length for BLOB data. Read-only.	Boolean
Maximum Sort Columns	The maximum number of columns that can be supported in a View Sort. This is 0 if there is no specified limit or the limit is unknown. Read-only.	Long
Maximum Tables in SELECT	The maximum number of tables allowed in the FROM clause of a SELECT statement. This is 0 if there is no specified limit or the limit is unknown. Read-only.	Long

Table Continued on Following Page

Property Name	Description	DataType
Mode	Specifies the access permissions. Read/Write.	DB_MODE
Multi-Table Update	Identifies whether the provider can update rowsets derived from multiple tables. Read-only.	Boolean
Multiple Connections	Identifies whether the provider silently creates additional connections to support concurrent `Command`, `Connection` or `Recordset` objects. This only applies to providers that have to spawn multiple connections, and not to providers that support multiple connections natively. Read/Write.	Boolean
Multiple Parameter Sets	Identifies whether the provider supports multiple parameter sets. Read-only.	Boolean
Multiple Results	Identifies whether the provider supports multiple results objects and what restrictions it places on those objects. Read-only.	DBPROPVAL_MR
Multiple Storage Objects	Identifies whether the provider supports multiple, open storage objects at the same time. Read-only.	Boolean
Network Address	Identifies the network address of the SQL Server. Read/Write.	String
Network Library	Identifies the name of the Net-Library (DLL) used to communicate with SQL Server. Read/Write.	String
NULL Collation Order	Identifies where NULLs are sorted in a list. Read-only.	DBPROPVAL_NC
NULL Concatenation Behavior	How the data source handles concatenation of NULL-valued character data type columns with non-NULL valued character data type columns. Read-only.	DBPROPVAL_CB
Numeric Functions	Identifies the numeric functions supported by the ODBC driver and data source. Read-only.	SQL_FN_NUM
OLE DB Services	Specifies the OLEDB services to enable. Read/Write.	DBPROPVAL_OS
OLE DB Version	Specifies the version of OLEDB supported by the provider. Read-only.	String

Property Name	Description	DataType
OLE Object Support	Specifies the way on which the provider supports access to BLOBs and OLE objects stored in columns. Read-only.	DBPROPVAL_OO
OLE Objects	Indicates the level of binding support for OLE Objects.	DBPROPVAL_OO
Open Rowset Support	Indicates the level of support for opening rowsets.	DBPROPVAL_ORS
ORDER BY Columns in Select List	Identifies whether columns in an ORDER BY clause must be in the SELECT list. Read-only.	Boolean
Outer Join Capabilities	Identifies the outer join capabilities of the ODBC data source. Read-only.	SQL_OJ
Outer Joins	Identifies whether outer joins are supported or not. Read-only.	Boolean
Outer Join Capabilities	Identifies the outer join capabilities of the ODBC data source. Read-only.	SQL_OJ
Output Parameter Availability	Identifies the time at which output parameter values become available. Read-only.	DBPROPVAL_OA
Packet Size	Specifies the network packet size in bytes. It must be between 512 and 32767. The default is 4096. Read/Write.	Long
Pass By Ref Accessors	Whether the provider supports the DBACCESSOR_PASSBYREF flag. Read-only.	Boolean
Password	The password to be used to connect to the data source. Read/Write.	String
Persist Encrypted	Whether or not the consumer requires that the data source object persist sensitive authentication information, such as a password, in encrypted form. Read/Write.	Boolean
Persist Format	Indicates the format for persisting data.	PersistFormatEnum
Persist Schema	Indicates whether or not the schema is persisted along with the data.	Boolean
Persist Security Info	Whether or not the data source object is allowed to persist sensitive authentication information, such as a password, along with other authentication information. Read/Write.	Boolean

Table Continued on Following Page

785

Property Name	Description	DataType
Persistent ID Type	Specifies the type of DBID that the provider uses when persisting DBIDs for tables, indexes and columns. Read-only.	DBPROPVAL_PT
Prepare Abort Behavior	Identifies how aborting a transaction affects prepared commands. Read-only.	DBPROPVAL_CB
Prepare Commit Behavior	Identifies how committing a transaction affects prepared commands. Read-only.	DBPROPVAL_CB
Procedure Term	Specifies the data source providers name for a procedure, e.g. 'database procedure' or 'stored procedure'. Read-only.	String
Prompt	Specifies whether to prompt the user during initialization. Read/Write.	DBPROMPT
Protection Level	The level of protection of data sent between client and server. This property applies only to network connections other than RPC. Read/Write.	DB_PROT_LEVEL
Protocol Provider	The protocol to use when using the IPP to connect to a resource. This should be WEC to use the FrontPage Web Extender Client protocol, and DAV to use the Web Distributed Authoring and Versioning (WebDAV) protocol.	String
Provider Friendly Name	The friendly name of the provider. Read-only.	String
Provider Name	The filename of the provider. Read-only.	String
Provider Version	The version of the provider. Read-only.	String
Quoted Catalog Names	Indicates whether or not quoted identifiers are allowed for catalog names.	Boolean
Quoted Identifier Sensitivity	Identifies how quoted identifiers treat case. Read-only.	DBPROPVAL_IC
Read-Only Data Source	Whether or not the data source is read-only. Read-only.	Boolean
Remote Provider	The data provide used to supply the data from a remote connection.	String
Remote Server	The name of the server supplying data from a remote connection.	String
Reset Datasource	Specifies the data source state to reset. Write only.	DBPROPVAL_RD

Property Name	Description	DataType
Rowset Conversions on Command	Identifies whether callers can enquire on a command and about conversions supported by the command. Read-only.	Boolean
Schema Term	The name the data source uses for a schema, e.g. 'schema' or 'owner'. Read-only.	String
Schema Usage	Identifies how schema names can be used in commands. Read-only.	DBPROPVAL_SU
Server Name	The name of the server. Read-only.	String
Sort on Index	Specifies whether the provider supports setting a sort order only for columns contained in an index. Read-only.	Boolean
Special Characters	Identifies the data store's special characters. Read-only.	String
SQL Grammar Support	Identifies the SQL grammar level supported by the ODBC driver. 0 represents no conformance, 1 indicates Level 1 conformance, and 2 represents Level 2 conformance. Read-only.	Long
SQL Support	Identifies the level of support for SQL. Read-only.	DBPROPVAL_SQL
SQLOLE execute a SET TEXTLENGTH	Identifies whether SQLOLE executes a SET TEXTLENGTH before accessing BLOB fields [*]. Read-only.	Boolean
Stored Procedures	Indicates whether stored procedures are available. Read-only.	Boolean
String Functions	Identifies the string functions supported by the ODBC driver and data source. Read-only.	SQL_FN_STR
Structured Storage	Identifies what interfaces the rowset supports on storage objects. Read-only.	DBPROPVAL_SS
Subquery Support	Identifies the predicates in text commands that support sub-queries. Read-only.	DBPROPVAL_SQ
System Functions	Identifies the system functions supported by the ODBC Driver and data source. Read-only.	SQL_FN_SYS
Table Term	The name the data source uses for a table, e.g. 'table' or 'file'. Read-only.	String

Table Continued on Following Page

Property Name	Description	DataType
Time/Date Functions	Identifies the time/date functions supported by the ODBC Driver and data source. Read-only.	SQL_SDF_CURRENT
Transact Updates	Indicates whether or not updates on the remote server are transacted. [*]	Boolean
Transaction DDL	Indicates whether Data Definition Language (DDL) statements are supported in transactions. Read-only.	DBPROPVAL_TC
Treat As Offline	Indicates whether or not the resource should treated as an offline resource.	Boolean
Unicode Comparison Style	Determines the sorting options used for Unicode data.	Long
Unicode Locale Id	The locale ID to use for Unicode sorting.	Long
Unique Reshape Names	Indicates whether or not the value of the Name property of a recordset would conflict with an existing name, resulting in a unique name being generated.	Boolean
URL Generation	Indicates whether the provider requires data store generated URLs.	DBPROPVAL_GU
Use Procedure for Prepare	Indicates whether SQL Server is to use temporary stored procedures for prepared statements. Read/Write.	SSPROPVAL_USEPROCFORPREP
User Authentication mode	Indicates whether Windows NT Authentication is used to access SQL Server. Read/Write.	Boolean
User ID	The User ID to be used when connecting to the data source. Read/Write.	String
User Name	The User Name used in a particular database. Read-only.	String
Window Handle	The window handle to be used if the data source object needs to prompt for additional information. Read/Write.	Long
Workstation ID	Identifies the workstation. Read/Write.	String

The Recordset Object's Properties

Property Name	Description	DataType
Access Order	Indicates the order in which columns must be accessed on the rowset. Read/Write.	DBPROPVAL_AO
Always use content index	Indicates whether or not to use the content index to resolve queries, even if the index is out of date.	Boolean
Append-Only Rowset	A rowset opened with this property will initially contain no rows. Read/Write.	Boolean
Asynchronous Rowset Processing	Identifies the asynchronous processing performed on the rowset. Read/Write.	DBPROPVAL_ASYNCH
Auto Recalc	Specifies when the MSDataShape provider updates aggregated and calculated columns. Read/Write.	ADCPROP_AUTORECALC_ENUM
Background Fetch Size	The number of rows to fetch in each batch, during asynchronous reads.	Long
Background thread Priority	The priority of the background thread for asynchronous actions. Read/Write.	ADCPROP_ASYCTHREADPRIORITY_ENUM
Batch Size	The number of rows in a batch. Read/Write.	Integer
BLOB accessibility on Forward-Only cursor	Indicates whether or not BLOB columns can be accessed irrespective of their position in the column list. If True then the BLOB column can be accessed even if it is not the last column. If False then the BLOB column can only be accessed if it the last BLOB column, and any non-BLOB columns after this column will not be accessible. Read/Write.	Boolean
Blocking Storage Objects	Indicates whether storage objects might prevent use of other methods on the rowset. Read/Write.	Boolean
Bookmark Information	Identifies additional information about bookmarks over the rowset. Read-only.	DBPROPVAL_BI
Bookmark Type	Identifies the bookmark type supported by the rowset. Read/Write.	DBPROPVAL_BMK
Bookmarkable	Indicates whether bookmarks are supported. Read-only.	Boolean
Bookmarks Ordered	Indicates whether boomarks can be compared to determine the relative position of their rows in the rowset. Read/Write.	Boolean

Table Continued on Following Page

Property Name	Description	DataType
Bulk Operations	Identifies optimizations that a provider may take for updates to the rowset. Read-only.	DBPROPVAL_BO
Cache Child Rows	Indicates whether child rows in a chaptered recordset are cached, or whether they are re-fetched when the rows are accessed. Read/Write.	Boolean
Cache Deferred Columns	Indicates whether the provider caches the value of a deferred columns when the consumer first gets a value from that column. Read/Write.	Boolean
Change Inserted Rows	Indicates whether the consumer can delete or update newly inserted rows. An inserted row is assumed to be one that has been transmitted to the data source, as opposed to a pending insert row. Read/Write.	Boolean
Column Privileges	Indicates whether access rights are restricted on a column-by-column basis. Read-only.	Boolean
Column Set Notification	Indicates whether changing a column set is cancelable. Read-only.	DBPROPVAL_NP
Column Writable	Indicates whether a particular column is writable. Read/Write.	Boolean
Command Time Out	The number of seconds to wait before a command times out. A value of 0 indicates an infinite timeout. Read/Write.	Long
Concurrency control method	Identifies the method used for concurrency control when using server based cursors. Read/Write.	SSPROPVAL_CONCUR
Cursor Engine Version	Identifies the version of the cursor engine. Read-only.	String
Defer Column	Indicates whether the data in a column is not fetched until specifically requested. Read/Write.	Boolean
Defer scope and security testing	Indicates whether or not the search will defer scope and security testing.	Boolean
Delay Storage Object Updates	Indicates whether, when in delayed update mode, if storage objects are also used in delayed update mode. Read/Write.	Boolean
Fastload Options	Indicates the options to use when in Fastload mode.	String

Property Name	Description	DataType
Fetch Backward	Indicates whether a rowset can fetch backwards. Read/Write.	Boolean
Filter Operations	Identifies which comparison operations are supported when using Filter on a particular column. Read-only.	DBPROPVAL_CO
Find Operations	Identifies which comparison operations are supported when using Find on a particular column. Read-only.	DBPROPVAL_CO
FOR BROWSE versioning columns	Indicates the rowset contains the primary key or a timestamp column. Only applicable with rowsets created with the SQL FOR BROWSE statement. Read/Write.	Boolean
Force no command preparation when executing a parameterized command	Identifies whether or not a temporary statement is created for parameterized commands. *. Read/Write.	Boolean
Force no command reexecution when failure to satisfy all required properties	Identifies whether or not the command is reexecuted if the command properties are invalid. *. Read/Write.	Boolean
Force no parameter rebinding when executing a command	Identifies whether or not the command parameters are rebound every time the command is executed *. Read/Write.	Boolean
Force SQL Server Firehose Mode cursor	Identifies whether or not a forward-only, read-only cursor is always created *. Read/Write.	Boolean
Generate a Rowset that can be marshalled	Identifies whether or not the rowset that is to be created can be marshalled across process boundaries *. Read/Write.	Boolean
Hidden Columns	Indicates the number of hidden columns in the rowset added by the provider to uniquely identify rows.	Long
Hold Rows	Indicates whether the rowset allows the consumer to retrieve more rows or change the next fetch position whilst holding previously fetched rows with pending changes. Read/Write.	Boolean
Immobile Rows	Indicates whether the rowset will reorder insert or updated rows. Read/Write.	Boolean

Table Continued on Following Page

Property Name	Description	DataType
Include SQL_FLOAT, SQL_DOUBLE, and SQL_REAL in QBU where clauses	When using a query-based update, setting this to True will include REAL, FLOAT and DOUBLE numeric types in the WHERE clause, otherwise they will be omitted. Read/Write.	Boolean
Initial Fetch Size	Identifies the initial size of the cache into which records are fetched. Read/Write.	Long
Jet OLEDB:Bulk Transaction	Determines whether bulk operations are transacted.	DBPROPVAL_BT
Jet OLEDB:Enable Fat Cursors	Indicates whether or not Jet caches multiple rows for remote row sources.	Boolean
Jet OLEDB:Fat Cursor Cache Size	The number of rows that should be cached if the dynamic property Jet OLEDB:Enable Fat Cursors is set to True.	Long
Jet OLEDB:Inconsistent	Indicates whether or not inconsistent updates are allowed on queries.	Boolean
Jet OLEDB:Locking Granularity	Identifies the lock mode used to open a table. This only applies if Jet OLEDB:Database Locking Mode is set to DBPROPVAL_DL_ALCATRAZ.	DBPROPVAL_LG
Jet OLEDB:ODBC Pass-Through Statement	Identifies the statement used for a SQL Pass through statement. Read/Write.	String
Jet OLEDB:Partial Bulk Ops	Indicates whether on not bulk operations will complete if some of the values fail.	
Jet OLEDB:Pass Through Query Bulk-Op	Indicates whether or not the pass-through query is a bulk operation.	Boolean
Jet OLEDB:Pass Through Query Connect String	Identifies the Connect string for an ODBC pass through query. Read/Write.	String
Jet OLEDB:Stored Query	Indicates whether or not the command should be interpreted as a stored query.	Boolean
Jet OLEDB:Validate Rules On Set	Indicates whether Jet validation rules are applied when the value in a column is set (True) or when the changes are commited (False).	Boolean

Property Name	Description	DataType
Keep Identity	Indicates whether or not IDENTITY columns should keep the values if supplied by the client during an INSERT. [*]	Boolean
Keep Nulls	Indicates whether or not NULL values supplied by the client should be kept if DEFAULT values exist on the columns.	Boolean
Literal Bookmarks	Indicates whether bookmarks can be compared literally, i.e. as a series of bytes. Read/Write.	Boolean
Literal Row Identity	Indicates whether the consumer can perform a binary comparison of two row handles to determine whether they point to the same row. Read-only.	Boolean
Lock Mode	Identifies the level of locking performed by the rowset. Read/Write.	DBPROPVAL_LM
Maintain Change Status	Indicates whether or not to maintain the status of a row if a conflict happens during row updates. [*]	Boolean
Maximum BLOB Length	Identifies the maximum length of a BLOB field. Read-only.	Long
Maximum Open Rows	Specifies the maximum number of rows that can be active at the same time. Read/Write.	Long
Maximum Pending Rows	Specifies the maximum number of rows that can have pending changes at the same time. Read/Write.	Long
Maximum Rows	Specifies the maximum number of rows that can be returned in the rowset. This is 0 if there is no limit. Read/Write.	Long
Memory Usage	Estimates the amount of memory that can be used by the rowset. If set to 0 the amount is unlimited. If between 1 and 99 it specifies a percentage of the available virtual memory. If 100 or greater it specifies the number of kilobytes. Read/Write.	Long
Notification Granularity	Identifies when the consumer is notified for methods that operate on multiple rows. Read/Write.	DBPROPVAL_NT
Notification Phases	Identifies the notification phases supported by the provider. Read-only.	DBPROPVAL_NP

Table Continued on Following Page

Property Name	Description	DataType
Objects Transacted	Indicates whether any object created on the specified column is transacted. Read/Write.	Boolean
ODBC Concurrency Type	Identifies the ODBC concurrency type. Read-only.	Integer
ODBC Cursor Type	Identifies the ODBC cursor type. Read-only.	Integer
Others' Changes Visible	Indicates whether the rowset can see updates and deletes made by someone other that the consumer of the rowset. Read/Write.	Boolean
Others' Inserts Visible	Indicates whether the rowset can see rows inserted by someone other than the consumer of the rowset. Read/Write.	Boolean
Own Changes Visible	Indicates whether the rowset can see its own updates and deletes. Read/Write.	Boolean
Own Inserts Visible	Indicates whether the rowset can see its own inserts. Read/Write.	Boolean
Position on the last row after insert	Identifies whether or not the cursor is placed on the last row after an insert. * Read-only.	Boolean
Preserve on Abort	Indicates whether, after aborting a transaction, the rowset remains active. Read/Write.	Boolean
Preserve on Commit	Indicates whether after committing a transaction the rowset remains active. Read/Write.	Boolean
Query Based Updates/Deletes/ Inserts	Identifies whether or not queries are used for updates, deletes, and inserts. * Read/Write.	Boolean
Quick Restart	Indicates whether RestartPosition is relatively quick to execute. Read/Write.	Boolean
Query Restriction	Indicates the restriction to use for a query.	String
Reentrant Events	Indicates whether the provider supports reentrancy during callbacks. Read-only.	Boolean
Remove Deleted Rows	Indicates whether the provider removes rows it detects as having been deleted from the rowset. Read/Write.	Boolean
Report Multiple Changes	Indicates whether an update or delete can affect multiple rows and the provider can detect that multiple rows have been updated or deleted. Read-only.	Boolean

Property Name	Description	DataType
Reshape Name	Indicates the name of the recordset that can be used in reshaping commands.	String
Resync Command	The command string that the `Resync` method will use to refresh data in the `Unique Table`.	String
Return PROPVARIANTs in variant binding	Indicates whether or not to return PROPVARIANTS when binding to variant columns.	Boolean
Return Pending Inserts	Indicates whether methods that fetch rows can return pending insert rows. Read-only.	Boolean
Row Delete Notification	Indicates whether deleting a row is cancellable. Read-only.	DBPROPVAL_NP
Row First Change Notification	Indicates whether changing the first row is cancellable. Read-only.	DBPROPVAL_NP
Row Insert Notification	Indicates whether inserting a new row is cancellable. Read-only.	DBPROPVAL_NP
Row Privileges	Indicates whether access rights are restricted on a row-by-row basis. Read-only.	Boolean
Row Resynchronization Notification	Indicates whether resynchronizing a row is cancellable. Read-only.	DBPROPVAL_NP
Row Threading Model	Identifies the threading models supported by the rowset. Read/Write.	DBPROPVAL_RT
Row Undo Change Notification	Indicates whether undoing a change is cancellable. Read-only.	DBPROPVAL_NP
Row Undo Delete Notification	Indicates whether undoing a delete is cancellable. Read-only.	DBPROPVAL_NP
Row Undo Insert Notification	Indicates whether undoing an insert is cancellable. Read-only.	DBPROPVAL_NP
Row Update Notification	Indicates whether updating a row is cancellable. Read-only.	DBPROPVAL_NP
Rowset Fetch Position Change Notification	Indicates whether changing the fetch position is cancellable Indicates whether changing the fetch position is cancellable. Read-only.	DBPROPVAL_NP
Rowset Release Notification	Indicates whether releasing a rowset is cancellable. Read-only.	DBPROPVAL_NP
Scroll Backward	Indicates whether the rowset can scroll backward. Read/Write.	Boolean

Table Continued on Following Page

Property Name	Description	DataType
Server Cursor	Indicates whether the cursor underlying the rowset (if any) must be materialized on the server. Read/Write.	Boolean
Server Data on Insert	Indicates whether, at the time an insert is transmitted to the server, the provider retrieves data from the server to update to update the local row cache. Read/Write.	Boolean
Skip Deleted Bookmarks	Indicates whether the rowset allows positioning to continue if a bookmark row was deleted. Read/Write.	Boolean
SQL Content Query Locale String	The locale string to use for queries.	String
Strong Row Identity	Indicates whether the handles of newly inserted rows can be compared. Read-only.	Boolean
Unique Catalog	Specifies the catalog, or database name containing the table named in the Unique Table property.	String
Unique Rows	Indicates whether each row is uniquely identified by it's column values. Read/Write.	Boolean
Unique Schema	Specifies the schema, or owner of the table named in the Unique Table property.	String
Unique Table	Specifies the name of the base table upon which edits are allowed. This is required when updateable recordsets are created from one-to-many JOIN statements.	String
Updatability	Identifies the supported methods for updating a rowset. Read/Write.	DBPROPVAL_UP
Update Criteria	Specifies which fields can be used to detect conflicts during optimistic updates. Read/Write.	ADCPROP_UPDATECRITERIA_ENUM
Update Operation	For chaptered recordsets, identifies the operation to be performed with a requery. Read/Write.	String
Update Resync	Specifies whether an implicit Resync method is called directly after an UpdateBatch method	CEResyncEnum
Use Bookmarks	Indicates whether the rowset supports bookmarks. Read/Write.	Boolean

The Field Object's Properties

The field properties names are different from the other properties because they are less readable and appear more like the schema column names.

Property Name	Description	DataType
BASECATALOGNAME	The name of the catalog. Read-only.	String
BASECOLUMNNAME	The name of the column. Read-only.	String
BASESCHEMANAME	The name of the schema. Read-only.	String
BASETABLENAME	The table name. Read-only.	String
CALCULATIONINFO	This is only available of client cursors.	Binary
CLSID	The class id of the field.	GUID
COLLATINGSEQUENCE	The locale ID of the sort sequence.	Long
COMPUTEMODE	Indicates the mode of recalculation for computed fields.	DBCOMPUTEMODE
DATETIMEPRECISION	The number of digits in the fraction seconds portion if a datetime column. Read-only.	Long
DEFAULTVALUE	The default value of the field.	Variant
DOMAINCATALOG	The name of the catalog containing this column's domain.	String
DOMAINNAME	The name of the domain of which this column is a member.	String
DOMAINSCHEMA	The name of the schema containing this column's domain.	String
HASDEFAULT	Indicates whether or not the field has a default value.	Boolean
ISAUTOINCREMENT	Identifies whether the column is an auto increment column, such as an Access Autonumber or a SQL Server IDENTITY column. Read-only.	Boolean
ISCASESENSITIVE	Identifies whether the contents of the column are case sensitive. Useful when searching. Read-only.	Boolean

Table Continued on Following Page

Property Name	Description	DataType
ISSEARCHABLE	Identifies the searchability of the column. Read-only.	DB_SEARCHABLE
ISUNIQUE	Indicates whether or not the field uniquely identifies the row.	Boolean
KEYCOLUMN	Identifies whether or not the column is a key column, used to uniquely identify the row. Read-only.	Boolean
OCTETLENGTH	The maximum column length in bytes, for character or binary data columns. Read-only.	Long
OPTIMIZE	Identifies whether the column is indexed locally. This is only available of client cursors. Read/Write.	Boolean
RELATIONCONDITIONS	Identifies the relationship between fields. This is only available on client cursors. [*]	Binary

Schemas

There are two terms that are important when dealing with schemas:

❑ A **Catalog** is like a normal paper catalog, but contains a list of schemas. It always contains a schema named INFORMATION_SCHEMA, which is the information schema. When dealing with Microsoft SQL Server and Access, a catalog is a database.

❑ A **Schema** is a collection of database objects that are owned, or have been created by, a particular user. Microsoft Access does not have an equivalent to a schema, and so all database objects appear in a single schema.

This appendix details the schema objects that can be accessed using the OpenSchema method of the Connection object.

The table below shows the main providers and the list of schemas supported by them:

Schema	ODBC Access 97	ODBC Access 2000	ODBC SQL Server 6.5	ODBC SQL Server 7	OLEDB Access 97	OLEDB Access 2000	OLEDB SQL Server 6.5	OLEDB SQL Server 7	Indexing Service	OLAP	Exchange
adSchemaAsserts											
adSchemaCatalogs	✓	✓	✓	✓				✓		✓	
adSchemaCharacterSets											
adSchemaCheckConstraints					✓	✓					
adSchemaCollations											
adSchemaColumnPrivileges			✓	✓			✓	✓			
adSchemaColumns	✓	✓	✓	✓	✓	✓	✓	✓		✓	
adSchemaColumnsDomainUsage											
adSchemaConstraintColumnUsage					✓	✓					
adSchemaConstraintTableUsage											
adSchemaCubes										✓	
adSchemaDBInfoKeywords	✓	✓	✓	✓	✓	✓	✓	✓	✓	✓	
adSchemaDBInfoLiterals	✓	✓	✓	✓	✓	✓	✓	✓	✓	✓	
adSchemaDimensions										✓	
adSchemaForeignKeys			✓	✓	✓	✓	✓	✓			
adSchemaHierarchies										✓	
adSchemaIndexes	✓	✓	✓	✓	✓	✓	✓	✓			
adSchemaKeyColumnUsage					✓	✓					
adSchemaLevels										✓	
adSchemaMeasures										✓	
adSchemaMembers										✓	
adSchemaPrimaryKeys			✓	✓	✓	✓	✓	✓			
adSchemaProcedureColumns	✓	✓									
adSchemaProcedureParameters	✓	✓	✓	✓			✓	✓			
adSchemaProcedures	✓	✓	✓	✓	✓	✓	✓	✓			
adSchemaProperties										✓	

Schema	ODBC Access 97	ODBC Access 2000	ODBC SQL Server 6.5	ODBC SQL Server 7	OLEDB Access 97	OLEDB Access 2000	OLEDB SQL Server 6.5	OLEDB SQL Server 7	Indexing Service	OLAP	Exchange
adSchemaProviderTypes	✓	✓	✓	✓	✓	✓	✓	✓		✓	✓
adSchemaReferentialContraints					✓	✓					
adSchemaSchemata			✓	✓			✓	✓			
adSchemaSQLLanguages											
adSchemaStatistics					✓	✓	✓	✓			
adSchemaTableConstraints					✓	✓	✓	✓			
adSchemaTablePrivileges							✓	✓			
adSchemaTables	✓	✓	✓	✓	✓	✓	✓	✓		✓	✓
adSchemaTranslations											
adSchemaTrustees											
adSchemaUsagePrivileges											
adSchemaViewColumnUsage											
adSchemaViews					✓	✓					
adSchemaViewTableUsage											

adSchemaAsserts

This identifies the assertions defined in the catalog.

Column name	Type	Description
CONSTRAINT_CATALOG	String	Catalog name, or Null if the provider does not support catalogs.
CONSTRAINT_SCHEMA	String	Schema name, or Null if the provider does not support schemas.
CONSTRAINT_NAME	String	Constraint name.
IS_DEFERRABLE	Boolean	**True** if the assertion is deferrable, **False** otherwise
INITIALLY_DEFERRED	Boolean	**True** if the assertion is initially deferred, **False** otherwise.
DESCRIPTION	String	Description of the assertion.

adSchemaCatalogs

This defines the physical attributes of the catalogs of a database. When using SQL Server the catalogs are the databases within the Server, and for Access the catalogs contain the current database.

Column name	Type	Description
CATALOG_NAME	String	Catalog name.
DESCRIPTION	String	Catalog description

adSchemaCharacterSets

This identifies the character sets supported by the catalog.

Column name	Type	Description
CHARACTER_SET_CATALOG	String	Catalog name, or Null if the provider does not support catalogs.
CHARACTER_SET_SCHEMA	String	Schema name, or Null if the provider does not support schemas.
CHARACTER_SET_NAME	String	Character set name.
FORM_OF_USE	String	Name of form-of-use of the character set.
NUMBER_OF_CHARACTERS	Big Integer	Number of characters in the character repertoire.
DEFAULT_COLLATE_CATALOG	String	Catalog name containing the default collation, or Null if the provider does not support catalogs or different collations.
DEFAULT_COLLATE_SCHEMA	String	Schema name containing the default collation, or Null if the provider does not support schemas or different collations.
DEFAULT_COLLATE_NAME	String	Default collation name, or Null if the provider does not support different collations.

adSchemaCheckConstraints

This identifies the check constraints available in the catalog. Check constraints identify the valid values allowed for columns.

Column name	Type	Description
CONSTRAINT_CATALOG	String	Catalog name, or Null if the provider does not support catalogs.
CONSTRAINT_SCHEMA	String	Schema name, or Null if the provider does not support schemas.
CONSTRAINT_NAME	String	Constraint name.
CHECK_CLAUSE	String	The WHERE clause specified in the CHECK constraint.
DESCRIPTION	String	Check constraint description.

adSchemaCollations

Collations identify how the catalog sorts data.

Column name	Type	Description
COLLATION_CATALOG	String	Catalog name, or Null if the provider does not support catalogs.
COLLATION_SCHEMA	String	Schema name, or Null if the provider does not support schemas.
COLLATION_NAME	String	Collation name.
CHARACTER_SET_CATALOG	String	Catalog name containing the character set on which the collation is defined, or Null if the provider does not support catalogs or different character sets.
CHARACTER_SET_SCHEMA	String	Schema name containing the character set on which the collation is defined, or Null if the provider does not support schema or different character sets.
CHARACTER_SET_NAME	String	Character set name on which the collation is defined, or Null if the provider does not support different character sets.
PAD_ATTRIBUTE	String	'NO PAD' if the collation being described has the NO PAD attribute, 'PAD SPACE' if the collation being described has the PAD SPACE attribute. This identifies whether variable length character columns are padded with spaces.

adSchemaColumnDomainUsage

This identifies the columns that use domains for integrity checking.

Column name	Type	Description
DOMAIN_CATALOG	String	Catalog name, or Null if the provider does not support catalogs.
DOMAIN_SCHEMA	String	Schema name, or Null if the provider does not support schemas.
DOMAIN_NAME	String	View name.
TABLE_CATALOG	String	Catalog name in which the table is defined, or Null if the provider does not support catalogs.
TABLE_SCHEMA	String	Unqualified schema name in which the table is defined, or Null if the provider does not support schemas.
TABLE_NAME	String	Table name.
COLUMN_NAME	String	Column name. This column, together with the COLUMN_GUID and COLUMN_PROPID columns, forms the column ID. One or more of these columns will be Null depending on which elements of the DBID structure the provider uses.
COLUMN_GUID	GUID	Column GUID.
COLUMN_PROPID	Long	Column property ID.

adSchemaColumnPrivileges

This identifies the privileges on table columns for a given user.

Column name	Type	Description
GRANTOR	String	User who granted the privileges on the table in TABLE_NAME.
GRANTEE	String	User name (or "PUBLIC") to whom the privilege has been granted.
TABLE_CATALOG	String	Catalog name in which the table is defined, or Null if the provider does not support catalogs.
TABLE_SCHEMA	String	Schema name in which the table is defined, or Null if the provider does not support schemas.
TABLE_NAME	String	Table name.
COLUMN_NAME	String	Column name.
COLUMN_GUID	GUID	Column GUID.

Column name	Type	Description
COLUMN_PROPID	Long	Column property ID.
PRIVILEGE_TYPE	String	Privilege type. One of the following: • SELECT • DELETE • INSERT • UPDATE • REFERENCES
IS_GRANTABLE	Boolean	**True** if the privilege being described was granted with the WITH GRANT OPTION clause, **False** if the privilege being described was not granted with the WITH GRANT OPTION clause.

adSchemaColumns

This identifies the columns of tables.

Column name	Type	Description
TABLE_CATALOG	String	Catalog name, or Null if the provider does not support catalogs.
TABLE_SCHEMA	Long	Schema name, or Null if the provider does not support schemas.
TABLE_NAME	String	Table name. This column cannot contain a Null.
COLUMN_NAME	String	The name of the column, or Null if this cannot be determined.
COLUMN_GUID	GUID	Column GUID, or Null for providers that do not use GUIDs to identify columns.
COLUMN_PROPID	Long	Column property ID, or Null for providers that do not associate PROPIDs with columns.
ORDINAL_POSITION	Long	The ordinal of the column, or Null if there is no stable ordinal value for the column. Columns are numbered starting from one.
COLUMN_HASDEFAULT	Boolean	**True** if column has a default value, **False** if the column does not have a default value or it is unknown whether the column has a default value.

Table Continued on Following Page

Column name	Type	Description
COLUMN_DEFAULT	String	Default value of the column.
COLUMN_FLAGS	Long	A bitmask that describes column characteristics. The DBCOLUMNFLAGS enumerated type specifies the bits in the bitmask. The values for DBCOLUMNFLAGS can be found in Appendix B. This column cannot contain a Null value.
IS_NULLABLE	Boolean	**True** if the column might be nullable, **False** if the column is known not to be nullable.
DATA_TYPE	Integer	The column's data type. If the data type of the column varies from row to row, this must be a **Variant**. This column cannot contain Null. For a list of valid Types, see DataTypeEnum in Appendix B.
TYPE_GUID	GUID	The GUID of the column's data type. Providers that do not use GUIDs to identify data types should return Null in this column.
CHARACTER_MAXIMUM_LENGTH	Long	The maximum possible length of a value in the column.
CHARACTER_OCTET_LENGTH	Long	Maximum length in octets (bytes) of the column, if the type of the column is character or binary. A value of zero means the column has no maximum length. Null for all other types of columns.
NUMERIC_PRECISION	Integer	If the column's data type is numeric, this is the maximum precision of the column. The precision of columns with a data type of **Decimal** or **Numeric** depends on the definition of the column If the column's data type is not numeric, this is Null.
NUMERIC_SCALE	Integer	If the column's Type is **Decimal** or **Numeric**, this is the number of digits to the right of the decimal point. Otherwise, this is Null.
DATETIME_PRECISION	Long	Datetime precision (number of digits in the fractional seconds portion) of the column if the column is a datetime or interval type. If the column's data type is not datetime, this is Null.
CHARACTER_SET_CATALOG	String	Catalog name in which the character set is defined, or Null if the provider does not support catalogs or different character sets.

Column name	Type	Description
CHARACTER_SET_SCHEMA	String	Schema name in which the character set is defined, or Null if the provider does not support schemas or different character sets.
CHARACTER_SET_NAME	String	Character set name, or Null if the provider does not support different character sets.
COLLATION_CATALOG	String	Catalog name in which the collation is defined, or Null if the provider does not support catalogs or different collations.
COLLATION_SCHEMA	String	Schema name in which the collation is defined, or Null if the provider does not support schemas or different collations.
COLLATION_NAME	String	Collation name, or Null if the provider does not support different collations.
DOMAIN_CATALOG	String	Catalog name in which the domain is defined, or Null if the provider does not support catalogs or domains.
DOMAIN_SCHEMA	String	Unqualified schema name in which the domain is defined, or Null if the provider does not support schemas or domains.
DOMAIN_NAME	String	Domain name, or Null if the provider does not support domains.
DESCRIPTION	String	Description of the column, or Null if there is no description associated with the column.
ORDINAL	Integer	The ordinal number of the column (only applicable to ODBC for Access).
SS_DATA_TYPE	Integer	SQL Server data type (only applicable to SQL Server).

CHARACTER_MAXIMUM_LENGTH will vary depending upon the data type of the column:

For character, binary, or bit columns, this is one of the following:

- The maximum length of the column in characters, bytes, or bits, respectively, if one is defined. For example, a CHAR(5) column in an SQL table has a maximum length of five (5).
- The maximum length of the data type in characters, bytes, or bits, respectively, if the column does not have a defined length.
- Zero (0) if neither the column nor the data type has a defined maximum length.

It will be Null for all other types of columns.

adSchemaConstraintColumnUsage

This identifies the columns used for referential integrity constraints, unique constraints, check constraints, and assertions.

Column name	Type	Description
TABLE_CATALOG	String	Catalog name in which the table is defined, or Null if the provider does not support catalogs.
TABLE_SCHEMA	String	Schema name in which the table is defined, or Null if the provider does not support schemas.
TABLE_NAME	String	Table name.
COLUMN_NAME	String	Column name.
COLUMN_GUID	GUID	Column GUID.
COLUMN_PROPID	Long	Column property ID.
CONSTRAINT_CATALOG	String	Catalog name, or Null if the provider does not support catalogs.
CONSTRAINT_SCHEMA	String	Schema name, or Null if the provider does not support schemas.
CONSTRAINT_NAME	String	Constraint name.

adSchemaConstraintTableUsage

This identifies the tables used for referential integrity constraints, unique constraints, check constraints, and assertions.

Column name	Type	Description
TABLE_CATALOG	String	Catalog name in which the table is defined, or Null if the provider does not support catalogs.
TABLE_SCHEMA	String	Schema name in which the table is defined, or Null if the provider does not support schemas.
TABLE_NAME	String	Table name.
CONSTRAINT_CATALOG	String	Catalog name, or Null if the provider does not support catalogs.
CONSTRAINT_SCHEMA	String	Schema name, or Null if the provider does not support schemas.
CONSTRAINT_NAME	String	Constraint name.

adSchemaCubes

Identifies the Cubes in an OLAP Catalog.

Column name	Type	Description
CATALOG_NAME	String	Catalog name in which the table is defined, or Null if the provider does not support catalogs.
SCHEMA_NAME	String	Schema name in which the table is defined, or Null if the provider does not support schemas.
CUBE_NAME	String	The name of the cube
CUBE_TYPE	String	Either CUBE to indicate a regular cube, or VIRTUAL CUBE to indicate a virtual cube.
CUBE_GUID	String	The GUID of the cube, or Null if no GUID exists.
CREATED_ON	Date	Date and time cube was created.
LAST_SCHEMA_UPDATE	Date	Date and time schema was last updated.
SCHEMA_UPDATED_BY	String	User ID of person who last updated the schema.
LAST_DATA_UPDATE	Date	Date and time data was last updated
DATA_UPDATED_BY	String	User ID of person who last updated the data.
DESCRIPTION	String	The cube description.

adSchemaDimensions

Identifies the Dimensions in an OLAP Catalog.

Column name	Type	Description
CATALOG_NAME	String	Catalog name in which the table is defined, or Null if the provider does not support catalogs.
SCHEMA_NAME	String	Schema name in which the table is defined, or Null if the provider does not support schemas.
CUBE_NAME	String	The name of the Cube to which this dimension belongs
DIMENSION_NAME	String	The name of the dimension
DIMENSION_UNIQUE_NAME	String	The fully qualified name of the dimension.

Table Continued on Following Page

Column name	Type	Description
DIMENSION_GUID	GUID	The GUID of the dimension, or Null if no GUID exists.
DIMENSION_CAPTION	String	The name of the dimension.
DIMENSION_ORDINAL	Long	The number of the ordinal. This is 0 based.
DIMENSION_TYPE	Integer	The type of the dimension. Can be one of MD_DIMTYPE_MEASURE, to indicate a measure dimension MD_DIMTYPE_TIME, to indicate a time dimension MD_DIMTYPE_OTHER, to indicate neither a measure nor a time dimension. MD_DIMTYPE_UNKNOWN, to indicate the type is unknown.
DIMENSION_CARDINALITY	Long	The number of members in the dimension. This figure is not guaranteed to be accurate.
DEFAULT_HIERARCHY	String	The default hierarchy for this dimension, or Null if no default exists.
DESCRIPTION	String	The description of the hierarchy.
IS_VIRTUAL	Boolean	True if the dimension is a virtual one, False otherwise.

adSchemaForeignKeys

This identifies the foreign key columns, as used in referential integrity checks.

Column name	Type	Description
PK_TABLE_CATALOG	String	Catalog name in which the primary key table is defined, or Null if the provider does not support catalogs.
PK_TABLE_SCHEMA	String	Schema name in which the primary key table is defined, or Null if the provider does not support schemas.
PK_TABLE_NAME	String	Primary key table name.
PK_COLUMN_NAME	String	Primary key column name.
PK_COLUMN_GUID	GUID	Primary key column GUID.
PK_COLUMN_PROPID	Long	Primary key column property ID.

Column name	Type	Description
FK_TABLE_CATALOG	String	Catalog name in which the foreign key table is defined, or Null if the provider does not support catalogs.
FK_TABLE_SCHEMA	String	Schema name in which the foreign key table is defined, or Null if the provider does not support schemas.
FK_TABLE_NAME	String	Foreign key table name.
FK_COLUMN_NAME	String	Foreign key column name.
FK_COLUMN_GUID	GUID	Foreign key column GUID.
FK_COLUMN_PROPID	Long	Foreign key column property ID.
ORDINAL	Long	The order of the column in the key. For example, a table might contain several foreign key references to another table. The ordinal starts over for each reference; for example, two references to a three-column key would return 1, 2, 3, 1, 2, 3.
UPDATE_RULE	String	The action if an UPDATE rule was specified. This will be Null only if the provider cannot determine the UPDATE_RULE. In most cases, this implies a default of NO ACTION.
DELETE_RULE	String	The action if a DELETE rule was specified. This will be Null if the provider cannot determine the DELETE_RULE. In most cases, this implies a default of NO ACTION.
PK_NAME	String	Primary key name, or Null if the provider does not support named primary key constraints.
FK_NAME	String	Foreign key name, or Null if the provider does not support named foreign key constraints.
DEFERRABILITY	Integer	Deferability of the foreign key. Value is one of the DBPROPVAL_DF types, as shown in Appendix B.

For UPDATE_RULE and DELETE_RULE, the value will be one of the following:

CASCADE	A referential action of CASCADE was specified.
SET NULL	A referential action of SET NULL was specified.
SET DEFAULT	A referential action of SET DEFAULT was specified.
NO ACTION	A referential action of NO ACTION was specified.

adSchemaHierarchies

Identifies the Hierarchies in an OLAP Catalog.

Column name	Type	Description
CATALOG_NAME	String	Catalog name in which the table is defined or Null if the provider does not support catalogs.
SCHEMA_NAME	String	Schema name in which the table is defined or Null if the provider does not support schemas.
CUBE_NAME	String	The name of the Cube to which this Hierarchy belongs
DIMENSION_UNIQUE_NAME	String	The fully qualified name of the Dimension to which this Hierarchy belongs.
HIERARCHY_NAME	String	The name of the Hierarchy.
HIERARCHY_UNIQUE_NAME	String	The fully qualified name of the Hierarchy
HIERARCHY_GUID	GUID	The GUID of the Hierarchy, or Null if no GUID exists.
HIERARCHY_CAPTION	String	The name of the Hierarchy.
DIMENSION_TYPE	Integer	The type of the dimension. Can be one of MD_DIMTYPE_MEASURE, to indicate a measure dimension MD_DIMTYPE_TIME, to indicate a time dimension MD_DIMTYPE_OTHER, to indicate neither a measure nor a time dimension MD_DIMTYPE_UNKNOWN, to indicate the type is unknown.
HIERARCHY_CARDINALITY	Long	The number of members in the Hierarchy. This figure is not guaranteed to be accurate.
DEFAULT_MEMBER	String	The default Level for this Hierarchy, or Null if no default exists.
ALL_MEMBER	String	The name of the default member if the first level is All, or Null if the first level is not All.
DESCRIPTION	String	The description of the hierarchy.

adSchemaIndexes

Identifies the list of indexes in the catalog.

Column name	Type	Description
TABLE_CATALOG	String	Catalog name, or Null if the provider does not support catalogs.
TABLE_SCHEMA	String	Unqualified schema name, or Null if the provider does not support schemas.
TABLE_NAME	String	Table name.
INDEX_CATALOG	String	Catalog name, or Null if the provider does not support catalogs.
INDEX_SCHEMA	String	Schema name, or Null if the provider does not support schemas.
INDEX_NAME	String	Index name.
PRIMARY_KEY	Boolean	Whether the index represents the primary key on the table, or Null if this is not known.
UNIQUE	Boolean	Whether index keys must be unique. This will be **True** if the index keys must be unique, and **False** if duplicate keys are allowed.
CLUSTERED	Boolean	Whether an index is clustered.
TYPE	Integer	The type of the index. One of the DBPROPVAL_IT constants as shown in Appendix B
FILL_FACTOR	Long	For a B+-tree index, this property represents the storage utilization factor of page nodes during the creation of the index.
INITIAL_SIZE	Long	The total amount of bytes allocated to this structure at creation time.
NULLS	Long	Whether null keys are allowed This will be one of the DBPROVAL_IN constants as shown in Appendix B.
SORT_BOOKMARKS	Boolean	How the index treats repeated keys. This will be **True** if the index sorts repeated keys by bookmark, and **False** if it doesn't.
AUTO_UPDATE	Boolean	Whether the index is maintained automatically when changes are made to the corresponding base table. This will be **True** if the index is automatically maintained, and **False** if it isn't.

Table Continued on Following Page

Column name	Type	Description
NULL_COLLATION	Long	How Nulls are collated in the index. This will be one of the DBPROPVAL_NC constants as shown in Appendix B.
ORDINAL_POSITION	Long	Ordinal position of the column in the index, starting with one.
COLUMN_NAME	String	Column name.
COLUMN_GUID	GUID	Column GUID.
COLUMN_PROPID	Long	Column property ID.
COLLATION	Integer	Identifies the sort order, and will be one of the DB_COLLATION constants as shown in Appendix B.
CARDINALITY	Unsigned Big Integer	Number of unique values in the index.
PAGES	Long	Number of pages used to store the index.
FILTER_CONDITION	String	The WHERE clause identifying the filtering restriction.
INTEGRATED	Boolean	Whether the index is integrated, that is, all base table columns are available from the index. This will be **True** if the index is integrated, and **False** if it isn't. Clustered indexes always set this value to **True**.

adSchemaInfoKeywords

This identifies a list of provider specific keywords.

Column name	Type	Description
Keyword	String	The Keyword supported by the provider

adSchemaInfoLiterals

This identifies a list of provider specific literals used in text commands.

Column name	Type	Description
LiteralName	String	The literal name.
LiteralValue	String	The literal value.
InvalidChars	String	Characters which are invalid as part of a literal.
InvalidStartingChars	String	Characters which the literal cannot start with.
Literal	Integer	The literal type. This can be one of the DBLITERAL constants described in Appendix B.
Supported	Boolean	True if the provider supports the literal.
Maxlen	Integer	Maximum length of the literal name.

adSchemaKeyColumnUsage

This identifies the key columns, and table names, in the catalog.

Column name	Type	Description
CONSTRAINT_CATALOG	String	Catalog name, or Null if the provider does not support catalogs.
CONSTRAINT_SCHEMA	String	Schema name, or Null if the provider does not support schemas.
CONSTRAINT_NAME	String	Constraint name.
TABLE_CATALOG	String	Catalog name in which the table containing the key column is defined, or Null if the provider does not support catalogs.
TABLE_SCHEMA	String	Schema name in which the table containing the key column is defined, or Null if the provider does not support schemas.
TABLE_NAME	String	Table name containing the key column.
COLUMN_NAME	String	Name of the column participating in the unique, primary, or foreign key.

Table Continued on Following Page

Column name	Type	Description
COLUMN_GUID	GUID	Column GUID.
COLUMN_PROPID	Long	Column property ID.
ORDINAL_POSITION	Long	Ordinal position of the column in the constraint being described.

adSchemaLevels

Identifies the Levels in an OLAP Catalog.

Column name	Type	Description
CATALOG_NAME	String	Catalog name, or Null if the provider does not support catalogs.
SCHEMA_NAME	String	Schema name, or Null if the provider does not support schemas.
CUBE_NAME	String	The Cube name to which the level belongs.
DIMENSION_UNIQUE_NAME	String	The unique name of the Dimension to which the level belongs.
HIERARCHY_UNIQUE_NAME	String	The unique name of the hierarchy to which the level belongs.
LEVEL_NAME	String	The level name.
LEVEL_UNIQUE_NAME	String	The unique level name.
LEVEL_GUID	String	The GUID of the level, or Null if no GUID exists.
LEVEL_CAPTION	String	The Caption of the level.
LEVEL_NUMBER	String	The index number of the level.
LEVEL_CARDINALITY	Long	The number of members in the level. This figure is not guaranteed to be accurate.
LEVEL_TYPE	Integer	The Type of the level. This can be one of the MDLEVEL constants, as described in Appendix L.
DESCRIPTION	String	The description of the level.

adSchemaMeasures

Identifies the Measures in an OLAP Catalog.

Column name	Type	Description
CATALOG_NAME	String	Catalog name, or Null if the provider does not support catalogs.
SCHEMA_NAME	String	Schema name, or Null if the provider does not support schemas.
CUBE_NAME	String	The Cube name to which the measure belongs.
MEASURE_NAME	String	The name of the measure.
MEASURE_UNIQUE_NAME	String	The unique name of the measure.
MEASURE_CAPTION	String	The caption of the measure.
MEASURE_GUID	GUID	The GUID of the measure, or Null if no GUID exists.
MEASURE_AGGEGATOR	Long	The type of aggregation for the measure. This can be one of the MDMEASURE_AGGR constants, as described in Appendix L.
DATA_TYPE	Integer	The data type that most closely matches the OLAP Provider type.
NUMERIC_PRECISION	Integer	The numeric precision of the data type.
NUMERIC_SCALE	Integer	The numeric scale of the data type.
MEASURE_UNITS	String	The unit of measurement for the measure.
DESCRIPTION	String	Description of the measure.
EXPRESSION	String	The expression which underlies a calculated measure.

adSchemaMembers

Identifies the Members in an OLAP Catalog.

Column name	Type	Description
CATALOG_NAME	String	Catalog name, or Null if the provider does not support catalogs.
SCHEMA_NAME	String	Schema name, or Null if the provider does not support schemas.

Table Continued on Following Page

Column name	Type	Description
CUBE_NAME	String	The Cube name to which the member belongs.
DIMENSION_UNIQUE_NAME	String	The unique name of the dimension to which the member belongs.
HIERARCHY_UNIQUE_NAME	String	The unique name of the hierarchy to which the member belongs.
LEVEL_UNIQUE_NAME	String	The unique name of the level to which the member belongs.
LEVEL_NUMBER	Long	The position of the member.
MEMBER_ORDINAL	Long	The ordinal of the member, indicating the sorting rank.
MEMBER_NAME	String	The name of the member.
MEMBER_UNIQUE_NAME	String	The unique name of the member.
MEMBER_TYPE	Integer	The type of the member. Can be one of the MDMEMBER_TYPE constants, as detailed in Appendix L.
MEMBER_GUID	GUID	The GUID of the member, or Null if no GUID exists.
MEMBER_CAPTION	String	The caption of the member.
CHILDREN_CARDINALITY	Long	The number of children that the member contains. This number is not guaranteed to be accurate.
PARENT_LEVEL	Long	The position, or level number, of the member's parent.
PARENT_UNIQUE_NAME	String	The unique name of the member's parent.
PARENT_COUNT	Long	The number of parents that this member has.
DESCRIPTION	String	The description of the member.
property members		A column for each property of the member.

adSchemaPrimaryKeys

This identifies the primary keys, and table name, in the catalog.

Column name	Type	Description
TABLE_CATALOG	String	Catalog name in which the table is defined, or Null if the provider does not support catalogs.
TABLE_SCHEMA	String	Schema name in which the table is defined, or Null if the provider does not support schemas.
TABLE_NAME	String	Table name.
COLUMN_NAME	String	Primary key column name.
COLUMN_GUID	GUID	Primary key column GUID.
COLUMN_PROPID	Long	Primary key column property ID.
ORDINAL	Long	The order of the column names (and GUIDs and property IDs) in the key.
PK_NAME	String	Primary key name, or Null if the provider does not support primary key constraints.

adSchemaProcedureColumns

This identifies the columns used in procedures.

Column name	Type	Description
PROCEDURE_CATALOG	String	Catalog name, or Null if the provider does not support catalogs.
PROCEDURE_SCHEMA	String	Schema name, or Null if the provider does not support schemas.
PROCEDURE_NAME	String	Table name.
COLUMN_NAME	String	The name of the column, or Null if this cannot be determined. This might not be unique.
COLUMN_GUID	GUID	Column GUID.
COLUMN_PROPID	Long	Column property ID.
ROWSET_NUMBER	Long	Number of the rowset containing the column. This is greater than one only if the procedure returns multiple rowsets.

Table Continued on Following Page

Column name	Type	Description
ORDINAL_POSITION	Long	The ordinal of the column. Columns are numbered starting from one, or Null if there is no stable ordinal value for the column.
IS_NULLABLE	Boolean	Will be **True** if the column might be nullable, or **False** if the column is known not to be nullable.
DATA_TYPE	Integer	The indicator of the column's data type. For a list of valid Types, DataTypeEnum in Appendix B.
TYPE_GUID	GUID	The GUID of the column's data type.
CHARACTER_MAXIMUM_LENGTH	Long	The maximum possible length of a value in the column.
CHARACTER_OCTET_LENGTH	Long	Maximum length in octets (bytes) of the column, if the type of the column is character or binary. A value of zero means the column has no maximum length. Null for all other types of columns.
NUMERIC_PRECISION	Integer	If the column's data type is numeric, this is the maximum precision of the column. If the column's data type is not numeric, this is Null.
NUMERIC_SCALE	Integer	If the column's Type is DBTYPE_DECIMAL or DBTYPE_NUMERIC, this is the number of digits to the right of the decimal point. Otherwise, this is Null.
DESCRIPTION	String	Column description

CHARACTER_MAXIMUM_LENGTH will vary depending upon the data type of the column:

For character, binary, or bit columns, this is one of the following:

- The maximum length of the column in characters, bytes, or bits, respectively, if one is defined. For example, a CHAR(5) column in an SQL table has a maximum length of five (5).
- The maximum length of the data type in characters, bytes, or bits, respectively, if the column does not have a defined length.
- Zero (0) if neither the column nor the data type has a defined maximum length.

It will be Null for all other types of columns.

adSchemaProcedureParameters

This identifies the parameters of stored procedures.

Column name	Type	Description
PROCEDURE_CATALOG	String	Catalog name, or Null if the provider does not support catalogs.
PROCEDURE_SCHEMA	String	Schema name, or Null if the provider does not support catalogs.
PROCEDURE_NAME	String	Procedure name.
PARAMETER_NAME	String	Parameter name, or Null if the parameter is not named.
ORDINAL_POSITION	Integer	If the parameter is an input, input/output, or output parameter, this is the one-based ordinal position of the parameter in the procedure call. If the parameter is the return value, this is zero.
PARAMETER_TYPE	Integer	The type (direction) of the parameter, which will be one of the DBPARAM_TYPE constants, as shown in Appendix B. If the provider cannot determine the parameter type, this is Null.
PARAMETER_HASDEFAULT	Boolean	**True** if the parameter has a default value, or **False** if it doesn't or the provider doesn't know whether it has a default value.
PARAMETER_DEFAULT	String	Default value of parameter. A default value of Null is a valid default.
IS_NULLABLE	Boolean	**True** if the parameter might be nullable, or **False** if the parameter is not nullable.
DATA_TYPE	Integer	The indicator of the parameter's data type. For a list of valid Types, see DataTypeEnum in Appendix B.
CHARACTER_MAXIMUM_LENGTH	Long	The maximum possible length of a value in the parameter.
CHARACTER_OCTET_LENGTH	Long	Maximum length in octets (bytes) of the parameter, if the type of the parameter is character or binary. A value of zero means the parameter has no maximum length. Null for all other types of parameters.
NUMERIC_PRECISION	Integer	If the column's data type is numeric, this is the maximum precision of the column. If the column's data type is not numeric, this is Null.

Table Continued on Following Page

Column name	Type	Description
NUMERIC_SCALE	Integer	If the column's Type is DBTYPE_DECIMAL or DBTYPE_NUMERIC, this is the number of digits to the right of the decimal point. Otherwise, this is Null.
DESCRIPTION	String	Parameter description
TYPE_NAME	String	Provider-specific data type name.
LOCAL_TYPE_NAME	String	Localized version of TYPE_NAME, or Null if the data provider does not support a localized name.

CHARACTER_MAXIMUM_LENGTH will vary depending upon the data type of the column:

For character, binary, or bit columns, this is one of the following:

- The maximum length of the column in characters, bytes, or bits, respectively, if one is defined. For example, a CHAR(5) column in an SQL table has a maximum length of five (5).
- The maximum length of the data type in characters, bytes, or bits, respectively, if the column does not have a defined length.
- Zero (0) if neither the column nor the data type has a defined maximum length.

It will be Null for all other types of columns.

adSchemaProcedures

This identifies the stored procedures or queries.

Column name	Type	Description
PROCEDURE_CATALOG	String	Catalog name, or Null if the provider does not support catalogs.
PROCEDURE_SCHEMA	String	Schema name, or Null if the provider does not support schemas.
PROCEDURE_NAME	String	Procedure name.
PROCEDURE_TYPE	Integer	Identifies whether there will be a return value or not, and will be one of the DB_PT constants as defined in Appendix B.
PROCEDURE_DEFINITION	String	Procedure definition.
DESCRIPTION	String	Procedures description.

Column name	Type	Description
DATE_CREATED	Date/Time	Date when the procedure was created or Null if the provider does not have this information.
DATE_MODIFIED	Date/Time	Date when the procedure definition was last modified or Null if the provider does not have this information.

adSchemaProperties

This identifies the properties for each level of a dimension.

Column name	Type	Description
CATALOG_NAME	String	The name of the catalog to which the property belongs.
SCHEMA_NAME	String	The name of the schema to which the property belongs.
CUBE_NAME	String	The name of the cube to which the property belongs.
DIMENSION_UNIQUE_NAME	String	The unique name of the dimension.
HIERARCHY_UNIQUE_NAME	String	The unique name of the hierarchy.
LEVEL_UNIQUE_NAME	String	The unique name of the level.
MEMBER_UNIQUE_NAME	String	The unique name of the member.
PROPERTY_TYPE	Integer	The type of the property. Can be one of: MDPROP_MEMBER to indicate the property relates to a member MDPROP_CELL, to indicate the property relates to a cell.
PROPERTY_NAME	String	The name of the property.
PROPERTY_CAPTION	String	The caption of the property.
DATA_TYPE	Long	The data type of the property. For a list of valid Types, see DataTypeEnum in Appendix B.
CHARACTER_MAXIMUM_LENGTH	Long	The maximum possible length of data in the property, or 0 to indicate no defined maximum.

Column name	Type	Description
CHARACTER_OCTET_LENGTH	Long	The maximum length in bytes of the property, for character and binary data types, or 0 to indicate no defined maximum.
NUMERIC_PRECISION	Integer	The numeric precision of the data type.
NUMERIC_SCALE	Integer	The numeric scale of the data type.
DESCRIPTION	String	The description of the property.

adSchemaProviderSpecific

The contents returned by this setting are dependent upon the provider, and you should consult the provider specific information for details regarding them.

adSchemaProviderTypes

This identifies the data types supported by the provider.

Column name	Type	Description
TYPE_NAME	String	Provider-specific data type name.
DATA_TYPE	Integer	The indicator of the data type.
COLUMN_SIZE	Long	The length of a non-numeric column or parameter refers to either the maximum or the defined length for this type by the provider. For character data, this is the maximum or defined length in characters. For datetime data types, this is the length of the String representation (assuming the maximum allowed precision of the fractional seconds component).
		If the data type is numeric, this is the upper bound on the maximum precision of the data type.
LITERAL_PREFIX	String	Character or characters used to prefix a literal of this type in a text command.
LITERAL_SUFFIX	String	Character or characters used to suffix a literal of this type in a text command.

Column name	Type	Description
CREATE_PARAMS	String	The creation parameters are specified by the consumer when creating a column of this data type. For example, the SQL data type DECIMAL needs a precision and a scale. In this case, the creation parameters might be the String "precision,scale". In a text command to create a DECIMAL column with a precision of 10 and a scale of 2, the value of the TYPE_NAME column might be DECIMAL() and the complete type specification would be DECIMAL(10,2).
IS_NULLABLE	Boolean	**True** if the data type is nullable, **False** if the data type is not nullable, and Null if it is not known whether the data type is nullable.
CASE_SENSITIVE	Boolean	**True** if the data type is a character type and is case sensitive, or **False** if the data type is not a character type or is not case sensitive.
SEARCHABLE	Long	Identifies whether the column can be used in WHERE clauses, and will be one of the DB_SEARCHABLE constants as shown in Appendix B.
UNSIGNED_ATTRIBUTE	Boolean	**True** if the data type is unsigned, **False** if the data type is signed, or Null if not applicable to data type.
FIXED_PREC_SCALE	Boolean	**True** if the data type has a fixed precision and scale, or **False** if the data type does not have a fixed precision and scale.
AUTO_UNIQUE_VALUE	Boolean	True if values of this type can be autoincrementing, or False if values of this type cannot be autoincrementing.
LOCAL_TYPE_NAME	String	Localized version of TYPE_NAME, or Null if a localized name is not supported by the data provider.
MINIMUM_SCALE	Integer	The minimum number of digits allowed to the right of the decimal point, for decimal and numeric data types. Otherwise, this is Null.
MAXIMUM_SCALE	Integer	The maximum number of digits allowed to the right of the decimal point, for a decimal and numeric data types. Otherwise, this is Null.
GUID	GUID	The GUID of the type. All types supported by a provider are described in a type library, so each type has a corresponding GUID.
TYPELIB	String	The type library containing the description of this type.

Table Continued on Following Page

Column name	Type	Description
VERSION	String	The version of the type definition. Providers may wish to version type definitions. Different providers may use different version schemes, such as a timestamp or number (integer or float), or Null if not supported.
IS_LONG	Boolean	**True** if the data type is a BLOB that contains very long data; the definition of very long data is provider-specific, or **False** if the data type is a BLOB that does not contain very long data or is not a BLOB.
BEST_MATCH	Boolean	**True** if the data type is the best match between all data types in the data source and the OLEDB data type indicated by the value in the DATA_TYPE column, or **False** if the data type is not the best match.
IS_FIXEDLENGTH	Boolean	**True** if columns of this type created by the DDL will be of fixed length. or **False** if columns of this type created by the DDL will be of variable length.
		If the field is Null, it is not known whether the provider will map this field with a fixed or variable length.

adSchemaReferentialConstraints

This identifies the referential integrity constraints for the catalog.

Column name	Type	Description
CONSTRAINT_CATALOG	String	Catalog name, or Null if the provider does not support catalogs.
CONSTRAINT_SCHEMA	String	Schema name, or Null if the provider does not support schemas.
CONSTRAINT_NAME	String	Constraint name.
UNIQUE_CONSTRAINT_CATALOG	String	Catalog name in which the unique or primary key constraint is defined, or Null if the provider does not support catalogs.
UNIQUE_CONSTRAINT_SCHEMA	String	Unqualified schema name in which the unique or primary key constraint is defined, or Null if the provider does not support schemas.
UNIQUE_CONSTRAINT_NAME	String	Unique or primary key constraint name.
MATCH_OPTION	String	The type of match that was specified.

Column name	Type	Description
UPDATE_RULE	String	The action if an UPDATE rule was specified. This will be Null only if the provider cannot determine the UPDATE_RULE. In most cases, this implies a default of NO ACTION.
DELETE_RULE	String	The action if a DELETE rule was specified. This will be Null if the provider cannot determine the DELETE_RULE. In most cases, this implies a default of NO ACTION.
DESCRIPTION	String	Human-readable description of the constraint.

For MATCH_OPTION, the values will be one of:

NONE	No match type was specified.
PARTIAL	A match type of PARTIAL was specified.
FULL	A match type of FULL was specified.

For UPDATE_RULE and DELETE_RULE, the value will be one of the following:

CASCADE	A referential action of CASCADE was specified.
SET NULL	A referential action of SET NULL was specified.
SET DEFAULT	A referential action of SET DEFAULT was specified.
NO ACTION	A referential action of NO ACTION was specified.

adSchemaSchemata

This identifies the schemas that are owned by a particular user.

Column name	Type	Description
CATALOG_NAME	String	Catalog name, or Null if the provider does not support catalogs.
SCHEMA_NAME	String	Unqualified schema name.
SCHEMA_OWNER	String	User that owns the schemas.
DEFAULT_CHARACTER_SET_CATALOG	String	Catalog name of the default character set for columns and domains in the schemas, or Null if the provider does not support catalogs or different character sets.

Table Continued on Following Page

Column name	Type	Description
DEFAULT_CHARACTER_SET_SCHEMA	String	Unqualified schema name of the default character set for columns and domains in the schemas, or Null if the provider does not support different character sets.
DEFAULT_CHARACTER_SET_NAME	String	Default character set name, or Null if the provider does not support different character sets.

adSchemaSQLLanguages

This identifies the conformance levels and other options supported by the catalog.

Column name	Type	Description
SQL_LANGUAGE_SOURCE	String	Should be "ISO 9075" for standard SQL.
SQL_LANGUAGE_YEAR	String	Should be "1992" for ANSI SQL92-compliant SQL.
SQL_LANGUAGE_CONFORMANCE	String	The language conformance level.
SQL_LANGUAGE_INTEGRITY	String	This will be **Yes** if optional integrity feature is supported, or **No** if optional integrity feature is not supported.
SQL_LANGUAGE_IMPLEMENTATION	String	Null for "ISO 9075" implementation.
SQL_LANGUAGE_BINDING_STYLE	String	"DIRECT" for C/C++ callable direct execution of SQL.
SQL_LANGUAGE_PROGRAMMING_LANGUAGE	String	Null.

SQL_LANGUAGE_CONFORMANCE will be one of the following values:

ENTRY   For entry level conformance
INTERMEDIATE   for intermediate conformance
FULL   for full conformance

adSchemaStatistics

This identifies the catalog statistics.

Column name	Type	Description
TABLE_CATALOG	String	Catalog name, or Null if the provider does not support catalogs.
TABLE_SCHEMA	String	Schema name, or Null if the provider does not support schemas.
TABLE_NAME	String	Table name.
CARDINALITY	Unsigned Big Integer	Cardinality (number of rows) of the table.

adSchemaTableConstraints

This identifies the referential table constraints.

Column name	Type	Description
CONSTRAINT_CATALOG	String	Catalog name, or Null if the provider does not support catalogs.
CONSTRAINT_SCHEMA	String	Schema name, or Null if the provider does not support schemas.
CONSTRAINT_NAME	String	Constraint name.
TABLE_CATALOG	String	Catalog name in which the table is defined, or Null if the provider does not support catalogs.
TABLE_SCHEMA	String	Unqualified schema name in which the table is defined, or Null if the provider does not support schemas.
TABLE_NAME	String	Table name.
CONSTRAINT_TYPE	String	The constraint type.
IS_DEFERRABLE	Boolean	**True** if the table constraint is deferrable, or **False** if the table constraint is not deferrable.
INITIALLY_DEFERRED	Boolean	**True** if the table constraint is initially deferred, or **False** if the table constraint is initially immediate.
DESCRIPTION	String	Column description

CONSTRAINT_TYPE will be one of the following values:

UNIQUE	for a unique constraint
PRIMARY KEY	for a primary key constraint
FOREIGN KEY	for a foreign key constraint
CHECK	for a check constraint

adSchemaTablePrivileges

This identifies the user privileges of tables.

Column name	Type	Description
GRANTOR	String	User who granted the privileges on the table in TABLE_NAME.
GRANTEE	String	User name (or "PUBLIC") to whom the privilege has been granted.
TABLE_CATALOG	String	Catalog name in which the table is defined, or Null if the provider does not support catalogs.
TABLE_SCHEMA	String	Unqualified schema name in which the table is defined, or Null if the provider does not support schemas.
TABLE_NAME	String	Table name.
PRIVILEGE_TYPE	String	Privilege type.
IS_GRANTABLE	Boolean	**False** if the privilege being described was granted with the WITH GRANT OPTION clause, or **True** if the privilege being described was not granted with the WITH GRANT OPTION clause.

PRIVILEGE_TYPE will be one of the following values:

SELECT	for SELECT privileges
DELETE	for DELETE privileges
INSERT	for INSERT privileges
UPDATE	for UPDATE privileges
REFERENCES	for REFERENCE privileges

adSchemaTables

This identifies the tables in a catalog.

Column name	Type	Description
TABLE_CATALOG	String	Catalog name, or Null if the provider does not support catalogs.
TABLE_SCHEMA	String	Schema name, or Null if the provider does not support schemas.
TABLE_NAME	String	Table name. This column cannot contain a Null.
TABLE_TYPE	String	Table type. This column cannot contain a Null.
TABLE_GUID	GUID	GUID that uniquely identifies the table. Providers that do not use GUIDs to identify tables should return Null in this column.
DESCRIPTION	String	Human-readable description of the table, or Null if there is no description associated with the column.
TABLE_PROPID	Long	Property ID of the table. Providers which do not use PROPIDs to identify columns should return Null in this column.
DATE_CREATED	Date/Time	Date when the table was created or Null if the provider does not have this information.
DATE_MODIFIED	Date/Time	Date when the table definition was last modified or Null if the provider does not have this information.

TABLE_TYPE will be one of the following, or a provider-specific value.

ALIAS	The table is an alias
TABLE	The table is a normal table
SYNONYM	The table is a synonym
SYSTEM TABLE	The table is a system table
VIEW	The table is a view
GLOBAL TEMPORARY	The table is a global, temporary table
LOCAL TEMPORARY	The table is a local, temporary table

Provider specific values should be defined in the provider documentation. For example, Access returns PASS-THROUGH for linked tables.

adSchemaTranslations

This identifies character translations that the catalog supports.

Column name	Type	Description
TRANSLATION_CATALOG	String	Catalog name, or Null if the provider does not support catalogs.
TRANSLATION_SCHEMA	String	Schema name, or Null if the provider does not support schemas.
TRANSLATION_NAME	String	Translation name.
SOURCE_CHARACTER_SET_CATALOG	String	Catalog name containing the source character set on which the translation is defined, or Null if the provider does not support catalogs.
SOURCE_CHARACTER_SET_SCHEMA	String	Unqualified schema name containing the source character set on which the translation is defined, or Null if the provider does not support schemas.
SOURCE_CHARACTER_SET_NAME	String	Source character set name on which the translation is defined.
TARGET_CHARACTER_SET_CATALOG	String	Catalog name containing the target character set on which the translation is defined, or Null if the provider does not support catalogs.
TARGET_CHARACTER_SET_SCHEMA	String	Unqualified schema name containing the target character set on which the translation is defined, or Null if the provider does not support schemas.
TARGET_CHARACTER_SET_NAME	String	Target character set name on which the translation is defined.

adSchemaUsagePrivileges

This identifies the usage privileges that are available to a user.

Column name	Type	Description
GRANTOR	String	User who granted the privileges on the object in OBJECT_NAME.
GRANTEE	String	User name (or "PUBLIC") to whom the privilege has been granted.
OBJECT_CATALOG	String	Catalog name in which the object is defined, or Null if the provider does not support catalogs.

Column name	Type	Description
OBJECT_SCHEMA	String	Unqualified schema name in which the object is defined, or Null if the provider does not support schemas.
OBJECT_NAME	String	Object name.
OBJECT_TYPE	String	Object type.
PRIVILEGE_TYPE	String	Privilege type.
IS_GRANTABLE	Boolean	**True** if the privilege being described was granted with the WITH GRANT OPTION clause, or **False** if the privilege being described was not granted with the WITH GRANT OPTION clause.

OBJECT_TYPE will be one of the following values:

DOMAIN	The object is a domain
CHARACTER SET	The object is a character set
COLLATION	The object is a collation
TRANSLATION	The object is a translation

adSchemaViewColumnUsage

This identifies the columns used in views.

Column name	Type	Description
VIEW_CATALOG	String	Catalog name, or Null if the provider does not support catalogs.
VIEW_SCHEMA	String	Schema name, or Null if the provider does not support schemas.
VIEW_NAME	String	View name.
TABLE_CATALOG	String	Catalog name in which the table is defined, or Null if the provider does not support catalogs.
TABLE_SCHEMA	String	Schema name in which the table is defined, or Null if the provider does not support schemas.
TABLE_NAME	String	Table name.
COLUMN_NAME	String	Column name.
COLUMN_GUID	GUID	Column GUID.
COLUMN_PROPID	Long	Column property ID.

adSchemaViewTableUsage

This identifies the tables used in views.

Column name	Type	Description
VIEW_CATALOG	String	Catalog name, or Null if the provider does not support catalogs.
VIEW_SCHEMA	String	Schema name, or Null if the provider does not support schemas.
VIEW_NAME	String	View name.
TABLE_CATALOG	String	Catalog name in which the table is defined, or Null if the provider does not support catalogs.
TABLE_SCHEMA	String	Schema name in which the table is defined, or Null if the provider does not support schemas.
TABLE_NAME	String	Table name.

adSchemaViews

This identifies the views in the catalog.

Column name	Type	Description
TABLE_CATALOG	String	Catalog name, or Null if the provider does not support catalogs.
TABLE_SCHEMA	String	Schema name, or Null if the provider does not support schemas.
TABLE_NAME	String	View name.
VIEW_DEFINITION	String	View definition. This is a query expression.
CHECK_OPTION	Boolean	**True** if local update checking only, or **False** for cascaded update checking (same as no CHECK OPTION specified on view definition).
IS_UPDATABLE	Boolean	**True** if the view is updateable, or **False** if the view is not updateable.
DESCRIPTION	String	View description
DATE_CREATED	Date/Time	Date when the view was created or Null if the provider does not have this information.
DATE_MODIFIED	Date/Time	Date when the view definition was last modified or Null if the provider does not have this information.

Schema Usage

Using schemas is quite easy, since all you need to do is use the `OpenSchema` method of the connection object. For example, to list all of the tables on a particular connection:

```
Set objRec = objConn.OpenSchema (adSchemaTables)
While Not objRec.EOF
  Print objRec("TABLE_NAME")
  objRec.MoveNext
Wend
```

This simply opens a recordset on the tables schema and loops through it printing each table name. You can use the `TABLE_TYPE` column to check for system tables:

```
Set objRec = objConn.OpenSchema (adSchemaTables)
While Not objRec.EOF
  If objRec("TABLE_TYPE") <> "SYSTEM TABLE" Then
    Print objRec("TABLE_NAME")
  End If
  objRec.MoveNext
Wend
```

You can use the `Restrictions` argument of `OpenSchema` to only return certain rows. This argument accepts an array that matched the column names. For example, to find only the system tables:

```
Set objRec = objConn.OpenSchema (adSchemaTables, _
                        Array (Empty, Empty, Empty, "SYSTEM_TABLE"))
```

Since the type is the fourth column in the recordset, you need to specify empty values for the columns you wish to skip.

For Multi-Dimensional providers using `adSchemaMembers`, the restrictions can either be the columns in the members schema, or one of the `MDTREEOP` constants, as defined in Appendix L.

When connecting to Microsoft Access, there are some interesting things you should be aware of. If you wish to see the queries, then you might have to use both `adSchemaProcedures` and `adSchemaViews` depending upon the query type. Normal select queries appear as Views, whereas action queries (Update, Delete, etc) and CrossTab queries appear as procedures. This is only for the native Jet provider. For the ODBC provider, select and crosstab queries appear as tables with a table type of **VIEW**.

E

ADO Data Types

You might find the large array of data types supported by ADO confusing, especially since your language or database might not support them all. This appendix details the DataTypeEnum constants and how they map to SQL and Access data types.

ODBC to Access 97

Database Type	ADO Type
Text	adVarChar
Memo	adLongVarChar
Number (Byte)	adUnsignedTinyInt
Number (Integer)	adSmallInt
Number (Long Integer)	adInteger
Number (Single)	adSingle
Number (Double)	adDouble
Number (Replication ID)	adGUID
Date/Time	adDBTimeStamp
Currency	adCurrency

Database Type	ADO Type
Long Integer	adInteger
Yes/No	adBoolean
OLE Object	adLongVarBinary
Hyperlink	adLongVarChar

ODBC to Access 2000

Database Type	ADO Type
Text	adVarWChar
Memo	adLongVarWChar
Number (Byte)	adUnsignedTinyInt
Number (Integer)	adSmallInt
Number (Long Integer)	adInteger
Number (Single)	adSingle
Number (Double)	adDouble
Number (Replication ID)	adGUID
Number (Decimal)	adNumeric
Date/Time	adDBTimeStamp
Currency	adCurrency
AutoNumber	adInteger
Yes/No	adBoolean
OLE Object	adLongVarBinary
Hyperlink	adLongVarWChar

ODBC to SQL 6.5

Database Type	ADO Type
binary	adBinary
bit	adBoolean
char	adChar
datetime	adDBTimeStamp
decimal	adNumeric
float	adDouble
image	adLongVarBinary
int	adInteger
money	adCurrency
numeric	adNumeric
real	adSingle
smalldatetime	adDBTimeStamp
smallint	adSmallInt
smallmoney	adCurrency
sysname	adVarChar
text	adLongVarChar
timestamp	adBinary
tinyint	adUnsignedTinyInt
varbinary	adVarBinary
varchar	adVarChar

ODBC to SQL 7.0

Database Type	ADO Type
binary	adBinary
bit	adBoolean
char	adChar
datetime	adDBTimeStamp
decimal	adNumeric
float	adDouble
image	adLongVarBinary
int	adInteger

Table Continued on Following Page

Database Type	ADO Type
money	adCurrency
nchar	adWChar
ntext	adLongVarWChar
numeric	adNumeric
nvarchar	adVarWChar
real	adSingle
smalldatetime	adDBTimeStamp
smallint	adSmallInt
smallmoney	adCurrency
text	adLongVarChar
timestamp	adBinary
tinyint	adUnsignedTinyInt
uniqueidentifier	adGUID
varbinary	adVarBinary
varchar	adVarChar

Native Jet Provider to Access 97

Database Type	ADO Type
Text	adVarWChar
Memo	adLongVarWChar
Number (Byte)	adUnsignedTinyInt
Number (Integer)	adSmallInt
Number (Long Integer)	adInteger
Number (Single)	adSingle
Number (Double)	adDouble
Number (Replication ID)	adGUID
Date/Time	adDate
Currency	adCurrency
Long Integer	adInteger
Yes/No	adBoolean
OLE Object	adLongVarBinary
Hyperlink	adLongVarWChar

Native Jet Provider to Access 2000

Database Type	ADO Type
Text	adVarWChar
Memo	adLongVarWChar
Number (Byte)	adUnsignedTinyInt
Number (Integer)	adSmallInt
Number (Long Integer)	adInteger
Number (Single)	adSingle
Number (Double)	adDouble
Number (Replication ID)	adGUID
Number (Decimal)	adNumeric
Date/Time	adDate
Currency	adCurrency
AutoNumber	adInteger
Yes/No	adBoolean
OLE Object	adLongVarBinary
Hyperlink	adLongVarWChar

Native SQL Provider to SQL Server 6.5

Database Type	ADO Type
binary	adBinary
bit	adBoolean
char	adChar
datetime	adDBTimeStamp
decimal	adNumeric
float	adDouble
image	adLongVarBinary
int	adInteger
money	adCurrency
numeric	adNumeric

Table Continued on Following Page

Database Type	ADO Type
real	adSingle
smalldatetime	adDBTimeStamp
smallint	adSmallInt
smallmoney	adCurrency
sysname	adVarChar
text	adLongVarChar
timestamp	adBinary
tinyint	adUnsignedTinyInt
varbinary	adVarBinary
varchar	adVarChar

Native SQL Provider to SQL Server 7.0

Database Type	ADO Type
binary	adBinary
bit	adBoolean
char	adChar
datetime	adDBTimeStamp
decimal	adNumeric
float	adDouble
image	adLongVarBinary
int	adInteger
money	adCurrency
nchar	adWChar
ntext	adLongVarWChar
numeric	adNumeric
nvarchar	adVarWChar
real	adSingle
smalldatetime	adDBTimeStamp
smallint	adSmallInt
smallmoney	adCurrency
text	adLongVarChar
timestamp	adBinary

Database Type	ADO Type
tinyint	adUnsignedTinyInt
uniqueidentifier	adGUID
varbinary	adVarBinary
varchar	adVarChar

Language Types

The following table lists the data types you should use in your programming language.

A blank value indicates that the language does not natively support the data type, although there may be support in other libraries, or other data types might be used instead. For example, the com.ms.wfc.data import library for J++ has support for dates and timestamp types, amongst others, but these are not supported by J++ natively.

Constant	Visual Basic	Visual C++	Visual J++
adBinary	Variant		
adBoolean	Boolean	bool	boolean
adChar	String	char[]	String
adCurrency	Currency		
adDate	Date		
adDBTimeStamp	Variant		
adDouble	Double	double	double
adGUID		char[]	String, char[]
adInteger	Long	int	int
adLongVarBinary	Variant		
adLongVarChar	String		
adNumeric			
adSingle	Single	float	float
adSmallInt	Integer	short	short
adUnsignedTinyInt	Byte	char	byte
adVarBinary		char[]	byte[]
adVarChar	String	char[]	String, byte[]
adVarWChar	String	char[]	String, byte[]

RDS Object Summary

The Remote Data Service (RDS) provides a series of objects that can be used to access data remotely from a client over HTTP protocol. This section lists the properties, methods and events for two RDS controls–the **RDS/ADC Data Source Object** (DSO) and the **Tabular Data Control** (TDC). It also lists the properties, methods, events and constants for the `DataSpace` and `DataFactory` objects that are used by the RDS/ADC control.

> **All properties are read/write unless otherwise stated.**

The RDS Advanced Data Control (RDS/ADC)

The RDS/ADC Data Control is used on the client to provide read/write access to a data store or custom business object on the server. To instantiate the control in a web page, an `<OBJECT>` tag is used:

```
<OBJECT CLASSID="clsid:BD96C556-65A3-11D0-983A-00C04FC29E33"
        ID="dsoBookList" HEIGHT=0 WIDTH=0>
  <PARAM NAME="Server" VALUE="http://www.yourserver.com">
  <PARAM NAME="Connect" VALUE="DSN=yourdsn;UID=anon;PWD=">
  <PARAM NAME="SQL" VALUE="SELECT * FROM BookList">
</OBJECT>
```

The <PARAM> elements are used to set the properties of the control at design time. They can be changed at run-time using script code. The following tables list the properties, methods and events for the control.

Properties

Name	Returns	Description
Connect	String	The data store connection string or DSN.
ExecuteOptions	Integer	Specifies if the control will execute asynchronously. Can be one of the ADCExecuteOptionEnum constants, as detailed in Appendix G.
FetchOptions	Integer	Specifies if the data will be fetched asynchronously. Can be one of the ADCFetchOptionEnum constants, as detailed in Appendix G.
FilterColumn	String	Name of the column to filter on.
FilterCriterion	String	The criterion for the filter, can be <, <=, >, >=, =, or <>.
FilterValue	String	The value to match values in FilterColumn with when filtering.
Handler	String	Specifies the server-side security handler to use with the control if not the default.
InternetTimeout	Long	Indicates the timeout (in milliseconds) for the HTTP connection.
ReadyState	Integer	Indicates the state of the control as data is received. Can be one of the ADCReadyStateEnum constants, as detailed in Appendix G. Read only.
Recordset	Object	Provides a reference to the ADO Recordset object in use by the control. Read only.
Server	String	Specifies the communication protocol and the address of the server to execute the query on.
SortColumn	String	Name of the column to sort on.
SortDirection	Boolean	The sort direction for the column. The default is ascending order (True). Use False for descending order.
SourceRecordset	Object	Can be used to bind the control to a different recordset object at run time. Write only.
SQL	String	The SQL statement used to extract the data from the data store.
URL	String	URL to the path of the file containing the data.

Methods

Name	Description
Cancel	Cancels an asynchronous action such as fetching data.
CancelUpdate	Cancels all changes made to the source recordset.
CreateRecordSet	Creates and returns an empty, disconnected recordset on the client.
MoveFirst	Moves to the first record in a displayed recordset.
MoveLast	Moves to the last record in a displayed recordset.
MoveNext	Moves to the next record in a displayed recordset.
MovePrevious	Moves to the previous record in a displayed recordset.
Refresh	Refreshes the client-side recordset from the data source.
Reset	Updates the local recordset to reflect current filter and sort criteria.
SubmitChanges	Sends changes to the client-side recordset back to the data store.

Syntax

datacontrol.Cancel
datacontrol.CancelUpdate
(Set) *object* = *datacontrol*.CreateRecordSet (*varColumnInfos As Variant*)
datacontrol.Recordset.MoveFirst
datacontrol.Recordset.MoveLast
datacontrol.Recordset.MoveNext
datacontrol.Recordset.MovePrevious
datacontrol.Refresh
datacontrol.Reset (*re-filter As Integer*)
datacontrol.SubmitChanges

Events

Name	Description
onerror	Occurs if an error prevents the data being fetched from the server, or a user action being carried out.
onreadystatechange	Occurs when the value of the ReadyState property changes.

Syntax

onError (*StatusCode, Description, Source, CancelDisplay*)
onReadyStateChange ()

The Tabular Data Control

The Tabular Data Control (TDC) uses a formatted text file that is downloaded to the client and exposed there as an ADO recordset. The control cannot be used to update the server data store. To instantiate the control in a Web page, an <OBJECT> tag is used:

```
<OBJECT CLASSID="clsid:333C7BC4-460F-11D0-BC04-0080C7055A83"
        ID="dsoBookList" WIDTH=0 HEIGHT=0>
  <PARAM NAME="DataURL" VALUE="/data/booklist.txt">
  <PARAM NAME="FieldDelim" VALUE=";">
  <PARAM NAME="UseHeader" VALUE="true">
  <PARAM NAME="Sort" VALUE="tCategory; -dReleasedate">
  <PARAM NAME="Filter" VALUE="tCode=16-1*" >
  <PARAM NAME="EscapeChar" VALUE="\">
</OBJECT>
```

The <PARAM> elements are used to set the properties of the control at design time. They can be changed at run-time using script code. The following tables list the properties, methods and events for the control.

Properties

Name	Returns	Description
AppendData	Boolean	If True, specifies that the Reset method will attempt to append returned data to the existing recordset rather than replacing the recordset. Default value is False.
CaseSensitive	Boolean	Specifies whether string comparisons will be case sensitive. Default is True.
CharSet	String	Specifies the character set for the data. Default is windows-1252 (Western).
DataURL	String	The URL or location of the source text data file.
EscapeChar	String	Single character string that is used to avoid the meaning of the other special characters specified by the FieldDelim, RowDelim, and TextQualifier properties.
FieldDelim	String	Specifies the character in the file that delimits each column (field). Default – if none specified – is a comma. Only a single character may be used.
Filter	String	Specifies the complete filter that will be applied to the data, such as "Name=Johnson". An asterisk acts as a wildcard for any set of characters.
FilterColumn	String	Name of the column to filter on. Not supported in all versions of the TDC.
FilterCriterion	String	The criterion for the filter, can be <, <=, >, >=, =, or <>. Not supported in all versions of the TDC.

Name	Returns	Description
FilterValue	String	The value to match values in FilterColumn with when filtering. Not supported in all versions of the TDC.
Language	String	Specifies the language of the data file. Default is en-us (US English).
ReadyState	Integer	Indicates the state of the control as data is received. Can be one of the ADCReadyStateEnum constants, as detailed in Appendix G. Read only.
RowDelim	String	Specifies the character in the file that delimits each row (record). Default if not specified is a carriage return. Only a single character may be used.
Sort	String	Specifies the sort order for the data, as a comma-delimited list of column names. Prefix column name with a minus sign (-) for descending order.
SortAscending	Boolean	The sort direction for the column. The default is ascending order (True). Use False for descending order. Not supported in all versions of the TDC.
SortColumn	String	Name of the column to sort on. Not supported in all versions of the TDC.
TextQualifier	String	The character in the data file used to enclose field values. Default is the double-quote (") character.
UseHeader	Boolean	If True, specifies that the first line of the data file is a set of column (field) names and (optionally) the field data type definitions.

Method

Name	Description
Reset	Updates the local recordset to reflect current filter and sort criteria.

Event

Name	Description
onreadystatechange	Occurs when the value of the ReadyState property changes.

The RDS DataSpace Object

The DataSpace object is responsible for caching the recordset on the client, and connecting it to a data source control. To instantiate the object in a web page, an <OBJECT> tag is used:

```
<OBJECT ID="dspDataSpace"
      CLASSID="CLSID:BD96C556-65A3-11D0-983A-00C04FC29E36">
</OBJECT>
```

A `DataSpace` object is also created automatically when a data source object (such as the RDS/ADC) is instantiated. The `DataSpace` object exposes one property and one method:

Property

Name	Returns	Description
InternetTimeout	Long	Indicates the timeout (in milliseconds) for the HTTP connection.

Method

Name	Description
CreateObject	Creates a data factory or custom object of type specified by a class string, at a location specified by the connection (address) parameter.

Syntax

variant = dataspace.CreateObject (*bstrProgId* As String, *bstrConnection* As String)

For a connection over HTTP, the connection parameter is the URL of the server, while over DCOM the UNC machine name is used. When the `CreateObject` method is used to create in-process objects, the connection should be a null string.

The RDS DataFactory Object

The `DataFactory` object handles transport of the data from server to client and vice versa. It creates a stub and proxy that can communicate over HTTP. To instantiate the object, the `CreateObject` method of an existing `DataSpace` control is used. The class string for the `DataFactory` object is `RDSServer.DataFactory`, and the address of the server on which the object is to be created must also be provided:

```
<OBJECT ID="dspDataSpace"
        CLASSID="CLSID:BD96C556-65A3-11D0-983A-00C04FC29E36">
</OBJECT>
. . .
<SCRIPT LANGUAGE="JavaScript">
  <myDataFactory = dspDataSpace.CreateObject("RDSServer.DataFactory",
                                      "http://servername.com");
</SCRIPT>
```

A `DataFactory` object is also created automatically when a data source object (such as the RDS/ADC) is instantiated. The `DataFactory` object provides four methods:

Methods

Name	Returns	Description
ConvertToString	String	Converts a recordset into a MIME64-encoded string.
CreateRecordSet	Object	Creates and returns an empty recordset.
Execute	Object	Execute a command and create a recordset
Query	Object	Executes a valid SQL query string over a specified connection and returns an ADO `Recordset` object.
SubmitChanges		Marshals the records and submits them to the server for updating the source data store.
Synchronize		Synchronize the recordset with the database in the connection string.

Syntax

string = *datafactory*.`ConvertToString`(*recordset* As `Object`)
(`Set`) *recordset* = *datafactory*.`CreateRecordSet`(*varColumnInfos* As `Variant`)
(`Set`) *recordset* = *datafactory*.Execute(*ConnectionString* As `String`, *HandlerString* As `String`, _
    QueryString As `String`, *MarshalOptions* As `Long`, *CommandPropertyString* As `String`, _
    TableId As `Variant`, *ExecuteOptions* As `Long`, *Parameters* As `Variant`)
(`Set`) *recordset* = *datafactory*.`Query`(*bstrConnection* As `String`, *bstrQuery* As `String`)
datafactory.`SubmitChanges`(*bstrConnection* As `String`, *pRecordset* As `Object`)
datafactory.`Synchronize`(*ConnectionString* As `String`, *HandlerString* As `String`, _
    SynchronizeOptions As `Long`, *Recordset* As `Object`, *StatusArray* As `Variant`)

G

RDS Constants

ADCPROP_UPDATECRITERIA_ENUM

Name	Value	Description
adCriteriaAllCols	1	Collisions should be detected if there is a change to any column.
adCriteriaKey	0	Collisions should be detected if there is a change to the key column.
adCriteriaTimeStamp	3	Collisions should be detected if a row has been accessed.
adCriteriaUpdCols	2	Collisions should be detected if there is a change to columns being updated.

RDS Constants

ADCExecuteOptionEnum

Name	Value	Description
adcExecAsync	2	The next `Refresh` of the recordset is executed asynchronously.
adcExecSync	1	The next `Refresh` of the recordset is executed synchronously.

ADCFetchOptionEnum

Name	Value	Description
adcFetchAsync	3	Records are fetched in the background and control is returned to the application immediately. Attempts to access a record not yet read will cause control to return immediately, and the nearest record to the sought record returned. This indicates that the end of the recordset has been reached, even though there may be more records.
adcFetchBackground	2	The first batch of records is read and control returns to the application. Access to records not in the first batch will cause a wait until the requested record is fetched.
adcFetchUpFront	1	The complete recordset is fetched before control is returned to the application.

ADCReadyStateEnum

Name	Value	Description
adcReadyStateComplete	4	All rows have been fetched.
adcReadyStateInteractive	3	Rows are still being fetched, although some rows are available.
adcReadyStateLoaded	2	The recordset is not available for use as the rows are still being loaded.

ADOX Object Summary

Microsoft ADO Ext. 2.1 for DDL and Security Reference

Objects

Name	Description
Catalog	Acts as a parent for the Tables, Groups, Users, Procedures and Views collections.
Column	An individual Column in a Table, Index or Key.
Columns	Contains one or more Column objects.
Group	An individual Group account describing data store permissions, and containing a Users collection describing the members of the group.
Groups	Contains one or more Group objects.
Index	An individual Index on a Table, containing a Columns collection describing the columns that comprise the index.

Table Continued on Following Page

Name	Description
Indexes	Contains one or more Index objects.
Key	An individual Key representing a primary or foreign key for a table, and containing a Columns collection to describe the columns that the Key comprises.
Keys	Contains one or more Key objects.
Procedure	Describes a stored procedure, and contains an ADO Command object to obtain the details of the procedure.
Procedures	Contains one or more Procedure objects.
Properties	Contains one or more Property objects.
Property	Describes an individual property of a particular object.
Table	Describes an individual data store table, and contains collections for Columns, Indexes, Keys and Properties.
Tables	Contains one or more Table objects.
User	An individual User account describing an authorized user of the data store, and containing a Groups collection to indicate the groups to which the user belongs.
Users	Contains one or more User objects.
View	Describes a virtual table, or a filtered set of records from the data store, and contains and ADO Command object to obtain the exact details of the view.
Views	Contains one or more View objects.

Catalog Object

Methods

Name	Returns	Description
Create	Variant	Creates a new catalog, using its argument as a connection string for the catalog.
GetObjectOwner	String	Obtains the name of the user or group that owns a particular catalog object.
SetObjectOwner		Sets the owner for a particular catalog object.

Properties

Name	Returns	Description
ActiveConnection	Object	Sets or returns the ADO Connection object or string to which the catalog belongs.
Groups	Groups	Contains one or more Group objects. Read only.
Procedures	Procedures	Contains one or more Procedure objects. Read only.
Tables	Tables	Contains one or more Table objects. Read only.
Users	Users	Contains one or more User objects. Read only.
Views	Views	Contains one or more View objects. Read only.

Column Object

Methods

The Column object has no methods.

Properties

Name	Returns	Description
Attributes	ColumnAttributesEnum	Describes the characteristics of the column.
DefinedSize	Long	Indicates the maximum size for a column.
Name	String	The name of the column.
NumericScale	Byte	The numeric scale of the column. Read only for existing columns.
ParentCatalog	Catalog	Indicates the Catalog to which the columns parent object belongs.
Precision	Integer	The maximum precision of data in the column. Read only for existing columns.
Properties	Properties	Contains one or more provider specific column properties. Read only.
RelatedColumn	String	For key columns this indicates the name of the related column in the related table. Read only for existing columns.
SortOrder	SortOrderEnum	Indicates the order in which the column is sorted. Only applies to columns in an Index.
Type	DataTypeEnum	Identifies the data type of the column. Read only once the column is appended to a collection.

Columns Collection

Methods

Name	Returns	Description
Append		Appends a `Column` object to the `Columns` collection.
Delete		Deletes a `Column` object from the `Columns` collection.
Refresh		Updates the `Column` objects in the `Columns` collection.

Properties

Name	Returns	Description
Count	Integer	Indicates the number of `Column` objects in the `Columns` collection. Read only.
Item	Column	Allows indexing into the `Columns` collection to reference a specific `Column` object. Read only.

Group Object

Methods

Name	Returns	Description
GetPermissions	RightsEnum	Obtains the permissions on a catalog object for the Group.
SetPermissions		Sets the permissions on a catalog object for the group.

Properties

Name	Returns	Description
Name	String	The name of the group.
Users	Users	Contains the `User` objects who belong to this group. Read only.

Groups Collection

Methods

Name	Returns	Description
Append		Appends a Group object to the Groups collection.
Delete		Deletes a Group object from the Groups collection.
Refresh		Updates the Group objects in the Groups collection.

Properties

Name	Returns	Description
Count	Integer	Indicates the number of Group objects in the Groups collection. Read only.
Item	Column	Allows indexing into the Groups collection to reference a specific Group object. Read only.

Index Object

Methods

The Index object has no methods.

Properties

Name	Returns	Description
Clustered	Boolean	Indicates whether or not the Index is clustered. Read only on Index objects already appended to a collection.
Columns	Columns	Contains one or more Column objects, which make up the Index. Read only.
IndexNulls	AllowNullsEnum	Indicates whether or not index entries are created for records that have null values. Read only on Index objects already appended to a collection.
Name	String	The name of the Index.
PrimaryKey	Boolean	Indicates whether or not the index is the primary key. Read only on Index objects already appended to a collection.
Properties	Properties	Contains provider-specific properties for the Index. Read only.
Unique	Boolean	Indicates whether or not the keys in the Index must be unique. Read only on Index objects already appended to a collection.

Indexes Collection

Methods

Name	Returns	Description
Append		Appends a Index object to the Indexes collection.
Delete		Deletes a Index object from the Indexes collection.
Refresh		Updates the Index objects in the Indexes collection.

Properties

Name	Returns	Description
Count	Integer	Indicates the number of Index objects in the Indexes collection. Read only.
Item	Column	Allows indexing into the Indexes collection to reference a specific Index object. Read only.

Key Object

Methods

The Key object has no methods.

Properties

Name	Returns	Description
Columns	Columns	Contains one or more Column objects that make up the Key. Read only
DeleteRule	RuleEnum	Indicates what happens to the key values when a primary key is deleted. Read only on Key objects already appended to a collection.
Name	String	The name of the Key.
RelatedTable	String	For foreign keys indicates the name of the foreign table.
Type	KeyTypeEnum	Specifies the type of the Key. Read only on Key objects already appended to a collection.
UpdateRule	RuleEnum	Indicates what happens to the key values when a primary key is updated. Read only on Key objects already appended to a collection.

Keys Collection

Methods

Name	Returns	Description
Append		Appends a Key object to the Keys collection.
Delete		Deletes a Key object from the Keys collection.
Refresh		Updates the Key objects in the Keys collection.

Properties

Name	Returns	Description
Count	Integer	Indicates the number of Key objects in the Keys collection. Read only.
Item	Column	Allows indexing into the Keys collection to reference a specific Key object. Read only.

Procedure Object

Methods

The Procedure object has no methods.

Properties

Name	Returns	Description
Command	Object	Specifies an ADO Command object containing the details of the procedure.
DateCreated	Variant	The date the procedure was created. Read only.
DateModified	Variant	The date the procedure was last modified. Read only.
Name	String	The name of the procedure. Read only

Procedures Collection

Methods

Name	Returns	Description
Append		Appends a Procedure object to the Procedures collection.
Delete		Deletes a Procedure object from the Procedures collection.
Refresh		Updates the Procedure objects in the Procedures collection.

Properties

Name	Returns	Description
Count	Integer	Indicates the number of Procedure objects in the Procedures collection. Read only.
Item	Column	Allows indexing into the Procedures collection to reference a specific Procedure object. Read only.

Properties Collection

Methods

Name	Returns	Description
Refresh		Updates the Property objects in the Properties collection.

Properties

Name	Returns	Description
Count	Integer	Indicates the number of Property objects in the Properties collection. Read only.
Item	Column	Allows indexing into the Properties collection to reference a specific Property object. Read only.

Property Object

Methods

The Property object has no methods

Properties

Name	Returns	Description
Attributes	Integer	Indicates one or more characteristics of the Property.
Name	String	The Property name. Read only.
Type	DataTypeEnum	The data type of the Property. Read only.
Value	Variant	The value assigned to the Property.

Table Object

Methods

The Table object has no methods.

Properties

Name	Returns	Description
Columns	Columns	One or more Column objects that make up the Table. Read only.
DateCreated	Variant	The date the table was created. Read only.
DateModified	Variant	The date the table was last modified. Read only.
Indexes	Indexes	Zero or more Index objects that belong to the Table. Read only.
Keys	Keys	Zero or more Key objects that the Table contains. Read only.
Name	String	The name of the Table.
ParentCatalog	Catalog	The Catalog to which the Table belongs.
Properties	Properties	One or more Property objects describing provider-specific properties. Read only.
Type	String	Indicates whether the table is a permanent, temporary, or system table. Read only.

Tables Collection

Methods

Name	Returns	Description
Append		Appends a Table object to the Tables collection.
Delete		Deletes a Table object from the Tables collection.
Refresh		Updates the Table objects in the Tables collection.

Properties

Name	Returns	Description
Count	Integer	Indicates the number of Table objects in the Tables collection. Read only.
Item	Column	Allows indexing into the Tables collection to reference a specific Table object. Read only.

User Object

Methods

Name	Returns	Description
ChangePassword		Changes the password for a User.
GetPermissions	RightsEnum	Gets the permissions on a Catalog object for a User.
SetPermissions		Sets the permissions on a Catalog object for a User.

Properties

Name	Returns	Description
Groups	Groups	One or more Group objects, to which the user belongs. Read only.
Name	String	The user name.

Users Collection

Methods

Name	Returns	Description
Append		Appends a User object to the Users collection.
Delete		Deletes a User object from the Users collection.
Refresh		Updates the User objects in the Users collection.

Properties

Name	Returns	Description
Count	Integer	Indicates the number of User objects in the Users collection. Read only.
Item	Column	Allows indexing into the Users collection to reference a specific User object. Read only.

View Object

Methods

The View object has no methods.

Properties

Name	Returns	Description
Command	Object	Specifies an ADO Command object containing the details of the view.
DateCreated	Variant	The date the view was created. Read only.
DateModified	Variant	The date the view was last modified. Read only.
Name	String	The name of the view. Read only.

Views Collection

Methods

Name	Returns	Description
Append		Appends a View object to the Views collection.
Delete		Deletes a View object from the Views collection.
Refresh		Updates the View objects in the Views collection.

Properties

Name	Returns	Description
Count	Integer	Indicates the number of View objects in the Views collection. Read only.
Item	Column	Allows indexing into the Views collection to reference a specific View object. Read only.

Method Calls

Catalog Object

```
Variant = Catalog.Create(ConnectString As String)
String = Catalog.GetObjectOwner(ObjectName As String, _
    ObjectType As ObjectTypeEnum, [ObjectTypeId As Variant])
Catalog.SetObjectOwner(ObjectName As String, _
    ObjectType As ObjectTypeEnum, UserName As String, _
    [ObjectTypeId As Variant])
```

Columns Collection

```
Columns.Append(Item As Variant, Type As DataTypeEnum, _
    DefinedSize As Integer)
Columns.Delete(Item As Variant)
Columns.Refresh
```

Group Object

```
RightsEnum = Group.GetPermissions(Name As Variant, _
    ObjectType As ObjectTypeEnum, [ObjectTypeId As Variant])
Group.SetPermissions(Name As Variant, ObjectType As ObjectTypeEnum, _
    Action As ActionEnum, Rights As RightsEnum, _
    Inherit As InheritTypeEnum, [ObjectTypeId As Variant])
```

Groups Collection

```
Groups.Append(Item As Variant)
Groups.Delete(Item As Variant)
Groups.Refresh
```

Indexes Collection

```
Indexes.Append(Item As Variant, [Columns As Variant])
Indexes.Delete(Item As Variant)
Indexes.Refresh
```

Keys Collection

```
Keys.Append(Item As Variant, Type As KeyTypeEnum, Column As Variant, _
    RelatedTable As String, RelatedColumn As String)
Keys.Delete(Item As Variant)
Keys.Refresh
```

Procedures Collection

```
Procedures.Append(Name As String, Command As Object)
Procedures.Delete(Item As Variant)
Procedures.Refresh
```

Properties Collection

```
Properties.Refresh
```

Tables Collection

```
Tables.Append(Item As Variant)
Tables.Delete(Item As Variant)
Tables.Refresh
```

User Object

```
User.ChangePassword(OldPassword As String, NewPassord As String)
RightsEnum = User.GetPermissions(Name As Variant, _
    ObjectType As ObjectTypeEnum, [ObjectTypeId As Variant])
User.SetPermissions(Name As Variant, ObjectType As ObjectTypeEnum, _
    Action As ActionEnum, Rights As RightsEnum, _
    Inherit As InheritTypeEnum, [ObjectTypeId As Variant])
```

Users Collection

```
Users.Append(Item As Variant, [Password As String])
Users.Delete(Item As Variant)
Users.Refresh
```

Views Collection

```
Views.Append(Name As String, Command As Object)
Views.Delete(Item As Variant)
Views.Refresh
```

ADOX Constants

ActionEnum

Constant Name	Value	Description
adAccessDeny	3	Deny the specific permissions to the Group or User.
adAccessGrant	1	Grant the specific permissions to the Group or User. Other permissions may remain in effect.
adAccessRevoke	4	Revoke any specific access rights to the Group or User.
adAccessSet	2	Set the exact permissions for the Group or User. Other permissions will not remain in effect.

Note: The documentation indicates that adAccessAuditSuccess and adAccessAuditFailure are allowable values for the Action. This is incorrect – these constants are not supported.

AllowNullsEnum

Constant Name	Value	Description
adIndexNullsAllow	0	Key columns with null values have index values.
adIndexNullsDisallow	1	Do not allow index entries if the key columns are null.
adIndexNullsIgnore	2	Null values in key columns are ignored and an index entry is not created.
adIndexNullsIgnoreAny	4	Null values in any part of the key (for multiple columns) are ignored, and an index entry is not created.

ColumnAttributesEnum

Constant Name	Value	Description
adColFixed	1	The column is of a fixed length.
adColNullable	2	The column may contain null values.

DataTypeEnum

The ADOX data type constants are the same as the ADO data type constants. See the listing for DataTypeEnum in Appendix B.

InheritTypeEnum

Constant Name	Value	Description
adInheritBoth	3	Permissions for the object are inherited by both objects and other containers.
adInheritContainers	2	Permissions for the object are inherited by other containers.
adInheritNone	0	No permissions are inherited.
adInheritNoPropogate	4	The adInheritObjects and adInheritContainers permissions are not propagated to child objects.
adInheritObjects	1	Permissions are only inherited by objects that are not containers.

Note: The documentation states that adInheritOnly is an allowable option for the InheritType. This is incorrect – this constant is not supported.

KeyTypeEnum

Constant Name	Value	Description
adKeyForeign	2	The key is a foreign key.
adKeyPrimary	1	The key is a primary key.
adKeyUnique	3	The key is unique.

ObjectTypeEnum

Constant Name	Value	Description
adPermObjColumn	2	The object is a column.
adPermObjDatabase	3	The object is a database.
adPermObjProcedure	4	The object is a procedure.
adPermObjProviderSpecific	-1	The object is of a provider-specific type.
adPermObjTable	1	The object is a table.
adPermObjView	5	The object is a view.

Note: The documentation mentions adPermObjSchema, adPermObjDomain, adPermObjCollation, adPermObjSchemaRowset, adPermObjCharacterSet, adPermObjTranslation as allowable options for the object type. This is incorrect – these constants are not supported.

RightsEnum

Constant Name	Value	Description
adRightCreate	16384	The User or Group has permission to create the object.
adRightDelete	65536	The User or Group has permission to delete the object.
adRightDrop	256	The User or Group has permission to drop the object.
adRightExclusive	512	The User or Group has permission to obtain exclusive access to the object.

Table Continued on Following Page

Constant Name	Value	Description
adRightExecute	536870912	The User or Group has permission to execute the object.
adRightFull	268435456	The User or Group has full permissions on the object.
adRightInsert	32768	The User or Group has permission to insert the object.
adRightMaximumAllowed	33554432	The User or Group has the maximum number of permissions allowed by the provider.
adRightNone	0	The User or Group has no permissions on the object.
adRightRead	-2147483648	The User or Group has permission to read the object.
adRightReadDesign	1024	The User or Group has permission to read the design of the object.
adRightReadPermissions	131072	The User or Group has permission to read the permissions of the object.
adRightReference	8192	The User or Group has permission to reference the object.
adRightUpdate	1073741824	The User or Group has permission to update the object.
adRightWithGrant	4096	The User or Group has permission to grant permissions to other users or groups.
adRightWriteDesign	2048	The User or Group has permission to change the design of the object.
adRightWriteOwner	524288	The User or Group has permission to change the owner of the object.
adRightWritePermissions	262144	The User or Group has permission to change the permissions of the object.

RuleEnum

Constant Name	Value	Description
adRICascade	1	Updates and deletes are cascaded.
adRINone	0	Updates and deletes are not cascaded.
adRISetDefault	3	Set the foreign key to its default value for updates and deletes.
adRISetNull	2	Set the foreign key to null for updates and deletes.

SortOrderEnum

Constant Name	Value	Description
adSortAscending	1	The key column is in ascending order.
adSortDescending	2	The key column is in descending order.

DBPROPVAL_NC

Constant Name	Value	Description
DBPROPVAL_NC_END	1	Null values are collated at the end of the list, irrespective of the collation order.
DBPROPVAL_NC_HIGH	2	Null values are collated at the high end of the list.
DBPROPVAL_NC_LOW	4	Null values are collated at the low end of the list.
DBPROPVAL_NC_START	8	Null values are collated at the start of the list, irrespective of the collation order.

DBPROPVAL_IN

Constant Name	Value	Description
DBPROPVAL_IN_DISALLOWNULL	1	Keys containing NULL values are not allowed. Generate an error if an attempt is made to insert a key that contains NULL.
DBPROPVAL_IN_IGNORENULL	2	Keys containing NULL values are allowed, but are ignored and not added to the index. No error is generated.
DBPROPVAL_IN_IGNOREANYNULL	4	Keys consisting of multi-columns will allow a NULL in any column, but the key is ignored and not added to the index. No error is generated.

DBPROPVAL_IT

Constant Name	Value	Description
DBPROPVAL_IT_BTREE	1	The index is a B+ tree.
DBPROPVAL_IT_CONTENT	3	The index is a content index.
DBPROPVAL_IT_HASH	2	The index is a hash file using linear or extensible hashing.
DBPROPVAL_IT_OTHER	4	The index is some other type of index.

ADOX Properties Collection

Property Support

The following table shows a list of all OLE DB dynamic properties for ADOX, and indicates which of them Microsoft Access and Microsoft SQL Server support. Since this list contains dynamic properties, not every property may show up under all circumstances. Other providers may also implement properties not listed in this table.

A tick indicates the property is supported, and a blank space indicates it is not supported.

Property Name	Object	Jet	SQL
Auto-Update	Index	✓	
Autoincrement	Column	✓	✓
Clustered	Index	✓	✓
Default	Column	✓	✓
Description	Column	✓	
Fill Factor	Index	✓	✓
Fixed Length	Column	✓	✓

Table Continued on Following Page

Property Name	Object	Jet	SQL
Increment	Column	✓	
Index Type	Index	✓	
Initial Size	Index	✓	
Jet OLEDB:Allow Zero Length	Column	✓	
Jet OLEDB:AutoGenerate	Column	✓	
Jet OLEDB:Cache Link Name/Password	Table	✓	
Jet OLEDB:Column Validation Rule	Column	✓	
Jet OLEDB:Column Validation Text	Column	✓	
Jet OLEDB:Compressed UNICODE Strings	Column	✓	
Jet OLEDB:Create Link	Table	✓	
Jet OLEDB:Exclusive Link	Table	✓	
Jet OLEDB:Hyperlink	Column	✓	
Jet OLEDB:IISAM Not Last Column	Column	✓	
Jet OLEDB:Link Datasource	Table	✓	
Jet OLEDB:Link Provider String	Table	✓	
Jet OLEDB:One BLOB per Page	Column	✓	
Jet OLEDB:Remote Table Name	Table	✓	
Jet OLEDB:Table Hidden In Access	Table	✓	
Jet OLEDB:Table Validation Rule	Table	✓	
Jet OLEDB:Table Validation Text	Table	✓	
NULL Collation	Index	✓	
NULL Keys	Index	✓	
Nullable	Column	✓	✓
Primary Key	Column		✓
Primary Key	Index	✓	✓
Seed	Column	✓	
Sort Bookmarks	Index	✓	
Temporary Index	Index	✓	
Temporary Table	Table	✓	✓
Unique	Column		✓
Unique	Index	✓	✓

Column Object

Name	Description	DataType
Autoincrement	Indicates whether or not the column is autoincrementing.	Boolean
Default	Specifies the default value for the column, to be used if no explicit value is supplied.	Variant
Description	The column description.	String
Fixed Length	Indicates whether or not the column holds fixed length data.	Boolean
Increment	The value by which auto-increment columns are increased.	Long
Jet OLEDB:Allow Zero Length	Indicates whether or not zero length strings can be inserted into the field.	Boolean
Jet OLEDB:Autogenerate	Indicates whether or not, for a GUID data type, a GUID should be automatically created.	Boolean
Jet OLEDB:Column Validation Rule	The validation rule to apply to column values before allowing the column to be set.	String
Jet OLEDB:Column Validation Text	Errors string to display if changes to a row do not meet the column validation rule.	String
Jet OLEDB:Compressed UNICODE Strings	Indicates whether or not Jet should compress UNICODE strings. Only applicable to Jet 4.0 databases.	Boolean
Jet OLEDB:Hyperlink	Indicates whether or not the column is a hyperlink.	Boolean
Jet OLEDB:IISAM Not Last Column	When creating columns (or a table) for installable IISAMS, this indicates whether or nor this is the last column.	Boolean
Jet OLEDB:One BLOB Per Page	Indicates whether or not BLOB columns can share data pages.	Boolean
Nullable	Indicates whether or not the column can contain NULL values.	Boolean
Primary Key	Indicates whether or not the column is part of the primary key.	Boolean
Seed	The initial seed value of an auto-increment column.	Long
Unique	Indicates whether or not the column allows unique values.	Boolean

Index Object

Property Name	Description	DataType
Auto-Update	Indicates whether or not the index is maintained automatically when changes are made to rows.	Boolean
Clustered	Indicates whether or not the index is clustered.	Boolean
Fill Factor	Identifies the fill-factor of the index. This is the storage use of page-nodes during index creation. It is always 100 for the Jet provider.	Long
Index Type	The type of the index.	DBPROPVAL_IT
Initial Size	The total number of bytes allocated to the index when it is first created.	Long
NULL Collation	Specifies how NULL values are collated in the index.	DBPROPVAL_NC
NULL Keys	Specifies whether key values containing NULLs are allowed.	DBPROPVAL_IN
Primary Key	Indicates whether or not the index represents the primary key on the table.	Boolean
Sort Bookmarks	Indicates whether or not repeated keys are sorted by bookmarks.	Boolean
Temporary Index	Indicates whether or not the index is temporary.	Boolean
Unique	Indicates whether or not index keys must be unique.	Boolean

Table Object

Property Name	Description	DataType
Jet OLEDB:Cache Link Name/Password	Indicates whether or not the authentication information for a linked table should be cached locally in the Jet database.	Boolean
Jet OLEDB:Create Link	Indicates whether or not a link is create is created to a remote data source when creating a new table.	Boolean
Jet OLEDB:Exclusive Link	Indicates whether or not the remote data source is opened exclusively when creating a link.	Boolean
Jet OLEDB:Link Datasource	The name of the remote data source to link to.	String
Jet OLEDB:Link Provider String	The connection string to the remote provider.	String
Jet OLEDB:Remote Table Name	The name of the remote table in a link.	String
Jet OLEDB:Table Hidden In Access	Indicates whether or not the table is shown in the Access user interface.	Boolean
Jet OLEDB:Table Validation Rule	The validation rule to apply to row values before committing changes to the row.	String
Jet OLEDB:Table Validation Text	Errors string to display if changes to a row do not meet the table validation rule.	String
Temporary Table	Indicates whether or not the table is a temporary table.	Boolean

ADOMD Object Summary

Microsoft ActiveX Data Objects (Multi-dimensional) 2.5 Library Reference

The ADOMD Objects

Name	Description
Axes	Contains an Axis object for each axis in the Cellset.
Axis	An Axis of a Cellset, containing members of one or more dimensions.
Catalog	Contains the multi-dimensional schema information.
Cell	The data at an intersection of Axis coordinates.
Cellset	The results of a multi-dimensional query.
CubeDef	A Cube from a multi-dimensional schema, containing related Dimension objects.
CubeDefs	One or more CudeDef objects contained within a Catalog.

Name	Description
Dimension	A dimension of a multi-dimensional cube, containing one or more Hierarchy objects.
Dimensions	One or more Dimension objects, making up the dimensions of a CubeDef.
Hierarchies	One or more Hierarchy objects, representing the ways a Dimension can be aggregated.
Hierarchy	Indicates one way in which aggregation of a Dimension can take place.
Level	Contains the members which make up the Hierarchy.
Levels	Contains one or more Level objects contained within the Hierarchy.
Member	An individual member of a the Members collection
Members	A collection of Members for the level.
Position	A position in the cellset.
Positions	A collection of Position objects in the cellset.

Axes Collection

Methods

Name	Returns	Description
Refresh		Refreshes the collection with details from the provider.

Properties

Name	Returns	Description
Count	Long	The number of Axis objects in the collection. Read only.
Item	Axis	The default property, allowing indexing into the collection. Read only.

Axis Object

Properties

Name	Returns	Description
DimensionCount	Long	The number of Dimensions on this Axis. Read only.
Name	String	The name of the Axis. Read only.
Positions	Positions	A collection of Position objects in the Axis. Read only.
Properties	Properties	A collection of provider specific properties for the Axis. Read only.

Catalog Object

Properties

Name	Returns	Description
ActiveConnection	Object	The ADO Connection object or string, indicating the data provider to which the catalog is attached.
CubeDefs	CubeDefs	A collection of CubeDef objects available in the catalog. Read only.
Name	String	The name of the Catalog. Read only.

Cell Object

Properties

Name	Returns	Description
FormattedValue	String	The formatted value of the cell.
Ordinal	Long	The unique number identifying a cell. Read only.
Positions	Positions	A collection of Position objects available for the cell. Read only.
Properties	Properties	A collection of provider specific properties for the cell. Read only.
Value	Variant	The value of the cell.

Cellset Object

Methods

Name	Returns	Description
Close		Opens the cellset.
Open		Closes the cellset.

Properties

Name	Returns	Description
ActiveConnection	Object	The ADO Connection object or string, indicating the data provider to which the catalog is attached.
Axes	Axes	A collection of Axis objects in the cellset. Read only.
FilterAxis	Axis	Indicates the filtering information for the cellset. Read only.
Item	Cell	The default property, which allows indexing into the cellset. Read only.
Properties	Properties	A collection of provider specific properties for the cellset. Read only.
Source	Variant	The multi-dimensional query used to generate the cellset.
State	Long	Indicates whether the cellset is open or closed. Read only.

CubeDef Object

Properties

Name	Returns	Description
Description	String	Text describing the cube. Read only.
Dimensions	Dimensions	A collection of Dimensions available in the cube. Read only.
Name	String	The name of the cube. Read only.
Properties	Properties	A collection of provider specific properties for the CubeDef. Read only.

CubeDefs Collection

Methods

Name	Returns	Description
Refresh		Refreshes the CubeDef objects from the provider.

Properties

Name	Returns	Description
Count	Long	Indicates the number of CubeDef objects in the collection. Read only.
Item	CubeDef	The default property, which allows indexing into the collection. Read only.

Dimension Object

Properties

Name	Returns	Description
Description	String	A description of the dimension. Read only.
Hierarchies	Hierarchies	A collection of hierarchies available in the dimension. Read only.
Name	String	The name of the dimension. Read only.
Properties	Properties	A collection of provider specific properties for the dimension. Read only.
UniqueName	String	The unique name of the dimension. Read only.

Dimensions Collection

Methods

Name	Returns	Description
Refresh		Refreshes the Dimensions collection from the provider.

Properties

Name	Returns	Description
Count	Long	The number of Dimension objects in the collection. Read only.
Item	Dimension	The default property, which allows indexing into the collection. Read only.

Hierarchies Collection

Methods

Name	Returns	Description
Refresh		Refreshes the Hierarchies collection from the provider.

Properties

Name	Returns	Description
Count	Long	The number of Hierarchy objects in the collection. Read only.
Item	Hierarchy	The default property, which allows indexing into the collection. Read only.

Hierarchy Object

Properties

Name	Returns	Description
Description	String	The description of the hierarchy. Read only.
Levels	Levels	A collection of levels in the hierarchy. Read only.
Name	String	The name of the hierarchy. Read only.
Properties	Properties	A collection of provider specific properties for the hierarchy. Read only.
UniqueName	String	The unique name of the hierarchy. Read only.

Level Object

Properties

Name	Returns	Description
Caption	String	The caption of the level. Read only.
Depth	Integer	How deep in the hierarchy this level is. Read only.
Description	String	The description of the level. Read only.
Members	Members	A collection of Member objects available in this level. Read only.
Name	String	The name of the level. Read only.
Properties	Properties	A collection of provider specific properties for the level. Read only.
UniqueName	String	The unique name of the level. Read only.

Levels Collection

Methods

Name	Returns	Description
Refresh		Refreshes the Levels collection from the provider.

Properties

Name	Returns	Description
Count	Long	The number of Level objects in the collection. Read only.
Item	Level	The default property, which allows indexing into the collection. Read only.

Member Object

Properties

Name	Returns	Description
Caption	String	The caption of the member. Read only.
ChildCount	Long	The number of children belonging to this member. Read only.
Children	Members	A collection of Member objects which are children of this member. Read only.
Description	String	A description of the member. Read only.
DrilledDown	Boolean	Indicates whether or not this is a leaf node (contains children). Read only.
LevelDepth	Long	How deep in the collection this member is. Read only.
LevelName	String	The name of the Level to which this member belongs. Read only.
Name	String	The name of the member. Read only.
Parent	Member	The Member object which is the parent of this member. Read only.
ParentSameAsPrev	Boolean	Indicates whether the parent Member is the same as the Parent member of the previous member in the collection. Read only.
Properties	Properties	A collection of provider specific properties for the member. Read only.
Type	MemberTypeEnum	The type of the member. Read only.
UniqueName	String	The unique name of the member. Read only.

Members Collection

Methods

Name	Returns	Description
Refresh		Refreshes the Members collection from the provider.

Properties

Name	Returns	Description
Count	Long	The number of Member objects in the collection. Read only.
Item	Member	The default property, which allows indexing into the collection. Read only.

Position Object

Properties

Name	Returns	Description
Members	Members	A collection of Member objects in this position. Read only.
Ordinal	Long	A unique identifier, indicating the location of the position in the collection. Read only.

Positions Collection

Methods

Name	Returns	Description
Refresh		Refreshes the Positions collection from the provider.

Properties

Name	Returns	Description
Count	Long	The number of Position objects in the collection. Read only.
Item	Position	The default property, which allows indexing into the collection. Read only.

Method Calls

Axes Collection

    Axes.Refresh

CubeDefs Collection

    CubeDefs.Refresh

Dimensions Collection

    Dimensions.Refresh

Hierarchies Collection

    Hierarchies.Refresh

Cellset Object

    Cellset.Close
    Cellset.Open([DataSource As Variant], [ActiveConnection As Variant])

Levels Collection

    Levels.Refresh

Members Collection

    Members.Refresh

Positions Collection

    Positions.Refresh

ADOMD Constants

MemberTypeEnum

Name	Value	Description
adMemberAll	2	The member is the All member, at the top of the members hierachy.
adMemberFormula	4	The member identifies a formula.
adMemberMeasure	3	The member identifies a Measure.
adMemberRegular	1	The member identifies a regular member.
adMemberUnknown	0	The type of member is unknown.

MDMEASURE_AGGR

Name	Value	Description
MDMEASURE_AGGR_SUM	1	The aggregate function is SUM.
MDMEASURE_AGGR_COUNT	2	The aggregate function is COUNT.

Table Continued on Following Page

Name	Value	Description
MDMEASURE_AGGR_MIN	3	The aggregate function is MIN.
MDMEASURE_AGGR_MAX	4	The aggregate function is MAX.
MDMEASURE_AGGR_AVG	5	The aggregate function is AVG.
MDMEASURE_AGGR_VAR	6	The aggregate function is VAR.
MDMEASURE_AGGR_STD	7	The aggregate function is one of SUM, COUNT, MIN, MAX, AVG, VAR, STDEV.
MDMEASURE_AGGR_CALCULATED	127	The aggregate function is derived from formula that is not a standard one.
MDMEASURE_AGGR_UNKNOWN	0	The aggregate function is not known.

MDLEVEL_TYPE

Name	Value	Description
MDLEVEL_TYPE_REGULAR	0	The level is a regular level
MDLEVEL_TYPE_ALL	1	The level identifies the top of the hierarchy, or All levels.
MDLEVEL_TYPE_CALCULATED	2	The level is a calculated level.
MDLEVEL_TYPE_TIME	4	The level is a time level.
MDLEVEL_TYPE_TIME_YEARS	20	The level is a time level, based on years.
MDLEVEL_TYPE_TIME_HALF_YEAR	36	The level is a time level, based on half-years.
MDLEVEL_TYPE_TIME_QUARTERS	68	The level is a time level, based on quarters.
MDLEVEL_TYPE_TIME_MONTHS	132	The level is a time level, based on months.
MDLEVEL_TYPE_TIME_WEEKS	260	The level is a time level, based on weeks.
MDLEVEL_TYPE_TIME_DAYS	516	The level is a time level, based on days.
MDLEVEL_TYPE_TIME_HOURS	772	The level is a time level, based on hours.
MDLEVEL_TYPE_TIME_MINUTES	1028	The level is a time level, based on minutes.
MDLEVEL_TYPE_TIME_SECONDS	2052	The level is a time level, based on seconds.
MDLEVEL_TYPE_TIME_UNDEFINED	4100	The level type is not defined.
MDLEVEL_TYPE_UNKNOWN	0	The level type is unknown.

MDTREEOP

Name	Value	Description
MDTREEOP_ANCESTORS	32	Show only members that are ancestors of the selected member.
MDTREEOP_CHILDREN	1	Show only members that are children of the selected member.
MDTREEOP_SIBLINGS	2	Show only members that are siblings of the selected member.
MDTREEOP_PARENT	4	Show only members that are parents of the selected member.
MDTREEOP_SELF	8	Show the selected member in the list.
MDTREEOP_DESCENDANTS	16	Show only members that are descendants of the selected member.

MDPROPVAL_AU

Name	Value	Description
MDPROPVAL_AU_UNSUPPORTED	0	Updating of aggregated cells is not supported.
MDPROPVAL_AU_UNCHANGED	1	Aggregated cells can be changed, but the cells that make up the aggregation remain unchanged.
MDPROPVAL_AU_UNKNOWN	2	Aggregated cells can be changed, but the cells that make up the aggregation remains undefined.

MDPROPVAL_FS

Name	Value	Description
MDPROPVAL_FS_FULL_SUPPORT	1	The provider supports flattening.
MDPROPVAL_FS_GENERATED_COLUMN	2	The provider supports flattening by using dummy names.
MDPROPVAL_FS_GENERATED_DIMENSION	3	The provider supports flattening by generating one column per dimension.
MDPROPVAL_FS_NO_SUPPORT	4	The provider does not support flattening.

MDPROPVAL_MC

Name	Value	Description
MDPROPVAL_MC_SINGLECASE	1	The provider supports simple case statements.
MDPROPVAL_MC_SEARCHEDCASE	2	The provider supports searched case statements.

MDPROPVAL_MD

Name	Value	Description
MDPROPVAL_MD_BEFORE	2	The BEFORE flag is supported.
MDPROPVAL_MD_AFTER	4	The AFTER flag is supported.
MDPROPVAL_MD_SELF	1	The SELF flag is supported.

MDPROPVAL_MF

Name	Value	Description
MDPROPVAL_MF_WITH_CALCMEMBERS	1	Calculated members are supported by use of the WITH clause.
MDPROPVAL_MF_WITH_NAMEDSETS	2	Named sets are supported by use of the WITH clause.
MDPROPVAL_MF_CREATE_CALCMEMBERS	4	Named calculated members are supported by use of the CREATE clause.
MDPROPVAL_MF_CREATE_NAMEDSETS	8	Named sets are supported by use of the CREATE clause.
MDPROPVAL_MF_SCOPE_SESSION	16	The scope value of SESSION is supported during the creation of named sets and calculated members.
MDPROPVAL_MF_SCOPE_GLOBAL	32	The scope value of GLOBAL is supported during the creation of named sets and calculated members

MDPROPVAL_MJC

Name	Value	Description
MDPROPVAL_MJC_IMPLICITCUBE	4	An empty FROM clause is supported, and the cube is implictly resolved.
MDPROPVAL_MJC_SINGLECUBE	1	Only one cube is supported in the FROM clause.
MDPROPVAL_MJC_MULTICUBES	2	More than one cube is supported in the FROM clause.

MDPROPVAL_MMF

Name	Value	Description
MDPROPVAL_MMF_COUSIN	1	The COUSIN function is supported.
MDPROPVAL_MMF_PARALLELPERIOD	2	The PARALLELPERIOD function is supported.
MDPROPVAL_MMF_OPENINGPERIOD	4	The OPENINGPERIOD function is supported.
MDPROPVAL_MMF_CLOSINGPERIOD	8	The CLOSINGPERIOD function is supported.

MDPROPVAL_MNF

Name	Value	Description
MDPROPVAL_MNF_MEDIAN	1	The MEDIAN function is supoprted.
MDPROPVAL_MNF_VAR	2	The VAR function is supported.
MDPROPVAL_MNF_STDDEV	4	The STDDEV function is supported.
MDPROPVAL_MNF_RANK	8	The RANK function is supported.
MDPROPVAL_MNF_AGGREGATE	16	The AGGREGATE function is supported.
MDPROPVAL_MNF_COVARIANCE	32	The COVARIANCE function is supported.
MDPROPVAL_MNF_CORRELATION	64	The CORRELATION function is supported.
MDPROPVAL_MNF_LINREGSLOPE	128	The LINREGSLOPE function is supported.
MDPROPVAL_MNF_LINREGVARIANCE	256	The LINREGVARIANCE function is supported.

Table Continued on Following Page

Name	Value	Description
MDPROPVAL_MNF_LINREGR2	512	The LINREGR2 function is supported.
MDPROPVAL_MNF_LINREGPOINT	1024	The LINREGPOINT function is supported.
MDPROPVAL_MNF_DRILLDOWNLEVEL	2048	The DRILLDOWNLEVEL function is supported.
MDPROPVAL_MNF_DRILLDOWNMEMBERTOP	4096	The DRILLDOWNMEMBERTOP function is supported.
MDPROPVAL_MNF_DRILLDOWNMEMBERBOTTOM	8192	The DRILLDOWNMEMBERBOTTOM function is supported.
MDPROPVAL_MNF_DRILLDOWNLEVELTOP	16384	The DRILLDOWNLEVELTOP function is supported.
MDPROPVAL_MNF_DRILLDOWNLEVELBOTTOM	32768	The DRILLDOWNLEVELBOTTOM function is supported.
MDPROPVAL_MNF_DRILLUPMEMBER	65536	The DRILLUPMEMBER function is supported.
MDPROPVAL_MNF_DRILLUPLEVEL	131072	The DRILLUPLEVEL function is supported.

MDPROPVAL_MO

Name	Value	Description
MDPROPVAL_MO_TUPLE		The tuple.[VALUE] clause can be qualified by a cube name as an argument.

MDPROPVAL_MOQ

Name	Value	Description
MDPROPVAL_MOQ_DATASOURCE_CUBE	1	Cubes can be qualified by the data source name.
MDPROPVAL_MOQ_CATALOG_CUBE	2	Cubes can be qualified by the catalog name.
MDPROPVAL_MOQ_SCHEMA_CUBE	4	Cubes can be qualified by the schema name.
MDPROPVAL_MOQ_CUBE_DIM	8	Dimensions can be qualified by the cube name.
MDPROPVAL_MOQ_DIM_HIER	16	Hierarchies can be qualified by the dimension name.

Name	Value	Description
MDPROPVAL_MOQ_DIMHIER_LEVEL	32	Levels can be qualified by the schema name, and/or the hierarchy name.
MDPROPVAL_MOQ_LEVEL_MEMBER	64	Members can be qualified by a level name.
MDPROPVAL_MOQ_MEMBER_MEMBER	128	Members can be qualified by their ancestor names.

MDPROPVAL_MS

Name	Value	Description
MDPROPVAL_MS_SINGLETUPLE	2	Only one tuple is supported in the WHERE clause.
MDPROPVAL_MS_MULTIPLETUPLES	1	Multiple tuples are supported in the WHERE clause.

MDPROPVAL_MSC

Name	Value	Description
MDPROPVAL_MSC_LESSTHAN	1	The provider supports the less than operator.
MDPROPVAL_MSC_GREATERTHAN	2	The provider supports the greater than operator.
MDPROPVAL_MSC_LESSTHANEQUAL	4	The provider supports the less than or equal to operator.
MDPROPVAL_MSC_GREATERTHANEQUAL	8	The provider supports the greater than or equal to operator.

MDPROPVAL_MSF

Name	Value	Description
MDPROPVAL_MSF_TOPPERCENT	1	The TOPPERCENT function is supported.
MDPROPVAL_MSF_BOTTOMPERCENT	2	The BOTTOMPERCENT function is supported.

Table Continued on Following Page

Name	Value	Description
MDPROPVAL_MSF_TOPSUM	4	The TOPSUM function is supported.
MDPROPVAL_MSF_BOTTOMSUM	8	The BOTTOMSUM function is supported.
MDPROPVAL_MSF_DRILLDOWNLEVEL	2048	The DRILLDOWNLEVEL function is supported.
MDPROPVAL_MSF_DRILLDOWNMEMBER	1024	The DRILLDOWNMEMBER function is supported.
MDPROPVAL_MSF_DRILLDOWNMEMBERTOP	4096	The DRILLDOWNMEMBERTOP function is supported.
MDPROPVAL_MSF_DRILLDOWNMEMBERBOTTOM	8192	The DRILLDOWNMEMBERBOTTOM function is supported.
MDPROPVAL_MSF_DRILLDOWNLEVELTOP	16384	The DRILLDOWNLEVELTOP function is supported.
MDPROPVAL_MSF_DRILLDOWNLEVELBOTTOM	32768	The DRILLDOWNLEVELBOTTOM function is supported.
MDPROPVAL_MSF_DRILLUPMEMBER	65536	The DRILLUPMEMBER function is supported.
MDPROPVAL_MSF_DRILLUPLEVEL	131072	The DRILLUPLEVEL function is supported.
MDPROPVAL_MSF_PERIODSTODATE	16	The PERIODSTODATE function is supported.
MDPROPVAL_MSF_LASTPERIODS	32	The LASTPERIODS function is supported.
MDPROPVAL_MSF_YTD	64	The YTD function is supported.
MDPROPVAL_MSF_QTD	128	The QTD function is supported.
MDPROPVAL_MSF_MTD	256	The MTD function is supported.
MDPROPVAL_MSF_WTD	512	The WTD function is supported.
MDPROPVAL_MSF_TOGGLEDRILLSTATE	262144	The provider supports toggling of the drilled down state.

MDPROPVAL_NL

Name	Value	Description
MDPROPVAL_NL_NAMEDLEVELS	1	The provider supports named levels
MDPROPVAL_NL_NUMBEREDLEVELS	2	The provider supports numbered levels.
MDPROPVAL_NL_SCHEMAONLY	4	The provider supports 'dummy' levels, for display only.

MDPROPVAL_RR

Name	Value	Description
MDPROPVAL_RR_NORANGEROWSET	1	The provider does not support range rowsets.
MDPROPVAL_RR_READONLY	2	The provider supports read-only range rowsets.
MDPROPVAL_RR_UPDATE	4	The provider supports updatable range rowsets.

MD_DIMTYPE

Name	Value	Description
MD_DIMTYPE_UNKNOWN	0	The dimension type is unknown.
MD_DIMTYPE_TIME	1	The dimension is a time dimension.
MD_DIMTYPE_MEASURE	2	The dimension is a measure dimension.
MD_DIMTYPE_OTHER	3	The dimension is neither a time nor a measure dimenstion.

ADOMD Properties Collection

The following table shows a list of all OLE DB properties for the Microsoft OLAP Provider.

Cell Object

Name	Description	Type
CELL_ORDINAL	The ordinal number of the cell.	Long
FORMATTED_VALUE	The formatted value of the cell.	String
VALUE	The unformatted value of the cell.	String

Connection Object

Name	Description	Type
Active Sessions	The maximum number of sessions allowable. Zero indicates no limit.	Long
Asynchable Abort	Whether transactions can be aborted asynchronously. Read-only.	Boolean
Asynchable Commit	Whether transactions can be committed asynchronously. Read-only.	Boolean

Table Continued on Following Page

Name	Description	Type
Asynchronous Initialization	Indicates the asynchronous initialization setting. This can only be DBPROPVAL_ASYNCH_INITIALIZE from the ADO constants.	Long
Auto Synch Period	Identifies the time (in milliseconds) of the synchronization between the client and the server. The default value is 10,000 (10 seconds).	Long
Autocommit Isolation Levels	Indicates the transaction isolation level when in auto-commit mode. Can be one of the DBPROPVAL_TI constants from ADO.	Long
Cache Policy	Reserved for future use.	Long
Catalog Location	The position of the catalog name in a table name in a text command. The value can be on of the DBPROPVAL_CL constants from ADO.	Long
Catalog Term	The name the data source uses for a catalog, e.g., 'catalog' or 'database'. Read/Write.	String
Catalog Usage	Specifies how catalog names can be used in text commands. Can be zero or more of DBPROPVAL_CU constants from ADO.	Long
Client Cache Size	The amount of memory used by the cache on the client. A value of 0 means there is no limit on the client memory that can be used. A value of 1-99 indicates the percentage of virtual memory to use for the cache. A value above 100 indicates the amount in Kb that can be used by the cache.	Long
Column Definition	Defines the valid clauses for the definition of a column. Can be one of the DBPROPVAL_CD constants from ADO.	Long
CompareCaseNotSensitiveStringFlags	Identifies the type of comparison to perform for case-insensitive strings.	Long
CompareCaseSensitiveStringFlags	Identifies the type of comparison to perform for case-sensitive strings.	Long

Name	Description	Type
Connect Timeout	The amount of time, in seconds, to wait for the initialization to complete. Read/Write.	Long
Connection Status	The status of the current connection. Can be one of the DBPROPVAL_CS constants from ADO.	Long
CREATECUBE	The statement used to create a cube.	String
Current Catalog	The name of the current catalog.	String
Data Source	The name of the data source to connect to.	String
Data Source Name	The name of the data source.	String
Data Source Object Threading Model	Specifies the threading models supported by the data source object.	Long
Data Source Type	The type of data source.	Long
DBMS Name	The name of the product accessed by the provider.	String
DBMS Version	The version of the product accessed by the provider.	String
Default Isolation Mode	Identifies whether the isolation mode is 'isolated', or the mode requested by the rowset properties. Isolated mode will be used if this value starts with Y, T or a number other than 0.	String
Execution Location	Identifies whether the query is resolved. Values can be: 0, for automatic selection. This is the default. 1, for automatic selection. 2, to execute the query on the client 3, to execute the query on the server.	Long
Extended Properties	Contains provider specific, extended connection information	String
Flattening Support	Indicates the level of support by the provider for flattening.	MDPROPVAL_FS

Table Continued on Following Page

Name	Description	Type
GROUP BY Support	The relationship between the columns in a GROUP BY clause and the non-aggregated columns in the select list. Can be one of the DBPROPVAL_GB constants from ADO.	Long
Heterogeneous Table Support	Specifies whether the provider can join tables from different catalogs or providers. Can be one of the DBPROPVAL_HT constants from ADO.	Long
Identifier Case Sensitivity	How identifiers treat case sensitivity. Can be one of the DBPROPVAL_IC constants from ADO	Long
Initial Catalog	The name of the initial, or default, catalog to use when connecting to the data source. If the provider supports changing the catalog for an initialized data source, a different catalog name can be specified in the Current Catalog property.	String
INSERTINTO	The statement used for inserting data into a local cube.	String
Integrated Security	Contains the name of the authentication service used by the server to identify the user.	String
Isolation Levels	Identifies the supported transaction isolation levels. Can be one of the DBPROPVAL_TI constants from ADO	Long
Isolation Retention	Identifies the supported transaction isolation retention levels. Can be one of the DBPROPVAL_TR constants from ADO.	Long
Large Level Threshold	Defines the number of levels a Dimension can have before it is deemed to be a 'large' dimension. A large level Dimension will have the levels sent from the server in increments, rather than all at once.	Long
Locale Identifier	The locale ID of preference for the consumer.	Long

Name	Description	Type
Location	The location of the data source to connect to. Typically this will be the server name	String
Maximum Index Size	The maximum number of bytes allowed in the combined columns of an index. This is 0 if there is no specified limit or the limit is unknown	Long
Maximum Row Size	The maximum length of a single row in a table. This is 0 if there is no specified limit or the limit is unknown.	Long
Maximum Row Size Includes BLOB	Identifies whether Maximum Row Size includes the length for BLOB data.	Boolean
Maximum Tables in SELECT	The maximum number of tables allowed in the FROM clause of a SELECT statement. This is 0 if there is no specified limit or the limit is unknown.	Long
MDX DDL Extensions	Defines any DDL extensions supported by the provider.	Long
MDX USE Extensions	Defines the USE extensions supported by the provider, allowing creation of user defined functions.	Long
Mode	Specifies the access permissions. Can be one of the DB_MODE constants from ADO.	Long
Multiple Results	Identifies whether the provider supports multiple results objects and what restrictions it places on those objects.	Long
Multiple Storage Objects	Identifies whether the provider supports multiple, open storage objects at the same time.	Boolean
Multi-Table Update	Identifies whether the provider can update rowsets derived from multiple tables.	Boolean
NULL Collation Order	Identifies where NULLs are sorted in a list.	Long

Table Continued on Following Page

Name	Description	Type
NULL Concatenation Behavior	How the data source handles concatenation of NULL-valued character data type columns with non-NULL valued character data type columns.	Long
Number of axes in the dataset	Maximum number of axes that the provider supports.	Long
OLE DB Services	Specifies the OLE DB services to enable.	Long
OLE DB Version	Specifies the version of OLE DB supported by the provider.	String
OLE Object Support	Specifies the way on which the provider supports access to BLOBs and OLE objects stored in columns.	Long
ORDER BY Columns in Select List	Identifies whether columns in an ORDER BY clause must be in the SELECT list.	Boolean
Output Parameter Availability	Identifies the time at which output parameter values become available. Can be one of the DBPROPVAL_AO constants in ADO.	Long
Pass By Ref Accessors	Whether the provider supports the DBACCESSOR_PASSBYREF flag.	Boolean
Password	The password to be used to connect to the data source.	String
Persist Security Info	Whether or not the consumer requires that the data source object persist sensitive authentication information, such as a password, in encrypted form.	Boolean
Persistent ID Type	Specifies the type of DBID that the provider uses when persisting DBIDs for tables, indexes and columns. Can be one of the DBPROPVAL_PT constants in ADO.	Long
Prepare Abort Behavior	Identifies how aborting a transaction affects prepared commands. Can be one of the DBPROPVAL_CB constants in ADO.	Long

Name	Description	Type
Prepare Commit Behavior	Identifies how committing a transaction affects prepared commands. Can be one of the DBPROPVAL_CB constants in ADO.	Long
Procedure Term	Specifies the data source providers name for a procedure, e.g., 'database procedure', 'stored procedure'.	String
Prompt	Specifies whether to prompt the user during initialization.	Integer
Provider Friendly Name	The friendly name of the provider.	String
Provider Name	The filename of the provider.	String
Provider Version	The version of the provider.	String
Provider's ability to qualify a cube name	Identifies how object names in a schema can be qualified in an MDX expression.	MDPROPVAL_MOQ
Quoted Identifier Sensitivity	Identifies how quoted identifiers treat case. Can be one of the DBPROPVAL_IC constants from ADO.	Long
Read Only Session	Reserved for future.	String
Read-Only Data Source	Whether or not the data source is read-only.	Boolean
Reset Datasource	Specifies the data source state to reset. Can be one of the DBPROPVAL_RD constants from ADO.	Long
Rowset Conversions on Command	Identifies whether callers can enquire on a command and about conversions supported by the command.	Boolean
Schema Usage	Identifies how schema names can be used in commands. Can be one of the DBPROPVAL_SU constants from ADO.	Long
Server Name	The name of the server.	String
SOURCE_DSN	The connection string for the source data store.	String

Table Continued on Following Page

Name	Description	Type
SOURCE_DSN_SUFFIX	The suffix to append to the SOURCE_DSN property for a local cube.	String
SQL Support	Identifies the level of support for SQL. Can be one of the DBPROPVAL_SQL constants from ADO.	Long
Structured Storage	Identifies what interfaces the rowset supports on storage objects. Can be one of the DBPROPVAL_SS constants from ADO.	Long
Subquery Support	Identifies the predicates in text commands that support sub-queries. Can be one of the DBPROPVAL_SQ constants from ADO.	Long
Support for cell updates	Indicates whether the provider supports updating of the cells.	MDPROPVAL_PR
Support for creation of named sets and calculated members	Indicates the level of support for named sets and calculated members.	MDPROPVAL_MF
Support for MDX case statements	The level of support for case statements.	MDPROPVAL_MC
Support for named levels	The level of support for named and/or numbered levels.	MDPROPVAL_NL
Support for outer reference in an MDX statement	The level of support for outer references.	MDPROPVAL_MO
Support for query joining multiple cubes	The level of support for joining multiple cubes.	MDPROPVAL_MJC
Support for querying by property values in an MDX statement	Indicates whether or not the provider supports the query of property statements.	Boolean
Support for string comparison operators other than equals and not-equals operators	The level of support for complex string comparison operators.	MDPROPVAL_MSC
Support for updating aggregated cells	The level of support for updating aggregated cells.	MDPROPVAL_AU
Support for various <desc_flag> values in the DESCENDANTS function	The level of support for flags when describing descendants.	MDPROPVAL_MD

Name	Description	Type
Support for various member functions	The level of support for functions that act on members.	MDPROPVAL_MMF
Support for various numeric functions	The level of support for numeric functions.	MDPROPVAL_MNF
Support for various set functions	The level of support for set functions.	MDPROPVAL_MSF
Table Term	The name the data source uses for a table, eg, 'table' or 'file'.	String
The capabilities of the WHERE clause of an MDX statement	The WHERE clause support for tuples.	MDPROPVAL_MS
Transaction DDL	Indicates whether Data Definition Language (DDL) statements are supported in transactions. Can be one of the DBPROPVAL_TC constants from ADO.	Long
USEEXISTINGFILE	When using CREATE CUBE or INSERT INTO, indicates whether an existing local cube file is overwritten. If the value starts with Y, T or a number other than 0, the existing file is used. If the value starts with any other character the existing cube file is overwritten.	String
User ID	The User ID to be used when connecting to the data source.	String
User Name	The User Name used in a particular database.	String
Window Handle	The window handle to be used if the data source object needs to prompt for additional information.	Long
Writeback Timeout	The maximum amount of time (in seconds) to wait whilst committing changes back to the server.	Long

CubeDef Object

Name	Description	Type
CATALOG_NAME	The name of the catalog to which the cube belongs.	String
CREATED_ON	The date the cube was created.	Date/Time
CUBE_GUID	The GUID of the cube.	GUID
CUBE_NAME	The cube name.	String
CUBE_TYPE	Will be CUBE for a standard cube and VIRTUAL CUBE for a virtual cube.	String
DATA_UPDATED_BY	The ID of the person who last update data in the cube.	String
DESCRIPTION	The cube description.	String
LAST_DATA_UPDATE	The date the cube data was last updated.	Date/Time
LAST_SCHEMA_UPDATE	The date the cube schema was last updated.	Date/Time
SCHEMA_NAME	The name of the schema to which this cube belongs.	String
SCHEMA_UPDATED_BY	The ID of the person who last updated the schema.	String

Dimension Object

Name	Description	Type
CATALOG_NAME	The name of the Catalog to which this Dimension belongs.	String
CUBE_NAME	The name of the Cube to which this Dimension belongs.	String
DEFAULT_HIERARCHY	The unique name of the default Hierarchy for this Dimension.	String
DESCRIPTION	The description of the Dimension.	String
DIMENSION_CAPTION	The caption of the Dimension.	String
DIMENSION_CARDINALITY	The number of members in the Dimension. This figure is not guaranteed to be accurate.	Long

Name	Description	Type
DIMENSION_GUID	The GUID of the Dimension, or Null if no GUID exists.	GUID
DIMENSION_NAME	The name of the Dimension.	String
DIMENSION_ORDINAL	The number or the ordinal of the Dimension. This is zero-based.	Long
DIMENSION_TYPE	The type of the Dimension.	MD_DIMTYPE
DIMENSION_UNIQUE_NAME	The unique name of the Dimension.	String
IS_VIRTUAL	Indicates whether or not the Dimension is a virtual dimension.	Boolean
SCHEMA_NAME	The schema name to which this Dimension belongs.	String

Hierarchy Object

Name	Description	Type
ALL_MEMBER	The name of the default member if the first level is All, or Null if the first level is not All.	String
CATALOG_NAME	Catalog name in which the table is defined or Null if the provider does not support catalogs.	String
CUBE_NAME	The name of the Cube to which this Hierarchy belongs	String
DEFAULT_MEMBER	The default Level for this Hierarchy, or Null if no default exists.	String
DESCRIPTION	The description of the hierarchy.	String
DIMENSION_TYPE	The type of the dimension.	MD_DIMTYPE
DIMENSION_UNIQUE_NAME	The fully qualified name of the Dimension to which this Hierarchy belongs.	String
HIERARCHY_CAPTION	The caption of the Hierarchy.	String
HIERARCHY_CARDINALITY	The number of members in the Hierarchy. This figure is not guaranteed to be accurate.	Long
HIERARCHY_GUID	The GUID of the Hierarchy, or Null if no GUID exists.	GUID

Table Continued on Following Page

Name	Description	Type
HIERARCHY_NAME	The name of the Hierarchy.	String
HIERARCHY_UNIQUE_NAME	The fully qualified name of the Hierarchy.	String
SCHEMA_NAME	Schema name in which the table is defined or Null if the provider does not support schemas.	String

Level Object

Name	Description	Type
CATALOG_NAME	Catalog name, or Null if the provider does not support catalogs.	String
CUBE_NAME	The Cube name to which the level belongs.	String
DESCRIPTION	The description of the level.	String
DIMENSION_UNIQUE_NAME	The unique name of the Dimension to which the level belongs.	String
HIERARCHY_UNIQUE_NAME	The unique name of the Hierarchy to which the level belongs.	String
LEVEL_CAPTION	The Caption of the level.	String
LEVEL_CARDINALITY	The number of members in the level. This figure is not guaranteed to be accurate.	Long
LEVEL_GUID	The GUID of the level, or Null if no GUID exists.	GUID
LEVEL_NAME	The level name.	String
LEVEL_NUMBER	The index number of the level.	Long
LEVEL_TYPE	The Type of the level.	MDLEVEL_TYPE
LEVEL_UNIQUE_NAME	The unique level name.	String
SCHEMA_NAME	Schema name, or Null if the provider does not support schemas.	String

Member Object

Name	Description	Type
EXPRESSION	The expression which underlies a calculated measure.	String
column	A column for each member	String

ADO Error Numbers

The following table lists the standard errors than might get returned from ADO operations:

Constant name	Number	Description
adErrInvalidArgument	3001	The application is using arguments that are of the wrong type, are out of acceptable range, or are in conflict with one another.
adErrNoCurrentRecord	3021	Either BOF or EOF is True, or the current record has been deleted; the operation requested by the application requires a current record.
adErrIllegalOperation	3219	The operation requested by the application is not allowed in this context.
adErrInTransaction	3246	The application cannot explicitly close a Connection object while in the middle of a transaction.
adErrFeatureNotAvailable	3251	The operation requested by the application is not supported by the provider.
adErrItemNotFound	3265	ADO could not find the object in the collection corresponding to the name or ordinal reference requested by the application.
adErrObjectInCollection	3367	Can't append. The object is already in the collection.

Constant name	Number	Description
adErrObjectNotSet	3420	The object referenced by the application no longer points to a valid object.
adErrDataConversion	3421	The application is using a value of the wrong type for the current operation.
adErrObjectClosed	3704	The operation requested by the application is not allowed if the object is closed.
adErrObjectOpen	3705	The operation requested by the application is not allowed if the object is open.
adErrProviderNotFound	3706	ADO could not find the specified provider.
adErrBoundToCommand	3707	The application cannot change the ActiveConnection property of a Recordset object with a Command object as its source.
adErrInvalidParamInfo	3708	The application has improperly defined a Parameter object.
adErrInvalidConnection	3709	The application requested an operation on an object with a reference to a closed or invalid Connection object.

The following lists the extended ADO errors and their descriptions:

Error Number	Description
-2147483647	Not implemented.
-2147483646	Ran out of memory.
-2147483645	One or more arguments are invalid.
-2147483644	No such interface supported.
-2147483643	Invalid pointer.
-2147483642	Invalid handle.
-2147483641	Operation aborted.
-2147483640	Unspecified error.
-2147483639	General access denied error.
-2147483638	The data necessary to complete this operation is not yet available.
-2147467263	Not implemented.
-2147467262	No such interface supported.
-2147467261	Invalid pointer.

Error Number	Description
-2147467260	Operation aborted.
-2147467259	Unspecified error.
-2147467258	Thread local storage failure.
-2147467257	Get shared memory allocator failure.
-2147467256	Get memory allocator failure.
-2147467255	Unable to initialize class cache.
-2147467254	Unable to initialize RPC services.
-2147467253	Cannot set thread local storage channel control.
-2147467252	Could not allocate thread local storage channel control.
-2147467251	The user supplied memory allocator is unacceptable.
-2147467250	The OLE service mutex already exists.
-2147467249	The OLE service file mapping already exists.
-2147467248	Unable to map view of file for OLE service.
-2147467247	Failure attempting to launch OLE service.
-2147467246	There was an attempt to call `CoInitialize` a second time while single threaded.
-2147467245	A Remote activation was necessary but was not allowed.
-2147467244	A Remote activation was necessary but the server name provided was invalid.
-2147467243	The class is configured to run as a security id different from the caller.
-2147467242	Use of OLE1 services requiring DDE windows is disabled.
-2147467241	A RunAs specification must be `<domain name>\<user name>` or simply `<user name>`.
-2147467240	The server process could not be started. The pathname may be incorrect.
-2147467239	The server process could not be started as the configured identity. The pathname may be incorrect or unavailable.
-2147467238	The server process could not be started because the configured identity is incorrect. Check the username and password.
-2147467237	The client is not allowed to launch this server.
-2147467236	The service providing this server could not be started.
-2147467235	This computer was unable to communicate with the computer providing the server.

Table Continued on Following Page

Error Number	Description
-2147467234	The server did not respond after being launched.
-2147467233	The registration information for this server is inconsistent or incomplete.
-2147467232	The registration information for this interface is inconsistent or incomplete.
-2147467231	The operation attempted is not supported.
-2147418113	Catastrophic failure.
-2147024891	General access denied error.
-2147024890	Invalid handle.
-2147024882	Ran out of memory.
-2147024809	One or more arguments are invalid.

Listed below are the OLE DB errors, and whilst they might not be relevant for some of the ADO work, they are included for completeness:

Error Number	Description
-2147217920	Invalid accessor.
-2147217919	Creating another row would have exceeded the total number of active rows supported by the rowset.
-2147217918	Unable to write with a read-only accessor.
-2147217917	Given values violate the database schema.
-2147217916	Invalid row handle.
-2147217915	An object was open.
-2147217914	Invalid chapter.
-2147217913	A literal value in the command could not be converted to the correct type due to a reason other than data overflow.
-2147217912	Invalid binding info.
-2147217911	Permission denied.
-2147217910	Specified column does not contain bookmarks or chapters.
-2147217909	Some cost limits were rejected.
-2147217908	No command has been set for the command object.
-2147217907	Unable to find a query plan within the given cost limit.
-2147217906	Invalid bookmark.

Error Number	Description
-2147217905	Invalid lock mode.
-2147217904	No value given for one or more required parameters.
-2147217903	Invalid column ID.
-2147217902	Invalid ratio.
-2147217901	Invalid value.
-2147217900	The command contained one or more errors.
-2147217899	The executing command cannot be cancelled.
-2147217898	The provider does not support the specified dialect.
-2147217897	A data source with the specified name already exists.
-2147217896	The rowset was built over a live data feed and cannot be restarted.
-2147217895	No key matching the described characteristics could be found within the current range.
-2147217894	Ownership of this tree has been given to the provider.
-2147217893	The provider is unable to determine identity for newly inserted rows.
-2147217892	No non-zero weights specified for any goals supported, so goal was rejected; current goal was not changed.
-2147217891	Requested conversion is not supported.
-2147217890	lRowsOffset would position you past either end of the rowset, regardless of the cRows value specified; cRowsObtained is 0.
-2147217889	Information was requested for a query, and the query was not set.
-2147217888	Provider called a method from IrowsetNotify in the consumer and the method has not yet returned.
-2147217887	Errors occurred.
-2147217886	A non-NULL controlling IUnknown was specified and the object being created does not support aggregation.
-2147217885	A given HROW referred to a hard- or soft- deleted row.
-2147217884	The rowset does not support fetching backwards.
-2147217883	All HROWs must be released before new ones can be obtained.
-2147217882	One of the specified storage flags was not supported.
-2147217881	Invalid comparison operator.

Table Continued on Following Page

Error Number	Description
-2147217880	The specified status flag was neither DBCOLUMNSTATUS_OK nor DBCOLUMNSTATUS_ISNULL.
-2147217879	The rowset cannot scroll backwards.
-2147217878	Invalid region handle.
-2147217877	The specified set of rows was not contiguous to or overlapping the rows in the specified watch region.
-2147217876	A transition from ALL* to MOVE* or EXTEND* was specified.
-2147217875	The specified region is not a proper subregion of the region identified by the given watch region handle.
-2147217874	The provider does not support multi-statement commands.
-2147217873	A specified value violated the integrity constraints for a column or table.
-2147217872	The given type name was unrecognized.
-2147217871	Execution aborted because a resource limit has been reached; no results have been returned.
-2147217870	Cannot clone a command object whose command tree contains a rowset or rowsets.
-2147217869	Cannot represent the current tree as text.
-2147217868	The specified index already exists.
-2147217867	The specified index does not exist.
-2147217866	The specified index was in use.
-2147217865	The specified table does not exist.
-2147217864	The rowset was using optimistic concurrency and the value of a column has been changed since it was last read.
-2147217863	Errors were detected during the copy.
-2147217862	A specified precision was invalid.
-2147217861	A specified scale was invalid.
-2147217860	Invalid table ID.
-2147217859	A specified type was invalid.
-2147217858	A column ID occurred more than once in the specification.
-2147217857	The specified table already exists.
-2147217856	The specified table was in use.

Error Number	Description
-2147217855	The specified locale ID was not supported.
-2147217854	The specified record number is invalid.
-2147217853	Although the bookmark was validly formed, no row could be found to match it.
-2147217852	The value of a property was invalid.
-2147217851	The rowset was not chaptered.
-2147217850	Invalid accessor.
-2147217849	Invalid storage flags.
-2147217848	By-ref accessors are not supported by this provider.
-2147217847	Null accessors are not supported by this provider.
-2147217846	The command was not prepared.
-2147217845	The specified accessor was not a parameter accessor.
-2147217844	The given accessor was write-only.
-2147217843	Authentication failed.
-2147217842	The change was canceled during notification; no columns are changed.
-2147217841	The rowset was single-chaptered and the chapter was not released.
-2147217840	Invalid source handle.
-2147217839	The provider cannot derive parameter info and `SetParameterInfo` has not been called.
-2147217838	The data source object is already initialized.
-2147217837	The provider does not support this method.
-2147217836	The number of rows with pending changes has exceeded the set limit.
-2147217835	The specified column did not exist.
-2147217834	There are pending changes on a row with a reference count of zero.
-2147217833	A literal value in the command overflowed the range of the type of the associated column.
-2147217832	The supplied `HRESULT` was invalid.
-2147217831	The supplied `LookupID` was invalid.
-2147217830	The supplied `DynamicErrorID` was invalid.

Table Continued on Following Page

Error Number	Description
-2147217829	Unable to get visible data for a newly inserted row that has not yet been updated.
-2147217828	Invalid conversion flag.
-2147217827	The given parameter name was unrecognized.
-2147217826	Multiple storage objects cannot be opened simultaneously.
-2147217825	Cannot open requested filter.
-2147217824	Cannot open requested order.
-2147217823	Invalid tuple.
-2147217822	Invalid coordinate.
-2147217821	Invalid axis for this dataset.
-2147217820	One or more cell ordinals is invalid.
-2147217819	Invalid columnID.
-2147217817	Command does not have a DBID.
-2147217816	DBID already exists.
-2147217815	Maximum number of sessions supported by the provider already created. Consumer must release one or more currently held sessions before obtaining a new session object.
-2147217814	Invalid trustee value.
-2147217813	Trustee is not for the current data source.
-2147217812	Trustee does not support memberships/collections.
-2147217811	Object is invalid or unknown to the provider.
-2147217810	No owner exists for the object.
-2147217809	Invalid access entry list.
-2147217808	Trustee supplied as owner is invalid or unknown to the provider.
-2147217807	Invalid permission in the access entry list.
-2147217806	Invalid index ID.
-2147217805	Initialization string does not conform to specification.
-2147217804	OLE DB root enumerator did not return any providers that matched any requested SOURCES_TYPE.
-2147217803	Initialization string specifies a provider that does not match the currently active provider.

Error Number	Description
-2147217802	Invalid DBID.
-2147217801	ConstraintType is invalid or not supported by the provider.
-2147217800	ConstraintType is not DBCONSTRAINTTYPE_FOREIGNKEY and cForeignKeyColumns is not zero.
-2147217799	Deferrability is invalid or the value is not supported by the provider.
-2147217798	MatchType is invalid or the value is not supported by the provider.
-2147217782	UpdateRule or DeleteRule is invalid or the value is not supported by the provider.
-2147217781	pConstraintID does not exist in the data source.
-2147217780	Invalid dwFlags.
-2147217779	rguidColumnType points to a GUID that does not match the object type of this column, or this column was not set.
-2147217778	URL is out of scope.
-2147217776	Provider cannot drop the object.
-2147217775	No source row.
-2147217774	OLE DB object represented by this URL is locked by one or more other processes.
-2147217773	Client requested an object type that is valid only for a collection.
-2147217772	Caller requested write access to a read-only object.
-2147217771	Provider does not support asynchronous binding.
-2147217770	Provider cannot connect to server for this object.
-2147217769	Attempt to bind to the object timed out.
-2147217768	Provider cannot create an object at this URL because an object named by this URL already exists.
-2147217767	Constraint already exists.
-2147217766	Provider cannot create an object at this URL because the server is out of physical storage.
-2147217765	Unsafe operation was attempted in safe mode. Provider denied this operation.
265920	Fetching requested number of rows would have exceeded total number of active rows supported by the rowset.
265921	One or more column types are incompatible; conversion errors will occur during copying.

Table Continued on Following Page

Error Number	Description
265922	Parameter type information has been overridden by caller.
265923	Skipped bookmark for deleted or non-member row.
265924	Errors found in validating tree.
265925	There are no more rowsets.
265926	Reached start or end of rowset or chapter.
265927	The provider re-executed the command.
265928	Variable data buffer full.
265929	There are no more results.
265930	Server cannot release or downgrade a lock until the end of the transaction.
265931	Specified weight was not supported or exceeded the supported limit and was set to 0 or the supported limit.
265932	Consumer is uninterested in receiving further notification calls for this operation.
265933	Input dialect was ignored and text was returned in different dialect.
265934	Consumer is uninterested in receiving further notification calls for this phase.
265935	Consumer is uninterested in receiving further notification calls for this reason.
265936	Operation is being processed asynchronously.
265937	In order to reposition to the start of the rowset, the provider had to re-execute the query; either the order of the columns changed or columns were added to or removed from the rowset.
265938	The method had some errors; errors have been returned in the error array.
265939	Invalid row handle.
265940	A given HROW referred to a hard-deleted row.
265941	The provider was unable to keep track of all the changes; the client must re-fetch the data associated with the watch region using another method.
265942	Execution stopped because a resource limit has been reached; results obtained so far have been returned but execution cannot be resumed.
265943	Method requested a singleton result but multiple rows are selected by the command or rowset. First row is returned.
265944	A lock was upgraded from the value specified.

Error Number	Description
265945	One or more properties were changed as allowed by provider.
265946	Errors occurred.
265947	A specified parameter was invalid.
265948	Updating this row caused more than one row to be updated in the data source.
265948	Row has no row-specific columns.

Index

Symbols

A

Index

wrox

PROGRAMMER TO PROGRAMMER™

Wrox writes books for you. Any suggestions, or ideas about how you want information given in your ideal book will be studied by our team. Your comments are always valued at Wrox.

Free phone in USA 800-USE-WROX
Fax (312) 893 8001

UK Tel. (0121) 687 4100   Fax (0121) 687 4101

Professional ADO 2.5 Programming - Registration Card

Name _____

Address _____

_____

_____

_____

City_____ State/Region _____

Country_____ Postcode/Zip _____

E-mail _____

Occupation _____

How did you hear about this book? _____

☐ Book review (name) _____

☐ Advertisement (name) _____

☐ Recommendation _____

☐ Catalog _____

☐ Other _____

Where did you buy this book? _____

☐ Bookstore (name)_____ City _____

☐ Computer Store (name)_____

☐ Mail Order _____

☐ Other _____

What influenced you in the purchase of this book?

☐ Cover Design
☐ Contents
☐ Other (please specify) _____

How did you rate the overall contents of this book?

☐ Excellent   ☐ Good
☐ Average   ☐ Poor

What did you find most useful about this book? _____

What did you find least useful about this book? _____

Please add any additional comments. _____

What other subjects will you buy a computer book on soon? _____

What is the best computer book you have used this year?

_____

Note: This information will only be used to keep you updated about new Wrox Press titles and will not be used for any other purpose or passed to any other third party.

Check here if you DO NOT want to receive support for this book ▮

wrox

PROGRAMMER TO PROGRAMMER™

NB. If you post the bounce back card below in the UK, please send it to:

Wrox Press Ltd., Arden House, 1102 Warwick Road,
Acocks Green, Birmingham B27 6BH. UK.

Computer Book Publishers